THE PAPERS OF ALEXANDER HAMILTON

THE PAPERS OF
Alexander Hamilton

VOLUME XXVI

MAY 1, 1802–OCTOBER 23, 1804

ADDITIONAL DOCUMENTS 1774–1799

ADDENDA AND ERRATA

HAROLD C. SYRETT, EDITOR

Associate Editors

BARBARA A. CHERNOW

IRENE R. DIAMANT   RICHARD J. MORRIS

SARA SOLBERG   PATRICIA SYRETT

 COLUMBIA UNIVERSITY PRESS

NEW YORK, 1979

FROM THE PUBLISHER

The preparation of this edition of the papers of
Alexander Hamilton has been made possible by the
support received for the work of the editorial and
research staff from the generous grants of the Rocke-
feller Foundation, Time Inc., the Ford Foundation,
and the Editing Program of the National Endow-
ment for the Humanities, and by the far-sighted co-
operation of the National Historical Publications and
Records Commission, which administered the Ford
Foundation grant during its ten years of existence,
has continued its support of research and editing, and
in addition, has provided funds toward the cost of
publication of this volume and five earlier volumes.

Funds to assist in meeting editorial costs were ap-
propriated during the early years of research by
Columbia University. The Sloan Foundation, the
New York Foundation, the Bank of New York, the
Kidder Peabody Foundation, the Charles E. Merrill
Trust, and Mr. Thomas S. Brush among them gave
substantial aid in meeting the publication costs of
eight volumes.

To all of those named, organizations and individual alike, the publisher expresses gratitude on behalf of all who are concerned about making available
the record of the founding of the United States.

Columbia University Press
New York   Guildford, Surrey
Copyright © 1979 Columbia University Press
International Standard Book Number: 0-231-08925-2
Library of Congress Catalog Card Number: 61-15593
Printed in the United States of America

CONTENTS

ACKNOWLEDGMENTS

Since the publication in 1976 of Volume XXIII of *The Papers of Alexander Hamilton*, the editors have incurred new obligations which they wish to take this opportunity to acknowledge. Of the many individuals who generously shared their specialized information or provided assistance, the editors are especially indebted to

Professor Joseph Baromé, City College, City University of New York

Dr. Kenneth R. Bowling, Madison, Wisconsin

Dr. Julian P. Boyd, The Papers of Thomas Jefferson, Princeton University

Ms. Nancy Burkett, Assistant Manuscripts Curator, American Antiquarian Society, Worcester, Massachusetts

Professor Joseph M. Conant, Emory University, Atlanta, Georgia

Mr. Allan N. Degutis, American Antiquarian Society, Worcester, Massachusetts

Miss Mary Jane Dowd, Silver Spring, Maryland

Professor Don R. Gerlach, The University of Akron, Akron, Ohio

Ms. Mary A. Giunta, Archivist, National Historical Publications and Records Commission, Washington, D.C.

Dr. Allen Hazen, Jr., New York City

Professor Jacob Judd, Sleepy Hollow Restorations, Inc., Tarrytown, New York

Dr. Mary-Jo Kline, The Papers of Aaron Burr, New-York Historical Society, New York City

Mr. John Knowlton, Washington, D.C.

Mr. E. M. Kolly, Archive Section, Bank of England, London

Mrs. Ruth Lester, The Papers of Thomas Jefferson, Princeton University

Mr. Kenneth H. MacFarland, Librarian Emeritus, Albany Institute of History and Art, Albany, New York

Professor John H. Middendorf, Columbia University

Mrs. Katherine Peckham, Middletown, Rhode Island

Dr. Richard K. Showman, The Nathanael Greene Papers, Rhode Island Historical Society, Providence

Mr. Edward T. Sullivan, Milton, Massachusetts

Miss Betty J. Thomas, Associate Editor, The Law Practice of Alexander Hamilton

Dr. and Mrs. Albert E. Van Dusen, The Papers of Jonathan Trumbull, Connecticut State Library, Hartford

PREFACE

This edition of Alexander Hamilton's papers contains letters and other documents written by Hamilton, letters to Hamilton, and some documents (commissions, certificates, etc.) that directly concern Hamilton but were written neither by him nor to him. All letters and other documents have been printed in chronological order. Two volumes of Hamilton's legal papers, entitled *The Law Practice of Alexander Hamilton*, have been published by the Columbia University Press under the editorial direction of the late Julius Goebel, Jr. The forthcoming volumes of this distinguished work are being completed by Joseph H. Smith, George Welwood Murray Professor of Legal History of the School of Law, Columbia University.

Many letters and documents have been calendared. Such calendared items include routine letters and documents by Hamilton, routine letters to Hamilton, some of the letters or documents written by Hamilton for someone else, letters or documents which have not been found but which are known to have existed, letters or documents which have been erroneously attributed to Hamilton, and letters to or by Hamilton that deal exclusively with his legal practice.

Hamilton's significant legal opinions appear in *The Law Practice of Alexander Hamilton*, and they have accordingly been omitted from these volumes.

Certain routine documents which Hamilton wrote and received as Secretary of the Treasury have not been printed. The documents that fall within this category are warrants or interest certificates; letters written by Hamilton acknowledging receipts from banks, endorsing margins of certificate of registry, and enclosing sea letters; letters to Hamilton transmitting weekly, monthly, and quarterly accounts, or enclosing certificates of registry and other routine Treasury forms; and drafts by Hamilton on the treasurer. Statements of facts from the judges of the District Courts on cases concerning violations of the customs laws and warrants of remission of forfeiture issued by Hamilton have generally been omitted unless they pertain to cases discussed in Hamilton's correspondence.

The notes in these volumes are designed to provide information concerning the nature and location of each document, to identify Hamilton's correspondents and the individuals mentioned in the text, to explain events or ideas referred to in the text, and to point out textual variations or mistakes. Occasional departures from these standards can be attributed to a variety of reasons. In many cases the desired information has been supplied in an earlier note and can be found through the use of the index. Notes have not been added when in the opinion of the editors the material in the text was either self-explanatory or common knowledge. Finally, the editors on some occasions have been unable to find the desired information, and on other occasions the editors have been remiss.

PREFACE TO THIS VOLUME

This volume of *The Papers of Alexander Hamilton,* unlike its predecessors, consists of four distinct parts. The first section completes the chronology of earlier volumes and also includes a few documents which were written after Hamilton's death and which are directly related to that event.

The second section is entitled "Additional Letters and Documents," and, as the title indicates, it contains those letters and documents which for a variety of reasons do not appear in earlier volumes. In some instances these materials have only recently been made available to scholars; in other cases they could not be dated properly without information which has subsequently come to light; and finally there are those letters and documents which the editors did not discover during their earlier searches for manuscripts and printed sources.

The third section is entitled "Undated Letters and Documents."

The fourth section, entitled "Addenda and Errata," covers the preceding volumes of *The Papers of Alexander Hamilton* and consists of the following:

1. Additional sources for letters and documents which have been printed in the preceding volumes. Transcripts, including the George Bancroft, Jared Sparks, John Church Hamilton, Francis Baylies, and William A. Oldridge transcripts, have not been listed.
2. Additions to a relatively small number of footnotes.
3. Corrections of mistakes in the text of letters and documents.
4. Corrections of mistakes, ranging from typographical errors to mistakes in fact, in footnotes and introductory notes.

No attempt has been made to correct the indexes to the preceding volumes, for any such changes will appear in a cumulative index which will be the concluding volume in this edition of Alexander Hamilton's papers.

The editors are under no illusions that they have discovered all the errors in the preceding twenty-five volumes of *The Papers of Alexander Hamilton*. They can state only that they have done their best and that they have been helped immeasurably by reviewers, friends, and strangers who have called omissions or errors to their attention.

GUIDE TO EDITORIAL APPARATUS

I. SYMBOLS USED TO DESCRIBE MANUSCRIPTS

AD   Autograph Document
ADS   Autograph Document Signed
ADf   Autograph Draft
ADfS   Autograph Draft Signed
AL   Autograph Letter
ALS   Autograph Letter Signed
D   Document
DS   Document Signed
Df   Draft
DfS   Draft Signed
LS   Letter Signed
LC   Letter Book Copy
[S]   [S] is used with other symbols (AD[S], ADf[S], AL[S], D[S], Df[S], L[S]) to indicate that the signature on the document has been cropped or clipped.

II. SHORT TITLES AND ABBREVIATIONS

Annals of Congress   *The Debates and Proceedings in the Congress of the United States; with an Appendix, Containing Important State Papers and Public Documents, and all the Laws of a Public Nature* (Washington, 1834–1852).

Arch. des Aff. Etr., Corr. Pol., Transcripts or photostats from the
    Etats-Unis   French Foreign Office deposited
                                      in the Library of Congress.

ASP   *American State Papers, Documents,*
                                     Legislative and Executive, of the
                                     Congress of the United States
                                     (Washington, 1832–1861).

Boyd, *Papers of Thomas Jefferson*   Julian P. Boyd, ed., *The Papers of*
                                     Thomas Jefferson (Princeton,
                                     1950–   ).

Burnett, *Letters*   Edmund C. Burnett, ed., *Letters*
                                     of Members of the Continental
                                     Congress (Washington, 1921–
                                     1938).

Carter, *Territorial Papers*   Clarence E. Carter, ed., *The Ter-*
                                     ritorial Papers of the United
                                     States (Washington, 1934–1952).

Davis, *Essays*   Joseph Stancliffe Davis, *Essays in*
                                     the Earlier History of American
                                     Corporations "Harvard Eco-
                                     nomic Studies," XVI [Cam-
                                     bridge, 1917]).

Executive Journal, I   *Journal of the Executive Proceed-*
                                     ings of the Senate of the United
                                     States of America (Washington,
                                     1828), I.

Goebel, *Law Practice*   Julius Goebel, Jr., and Joseph H.
                                     Smith, eds., *The Law Practice of*
                                     Alexander Hamilton: Documents
                                     and Commentary (New York
                                     and London, 1964–   ).

GW   John C. Fitzpatrick, ed., *The*
                                     Writings of George Washing-
                                     ton (Washington, 1931–1944).

Hamilton, *History*   John C. Hamilton, *Life of Alex-*
                                     ander Hamilton, a History of the
                                     Republic of the United States of
                                     America (Boston, 1879).

Hamilton, *Intimate Life*   Allan McLane Hamilton, *The In-*
                                     timate Life of Alexander Hamil-
                                     ton (New York, 1910).

Hamilton, *Reminiscences*   James A. Hamilton, *Reminiscences*
                                     of James A. Hamilton: or Men
                                     and Events, at Home and

	Abroad, During Three Quarters of a Century (New York, 1869).
HCLW	Henry Cabot Lodge, ed., *The Works of Alexander Hamilton* (New York, 1904).
JCC	*Journals of the Continental Congress, 1774–1789* (Washington, 1904–1937; Reprinted, New York, 1968).
JCH Transcripts	John C. Hamilton Transcripts, Columbia University Libraries.
JCHW	John C. Hamilton, ed., *The Works of Alexander Hamilton* (New York, 1851–1856).
Journal of the House, I, II, III, IV	*Journal of the House of Representatives of the United States* (Washington, 1826), I, II, III, IV.
King, *The Life and Correspondence of Rufus King*	Charles R. King, ed., *The Life and Correspondence of Rufus King* (New York, 1894–1900).
Miller, *Treaties*, II	Hunter Miller, ed., *Treaties and Other International Acts of the United States of America* (Washington, 1931), II.
Minutes of the Common Council	*Minutes of the Common Council of the City of New York, 1784–1831* (New York, 1917).
Mix, *Catalogue: Maps and Surveys*	David E. E. Mix, ed., *Catalogue: Maps and Surveys in the Offices of the Secretary of State, State Engineer and Surveyor, and Comptroller, and the New York State Library* (Albany, 1859).
Naval Documents, Barbary Powers, II	*Naval Documents Related to the United States Wars With the Barbary Powers* (Washington, 1940), II.
PAH	Harold C. Syrett, ed., *The Papers of Alexander Hamilton* (New York and London, 1961-).
PRO: F.O., or PRO: C.O.	Public Record Office of Great Britain.
1 *Stat.*; 2 *Stat.*	*The Public Statutes at Large of*

	the United States of America, I (Boston, 1845); II (Boston, 1850).
6 Stat.	The Public Statutes at Large of the United States of America [Private Statutes] (Boston, 1846).
Syrett and Cooke, Interview in Weehawken	Harold C. Syrett and Jean G. Cooke, eds., Interview in Weehawken. The Burr-Hamilton Duel as Told in the Original Documents (Middletown, Conn., 1960).
Winfield, Jersey City	Charles H. Winfield, A Monograph on the Founding of Jersey City (New York, 1891).

III. INDECIPHERABLE WORDS

Words or parts of words which could not be deciphered because of the illegibility of the writing or the mutilation of the manuscript have been indicated as follows:

1. ⟨-----⟩ indicates illegible words with the number of dashes indicating the estimated number of illegible words.
2. Words or letters in broken brackets indicate a guess as to what the words or letters in question may be. If the source of the words or letters within the broken brackets is known, it has been given a note.

IV. CROSSED-OUT MATERIAL IN MANUSCRIPTS

Words or sentences crossed out by a writer in a manuscript have been handled in one of the three following ways:

1. They have been ignored, and the document or letter has been printed in its final version.
2. Crossed-out words and insertions for the crossed-out words have been described in the notes.
3. When the significance of a manuscript seems to warrant it, the crossed-out words have been retained, and the document has been printed as it was written.

V. TEXTUAL CHANGES AND INSERTIONS

The following changes or insertions have been made in the letters and documents printed in these volumes:

1. Words or letters written above the line of print (for example, 9th) have been made even with the line of print (9th).

2. Punctuation and capitalization have been changed in those instances where it seemed necessary to make clear the sense of the writer. A special effort has been made to eliminate the dash, which was such a popular eighteenth-century device.

3. When the place or date, or both, of a letter or document does not appear at the head of that letter or document, it has been inserted in the text in brackets. If either the place or date at the head of a letter or document is incomplete, the necessary additional material has been added in the text in brackets. For all but the best known localities or places, the name of the colony, state, or territory has been added in brackets at the head of a document or letter.

4. In calendared documents, place and date have been uniformly written out in full without the use of brackets. Thus "N. York, Octr. 8, '99" becomes "New York, October 8, 1799." If, however, substantive material is added to the place or date in a calendared document, such material is placed in brackets. Thus "Oxford, Jan. 6" becomes "Oxford [Massachusetts] January 6 [1788]."

5. When a writer made an unintentional slip comparable to a typographical error, one of the four following devices has been used:

   a. It has been allowed to stand as written.

   b. It has been corrected by inserting either one or more letters in brackets.

   c. It has been corrected without indicating the change.

   d. It has been explained in a note.

6. Because the symbol for the thorn was archaic even in Hamilton's day, the editors have used the letter "y" to represent it. In doing this they are conforming to eighteenth-century manuscript usage.

THE PAPERS OF ALEXANDER HAMILTON

1 8 0 2

To Simeon Baldwin [1]

[*New York, May 1, 1802.* "Capt. Du Buisson who has obtained a decree of restitution of his vessel & cargo tells me that there are some obstacles, which he cannot explain, to his receiving the moiety of the proceeds reserved for the Captors, and remaining as he understands it in deposit with you. As he has solicited my aid which I have promised, you will oblige me by explaining as early as may be the situation of the business." [2] *Letter not found.*]

1. ALS, listed by Thomas Madigan, New York City, in *A Catalogue of Autographs* (n.d.), Item 98.
Baldwin, a lawyer in New Haven, Connecticut, was clerk of the United States Circuit and District Courts for Connecticut from 1789 to 1806.
For background to this letter, which concerns the case of the *United States v Schooner Peggy, Joseph Buisson, claimant,* see H to Jedediah Huntington, November 12, 1801, note 2; Robert Smith to H, November 20, 1801; H to Aaron Burr, April 1, 1802.
2. Extract taken from the dealer's catalogue.

Election by the Triennial General Meeting of the Society of the Cincinnati [1]

Washington, May 3, 1802. "A Ballot was accordingly had; and on counting the Votes it appeared that the following Gentlemen were unanimously Elected to fill the Offices annexed to their names, respectively. Major General Alexander Hamilton, President General. . . ." [2]

"Journals of the Cincinnati, 1784–1787, Vol. I," 105, Library of Congress.
1. See William Jackson to H, March 12, 1802.
2. H, who was not present at this meeting, served as president of the Society of the Cincinnati from 1800 until his death in 1804. See "Election by the Adjourned General Meeting of the Society of the Cincinnati," May 5, 1800.

From Charles Cotesworth Pinckney [1]

Charleston [South Carolina] May 3d. 1802

Dear Sr:

I was in Georgia when your favour of the 15th: of March arrived in Charleston, & when I received it, it was too late to set out for Washington to be there at the time mentioned even if I had been prepared for such a jaunt. I agree entirely with you in your sentiments of the act repealing the act of the last session for the better organization of the Judiciary department; but it was natural to expect that Persons who have been always hostile to the Constitution would when they had power endeavour to destroy a work whose adoption they opposed, and whose execution they have constantly counteracted. But I do not imagine they will stop here, they will proceed in their mad & wicked career, and the Peoples' eyes will be opened. If you have been able to effect a meeting I should be glad to hear of the result. I did not write to Genl: Davie [2] as I knew he had lately met with a loss in his family which would prevent his being with you even if he had time. [3]

Be so obliging as to acquaint the Editor of the Herald [4] that none of his South Carolina Subscribers have received more than three parcels of papers from him. If he was regular in the transmitting them I am sure he would receive encouragement in this State; but the irregularity & negligence of the persons who put them up will occasion most of those who now subscribe to withdraw their names another year. From Boston, Philadelphia & Washington I get the papers punctually. I am obliged to you for making me acquainted with Prince Ruspoli, [5] I found him well informed. He sails for Europe tomorrow. I always am

Your affectionate friend   Charles Cotesworth Pinckney

Genl: Hamilton

ALS, Hamilton Papers, Library of Congress.
    1. A Federalist from South Carolina and a veteran of the American Revolution, Pinckney was United States Minister Plenipotentiary to France in 1796, a

member of the XYZ mission in 1798, and a major general in the United States Army during the undeclared war with France. In 1800 he was the Federalist candidate for President or Vice President. After the election, he continued to practice law in Charleston and represented that city in the state Senate.

2. William R. Davie, former governor of North Carolina, was a member of the three-man peace commission which negotiated the Convention of 1800 (Treaty of Môrtefontaine) with France. In January, 1802, he was appointed a commissioner to negotiate a treaty between the state of North Carolina and the Tuscaroras.

3. On August 20, 1802, Davie wrote to John Steele: "The death of Mrs. Davie [Sarah Jones Davie] has devolved upon me the whole care of my children; I am therefore at present confined to this spot [Halifax, North Carolina], and my health has been bad ever since my return from So. Carolina in the spring" (J. G. de Rouhlac Hamilton, "William Richardson Davie: A Memoir," *James Sprunt Historical Monograph No.* 7 [Chapel Hill: Published by the University, 1907], 54–55).

4. William Coleman, editor of the *New-York Evening Post,* also edited a semi-weekly edition of the *Post,* entitled the *New-York Herald,* the first issue of which appeared on January 2, 1802.

5. Bailli Barthélemy Ruspoli. See H to James McHenry, November 21, 1801.

From Rufus King [1]

secret and Confidential   London May 7th. 1802.

Dear Sir

As I know of no measure from abroad, which is capable of such extensive and injurious effects as the cession of Louisiana and the Floridas to France, it has been a subject of my unremitted solicitude and attention from the moment of our first suspicions concerning it. Its importance was fully and repeatedly developed to the Ministers of this Country before the conclusion of the Preliminaries, and during the negotiation at Amiens;[2] but no explanation was demanded of France, lest it should embarrass the conclusion of Peace.[3]

LS, New-York Historical Society, New York City; LC, New-York Historical Society, New York City.

1. For background to this letter, see William Constable to H, March 23, 1801. King was United States Minister to Great Britain.

In King's "Memorandum of private Letters, &c., dates & persons from 1796 to Augt 1802," owned by Mr. James G. King, New York City, King dates this letter "May 5, 1802," and describes its contents as "Secret and confidential—Louisiana."

2. See King to H, April 8, 1802, note 6.

3. See King to Robert R. Livingston, January 16, 1802 (King, *The Life and Correspondence of Rufus King,* IV, 57–58).

On March 5, 1801, Thomas Jefferson appointed Livingston, who had been Chancellor of New York from 1777 to 1801, Minister Plenipotentiary to the

Mr. Pinkney [4] absurdly enough is *offering* to purchase the Floridas
of Spain, which has already disposed of them.[5] Mr. Livingston can
obtain no answer whatever to his repeated Notes upon this subject at
Paris; [6] while we learn for a certainty that an Expedition to be commanded by Bernadotte [7] is already preparing in the Ports of France,
and will go directly to the Mississippi, unless the bad state of the
affairs of St Domingo [8] should alter its destination.[9] In these circumstances I have thought it prudent to ask this Government to explain
itself upon this important measure, and I send you in entire confidence copies of my Letter and of the answer which I have received and transmitted to the Department of State.[10]

In Thornton's last Dispatches, which I have seen, he reports a

---

Republic of France. He sailed for Europe on October 15, 1801, arrived in
France on November 13, and was formally presented to Napoleon Bonaparte
on December 6.

4. Jefferson appointed Charles Pinckney of South Carolina Minister Pleni-
potentiary at Madrid in March, 1801 (Jefferson to Pinckney, March 17, 1801
[ALS, letterpress copy, Thomas Jefferson Papers, Library of Congress]), and
Pinckney sailed for Europe in July, 1801.

5. On September 25, 1801, Secretary of State James Madison wrote to
Pinckney, instructing him to cooperate with Livingston in an effort to dissuade
Spain from ceding Louisiana to France and if possible to obtain the cession of
the Floridas to the United States (LC, RG 59, Diplomatic and Consular In-
structions of the Department of State, December 3, 1798–September 28, 1801,
"Despatches to Consuls," October 4, 1800–February 26, 1817, Vol. I, National
Archives). Pinckney conducted negotiations for the purchase of the Floridas
with Pedros Cevallos, the Spanish Secretary of State, until October, 1802, when
Madison, having received confirmation of the fact that Spain had ceded
Louisiana to France, instructed Pinckney to end the negotiation (Pinckney to
Madison, April 20, July 6, August 15, October 10, 1802 [LS, RG 59, Des-
patches from United States Ministers to Spain, 1792–1825, Vol. 6, September 14, 1801–May 2, 1803, National Archives]; Madison to Pinckney, July 26,
1802 [*ASP, Foreign Relations*, II, 519]).

6. See Livingston to King, March 10, 1802 (*ASP, Foreign Relations*, II 515).

7. On May 8, 1800, Napoleon appointed Jean Baptiste Jules Bernadotte, a
French general and officeholder under the Directory and Consulate, commander of the Army of the West. Under the terms of the Treaty of Amiens,
the Army of the West was dissolved in April, 1802, and Bernadotte was re-
called to Paris from Rennes, where he had been stationed.

8. French forces under the command of Charles Victor Emmanuel Leclerc
were attempting to regain control of Santo Domingo, the French colony which
had achieved *de facto* independence under François Dominique Toussaint
L'Ouverture.

9. The expedition never materialized because Napoleon refused to comply
with Bernadotte's demands for men and supplies.

10. See King to Madison, May 7, 1802, and its enclosures (LS, RG 59, Despatches from United States Ministers to Great Britain, 1791–1906, Vol. 10,
January 9, 1802–July 30, 1803, National Archives).

Conversation between him and the President in which the latter is represented to have said that this cession would inevitably change the political System of the United States in respect to their foreign Relations, inasmuch as it would lead to jealousies irritation and hostility: and, alluding to the north west boundary of the United States, suggested the expediency of an immediate settlement of it by an agreement to close the boundary by taking for that purpose the shortest line between lake superior and any part of the Mississippi.[11]

With sincere regards   I am, Dear sir,   Your obedient servant

Rufus King

[ENCLOSURE]

Rufus King to Lord Hawkesbury [12]

Confidential.   London Ap. 21. 1802

My Lord,

By the Treaty of Alliance concluded at Paris in 1778, between the United States of America and France, with the Exception of New orleans the latter renounced for ever the possession of every part of the Continent of america lying to the East of the course of the River Mississippi.[13] This renunciation, confirming that which had been previously made in the Treaty of 1763,[14] between Great Britain and France, authorized the expectation that France, content with her widely spread dominions, would abstain from seeking an extension of them on this part of the American Continent: an expectation that appeared the more reasonable, inasmuch as the motives to such Extension could not be satisfactorily reconciled with a just Regard to the Rights and security of those Powers, between which this Portion

11. See Edward Thornton, British chargé d'affaires at Washington, to Robert Banks Jenkinson, Lord Hawkesbury, British Foreign Secretary, March 6, 1802 (ALS, PRO: F.O., 5/96–99).

12. LS, PRO: F.O., 5/105–106; copy, RG 59, Despatches from United States Ministers to Great Britain, 1791–1906, Vol. 10, January 9, 1802–July 30, 1803, National Archives; typed copy, New-York Historical Society, New York City.

13. Article 6 of the Treaty of Alliance, signed at Paris on February 6, 1778 (Miller, *Treaties*, II, 38).

14. Article VII of the Treaty of Paris of 1763 (*The Parliamentary History of England, From the Earliest Period to the Year 1803* [London, 1806–1820], XV, 1296).

of america is divided, and by which the same is at present possessed.

Contrary, nevertheless, to expectations which have been entertained on this subject, if credit be due to uniform and uncontradicted Reports, the Government of France has prevailed upon his Catholic Majesty to cede to France both the Provinces of Louisiana and the Floridas, and having thus acquired a station at the Mouth, and on both sides of the Mississippi, may be inclined to interfere with and interrupt the open Navigation of the Same.

By the Treaty of Peace, concluded at Paris in 1783, between the United States of america and Great Britain, it is mutually stipulated that "the Navigation of the River Mississippi from its source to the Ocean shall for ever remain free and open to the subjects of Great Britain and the Citizens of the United States." [15] Without enlarging upon the great and peculiar importance of this Navigation to the United States, a large and increasing Portion of whose People can conveniently communicate with each other, and with foreign Countries, by no other route, I take the liberty thro' your Lordship to request that the British Government will in confidence explain itself upon this subject, and especially that it will explicitly declare whether any Communication has been received by it from the Government of France or Spain respecting the said Cession, or whether his Britannic Majesty has in any manner acquiesced in or sanctioned the same, so as to impair or affect the Stipulation above referred to concerning the free Navigation of the Mississippi: in a word I entreat your Lordship to open yourself on this occasion with that freedom which, in matters of weighty concern, is due from one friendly Nation to another, and which, in the present instance, will have the effect to do away all those misconceptions that may otherwise prevail in respect to the Privity of Great Britain to the cession in question.

With the highest consideration and respect   I have the honour to be,   Your Lordship's obedient & most humble servant   Rufus King.

15. Article 8 of the Treaty of Paris of 1783 (Miller, *Treaties*, II, 155).

[E N C L O S U R E]

Lord Hawkesbury to Rufus King [16]

Confidential   Downing Street [London]
                                                 7th: May, 1802.

Sir,

I have the Honour to acknowledge the Receipt of your Confidential Letter of the 21st: Ultimo. It is impossible that so important an Event, as the Cession of Louisiana by Spain to France, should be regarded by the King in any other Light, than as highly interesting to His Majesty and to the United States, and should render it more necessary than ever, that there should subsist between the two Governments that Spirit of Confidence, which is become so essential to the Security of Their respective Territories and Possessions.

With regard to the free Navigation of the Mississippi, I conceive that it is perfectly clear, according to the Law of Nations, that in the Event of the District of Louisiana being ceded to France, that Country would come into the Possession of it, subject to all the Engagements which appertained to it at the Time of Cession; and that the French Government could consequently alledge no colourable Pretext for excluding His Majesty's Subjects, or the Citizens of the United States, from the Navigation of the River Mississippi.

With regard to the second Question in Your Letter, I can have no Difficulty in informing you that no Communication whatever has been received by His Majesty from the Government of France or Spain, relative to any Convention or Treaty for the Cession of Louisiana or of the Floridas; and I can at the same Time most truly assure you that His Majesty has not in any Manner, directly or indirectly acquiesced in or sanctioned this Cession.

In making this Communication to you for the Information of the Government of the United States, I think it right to acquaint you that His Majesty will be anxious to learn their Sentiments on every Part of this Subject, and the Line of Policy which they will be inclined to adopt, in the Event of this Arrangement being carried into Effect.

16. LC, PRO: F.O., 5/111–113; copy, RG 59, Despatches from United States Ministers to Great Britain, 1791–1906, Vol. 10, January 9, 1802–July 30, 1803, National Archives; typed copy, New-York Historical Society, New York City.

From Simeon Baldwin [1]

[*New Haven, Connecticut, May 8, 1802*. The dealer's description
of this letter reads: "Legal." *Letter not found*.]

The Collector: A Magazine for Autograph and Historical Collectors, LIX,
No. 1 (January, 1946), 20.
    1. Baldwin wrote this letter in reply to H to Baldwin, May 1, 1802.

To Louis André Pichon [1]

New York May 10. 1802

Sir

    The inclosed was put into my hands by Capt Du Buisson, when
lately I was about to make a journey to the City of Washington,[2]
with the suggestion that you had desired it as a voucher for his
right to receive 3000 francs from the *Armateurs* of the *Peggy* and
which sum he informed me you would be willing to pay out of
funds in deposit with you on account of that Vessel and her Cargo.[3]
The interruption of my journey, by an accident, has deprived me
of the pleasure of delivering you the paper myself. I therefore now
forward it by post.

    If you think fit to remit to me the sum claimed it shall be paid
to Captain Du Buisson and a receipt from him shall be transmitted
to you.

    Do me the favour to present my respectful Compliments to
Madame Pichon [4] and to accept yourself the assurances of the distinguished consideration with which

    I have the honor to be   Sir   Yr. very obed. servt   A Hamilton

Mr. De Pichon &c.[5]

ALS, Hamilton Papers, Library of Congress.
    1. For background to this letter, see H to Jedediah Huntington, Novem-
ber 12, 1801; Robert Smith to H, November 20, 1801; H to Aaron Burr,

April 1, 1802; H to Simeon Baldwin, May 1, 1802; Baldwin to H, May 8, 1802.

Pichon was consul general and chargé d'affaires from the French Republic to the United States. He also served as commissary general of commercial relations for France.

2. H had been planning to attend the triennial general meeting of the Society of the Cincinnati which was held in Washington on May 3, 1802. See H to Charles Cotesworth Pinckney, March 15, 1802; "Election by the Triennial General Meeting of the Society of the Cincinnati," May 3, 1802, note 2.

3. See H to Burr, April 1, 1802, note 4.

4. A. Emilie Brongniart Pichon.

5. The endorsement on this letter reads: "Repue Le 21 mai." Letter not found.

To Jeremiah Wadsworth [1]

New York May 19. 1802

My Dear Sir

I have the pleasure of receiving your letter of the 26th. of April [2] and with it the half barrel of Mess Pork. It is excellent. Nothing could have been more acceptable to me. It is an article I am particularly fond of—& the gift deserves additional value from the *Giver*. Receive my thanks & believe me always

Yr. sincere & Affect friend   A Hamilton

Col Wadsworth

ALS, Connecticut Historical Society, Hartford.

1. Wadsworth, a resident of Hartford and a Federalist, was deputy commissary general and commissary general of purchases during the American Revolution and a member of the House of Representatives from 1789 to 1795. He was a member of the executive council of Connecticut from 1795 to 1801.

2. Letter not found.

From Louis André Pichon

[*Washington, May 21, 1802.* The endorsement on Hamilton to Pichon, May 10, 1802, reads: "Repue Le 21 mai." *Letter not found.*]

From Peter W. Yates [1]

[*Albany, May, 1802.*] "The Argument on the inclosed case [2] is to be the next term in new York. I cannot attend. I request you to pay particular attention to this Case & prepare for the argument. The deft. claims under my Br in Law Anthony Bries [3] the eldest son and heir of old Hendrick Bries their father. . . ."

ALS, Hamilton Papers, Library of Congress.
  1. Yates, an Albany lawyer, was a regent of the University of the State of New York in 1784 and a member of the New York Assembly in 1784 and 1785. He was a member of the Continental Congress from 1785 to 1787, after which he resumed the practice of law.
  2. AD, Hamilton Papers, Library of Congress.
  This document is an argument for a motion for a new trial prepared by defendant's counsel in *James Jackson ex dem. Gerrit T. Van Den Bergh* v *Frederick Breese et al.* in the New York Supreme Court. The first sentence of this "case" reads: "This is an Action of Ejectment for Lands in the patent of Hosick which was tried before his Honor the Chief Justice at the Rensselaer Circuit in May 1802." No record of this case has been found in the minutes of the New York Supreme Court for July, 1802, but for similar or related cases concerning the partition of the Hoosick patent, see George Caines, *Cases Argued and Determined in the Court for the Trial of Impeachments and Correction of Errors, in the State of New-York* (New York, 1810), II, 326–36; Caines, *New-York Term Reports of Cases Argued and Determined in the Supreme Court of That State* (New York, 1805), II, 169–76.
  3. Bries (Brees or Breese) was a resident and officeholder in Albany. Born in 1727, he married Catharyntie Yates, the older sister of Peter Yates, shortly before 1760.

To James M. Hughes [1]

[New York, June 3, 1802]

Mr. Hughes will please to execute the above order as follows— After deducting the Costs he will pay their proportions to the respective parties except that to Joseph Caste which I will receive.

New York June 3. 1802
Alex Hamilton

ALS, Emmett Collection, MS Division, New York Public Library.
  1. Hughes, a New York City lawyer, was a master of the New York Court of Chancery.
  This letter concerns the case of *Benjamin Taylor* v *Charles Bridgen,*

Thomas B. Bridgen, Anthony Ernest, Andrew Morris, Mark Tier, Maturin Livingston, Peter R. Livingston, Jean Cadiot, and Francis DelaCroix, which involved a mortgage foreclosure against the defendants. See MS Minutes, New York Court of Chancery, 1801–1804, 1804–1807, under the dates of February 18, 23, May 6, 1801 (Hall of Records, New York City).

H wrote on this letter: "Order of Court in Case of Bridgen Mortgages."

To Rufus King

By duplicate   New York June 3. 1802

My Dear Sir

I have been long very delinquent towards you, as a correspondent, and am to thank you that you have not cast me off altogether as an irretrievable reprobate. But you knew how to appreciate the causes and you have made a construction equally just and indulgent.

In your last you ask my opinion about a matter delicate and important both in a public and in a personal view.[1] I shall give it with the frankness to which you have a right, and I may add that the impressions of your other friends, so far as they have fallen under my observation do not differ from my own. While you were in the midst of a negotiation interesting to your country, it was your duty to keep your post. You have now accomplished the object[2] and have the good fortune not very common of having the universal plaudit.[3] This done, it seems to me most adviseable that you return home. There is little probability that your continuance in your present station will be productive of much positive good. Nor are circumstances such as to give reason to apprehend that the substitute for you, whoever he may be, can do much harm. Your stay or return

ALS, New-York Historical Society, New York City.

1. See King to H, April 8, 1802.

2. The Convention Regarding Articles 6 and 7 of the Jay Treaty and Article 4 of the Definitive Treaty of Peace was signed by Rufus King and Robert Banks Jenkinson, Lord Hawkesbury, at London on January 8, 1802 (Miller, *Treaties*, II, 488–91). For the documents on King's negotiations with the British government, see ASP, *Foreign Relations*, II, 382–428.

3. The Senate ratified the Convention with Great Britain by a vote of nineteen to two on April 26, 1802 (*Executive Journal*, I, 421–22). On May 3, 1802, Congress passed "An Act making an appropriation for carrying into effect the Convention between the United States of America and His Britannic Majesty" (2 *Stat.* 192), which appropriated $2,664,000 to carry out the provisions of the Convention.

ripening into a more bitter animosity between the partizans of the
two men than ever existed between the Fœderalists and Antifœder-
alists.

Unluckily we are not as neutral to this quarrel as we ought to be.
You saw how far our friends in Congress went in polluting themselves with the support of the second personage for the presidency.[8]
The Cabal did not terminate there. Several men, of no inconsiderable importance among us, like the enterprising and adventurous
character of this man, and hope to soar with him to power. Many
more through hatred to the Chief and through an impatience to
recover the reins are linking themselves with the vice-Chief, almost
without perceiving it and professing to have no other object than
to make use of him; while he knows that he is making use of them.
What this may end in, it is difficult to foresee.

Of one thing only I am sure, that in no event will I be directly or
indirectly implicated in a responsibility for the elevation or support
of either of two men, who in different senses, are in my eyes equally
unworthy of the confidence of intelligent or honest men.

Truly, My dear Sir, the prospects of our Country are not brilliant. The mass is far from sound. At headquarters a most visionary
theory presides. Depend upon it this is the fact to a great extreme.
No army,[9] no navy [10] no *active* commerce [11]—national defence, not

---

Finally, James Cheetham, Republican editor of the [New York] *American
Citizen and General Advertiser*, began a vituperative and sustained attack
against Burr in December, 1801 ("Some account of the plans and views of
aggrandisement of a faction in the City of New York, Respectfully Sub-
mitted to the Consideration of the President of the United States" [ADS,
Jefferson Papers, Library of Congress], enclosed in Cheetham to Jefferson,
December 10, 1801 [AL, Jefferson Papers, Library of Congress]; Cheetham to
Jefferson, December 29, 1801 [ALS, Jefferson Papers, Library of Congress];
American Citizen and General Advertiser, May 26, 1802; Cheetham, *A Narra-
tive of the Suppression by Col. Burr of the History of the Administration of
John Adams* [New York: Printed by Denniston and Cheetham, 1802];
Cheetham, *A View of the Political Conduct of Aaron Burr, Esq. Vice-
President of the United States* [New York: Printed by Denniston and
Cheetham, 1802]).

8. See H to Oliver Wolcott, Jr., December 16, 1800, note 1.

9. At the time Jefferson became President the United States Army consisted
of the general staff, four regiments of infantry, two regiments of artillerists
and engineers, and two troops of light dragoons, all of which totaled 4,436
men (Francis B. Heitman, *Historical Register and Dictionary of the United
States Army, From Its Organization, September 29, 1789, to March 2, 1903*
[Washington, 1903], II, 568). See also "An Act supplementary to the act to
suspend part of an act, intituled 'An act to augment the Army of the United

by arms but by embargoes,[12] prohibition of trade &c.—as little government as possible within—these are the pernicious dreams which as far and as fast as possible will be attempted to be realized. Mr. Jefferson is distressed at the codfish having latterly emigrated to the Southern Coast lest the people there should be tempted to catch them, and commerce of which we have already too much receive an accession. Be assured this is no pleasantry, but a very sober anecdote.

Among Fœderalists old errors are not cured. They also continue to dream though not quite so preposterously as their opponents. "All will be very well (say they) when the power once more gets back into Fœderal hands. The people convinced by experience of their

---

States, and for other purposes' " (2 *Stat.* 85–86 [May 14, 1800]). In his first annual message to Congress on December 8, 1801, Jefferson stated: "A statement has been formed by the Secretary of War, on mature consideration, of all the posts and stations where garrisons will be expedient, and of the number of men requisite for each garrison. The whole amount is considerably short of the present Military Establishment. . . . the only force which can be ready at every point, and competent to oppose them, is the body of neighboring citizens, as formed into a militia" (*Annals of Congress*, XI, 14). On March 16, 1802, Congress passed "An Act fixing the military peace establishment of the United States" (2 *Stat.* 132–37), which provided for an army composed of one regiment of artillerists, two regiments of infantry, and a corps of engineers, not to exceed twenty men including officers, and fixed the number of officers and men in the Army at 3,287 (Heitman, *United States Army*, II, 569).

10. On February 16, 1802, Jefferson sent to Congress a "roll of persons having employment under the United States," which contains a list of three hundred and nineteen naval offices that he had abolished (*ASP, Miscellaneous*, I, 260–319). These cutbacks were reflected in the appropriation which Congress made for the Navy for the year 1802, amounting to nine hundred thousand dollars, or less than one-third of the amount appropriated for the Navy for 1801. See "An Act making appropriations for the Navy of the United States, for the year one thousand eight hundred and one" (2 *Stat.* 122 [March 3, 1801]); "An Act making an appropriation for the support of the Navy of the United States, for the year one thousand eight hundred and two" (2 *Stat.* 178–79 [May 1, 1802]).

11. The value of United States exports had declined from $94,115,925 in 1801 to $72,483,160 in 1802. The value of imports had declined from $111,363,511 in 1801 to $76,330,000 in 1802. By 1805, however, the value of both exports and imports exceeded that of any single year when the Federalists were in office (Timothy Pitkin, *A Statistical View of the Commerce of the United States of America* . . . [New Haven: Durrie & Peck, 1835], 51, 259; Emory R. Johnson, et al., *History of Domestic and Foreign Commerce of the United States* [Washington, 1915], II, 20).

12. For Jefferson's earlier views on embargoes, see his report on "The Privileges and Restrictions on the Commerce of the United States . . . ," which he presented to the House of Representatives on December 16, 1793 (*ASP, Foreign Relations*, I, 300–04).

error will repose a *permanent* confidence in good men." Rescum
teneatis—Adieu.

Yrs. ever   A H

R King Esq

P.S. The bearer our acquaintance Wm Bayard [13] continues worthy
of high esteem & regard.   A H

13. Bayard, a New York City merchant, was a member of the firm of
Herman LeRoy, Bayard, and James McEvers, which represented the Holland
Land Company in the United States.

Account with Louis Le Guen [1]

[New York, June 6, 1802]

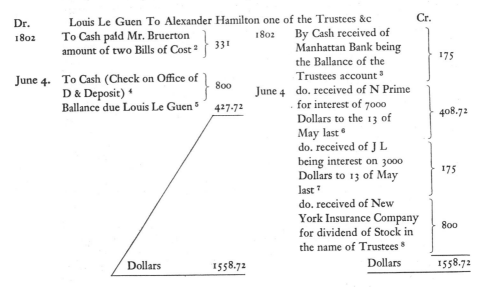

Dr.	Louis Le Guen To Alexander Hamilton one of the Trustees &c		Cr.
1802	To Cash paid Mr. Bruerton amount of two Bills of Cost [2]	331	1802 By Cash received of Manhattan Bank being the Ballance of the Trustees account [3] ... 175
June 4.	To Cash (Check on Office of D & Deposit) [4]	800	June 4 do. received of N Prime for interest of 7000 Dollars to the 13 of May last [6] ... 408.72
	Ballance due Louis Le Guen [5]	427.72	do. received of J L being interest on 3000 Dollars to 13 of May last [7] ... 175
			do. received of New York Insurance Company for dividend of Stock in the name of Trustees [8] ... 800
	Dollars	1558.72	Dollars 1558.72

E E   New York June 6. 1802
                A H [9]

ADS, Yale University Library.
    1. This document describes the management of some of the funds entrusted
by Le Guen to H, Richard Harison, and Aaron Ogden under an antenuptial
contract drawn up in February, 1799. See Le Guen to H, December 27, 1800,
note 7; "Receipt to Louis Le Guen," January 15, 1801; Ogden to H, January 15, 1801; "Indenture between Alexander Hamilton of the First Part and
Richard Harison and Aaron Agden of the Second Part," July 1, 1801; "Bond
to Richard Harison and Aaron Ogden," July 1, 1801.

2. Henry Brewerton was a New York City lawyer. For his earlier services on Le Guen's behalf, see H to Ezra L'Hommedieu, April 4, 1799, note 3.

3. See Le Guen to H, January 15, 1801.

4. See H to Jonathan Burrall, May 17, 1798.

5. An entry in H's Cash Book, 1795–1804, under the date of June 7, 1802, reads: "Interest &c (L L Guen) 427.72" (AD, Hamilton Papers, Library of Congress).

6. Although Le Guen originally intended to place ten thousand dollars at Nathaniel Prime's disposal for investment (Le Guen to H, January 15, 1801), this figure, as the document printed above indicates, was subsequently reduced to seven thousand dollars. See also "Description of Account with Louis Le Guen," June 8, 1802. In addition, the document printed above indicates that H had loaned the remaining three thousand dollars to John Laurance.

7. Laurance, a veteran of the American Revolution and one of H's closest friends, was a delegate to the Continental Congress from 1785 to 1787, a member of the House of Representatives from 1789 to 1793, United States judge for the District of New York from 1794 to 1796, and a member of the United States Senate from 1796 until his resignation in August, 1800.

8. See "Description of Account with Louis Le Guen," June 8, 1802.

9. At the bottom of this document is a receipt in H's handwriting for $424.72, dated June 7, 1802, which Louis Le Guen signed.

Description of Account with Louis Le Guen [1]

[New York, June 8, 1802]

I acknowlege to have received of Louis Le Guen Esquire in deposit for the purposes of his marriage contract with his present wife Mary Le Guen [2] the sum of Twenty Five thousand Dollars which with his consent have been disposed of as follows say Five thousand Dollars in the Stock of the New York Insurance Company standing in the name of the Trustees Five thousand Dollars in a loan to Richard Harrison [3] secured by his Bond and a mortgage on his house in the city of New York (which bond and mortgage are in my possession), five thousand Dollars in a loan to Alexander Hamilton secured by his bond and a mortgage on his house and farm at Haerlem (which bond and mortgage are in the possession of Louis Le Guen) seven thousand Dollars in a loan to Nathaniel Prime secured by a transfer to me of Stock in the Columbian Insurance Company (say one hundred and forty shares) the remaining three thousand Dollars kept at interest at my discretion [4] till further order.

A Hamilton
New York June 8, 1802

NB The Stock in the New York Insurance Company consists of one hundred shares which cost five thousand five hundred Dollars being five hundred Dollars more than are due to the fund for the marriage Contract. I have also in my hands belonging to the said Louis Le Guen a bond of Aaron Burr conditioned for the payment of six thousand seven hundred & thirty Dollars and thirteen Cents secured by the Assignment of certain leases also two promissory notes of the said Aaron which are included in the amount of the said bond.[5]

A H[6]

ADS, Hamilton Papers, Library of Congress.

1. For background to this document, see "Account with Louis Le Guen," June 6, 1802.

2. For this contract, see Le Guen to H, December 27, 1800, note 7.

3. Although no documents relating to this transaction have been found, it was obviously similar to the mortgage which H had obtained from his fellow trustees. See "Indenture between Alexander Hamilton of the First Part and Richard Harison and Aaron Ogden of the Second Part," July 1, 1801; "Bond to Richard Harison and Aaron Ogden," July 1, 1801.

4. See "Account with Louis Le Guen," June 6, 1802, notes 5 and 7.
An entry in H's Cash Book, 1795–1804, under the heading "Louis Le Guen" and dated October 11, 1802, reads: "This sum paid him on acct of Insurance Stock   200   order to received interest of Prime" (AD, Hamilton Papers, Library of Congress).

5. See Le Guen to H, December 27, 1800; "Receipt to Louis Le Guen," January 15, 1801, notes 2 and 3.

6. H wrote opposite this paragraph: "surrendered & a new acknowlegement given the 20th of May 1803. AH."
Opposite the end of this paragraph Le Guen wrote: "$—6730. Due a la dite Epoque du 8. Juin 1802. Non Compris—Les interets *due*, et Cinq % le futurs."

From John B. Graves [1]

New York, June 8, 1802. Requests Hamilton's opinion concerning his claim for reimbursement on a premium that he had paid to insure his cargo aboard the schooner *Alert*.[2]

ALS, Montague Collection, MS Division, New York Public Library.

1. Graves was a New York City merchant.

2. For the full text of this letter, related documents, and an explanation of their contents, see Goebel, *Law Practice*, II, 724–30.

From Philip Schuyler [1]

Junction of Canada with wood
Creek [Verona, New York] Tuesday [June] [2] 15 1802

My Dear Sir

On Sunday a letter from Mrs. Church [3] announced the happy delivery of My Dear Eliza, and that She and the child,[4] were in as good health as could be expected and wished for. On this Event, I must Sincerely congratulate you and her. May I soon learn that she is perfectly restored.

It is more than probable that soon after my return to albany I shall have the pleasure of seeing [you] at New York.

The very heavy rains which fell in the two preceeding weeks to this, has injured the country to a very extensive Amount, and retarded the progress of the works for improving the navigation of Wood Creek. I hope nevertheless to finish one lock and Its dam, by the 10th of next month, when I shall return to Albany—passing in my boat thro the lock.[5]

I have been so actively employed since my arrival here on the 2d Instant, that I enjoy perfect health.

We have excellent Mutton here, and as fine and fat Salmon as ever was dished, and I believe as cheap as cod at the New York Market. I gave half a dollar for a very fine one weighing more than 19lt. They are taken four miles and an half from this.

You My beloved Eliza & the Children all participate in my warmest Affections.

Adieu My Dear Sir   Most truly yours   Ph: Schuyler

General Hamilton

ALS, Lloyd W. Smith Collection, Morristown National Historical Park, Morristown, New Jersey.

1. For background to this letter, see Schuyler to H, March 28, April 5, 1802.
2. Schuyler wrote "July 15." The letter is postmarked "Albany June 21."
3. Angelica Church.
4. H's last child, a boy named Philip, was born on June 2, 1802.

5. Schuyler was president of the Western Inland Lock Navigation Company, which was incorporated by the New York legislature in 1792 to facilitate water transportation from the Hudson River to Lake Ontario and Lake Seneca. See Théophile Cazenove to Egbert Benson and H, May 29, 1797, note 3; Schuyler to H, April 5, 1802.

From Charles Cotesworth Pinckney

Charleston [South Carolina] July 2d: 1802

Dear Sir:

My Brother [1] is desirous that his son who in the late Army was one of my Aids [2] should qualify himself for the profession of the Law: for this purpose he has been some time studying with Mr: De Saussure [3] of this State. Our City has been for several years past fatal to many strangers who have attempted to spend their summer in it; my nephew has not been here in that season since his return from Europe, on this account my Brother is unwilling that he should be here this summer, but intends that he should spend six Months at the Northward; and as he is informed the practice in the Courts of Law & Equity in New York, is very similar to the practice in our state, he wishes him to study for that term in the office of some gentleman of Eminence at the Bar in New York. His desire was that he should have been under your auspices, but I told him I understood you confined yourself totally to the business of a Counsellor, and did not practice as an attorney,[4] but that Mr: Troup [5] & many other eminent gentlemen did, that I however would write to you by my nephew and if you did not take Students into your office, that I would request you to place him in one where he would be, if diligent, much benefitted. Whatever fee is customary or proper on such an occasion my Brother will transmitt as soon as you inform me of it.

I enclose Mr: Troup's Letter to you which we had before us in Decr: 1798, and which being confidential, I obtained, after the decease of our ever lamented friend, to transmitt to you.[6]

The Vice President when here & in Georgia was received with great politeness & hospitality both by federalists & antifederalists.[7] It was a compliment to the office. I was at a plantation a considerable distance from his rout, & did not see him.

My friend Mr: De Saussure with whom you are acquainted, spends his summer in the northern States and can inform you accurately of every thing relating to this State.

Mrs: Pinckney unites with me in best respects to Mrs: Hamilton and I always am

Your affectionate friend   Charles Cotesworth Pinckney

Genl: Hamilton

ALS, Hamilton Papers, Library of Congress.

1. Thomas Pinckney.

2. Thomas Pinckney, Jr., who was twenty-two years old in 1802, was a lieutenant in the First Regiment of Artillerists and Engineers and an aide to Charles Cotesworth Pinckney from 1799 to 1801.

3. Henry William De Saussure, a Federalist and lawyer from Charleston, who had been director of the United States Mint in 1795, was a member of the lower house of the General Assembly of South Carolina in 1802.

4. The functions of counsel and attorney were distinct, although it was possible for a lawyer to act in both capacities. The attorney's responsibilities were primarily procedural and involved the preparation of a case for trial. The counsel was retained by the attorney and was responsible for arguing the case in court and handling pleadings between the verdict and the judgment.

In 1795, when H resigned as Secretary of the Treasury and returned to the practice of law, he at first acted as his own attorney. Gradually, as his practice grew, he relinquished the role of attorney and served primarily as counsel. See Goebel, *Law Practice*, II, 1–28.

5. Robert Troup, a New York City and Albany lawyer, had been a close friend of H since the time when they had been students at King's College. A veteran of the American Revolution, Troup served briefly as secretary of the Board of War and was secretary of the Board of Treasury in 1779 and 1780. In 1786 he was a member of the New York Assembly, and from 1796 to 1798 he was United States judge for the District of New York. Troup was involved in land speculation in western New York and was associated with Charles Williamson in the development of the Pulteney Purchase in the Genesee country.

6. Letter not found.

In November and December, 1798, H, Pinckney, James McHenry, and George Washington were in Philadelphia to make plans for the Army. See H to McHenry, November 9, 1798; H to Elizabeth Hamilton, November 10, 1798.

7. In April, 1802, Aaron Burr made a trip to Charleston to visit his daughter Theodosia, who was the wife of Joseph Alston, a lawyer, planter, and member of the lower house of the South Carolina legislature.

On April 16 Burr excused himself from presiding over the Senate (*Annals of Congress*, XI, 264) and made plans to leave Washington on April 20. On his way south he was met on April 27 at Raleigh, North Carolina, by a group of "Federal Republican gentlemen" who "saluted him with SIX GUNS, emblematical of the six states which supported Mr. Burr, when the election of President of the United States was finally decided in the House of Representatives" ([New York] *American Citizen and General Advertiser*, May 14, 1802). From Raleigh, Burr passed through Fayetteville and Lumberton, in which he was reported to have "accepted of a dinner from Mr. Peter John Blink[le]y, at which there were one or two federalists" ([New York] *American Citizen and General Advertiser*, May 28, 29, June 2, 1802). On May 6 Burr arrived in Charleston (*The* [Charleston] *Carolina Gazette*, May 13, 1802). On the same day Robert Troup wrote: "The real object of the visit is well understood, and it is supposed to occasion at least a sigh to Jefferson" (King, *The Life and Correspondence of Rufus King*, IV, 120–21). On May 13 Burr attended a public dinner held at the Carolina Coffee-House, and from Charleston he made a side trip to Savannah, Georgia, where he arrived on May 20 and was given a public reception (*The* [Charleston] *Carolina Gazette*, Supplement, May 27, 1802). On May 27 the following article appeared in *The* [Charleston] *Carolina Gazette:* "The idea of party—of who was federalist, or who was republican—was on this occasion forgotten; to honour the second chief magistrate of our country, was the 'order of the day.'" On June 6 Troup again wrote: "Burr is now at Savannah doing what he can *to render Jefferson more popular and promote his re-election.* . . . we have reason to think that Burr has been caballing with some of our friends to the southward" (King, *The Life and Correspondence of Rufus King*, IV, 135–36). Burr left Savannah on May 25 ([Savannah] *Georgia Gazette*, May 27, 1802) and returned to Charleston. On June 17 he sailed for New York City on the brig *Comet* accompanied by his daughter (*The* [Charleston] *Carolina Gazette*, June 17, 1802), and he arrived in New York on June 23.

From Thomas Truxtun [1]

Perth Amboy [New Jersey] 10th July 1802.

Dear Sir

I pray you to accept a Copy of the medal voted me by Congress [2] as a Small token of the great Respect and esteem with which I have the honor to be

Dear Sir   Your very obt. st.   Thomas Truxtun

Honorable General Hamilton
New York

ALS, Hamilton Papers, Library of Congress.
    1. Truxtun was appointed a captain in the United States Navy in 1794 and ranked fifth among the six captains appointed at that time. During the undeclared war with France, he commanded the U.S. frigate *Constellation* and a squadron of ships in the Caribbean, where he won two important naval engagements against the French ships *L'Insurgente* and *La Vengeance.* After peace with France was established in 1800, Truxtun was retained as one of nine captains provided for in the Naval Peace Establishment of 1801. On March 3, 1802, Truxtun resigned from the Navy as a result of a disagreement with Secretary of the Navy Robert L. Smith (Truxtun to H, March 26, 1802).
    For Truxtun's earlier career in the Navy, see Henry Knox to H, June 23,

1794; Silas Talbot to H, January 15, May 13, 1799; Benjamin Stoddert to H, May 3, July 19, 1799.

2. See Truxtun to H, March 26, 1802, note 14.

From Gilbert McClaghry

July 15, 1802. States that he is destitute and asks Hamilton to help him collect the commutation and ration money of his brother, John McClaghry,[1] who died while serving in the Continental Army.

ALS, Hamilton Papers, Library of Congress.

1. John McClaghry (McLaughry) became an ensign in the Fifth New York Regiment on November 21, 1776. He was taken prisoner at Fort Montgomery on October 6, 1777, released in 1778, and became a lieutenant on March 30, 1780. He was transferred to the Second New York Regiment on January 1, 1781, and died on October 27, 1781.

Account with Ezra Weeks [1]

[New York, July 16, 1802]

Dr		Genl. Alexander Hamilton in Account with E Weeks		Cr
1802			1802	
To Balance of Acct. of work & Materials rend. up to 15th. may	£ 158.14. 1	May 27th. By Cash £ 120.[2] July 3 Balance	276. 3. 6	
" Acct. of work & Materials up to July 3d	197.13.11			
" Danl. Hitchock [3] Bill of Boards	3.13.			
" Aymar & Prides [4] Bill of Joist	1.19.			
" John Aymars do of Do and Shingles	6. 3. 6			
" A. Freelons [5] Bill of Fans & Side lights	28.			
	£ 396. 3. 6		£ 396. 3. 6	

1802
July 3 To Balance 276. 3. 6

Received New York July 16. 1802
Received of A Hamilton Three
hundred & Ninety six Dollars
& 83 Cents on account.[6]

E. Weeks

The Amount of Mr. J B: Dashes' Bill was Credited on a Statement rendered May 15.[7]

AD, Hamilton Papers, Library of Congress.

1. Weeks submitted this bill to H for work he had done as builder of the Grange. See the introductory note to Philip Schuyler to H, July 17, 1800.

2. An entry in H's Cash Book, 1795–1804, under the date of May 27, 1802, reads: "paid E Weeks (Grange) 300" (AD, Hamilton Papers, Library of Congress).

3. Daniel Hitchcock was a lumber merchant in New York City.

4. John Aymar and John and Peter Pride owned a lumberyard in New York City.

5. Abraham Freelon was a fanlight maker in New York City.

6. This receipt is in H's handwriting and is signed by Weeks. In H's Cash Book, 1795–1804, under the date of July 18, 1802, H wrote: "Expence (Weeks) 396.83" (AD, Hamilton Papers, Library of Congress). In 1802 three hundred and ninety-six dollars equaled approximately one hundred and fifty-eight pounds. H's payment was therefore equal to the balance of his account with Weeks on May 15 as stated in the first item in this bill.

For subsequent payments to Weeks, amounting to four hundred dollars, see H's Cash Book, 1795–1804, under the dates of January 1, 1803, and February 1, 1804.

7. See Dash's account in H's Cash Book, 1795–1804 (AD, Hamilton Papers, Library of Congress). See also H's Cash Book, 1795–1804, for the following receipt: "Received New York April 10th. 1802 from Alexr. Hamilton Esqr two hundred and fifty dollars on account for John B. Dash Jr.   John G. Carpender." John B. Dash, Jr., was a New York City ironmonger.

To ————

[*July 23, 1802*. The description of this letter in the dealer's catalogue reads: "enclosing a letter of introduction [1] to 'Mr. Lowel,[2] Son of Judge Lowel deceased, who is a very respected member of the Essex Junto'[3] & mentioning a financial matter." *Letter not found.*]

ALS, sold at Swann Auction Galleries, April 27, 1944, Lot 132.

1. Letter not found.

2. John Lowell, Jr., a Federalist lawyer from Newburyport, represented Boston in the Massachusetts General Court from 1798 to 1800.

3. John Lowell, a Federalist lawyer in Newburyport who moved to Boston, was a member of the Continental Congress in 1782, 1783, and 1784, a member of the commission to settle the boundary dispute between Massachusetts and New York in 1784, United States judge for the District of Massachusetts from 1789 to 1801, and chief judge of the First Circuit under the Judiciary Act of 1801 from 1801 until his death on May 6, 1802. For Lowell and the Essex Junto, see H to Benjamin Stoddert, June 6, 1800, note 7.

From Rufus King

[*London, July 23, 1802*. King's description of this letter reads: "General Hamilton. Determination to return home &c." [1] *Letter not found.*]

1. Rufus King's "Memorandum of private Letters, &c., dates & persons from 1796 to Augt 1802," owned by Mr. James G. King, New York City.

From Rufus King

London August 5 1802

Dear Sir

I have received your obliging letter in duplicate of June [1]—enclosed I have now the pleasure to send you a copy of my letter to the Secretary of State resigning my mission, and requesting to be relieved in season to return home in may next.[2]

In a few days I purpose to avail my self of the leave of temporary absence which I have received [3] to visit the continent. My plan is to go to Holland, and thence thro' the Netherlands to Paris, whose collections of various sorts, excite my curiosity more than either the men or systems which chance at present to prevail there—the former are worthy to be seen and admired, the latter may be as well, perhaps better, understood at a Distance.

With sincere Regards   I am most faithfully yr. ob. ser

Rufus King

General Hamilton
New york

ALS, Hamilton Papers, Library of Congress.
1. H to King, June 3, 1802.
2. Copy, Hamilton Papers, Library of Congress; LS, RG 59, Despatches from United States Ministers to Great Britain, 1791–1906, Vol. 10, January 9, 1802–May 14, 1803, National Archives.
3. See King to H, April 8, 1802, note 8.

To Ernst Frederich von Walterstorff [1]

[*New York, August 5, 1802.* On April 20, 1803, Walterstorff wrote to Hamilton and referred to "Your favr. of the 5th. August." *Letter not found.*]

1. Walterstorff was governor general of the Danish West Indies from 1787 to July 25, 1794. On leaving office he went to the United States where he remained until 1796, at which time he returned to Denmark. He served again as governor general from February 16, 1802, to February 16, 1803. See also *New-York Evening Post*, March 9, 1802.

Egbert Benson, Richard Harison, and Alexander Hamilton to Charles Williamson [1]

New York, August 6, 1802. Propose that Williamson go to England to settle his dispute with William Hornby and Patrick Colquhoun.

Copy, Rochester Historical Society, Rochester, New York.
1. Benson, Harison, and H were Williamson's attorneys. See William Hornby to H, September 15, 1801.

Benson, a Federalist, was attorney general of New York from 1777 to 1788, a member of the New York Assembly from 1777 to 1781 and in 1788, a member of the Continental Congress from 1784 to 1788, a member of the House of Representatives from 1789 to 1793, and an associate justice on the New York Supreme Court from 1794 to 1801. In 1801 John Adams appointed him chief judge of the Second Circuit of the United States Circuit Courts.

Harison was a delegate to the New York Ratifying Convention in 1788, a member of the New York Assembly in 1788 and 1789, United States attorney for the District of New York from 1789 to 1802, and recorder for New York City from 1798 to 1801.

To Albert Gallatin

[*New York, August 6, 1802.* On August 13, 1802, Gallatin wrote to Hamilton: "I had the honor to receive your letter of the 6th instt." *Letter not found.*]

From Rufus King [1]

London August 6th. 1802

Dear Sir

I wrote to you two days ago [2] by a private ship, as the Packet goes in a day or two I avail myself of the Opportunity to inform you that I have sent to the Secy of State my Resignation, and requested to be relieved in time to return home in April next. As there is reason to apprehend that we may be at war with all the barbary powers, as well as morocco I have asked for a Passage home in a Frigate or other public vessel; in case this accomodation be refused, I have decreed my Agent Mr Low [3] to ingage & send me a vessel from New york.[4]

The grounds or reason of the morocco war is said to be our refusal to allow the morocco merchants & Govt. to supply Tripoli with corn; [5] the same claim has been made & refused by our consul at Tunis,[6] and may be followed by a similar Conduct as has been adopted by Morocco. Add to this, intelligence is just in (how authentic I am at present unable to determine) that two of our merchant ships have been carried into Algiers.[7] This Regency is elated with the late success of its cruisers against the portuguese,[8] and is likely to incur a formidable attack from France, which certainly has the prospect of embarking a powerful army in the Ports of Spain to attack and destroy Algiers! [9]

with sincere respect   yr's &c   R King

I am going next week to Holland, thence thro the low Countries to Spa on my way to Paris where we shall spend four or six weeks & return at the meeting of Parliament in Novr. How happy shd. we be if you & Mrs. H. could be of our party. I shd. add that I have leave to make this Excursion.

ALS, Hamilton Papers, Library of Congress.
    1. For background to this letter, see King to H, August 5, 1802.
    2. King was mistaken; his letter to H is dated August 5, 1802.
    3. Nicholas Low, a New York City merchant and land speculator, had been a director of the Bank of New York and of the Society for Establishing Useful Manufactures. He was also director of the New York Office of Discount and Deposit of the Bank of the United States. From 1793 to 1801 he was supervisor of the revenue for New York.
    4. See King to James Madison, private letter of August 5, 1802 (King, *The Life and Correspondence of Rufus King*, IV, 156). See also Low to King, October 23, 1802 (King, *The Life and Correspondence of Rufus King*, IV, 200).
    5. When James Simpson, United States consul for the Kingdom of Morocco, refused to issue passports requested by the Emperor of Morocco for two Tripolitan vessels to carry cargoes of wheat from Gibraltar to Tripoli, which the United States was blockading, the Emperor on June 22, 1802, expelled Simpson and declared war on the United States. On July 26, 1802, the Emperor invited Simpson to return to his post, and peace was temporarily

restored (*ASP, Foreign Relations*, II, 465, 466; *Naval Documents, Barbary Powers*, II, 181–83, 184, 231).

6. On April 26, 1802, William Eaton, United States consul for Tunis, wrote to James Cathcart, former United States consul to Tripoli, that he had refused "to countenance his [the Bey of Tunis] commercial intercourse with Tripoli. . . . I . . . forbade my secretary filling any more passports for Tunisian Cruisers" (*Naval Documents, Barbary Powers*, II, 134).

7. See King to H, second letter of August 6, 1802.

8. King is referring to the capture of the *Cisne*, a forty-four gun Portuguese frigate, by an Algerian vessel in May, 1802, while Algiers was at war with Portugal. See *Naval Documents, Barbary Powers*, II, 155, 156, 163, 173, 180). 180).

9. On September 8, 1802, Charles Pinckney, United States Minister Plenipotentiary to Spain, wrote to Madison: ". . . I am to inform you I have this day received intelligence from Algiers that France by sending some 74 Gun ships & other armed Vessels to that Place with a Plenipotentiary on board has forced the Dey to submit to such Terms as Bonaparte thought proper to prescribe . . . at the time the French Envoy demanded & the Dey was obliged to submit to these Terms, that the Envoy told him he was charged by Bonaparte to inform him, if ever Algiers committed the least outrage or in any degree insulted the flag or injured the commerce of France, he would erase his name from the list of nations" (ALS, RG 59, Despatches from United States Ministers to Spain, 1792–1906, Vol. 6, June 11, 1795–April 2, 1803, National Archives).

From Rufus King [1]

London Aug 6. 1802

After further enquiry, I annex little credit to the notice posted at Loyds', that two american vessels had been carried into Algiers. Two vessels the Franklin morris master, and the Rose (master not known) said to be of Philadelphia, are reported to have been taken by the cruisers of morocco or some other of the Barbary Powers. These are also the vessels which are mentioned at Loyds as having been carried into Algiers.[2]

Having no late intelligence, which affords reason to believe that Algiers is disposed immediately to break with the U S, I am inclined to suppose these captures, if made, have been made by some of the other pirates.

The Project of France is to embark her Army going agt. Algiers in the spanish ports, and it is quite probable that Spain will be called upon to assist in defraying the Expences of marching and embarking, as well as in transporting this army to Africa, notwithstanding she has as we understand very recently expended a large sum to confirm her Peace with this Regency.

If the fortune of France prevail on the Shores of Africa, these regencies will become more reasonable, if they be not extirpated. A part of Bonapartes Egyptian Plan, was to have colonized the Shores of Africa, and although the acquiring the treasure, which is said (tho I suspect erroneously) to be accumulated there, are assigned as the leading motives of the Expedition, it is more likely to be a step towards the accomplishment of the Project in which the chief Consul was foiled in Egypt.

very faithfully yrs   Rufus King

ALS, Hamilton Papers, Library of Congress.
1. For background to this letter, see King to H, August 5, first letter of August 6, 1802.
2. On June 17, 1802, a Tripolitan corsair captured the brig *Franklin,* under Captain Andrew Morris, which belonged to the Philadelphia merchant firm of Joseph Sommerl (Summerl) and Israel Brown and which had sailed from Marseilles on June 8 for the West Indies. The *Franklin's* crew was sent to Tripoli, and the vessel was sold at auction on July 8, 1802, in Tunis. The *Rose,* which was also captured, was released (*Naval Documents, Barbary Powers,* II, 176–78, 187, 194–97, 208).

To Louis André Pichon [1]

New York Aug 6. 1802

Sir

At the request of Capt Du Buisson, I have the honor to send you two documents one of which is the copy of an Arbitration Bond between Mr. Roget and himself, the other the copy of an award, which has been made pursuant to the submission.

As Mr. Roget makes difficulties about the performance of the award (though given unanimously and under circumstances very obligatory upon his candour) Capt du Buisson is anxious that the result may be known to you—in the hope that it may interest your good offices to secure him satisfaction out of the fund still remaining of the proceeds of the Peggy and her Cargo.

He desires it to be understood that he opposes as far as the law will permit the payment in future of any part of that fund to

Mr. Roget or to any other person except himself 'till he shall have been satisfied agreeably to his rights under the award.

I regretted very much that the expectation you gave us of a visit to this City was not fulfilled. It would have given Mrs. Hamilton & myself particular pleasure to have received Madame Pichon and yourself at our Country seat [2] where we can promise you at least cool and wholesome air.[3]

With much esteem & consideration   I have the honor to be   Sir Yr. Obed servt   A Hamilton

Mr. De Pichon &c

ALS, Hamilton Papers, Library of Congress.
    1. This letter concerns the case of *Joseph Buisson* v *Brigantine Peggy, libel,* which was related to the earlier case of *United States* v *Schooner Peggy, Joseph Buisson, claimant* (H to Jedediah Huntington, November 12, 1801; Robert Smith to H, November 20, 1801; H to Aaron Burr, April 1, 1802; H to Pichon, May 12, 1802; H to Simeon Baldwin, May 1, 1802; Baldwin to H, May 8, 1802). While the case of the schooner *Peggy* was being heard on appeal before the United States Circuit Court for Connecticut, William Cushing, associate justice of the Supreme Court of the United States, ordered an appraisal of the schooner and its cargo. Subsequently, Isaac Roget, a New York City merchant, deposited a security with the court for the amount of the appraisal, and the vessel was restored to Buisson. Buisson sailed the *Peggy* from New London to New York City, where he arrived on August 9, 1800. Meanwhile, Roget had sold the vessel at auction to John Blagge, who in turn had sold it to Jacob Furtado. Both Blagge and Furtado were New York City merchants. Buisson, a part-owner of the vessel, brought suit in the United States District Court for the Southern District of New York asking the court to prevent the *Peggy* from sailing unless he received a security on the vessel. On May 26, 1802, the Court attached the *Peggy* and proceeded to trial. The case papers for this trial are incomplete (RG 21, United States District Court for the Southern District of New York. Case Files. *Joseph Buisson or Libellants* v *The Brigantine Peggy,* National Archives).
    2. The Grange. See the introductory note to Philip Schuyler to H, July 17, 1800.
    3. This letter is endorsed: "Repue Le 12." Letter not found.

To the Editor of the Evening Post [1]

New-York, August 10, 1802.

Sir,

Finding that a story long since propagated under circumstances, which it was expected would soon consign it to oblivion, (and by which I have been complimented at the expence of Generals Washington and La Fayette) has of late been revived and has acquired a degree of importance by being repeated in different publications as well as in Europe as America—it becomes a duty to counteract its currency and influence by an explicit disavowal.[2]

The story imports in substance, that General La Fayette, with the approbation or connivance of General Washington, ordered me, as the officer who was to command the attack on a British redoubt, in the course of the siege of York-Town, to put to death all those of the enemy who should happen to be taken in the redoubt; and that through motives of humanity I forbore to execute the order.

Positively and unequivocally I declare, that no such nor similar order, nor any intimation nor hint resembling it, was ever by me received or understood to have been given.

It is needless to enter into an explanation of some occurrences on the occasion alluded to, which may be conjectured to have given rise to the calumny. It is enough to say that they were entirely unconnected with any act of either of the Generals who have been accused.

With esteem, I am, Sir,   Your obedient servant,   A. Hamilton

New York Evening Post, August 11, 1802.

1. William Coleman, editor of the *New-York Evening Post*, was a Federalist lawyer originally from Boston who had practiced in Greenfield, Massachusetts, and served in the Massachusetts General Court in 1795 and 1796. Following major financial losses as a result of speculation in the Yazoo lands, he moved to New York City to practice law. In early 1800 H secured Coleman's appointment as clerk of the circuit of the Supreme Court of New York State (H to John Jay, March 4, 1800; Jay to H, March 13, 1800). In November, 1801, Coleman became the editor of the *New-York Evening Post*, which H had helped to found.

H's letter was preceded by the following statement: "The following letter will doubtless receive an insertion in the several newspapers in the United States. It was not without much regret we once saw the slander which is here meant to be destroyed, find its way into one of our most respectable public prints, from the *Anti-Jacobin Review*—a work of great literary merit, but in whatever relates to this country discoloured with gross, unjustifiable misrepresentation."

2. In 1788 William Gordon, an English clergyman who supported American independence and lived in America from 1779 to 1786, published a history of the American Revolution in which he wrote: "The marquis [de Lafayette] said to gen. Washington—'The troops should retaliate on the British, for the cruelties they have practised.' The general answered—'You have full command, and may order as you please.' The marquis ordered the party to remember New London [burned by the British on September 6, 1781], and to retaliate, by putting the men in the redoubt to the sword after having carried it. The

men marched to the assault with unloaded arms, at dark on the night of the 14th [October, 1781], passed the abbatis and palisades, and attacking on all sides carried the redoubt in a few minutes. . . . Lieut. col. [John] Laurens personally took the commanding officer. The colonel's humanity and that of the Americans so overcame their resentments, that they spared the British. . . . Col. Hamilton, who conducted the enterprise with much address and intrepidity, in his report to the marquis mentioned to the honor of his detachment—'that, incapable of imitating examples of barbarity, and forgetting recent provocations, they spared every man that ceased to resist'" (*The History of the Rise, Progress and Establishment, of the Independence of the United States of America: Including an Account of the Late War; And of the Thirteen Colonies, From Their Origin to That Period*, IV [London: Printed for the Author, 1788], 192–93). For H's report to Lafayette, see H to Lafayette, October 15, 1781. In 1802 John Wood, a native of Scotland who had emigrated to the United States in 1800, revived this story in a pamphlet in which he attempted to discredit John Adams's administration. See Wood, *The history of the administration of John Adams* (New York: Barlas and Ward, Naphtali Judah, 1802).

During the American Revolution, H had challenged Gordon to a duel because of statements Gordon had made concerning H's political views. See John Brooks to H, July 4, 1779; Francis Dana to H, July 25, August 25, 1779; H to Gordon, August 10, September 5, December 10, 1779; Gordon to H, August 25, September 23, 1779; David Henley to H, September 1, 22, 1779; George Washington to H, May 2, 1780.

To Louis André Pichon

[*Washington, August 12, 1802.* The endorsement on Hamilton to Pichon, August 6, 1802, reads: "Repue Le 12." *Letter not found.*]

From Albert Gallatin [1]

Treasury department Aug. 13th 1802

Sir

I had the honor to receive your letter of the 6th instt.,[2] and have directed the documents therein enclosed to be filed with the other papers relative to the French prize "Peggy."

The enclosed papers[3] will show, however, that the President does not intend that any further payments should be made, out of the Treasury, on account of that vessel; and that, even in case of such payment being made, Mr Pichon will be authorized to receive the amount, unless Capt Buisson shall revoke his former powers, & shall transmit an instrument to that effect to this department.

For the information of your client, it may be proper to add, that the order of distribution of the circuit court for the district of Connecticut, bears date the 15th April 1801, so far as relate to the moiety of the captors, & the 23d do. for the share of the United States. This has been paid to Mr Pichon, as attorney of Buisson & Roget, not under the treaty, but by virtue of the decree of the supreme court. The other moiety amounting to Drs. 9,139$^{93}/_{100}$ was, on the 20th Ap. 1801, paid by S. Baldwin clerk of the aforesaid court to Joseph Howland agent for the officers and crew of the United States ship "Trumbull."

I have the honor to be with respect   Sir   Your obedt. Servt.

Albert Gallatin

Alexander Hamilton Esqre
New York

ALS, Hamilton Papers, Library of Congress.
   1. For background to this letter, see H to Jedediah Huntington, November 12, 1801; Robert Smith to H, November 20, 1801; H to Aaron Burr, April 1, 1802, note 4; H to Louis André Pichon, May 10, August 6, 1802; H to Simeon Baldwin, May 1, 1802; Baldwin to H, May 8, 1802.
   2. Letter not found.
   3. Gallatin to James Madison, June 9, 1802 (copy, Hamilton Papers, Library of Congress); Madison to Pichon, July 19, 1802 (copy, Hamilton Papers, Library of Congress); "List of Powers of Attorney, by which L. A. Pichon, is authorized to receive the proceeds of the French prize Schooner 'Peggy' Lodged in the Treasury of the United States" (D, undated, Hamilton Papers, Library of Congress).

To Oliver Wolcott, Junior [1]

Grange [New York] August 14. 1802

My Dear Sir

When you were last in Town I promised to communicate to you the outline of a project by which I think you may enter upon a career of business beneficial to yourself and friends. My almost constant attendance at Court ever since you were here has retarded its communication, which I shall now make.

Let a commercial Capital be formed to consist of 100 000 Dollars divided into shares of 1000 Dollars each.

1/10   A subscriber to pay in Cash *one tenth* of his subscription and for the residue 7 ℔ Centum per annum. It will then be his interest to pay up as soon as he can.

The subscribers to form a Partnership under the firm of Oliver Wolcott & Co., Oliver Wolcott alone to have the signature of the firm and the active management of the affairs of the Company; with an allowance of 1500 Dollars per annum out of the profits for the trouble of management besides his share of profits as a Partner.

Oliver Wolcott and two others of the partners to form a board of Direction, to *plan* &c.

Clerks and all incidental expences to be paid out of the fund.

The objects of the Company—

1 Agencies for purchase & sales of lands *Stock* &c.

2 Factorage of Cargoes consigned on commission purchases of goods on Commission &c in brief "the business of a Commission Merchant merely."

3 Purchases at Auction and sales of the articles purchased.

4 Loans of money on deposit of goods with a right if not redeemed in time to sell on commission—*Perhaps*

Speculative enterprises in navigation and com⟨merce⟩ to be excluded.

In a company thus formed under your management I should be willing to become a partner for from 5 to 10 000 Ds. and I have no doubt that the Capital will be readily formed of confidential and trust worthy characters who would ensure great credit to the House.

I am also confident that when it should be known in Europe that certain characters were of the Company, it would attract a good portion of profitable employment.

I will enter into no further detail. If the project impresses you favourably, come to New York & we will give it form & finish & prepare for the Execution.[2] Do not lightly reject it.

Yrs.   very truly   A Hamilton

Oliver Wolcott Esq

ALS, Connecticut Historical Society, Hartford.
   1. Following his resignation as Secretary of the Treasury on December 31,

1801, Wolcott served as a judge for the Second Circuit of the United States from February, 1801, to March, 1802, when the position was abolished by "An Act to repeal certain acts respecting the organization of the Courts of the United States; and for other purposes" (2 *Stat.* 132 [March 8, 1802]).

2. On February 3, 1803, Wolcott signed an agreement which was similar to that proposed by H and under which James Watson, Moses Rogers, Archibald Gracie, and William W. Woolsey, all merchants of New York City, were "to form a commercial Partnership, and to transact business in the manner hereafter mentioned, under the style and firm of OLIVER WOLCOTT & COMPANY." According to the terms of this agreement; each partner contributed fifteen thousand dollars, except Wolcott, whose share "shall be advanced in whole or in part, when it shall suit his convenience." Wolcott, as the managing partner, received three thousand dollars as salary as well as one-fifth of the annual profits. The business of the firm included: "the execution of all Agencies and Commissions for the purchase or sale of Merchandize, Stock or other property: Purchases and Sales in the market of the United States: Loans of money on deposits of goods for sale: and generally all money negociations for good and lawful considerations: but that no concern in navigation or for the importation or exportation of Goods or Merchandize to or from foreign Countries, is to be undertaken on account of the Company, without the consent of all the Parties" (DS, Connecticut Historical Society, Hartford).

On February 7, 1803, Wolcott wrote from his home in Litchfield, Connecticut, to George Cabot: ". . . I have determined on a removal to New York immediately. My family will remain in the country till next autumn. To this change of situation I am impelled by a kind of *necessity.* I have been contented here; but my property is not sufficient to employ my time, or to furnish the means of educating and providing for my family as I wish. This State furnishes no employments in which I can engage, except those of a public nature, and with those I have been satiated.

"The terms on which I have concluded to enter upon a new career of active business are beneficial and as safe as possible; and the gentlemen associated with me are all men of ample fortunes and respectability. Where prior engagements and connections do not interfere, I hope to experience the patronage and encouragement of my acquaintance." (Henry Cabot Lodge, *Life and Letters of George Cabot* [Boston, 1878; reprinted New York, 1974], 329–30).

Wolcott's company was not successful, and it was dissolved in 1805 (Wolcott to Sir Francis Baring and Company, August 6, 1805 [LC, in Wolcott's handwriting, MS Division, New York Public Library]). The account books of the company may be found in the New-York Historical Society, New York City.

From Philip Schuyler [1]

Albany August 19 1802

My Dear Sir

On Monday evening I returned to my family.

Days of constant activity, and some of fatigue were succeeded by nights of sound sleep. This with a good appetite, and good food to satisfy it, afforded me as good health as I ever enjoyed, and which I still retain.

My labours have been crowned with Success & one of the Locks in Wood Creek is contemplated, a Second greatly advanced and a third will be compleated in the present season as also two Small Sluices. These are all the works contemplated in the present year, but to compleat the navigation to the Oneida Lake four more Locks must be constructed, preparations are making for two, and directions ought to be given to provide the materials for the other two.

How is your health, that of my Beloved Eliza, and my Dear GrandChildren? I hope all well, embrace them tenderly for me, they share with you in my warmest affections, and in those of Mrs. Schuyler. Catherine [2] is either at Still water,[3] Ballston [4] or Lake George.

If Mr Jefferson has really encouraged that wretch Callender to Vent his calumny against you, and his predecessors in office,[5] the head of the former must be abominably wicked, and weak. I feel for the reputation of my Country which must suffer, when Its Citizens can be brought to Elevate such a Character to the first office in the republic. May Indulgent heaven avert the Evils, with which we are threatened from such a ruler, and the miscreants who guide his councils.

Adieu My Dear Sir, may you enjoy health and happiness, and that peace of mind which results from a rectitude of Conduct.

I am Ever most affectionately Yours   Ph: Schuyler

Alexander Hamilton Esq

ALS, Hamilton Papers, Library of Congress.
    1. For background to this letter, see Schuyler to H, April 5, July 15, 1802.
    2. Catherine Schuyler was Schuyler's youngest child. In 1802 she was twenty-one years old.
    3. Stillwater, Saratoga County, New York.
    4. Ballston Spa, Saratoga County, New York.
    5. James Thomson Callender, a native of Scotland, fled to the United States after he was indicted for sedition in January, 1793, because of his pamphlet *The political progress of Britain; or, An impartial account of the principal abuses in the government of the Country, From the Revolution in 1688; the whole tending to prove the ruinous consequences of the popular system of war and conquest* . . . Part I (London: Printed for T. Kay, 1792). Until the spring of 1796 he reported on congressional debate for *The Philadelphia Gazette and Universal Daily Advertiser*. In 1797 he published *The*

History of the United States for 1796; Including a Variety of Interesting Particulars Relative to the Federal Government Previous to That Period (Philadelphia: Snowden and McCorkle, 1797), which was the first phase of the public discussion of the "Reynolds affair." See the introductory note to Oliver Wolcott, Jr., to H, July 3, 1797. In 1798 Challender went to Virginia, and in 1799 he became associated with the [Richmond] *Examiner,* a Republican newspaper. In May and June, 1800, he was tried, fined two hundred dollars, and sentenced to prison for nine months under the Sedition Law for comments he had made about John Adams in a pamphlet entitled *The Prospect Before Us.* Volume I (Richmond, Virginia: Printed for the Author, and sold by M. Jones, S. Pleasants, jun. and J. Lyon, 1800). The second volume of Callender's pamphlet was published in 1801 (*The Prospect Before Us.* Vol. II. Part II [Richmond: Printed by H. Pace, And sold by M. Jones, Printer to the Commonwealth; by S. Pleasants, jun. at the Office of the Virginia Argus; by T. Field, Petersburg; and by the Author, in the Jail of Richmond, 1801]). In 1801 Thomas Jefferson pardoned Callender and remitted his fine.

During the summer of 1802 Callender wrote a series of letters to the [Richmond] *Recorder* in which he stated that on two occasions in 1799 and 1800 Jefferson had given him fifty dollars to help him publish two volumes of *The Prospect Before Us.* Jefferson maintained that his payments to Callender were based on "mere motives of charity" (Jefferson to James Monroe, July 15, 1802 [ALS, letterpress copy, Thomas Jefferson Papers, Library of Congress]). For correspondence concerning these payments, see Callender to Jefferson, August 10, 1799 (ALS, Thomas Jefferson Papers, Library of Congress); Jefferson to Callender, September 6, 1799 (ALS, letterpress copy, Thomas Jefferson Papers, Library of Congress); Thomas Jefferson to George Jefferson, October 24, 1800 (ALS, Massachusetts Historical Society, Boston); George Jefferson to Thomas Jefferson, January 12, 1801 (ALS, Massachusetts Historical Society, Boston). George Jefferson was a distant cousin of Thomas Jefferson and a partner in the mercantile firm of Gibson and Jefferson in Richmond. From 1797 to 1811 George Jefferson served as Thomas Jefferson's principal agent in Richmond.

Schuyler's comment may have been prompted by a series of twelve articles entitled "Jefferson and Callender," which appeared in the *New-York Evening Post* on August 3, 4, 5, 7, 9, 10, 11, 12, 13, 14, 16, and September 6, 1802. The writer accused Jefferson of treachery and moral turpitude as well as violation of the Sedition Law for having made payments to Callender.

On September 29, 1802, William Coleman wrote in the *New-York Evening Post:* "The batteries of scandal from Georgia to the Province of Maine have been turned on General Hamilton, in consequence of the numbers of '*Jefferson & Callender*' which originally appeared in this paper, and of the private disreputable tale copied from the Richmond Recorder [*New-York Evening Post,* July 12, 1802]. I think it proper and I think it a justice due to General Hamilton, to declare, that he never saw either of the publications which have created so much sensibility in the friends of Mr. Jefferson, till after he saw them in print in common with other readers; nor knew of their intended appearance, excepting the 12th number, containing the constitutional argument; as to the soundness of which, I consulted him in company with another gentleman of the bar, before I committed it to the press. This I thought due to the importance of the subject. And as to the extract from the Recorder, the first time I saw him afterwards he expressed his regret that my deference to the judgment, or complaisance for the wishes of others, however respectable, had induced me to deviate for a moment from my established plan of conducting my paper. He declared his sentiments to be averse to all personalities, not immediately connected with public considerations. . . ."

Mortgage by John Laurance, John B. Church, and Alexander Hamilton to Robert Gilchrist [1]

New York, August 21, 1802. Laurance, Church, and Hamilton give a mortgage to Gilchrist on an undivided one-half of Townships 9, 10, a portion of 17, and certain lots in Townships 21 and 15, all located in Scriba's Patent, as security for the payment of $21,765. By the terms of the mortgage each is to pay Gilchrist $7,255 in five equal annual payments with interest from May 18, 1802.

Copy, Oneida County Clerk's Office, Mortgages, Vol. III, 500–01, Utica, New York.

    1. Gilchrist, a resident of Westchester County, New York, was a partner in land speculation with Theodosius Fowler, a veteran of the American Revolution and a resident of New York City.

    This document concerns a purchase by H, John Laurance, and John B. Church of lands in Scriba's Patent. On January 5, 1795, George Scriba had sold this land to Jacob Mark and Company ("Partition Deed among John Laurance, John B. Church, and Alexander Hamilton," June 28, 1804). On January 8, 1795, Mark, who was indebted to Gilchrist and Fowler in the amount of $70,000, gave them a mortgage on Townships 21, 15, 9, 10, and a portion of 17 (Bill in Chancery, *Robert Gilchrist v Jacob Mark, John Laurance, and others*, May 20, 1801 [Chancery Papers, Copied Libers, Vol. 128, 469–85, Hall of Records, New York City]; Fowler's Account Book, Stevens Family Papers, New Jersey Historical Society, Newark). On January 15, 1796, Laurance purchased for H, Church, and himself Townships 21 and 15, in which Mark retained an undivided one-fourth interest to be held in trust (Conveyance, Mark and wife to Laurance, January 15, 1796 [Chancery Papers, Copied Libers, Vol. 128, 507–10, Hall of Records, New York City]; Jacob Mark and Company to Church, H, and Laurance, May 30, 1797; Laurance to H, June 3, December 10, 1797, December 28, 1798; H to Laurance, December 26, 1798). On January 20, 1796, H made the following entry in his Cash Book, 1795–1804: "John Laurance Dr. to Cash   for this sum dld John Laurance towards my share of two Townships of Land No. 21 & No. 15 in Rosevelts purchase, purchased of Mr. Mark   1000" (AD, Hamilton Papers, Library of Congress). H recorded additional payments for this land of $5,000 on January 21, 1796; $88.90 on March 30, 1796; and $5,326.65 on December 12, 1796 (AD, Hamilton Papers, Library of Congress). See also "Account with John Barker Church," June 15, 1797. In May, 1799, Laurance executed deeds to H and Church for their shares in this land ("John B. Church and Alexander Hamilton Esqrs for their Interest in Towns No 15 and 21 in Account with John Laurance," n. d., and endorsed by H: "This the last accots. & ballance still due. I have never examined whether the principles of the account are correct. A H" [DS, New-York Historical Society, New York City]). By 1800, however, Mark had failed to make his payments to Gilchrist under the mortgage, was in debt to numerous other creditors, and was declared a bankrupt. In 1801 Gilchrist brought suit in Chancery to foreclose on the mortgage he held on which Mark still owed $41,000 (Bill in Chancery, May 20, 1801; Joint and Several Answers of Jacob Mark and others, May 17, 1802; Answer of John Lawrance, May 17, 1802 [Chancery Papers, Copied Libers, Vol. 128, 469–85, 486–97, 499–516, Hall of Records, New York City]). In order to protect the investment they had made on January 15, 1796, in Townships 21 and 15, H, Church, and Laurance redeemed the lands that remained subject to mortgage to Gilchrist by purchasing the residue of Mark's holdings (Townships 9, 10, and part of 17, and one-fourth interest in Townships 21 and 15) for $43,530.33, the amount of principal and interest due to Gilchrist as determined by a master in Chancery (Master's Report, May 18, 1802; Decree, May 31, 1802 [Chancery Papers, Copied Libers, Vol. 420, 401–03, 404–06, Hall of Records, New York City]; Final Decree, March 7, 1803 [Chancery Papers, Copied Libers, Vol. 128, 522–33, Hall of Records, New York City]; MS Minutes, 1801–1804, under dates of January 18, May 11, 17, 18, 31, 1802; March 4, 5, 1803 [Chancery Papers, Hall of Records, New York City]).

In the document printed above, H, Church, and Laurance gave a mortgage to Gilchrist on an undivided moiety of the lands as security for payment of $21,765, or one-half of the purchase price. A statement at the bottom of the document records that Gilchrist gave proof of satisfaction to a master in Chancery on August 13, 1805, and the mortgage was canceled. A bond and mortgage on the other moiety on similar terms was executed with Theodosius Fowler ("Promissory Note to Theodosius Fowler," August 21, 1802).

Promissory Note to Theodosius Fowler [1]

New York, August 21, 1802. ". . . Alexander Hamilton . . . shall pay to . . . Theodosius Fowler . . . the sum of One thousand four hundred and fifty one Dollars lawful Money aforesaid on or before the eighteenth day of May next with lawful Interest for the same from the eighteenth day of May last then the Obligation to be Void. . . ." [2]

DS, New-York Historical Society, New York City.

1. For information on the contents of this document, see "Mortage by John Laurance, John B. Church, and Alexander Hamilton to Robert Gilchrist," August 21, 1802.

2. Gilchrist endorsed this document: "New York 18 May 1803 Recd. the within in full for Theo Fowler. Rob. Gilchrist."

To Gouverneur Morris [1]

[Grange, New York, August 25, 1802]

Dear Sir

It was my intention to have come to see you this afternoon, among other things to confer about the affair of the loan.[2] But the uncertain state of the weather & some bodily indisposition prevent me.

As to the security for the loan: I hold it to be the better opinion that no foreigner can be in any form a *cestuy que trust* [3] of land— that consequently no conveyance directly for the security of the money lender will be legal. But Mr chaumont is Guarantor & He is a Citizen. A conveyance to countersecure him will be valid, which in the result will protect the money lender. This therefore is the form I propose to give the business.

As to *Tillier* [4] I want your definitive.

Have the *Clerk* brought down and engage to pay what ballance may be due from the *Company* [5]—he shall immediately deliver up the maps & field books & shall deposit with the Master the bill of Exchange & shall give every facility possible on his part to accelerate a final settlement. Surely this is the best course in the view of interest & humanity.

Mr. Church [6] requests you to renew the inclosed, & send it to him. If you forward the renewed note by the bearer, I will take it to Town with me in the morning.

Yrs. very truly   A H

Aug 25
G Morris Esq

ALS, Hamilton Papers, Library of Congress.
    1. Morris was a United States Senator from New York.
    2. This was a loan of two hundred thousand Swiss livres from Jean Frederick Houst de Grandson, a European banker, to William Constable, a New York City merchant who had been a partner in Alexander Macomb's purchase of land in northern New York. James Donatien Le Ray de Chaumont was the guarantor of the loan, and H and Morris had agreed to serve as trustees and counter-guarantors. As security for the loan, Constable offered 137,214⅔ acres of land in Great Tracts Nos. 1 and 2 of Macomb's Purchase.

Le Ray de Chaumont was the son of Jacques Donatien Le Ray de Chaumont, a French merchant who had allowed Benjamin Franklin to use his estate at Passy and had advanced money to the colonies during the American Revolution. James Donatien Le Ray de Chaumont came to the United States to press his father's Revolutionary War claims and became involved in land speculation in northern New York. He was a commissioner of Castorland, a colony for French émigrés established on the Black River on land purchased from Macomb.

3. Black defines *cestui que trust* as "the person who possesses the equitable right to property and receives the rents, issues, and profits thereof, the legal estate of which is vested in a trustee" (Henry Campbell Black, *Black's Law Dictionary: Definitions of the Terms and Phrases of American and English Jurisprudence, Ancient and Modern* [St. Paul, Minnesota, 1951], 289).

4. Rodolphe Tillier, native of Berne, Switzerland, replaced Simon Déjardines as head of the Castorland colony in May, 1796. On May 1, 1798, the commissaries of *La Compagnie de New York*, the Paris association that founded the colony, appointed Morris to investigate Tillier's accounts, and in March, 1800, Morris succeeded Tillier. In 1799 Morris instituted two suits in the names of Le Ray de Chaumont and Pierre Chassanis, the director of the colony, against Tillier in the New York Court of Chancery for mismanagement of the colony during Tillier's agency. In these suits H was Tillier's attorney. The suits were heard before the Chancery Court on March 7, May 7, November 7, 1800, March 3, May 11, 1801, May 9, 18, 29, 1802, February 23, 1803, April 8, 10, and May 23, 1805 (MS Minutes of the New York Court of Chancery, 1797–1800, 1801–1805 [Hall of Records, New York City]). For the documents concerning these suits, see Chancery Papers, BM-600-C, BM-710-L, BM-744-L, BM-1679-L, Parchment 248-B-2 (Hall of Records, New York City), and Chancery Decrees Before 1800, C-228 (Historical Documents Collection, on deposit in Queens College, City University of New York). Tillier defended his agency in *Mémoire pour Rodolphe Tillier, Commissaire-Gérant de la Campagnie de New York* (New York: De l'Imprimerie de J. C. Parisot, 1800). Part of Chassanis's reply to Tillier's pamphlet is printed in Franklin B. Hough, *A History of Lewis County, in the State of New York, from the Beginning of its Settlement to the Present Time* (Albany: Munsell and Rowland, 78 State Street, 1860), 65–67.

On September 7, 1802, Tillier wrote to Morris: "Disposed to every advisable measure by General Hamilton conciliatory, I adress you Honord Sir! with the assurances in my intended Journey to Black river I will obstruct nothing that may be pleasing to your Agency, in returne expecting from your Sub Agent Mr. R. Coxe an analoguos behaviour and Conduct" (ALS, Hamilton Papers, Library of Congress). Richard Coxe of New Jersey was Morris's agent.

An entry in H's Cash Book, 1795–1804, for May 11, 1803, reads: "Tillier 100" (AD, Hamilton Papers, Library of Congress).

5. *La Compagnie de New York*.

6. John B. Church was married to Angelica Schuyler, Elizabeth Hamilton's sister.

From Gouverneur Morris [1]

Alexander Hamilton Esqr.   Morrisania [New York] 31 Aug. 1802
New York

My dear Sir

Enclosed you have a Letter for you I have this Instant received from Leray.[2] I must add a word respecting that same Bill of Exchange. I have agreed to pay to Mr. Tillier [3] whatever the Company shall owe him and Thereby confirm what I have said to you upon that Subject but it is upon the express Condition that the Bill in Question be deposited, in your Hands if you please, so that I may be possest of it eventually as Assets of the Company. I am fully convinced that they can owe Nothing to Mr. Tillier but in any and every Case that Bill must come at last into my Hands. Leray will be here on Saturday Morning and will expect to meet you and receive from you the field Books of No. four.[4] I wish you could contrive to come over early in the Day so as to a Business I will mention and which he did not because it was not then matur'd and he is obliged to leave this on Sunday Morning. It relates to our friend who is now with me.[5]

LC, Gouverneur Morris Papers, Library of Congress.

1. For background to this letter, see H to Morris, August 25, 1802.

2. The letter from James Donatien Le Ray de Chaumont has not been found.

3. Rodolphe Tillier.

4. For the field notes for the survey of this tract, see Mix, *Catalogue: Maps and Surveys*, 297.

5. This is the first mention of Gouverneur Morris's efforts to provide an annuity for Robert and Mary Morris.

By the time that Robert Morris was released from debtors' prison on August 31, 1801, the Holland Land Company had agreed to pay an annuity of fifteen hundred dollars to Mary Morris in return for Gouverneur Morris's surrender of any conflicting claims to the company's title to the one-and-one-half-million-acre tract of land in New York's Genesee country originally owned by Robert Morris (David A. Ogden to Paul Busti, April 16, 1800, April 10, 1801; Busti to P. and C. Van Eeghen, January 28, 1801 [ALS, Gemeentearchief Amsterdam, Holland Land Company. These documents were transferred in 1964 from the Nederlandsch Economisch-Historisch Archief, Amsterdam]). For the Holland Land Company's purchase of this tract from Robert Morris, see H to Robert Morris, March 18, 1795, note 29; H to

Théophile Cazenove, October 14, 1797. This annuity, however, was apparently never paid, and in 1802, H and Gouverneur Morris arranged for a second annuity of sixteen hundred dollars which was to be paid by Le Ray de Chaumont and secured against land in St. Lawrence County, New York.

On April 19, 1802, Robert Morris wrote to his son Thomas: "[A]s to money I will not trouble you if I can help it, I am meditating on a business which if I can bring to bear will afford me sufficient supplies of that necessary Article not only for current use but to lay by annually something for the support of your Mother after my death . . ." (ALS, Robert Morris Papers, The Huntington Library, San Marino, California). During the summer of 1802, Robert and Mary Morris visited Gouverneur Morris at Morrisania, his home in the Bronx. On August 22, 1802, Gouverneur Morris wrote in his diary: "Leray [and the Chevalier] d'orleans and Hamilton dined with us. Last Evening spoke to R.M. about his Situation and recommended an Annuity to which he agreed, Spoke to Leray on the Subject of granting one for a present value of $1500. It is to be arranged between them" (AD, Gouverneur Morris Papers, Library of Congress). On September 29, 1802, Robert Morris again wrote to his son Thomas: "Mr G Morris has settled that affair of business respecting your mother to her satisfaction in a way that I will explain to you when we meet . . ." (ALS, Robert Morris Papers, The Huntington Library, San Marino, California). On January 14, 1803, Gouverneur Morris wrote concerning Robert Morris to John Parish, an English merchant who had served as United States vice consul and consul to Hamburg in the early seventeen-nineties: "He came to me lean, low spirited, and as poor as a commission of bankruptcy can make a man, whose effects will, it is said, not pay a shilling on the pound. Indeed the assignees will not take the trouble of looking after them. I sent him home fat, sleek, in good spirits, and possessed of the means of living comfortably for the rest of his days" (LC, Gouverneur Morris Papers, Library of Congress).

From Oliver Wolcott, Junior

Litchfield [Connecticut] Aug 31. 1802.

My Dear Sir,

I have recd. your favour of the 14th. instant & I sincerely thank you for the friendly attention to my Interests therein manifested. It is certain that I must immediately engage in some active business, or wholly confine my expences to the prospects of my family, to what can be produced from a small farm. A removal from this place, considering the state of Mrs. Ws. health & that my children are of very tender age, is the circumstance which constitutes the principal difficulty in forming an immediate decision. I will come to New York some time during the fall months, when the whole subject can be maturely considered. In the plan you propose, that part, which includes commercial speculations attended with hazard, would be insisted on by me, as an indispensable requisite.

I have written a reply to the Report of the Committee of Investigation, which is in the Press at Boston, and of which a Copy, will be sent you by my request.[1] This pamphlet will I trust furnish several useful Trut[h]s to those who wish comment upon the conduct of our present administration.

Since my return from Boston after my answer was committed to the Press, I have discovered a *second edition* of the Report of the Committee,[2] with several documents, which were not annexed to the *first*,[3] has been printed & sent to the members of Congress. As I had intimated an opinion that there was an impropriety in publishing the report without the Vouchers to which it refers [4]—& as some of these Vouchers have been since published, the democratic printers may possibly cavil at my observations. If this should happen, I wish that it may be immediately stated by Mr. Coleman, *that even in the second Edition, the whole of the Letter of Mr. Gallatin of March 2d. 1802, with the explanatory statements, favourable to Mr. Pickering, & adverse to Mr. Randolph, are omitted.*[5] When he sees my pamphlet, he will readily perceive the importance of rendering this fact as prominent as possible.[6]

I am Dr Sir truly yours   Oliv Wolcott.

Alexander Hamilton Esq

ADfS, Connecticut Historical Society, Hartford.
    1. On April 22, 1802, a report was submitted to the House of Representatives by a committee which had been appointed on December 14, 1801, "to inquire and report, whether moneys drawn from the Treasury have been faithfully applied to the objects for which they were appropriated, and whether the same have been regularly accounted for; and to report, likewise, whether any further arrangements are necessary to promote economy, enforce adherence to legislative restrictions, and secure the accountability of persons entrusted with the public money" (*Annals of Congress*, XI, 319). For the text of this report and related documents, see *ASP, Finance*, I, 752–821.
    On October 8, 1802, John Quincy Adams wrote to Rufus King: "It [the committee report] has since been analysed and refuted by several publications in various parts of the Union, but most effectually by a pamphlet of Mr Wolcott . . ." (LC, Adams Family Papers, deposited in the Massachusetts Historical Society, Boston).
    Wolcott's pamphlet is entitled *An Address to the People of the United States, on the Subject of the Report of a Committee of the House of Representatives, Appointed to "Examine and Report, Whether Monies Drawn from*

the Treasury, Have Been Faithfully Applied to the Objects for Which They Were Appropriated, and Whether the Same Have Been Regularly Accounted For," Which Report was Presented on the 29th of April, 1802 (Boston: Printed by Russell and Cutler, 1802).

2. *Report of the Committee Appointed to Examine and Report Whether Monies, Drawn from the Treasury, Have been faithfully applied to the objects for which they were appropriated, and whether the same have been regularly accounted for; and to report likewise whether any further arrangements are necessary to promote economy, enforce adherence to legislative restrictions, and secure the accountability of persons entrusted with public money. April 29, 1802. Read, and ordered to lie on the table. 1st May, 1802. Motion to recommit the Report to the same select Committee, further to consider and report thereon to the House, negatived* (Washington: Printed by William Duane, 1802).

3. *Report of the Committee, Appointed to Examine and Report Whether Monies, Drawn from the Treasury, Have been faithfully applied to the objects for which they were appropriated, and whether the same have been regularly accounted for; and to report likewise whether any further arrangements are necessary to promote economy, enforce adherence to legislative restrictions, and secure the accountability of persons entrusted with public money. April 29, 1802. Read, and ordered to lie on the table* (Washington: Printed by William Duane, 1802).

4. See Wolcott, *An Address to the People of the United States, on the Subject of the Report of a Committee of the House of Representatives,* 52–53.

5. On March 2, 1802, Secretary of the Treasury Albert Gallatin submitted a report to the House committee investigating the disbursement of public money. This report contained answers to queries that the committee had sent to him on January 21, 1802. For Gallatin's letter and supporting documents, see *ASP, Finance,* I, 755–821. Gallatin's letter was also published as a pamphlet (*Communication from the secretary of the Treasury to the chairman of the committee, appointed to investigate the state of the Treasury, in answer to the enquiries made by the Committee* [Washington City: Printed by William Duane, 1802]).

6. See the *New-York Evening Post,* September 16, 1802.

To Gouverneur Morris [1]

[Grange, New York, September 4, 1802]

My Dear Sir

I fully intended to have dined with you to day but going to Town the two last days & forgetting that I ought to observe a regimen, I have brought back in some degree the complaint which lately annoyed me & which requires to be well watched. This must deprive me of the pleasure of seeing you.

I send Schedules of the papers [2] required of Tillier, all which have been put into my hands—the bill to remain 'till the close of the affair, the other documents to be delivered to your order.

I also send a draft of the Trust deed. It endeavours to comply with your suggestion as far as can be done without running foul of the danger desired to be avoided.

Yrs. very truly   A H

Grange Sep 4th.

Your guests [3] are invited to dine with us Thursday next. Will you make one?

ALS, Hamilton Papers, Library of Congress.
    1. For an explanation of the contents of this letter, see H to Morris, August 25, 1802; Morris to H, August 31, 1802.
    2. None of the documents mentioned in this and the succeeding paragraph has been found.
    3. Robert and Mary Morris.

Indenture: James Donatien Le Ray de Chaumont, Gouverneur Morris, and Alexander Hamilton [1]

[New York, September 4–5, 1802]

This Indenture made the fourth Day of September in the year of our Lord one thousand eight hundred and two Between James Donatianus Le Ray de Chaumont of the first Part, Gouverneur Morris of the second Part and Alexander Hamilton of the third Part.

Whereas it hath been agreed by and between the Parties of the first and second Part that the said Party of the second Part shall pay to the said Party of the first Part the Sum of fifteen thousand Dollars Money of the United States of America in Consideration whereof the said Party of the first Part hath agreed to pay to Alexander Hamilton the Party of the third Part the annual Sum of one thousand five hundred Dollars of like Money as aforesaid every Year during the Life of Robert Morris of Philadelphia in the State of

DS, Columbia University Libraries.
    1. For an explanation of the contents of this document, see Gouverneur Morris to H, August 31, 1802, note 5.

Pennsylvania Esquire and Mary his wife and during the Life of the Survivor of them in four equal quarter Yearly Payments the first of the said Payments to be made on the Day of the Date hereof and every quarterly Payment thereafter to be made three Months in Advance, Upon the Trust Nevertheless and for the Uses and Purposes herein after mentioned—and in order to secure the Payment of the said annual Sum of one thousand five hundred Dollars in quarter yearly Payments as aforesaid, the said Party of the first Part hath agreed to mortgage to the said Party of the third Part, the Tract of Land herein after particularly described.

Now therefore this Indenture witnesseth that the said James Donatianus Le Ray, the Party of the first part together with Grace [2] his Wife in consideration of the Sum of fifteen thousand Dollars of like Money as aforesaid to him in Hand paid by the said Party of the second Part at the Time of the Execution of these Presents, the Receipt whereof is hereby acknowledged, and also in consideration of the Sum of one Dollar to him in Hand paid by the Party of the third part at the time of the Execution of these Presents the Receipt whereof is also hereby acknowledged, *Hath* granted, bargained, sold, aliened, released and conveyed and by these Presents *Doth* grant, bargain, sell, alien, release and convey to the said Party of the third Part and to his Heirs and assigns: forever all that certain Tract of Land situate, lying and being in the County of St Laurence,[3] formerly Clinton in the State of New York, being designated on a certain Map of a Tract of Land commonly called Macombs Purchase, by Township Number thirteen in Lot Number thirteen, being bounded as follows, Beginning at the north East Corner of Town Number Twelve at a Spruce standing in a Swamp marked ☩. No. 9, 10, 12, 13 and running thence East five hundred and fifty Chains to a large Hemlock standing in the East Line of great Lot No 3 marked ☩ No 10, 13—thence South as run in the year 1796 by M. Mitchell,[4] five hundred and fifty six Chains to a Stake fifteen

2. Le Ray de Chaumont married Grace Coxe, the daughter of Charles Davenport Coxe of Sidney, New Jersey.

3. St. Lawrence County was formed out of Clinton County on March 3, 1802.

4. For the survey by Medad Mitchell, see Mix, *Catalogue: Maps and Surveys*, 297, and Franklin B. Hough, *A History of St. Lawrence and Franklin Counties, New York, from the Earliest Period to the Present Time* (Albany: Little & Company, 53 State Street, 1853), 261.

Links North East of a Beech marked ⚹ No 13, 15—Thence west
five hundred and forty eight Chains to an Hemlock marked ⚹
No 12, 13, 14, 15—Thence North five hundred and sixty Chains to
the Place of Beginning Containing thirty thousand six hundred and
twenty seven acres,[5] be the same more or less; And also all the
Estate, Right, Title, Interest, Claim and Demand both in Law and
Equity of the said Party of the first Part, and all Dower and Right
of Dower of the said Grace his Wife, of in and to the same, and
the Reversion and Reversions, Remainder and Remainders, Rents,
Issues and Profits thereof, To have and to hold unto the said Party
of the third Part his Heirs and assigns forever—*Upon Condition
Nevertheless* that if the said Party of the first Part or his Heirs,
executors, administrators or assigns shall pay annually and every
year during the Life of the said Robert Morris and Mary his Wife
and during the Life of the Survivor of them, to the said Party of
the third Part or to his Executors or administrators the Sum of one
thousand five hundred Dollars of like Money as aforesaid in four
equal quarter yearly Payments, the first Payment to be made on the
Day of the Date hereof—and each and every succeeding Payment
to be made three months in advance; and if Default shall be made
in the Payment of any of the said Sums of Money, legal Interest
thereon from the Time the Payment ought to have been made; *or*
if the said Party of the first Part or his Heirs, Executors, administrators or assigns shall at any Time hereafter transfer to the said
Alexander Hamilton the Party of the third Part or to his Executors
or administrators so much of the Debt of the United States of
America bearing an Interest of three per Cent per Annum as that
the annual Interest thereof shall amount to the Sum herein and
hereby intended to be secured to be paid to the said Party of the
third Part his Executors and administrators in Manner as aforesaid
every Year during the Life of the said Robert Morris and Mary his
wife and during the Life of the Survivor of them, to be held by the
said Party of the third Part his Executors and Administrators in
Trust to receive the Interest thereon as it shall accrue and to apply
the same in the Manner herein directed in and by the Trust hereby

5. The land described was located in Lot 13 on the eastern boundary of
Great Tract No. 3 of Macomb's Purchase. See Hough, *St. Lawrence and
Franklin Counties,* 254–58.

created and after the Decease of the said Robert Morris and Mary his Wife, in Trust to transfer the same back again to the said Party of the first Part or to his Executors, administrators or assigns. *Then* and in either of the above Cases this present Indenture and the Estate therein and thereby created and conveyed and every Article Matter and Thing therein contained, shall cease and become void, any Thing therein contained to the contrary notwithstanding.

And if Default shall be made by the said James Donatianus Le Ray, his Heirs, Executors or administrators in the Payment of any of the Sums of Money herein and hereby intended to be secured, then and in such Case the said James Donatianus Le Ray hereby authorises and empowers the said Party of the Third Part his Executors or Administrators to sell all or any Part or Parts of the above described Premises at Public Auction for the best Price or Prices that can be gotten for the Same and out of the monies arising from such Sale or Sales in the first Place to receive the amount of such Sums of Money herein secured to be paid as may be in arrear and unpaid, with Interest thereon from the Periods when the same respectively ought to have been paid; and with the Residue of the Monies arising from such Sale or Sales to purchase so much of the Debt of the United States, bearing an Interest of three per Cent per annum as that the annual Interest thereof will amount to the said Sum of one thousand five hundred Dollars herein intended to be secured to be paid every year in Manner as aforesaid during the Life of the said Robert Morris and Mary his Wife and during the Life of the Survivor of them rendering the overplus if any, after deducting the Costs and Expences of such Sale or Sales, to the said James Donatianus Le Ray, his Executors or Administrators. And if such Purchase of the Debt aforesaid shall be made, the said Party of the third Part his Executors and administrators are hereby authorised and empowered by the said Party of the first Part to hold the same for the Purpose of receiving the Interest thereon as it shall become due, to be applied in the Manner directed in and by the Trust herein and hereby created; and after the Decease of the said Robert Morris and Mary his Wife in Trust to transfer the same to the said James Donatianus Le Ray, his Executors, administrators or assigns.

And the said Parties to these Presents hereby declare the Trust upon which the Party of the third Part and his Executors and administrators shall receive the Monies herein before secured to be paid to him and them, to be as follows, to wit, In Trust to pay the said Monies as he or they shall receive the same to the said Mary Morris during the Time of her Natural Life, for the use and Purpose of her Maintenance and Support and to be applied by her when so received for such Purpose, in such Manner as she may elect and deem most convenient; and after her Decease, if the said Robert Morris her Husband shall survive her, upon the farther Trust to pay the said Monies so as aforesaid to be received to the said Robert Morris for his Maintenance and Support to be applied by him the said Robert Morris, when so received for such Purpose, in such Manner as he may elect and deem most convenient.

And the said James Donatianus Le Ray for himself, his Heirs, Executors and Administrators covenants to and with the said Alexander Hamilton, his Executors and Administrators that he the said James Donatianus Le Ray, his Heirs, Executors or Administrators shall and will pay to the said Alexander Hamilton or to his Executors or Administrators the said Sum of one thousand five hundred Dollars every Year during the Life of the said Robert Morris and Mary his Wife and during the Life of the Survivor of them in four equal quarter Yearly Payments and will make the first Payment on the Day of the Date hereof and each and every succeeding Payment three Months in Advance; and also shall and will pay Interest at the Rate aforesaid upon all and every of the said Sums of Money in the Payment of which Default shall be made, from the respective Periods at which the said Payments ought to have been made—and for the true and faithful Performance of this Covenant and of every article and Matter herein contained on the Part of the said James Donatianus Le Ray or of his Executors, Heirs or Administrators to be performed and kept, he hereby binds himself, his Heirs, Executors and Administrators unto the said Alexander Hamilton his Executors & Administrators in the penal Sum of thirty thousand Dollars.

And the said Alexander Hamilton for himself, his Heirs, Executors and Administrators hereby covenants to and with the said Gouverneur Morris his Executors and Administrators that he the said Alexander Hamilton, his Executors or administrators shall and will pay over the said Monies herein and hereby secured to be paid to him and them every Year in the Manner herein before specified, during the Life of the said Robert Morris and Mary his Wife and during the Life of the Survivor of them, as he the said Alexander Hamilton or his Executors or administrators shall receive the same to the said Mary Morris during her Life for the uses and Purposes herein before expressed; and after her Decease to the said Robert Morris her Husband, if he shall survive her, to and for the Uses and Purposes also herein before expressed—and also if Default shall be made in the Payment of the said Sum of one thousand five hundred Dollars every Year during the Life of the said Robert Morris and Mary his Wife and during the Life of the Survivor of them in quarter yearly Payments in Manner as is above provided, and as Default shall be made in any of the said Payments, he the said Alexander Hamilton, his Executors or Administrators will use due Diligence and take all reasonable and legal Measures to recover the same from the said James Donatianus Le Ray, his Heirs, Executors or Administrators; and shall and will in all Things well and faithfully execute the Trust herein and hereby created.

And the said Alexander Hamilton for himself, his Heirs, Executors and Administrators covenants to and with the said James Donatianus Le Ray, his Executors, Administrators and assigns that if it shall so happen in the Execution of the Trust herein and hereby created, that any of the Debt of the United States shall become vested in him the said Alexander Hamilton, his Executors or Administrators by any of the Provisions herein contained then and in such Case he the said Alexander Hamilton or his Executors or Administrators, after the Purposes of such Trust as is herein and hereby created shall have been completed, and after the Decease of the said Robert Morris and Mary his Wife, shall and will transfer the said Debt to the said James Donatianus Le Ray or to his Executors, administrators or assigns.

In Witness whereof the Parties to these Presents have hereunto set their Hands and Seals the Day and Year first above written.

Le Ray
Gouv. Morris

Received on the Day of the Date of the within Indenture from Mr. Gouverneur Morris the Sum of fifteen thousand Dollars being the Sum within agreed to be paid by the said Gouverneur Morris to me on the Day of the Date of the said within Indenture.

Le Ray

Witnessed by
Thomas Cooper [6]

J. Leray agrees in Consideration of one thousand Dollars pd to him by Gouverneur Morris that the within mentioned Annuity shall be sixteen hundred instead of fifteen hundred Dollars he having received sixteen thousand 5 Sepr. 1802.

Le Ray

6. Cooper, a New York City lawyer, was a master of the New York Court of Chancery.

To William Cooper [1]

New York September 6. 1802

Dear Sir

I congratulate you and myself on your victory over Brockholst.[2] Whether your interest is much promoted by it or not is of small consequence—In the triumph of vanquishing such an enemy. That *you know* was your principal inducement and *I know* that you will be willing to pay well for it.

I have been deliberating whether to charge you 200 or 100 pounds for my services in this cause. In fixing upon the latter I am afraid I shall offend you. But I love to show my moderation & therefore whether you are angry or not I will only have One hundred.[3]

This I beg you to remit without delay. I have been building a fine house [4] and am very low in Cash; so that it will be amazingly convenient to me to touch your money as soon as possible.[5]

I wish you many pleasant moments & that you may be able to steer clear of the Court of Errors. I have fought so hard for you that I am entirely exhausted.

Yrs. with great regard   A Hamilton

Typescript, anonymous donor.

1. Cooper, the founder of Cooperstown, New York, was one of the largest landholders in New York State. H was Cooper's attorney in many of his land transactions. In 1791 Cooper became the first judge of the Court of Common Pleas for Otsego County. From 1795 to 1797 and from 1799 to 1801 he was a Federalist member of the House of Representatives.

2. H is referring to the case of *Brockholst Livingston v William Cooper,* which involved a dispute over seventy-five thousand acres of land known as the Brantingham Tract in the Macomb Purchase in northern New York. H served as counsel to Cooper as well as an arbitrator between the two disputing parties. See Goebel, *Law Practice,* forthcoming volumes.

3. For an earlier fee from Cooper, see the entry in H's Cash Book, 1795–1800, under the date of May, 1800, which reads: "William Cooper services in his suit with B Livingston   100" (AD, Hamilton Papers, Library of Congress).

4. See the introductory note to Philip Schuyler to H, July 17, 1800.

5. On April 9, 1802, Robert Troup wrote to Rufus King: "Hamilton is closely pursuing the law, and I have at length succeeded in making him somewhat mercenary. I have known him latterly to dun his clients for money, and in settling an account with me the other day, he reminded me that I had received a fee for him in settling a question referred to him and me jointly. These indications of regard to property give me hopes that we shall not be obliged to raise a subscription to pay for his funeral expenses" (King, *The Life and Correspondence of Rufus King,* IV, 104).

From James Donatien Le Ray de Chaumont [1]

General Alex. Hamilton Esq   Morisiana [New York] Sepr. 6. 1802

Sir

I Regret very much that I have not had the pleasure to see you at Morisiana, and hope at the Same time that this Cool weather will have restored your health.

I include here a receipt for the papers which belong to me and which are absolutely necessary to take with me in the Journey I am going to undertake. As I am to be at particular day at Albany I send you an express to desire you in case you cant go to town today to give him an order that he may get the papers in your office. I must set of this afternoon else I will not arrive in time & Mr. Constable [2] will be gone to Montreal &c &c.

I am going to make him sign the paper you had drawn and which I think will answer all purposes.

With great regard   I remain   Sir   Your most humble & obedient Servant

Le Ray

Mr. T. Cooper [3] is Kind enough to take charge of this and will give you the receipt on receiving the papers.

ALS, Hamilton Papers, Library of Congress.
1. For an explanation of the contents of this letter, see H to Gouverneur Morris, August 25, 1802.
2. William Constable.
3. Thomas Cooper.

From Lewis Tousard [1]

Cap-Français [*Santo Domingo*], *September 6–9, 1802.* States that he has returned to General Charles Victor Emmanuel Leclerc's staff in Santo Domingo.[2] Describes Leclerc's campaign to restore French rule on the island and replies to criticism in the United States of Leclerc's conduct.[3]

ALS, Hamilton Papers, Library of Congress.
1. Tousard, a former captain of artillery in the French army, was an aide to the Marquis de Lafayette during the American Revolution and a lieutenant colonel in the Continental Army. After the war he served with the French forces in Santo Domingo until 1792 and then returned to France, where he was imprisoned. In 1793 he returned to the United States, and in 1795 he became a major in the United States Army. On May 26, 1800, Tousard received his commission as a lieutenant colonel and was named inspector of the artillery. He was honorably discharged from the Army on June 1, 1802.
2. Leclerc, the husband of Napoleon Bonaparte's sister, Pauline, was the commanding officer of an army of thirty-three thousand men which successfully subdued the rebellion on Santo Domingo led by François Dominque Touissant L'Ouverture. See Rufus King to H, May 7, 1802, note 8. By November, 1802, nearly three-quarters of the army, including Leclerc, had died of yellow fever.
3. For examples of criticism of Leclerc, see the *New-York Evening Post*, April 9, 17, 29, May 8, 10, 1802.

Receipt from Louis Le Guen [1]

[Morrisville, Pennsylvania, September 10, 1802]

Jai Ce Jour: 10. Septembre 1802. recu du General Hamilton *trois Cents* cinquante d'ollars, Pour Linterest d'un ân sur La Somme de Cinq milles dollars, mentionnee au dit Bond. Morris Ville 10 Septe. 1802.

L Le Guen

ADS, Yale University Library
1. For an explanation of the contents of this document, see "Indenture be-tween Alexander Hamilton of the First Part and Richard Harison and Aaron Ogden of the Second Part," July 1, 1801; "Bond to Richard Harison and Aaron Ogden," July 1, 1801; "Description of Account with Louis Le Guen," June 8, 1802.

To Herman LeRoy [1]

Grange [*New York*], *September 19, 1802.* Informs LeRoy of an arrangement he has concluded with Henry Sands [2] to assign Sands's mortgage on lots in Brooklyn to the Bank of New York, which, in turn, would sell the mortgaged property and use the proceeds to discharge Comfort Sands's debts.[3] States: "Going tomorrow morning to attend the W Chester Circuit [4] which may occasion an absence of three or four days."

ALS, Bank of New York, New York City.
1. LeRoy, William Bayard, and James McEvers were partners in a New York City mercantile firm which represented the Holland Land Company in the United States. LeRoy was a director of the Bank of New York.
2. Sands, the second son of Comfort Sands, a New York City merchant, was a lawyer in New York City.
3. This letter concerns the case of *The President, Directors, and Company of the Bank of New York* v *Comfort Sands, Henry Sands, and Isaac Kibbee,* one of several cases that resulted from the bankruptcy of Comfort Sands. Kibbee, a New York City merchant, was chosen by a commission of bank-ruptcy in July, 1802, as assignee of Sands's real property. Sands owned land in New York City, Brooklyn, upstate New York, the city of Washington, and Georgia. H acted as counsel for the complainants.
   In 1797 Comfort Sands, who owed money to several prominent merchants in New York City, suffered financial misfortunes, stopped payments to his creditors, and refused to give them an account of his affairs. On June 15, 1797, he mortgaged his estate of one hundred and sixty acres in Brooklyn to the Bank of New York for a payment of fifty thousand dollars plus interest. In July, 1798, shortly after the first judgment was made against him by one of his many creditors, Sands conveyed the property in Brooklyn to his son, Henry, for sixty thousand dollars. From this sum, fifty-six thousand dollars was to be paid to the Bank of New York, which included the amount Com-fort Sands owed the bank, and four thousand dollars was to be paid to Comfort Sands. Despite the sale of the land to his son, Comfort Sands con-tinued to exercise his rights of ownership over the property in Brooklyn. Sands was imprisoned in Kings County for nonpayment of debts from August, 1798, to July, 1801. On June 22, 1801, according to provisions of the Uniform Bankruptcy Act ("An Act to establish an uniform System of Bankruptcy throughout the United States" [2 *Stat.* 19–36 (April 4, 1800)]), he was de-clared a bankrupt.
   On November 4, 1802, the Bank of New York filed a bill in the New York

Chancery Court against Comfort Sands, Henry Sands, and Isaac Kibbee, requesting foreclosure of the mortgage on the estate in Brooklyn and sale of the property. On December 9, 1803, the land was sold at public auction in New York City to Lewis Sands, another son of Comfort Sands, who agreed to purchase it for ninety-four thousand dollars. When Abraham Bancker, master of the Chancery Court, tendered the deed for the land to Lewis Sands on May 22, 1804, Lewis Sands stated that he could not conform to the conditions of the sale. On June 4, 1804, the court ordered a second sale of the land. Between July 3, 1804, and November 5, 1806, Thomas Cooper, master of the Chancery Court, sold the land at public auction in several parcels to separate purchasers for a total price of $73,363.23. On July 29, 1808, Cooper filed a report in Chancery Court in which he stated that he had paid the Bank of New York $56,366.81 from the sale of the land. The remaining surplus was brought into court to be applied to Comfort Sands's other creditors (Chancery Papers, Copied Libers, Vol. 106, 1–97, Hall of Records, New York City; William Johnson, *Reports of Cases Argued and Determined in the Supreme Court of Judicature; and in the Court for the Trial of Impeachments and the Correction of Errors, in the State of New York,* IV [New York, 1809], 536–43).

See H's "Memorandum of what is understood to be the intention of the Bank of New York communicated by Mr. Hamilton their counsel to Mr. [Nathaniel] Pendleton the counsel of Mr. H Sands in relation to the mortgage on certain lots at Brooklyn . . . ," August 1, 1803 (ADS, Bank of New York, New York City).

An entry in H's Cash Book, 1795–1804, under the date of January 31, 1799, reads: "Bank of New York for opinion concerning the Mortgage from Sands 20" (AD, Hamilton Papers, Library of Congress).

4. The Circuit Court of Westchester County, New York, met on September 20, 1802.

To Oliver Wolcott, Junior

New York October 3. 1802

My Dear Sir

I lately received a letter from you, transmitting a pamphlet.[1] The latter, I have read with much pleasure. If party spirit admitted of candor, I should say that it was calculated to satisfy candid men of whatever party. Pains will be taken to disseminate it.

You may remember that when you were last in this City, I spoke to you about some lands which I owned in the Ohio Company tracts.[2] Inclosed is an extract from my deed which contains the only description of it in my possession. In a plan communicated to me for the sale of such of the shares as belonged to non resident proprietors, I find the following tariff of values—(viz)

8 acre lots at 10 Dollars ℔ acre		80
3 do at 3 do		9
House lots		20
160 acre lots at 2½ do		400
100 do a 3 do		300
640 do a 1½		960
262 do a 2		524
1173	Total of a right.	2293

This tariff was formed by Judge Putnam,[3] who appears to have thought it not exaggerated.

My hope has been that an exchange may be made of these lands for settled farms in Connecticut. If this could be done so as to realise to me the price of *a dollar* per acre round in *intrinsic* value, I should be content. You encouraged me by your opinion, that the plan might possibly succeed. If so I authorise you on my part to give it effect; relying upon your care that the value I mentioned will be obtained & that the titles will be unexceptionable.[4] I do not mean to sell speedily the lands which may be procured in exchange.

Our friends are of opinion that the Fœderal cause looks up in this state.[5] How is it in Connecticut?

Yrs. very truly   A Hamilton

O Wolcott Esq

[ENCLOSURE][6]

five compleat shares of Land [7] (including the several lots heretofore drawn for the said shares in the name of the said Alexander Hamilton Esqr.) in two several tracts of land situate in the county of Washington, in the Territory of the United States, north west of the river Ohio, and in that part thereof purchased by the aforesaid Compy of associates, the said two tracts of Land in which the shares hereby granted and conveyed are located, are the same two tracts granted and conveyed to us the aforesaid Grantors, in trust as aforesaid by the said Letters Patent, bearing date the Tenth day of May, in the year of our Lord one Thousand seven hundred and ninety Two.[8] One of the said Tracts contains besides the Several lots and parcels of land reserved & appropriated to particular purposes, seven Hundred and fifty thousand acres, and the other said Tracts contain two hundred fourteen Thousand, two hundred and Eighty five acres; as by reference to the said letters patent will more at large appear. The whole number of shares in the aforesaid company are Eight Hundred and twenty two.

ALS, Connecticut Historical Society, Hartford.

1. See Wolcott to H, August 31, 1802, note 3.

2. See "Receipt to Rufus Putnam," May 21, 1792 (printed in this volume); Benjamin Tallmadge to H, June 20, 1795, note 2; Rufus Putnam to H, November 19, 1796; H to William R. Putnam, July, 1800.

3. Rufus Putnam, a veteran of the American Revolution, was one of the founders of the Ohio Company in 1786 and became its superintendent. The company owned one and one-half million acres of land on the north bank of the Ohio River. Putnam was a judge in the Territory Northwest of the River Ohio from 1790 to 1792, brigadier general in the United States Army from 1792 to 1793, and surveyor general of the United States from 1796 to 1803.

4. H did not exchange his lands in the Ohio Company for lands in Connecticut. According to a statement which he prepared shortly before his death, he estimated the value of his shares in the Ohio Company at six thousand dollars. See "Statement of my property and Debts July 1. 1804." In 1806 H's executors sold some of his Ohio Company property for seventeen hundred dollars (two conveyances, April 25, 1806 [DS, Hamilton Papers, Library of Congress]).

5. On August 24, 1802, Robert Troup wrote to Rufus King: "Federalism is looking up. At the last 4th of July the toasts everywhere given prove that Hamilton is regaining that general esteem and confidence, which he seems to have lost, and his standing is very much our political thermometer" (King, *The Life and Correspondence of Rufus King*, IV, 161).

Contrary to Troup's optimism, the election results in New York were favorable to the Republican party. See "Speech on Congressional Election in New York City," April 21, 1802.

6. Extract, Connecticut Historical Society, Hartford.

7. According to the records of the Ohio Company, H owned five and one-half shares (Archer Butler Hulbert, *The Records of the Original Proceedings of the Ohio Company* [Marietta, Ohio, 1917], II, 238).

8. For this deed, see "Receipt to Rufus Putnam," May 21, 1792 (printed in this volume).

To Elizabeth Hamilton [1]

Peeks Kill [2] [New York] October 16 [1802] Saturday.

I have just arrived here and shall stay till tomorrow.

It has always appeared to me that the ground on which our Orchard stands is much too moist. To cure this a ditch round it would be useful, perhaps with a sunken fence as a guard. But this last may be considered at a future time.

If you can obtain one or two more labourers, it may be adviseable to cut a ditch round the Orchard—three feet deep by three feet wide at the bottom. The clay that comes out of the ditch will be useful to give firmness to our roads and may be used for this purpose.

Yet you will consider this merely as a suggestion & do as you shall think best after you shall have ascertained whether you can procure any better materials for the purpose. But remember that mere *sand* & stones will not answer.[3]

Very Affectionately My beloved   Yrs.   A H

Mrs. H

ALS, Hamilton Papers, Library of Congress.

1. For background to this letter, see the introductory note to Philip Schuyler to H, July 17, 1800.

2. H was on his way to Albany to attend the October term of the New York Supreme Court which met from October 19 to October 30, 1802.

3. H addressed this letter to his wife at "No. 58 Partition Street" where the Hamilton family lived in 1802. Partition Street is the present-day Fulton Street in New York City.

To Elizabeth Hamilton

Monday Morning [October 18, 1802]
Rhinebeck Flatts [New York]

Dear Eliza

I am thus far on my journey in good health. Tomorrow by eleven oClock I hope to reach Albany. This is the third letter I have written to you since we parted.[1]

I passed last night at Doctor Bards.[2] The young couple [3] seemed as usual in the like circumstances happy, and the rest of the company were in good spirits. Betsey Church [4] talked of paying a visit to day to her uncle Philip.[5]

My former letters were full of advice about our little farm. This is merely to inform you of my progress in safety and health, and that I shall be very glad to get back to you.

My love to all my children. Adieu beloved   A H

Mrs. H

ALS, Hamilton Papers, Library of Congress.

1. Only one letter written by H to his wife at this time has been found. See H to Elizabeth Hamilton, October 16, 1802.

H arrived in Albany on October 19 (Philip Schuyler to Elizabeth Hamilton, October 20, 1802 [ALS, Schuyler Papers, MS Division, New York Public Library]).

H addressed this letter to his wife: "To the care of Mr. T L Ogden No. 69 Stone Street New York." H and Thomas L. Ogden, a New York City lawyer, had their law offices at this address in 1801 and 1802.

2. Samuel Bard, a native of Philadelphia, received his medical degree from the University of Edinburgh in 1765 and subsequently practiced medicine in New York. He was professor of the theory and practice of physic and dean of the faculty of Columbia College until he retired to Hyde Park in 1798. He and Dr. David Hosack, who became Bard's partner in 1796, were physicians to H and his family. See H's Cash Book, 1795–1804, for entries under the dates of February 1, 1797, June 7, 1798, November 16, 1802, July 3, 1804 (AD, Hamilton Papers, Library of Congress).

3. On October 7, 1802, William Bard, Samuel Bard's son, married Catherine Cruger, daughter of Nicholas Cruger, a New York City merchant. In the seventeen-sixties and seventeen-seventies Cruger was a partner in the mercantile firm of Beekman and Cruger in Christiansted, St. Croix. H had worked as a clerk for this firm in his youth (Walton and Cruger to H, October 19, 1771).

4. Elizabeth Church, who was born in 1786, was the second daughter of John B. Church and Angelica Schuyler Church, Elizabeth Hamilton's older sister.

5. Philip Jeremiah Schuyler was Elizabeth Hamilton's younger brother. He married Sarah Rutsen in 1788, and in 1802 he was living in Rhinebeck, New York.

Indenture: William Constable, Ann Constable, Alexander Hamilton, and Gouverneur Morris [1]

[New York, October 20, 1802]

This Indenture made the twentieth day of October in the year of our Lord one thousand eight hundred and two Between William

Copy, Division of Corporations and State Records, Department of State, Albany; two copies, Constable Papers, MS Division, New York Public Library.

1. For background to this document, see H to Gouverneur Morris, August 25, 1802. For the part played by this agreement in the settlement of Constable's estate, see Goebel, *Law Practice*, forthcoming volumes.

Constable of the City of New York in the State of New York Gentleman and Ann his wife of the first part and Alexander Hamilton
and Gouverneur Morris of the same State Esquires of the second
part. Whereas by a certain agreement entered into and made before
Mr. Lewis Fevot Notary public residing at Lausanne in Switzerland
on the twenty fifth day of March last [2] past between Mr. George
De Ribaupierre de Grandson of Lausanne aforesaid Banker acting
for and in the name of the said William Constable, and also for and
in the name of Mr. James Donatien LeRay de Chaumont Citizen of
the United States in virtue of their respective powers of the one part
and Mr. Jean Frederick Houst de Grandson of the Canton of Leman
in Switzerland of the other part,[3] the said George de Ribaupierre
de Grandson for and in the name of the said William Constable did
acknowledge himself to be indebted to the said Jean Frederick Houst
de Grandson in the Sum of two Hundred thousand Livres of Switzerland (four Livres of Switzerland being equal in value to one
Crown of six Livres of France) to be paid in Gold or Silver according to the value weight and exchange of that day within the period
of ten years computing from the first day of April then next ensuing
with the Interest from the same date at the rate of six ℔ centum ℔
annum payable at the House of the said Jean Frederick Houst de
Grandson at Lausanne aforesaid or at such other place whether in
France or Switzerland as he should by one years previous notice direct, and in half yearly payments that is to say on the first days of
October and April in each and every of the said years, the first of
the said half yearly payments to be made on the first day of October
then next ensuing. And whereas by the same agreement the said
George de Ribaupierre de Grandson for and in the name of the said
William Constable in order to secure to the said Jean Frederick
Houst de Grandson the payment of the said Sum of two hundred
thousand Livres of Switzerland with the Interest for the same at the
Rate, and at the times, and in the manner aforesaid did engage and
agree to pledge and Hypothecate the several Tracts or Towns of
Land hereinafter described, and for this purpose to make and execute
in the said State of New York all such acts conveyances and assur-

---

2. Two copies of this agreement are in the Constable Papers, MS Division,
New York Public Library.

3. From 1798 to 1813, Leman was part of the French empire.

ances as by counsel learned in the Laws of the said State should be deemed and pronounced to be most valid and effectual. And whereas by the same agreement as a further security for the payment of the same principal Sum, and of the Interest thereupon in manner aforesaid the said James Donatien LeRay de Chaumont acting by the said George De Ribaupierre de Grandson duly authorised for that purpose did become the Guarrantor and Surety of the said William Constable thereby binding and pledging himself his heirs Executors and Administrators for the payment of the said principal Sum and Interest in case default should be made in the payment of either on the part of the said William Constable as by the said agreement a true copy whereof is hereunto annexed may appear. And whereas in order to fulfil the objects of the said agreement and to give effect to the intentions of the parties thereto in respect to the security intended to be provided by the Hypothecation of the said several Tracts of Land in the manner the most valid and effectual which the existing Laws of the said State of New York do permit it has been advised and recommended by counsel learned in those Laws that the said Lands shall be granted and conveyed to Trustees upon Trust to enure and serve as a Counter Guaranty to the said James Donation LeRay de Chaumont his heirs Executors and Administrators to the end that if default shall be made in the payment of the said principal Sums or Interest in and by the said contract or agreement secured to be paid or any part thereof on the part of the said William Constable his heirs Executors and Administrators the said James Donatien LeRay de Chaumont his heirs Executors and administrators may be fully reimbursed and indemnified for and against all payments losses and damages whatsoever in consequence of such default and enabled to fulfil his Guaranty to the said Jean Frederick Houst de Grandson without detriment to himself or themselves respectively. And for this purpose with powers to the said Trustees forthwith upon such default to Grant bargain sell and convey the same premises or such part thereof as may be necessary. And the monies thence arising to pay and apply towards the reimbursement amd exoneration of the said James Donation LeRay de Chaumont as such Guarantor and Surety. And whereas the said Alexander Hamilton and Gouverneur Morris have been named and appointed as such Trustees and they have respectively consented to accept the Trust.

Now therefore This Indenture Witnesseth that the said William Constable and Ann his wife in consideration of the premises, and also in consideration of the Sum of One Dollar to them in hand paid by the said Alexander Hamilton and Gouverneur Morris the receipt whereof is hereby acknowledged Have Granted, bargained, sold, released conveyed and confirmed, and by these presents Do Grant bargain, sell, release convey and confirm unto the said Alexander Hamilton and Gouverneur Morris their heirs and assigns All those certain Tracts pieces and parcels of Land situate lying and being in the County of Clinton, the county of Saint Lawrence and State of New York being part of the Great allotments Number One and Two of Macombs purchase from the said State, to wit, Town Number Seven of the said Great allotment Number One, which said Town Number Seven in the Map, Survey and Subdivision of the said Great allotments Number One and Two made by Benjamin Wright in the year of our Lord one thousand eight hundred [4] and filed according to Law in the Office of the Surveyor General of the said State is described as follows viz. Bounded Westerly by the division line of Great allotments Number One and Two, Northerly by Town Number Four, Easterly by Town Number Eight, and Southerly by Town Number Ten and contains twenty seven thousand nine hundred and thirteen acres of Land. The North third of Town Number Nine of the said Great allotment Number One Containing ten thousand seven hundred and twenty six acres, which Town Number nine in the said Map Survey and Subdivision is described as follows viz. Bounded Easterly by the Eastern boundary of the said Great allotment Number One, northerly by Town Number Six Westerly by Town Number Eight, and Southerly by Town Number Twelve and contains thirty two thousand one hundred and seventy eight acres of Land. Town Number Ten of the said Great allotment Number One, which said Town in the said Map Survey and Subdivision is described as follows viz. Bounded Westerly by the division line of Great allotments Number One and Two, Northerly by Town Number Seven, Easterly by Town Number Eleven and Southerly by Town Number Thirteen and contains Twenty

---

4. For this survey, see Franklin B. Hough, *A History of St. Lawrence and Franklin Counties, New York, from the Earliest Period to the Present Time* (Albany: Little & Company, 53 State Street, 1853), 261–65.

seven thousand six hundred and eleven acres of Land. Town Number Sixteen of the said Great allotment Number One, which said Town in the said Map, Survey and Subdivision is described as follows viz Bounded Westerly by the Division lines of Great allotments Number One and Two, Northerly by Town Number Thirteen, Easterly by Town Number Seventeen, and Southerly by Town Number Nineteen and contains twenty six thousand six hundred and forty two acres of Land. The Southwest quarter of Town Number Twenty Three of the said Great allotment Number One Containing seven thousand five hundred and twenty one acres of Land, which said Town Number Twenty three in the said Map Survey and Subdivision is described as follows viz. Bounded Easterly by Town Number Twenty four, Northerly by Town Number Twenty, Westerly by Town Number Twenty two and Southerly by Town Number Twenty six and contains twenty two thousand five hundred and sixty three acres of Land. The Middle third of Town Number Twenty five of the said Great allotment Number One containing eight thousand six hundred and fifty four acres and two thirds of an acre of Land which said Town Number Twenty five in the said Map Survey and Subdivision is described as follows viz bounded Westerly by the division line of Great allotments Number One and Two, Northerly by Town Number Twenty two, Easterly by Town Number Twenty six, and Southerly by the Southern boundary of Great allotment Number One adjoining to Totten & Crossfields purchase and contains Twenty five thousand nine hundred and sixty four acres of Land. And Town Number Eleven of the said Great allotment Number Two, which said Town in the said Map, Survey and Subdivision is described as follows viz Bounded Easterly by Town Number Twelve Northerly by Town Number Fourteen, Westerly by Town Number Ten, and Southerly by Town Number Eight, and contains twenty eight thousand one hundred and forty seven acres of Land making together One hundred and thirty seven thousand two hundred and fourteen acres and two thirds of an acre of Land with the Hereditaments and appurtenances to the same several Tracts pieces or parcels of Land belonging or in any wise appertaining. To have and to hold all and singular the said premises with the appurtenances unto the said Alexander Hamilton and Gouverneur Morris their heirs and assigns to the proper use and behoof of them the said Alexander Hamilton and Gouverneur Morris their heirs and assigns forever as joint Tenants and not as Tenants in common. In Trust nevertheless for the uses and purposes following that is to say, upon Trust whenever and as often as default shall be made by the said William Constable his heirs Executors or administrators in the payment of the said principal Sum and Interest or any part thereof according to the Tenor true intent and meaning of the said Contract (whereof a Copy is hereunto annexed as aforesaid) forthwith after any and every such default to bargain and sell (at a public vendue or otherwise at their discretion) the whole or so much of the premises hereby granted and conveyed as shall be at any time and from time to time sufficient and necessary to pay the said principal Sum and Interest or such part thereof in respect to which default shall have been at any time made and thereupon in their own right as Trustees or if need be as the Attornies or Attorney of the said William Constable and Ann his wife for that purpose constituted by these presents by one or more good and sufficient deed or deeds conveyance or conveyances in the Law to Grant and Convey the same to purchaser or purchasers thereof in fee simple. And the monies arising from such Sale or Sales first deducting the reasonable charges and expences attending the same to pay and apply to and for the exoneration and reimbursement of the said James Donatien LeRay de Chaumont his heirs Executors and Administrators in respect to the Guarantee aforesaid and in conformity with the agreement or contract aforesaid so that the said James Donatian LeRay de Chaumont his heirs Executors or administrators may in no event be subjected to any loss damage or detriment by reason of his said Guaranty. And upon this further Trust to pay the over plus monies to arise from such Sale or Sales if any there shall be after satisfying the whole of the said principal Sum with the Interest thereupon, and the costs and charges of such Sale or Sales to the said William Constable his Executors or administrators, but in case the said William Constable his heirs Executors or Administrators shall well and truly pay and discharge the said principal Sum, and the Interest thereupon and every part thereof according to the Tenor true intent and meaning of the said contract or agreement or in case any part of the said premises shall remain unsold after the said principal Sum and Interest shall have been fully paid and discharged and the said James Donatien Le Ray de Chaumont his heirs Executors and Administrators fully exonerated and indemnified for and on account of the said Guaranty by the said William Constable his heirs Executors or administrators, then upon this Further Trust, that is to say to Grant release and convey so much of the said premises as shall remain so unsold to William Constable his heirs and assigns in fee simple. In Witness whereof the parties to these presents have hereunto set their hands and Seals the day and year before written.

Alexander Hamilton
Gouvr. Morris
Wm. Constable
Ann Constable

To Elizabeth Hamilton [1]

[Albany, October 27, 1802]

I was made happy My beloved Eliza by the receipt of two letters from you [2] which gave me the delightful intelligence that you & my dear Children were well. I shall be glad to come and receive the assurance in person.

This moment I came from Court & I fear I shall not be disengaged from it before Saturday. Judge of my impatience by your own.

Adieu My darling Eliza   A H

I am quite well

Wednesday Evening
Octo⟨ber 2⟩7

ALS, Hamilton Papers, Library of Congress.
  1. For background to this letter, see H to Elizabeth Hamilton, October 16, 1802.
  2. Letters not found.

To John V. Henry [1]

Pitts Field [Massachusetts] Oct 31. 1802 [2]

Dr. Sir

I left with a Watchmaker at Albany my watch to be put in order & forgot it when I came away. I believe the name of the Watchmaker is *Howal*.[3] He lives near the Court House, obliquely South-West.

Do me the favour to get it from him and send it to me by a safe opportunity; paying the expence.[4]

Yrs. with much esteem   A Hamilton

John V Henry Esqr

ALS, Massachusetts Historical Society, Boston.

1. Henry, an Albany lawyer, was comptroller of New York State from March, 1800, to August, 1801, a member of the Assembly in 1800 and 1802, and a delegate to the state convention which met in Albany in October, 1801, to settle the controversy between the Council of Appointment and the governor over the power of appointment.

2. After the October term of the New York Supreme Court in Albany had adjourned on October 30, 1802, H did not return directly to New York City, but made a side trip, which included stops at Pittsfield and Stockbridge in western Massachusetts. On October 8, 1802, Henry Van Schaack, a Loyalist, who following his banishment from New York State during the American Revolution had settled in Pittsfield, wrote to his brother, Peter Van Schaack, a former Tory and a lawyer in Kinderhook, New York: "General Hamilton, according to [Egbert] Benson's message to me, is to spend a day or two with me, on his way from Connecticut to Albany" (Henry Cruger Van Schaack, *Memoirs of the Life of Henry Van Schaack* [Chicago, 1892], 199). Van Schaack's information was not correct, because H's correspondence earlier in October (H to Elizabeth Hamilton, October 27, 1802) indicates that he would be detained in Albany until Saturday, October 30. For H's trip to Massachusetts, see also Theodore Sedgwick to H, January 27, 1803.

3. Silas White Howell was a silversmith and watchmaker in Albany from 1798 to 1803, when he moved to New Brunswick, New Jersey. His business, according to his advertisements, was "opposite City Hall, Court Street."

4. This letter is endorsed: "1802 Novr 9 Sent by Peter R Ludlow pd for repairs to Howell 6/."

Ludlow, an attorney and friend of H, lived on an estate near Goshen, New York. He was in Albany to attend either the New York Supreme Court or the Court of Errors.

From William Constable [1]

[New York] 30 Novr. 1802

Genl. Hamilton.

I have conversed with Mr G M since I had the Pleasure of seeing you relative to my being authorized to settle the Lands contained in the Deed of Trust. He sees no possible Objection to my having such Authority, the Money & Bonds received being paid over for the Use of the Lenders & will execute any Thing that you will order made out for the Purpose. May I request that you will direct Mr Ogden [2] to have such Power made that I may have it completed before Mr Morris goes to Washington.[3]

LC, William Constable Letter Book, 1797–1830, MS Division, New York Public Library.
    1. For background to this letter, see H to Gouverneur Morris, August 25, 1802; "Indenture: William Constable, Ann Constable, Alexander Hamilton, and Gouverneur Morris," October 20, 1802.
    2. Either Thomas L. or David A. Ogden, New York City lawyers.
    3. Although the United States Senate convened on December 6, 1802, Gouverneur Morris left for Washington on December 13 and arrived on December 23, 1802 (*Annals of Congress,* XII, 9, 17; Morris's diary [AD, Gouverneur Morris Papers, Library of Congress]).

To William R. Putnam [1]

New York Decr 6. 1802

Dr. Sir

The multiplicity of my engagements has diverted my attention from a remittance to you on account of the taxes of my lands in your quarter.[2] I count upon your good will that no inconvenience will have ensued & I now enclose Fifty Dollars. It will be satisfactory to me to know that it has reached you and whether any further supply will be promptly requisite; also what are the present prospects as to the sale of these lands.

With great esteem & regard   I remain Dr Sir   Yr Obliged & obedt servant   A Hamilton

Wm. R Putnam Esq

ALS, Dawes Memorial library, Marietta College, Marietta, Ohio.
1. Putnam, the son of Rufus Putnam, was appointed a surveyor for the Ohio Company in 1794, and he subsequently worked for his father on surveys for the United States Government.
2. See H to Oliver Wolcott, Jr., October 3, 1802.

Account with John McComb, Junior [1]

[New York, December 8, 1802]

State of acct. between Genl. Hamilton and John McComb Junr.

amt. of Contract for finishing the Dwelling House		$1875–0
571 ds board as pr. agreement @ 3/ (done Last Year)		214–
amt. of Extra work is uncertain		
	Dolls	2089–

1802	Cr		
June 2d	By Cash recd	$400	
July	By Cash	400	
Sept. 12th	" Cash	400	
Decm. 8th	" Cash	150	
			1350–

AD, Hamilton Papers, Library of Congress.
1. McComb designed and supervised the construction of the Grange, H's country house in upper Manhattan. See the introductory note to Philip Schuyler to H, July 17, 1800; McComb to H, June 22, 1801.

To Richard Peters [1]

New York December 29
1802

Dear Sir

A disappointed politician you know is very apt to take refuge in a Garden. Accordingly I have purchased about thirty acres nine miles from Town, have built a house, planted a garden, and entered upon some other simple improvements.[2]

In this new situation, for which I am as little fitted as Jefferson to guide the helm of the UStates, I come to you as an Adept in rural science for instruction. The greatest part of my little farm will be dedicated to Grass. The soil is a sandy loam, in which there is rather too large a dose of Sand. Yet every thing has hitherto thriven well.

What will be my best plan as to the raising of Grass and what kinds ought I to prefer; and what season for sowing the seed? You have heard that on Long Island the plaister of Paris [3] has absolutely failed and that on this Island its success is very problematical. Yet in my neighbourhood it has been lately tried with some success; and an opinion is growing that if applied in a pretty smart shower of rain, it will answer the purpose. The rain is supposed to purify the air of the sea salts which are believed to be the obstacle to the salutary operation of the Gypsum. What say you to all this? What mode of experiment would you prescribe?

It has been mentioned to me that you have in your quarter a species of red clover, the stock of which is less coarse than ours, and the quality very good. If this be so, and you think well of it, you will oblige me by procuring & sending me a couple bushels of the seed. In asking such favours you will please to understand that I insist upon being informed how much any articles sent me, whether more or less, shall cost. For it is too much to draw upon the time and pockets too of our friends.

Adieu My Dear Sir. Mrs. Hamilton joins in high compliments to Mrs. Peters.

Yrs. truly

AH

R Peters Esq

ALS, Harvard College Library.
1. Peters, a lawyer from Philadelphia, was secretary of the Board of War from 1776 to 1781 with a few interruptions, a member of the Pennsylvania Assembly from 1787 to 1790, a member of the state Senate from 1791 to 1792, and United States judge for the District of Pennsylvania from 1792 until his death in 1828.
Peters was also a farmer who experimented with scientific farming methods. He was the first president of the Philadelphia Society for Promoting Agriculture, which was founded in 1785, and he was the author of more than one hundred articles on agriculture (*Memoirs of the Philadelphia Society for Promoting Agriculture* [Philadelphia, 1808–1939]).
2. H is referring to his country house, the Grange, which he built between 1800 and 1802 in upper Manhattan. See the introductory note to Philip Schuyler to H, July 17, 1800.

3. Peters was the author of *Agricultural enquiries on plaister of Paris. Also facts observations and conjectures on that substance, when applied as manure. Collected chiefly from the practice of farmers in Pennsylvania, and published as much with a view to incite as to give information* (Philadelphia: Printed by C. Cist, 1797).

To Charles Cotesworth Pinckney

Grange (NY)
Decr. 29. 1802 [1]

My Dear Sir

A garden, you know, is a very usual refuge of a disappointed politician. Accordingly, I have purchased a few acres about 9 Miles from Town, have built a house and am cultivating a Garden. The melons in your country are very fine. Will you have the goodness to send me some seed both of the Water & Muss Melons?

My daughter [2] adds another request, which is for three or four of your peroquets. She is very fond of birds. If there be any thing in this quarter the sending of which can give you pleasure, you have only to name them. As Farmers a new source of sympathy has risen between us; and I am pleased with every thing in which our likings and tastes can be approximated.

Amidst the triumphant reign of Decomocracy, do you retain sufficient interest in public affairs to feel any curiosity about what is going on? In my opinion the follies and vices of the Administration have as yet made no material impression to their disadvantage. On the contrary, I think the malady is rather progressive than upon the decline in our Northern Quarter.[3] The last *lullaby* message,[4] instead of inspiring contempt, attracts praise. Mankind are forever destined to be the dupes of bold & cunning imposture.

But a difficult *knot* has been twisted by the incident of the cession of Louisian [5] and the interruption of the Deposit at New Orleans.[6] You have seen the soft tun given to this in the message.[7] Yet we are told the President in conversation is very stout.[8] The great embarrassment must be how to carry on war without taxes. The pretty scheme of substituting œconomy to taxation will not do here; and a war would be a terrible comment upon the abandonment of the Internal Revenue. Yet how is popularity to be preserved with the

Western partisans if their interests are tamely sacrificed? Will the artifice be for the Chief to hold a bold language and the subalters to act a public part? Time must explain.

You know my general theory as to our Western affairs. I have always held that the Unity of our empire and the best interests of our Nation require that we should annex to the UStates all the territory East of the Mississippia, New Orleans included.[9] Of course I infer that in an emergency like the present, Energy is Wisdom.

Adieu My Dear Sir   Ever Yrs   A H

Mrs. H joins me in affectionate Compliments to Mrs. Pinckney.

General Pinckney

ALS, Charleston Library Society, Charleston, South Carolina.

1. In Hamilton, *Intimate Life,* 346, this letter is dated "December 20, 1802."

2. Angelica Hamilton, H's older daughter, was eighteen years old in 1802. According to Allan McLane Hamilton, "Upon receipt of the news of her brother's death in the Eacker duel, she suffered so great a shock that her mind became permanently impaired, and although taken care of by her devoted mother for a long time there was no amelioration in her condition, and she was finally placed under the care of Dr. [James] MacDonald of Flushing, and remained in his charge until her death at the age of seventy-three" (Hamilton, *Intimate Life,* 219). For information on the duel between Philip Hamilton and George I. Eacker, see Benjamin Rush to H, November 26, 1801.

3. On November 6, 1802, George Cabot wrote to Rufus King: "The failure of the Federalists in the Election of J. Q. Adams may be attributed to negligence or rather weariness. . . . but the failure of Mr. Pickering proves the decline of good influence in that district" (King, *The Life and Correspondence of Rufus King,* IV, 181). In November, 1802, Adams and Timothy Pickering were unsuccessful candidates for the House of Representatives from Massachusetts.

4. H is referring to Thomas Jefferson's second annual message, which Jefferson sent to Congress on December 15, 1802 (*Annals of Congress,* XII, 12–15).

5. See William Constable to H, March 23, 1801, note 2.

6. Under the provisions of Article XXII of the Treaty of Friendship, Limits, and Navigation, which the United States and Spain had signed at San Lorenzo el Real on October 27, 1795, United States traders had the right to store goods at New Orleans for shipment to other ports (Miller, *Treaties,* II, 318–38). This article reads in part: ". . . his Catholic Majesty will permit the Citizens of the United States for the space of three years from this time to deposit their merchandize and effects in the Port of New Orleans, and to export them from thence without paying any other duty than a fair price for the hire of the stores, and his Majesty promises either to continue this permission if he finds during that time that it is not prejudicial to the interests of Spain, or if he should not agree to continue it there, he will assign to them on another part of the banks of the Mississipi an equivalent establishment" (Miller, *Treaties,* II, 337).

The deposit was formally established in 1798. On October 18, 1802, Juan

Ventura Morales, acting intendant of Louisiana, adhering to secret orders from the Spanish crown, published a proclamation ending the right of American deposit. News of the proclamation reached New York City on November 22, 1802 (*The* [New York] *Daily Advertiser*, November 23, 1802; *New-York Evening Post*, November 25, 1802). An English translation of part of Morales's proclamation appeared in both newspapers on November 26.

7. Jefferson made no mention in his message of the ending of the right of deposit at New Orleans. Concerning the cession of Louisiana, Jefferson stated: "The cession of the Spanish province of Louisiana to France, which took place in the course of the late war, will, if carried into effect, make a change in the aspect of our foreign relations, which will doubtless have just weight in any deliberations of the Legislature connected with that subject" (*Annals of Congress*, XII, 14).

8. On January 2, 1802, Louis André Pichon wrote to Charles Maurice de Talleyrand-Périgord: "J'ai eû il y a quelques jours avec M. Jefferson une longue conversation où il a été question de la Louisiana et des relations de commerce à lier entre les deux Nations. . . . La prise de possession de la Louisiana lui parait toujours de notre pais une grande faute politique et qui dois produire à la première guerre d'Europe une rupture entre nous et les Etats-unis et amener entre ceux-ci et l'Angleterre une Alliance. Nous n'y resterons, dit-il, qu-autans qu'il plaira aux Etats-unis; il ne pense pas que la chose vaille une guerre, mais ce sera un evenemens qu'on ne pourra pas émpeché" (copy, *Arch. des Aff. Etr., Corr. Pol., Etats-Unis*).

On March 6, 1802, Edward Thornton, British chargé d'affaires at Washington, wrote to Robert Banks Jenkinson, Lord Hawkesbury, British Foreign Secretary: "Mr. Jefferson used the ⟨same⟩ language to me which I heard he had ⟨held⟩ to other persons on the subject. He said that the occupation of this country by ⟨France⟩ gave an entirely new character to all the American relations with her—that hither⟨to⟩ he had regarded her as so removed by ⟨her⟩ situation and absolute want of contact ⟨for⟩ any collision with the United States, that it was not easy to foresee any mode of disturb⟨ing⟩ the mutual tranquillity of the two countries—that his wish for peace and harmony con⟨tinued⟩ equally sincere and ardent; but the inevitable consequences of such a neighborhood must ⟨provoke⟩ jealousy, irritation, and finally hostilities. He had mentioned this, he observed, with the same frankness to the Spanish and French Agents, and had frequently suggested to both ⟨of⟩ them, as the only mean of averting future quarrels, the *voluntary cession* of the Island of Orleans to the United States ⟨which as ample stipulations for its freedom even in time of war as could be devised) because it could not fail to come into their hands, whenever the arrival of that calamity should oblige them to exert their force" (ALS, PRO: F.O., 5/96–99).

9. See H to George Washington, September 15, 1790; "Conversation with George Beckwith," September 25–30, 1790, October 15–20, 1790; H to Pickering, March 27, 1798; H to James McHenry, January 27–February 11, 1798.

From William R. Putnam

[*Marietta, Territory Northwest of the River Ohio, December, 1802.* On January 17, 1803, Putnam wrote to H and itemized H's account, which contained: "1802 Decmr to postage of a letter." *Letter not found.*]

1 8 0 3

From Richard Peters

Philada. 8. Jany. 1803

Dear Sir

Yours of the 29 Decr. I did not receive 'till the Day before Yesterday. I *marvel* that you should be a *dissappointed* Politician. I am a mortified but not dissappointed one. You must have foreseen the Catastrophe which has befallen us. I was a Cassandra because more of a Looker on, than one playing the Game. Much useless Pains did I take in the Case of the House Tax &c &c to earn among my zealous Brother Feds the Character of a *Half paced* halting Politician.[1] But I saw the Race would not be to the Swift; tho' no one laments more than I do their being distanced.

A Garden is too sequestered a Position for one whose Mind cannot be confined within its Limits. A strong Passion for horticultural or rural Persuits has sometimes lulled, but has never yet eradicated the stronger Propensities for political Operations. In old Times it was more the Fashion for People to quit great public Scenes, for the Still-Life of the Country. Yet I believe there were few, when Time was younger, who did not cast "a longing lingering Look behind." [2] Make your little Farm your Plaything—but see that you have other Business, that you may afford to pay for the Rattle. It is well you have anything to withdraw you from unpleasant Contemplations. I should be very happy to give you Instructions, in one of the few Subjects you do not know better than I do. I wish your Retreat was not so distant from the City; both on Account of your frequent Calls to it, & because it would be serviceable both to your Farm & the Town, to remove *the Filth* with which it abounds. You must depend on Manure from more proximate Sources. Your Soil is the one calculated for Plaister of Paris; but if the Sea Air mixes with its Atmosphere, it will not succeed. The Theory of Plaister I started in my little Publication [3] some Years ago, I find from many Experiments, perfectly correct. The least Mixture of marine saline Particles with the Gypsum, neutralizes that Substance; & converts the Mass into Sulphate of Soda, or Glauber Salts. The operative Principle is the Sulphuric Acid, a Mixture of common Salt with this, will render it totally or paritally inefficacious, for agricultural Purposes. Accident, or Absence of Sea Air, may have permitted the operation of the Plaister occasionally. But do not believe those who tell you about the Magic of sowing it in Rain, in Preference to Sunshine. The Plaister does not vanish; & is subject to the Influence of the Air, & all it brings along with it, after the Clouds have shut their Flood Gates. It is no great Expence to make Trials on your Land. Read my little Collection; which you may get in New York, if the Pastry Cooks have not singed it away. It contains all I can say on that Subject. I have strewed Plaister more than 30 years & was the first who applied it extensively. I have often failed, but in general I have succeeded. Therefore be not discouraged by a Failure or two.

If you dedicate your Farm to Grass, divided it into small Fields; say 5 or 6 Acres each. Let them be well cultivated with cleaning Crops, so as to destroy all the noxious Weeds or Grasses. The great Mistake of young Farmers, & the Disgrace of slovenly old ones, is to be in too great a Hurry in laying their Grounds for Grass. The Pests of bad precedent farming choak all their Crops. Spare no Expence to destroy Weeds, by cutting them before ripe, & frequent deep ploughing, with covering Crops. Weeds are the Jacobins of Agriculture. If you do not destroy them, they will certainly ruin you. Trench ploughing is the surest Way to get rid of them. If I can find a little Essay I wrote many Years ago on this Subject,[4] I will send it to you. You must make compost of all the Trash of your Farm, mixed with what little Dung you have & Lime or Cystic Shells. Have you any Pond or River Mud? This with Ashes to give it Stimulus is good for your Land.

I sow my Grass Seeds at all Seasons, as Circumstances require. On my Wheat Fields in February—with Oats or Barley in the Spring also then with Flax—With Buckwheat in July—with Turnips in August. Timothy succeeds best in the Autumn. I cannot tell what is the best Seed for your Ground—if wet, Timothy or Hard Grass—if dry red clover mixed with Timothy or orchard Grass according to Situation. The latter absorb the superabundant Juices of the Clover, & while growing preserve the Crop from lodging or laying

down. Salt your Clover when you are putting it into the Stack or
Mow. A Bushell to 4 or 5 Tons. I would chearfully send you Clover
Seed; but we have none better than your own. Sowing it thick or
thin makes it fine or coarse. I generally sow 8 Pounds or Pints to
the Acre & I find it fine enough. I have tried Luzerne, Onobrychis
or Sainfoin, Burnet &c &c, but I stick to the red clover because it
sticks to me. The others cost more than they come to.

I am glad you have this little Syren to seduce you from public
Anxieties. But take Care that the meretricious Charms of this new
Flame does not make too great Drafts on your Purse. I wish she
may often bring me into your Memory. If any of your Details
should require any Advice I can give, it will always be at your Service. This Advice, however otherwise useless, will give me Opper-
tunities of repeating the sincere Assurances of Esteem, with which
I always am

 very affectionately yours   Richard Peters [5]

Mrs P & my whole House desire to be remembered with Affection
to Mrs H and your Family.

Genl Hamilton

ALS, Hamilton Papers, Library of Congress.
 1. "An Act to provide for the valuation of Lands and Dwelling-Houses, and
the enumeration of Slaves within the United States" (1 *Stat.* 580–91 [July 9,
1798]); "An Act to lay and collect a direct tax within the United States" (1
Stat. 597–604 [July 14, 1798]). See Oliver Wolcott, Jr., to H, April 1, 1799;
James McHenry to H, March 13, 1799, note 12.
 Peters was one of the presiding judges at the two trials of John Fries in
1799 and 1800 (William Lewis to H, October 11, 1800, note 1). At Fries's trial
in 1799 Peters objected to a motion by the defendant's attorney for a new trial,
but yielded to the opinion of James Iredell, the other presiding judge (Francis
Wharton, *State Trials of the United States During the Administrations of
Washington and Adams* [Philadelphia, 1849], 608–09).
 2. The full quotation reads:
 "For who, to dumb forgetfulness a prey,
  This pleasing anxious being e'er resign'd,
  Left the warm precincts of the cheerful day,
   Nor cast one longing ling'ring look behind?"   (Thomas Gray, *Elegy in a
Country Churchyard*, Stanza 22).
 3. See H to Peters, December 29, 1802, note 3.
 4. On March 8, 1808, Peters read a paper before the Philadelphia Society for
Promoting Argiculture entitled "On Trench Ploughing" in which he stated:
"Many years ago I gave an account of my process, and its results. It was not

theory, but the actual product of repeated and successful practice" (*Memoirs of the Philadelphia Society for Promoting Agriculture. Containing Communications on Various Subjects in Husbandry & Rural Affairs*, I [Philadelphia, 1808], 240–48). Peters's earlier "account" has not been found.

5. On the back of this letter H wrote:
"1 Appeal to Circuit Courts
2 *Woodhams*
    Whether previous certificate requisite
3 Gouverneur & *Kemble*."
For information concerning the cases of *The United States* v *The Ship Two Marys* and *The United States* v *The Ship Liberty*, in both of which Captain James Woodham of New York City was the claimant, see Goebel, *Law Practice*, II, 826–27.

From William R. Putnam

[Territory Northwest of the River Ohio]
Marietta January 17th 1803

Dr Sir

Your favor of December 6th has been duly receiv'd. You mention inclosing fifty dollars, the letter contained but thirty, consisting of one twenty, and one ten dollar bill; the letter and seal appeared in good order. Inclosed you'll find the receipt for the payment of your taxes for the year 1802 and here follows a statement of my acct.

A Hamilton Esqr Dr

1802 July to ballance of a/c for 1801	$8.23	
Decmr to postage of a letter	25 [1]	
to cash paid for taxes	20.09 [2]	
to my commission	4	
	33.57	$33.57
Pr Conr. Supr Cr By cash per post Decmr 1802		30.
Ballance debt		3.57

This ballance will be included in the statement for 1803—when the amount of taxes is known. The prospect of sale of land in the Ohio Companys purchase is not very flattering at present—owing to two circumstances—the United States have such quantities for sale in small tracts upon credit [3]—And as yet the proprietors of the Company have not generally been disposed to sell at all—and many of those who are disposed to sell, choose to do it in whole shares than in parts. Most of the persons coming to settle in our country are unable to purchase a share, and were they able, they would not as the parts of a share are as disconnected as any other lands in the country. Untill it is known that the proprietors will generally sell their lands in seperate tracts, and partly upon credit, it cannot be expected settlers will apply for them. Most of the land composing your five shares [4] may be said to be of a good quality—and some day will command both price & settlement. Your taxes have been augmented for the want of payment on the first of Novr last fifty per Centum which was not convenient for me to prevent—expecting daily to have receiv'd your money. I have the honor to be

Dear Sir your most obedient Hb Servt   Wm Rufus Putnam

The Honl A Hamilton Esqr.

ALS, Yale University Library.
1. Letter not found.
2. In the Yale University Library there is a receipt which reads:
"Rec'd of Wm Rufus Putnam
A Hamilton Esq his taxes upon his land for the year 1803 amounting to twenty dollars & nine Cents.
This 12th of January
AD 1803   Ebr. Sprout Sheriff
                                                      & Co."
3. See "An Act to amend the act intituled 'An act providing for the sale of the lands of the United States, in the territory northwest of the Ohio, and above the mouth of Kentucky river' " (2 *Stat.* 73–78 [May 10, 1800]).
4. See H to Oliver Wolcott, Jr., October 3, 1802, note 7.

From Theodore Sedgwick [1]

Stockbridge [Massachusetts] 27. Jany. 1803.[2]

Dear Sir,

This will be handed to you by a Mr. Thomas Fitch; [3] and, at his desire, is addressed to his case. He wishes for the honor of being known to you, and he hopes for the aid of your patronage, in the persuit of some object, of which I have no distinct knowledge. He is of an obscure, tho' respectable family in this neighbourhood. The President of the college where he was educated,[4] a good & respectable man, has spoken to me of his talents and acquirements in terms above the degree which would be expressed by the epithet *decent,* and of his moral character as perfectly pure.

I regret, exceedingly, that I had not the pleasure to see you here the last autumn.[5] There is not a man, on the earth, whose company would have given me more pleasure. Of this enough, because you know the fact to be so without my affirmation.

What think you of democracy? Will it not progress successfully until its evils are felt? For myself I have no doubt that it will. Even in this state great sacrafices are made to popular passions & prejudices, and they are deemed necessary to retain the powers of our government in federal hands. There is one consolation, under all the humiliation which we endure, from a sense of the degradation of our national character—this state of things cannot long exist. The disorganization which is the inevitable effect, of the enfeebling policy of democracy, will produce such intolerable evils as will necessarily destroy their cause. All that good & enlightened men can hope is to be in such a state, as that their talents and experience, at that period, may be applied to the public benefit. For that purpose, union of conduct & sympathy of sentiment ought now to be cultivated. It is of the utmost importance that the conduct of certain men should be constantly regulated by these important considerations. Hence it was that I was pleased with the idea, which you suggested, when I last had the pleasure of seeing you, of a confidential meeting,[6] and I have very much regreted that it did not take place.

It is very important that the federalists should retain and acquire the possession of state governments wherever in their power. For this reason, and indeed for many other I am glad Mr King is about to return home.[7] With wisdom and prudence I think it probable that he may be placed at the head of the government of New York. He may there do infinitely more good than in the inefficient office of Vice-president. General Pinckney [8] must, in all events, be considered as our candidate for the first office. I have been inexpressibly disgusted with some of our friends who have suggested that we ought to consider him only as designed for the second.[9] There is, however, another consideration on this subject which ought to be considered as conclusive—we shall most certainly not succeed at the next election; nor is it, in my mind, desirable that we should. Should Mr. King be holden up for this office it would lessen, at least, the probability of his success for the government of New York.

There seems to me an inexcusable indolence, or a want of ability among our friends at Washington. The public interest has been shamefully neglected, or profligately sacraficed, in the affair of Louisiana,[10] the compromise with Georgia,[11] and in the attempt made to break down our system of navigation.[12] These subjects either are not understood, or there is a criminal inattention to them.

Next week I go to Boston, where I wish you would have the goodness to address a letter to me. Present my sincere regards to Mrs. Hamilton, & believe as I truly am your friend,

Theodore Sedgwick

Genl Hamilton.

ALS, Hamilton Papers, Library of Congress.

1. Sedgwick, a Massachusetts lawyer and Federalist, was a member of the House of Representatives from 1789 to 1796 and from 1799 to 1801. He was a member of the United States Senate from 1796 to 1799. In 1802 Sedgwick was appointed for life to the Supreme Court of Massachusetts.

2. In a list entitled "Letters from T. S. [Theodore Sedgwick] to Genl. A. Hamilton" (William Livingston Papers, Massachusetts Historical Society, Boston), this letter is dated January 27, 1801.

3. Fitch, a native of Salisbury, Connecticut, and a grandson of Thomas Fitch, who served as governor of Connecticut from 1756 to 1766, was graduated in 1798 from Williams College, of which Sedgwick was a trustee. He became a merchant, first in Vermont and later in Schoharie County, New York, and Vernon, New York.

4. The Reverend Ebenezer Fitch was graduated from Yale in 1777 and served as a tutor in religion at Yale from 1780 to 1783 and from 1786 to 1791. In 1791 he became preceptor of a new academy in Williamstown, Massachusetts, which was chartered as Williams College in June, 1793. Fitch was president of Williams from 1793 to 1815. Ebenezer Fitch was not related to Thomas Fitch.

5. See H to John V. Henry, October 31, 1802, note 2.

6. See H to Charles Cotesworth Pinckney, March 15, 1802; James A. Bayard to H, April 12, 1802.

7. See Rufus King to H, April 8, August 5, first letter of August 6, 1802; H to King, June 3, 1802.

8. Charles Cotesworth Pinckney.

9. Although most Federalist leaders had generally agreed that Pinckney and King should be the party's candidates in 1804, they had given little thought to the question of which one should head the ticket. On November 12, 1802, William Vans Murray reported to King: "For some time the Feds. have talked of running you & Genl. Pinckney as P. & V. P. fairly & side by side" (King, *The Life and Correspondence of Rufus King*, IV, 181). On December 12, 1802, Robert Troup wrote to King: "The project on foot here seems to be

to run you at the next election for Vice-President or President—which of the two is not determined" (King, *The Life and Correspondence of Rufus King*, IV, 193). On the other hand, on November 21, 1802, William Hindman, a Federalist Senator from Maryland, wrote to King: ". . . your Friends . . . are anxious that you should be the next President . . ." (King, *The Life and Correspondence of Rufus King*, IV, 183).

10. This is a reference to the Federalist position that Thomas Jefferson should have opposed by force the cession of Louisiana to France. See *Annals of Congress*, XII, 83–89, and "For the *Evening Post*," February 8, 1803.

11. On April 24, 1802, three commissioners representing the United States (Secretary of State James Madison, Secretary of the Treasury Albert Gallatin, and Attorney General Levi Lincoln) and six commissioners from Georgia, all of whom were Republicans, signed an agreement entitled "The Articles of Agreement and Cession" (Carter, *Territorial Papers*, V, 142–46). Under this agreement, which is often referred to as the Georgia Compact, Georgia ceded fifty-four million acres of land between the state's western boundary and the Mississippi River. The land in question, which formed part of the Mississippi Territory that had been organized in 1798, had been claimed by both Georgia and the United States. As compensation for the land cession, the Federal Government paid the state one and one-half million dollars, promised to extinguish Indian titles to the land within Georgia, and agreed to reserve five million acres to satisfy unsettled claims within the ceded area. Most such claims grew out of land sales by the state to land companies under the terms of the Yazoo Act of 1795 (H to James Greenleaf, October 9, 1795, note 3).

Federalists objected to the agreement on the ground that it was too favorable to the state's interests (*New-York Evening Post*, May 14, 18, 20, 22, 25, 26, 1802). On May 3, 1802, Federalists in the House of Representatives unsuccessfully attempted to prevent the cession from going into effect before the next session of Congress (*Annals of Congress*, XI, 1295).

12. This is a reference to the Federalist reaction to the failure of the Jefferson administration to act aggressively following the Spanish withdrawal of the right of deposit at New Orleans on October 18, 1802. See H to Pinckney, December 29, 1802, notes 6 and 7; Troup to King, January 8, 1803 (King, *The Life and Correspondence of Rufus King*, IV, 203).

Election by a Meeting of the Society for Promoting the Manumission of Slaves [1]

New York, February 1, 1803. ". . . The Society proceeded to Ballot for their ann[u]al officers, when, on Counting the votes, the following persons appeared duly elected vizt . . . Alexander Hamilton . . . Consellor. . . ."

Ms "Minutes of the Society for Promoting the Manumission of Slaves," New-York Historical Society, New York City.

1. H was one of the original sponsors of the Society for Promoting the Manumission of Slaves and Protecting Such of Them as have been, or may be, Liberated, which was founded in 1785. H remained a member until his death. See "Attendance at a Meeting of the Society for Promoting the Manumission of Slaves," February 4, 1785, note 1.

For the Evening Post [1]

[New York, February 8, 1803] [2]

Since the question of Independence, none has occurred more deeply interesting to the United States than the cession of Louisiana

New-York Evening Post, February 8, 1803; JCH Transcripts.

1. H wrote this article in response to Thomas Jefferson's appointment of James Monroe as United States Minister Extraordinary and Plenipotentiary to France and Spain on January 11, 1803. Jefferson gave Monroe the power to act independently or jointly with Robert R. Livingston, United States Minister Plenipotentiary to France, and Charles Pinckney, United States Minister Plenipotentiary at Madrid, "to enter into a treaty or convention . . . for the purpose of enlarging, and more effectually securing our rights and interests in the river Mississippi, and in the territories eastward thereof" (*Executive Journal*, I, 431–32). On January 12, 1803, the Senate confirmed Monroe's nomination by a vote of fifteen to twelve, with all the Federalist senators voting against it (*Executive Journal*, I, 436).

Monroe left the United States on March 8 and arrived in France on April 8. On April 30 he, Livingston, and François, marquis de Barbé-Marbois, Minister of the Public Treasury of the French Republic, signed the Treaty of the Cession of Louisiana and two accompanying conventions. These three documents provided for the sale of the territory of Louisiana, including New Orleans, to the United States for sixty million francs or eleven million two hundred and fifty thousand dollars. The United States also assumed payment of debts owed by France to United States citizens which had been incurred before the Convention of 1800 (Treaty of Môrtefontaine) and which amounted to no more than twenty million francs, or approximately three and one-half million dollars (Miller, *Treaties*, II, 498–528).

In the *New-York Evening Post* the article printed above is preceded by the following paragraph: "*Louisiana*. A writer who some time past addressed the public in a series of spirited numbers under the signature of CORIOLANUS, in the [New York] Morning Chronicle [December 20, 21, 22, 24, 27, 30, 1802; January 1, 10, 11, 12, February 8, 1803], finds himself at last disposed to slide fully into the views of the administration. He ascribes his former sentiments to haste, and recommends negociation, by Mr. Munro, as preferable to *war*, which he now deplores as the greatest calamity which can befall a nation. We, however, see no reason to alter our former opinions, nor shall we retract any thing that has been said in this paper. War is undoubtedly a calamity, but national degradation is a greater, and besides, is always inevitably followed by war itself. But not to dilate here, we feel no scruples in declaring, that in our opinion, the appointment of an Envoy Extraordinary, at this time, and under present circumstances, is in every respect the weakest measure that ever disgraced the administration of any country. And it requires not the gift of prophecy to foretel that the time is coming when there will be but one opinion on this subject. The following letter received this morning from a correspondent, merits serious perusal of every reader."

H's article reflected the belief of many Federalist party leaders that war with Spain or France was more desirable than negotiation. See *Annals of Congress*, XII, 83–88, 91–96, 107–19, 136–39, 153–57, 171–84, 185–206.

2. In *HCLW*, VI, 333–36, this document is dated "1803."

to France.[3] This event threatens the early dismemberment of a large portion of our country: more immediately the safety of all the Southern States; and remotely the independence of the whole union. This is the portentous aspect which the affair presents to all men of sound and reflecting minds of whatever party, and it is not to be concealed that the only question which now offers itself, is, how is the evil to be averted?

The strict right to resort at once to WAR, if it should be deemed expedient cannot be doubted. *A manifest and great danger* to the nation: the nature of the cession to France, extending to ancient limits without respect to our rights by treaty; [4] the direct infraction of an important article of the treaty itself in withholding the deposit of New-Orleans; [5] either of these affords justifiable cause of WAR and that they would authorize immediate hostilities, is not to be questioned by the most scrupulous mind.

The whole is then a question of expediency. Two courses only present. First, to negociate and endeavour to purchase, and if this fails to go to war. Secondly, to seize at once on the Floridas and New-Orleans, and then negociate.

A strong objection offers itself to the first. There is not the most remote probability that the ambitious and aggrandizing views of Bonaparte will commute the territory for money. Its acquisition is of immense importance to France, and has long been an object of her extreme solicitude.[6] The attempt therefore to purchase, in the first instance, will certainly fail, and in the end, war must be resorted to, under all the accumulation of difficulties caused by a previous and strongly fortified possession of the country by our adversary.

3. See William Constable to H, March 23, 1801, notes 2 and 3; H to Charles Cotesworth Pinckney, December 29, 1802.

4. The Treaty of Friendship, Limits, and Navigation, signed at San Lorenzo el Real on October 27, 1795, between Spain and the United States (Miller, *Treaties*, II, 318–45).

5. For Article XXII of the Treaty of Friendship, Limits, and Navigation between the United States and Spain, to which H is referring, see H to Pinckney, December 29, 1802, note 6.

6. See Timothy Pickering to H, March 25, 1798; "The Stand No. IV," April 12, 1798; H to Harrison Gray Otis, January 26, 1799.

For detailed discussions of French involvement in Louisiana during the last third of the eighteenth century, see Mildred Stahl Fletcher, "Louisiana as a Factor in French Diplomacy From 1763 to 1800," *Mississippi Valley Historical Review*, XVII (December, 1930), 367–76; E. Wilson Lyon, *Louisiana in French Diplomacy 1795–1804* (Norman, Oklahoma, 1934).

The second plan is, therefore, evidently the best. First, because effectual: the acquisition easy; the preservation afterwards easy: The evils of a war with France at this time are certainly not very formidable: Her fleet crippled and powerless, her treasury empty, her resources almost dried up, in short, gasping for breath after a tremendous conflict which, though it left her victorious, left her nearly exhausted under her extraordinary exertions.[7] On the other hand, we might count with certainty on the aid of Great Britain with her powerful navy.

Secondly, this plan is preferable because it affords us the only chance of avoiding a long-continued war. When we have once taken possession, the business will present itself to France in a new aspect. She will then have to weigh the immense difficulties, if not the utter impracticability of wresting it from us. In this posture of affairs she will naturally conclude it is her interest to bargain. Now it may become expedient to terminate hostilities by a purchase, and a cheaper one may reasonably be expected.

To secure the better prospect of final success, the following auxiliary measures ought to be adopted.

The army should be increased to ten thousand men,[8] for the purpose of insuring the preservation of the conquest. Preparations for increasing our naval force should be made.[9] The militia should be classed, and effectual provision made for raising on an emergency, 40,000 men.[10] Negociations should be pushed with Great-Britain, to

7. France and Great Britain had been at peace since March, 1802, when both countries signed the Treaty of Amiens.

8. For the strength and organization of the United States Army while Jefferson was President, see H to Rufus King, June 3, 1802, note 9.

9. When Jefferson became President, the United States naval force consisted of six active frigates and seven reserve frigates, as well as nine captains, thirty-six lieutenants, and one hundred and fifty midshipmen. See "An Act providing for a Naval peace establishment, and for other purposes" (2 *Stat.* 110–11 [March 3, 1801]). See also H to King, June 3, 1802, note 10.

10. Shortly after H's article was published, John Breckenridge, Republican Senator from Kentucky, introduced a series of resolutions, on February 23, 1803, one of which authorized the President "to require of the Executives of the several States to take effectual measures to organize, arm and equip, according to law, and hold in readiness to march at a moment's warning, eighty thousand effective militia, officers included" (*Annals of Congress*, XII, 119). On February 28 a bill containing these resolutions passed the Senate and was sent to the House, where it was passed on March 3, 1803 (*Annals of Con-*

induce her to hold herself in readiness to co-operate fully with us, at a moment's warning.

This plan should be adopted and proclaimed before the departure of our envoy.

Such measures would astonish and disconcert Bonaparte himself; our envoy would be enabled to speak and treat with effect; and all Europe would be taught to respect us.

These ideas have been long entertained by the writer, but he has never given himself the trouble to commit them to the public, because he despaired of their being adopted. They are now thrown out with very little hope of their producing any change in the conduct of administration, yet, with the encouragement that there is a strong current of public feeling in favour of decisive measures.

If the President would adopt this course, he might yet retrieve his character; induce the best part of the community to look favorably on his political career, exalt himself in the eyes of Europe, save the country, and secure a permanent fame. But for this, alas! Jefferson is not destined!

PERICLES.

---

gress, XII, 255, 256, 258–60, 261, 610, 643). See "An Act directing a detachment from the Militia of the United States, and for erecting certain Arsenals" (2 Stat. 241 [March 3, 1803]). See also "An Act in addition to an act, intituled 'An act more effectually to provide for the National defence, by establishing an uniform Militia throughout the United States'" (2 Stat. 241 [March 2, 1803]).

Account with John McComb, Junior [1]

[New York, February 10, 1803]

Alexander Hamilton Esquire in acct. with John McComb Junr.

Dr.			Cr.
1802		1801	
To amt. for finishing House at Bloomingdale		By Cash receiv'd on Ac(ct — ‹—›	
as p Contract	$1875	July " Cash ‹—›	
750 days board as p. agreement 3/	281.25	Sep 18 " Cash ‹—›	
Securing Cellar floor agt. Rats	25.	Dec. 6th. " Cash ‹—›	
2 load Stone had by the Carpenters	1.25	1802	
Paving the Cool Cellar	10.	Apl. 24 " Cash ‹—›	
Ash House and 2 Iron doors &c.	14	30 " Cash ‹—›	
Cess Pool	30	July 23d. " Cash ‹—›	
Rough Casting the foundation	13	" 62½ ds. Board ‹—›	
Foundation for 8 Peirs	8	" Ballance due J McC(omb —›	
Foundation for Stoops	8		
Inrichments for Cornice	30		
June 21st. 3 Casks Lime	4.50		
28 2 do Lime	2.75		
20 Loads Stone	12.50		
24 days Mason work 13/	39.		
26½ ds Laborers do 8/	26.50		
1 Cast Iron plate for Stew Holes	7.50		
1 Iron bar for Ironing room chimy.	1.		
Freight of the Lime	5.		

		3/ }	
6¾ days mason work plasterg. necessary House & flagging			10.96
milk House			
Octr. 27	2 casks Lime		3.81
Novm. 5th.	2 do do		3.25
	6½ ds. Mason Setting Grates &c		10.56
	6½ ds. Labor		6.50
	12 lb. Nails		2.
1803			
Feby. 9th	2 ds Mason taking down the Kitchen range		3.25
	Shed and Scaffold plank		20.
		Dolls	2456.83

New York 10th February 1803

AD, Hamilton Papers, Library of Congress.

1. For background to this document, see the introductory note to Philip Schuyler to H, July 17, 1800; McComb to H, June 22, 1801; "Account with John McComb, Jr.," December 8, 1802.

2. On the back of this document H wrote:

"Ballance due J McComb brought over ⟨Interest from⟩ 10 Feby. 1803 to 23 of ⟨May 1804⟩ is (one) year 3 Months & 13 days

583:33

11.67

595.00

1803
May 23 Cash   250.

Ds.   345.00

1803
Interest from May 23 to July 1 1804   26.70

Ds   371.70."

Below H's computation of the amount he owed to McComb, he wrote and McComb signed: "Received New York March 23. 1804 Received of Alexander Hamilton his note for the above Ballance payable on the first of June next which when paid will be in full of all demands.
John McComb Junr."

In H's Cash Book, 1795–1804, under the date of June 14, 1804, H wrote: "Grange ⟨McCombe⟩ 371.70" (AD, Hamilton Papers, Library of Congress).

From John Guillemard [1]

Gower Street. [London] 22 feb. 1803.

Sir

I take the liberty of introducing to your acquaintance and recommending to your attentions the Earl of Selkirk [2] a young Nobleman whose merits you will soon be able to appreciate and respect. I shall be excused for my motive's sake, which is not only to render him Service but to assure you that neither time nor distance have diminished the high sense I entertain of the attentions with which you sometimes honoured me during my residence in the United States. I have the honour to be Sir your obliged and obedt. humble servant.

J. Guillemard.

Gen. A. Hamilton &c &c

ALS, Hamilton Papers, Library of Congress.

1. Guillemard, a member of a family of Huguenot silk merchants who had settled in England, was born in England on August 31, 1764, and was graduated from St. John's College, Oxford, in 1786. On May 25, 1797, while in Philadelphia, he was chosen as the fifth commissioner to settle pre-Revolutionary War debts under Article 6 of the Jay Treaty (John Bassett Moore, ed., *International Adjudications: Ancient and Modern, History and Documents, Together with Mediatorial Reports, Advisory Opinions, and the Decisions of Domestic Commissions, on International Claims* [New York, 1929–1936], III, 18, 22). See Oliver Wolcott, Jr., to H, August 9, 1798, note 3.

2. Thomas Douglas, fifth Earl of Selkirk, Baron Daer and Shortcleuch, was a student at Edinburgh University between 1768 and 1790. While on a tour of the Scottish Highlands in 1792 he became interested in the plight of Scottish peasants who were being forced off the land as a result of the growth of sheep raising. In 1802 Selkirk obtained a large grant of crown lands on Prince Edward Island to provide a settlement for Scottish emigrants. He arrived on the island in August, 1803, and in September began a tour of the United States and Canada.

From Jonathan Lawrence and Jonathan Dayton [1]

New York, March 4, 1803. "The foregoing are Copies of our letters [2] to Meeker Denman & Co [3] on the subject of Insurance. . . ."

AL, Hamilton Papers, Library of Congress.

1. Lawrence and Dayton were partners in a mercantile firm at 94 Greenwich Street, New York City.

2. Copies, Hamilton Papers, Library of Congress.

This letter and its enclosures, which concern the case of *Lawrence and Dayton* v *Columbian Insurance Company, Brig Molly,* are printed in Goebel, *Law Practice,* II, 424–26. See also Goebel, *Law Practice,* forthcoming volumes.

3. The firm of Meeker, Denman, and Company, headed by Samuel Meeker, was located at 20 South Front Street, Philadelphia.

From Charles Cotesworth Pinckney

[*Charleston, South Carolina, March 5, 1803.* On March 6, 1803, Pinckney wrote to Hamilton: "I wrote you a few lines yesterday." *Letter not found.*]

From Madame de Caradeux Lecaye

Duplicata   Puorto-Rico Ce 6 mars *1803*

Qu'il m'est peinible d'avoir à vous apprendre par Cette lettre, Monsieur le Général, que je N'ai plus l'éspoire de revoir mes Amis de l'Amérique comme je m'en flattois pour ce Printems; Vous qui avez été témoins de mes regrets en les quittant, Vous jugerez aisement de mon Chagrin d'être obligée de renoncer au doux espoire de ma réunion avec eux, je ne Croyois pas pouvoir le Sentir aussi vivement, après avoir eu l'ame froissée par tous les malheurs que j'ai éprouvés depuis que j'ai quitté votre Pays, mais mon Amitié pour eux, me rappelle en ce moment, toute ma Sensibilité et me laisse à peine le Courage de leur anoncer cette Nouvelle. Vous Savez, Monsieur, les Mesures que je devois prendre pour m'assurer un Sort à l'abrit du besoin et exempt d'inquiétudes relativement aux affaires de mon Mari. il faloit pour Cela que je me rendisses à St Domingue, mais les Cruels évenements qui se Sont encore passés dans ce trop malheureux Pays,[1] ont empêchés mon Voyage: j'étois à la Veille de l'effectuer quand j'ai Su à tems le danger que j'allois Courir. Ma Séparation de Biens avec mon Mari [2] N'ayant pu avoir lieu par l'impossibilité de me rendre près de lui, je reste donc dans la même position relativement à ses Créanciers. Mrs Kemble [3] et Gouverneur,[4] Murray,[5] Jobert,[6] de New-york, Sont de ce Nombre pour quinze à Seize mille gourdes. Si j'allois vivre dans la même Ville qu'eux, j'aurois Continuellement à Craindre qu'ils prissent de l'humeur de ne point voir arriver un terme à leur payement et que je n'en devinsses Victime, pour ce qui assure mon existance en ce moment; j'y

tiens plus que jamais étant persuadée maintenant, que St. Domingue
est entierement perdu pour Cette génération, et que je N'aurai
plus rien de ma fortune. je me résigne en conséquance à vivre ig-
norée dans mes bois de Puorto-rico, plutôt que d'aller ecxiter la pitié
de mes amis, Soit par une jeune humilliante ou par les risques des
désagréments que je Serois dans le Cas dessuyer: Vous me Con-
noissez assez pour Savoir ce que je Souffrirois d'une pareille position.
je N'ai pu avoir que deux mille cinq Cents gourdes de mon frere;
je vais les employer avec les dix que j'ai en Amerique pour établir
une terre, Sous le nom de mon beau frere: [7] ce moïen m'assure une
jolie fortune dans trois ans. C'est Sans doute l'achetter bien Cher,
par Cette exile, mais la nécéssité est un Maître bien impérieux. Si
vous Connaissiez ma vie dans ce Pays vous m'en pleindriez, car elle
est très triste. je Suis absolument retirée du peu de Société qu'il y
auroit à voir, je m'occupes beaucoup de mes affaires et des Soins
Nécéssaire à mes malheureux Neveux et Niece et Voilà comme je
passe mon tems; aussi vous ne reconnoitriez pas mon Caractaire, je
Suis aussi triste que vous m'avez Connue gay. Donnez-moi je vous
prie, quelques-fois des marques de votre Souvenir, elles me Seront
Toujours précieuses, je ne puis jamais oublier les marques d'interet,
que vous et Votre famille m'avez témoigné avec tant de bonté.
Veuillez Monsieur, parler Souvent de moi à ma chere Kitty; [8] dites-
lui bien que je ne l'oublierai jamais, elle et Son bonheur m'occupes
plus qu'elle ne pense peut être. je ne vous dis rien pour Mme hamilton, lui écrivant par Cette même occasion. une des grandes peines
que j'éprouve ici est de ne pouvoir pas donner de mes Nouvelles à
mes amis Sans les plus grandes difficultées, et d'être si entierrement
privée des leurs. les Amériquins N'ont aucunes relations avec ce
Paÿs. je Suis obligée d'envoyer mes lettres à St. Thomas et Ste. Croix.
on est je vous assure mort au monde ici: je ne vous parlerai pas
davantage de ce Peuple, il n'en mérite pas la piene, mais le Paÿs est
parfaitement tranquil et offre de grandes ressources pour faire fortune, quant on a Cependant quelques moïens. on dit ici que vous
allez avoir une guerre avec les français; C'est nous la déclarer aussi:
on prétend que nous ne pouvons qu'y gagner dans Cette îsle, je ne
dois donc pas vous en faire de reproches. Comment va Votre Politique? je voudrois bien apprendre un grand Succès pour vous et
votre Parti. nous ne lisons pas une gazette dans ce Paÿs, ou n'en fait

même pas l'apparance d'une; on ne parle que Caffé et Sucre, jugez de notre Stupidité? que je regrette l'amérique, Monsieur! il ne Se passe pas de jours que je n'y pense dix fois et ne lui donnes autant de regrets. pouvois-je Croire tout ce qui S'est passé depuis que je l'ai quitté! je ne pouvois pas Croire que les français qui avoient Conquis tous les peuples, Succomberoient à la Conquête de St. Domingue. Adieu, Monsieur le Général, Voilà une longue lettre; je Crains de m'être trop livrée au plaisir de Causer avec vous Sans avoir assez Consultez vos affaires, mais je Compte Sur votre indulgance comme Sur Votre Amitié, quand à la mienne, elle vous est acquise pour la vie, par beaucoup de droits: je vous prie d'en recevoir l'assurance Sincère ainsi que Celle de mon estime distinguée.

P.S. je vais écrire cette lettre par duplicata dans l'éspoire qu'il vous en arrivera une: depuis mon départ de New york, je n'ai eu la Satisfaction d'en recevoir qu'une de vous, quoique je vous en aye ecrit au moins dix.[9] adressez moi vos lettres chez Messieurs *Rio Deville et Cie.* à St. Thomas.

AL, Hamilton Papers, Library of Congress.

1. See H to Madame de Caradeux Lecaye, November, 1800–1803; Rufus King to H, May 7, 1802, note 8; Lewis Tousard to H, September 6–9, 1802.

2. Comte Laurent Caradeux Lecaye was a French planter and a member of the colonial assembly who owned a plantation at Cul de Sac near Port-au-Prince in Santo Domingo. In 1792, as a result of the slave revolt against French rule on the island, he fled with fifty slaves and came to the United States, where he settled near Charleston, South Carolina. In 1799 François Dominique Toussaint L'Ouverture, the black ruler of Santo Domingo, invited the French colonists to return, and on August 14, 1799, Caradeux received a passport from the State Department allowing him to return to Cap-Français (RG 59, General Records of the Department of State, Cashbook, 1785–95, National Archives). See also Timothy Pickering to James Simon, collector of customs at Charleston, South Carolina, August 15, 1799 (LS, Massachusetts Historical Society, Boston).

3. Peter Kemble was a New York City merchant and a partner in the firm of Gouverneur and Kemble.

4. Madame de Caradeux Lecaye is referring either to Isaac Gouverneur, a New York City merchant and a partner in the firm of Gouverneur and Kemble, who died in February, 1800, or to Nicholas Gouverneur, Isaac Gouverneur's brother and also a New York City merchant. Kemble was a brother-in-law of the Gouverneurs.

5. There were several merchants in New York City named Murray, including John B. Murray, John Murray, Jr., Robert Murray, James V. Murray, George W. Murray, and John S. Murray.

6. Charles Gobert was a New York City merchant.

7. Captain-General Jean-Baptiste Caradeux Lecaye, Comte Laurent Caradeux

Lecaye's older brother, had been a planter in Santo Domingo until 1792, when he came to the United States and settled in Charleston, South Carolina, with his wife Louise Agathe and their two sons, John Baptiste and Jacques Joseph. He died in South Carolina in 1810.

8. Catherine Church Cruger, the daughter of Angelica and John B. Church and the wife of Peter Bertram Cruger, or Catherine Van Rensselaer Schuyler, Elizabeth Hamilton's younger sister.

9. Letter not found.

From Charles Cotesworth Pinckney [1]

Charleston [South Carolina] March 6th: 1803

My dear Sir:

I wrote you a few lines yesterday, and sent you some water melon seeds & musk melon seeds by the brig Charleston packett Samuel Wasson master which sails this morning.[2] I intend sending you some more by the Sloop Industry Capt: Mattocks who will sail on tuesday next.[3] I formerly sent some to Mrs: Washington at Mount Vernon;[4] but she told me they did not answer so well as some she got in the neighbourhood: perhaps had she planted the seeds from the melons which were produced from the Carolina seed the subsequent year, they would have adapted themselves to the Climate and produced good fruit. It was by this means we obtained our fine Cotton which has been of such advantage to our state; the first year it produced but three or four pods, by planting the seeds of those pods the second year, they produced thirty, & by following the same method the third year they were thoroughly naturalized & bore from 150 to 200 pods. I will also send you by the Industry a few seeds of the salvia coccinea or scarlet sage which I believe you have not with you, and of the Erythrina herbacea or coral shrub, also a few seeds of the Ipomoea quamoclit or Indian Creeper, & some of a beautiful purple convolvulus.

I will endeavour to obtain some Peroquets for Miss Hamilton; I have not seen any for some years; ours are the large kind, by no means equal in beauty to the small african species.

Does there not appear to be a great want of nerve & energy in the measures our Rulers are adopting? They are not calculated to avoid war, & we shall have to encounter it in a shameful state of unpreparedness. Yet such is the infatuation of the people that antifederalism certainly gains ground in this state,[5] which can only exist by a strong union & firm government.

Mrs: Pinckney unites with me in best respects to Mrs: Hamilton, and I always am

　　Yrs very sincerely　　　　　　　　Charles Cotesworth Pinckney

General Hamilton

The musk-melon seed by the Industry are a variety of different seeds which I have collected from different persons & are very fine.

ALS, Hamilton Papers, Library of Congress.
　　1. This letter was written in reply to H to Pinckney, December 29, 1802.
　　2. See the *Charleston Courier*, March 7, 1803.
　　3. See the *Charleston Courier*, March 8, 1803.
　　4. See Martha Washington to Mary Pinckney, April 20, 1799 (ALS, George Washington Papers, Library of Congress).
　　5. See John Harold Wolfe, *Jeffersonian Democracy in South Carolina* (Chapel Hill, 1940), 166–202.

To Elizabeth Hamilton [1]

Grange [New York] Sunday [March 13, 1803]

Captain Church,[2] My Dear Betsy, has just arrived & brings me favourable accounts of your journey hitherto and prospects. It is a great comfort to me and I hope will not be marred by bad weather; so that you may all speedily arrive and without too much fatigue to sooth and console your affected Father. Now you are all gone and I have no effort to make to keep up your spirits, my distress on his account and for the loss we have all sustained is very poignant. God grant that no new disaster may befal us; entreat your father to take care of himself for our sakes, and do you take care of yourself for mine.

　　Love to your sisters & much love for yourself　　　　　A H

I write your father by this opportunity & press him to accompany you back with Kitty.[3] This appears to me a *sine qua non*. Your Sister & you must not be refused.

　　　　　　　　　　　　　　　　　　　　　　　　Adieu

ALS, Hamilton Papers, Library of Congress.

1. Elizabeth Hamilton was on her way to Albany to be with her father, Philip Schuyler, after the death of her mother, Catherine Van Rensselaer Schuyler on March 7, 1803. For the notice of Mrs. Schuyler's death, see *The Albany Centinel*, March 15, 1803.

2. Philip Church, the son of John B. and Angelica Schuyler Church, was Elizabeth Hamilton's nephew. He attended Eton for six years and studied law at the Middle Temple in London. After the Church family returned to the United States in 1797, Philip Church entered the law office of Nathaniel Pendleton. On January 8, 1799, he was commissioned a captain in the Twelfth Regiment of Infantry (*Executive Journal*, I, 299, 303), and on January 12, 1799, he became an aide-de-camp to H (H to Church, January 12, 1799). In 1800, at a sale ordered by Chancellor Robert R. Livingston, he purchased for his father the Genesee tract that Robert Morris had mortgaged to John B. Church as security for a debt. He agreed to manage the land for his father and named the first town in the tract Angelica for his mother (see the introductory note to Morris to H, June 7, 1795).

3. Catherine Van Rensselaer Schuyler was Elizabeth Hamilton's youngest sister.

To Philip Schuyler

[*New York, March 13, 1803*. On March 13, 1803, Hamilton wrote to Elizabeth Hamilton: "I write your father by this opportunity." *Letter not found.*]

To Elizabeth Hamilton [1]

[New York] March [16–17] [2] 1803

I thank you My Betsy for your letter from Fish Kill.[3] I hope the subsequent part of your journey has proved less fatiguing than the two first days.

I have anticipated with dread your interview with your father. I hope your prudence and fortitude have been a match for your sensibility. Remember that the main object of visit is to console him; that his own burthen is sufficient, and that it would be too much to have it increased by the sorrows of his Children.

Arm yourself with resignation. We live in a world full of evil. In the later period of life misfortunes seem to thicken round us; and our duty and our peace both require that we should accustom ourselves to meet disasters with christian fortitude.

Kiss Kitty [4] for me & give my love to Angelica,[5] & all the friends & connections round you.

Adieu My excellent wife.   A H

Your Children are all well. I write your father by this oppy.[6]

ALS, Hamilton Papers, Library of Congress.
    1. For background to this letter, see H to Elizabeth Hamilton, March 13, 1803.
    2. H mistakenly dated this letter March 18. The letter is postmarked March 17.
    3. Letter not found.
    4. Catherine Van Rensselaer Schuyler.
    5. Angelica Schuyler Church.
    6. Letter not found.

To Philip Schuyler

[*New York, March 16–17, 1803.* On March 16–17, 1803, Hamilton wrote to Elizabeth Hamilton: "I write your father by this oppy." *Letter not found.*]

To Elizabeth Hamilton [1]

Sunday Evening March 20 [1803]
Grange [New York]

I am here my beloved Betsy with my two little boys *John* [2] & *William* [3] who will be my bed fellows to night. The day I have passed was as agreeable as it could be in your absence; but you need not be told how much difference your presence would have made. Things are now going on here pretty and pretty briskly. I am making some innovations which I am sure you will approve.

The remainder of the Children were well yesterday. Eliza [4] pouts and plays, and displays more and more her ample stock of Caprice.

I am anxious to hear of your arrival at Albany & shall be glad to be informed that Your Father and all of you are composed. I pray you to exert yourself & I repeat my exhortation that you will bear in mind it is your business to comfort and not to distress.

Remember me particularly to your Aunt Cochran [5] & to my good old friend the Doctor [6] if with you.

Adieu my precious Betsy   A H

Mrs. H

ALS, Hamilton Papers, Library of Congress.
    1. For background to this letter, see H to Elizabeth Hamilton, March 13, 16–17, 1803.
    2. John Church Hamilton, H's fifth child, was born on August 22, 1792.
    3. William Stephen Hamilton, H's sixth child, was born on August 4, 1797.
    4. H's other children were Angelica, who was born on September 25, 1784; Alexander, who was born on May 16, 1786; James Alexander, who was born on April 14, 1788; Eliza, who was born on November 20, 1799; Philip, who was born on June 2, 1802.
    5. Gertrude Schuyler Cochran was Philip Schuyler's older sister. Her first husband was her cousin, Peter Schuyler, Jr., the son of Peter Schuyler, Jr., and Catherine Groesbeck Schuyler. After her first husband's death, she married Dr. John Cochran in 1760 and settled in New Jersey. After the American Revolution, the Cochrans moved to New York City, where they remained until 1795, when they moved to Palatine, New York.
    6. John Cochran, a New Jersey physician and the husband of Gertrude Schuyler Cochran, collaborated with Dr. William Shippen during the American Revolution in preparing a plan of organization for all the military hospitals in the United Colonies. He served as physician and surgeon general in the middle department and later as chief physician and surgeon. In 1781 he became director general of all army hospitals in the United States. After the war, he moved to New York City, where he served as commissioner of loans from 1790 to 1795, when he retired.

To John V. Henry

New York March 20. 1803

My Dear Sir

I am afraid the frequency of my requests [1] may induce you to think me troublesome; but I do not know any one to whom I can with more confidence address myself; and if I trespass too much on your politeness I beg you will retaliate by commanding me freely in any matter in which I can render you service.

When I was last at Albany,[2] I applied to The Comptroller, Mr. Jenkins,[3] to ascertain the amount of a tax on certain lands which

Mr. Church [4] Mr. Laurance [5] and myself own say four Townships and part of a fifth in Rosevelts purchase.[6] I gave him a particular description of the land belonging to us. There had been some errors in the assessment which he promised to correct, and to advise me shortly of the precise amount of the tax, which he said I might pay into the Bank of New York to the Credit of the Treasurer. But it happens that I have not since heared a word from him on the subject which makes me rather uneasy as I know part of the tract was advertised for sale & chargeable as I understood from the Comptroller with an interest of fifteen per Cent.

Do me the favour to see the Comptroller without delay and to obtain from him a statement of the amount of the tax and fix the mode in which I shall remit or pay it.

There is another tract of upwards of 20000 acres in which also I am interested. Laurance Fish [7] & Troupe [8] are concerned with me.[9] The Comptroller could not discover whether this parcel had been taxed or not especially as I was not prepared at the time, sufficiently to identify it. At foot is an extract of the boundary. It formerly belonged to Arthur Noble [10] was either the whole or part of the tract called Nobleborough & is situate in Herkermer County. If these indications do not enable the Comptroller to pronounce with certainty whether it has been taxed or not, I will entreat you to take the trouble to write to S Breese [11] Esqr of Whites Town under whose superintendence it was not long since surveyed [12] and who doubtless can name the Town in which it lies and afford any auxiliary description which may be requisite.

I am not done troubling you. When at Albany, on the last day of the Court, I left on the Clerks Table a bundle containing a number of cases and some briefs, to which just before my departure, a friend promised me to attend but probably forgot it; for I have heared no more of the matter since that time, and indeed had temporarily forgotten it myself. Have the goodness to inquire for the bundle and forward it to me by some trusty & careful hand. It would be a good deal inconvenient to me not to recover it.

With great esteem & regard   I am Sir   Yr Obed   A Hamilton

"All those several pieces or parcels of land following being parts of a Township of Land designated by the name of Nobleborough situate &c. in the then County of Montgomery now County of

Herkema on the North side of the Mohawk River and to the Northward of a tract of land heretofore granted to Henry Glen [13] &
others, commonly called Jersey field [14] beginning on the East shore
of the Tioga or Canda Creek at the distance of three hundred Chains
measured on a course N 31° E   [15] from the N bounds of the
said tract called Jersey field and runs thence S 59 E Ninety one
chains and 24 links the[n] N 31° E 59° Chains then N 59 degrees W
694 Chains & 24 links then S 31° W 590 Chains and then S 59° E
600 Chains to the place of beginning containing the quantity of
Eight Miles square or 40960 acres (viz) Lots No. 2, 7 to 38, 50 to 71,
82 to 96, 98, 100, 101 part of 6 containing in the whole *21.800* acres.

Noble grants to J Laurance
Nichs Fish [16]

ALS, Mr. Hall Park McCullough, North Bennington, Vermont.
1. See H to Henry, October 31, 1802.
2. H had attended the January term of the Supreme Court of New York
State which convened in Albany on January 18, 1803, and adjourned on January 29, 1803.
3. Elisha Jenkins of Hudson, New York, was comptroller of New York
State from 1801 to 1806.
4. John B. Church.
5. John Laurance.
6. See Jacob Mark and Company to Church, H, and Laurance, May 30,
1797, note 2; "Mortgage by Laurance, Church, and H to Robert Gilchrist,"
August 21, 1802, note 1.
7. Nicholas Fish, a veteran of the American Revolution and a close friend of
H, was supervisor of the revenue for the District of New York.
8. Robert Troup.
9. For the purchase to which H is referring, see H to Troup, July 25, 1795,
note 13.
10. Noble, who had emigrated from Ireland to the United States in 1783,
was a speculator in New York State lands. In 1790 he settled on the Nobleborough tract of 40,960 acres in Herkimer County. Although he built a saw-
mill and attempted to colonize his lands, the project failed. The present town
of Nobleborough or Nobleboro was named for him.
11. Samuel Sidney Breese, who was born in Philadelphia and later moved to
Whitestown, Oneida County, New York, was the brother of Arthur Breese, a
prominent lawyer in Utica. Samuel Sidney Breese served as a delegate to the
New York State constitutional convention of 1821.
12. Nobleborough was surveyed on August 23, 1787 (Mix, *Catalogue: Maps
and Surveys,* 221).
13. Henry Glen, a Schenectady merchant, was a member of the House of
Representatives from 1793 to 1801. H and Glen were old friends. See H to
Richard Varick, May 12, 1795, note 2.
14. For the Jerseyfield Patent, see Mix, *Catalogue: Maps and Surveys,* 251;
Nathaniel S. Benton, *A History of Herkimer County, Including the Upper
Mohawk Valley* (Albany: J. Munsell, 1856), 200, 477.

15. Space left blank in MS.
16. Henry endorsed this letter: "Recd 26 ⟨ansd⟩ 29 ℔ mail." Henry's reply has not been found.

To Richard Hartshorne [1]

[New York, March 23, 1803]

I understand that our Supreme Court has decided that the Plaintiff is liable to the Sheriff for his poundage. The agents of Mr. Sansom are therefore to pay the above.[2]

A Hamilton
March 23. 1803

Mr. Richard Hartshorne

ALS, Columbia University Libraries.
1. Hartshorne, a New York City merchant, was acting as agent for Philip Sansom, a London merchant, who was bringing suit against the New York mercantile firm of Robert Murray and Company. In 1796 Hartshorne retained H as solicitor and counselor for Sansom. An entry in H's Law Register, 1795–1804, reads:

"Philip Sansom   £ 8500
        v   upon promise
Robert Murray
James V. Murray   C. I. Bogert
George W. Murray
& John R. Wheaton"

(D, partially in H's handwriting, New York Law Institute, New York City). Cornelius I. Bogert was a New York City lawyer.
An entry in H's Cash Book, 1795–1804, under the date of September 14, 1796, reads: "received of   V Robert Murray & Co 10" (AD, Hamilton Papers, Library of Congress).
For additional information concerning this case, see Goebel, *Law Practice*, forthcoming volumes.
2. H wrote the letter printed above at the bottom of the following document: "New York April 1797
Mr. Philip Sampson to Jacob Jn. Lansing Dr
To poundage on a Casa issued by Alexander Hamilton Esqr. vs Robert Murray on £8229–6–10   £104–2–3" (D, Hamilton Papers, Library of Congress).
Jacob John Lansing, who had been sheriff from September 29, 1795, to December 28, 1798, received the poundage. Lansing's receipt, written below H's note to Hartshorne printed above, reads: "Recd. Newyork the 19th January 1804 of Richd. Hartshorne one Hundred and four pounds 2/3 N. york Currency in full for the above claim of poundage for a Judgment obtained in the

name of Philip Sansom against Robert Murray & Co. in the Supreme Court of
this State

Jacob Jn Lansing
Late Sheriff of the
City & County of New York

218 Wm Street" (DS, Hamilton Papers, Library of Congress).

Poundage is defined as "an allowance to the sheriff of so much in the pound
upon the amount levied under an execution" (Henry Campbell Black, *Black's
Law Dictionary: Definitions of the Terms and Phrases of American and
English Jurisprudence, Ancient and Modern* [St. Paul, Minnesota, 1951], 1332).

From John V. Henry

[*Albany, March 29, 1803.* Henry's endorsement on Hamilton's
letter to him of March 20, 1803, reads: "Recd 26 ⟨ansd⟩ 29 ℔ mail."
Letter not found.]

From Marquis de Lafayette

Paris Germinal the 10th. 11th year
[March 31, 1803]

My dear hamilton

I would like by this opportunity to write to you a long letter, but
having been Laying on my back for two months past, and being for
three weeks to come, doomed to the same situation, I must confine
myself to a few lines written near my bed. The particulars of the
accident and his cure [1] will be given to you by General Bernadotte,[2]
whom I must particularly introduce and his lady [3] to Mrs. Hamilton
and to you. Politics I will not dwell upon. My sentiments are so well
Known to you that it were superfluous to say what I think of
senatus-consulta [4] at home, and settling colonies in North America.[5]
Yet I hope this late affair may still be arranged to mutual satisfaction, and I am sure nobody could have better personal disposition
than my friend General Bernadotte, who to those high and brilliant
abilities which have so much contributed to ⟨the⟩ triumph of the
french arms, joins one of the most civic, generous, ⟨and⟩ candid
hearts, it is possible to meet with. I Know he sets a great value by
the approbation of the citizens of America, and is particularly desirous of your acquaintance, and properly sensible of its advantages.

I have seen in the papers a letter from you relative to the transactions at our Yorktown redoubt [6] in which I have found my friend hamilton's whole caracter, and the more pleased I have been to receive it, as the attack had been for some time known to me, but on the proposal of some friends to write to you, I had answered you were on the spot, and would know better what was best for me to be done.

Adieu my dear friend, my best respects to Mrs. hamilton, remember me to our friends, I Know you are most friendly interested in my private concerns, and have ever depended upon it.

most affectionately I am your constant friend   Lafayette

Gen. hamilton

ALS, Hamilton Papers, Library of Congress.
1. On February 23, 1803, Lafayette slipped on the ice while he was in Paris and broke his left leg. The treatment which his physicians used left him permanently lame.
2. Jean Baptiste Jules Bernadotte was appointed Minister Plenipotentiary of France to the United States in January, 1803.
Bernadotte did not deliver this letter to H. In May, 1803, on the eve of his departure for the United States, Bernadotte received the news of war between France and England, and he gave up his appointment to return to military duty.
3. In 1798 Bernadotte married Désirée Clary, whose sister was the wife of Joseph Bonaparte.
4. The Senatus Consultum, dated August 4, 1802, radically amended the Constitution of the Year X through a series of decrees, the most significant of which gave the First Consul the right to choose his successor.
5. This is a reference to the cession of Louisiana to France by Spain.
6. See H to the Editor of the *Evening Post*, August 10, 1802.

Account of Louis Le Guen [1]

[New York, April 1, 1803]

Louis Le Guen Esqr.   To A Hamilton Dr
            For retainer to Van Vechten & Spencer [2]   100
                        Cr
            By interest received from J L [3] from the
            13 of May 1802 to the 1 of April 1803   185.50
                        Ballance due from L L Guen   Ds — 85.50

Recu. L. Le Guen

AD, signed by Le Guen, Yale University Library.

1. This document concerns the management of the funds established under the terms of Louis Le Guen's antenuptial contract. For background to this document, see Le Guen to H, December 27, 1800, note 7, January 15, 1801; "Receipt to Louis Le Guen," January 15, 1801; Aaron Ogden to H, January 15, 1801; "Indenture between Alexander Hamilton of the First Part and Richard Harison and Aaron Ogden of the Second Part," July 1, 1801; "Bond to Richard Harison and Aaron Ogden," July 1, 1801; "Account with Louis Le Guen," June 6, 1802; "Description of Account with Louis Le Guen," June 8, 1802; "Receipt from Louis Le Guen," September 10, 1802.

2. Abraham Van Vechten and Ambrose Spencer were lawyers and among the most prominent members of their profession in New York State.

Van Vechten, a native of Catskill and a Federalist, was appointed in 1796 as district attorney for the Fifth District of New York. In 1798 he declined appointment as associate justice of the Supreme Court of New York. He was a member of the state Senate from 1798 to 1805.

Spencer, a native of Connecticut and for many years a resident of Columbia County, New York, was appointed clerk of the city of Hudson in 1786. He was a member of the New York Assembly in 1794 and a member of the Senate from 1796 to 1802. In 1797 he was a member of the Council of Appointment. He was a Federalist until 1798, when he shifted to the Republican party.

3. John Laurance. See "Account with Louis Le Guen," June 6, 1802.

From Nathaniel Terry [1]

[*Hartford, April 2, 1803*. On April 21, 1803, Hamilton wrote to Terry and referred to "Your letter of the 2d instant." *Letter not found.*]

1. Terry was a Hartford, Connecticut, lawyer.

From Timothy Pickering [1]

Salem (Massachusetts) April 5. 1803.

Dear Sir,

The assertion of the Jacobins, that you are an aristocrat & a Monarchist, is not new: But at a late meeting of the *sect* in this town, one of their leaders declared "That General Hamilton proposed (&, it was understood, advocated) in the general Convention, That the President of the United States, and the Senators, should be chosen for life: That this was intended as an introduction to Monarchy: And that the Federalists of this county (Essex) had adopted General Hamilton's plan." [2]

Your friends here (who are the real friends of their country) are very desirous of knowing the fact. If you did not make and advocate that proposition, it will be useful to have it known, & the Jacobin lie contradicted. If the proposition *was* offered in the Convention, your friends will know to what motives to ascribe it; and that, whatever form of Government you may have suggested for consideration, the public welfare, and the permanent liberty of your country, were not less the objects of pursuit with you, than with the other members of the Convention.

Your answer will gratify me and your numerous friends here. Such use only shall be made of it as you shall prescribe. And as I shall be absent [for about] [3] four weeks from this time, have the goodness to direct your letter to me, under cover to my nephew Samuel Putnam Esqr. of Salem. [4]

I am, as ever,   truly & respectfully yours,   Timothy Pickering.

General Hamilton

Copy, in Pickering's handwriting, Essex Institute, Salem, Massachusetts; copy, Massachusetts Historical Society, Boston; copy, Hamilton Papers, Library of Congress.

1. Following his dismissal as Secretary of State on May 12, 1800, Pickering moved to Easton, Pennsylvania, where he owned land which he planned to cultivate. His Federalist friends subsequently purchased his land by subscription, and Pickering returned to his home in Essex County, Massachusetts. From March 4, 1803, to March 3, 1811, he was a member of the United States Senate.

2. On March 31, 1803, Republicans held a meeting at Rhust's Hall in Salem to nominate candidates for governor and state senators. On April 4, 1803, the *Salem Register*, a Republican newspaper, printed a report of the meeting, which reads in part: "*The following propositions were made by the celebrated* ALEXANDER HAMILTON, *in the Convention, and shew unequivocally his political opinions. Here we have a President and Senate* FOR LIFE. *Governors of the States chosen by this President and Senate, with an absolute* NEGATIVE *upon all laws. The whole Militia under* THE SOLE AND EXCLUSIVE *direction of the General Government. The State Governments reduced to mere corporations—All Courts instituted by the United States. The Senate with* SOLE *power to declare war; and in fine all the prerogatives of a monarch and nobility.*" The eleven propositions printed at the end of this article were the same as the provisions in H's first plan of government in the Constitutional Convention. See "Constitutional Convention. Plan of Government," June 18, 1787.

3. The words in brackets have been taken from the copy in the Hamilton Papers, Library of Congress.

4. Putnam, a lawyer in Salem, Massachusetts, was the husband of Sarah Gooll, a daughter of Pickering's sister, Lois Gooll.

To Edward Pennington [1]

[*New York, April 6, 1803.* Letter listed in dealer's catalogue. *Letter not found.*]

1. ALS, sold by M. Thomas & Sons, Philadelphia, February 8, 1859, Item 815.
Pennington (Penington) was a sugar refiner in Philadelphia.

Articles of Association of the Merchants' Bank [1]

[New York, April 7, 1803]

To all to whom these Presents shall come, or in any wise concern. Be it known and made manifest, that we, the Subscribers, have formed a Company or limited Partnership, and do hereby associate

Merchant's Bank Stockholders 1803 (n.p., n.d.).
1. Although no manuscript of the document printed above has been found, historians have generally agreed that H was its author (*JCHW*, VII, 838–44; I. N. Phelps Stokes, *The Iconography of Manhattan Island*, V [New York, 1926], 1405; Philip G. Hubert, Jr., *The Merchants' National Bank of the City of New York* [New York, 1903], 2; Bray Hammond, *Banks and Politics in America from the Revolution to the Civil War* [Princeton, 1957], 142–43; John C. Miller, *Alexander Hamilton: Portrait in Paradox* [New York, 1959], 546).
In addition H and Richard Harison served as attorneys for the new bank. See Isaac Bronson's account with the New York branch of the Bank of the United States in his account book under the dates of March 21, 25, 1803 (AD, Bronson Papers, MS Division, New York Public Library). See also *New-York Evening Post*, April 8, 1803.
On April 30, 1803, fourteen men (to whom two more were subsequently added from the board of directors) organized the bank with Oliver Wolcott, Jr., as president. During 1803 three hundred and ninety-one subscribers bought shares in the bank. The bank opened for business on June 3, 1803, with a capital of $1,246,250. On November 30 the bank paid a dividend of three percent—totaling $30,960.31—to all subscribers (Hubert, *Merchants' Bank*, 1, 2, 8, 22–23; *Merchant's Bank Stockholders 1803*).
During its first two years the bank operated without a charter from the legislature.

and agree with each other, to conduct business in the manner hereinafter specified and described, by and under the name and style of the "Merchants' Bank," and we do hereby mutually covenant, declare and agree, that the following are and shall be the fundamental Articles of this our Association and agreement with each other, by which we and all persons who at any time hereafter may transact business with the said Company, shall be bound and concluded.

I. The Capital Stock of the said Company shall consist of One Million Two Hundred and Fifty Thousand Dollars, in Money of the United States. The said Capital Stock shall be divided into Shares of Fifty Dollars each: two Dollars and fifty Cents on each Share shall be paid at the time of subscribing, and the remainder shall be paid at such times, and in such proportions as the board of Directors shall order and appoint, under pain of forfeiting to the said Company the said Shares, and all previous payments thereon: but no payment shall be required, unless by a notice to be published for at least fifteen days, in two newspapers printed in the City of New-York.

II. The affairs of the said company, shall be conducted by sixteen Directors, who shall elect one of their number to be the president thereof, and nine of the Directors shall form a board or quorum for transacting all the business of the company, except ordinary discounts, which it shall be in the power of any five of the Directors to perform, of whom the President shall always be one, except in case of his sickness or necessary absence, when his place may be supplied by any other Director, whom he by writing under his hand, shall nominate for that purpose; and until the second Tuesday in June, one thousand eight hundred and four, Oliver Wolcott, Richard Varick,[2] Peter Jay Munro,[3] Joshua Sands,[4] Thomas Storm,[5]

2. Varick, a veteran of the American Revolution, served as George Washington's recording secretary from 1781 to 1783. In 1784 he became recorder of the City of New York, and in 1786 he and Samuel Jones were appointed to codify New York State laws. He was speaker of the New York Assembly in 1787 and 1788, attorney general in 1788 and 1789, and mayor of New York City from 1789 to 1801.

3. Munro was a New York City lawyer.

4. Sands, a veteran of the American Revolution, a Federalist, and a New York City merchant, was a member of the New York Senate from 1792 to 1799 and collector of customs for the District of New York from 1797 to 1802.

5. Storm, a New York City merchant, held numerous municipal offices and served as a member of the Assembly from 1798 to 1802.

William W. Woolsey,[6] John Hone,[7] John Kane,[8] Joshua Jones,[9] Robert Gilchrist,[10] Wynant Van Zandt, Jun.,[11] Isaac Bronson,[12] James Roosevelt,[13] John Swartwout,[14] Henry I. Wyckoff,[15] and Isaac Hicks [16] shall be Directors of the said Company; the Directors from and after that period, shall be elected for one year by the Stockholders, for the time being, and each Director shall be a Stockholder at the time of his election, and shall cease to be a Director if he should cease to be a Stockholder: and the number of votes which each Stockholder shall be entitled to, shall be equal to the number of shares which he shall have held on the books of the company, for at least sixty days prior to the election; and all stockholders shall vote at elections by ballot, either personally or by proxy; to be made in such form as the board of Directors may appoint.

III. A General Meeting of the Stockholders of the Company shall be holden upon the first Tuesday of June, in every year, (excepting in June now next ensuing) at such place as the Board of Directors shall appoint, by notice, to be published in two newspapers printed in the City of New-York, at least fifteen days previous to such meeting, for the purpose of electing Directors for the ensuing year, who shall take their seats at the Board on the second Tuesday in the same month of June and immediately proceed to elect the President.

IV. The board of Directors, are hereby fully empowered to make, revise, and alter or amend, all such rules, bye laws, and regulations, for the government of the company, and that of their officers, servants and affairs, as they, or a majority of them, shall from time to time think expedient, not inconsistent with law, or these articles of

6. Woolsey was a New York City merchant and sugar refiner.

7. Hone, a merchant and auctioneer in New York City, was a partner with his brother Philip in the firm of J. and P. Hone.

8. Kane, a merchant, was head of the firm of Kane and Company in New York City.

9. Jones was a New York City merchant.

10. Gilchrist was a resident of Westchester County, New York.

11. Van Zandt, a New York City merchant, held a variety of municipal offices and was an alderman representing the First Ward from 1802 to 1807.

12. Bronson was a New York City merchant and moneylender.

13. Roosevelt was a New York City merchant.

14. Swartwout, a close political associate of Aaron Burr, was a member of the New York Assembly from 1798 to 1801. In 1802 Thomas Jefferson appointed him United States marshal for the District of New York.

15. Wyckoff was a New York City merchant.

16. Hicks, a New York City merchant, owned a store at 239 Water Street.

association; and to use, employ, and dispose of the joint stock, funds or property of the said Company (subject only to the restrictions hereinafter contained) as to them, or a majority of them, shall seem expedient.

V. All bills, bonds, notes, and every contract and engagement on behalf of the Company, shall be signed by the president; and countersigned or attested, by the cashier of the company; and the funds of the company shall in no case be held responsible for any contract or engagement whatever, unless the same shall be so signed and countersigned, or attested as aforesaid.

VI. The books, papers, correspondence and funds of the company, shall at all times, be subject to the inspection of the directors.

VII. The said board of Directors, shall have power to appoint a cashier, and all other officers and servants, for executing the business of the company; and to establish the compensations to be paid to the president and all other officers and servants of the company respectively; all which, together with all other necessary expenses, shall be defrayed out of the funds of the company.

VIII. A majority of the Directors, shall have power to call a general meeting of the Stockholders, for purposes relative to the concerns of the Company; giving at least thirty days notice, in two of the public Newspapers printed in the city of New-York, and specifying in such notice the object or objects of such meeting.

IX. The Shares of Capital Stock, at any time owned by any individual Stockholder, shall be transferable on the books of the Company, according to such rules, as conformable to law, may be established in that behalf, by the Board of Directors; but all debts actually due and payable to the Company, by a Stockholder requesting a transfer, must be satisfied before such transfer shall be made, unless the Board of Directors shall direct to the contrary.

X. No transfer of Stock in this Company, shall be considered as binding upon the Company, unless made in a book or books, to be kept for that purpose by the Company. And it is hereby further expressly agreed and declared, that any Stockholder, who shall transfer in manner aforesaid, all his Stock or Shares in this Company, to any other person or persons whatever, shall *ipso facto* cease to be a member of this Company; and that any person or persons whatever, who shall accept a transfer of any Stock or Share in this Company, shall *ipso facto* become and be a member of this Company, according to these articles of association.

XI. It is hereby expressly and explicitly declared, to be the object and intention of the persons who associate under the style or firm of the "Merchants' Bank," that the joint stock or property of the said Company (exclusive of dividends to be made in the manner hereinafter mentioned) shall alone be responsible for the Debts and engagements of the said Company. And that no person, who shall or may deal with this Company, or to whom they shall or may become in anywise indebted, shall on any pretence whatever have recourse against the separate property of any present or future member of this Company, or against their persons, further than may be necessary to secure the faithful application of the Funds thereof, to the purposes to which by these presents they are liable. But all persons accepting any Bond, Bill, Note or other Contract of this Company, signed by the President, and countersigned or attested by the Cashier of the Company, for the time being, or dealing with it in any other manner whatsoever, thereby respectively give credit to the said joint stock or property of the said Company, and thereby respectively disavow having recourse, on any pretence whatever, to the person or separate property of any present or future member of this Company, except as above mentioned. And all suits to be brought against this Company, (if any shall be) shall be brought against the President for the time being; and in case of his death or removal from office, pending any such suit against him, measures shall be taken at the expense of the Company for substituting his successor in office as a defendant; so that persons having demands upon the Company, may not be prejudiced or delayed by that event, or if the persons suing, shall go on against the person first named as defendant, (notwithstanding his death or removal from office) this Company shall take no advantage by writ of error, or otherwise, of such proceeding, on that account; and all recoveries had in manner aforesaid, shall be conclusive upon the Company, so far as to render the company's said joint stock or property liable thereby, and no further; and the Company shall immediately pay the amount of such recovery out of their joint stock, but not otherwise. And in case of any suit at law, the President shall sign his appearance upon the writ, or file common bail thereto; it being expressly understood and declared, that all persons dealing with the said Company, agree to these terms, and are to be bound thereby.

XII. Dividends of the profits of the Company, or of so much of the said profits as shall be deemed expedient and proper, shall be declared and paid half yearly during the months of May and November in every year, and shall from time to time be determined by a majority of the said Directors, at a meeting to be held for that purpose, and shall in no case exceed the amount of the net profits actually acquired by the Company; so that the Capital Stock of the Company shall never be impaired by Dividends; and at the expiration of every three years, from the first Tuesday of June next, a dividend of surplus profits shall be made, but the Directors shall be at liberty to retain at least one per cent upon the capital, as a fund for future contingencies.

XIII. If the said Directors shall at any time, wilfully and knowingly, make or declare, any dividend which shall impair the said Capital Stock, all the Directors present at the making or declaring such dividend, and consenting thereto, shall be liable, in their individual capacities, to the Company, for the amount or proportion of the said Capital Stock, so divided by the said Directors. And each Director who shall be present at the making or declaring of such dividend, shall be deemed to have consented thereto, unless he shall immediately enter, in writing, his dissent, on the minutes of the proceedings of the Board, and give public notice to the Stockholders, that such dividend has been declared.

XIV. These Articles of Agreement shall be published in at least three newspapers, printed in the City of New-York, for one month; and for the further information of all persons, who may transact business with, or in any manner give Credit to this Company, every Bond, Bill, Note, or other instrument or contract, by the effect or terms of which, the Company may be charged or held liable, for the payment of money, shall specially declare, in such form as the board of directors shall prescribe, *that payment shall be made out of the joint funds of the Merchants' Bank, according to the present articles of association, and not otherwise;* and a copy of the eleventh article of this association, shall be inserted in the bank book of every person depositing money, or other valuable property, with the Company, for safe custody, or a printed copy shall be delivered to every such person, before any such deposit shall be received from him. And it is hereby expressly declared, that no engagement can be legally made in the name of the said Company, unless it contain a limitation or restriction, to the effect above recited. And the Company hereby expressly disavow all responsibility, for any debt or engagement, which may be made in their name, not containing a limitation or restriction to the effect aforesaid.

XV. The Company shall in no case be owners of any ships or vessels, or directly or indirectly concerned in trade, or the importation or exportation, purchase or sale of any goods, wares, or merchandise whatever (bullion only excepted) unless by selling such goods, wares, and merchandise, as shall be truly pledged to them, by way of security for debts due to the said company.

XVI. If a vacancy shall at any time happen among the Directors, by death, resignation, or otherwise, the residue of the Directors, for the time being, shall immediately elect a Director, to fill the said vacancy, until the next election of Directors, to be made according to the second article of these presents.

XVII. This association shall continue until the first Tuesday of June, one thousand eight hundred and fifteen, and no longer; but the proprietors of two thirds of the capital stock of the Company, may by their concurring votes, at a general meeting to be called for that express purpose, dissolve the same at any prior period; provided, that notice of such meeting, and of its object, shall be published in at least three newspapers, to be printed in the City of New-York, for at least six months previous to the time appointed for such meeting.

XVIII. Immediately on any dissolution of this association, effectual measures shall be taken by the Directors then existing, for closing all the concerns of the Company, and for dividing the capital and profits, which may remain, among the Stockholders, in proportion to their respective interests.

IN WITNESS WHEREOF, we have hereunto set our names or firms the Seventh Day of April, one thousand eight hundred and three.

From John Hamilton [1]

Norfolk Virginia 16. April 1803.

Dear Sir

I take the liberty to introduce to your acquaintance, personally, the Honourable Captain John Murray of His Majesty's Navy, third Son of the Earl of Dunmore,[2] in whose favour I beg leave to request your particular Civilities; assuring you that you will find him perfectly to merit whatever attention and good Offices you may have the kindness to render him during his visit to New York.

I remain with much esteem and respect Dear Sir, Your most obedient humble servant   Jn. Hamilton

General Hamilton.

ALS, Hamilton Papers, Library of Congress.
  1. John Hamilton was the British consul at Norfolk, Virginia.
  2. John Murray, fourth Earl of Dunmore, sat in the House of Lords as a representative peer from Scotland from 1761 to 1769. He was governor of New York from 1770 to 1771 and governor of Virginia from 1772 to 1776. He was elected to the House of Lords in 1776, 1780, and 1784, and was governor of the Bahama Islands from 1787 to 1796.

From Philip Schuyler

Albany April 16th 1803

My Dear Sir

Every letter of yours affords a mean of consolation, and I am well aware that nothing lends so much [to] the alleviation of distress, as the personal intercourse with a sincere friend, and the endearing Attentions of children. I shall therefore delay no longer than is indispensibly necessary my visit to you—my trial has been severe.[1] I have attempted to sustain it with fortitude. I have I hope succeeded in a degree, but after giving and receiving for nearly half a century a series of mutual evidences of an affection and of a friendship which increased as we advanced in life, the shock to me was great & most Sensibly felt, to be thus suddenly deprived of a beloved wife, the Mother of my Children, and the Soothing companion of my declining days. But as I kiss the rod with humility, the being that inflicted the stroke will enable me to sustain the smart, and progressively restore peace to a wounded heart, and will make you & my Eliza and my other Children the instruments of Consolation.

There has not been the least indication of the gout rising to the vital parts. It continues in my foot, but with diminished force, and will probable soon be expelled as the season becomes more mild.

I have Obtained a copy of the Act, for the Adjustment of the Controversy in Hillsdale,[2] and shall transmit it to you, by the first person going to NYork in whose care I can have confidence.

Mr. Yates's [3] declining to stand as a candidate for the office of Senator in this district, altho It will give some more votes to Mr Lush,[4] will nevertheless tend to increase the number in favor of Mr. Taylor,[5] and I apprehend he will be returned.[6] The democratic infection has taken such deep root, and will continue to be cherished, as long as pecuniary means can be found to carry on Government without recourse to taxation, for the people are incapable of appreciating the injury the[y] sustain from a diminution of their Capital Stock. And this system will be prosecuted until all is expended, unless an exterior pressure should drive our rulers to the necessity of other means for supplies. Nor should I be much surprized in the Case of such a pressure, If the Interest on the national debt was diverted to the relief of the Moment. For there appears to me, no folly, no measure however Atrocious to which the wretches who could hire a miscreant [7] to defame Washington & his virtuos consellers, are unequal.

My Children are all in health, and unite with me In love to you to my Dear Eliza and my dear Grandchildren. I am My Dear Si

with the tenderest affection ever yours   Ph: Schuyler

General Hamilton

ALS, Lloyd W. Smith Collection, Morristown National Historical Park, Morristown, New Jersey.
1. See H to Elizabeth Hamilton, March 13, 1803.

2. "An Act for settling the disputes and controversies between the representatives of John Van Rensselaer the elder, deceased, and the possessors of
lands in the town of Hillsdale, in the County of Columbia" (*New York Laws,*
26th Sess., Ch. LXXVI [April 2, 1803]). This act provided for the appointment of commissioners by the state legislature to settle the dispute over lands
in Claverack, Columbia County, New York, between the heirs of Van
Rensselaer, Philip Schuyler's father-in-law, and those individuals whom Van
Rensselaer had charged with occupying his lands without acknowledging
themselves as his tenants. For information concerning this controversy and its
settlement, see Goebel, *Law Practice,* forthcoming volumes. See also Schuyler
to H, September 9, 1801.

3. John Van Ness Yates of Albany was a Republican, a lawyer, and a legal
scholar.

4. Stephen Lush, a veteran of the American Revolution a Federalist and an
Albany merchant, was a member of the New York Assembly in 1792, 1793,
1803, and of the state Senate in 1800, 1801, and 1802.

5. John Tayler, a Republican and an Albany merchant and land speculator,
was a member of the state Assembly from 1777 to 1779 and 1780 to 1781 and
in 1786 and 1787. From 1797 to 1803 he was a judge in the Court of Common
Pleas in Albany County.

6. On March 22, 1803, a meeting of Federalists at the City Tavern in
Albany nominated Lush for state senator from the Eastern District of New
York. Subsequently, Federalists in other towns in Albany County endorsed
Lush's nomination (*The Albany Centinel,* April 1, 5, 12, 26, 1803). During
March, various groups of Republicans in Albany County nominated Yates and
Tayler for the New York Senate. An article, which appeared in *The Albany
Centinel* on April 1, 1803, and is signed by "A True Republican," reads in
part: "It is a mortifying truth, that an officious committee of three persons,
sent from the city of Albany to Schenectady, have made an arrangement with
Mr. Yates to forego a competition with Mr. Tayler at the approaching election, upon the express condition, that he is to be supported by the republican
party as a candidate to fill the next vacancy in the Senate which may happen
in this county." See also *The Albany Centinel,* April 12, 1803; *New-York
Evening Post,* April 2, 1803. Tayler won the election for state senator, which
was held on April 26, 1803.

7. James Thomson Callender. See Schuyler to H, August 19, 1802, note 5.

Speech to Federalist Nominating Convention
for the City of New York [1]

[New York, April 20, 1803]

First Version

He took a brief view of the disgraceful measures of the general
government, and then descended to notice some of the acts of the
petty tyrants of our own state. He concluded his address by exhort-
ing his fellow-citizens to lay hold of the present occasion, and wrest

the dominion from hands so unfit to retain it. Speaking of the success of elections in New England,[2] he observed, that the "Wise men of the East" had lately arisen in their power, and put democracy to flight, and he could not but entertain the hope that their glorious example would be followed in this city. The trunk of federalism, he said, was evidently reviving; the sap was ascending, the buds began to put forth, and he doubted not, its leaves would soon over-shadow the land, and that we should be blessed with fruit more than ever abundant. The address was received with acclamations that made the "welkin ring," followed by three cheers to the success of the federal ticket.

Second Version [3]

After the business of the evening was completed, the gallant of Mrs. Reynolds [4] addressed the meeting in a speech fraught with misrepresentation and abuse of the State and General Governments. He reiterated all the train that has appeared in the Post.[5] He declared that the federal executive was too feeble to sustain the Government! But this restless & turbulent demagogue, this *croaker* of a *swampt* faction, assigned no reason for the assertion except that we ought to have gone to war with Spain instead of adopting measures for an amicable adjustment of our differences! Had the latter course been pursued; had we by war destroyed thousands of our citizens, suspended our commerce, increased our taxes, and augmented the national debt, which he has declared is a *national blessing*,[6] the Executive would, in the opinion of this demagogue, have been truly energetic! . . .

This *croaker*, (*croaker* is a word he always uses in his electioneering harangues) after vilifying the executive and congress for not going to war, declared that they had *destroyed* the *energies* of the country! And pray, reader, how are those *energies destroyed* in the opinion of this factious man? Why, said the declaimer, by *abolishing* the *internal* taxes,[7] and thereby lopping off from the revenue near *one million of dollars.* . . .

Turning his attention to this state, Hamilton, speaking of the measures of the last session, traduced, in terms the most false and inflammatory, the executive and the members of the legislature. This factious demagogue, called them *croakers*, accused them of attempts to subvert the government, declared contrary, I will venture to say, to his own opinion, that the act to increase and equalize the number of wards in this city was unconstitutional;[8] reprobated in terms of severity, the suffrage bill,[9] denominated it a *jacobin* scheme, and averred that property was unsafe where *republicans* ruled. . . .

But, said the CROAKER, not content with straining every nerve to subvert government and religion—the old thing over again—the legislature made a formal & vigorous attack on the *Ladies*—alluding to the Dower-bill.[10] This excited a smile, and many regretted the absence of Mrs. Reynolds, who could have best answered the general on this point. . . .

New-York Evening Post, April 21, 1803.
1. The two documents printed above are different versions of a speech which H made at a meeting of New York City Federalists on April 20, 1803. On April 15 a meeting of Federalists electors at the Tontine Coffee House had nominated Egbert Benson as state senator for the Southern District of New York, which consisted of New York, Kings, Queens, Richmond, Suffolk, and Westchester counties (*New-York Evening Post,* April 16, 1803). On April 20 the Federalists met again at City Hall to confirm Benson's nomination and to name nine candidates for the Assembly (*New-York Evening Post,* April 21, 1803). On the same day, the Republicans met at Adams Hotel and nominated John Broome, a New York City merchant, for the state Senate and a ticket for the Assembly ([New York] *American Citizen,* April 22, 1803). The election was held on April 26 (*New-York Evening Post,* April 26, 1803), and the Republicans elected their senatorial candidate and their entire Assembly slate (*New-York Evening Post,* April 29, 1803).
In the account in the *New-York Evening Post,* the report on H's speech is preceded by the following statement: "*Federalism reviving.* At a meeting of the Federalists, last evening, for the purpose of nominating suitable persons to represent the city in the Assembly of this state, it is believed there was a greater collection of persons than has been seen on a similar occasion, since the formation of the constitution. After a respectable ticket had been unanimously adopted by the meeting, and ward committees appointed to take all proper measures to ensure the success of the election, General Hamilton rose and addressed the electors in a speech the most eloquent and animating."
2. This is a reference to the gubernatorial elections which took place in New Hampshire, Massachusetts, and Connecticut in April, 1803, in which the respective governors (John Gilman, Caleb Strong, and Jonathan Trumbull), all of whom were Federalists, were re-elected (*New-York Evening Post,* April 11, 15, 1803).
3. [New York] *American Citizen,* April 22, 1803.
The parts of this account which have been omitted consist of the editor's comments on H's speech.
4. Maria Reynolds. See the introductory note to Oliver Wolcott Jr., to H, July 3, 1797.
5. For an explanation of the contents of the remainder of this paragraph, see "For the *Evening Post,*" February 8, 1803.

6. See H to Robert Morris, April 30, 1781; "Report Relative to a Provision for the Support of Public Credit," January 9, 1790.

7. "An Act to repeal the Internal Taxes" provided for the abolition of internal duties on stills, domestic distilled spirits, sugar, licenses to retailers, sales at auctions, carriages, and stamped vellum, parchment, and paper, which became effective on June 30, 1802 (2 *Stat.* 148–50 [April 6, 1802]). For the debates in Congress on the repeal of internal taxes, which the Federalists opposed, see *Annals of Congress*, XI, 210–50, 356–60, 1015, 1018–74.

8. "An Act to increase the number of Wards in the city of New-York, and equalize the same" changed the number of wards in New York City from seven to nine and redefined the boundaries of the existing wards (*New York Laws*, 26th Sess., Ch. XXIV [March 8, 1803]).

9. On February 15, 1803, William Few of New York City introduced into the New York Assembly a bill entitled "An Act for the better regulation of the election of charter officers in the city of New-York, and designating the qualifications of electors." This act revised the city charter by extending the franchise to all males twenty-one years old or over who were citizens of the state and residents of the city for at least six months and who had paid taxes and either rented or leased a house at a yearly value of twenty-five dollars. On March 16, 1803, the bill passed the Assembly and was sent to the Senate where it was submitted to a committee of the whole house. The bill was not reported out of committee before the end of the session (*Journal of the Assembly of the State of New-York. At Their Twenty-sixth Session, Begun and Held at the City of Albany, the Twenty-fifth Day of January, 1803* [Albany, n.d.], 65, 78, 145, 178, 180, 197; *Journal of the Senate of the State of New-York. At Their Twenty-sixth Session, Begun and Held at the City of Albany, the Twenty-fifth Day of January, 1803* [Albany, n.d.], 87, 89).

10. On February 5, 1803, Ambrose Spencer introduced a bill into the Assembly entitled "An Act amending the Act, entitled 'An Act concerning dower.'" This amended act in its final form provided "That no wife, whose husband is now alive, shall be entitled to or recover dower in any lands or tenements which her husband hath granted, sold or conveyed to any person or persons at any time before the passing of this act, and whereof he is not again reseized, at the time of the passing hereof." The act also prohibited a wife from recovering dower in any property of which her husband had been divested by "forfeiture, confiscation or judgment of law." On March 28 the dower bill passed the Assembly and was sent to the Senate where it was read the following day and committed to a committee of the whole house. The bill was not reported out of committee before the end of the session (*Journal of the Assembly of the State of New-York. 26th Sess.*, 36, 52, 54, 81, 92, 233, 240, 243–44; *Journal of the Senate of the State of New-York. 26th Sess.*, 116, 118).

From Ernst Frederich von Walterstorff

St. Croix 20th. April 1803

Dear General,

When I received Your favr. of the 5th August [1] I certainly did not think that I should postpone so long answering it and returning

You my thanks for this proof of Your kind remembrance. I shall offer You no appology for it because there is none that would be satisfactory to myself. I beg You only to be assured, dear General, that there is not a character in America for whom I feel a greater regard and respect than that of General Hamilton, whose talents will no doubt soon again be called into action to the honor and advantage of his Country.

Our amiable friend Madame de Caradeux [2] is at present at St. Thomas, but will soon return to Puerto rico, where She has made a purchase; it has not been in my power to pay her a visit at St. Thomas owing to my departure for Europe which is to take place to-morrow on board our frigate Fredericksteen. I shall do myself the pleasure of writing to You on my arrival in England and give You any ideas on the situation of public affairs and politics. [3]

You would oblige me very much by sending our friend Dr Stevens [4] a copy of Camillus's letters [5] and of Your later publications, the only copy of Camillus's letters which I had I once lent to the late Count Bernstorff, [6] who begged of me to let him keep it in his library *as a classical work*, these were his expressions.

Accept my sincerest wishes for Your happiness and that of Your family, and believe me to be with the greatest regard and the sincerest attachment

Dear General   Your most obedt. and most humble Servt

Walterstorff

General A. Hamilton
New York.

ALS, Hamilton Papers, Library of Congress.
    1. Letter not found.
    2. See Madame de Caradeux Lecaye to H, March 6, 1803.
    3. In *JCHW*, VI, 556, this paragraph is omitted.
    4. Edward Stevens was one of H's oldest and closest friends, for they had known each other well from the time they were young boys at St. Croix (H to Stevens, November 11, 1769). Stevens studied medicine at the University of Edinburgh and subsequently practiced in Philadelphia, where he treated H and Elizabeth Hamilton when they had yellow fever (H to the College of Physicians, September 11, 1793). Stevens was United States consul general at Santo Domingo from March 10, 1799, to September 25, 1801, when he returned to the United States for a short time before settling in St. Croix (Richard Harrison, auditor of the Treasury Department, to Gabriel Duvall, comptroller of the Treasury Department, January 11, 1804 [copy, Massa-

chusetts Historical Society, Boston], enclosed in William Thornton to Timothy Pickering, December 12, 1825 [ALS, Massachusetts Historical Society, Boston]).

5. For the "Camillus" letters, see the introductory note to "The Defence No. I," July 22, 1795.

6. Count Andreas Peter von Bernstorff, who died in 1797, had been Danish Minister for Foreign Affairs and president of the German Chancery.

To Nathaniel Terry

New York, April 21, 1803. States: "Your letter of the 2d instant [1] found me in the midst of a Circuit Court." [2] Discusses a case concerning Jeremiah Wadsworth, one of the executors of Nathanael Greene's estate.[3]

ALS, Hamilton Papers, Library of Congress.

1. Letter not found.

2. The Circuit Court of the City and County of New York met from March 29 to April 21, 1803.

3. For Greene's estate, see "Report on the Petition of Catharine Greene," December 26, 1791; Wadsworth to H, August 23, 1800, H to Wadsworth, March 25, May 8, 1801.

In the Hamilton Papers, Library of Congress, there is an undated document in H's handwriting, entitled "Memoranda," which contains a list of questions and answers concerning the case discussed in the letter printed above.

From Vincent Gray [1]

Havana 26. April 1803

Sir

The Ship Aspasia being about to depart for new york, I take leave to present to you this my friend Mr. Walden a small Turtle which I beg your acceptance as a small memento of my grateful recollection of your politeness while acting at the head of the Treasury Department.

I have resided here some time as agent of the United States, and shall in consequence of having many debts to collect for her citizens, have Occasion to remain here some time longer—during which time, if I can serve you or any of your friends in this quarter you will please to command my services.

I am Sir,   very respectfully   your mo: obt. Serv.   Vincent Gray

Genl. Alex. Hamilton
New York

ALS, Hamilton Papers, Library of Congress.
1. Gray was surveyor for the District of Alexandria, Virginia, and inspector of the revenue for the port of Alexandria from 1793 to 1798.

Receipt to Benjamin Tallmadge [1]

[New York, May 6, 1803]

I Alexander Hamilton of New York acknowledge to have received of BENJAMIN TALLMADGE, Treasurer of the OHIO COMPANY, ninety seven Dollars five cents being the third dividend payable on five Shares in said Company,[2] in the agency of Winthrop Sargent.[3] Dated at New York this sixth Day of May 1803.

A Hamilton

DS, Princeton University Library; DS (photostat), Benjamin Tallmadge Scrapbook, Library of Congress.
1. Tallmadge, who was brevetted a lieutenant colonel at the close of the American Revolution, was a merchant and deputy postmaster in Litchfield, Connecticut, and treasurer of the Ohio Company. In 1800 Tallmadge was elected to the House of Representatives as a Federalist and served in Congress until 1817.
2. See H to Oliver Wolcott, Jr., October 3, 1802, note 7.
3. Sargent, a veteran of the American Revolution, a native of Massachusetts, and a Federalist, was the surveyor of the Seven Ranges in Ohio in 1786 and in the same year helped to found the Ohio Company. In 1787 he became secretary of the Ohio Company and secretary of the Territory Northwest of the River Ohio. In 1798 he was appointed governor of the Mississippi Territory, a post which he held until 1801.

From Jacob Read [1]

Savannah 19th; May 1803

Sir

I have been applied to by some friends whom I very much regard, to give a few Letters of Introduction to Jas. Hume Esqr; now of this City and who intends in the Course of the summer to Visit the Northern & Eastern States, and I have had the Freedom to give him

a Letter to yourself.[2] The Wish I know Mr Hume entertained to
be made acquainted with a Gentleman so justly intitled to Celebrity,
as General Hamilton is, and the pleasure I know it gives you to receive Strangers of Worth & high Talent, were my Inducements to
take the liberty I have. I assure you it will ever give me great pleasure to reciprocate any attentions you may please to shew to my
Friend by the like Civilities to any Friend of your's that may visit
my residence whether in the southern states or Elsewhere and I beg
on any such occasion you will be pleased to Command me.

Mr Hume was for many years the King's Attorney General in
Georgia during the Royal Government—he was afterwards Chief
Justice of E. Florida & lastly Chief Justice of Georgia during the
time the State was a second-time under the Royal power.[3]

At the Commencement of the Revolution Mr; Hume being of the
King's Council, was ordered off by the Committee of safety & he
retired to England where he remained 'till appointed to the Bench
in Florida. Notwhthstanding his obedience to the mandate & a Conduct truly liberal mild & Correct Governor O'Howley,[4] (of whom
you may have heard & Who by the bye was as great a Scoundrel as
ever disgraced humanity) put this Gentleman on His Act of banishment[5] & Confiscated his Estates. This Act of Injustice to so good &
honorable a Man the Legislature have Corrected & Relieved Mr
Hume from the pains & penalties of Mr OHowley's Law.[6]

Mr Hume having acquired very large Estates in Lands & Negroes
in this State has lately come over from Scotland where he has many
years resided at his own Estate, Carroll Side, near Edinburgh & will
pass some time in the United States. He is now on his first Visit to
the Northern & Eastern States—for altho' a Carolinian by Birth Mr
Hume (as most of us formerly were) was Educated in Britain &
took his Degree at the Middle Temple. I have been thus Minute to
make you Acquainted with the whole Facts Relating to the Gentleman I have taken leave to introduce to your acquaintance, and I ask
for him a small share of that Notice & of those attentions which you
so readily bestow on Strangers of merit. Mr Hume is accompanied
by his Lady who is of one of the most reputable *old Families* of
Georgia. They have no family.

I hope in the Course of a few Weeks to have the pleasure of seeing you in New York, where I expect to join Mrs; Read, & of once

more assuring my Friends in person of My high Respect & Esteem for them.

I have the Honour to remain   Dear Sir   Your most obedt Huml. Srvt   Jacob Read

The Honl
Majr: Genl; Hamilton
New York

ALS, Hamilton Papers, Library of Congress.
1. Read, a South Carolina Federalist and a veteran of the American Revolution, was a delegate to the Continental Congress from 1783 to 1786 and a member of the United States Senate from 1795 to 1801. On February 23, 1801, John Adams nominated Read as judge of the District of South Carolina. Read's nomination was confirmed on February 24 (*Executive Journal*, I, 383, 385), but he never assumed the position because the Judiciary Act of 1801, which created his office, was repealed in March, 1802 (*Annals of Congress*, XI, 183, 982).
2. Letter not found.
3. The British temporarily re-established control over Georgia from 1779 to 1782.
4. Richard Howley became a member of the Georgia legislature in 1779 and was elected governor in 1780. He was a delegate to the Continental Congress from 1780 to 1782 and chief justice of Georgia from 1782 to 1783. He died in 1784.
5. "An Act for inflicting penalties on, and confiscating the estates of such persons as are therein declared guilty of treason, and for other purposes therein mentioned" (*Georgia Laws*, 1782 Sess. [May 4, 1782]).
6. "An Act to take off the Act of Confiscation and Banishment, the name of James Hume" (*Georgia Laws*, April-May, 1803, Sess. [May 9, 1803]).

Description of a Cipher [1]

[May 23, 1803]

Pour se servir de l'Echiquier cy inclus,[2] en place d'un Chiffre, afin d'empecher la decouverte de votre correspondance; employer la maniere suivante.

Ayant ecris votre lettre comme de coutume; vous prepárerez le papier sur lequel vous êtes intentioné a coucher votre copie secrete de la meme grandeur que le carré en Echiquier, lequel ētant placé sur le dit papier, vous l'y fixerez par les quatre coins avec des

Epingles—il est indifferent par quel coin vous commenciez, soit
A. B. C. ou *D.*, pourvu que vous fassiez attention de tourner l'Ex-
hiquier vers votre gauche. Ainsi si vous commencez par le coin *A.*
vous ecrirez votre communication en placeant sur le papier préparé
a cet effet, *une seule lettre* dans chaque *carré découpé*, allant de la
droit, à la gauche, ligne par ligne, ayant ecris de cette maniére
jusqu'a láfin de la page, détaché l'Echiquier, tournez le de la droite
a la gauche, l'*A* faisant place a *B.* fixez le avec des epingles par les
memes trous sur votre papier a lettre, continuez a copier votre lettre
ainsi qu'il est explique cy dessus, et ayant remplis tous les carrés
decoupés de la dite page, vous tournerez de rechef l'Echiquier en
sorte que *B.* fasse place a *C.* En suivant cette maniere jusqu'a ce que
vous ayez fait usage des quatre cotés de l'Echiquier, vous aurez remplis votre papier avec vingt six lignes, chaque contenant 26 letters.
Pour eviter toute difficulté et confusion, vous pouvez désigner par
quel coin de l'Echiquier vous avez commencé, en placeant au haut
de votre communication la lettre marquante le dit coin cy dessus
pour la lettre *A.*[3]

Copy, New-York Historical Society, New York City.
    1. According to endorsements on the cover of this document, it was first
sent to Robert Troup by Evan Jones, United States consul for the port of New
Orleans, who was acting as an intermediary. Jones endorsed the cover: "Received & forwarded by Your most obt. Ser E. Jones." Troup, in turn, sent
the document to H and later endorsed it: "Shewn to me this day by General
Hamilton within five minutes after I had sent it to him dated this 23 May
1803 Rob. Troup." Below the notations made by Jones and Troup is a third
endorsement, which reads: "The whole were put in another cover thus endorsed in the hand writing of Genl. Hamilton 'The Chancellor Lansing.' J.L."
    John Lansing, Jr., a veteran of the American Revolution and a lawyer, was a
member of the New York Assembly from 1780 to 1784 and in 1786 and 1788, a
member of the Continental Congress in 1784 and 1785, a delegate (with H and
Robert Yates) to the Constitutional Convention in 1787, and a member of the
New York Ratifying Convention in 1788. He was appointed judge of the New
York Supreme Court in 1790 and chief justice in 1798. In 1801 he became
chancellor and served in that capacity until 1814, when he returned to private
law practice.
    2. "L'Echiquier" referred to in the document printed above may be found
in the New-York Historical Society, New York City. It is a grid of empty
squares with twenty-six squares to a side. At the bottom of the grid is written:
"Endorsed with the initials of Chancellor Lansing thus J.L."
    3. On November 5, 1808, Nathaniel Pendleton, an executor of H's estate,
wrote to Jones: "Among General Hamiltons papers was found a packet containing a Cypher for carrying on a Secret correspondence with an Explanation
in the French Language, and directions as to the manner of using it. It was without a signature or any other means of ascertaining from whom it came. It was

Stated to be intended to open a secret correspondence with General Hamilton by means of this Cypher. It was enclosed under a blank cover to 'Robert Troup Esqr. Attorney at Law Newyork' and on the back of the *Enveloppe* was the following Endorsement 'New Orleans 13 Apl. 1803. Received and forwarded by your most obt Ser. E. Jones.' We are extreemly desirous of ascertaining, if possible from whom this proposal of a secret correspondence came. We hope therefore you will be able to recollect the circumstance of your having received and forwarded this packet addressed to Col Troup, and from whom you received it, so as to trace it to its author. It is possible you may have been acquainted with the author and with his motives for proposing a Secret correspondence with General Hamilton, and if so it would be a gratification to us to be informed of them. We have no object in view in asking the favor of these communications, but to obtain authentic and full information as to every transaction any way relating to our friend in order that such circumstances as are of sufficient importance to merit it, may be preserved as materials from which the Historian may be Enabled to transmit to posterity a Correct and just account of that great man" (ALS, New-York Historical Society, New York City).

From John B. Graves [1]

New York, May 31, 1803. States that he is acting on behalf of George Scriba [2] who wishes to procure a mortgage in Europe on land in New York State. Requests Hamilton's opinion on "whether European citizens can hold in their own right a mortgage on real Estate and likewise in case of purchase, if they can hold real Estate in their own name and dispose of it."

ALS, Hamilton Papers, Library of Congress.
  1. Graves was a New York City merchant.
  2. Scriba was a New York City merchant and land speculator.

From Ernst Frederich von Walterstorff

London 31st May 1803

Dear General,

I will now according to my promise when I left St: Croix [1] acquaint You of my safe arrival at Portsmouth the 27th. instant and write You a few lines about the present state of politics.

You may think of our surprize, Sir, when we learned from an English Brig of war in the Channel that England had declared war against France and that hostilities had actually commenced.[2] Who can foretell what will be the result of this war and to what extent it will go? I do not conceive it possible that the continental powers, particularly, Austria, with regard to Italy can avoid getting into it. Many people think that no cordial peace can be established between England and France as long as Bonaparte lives and is at the head of the french Government, because the English Govt. is afraid of his ambition. I fear the war will be carried on with great animosity. The neutral powers will, I think, be respected by the English, at least untill England has formed some strong continental connections. Both parties are now courting Russia and everybody must be anxious to know what plan the Court of St. Petersbourg will adopt. I do not think that the tranquillity of Denmark will be affected, at least not for the present. Denmark is on the most friendly term with Russia and the Danish Minister enjoys the greatest consideration at Petersburg.[3] I think however that the Neutral should act with the great prudence and circumspection and be very cautious in granting passes to Ships.

Give me leave, Sir, to introduce to Your acquaintance Mr Peterson,[4] who is appointed Danish Consul General in america; he is a well informed man, without any kind of pretentions, and will, I hope, be approved of by the Government of the United States. It is a great loss to Your Government that you have not Mr King[5] here in the present situation of affairs.

My best respects attend Mrs. Hamilton. Believe me to be with the greatest consideration and a very sincere attachment,

Dear Sir   Your Most obedt. humble Servant   Walterstorff

Major General Alexr. Hamilton
New York.

ALS, Hamilton Papers, Library of Congress.
    1. See Walterstorff to H, April 20, 1803.
    2. On May 14, 1803, Great Britain declared war on France because of a dispute between the two countries concerning the possession and occupation of the island of Malta. News of the war in Europe appeared in the *New-York Evening Post* on June 17, 1803.
    3. Niels Rosenkrantz was the Danish Envoy Extraordinary and Minister Plenipotentiary at St. Petersburg from June 11, 1802, to February 17, 1804.
    4. Peder Pedersen, a lawyer, became acting Danish consul in Tangiers in 1799. Later that year he was appointed consul at Tangiers and held that posi-

tion until 1801. In 1802 he was appointed secretary at the consulate, and later in 1802 was given the title of consul and sent to Philadelphia, where he served as chargé d'affaires until 1831.

5. Rufus King. See King to H, April 8, 1802, note 8.

To Henry William De Saussure

[*New York, June 9, 1803.* On August 6, 1803, De Saussure wrote to Hamilton: "I received your favor of the 9th June." *Letter not found.*]

To John B. Graves [1]

New York, June 9, 1803. Gives his opinion concerning Graves's legal questions and states: "Having myself lands in the vicinity of those of Mr. Scriba,[2] I have occasionally received some information concerning the latter. . . . Some of my lands are now selling to settlers at the rate of three Dollars per acre." [3]

ALS, Hamilton Papers, Library of Congress.
   1. This letter was written in reply to Graves to H, May 21, 1803.
   2. See Jacob Mark and Company to John B. Church, H, and John Laurance, May 30, 1797, note 2; "Mortgage by Laurance, Church, and H to Robert Gilchrist," August 21, 1802, note 1.
   3. For the sale of H's lands, see H to John V. Henry, March 20, 1803.

To Nicholas Low

[New York, June 17, 1803]

Dr. Sir

I send you the letter I have drafted to Mr. Ludlow.[1] Be so good as to sign and forward it. Retain carefully the copy on the other side.[2] Yrs. with esteem   A H

[ENCLOSURE]

Alexander Hamilton and Nicholas Low to Daniel Ludlow [3]

New York June 17th. 1803

Dr. Sir

It is now a considerable length of time since we became with you Trustees for the Creditors of Isaac Moses & Co and Samuel and Moses Meyers; [4] and we feel anxious that the affairs of this trust should be finally closed. We therefore request that you will be good enough to communicate to us the present situation of this business and especially a statement of the funds, if any, which may remain in your hands unapplied, together with the obstacles, if any, which are in the way of a definitive settlement of the Trust. The full confidence we have in your punctuality and care assures us that the wish we have expressed can be speedily complied with.

With great esteem & regard   We are Dr Sir   Yr Obed servts

Daniel Ludlow Esq

ALS, The Sol Feinstone Collection, Library of the American Philosophical Society, Philadelphia.

1. Daniel Ludlow, a former Loyalist and a New York City merchant, was one of the founders of the Manhattan Company in 1799. In 1801 he was appointed United States Navy agent at New York City.

2. Low endorsed this note: "Alexandr. Hamilton was a letter of which the inclosed is Copy Signed by him dated 27 June 1803 was signed by me on 21 Do & sent to Mr. Ludlow by George Cline on that Day." Cline was a New York City accountant.

3. L, in H's handwriting, The Sol Feinstone Collection, Library of the American Philosophical Society, Philadelphia.

4. Isaac Moses was an auctioneer and head of the firm of Isaac Moses and Company at 63 Wall Street, New York City. During the early seventeen-eighties Moses became involved in an international partnership with Marcus Elcan of Richmond, Virginia, and Samuel and Moses Myers of Amsterdam. Isaac Moses became a bankrupt in early 1785 (H to Jeremiah Wadsworth, April 7, 1785), and the dissolution of the firm was announced in a supplement to *The New-York Journal, or the Weekly Register*, June 23, 1785 (Wadsworth to H, April 3, 1785). For H's earlier activities as a trustee for Moses, see H's "Cash Book," March 1, 1782–1791, under the entry entitled "Trustees of Isaac Moses."

Daniel Ludlow to Alexander Hamilton and Nicholas Low

New York June 21st. 1803

A. Hamilton ⎫
N. Low   ⎬ Esqrs.
            ⎭

Sirs

Your favor of the 17th inst. I this day only received and have to assure you that the Settlement of the trust you mention committed to our joint care and under my particular management has been an object I have long had seriously at heart and nothing has prevented the completion thereof on my part but the want of time. The accounts are in hands and nearly arranged, little wanting but leisure to give them a proper examination, this I expect to have next week when they will be laid before you.

I am respectfully   Sirs   Your most obedt. Servt.   D Ludlow

ALS, New-York Historical Society, New York City.

From Thomas Stoughton [1]

New York, June 25, 1803. Requests Hamilton to inform Dominick Lynch [2] that "after waiting nearly Seven Years to procure a Settlement of our Copartnership Accots . . . it must now be determined either Amicably or through the medium of the Law." [3] States that he wrote to Hamilton on November 11, 1797,[4] with "a Statement of Facts, Copy of our Articles and my claims."

ALS, Hamilton Papers, Library of Congress.
   1. Stoughton, a New York City merchant, was the Spanish consul general in New York City.
   2. Lynch was a New York City merchant.
   3. An entry in H's Law Register, 1795–1804, reads:

"Thomas Stoughton
    v
Dom Lynch
Retainer expected suit
60 Ds" (D, partially in H's handwriting, New York Law Institute, New York City). See also H's Cash Book, 1795–1804, under the date of November 9, 1797 (AD, Hamilton Papers, Library of Congress). For additional information concerning this suit, see Goebel, *Law Practice*, forthcoming volumes.
   4. Letter not found.

To William Rawle [1]

[*New York, June 26, 1803.* On June 27–July 29, 1803, Rawle wrote to Hamilton: "This morning I received your favor of the 26th. inst." *Letter not found.*]

   1. A native of Philadelphia, Rawle studied law in England at the Middle Temple from 1781 to 1782. In 1782 he returned to America, and in 1789 he was elected to the Pennsylvania Assembly. He was United States attorney for the District of Pennsylvania from 1791 to 1799.

From William Rawle

Philadelphia, June 27–July 29, 1803. States: "This morning I received your favor of the 26th. inst." [1] Answers questions concerning certain aspects of William Duane's indictment and trial for libel.[2]

ALS, Hamilton Papers, Library of Congress.
   1. Letter not found.
   2. Duane had been indicted in 1800 under the Sedition Act for libel of the United States Senate. H needed the information concerning Duane's indictment and trial for his defense of Harry Croswell, Federalist editor of *The* [Hudson, New York] *Balance, and Columbian Repository*, who in January, 1803, had been indicted for seditious libel by the Grand Jury in Columbia County, New York. For H's role in *People* v *Croswell*, see Goebel, *Law Practice*, I, 775–848.
   Rawle did not send this letter to H until July 29, 1803, when he wrote at the bottom of the letter printed above: "The above was written sometime ago and no safe private conveyance occurring to my knowledge—& your letter not specifying within what particular time, it was necessary to send them, I kept the papers by me. . . ."

Purchase of Louisiana [1]

[New York, July 5, 1803]

Purchase of Louisiana. At length the business of New-Orleans has terminated favourably to this country.[2] Instead of being obliged to rely any longer on the force of treaties, for a place of deposit,[3] the jurisdiction of the territory is now transferred to our hands and in future the navigation of the Mississippi will be ours unmolested. This, it will be allowed is an important acquisition, not, indeed, as territory, but as being essential to the peace and prosperity of our Western country, and as opening a free and valuable market to our commercial states. This purchase has been made during the period of Mr. Jefferson's presidency, and, will, doubtless, give eclat to his administration. Every man, however, possessed of the least candour and reflection will readily acknowledge that the acquisition has been solely owing to a fortuitous concurrence of unforseen and unexpected circumstances, and not to any wise or vigorous measures on the part of the American government.

As soon as we experienced from Spain a direct infraction of an important article of our treaty, in withholding the deposit of New-Orleans, it afforded us justifiable cause of war, and authorised immediate hostilities. Sound policy unquestionably demanded of us to

New-York Evening Post, July 5, 1803.

1. For background to this document, see H to Charles Cotesworth Pinckney, December 29, 1802; "For the *Evening Post,*" February 8, 1803.

This document was first attributed to H in "Hamilton on the Louisiana Purchase: A Newly Identified Editorial from the *New-York Evening Post*" (*The William and Mary Quarterly,* 3rd ser., XII, No. 2 [April, 1955], 268–81]).

For H's earlier opinions concerning the strategic and economic importance of Louisiana, see H to George Washington, September 15, 1790; "Conversation with George Beckwith," September 25–30, October 15–20, 1790; H to James McHenry, January 27–February 11, 1798; H to Timothy Pickering, March 27, 1798.

2. News of the cession of Louisiana to the United States reached New York City on June 30, 1803 (*New-York Evening Post,* June 30, 1803), but the dispatches from Paris containing the treaty and the two conventions did not arrive in Washington until July 14 (Thomas Jefferson to Meriwether Lewis, July 15, 1803 [ALS, letterpress copy, Thomas Jefferson Papers, Library of Congress]).

3. See H to Pinckney, December 29, 1802, note 6.

begin with a prompt, bold and vigorous resistance against the injustice: to seize the object at once; and having this *vantage ground*, should we have thought it advisable to terminate hostilities by a purchase, we might then have done it on almost our own terms. This course, however, was not adopted, and we were about to experience the fruits of our folly, when another nation has found it her interest to place the French Government in a situation substantially as favourable to our views and interests as those recommended by the federal party here, excepting indeed that we should probably have obtained the same object on better terms.

On the part of France the short interval of peace [4] had been wasted in repeated and fruitless efforts to subjugate St. Domingo; and those means which were originally destined to the colonization of Louisiana, had been gradually exhausted by the unexpected difficulties of this ill-starred enterprize.[5]

To the deadly climate of St. Domingo, and to the courage and obstinate resistance made by its black inhabitants are we indebted for the obstacles which delayed the colonization of Louisiana, till the auspicious moment, when a rupture between England and France gave a new turn to the projects of the latter, and destroyed at once all her schemes as to this favourite object of her ambition.

It was made known to Bonaparte, that among the first objects of England would be the seizure of New-Orleans,[6] and that preparations were even then in a state of forwardness for that purpose. The First Consul could not doubt, that if an English fleet was sent thither, the place must fall without resistance; it was obvious, therefore, that it would be in every shape preferable that it should be placed in the possession of a neutral power; and when, besides, some millions of money, of which he was extremely in want, were offered him, to part with what he could no longer hold it affords a moral

4. Peace between France and Great Britain lasted from March 21, 1802, when both countries signed the Treaty of Amiens, until May, 1803, when Great Britain renewed hostilities (Ernst Frederich von Walterstorff to H, May 31, 1803, note 2).

5. See Rufus King to H, May 7, 1802, notes 8 and 9.

6. See François de Barbé-Marbois, *Histoire de la Louisiane et de la Cession de Cette Colonie par la France aux États-Unis de l'Amérique Septenrionale* . . . (Paris: Imprimerie de Firmin Didot, 1829) 258–88. See also King to Robert R. Livingston and James Monroe, May 7, 1803 (ALS, New-York Historical Society, New York City).

certainty, that it was to an accidental state of circumstances, and not
to wise plans, that this cession, at this time, has been owing. We
shall venture to add, that neither of the ministers through whose in-
strumentality it was effected,[7] will ever deny this, or even pretend
that previous to the time when a rupture was believed to be inevitable, there was the smallest chance of inducing the First Consul,
with his ambitious and aggrandizing views, to commute the territory for any sum of money in their power to offer. The real truth
is, Bonaparte found himself absolutely compelled by situation, to relinquish his darling plan of colonising the banks of the Mississippi:
and thus have the Government of the United States, by the unforseen operation of events, gained what the feebleness and pusillanimity
of its miserable system of measures could never have acquired. Let
us then, with all due humility, acknowledge this as another of those
signal instances of the kind interpositions of an over-ruling Providence, which we more especially experienced during our revolutionary war, & by which we have more than once, been saved from the
consequences of our errors and perverseness.

We are certainly not disposed to lessen the importance of this
acquisition to the country, but it is proper that the public should be
correctly informed of its real value and extent as well as of the
terms on which it has been acquired. We perceive by the newspapers that various & very vague opinions are entertained; and we
shall therefore, venture to state our ideas with some precision as to
the territory; but until the instrument of cession itself is published,
we do not think it prudent to say much as to the conditions on
which it has been obtained.[8]

Prior to the treaty of Paris 1763,[9] France claimed the country on
both sides of the river under the name of Louisiana, and it was her
encroachments on the rear of the British Colonies which gave rise

7. Robert R. Livingston and James Monroe.
8. On July 18, 1803, the *National Intelligencer and Washington Advertiser*
printed a summary of the provisions of the treaty and the conventions. On
October 24, 1803, three days after the Senate ratified the agreements (Miller,
Treaties, II, 506–07), the texts of the documents were published in the *New-
York Evening Post*.
9. The Definitive Treaty of Peace between Great Britain, France, and Spain
was signed in Paris on February 10, 1763 (*The Parliamentary History of
England, From the Earliest Period to the Year 1803* [London, 1806–1820], XV,
1291–1305).

to the war of 1755.[10] By the conclusion of the treaty of 1763, the limits of the colonies of Great Britain and France were clearly and permanently fixed; and it is from that and subsequent treaties that we are to ascertain what territory is really comprehended under the name of Louisiana. France ceded to Great-Britain all the country east and south-east of a line drawn along the middle of the Mississippi from its source to the Iberville, and from thence along that river and the Lakes Maurepas and Pontchartrain to the sea; France retaining the country lying west of the river, besides the town and Island of New-Orleans on the east side.[11] This she soon after ceded to Spain [12] who acquiring also the Floridas by the treaty of 1783,[13] France was entirely shut out from the continent of North America. Spain, at the instance of Bonaparte, ceded to him Louisiana, including the Town and Island (as it is commonly called) of New-Orleans.[14] Bonaparte has now ceded the same tract of country, and this only, to the United States.[15] The whole of East and West-Florida, lying south of Georgia and of the Mississippi Territory, and extending to the Gulf of Mexico, still remains to Spain, who will continue, therefore, to occupy, as formerly, the country along the southern frontier of the United States, and the east bank of the river, from the Iberville to the American line.

Those disposed to magnify its value will say, that this western region is important as keeping off a troublesome neighbour, and leaving us in the quiet possession of the Mississippi. Undoubtedly this has some force, but on the other hand it may be said, that the acquisition of New-Orleans is perfectly adequate to every purpose; for whoever is in possession of that, has the uncontrouled command of the river. Again, it may be said, and this probably is the most favourable point of view in which it can be placed, that although not valuable to the United States for settlement, it is so to Spain, and will become more so, and therefore at some distant period will form

10. The French and Indian War or the Seven Years War.

11. Article VII of the Treaty of Paris of 1763 (*The Parliamentary History of England*, XV, 1295–96).

12. France secretly ceded Louisiana to Spain in 1762 by the terms of the Treaty of Fontainebleau, but these terms were not made public in America until 1764.

13. Article V of the Definitive Treaty of Peace and Friendship between His Britannic Majesty and the King of Spain, signed at Versailles, September 3, 1783 (*The Parliamentary History of England*, XXIII, 1176).

14. See William Constable to H, March 23, 1801, note 2.

15. See "For the *Evening Post*," February 8, 1803, note 1.

an object which we may barter with her for the Floridas, obviously of far greater value to us than all the immense, undefined region west of the river.

It has been usual for the American writers on this subject to include the Floridas in their ideas of Louisiana, as the French formerly did, and the acquisition has derived no inconsiderable portion of its value and importance with the public from this view of it. It may, however, be relied on, that no part of the Floridas, not a foot of land on the east of the Mississippi, excepting New-Orleans, falls within the present cession. As to the unbounded region west of the Mississippi, it is, with the exception of a very few settlements of Spaniards and Frenchmen bordering on the banks of the river, a wilderness through which wander numerous tribes of Indians. And when we consider the present extent of the United States, and that not one sixteenth part of its territory is yet under occupation, the advantage of the acquisition, as it relates to actual settlement, appears too distant and remote to strike the mind of a sober politician with much force. This, therefore, can only rest in speculation for many years, if not centuries to come, and consequently will not perhaps be allowed very great weight in the account by the majority of readers. But it may be added, that should our own citizens, more enterprizing than wise, become desirous of settling this country, and emigrate thither, it must not only be attended with all the injuries of a too widely dispersed population, but by adding to the great weight of the western part of our territory, must hasten the dismemberment of a large portion of our country, or a dissolution of the Government. On the whole, we think it may with candor be said, that whether the possession at this time of any territory west of the river Mississippi will be advantageous, is at best extremely problematical. For ourselves, we are very much inclined to the opinion, that after all, it is the Island of N. Orleans by which the command of a free navigation of the Mississippi is secured, that gives to this interesting cession, its greatest value, and will render it in every view of immense benefit to our country. By this cession we hereafter shall hold within our own grasp, what we have heretofore enjoyed only by the uncertain tenure of a treaty,[16] which might be

16. The Treaty of Friendship, Limits, and Navigation between the United States and Spain, signed at San Lorenzo el Real on October 25, 1795 (Miller, *Treaties*, II, 318–38).

broken at the pleasure of another, and (governed as we now are) with perfect impunity. Provided therefore we have not purchased it too dear, there is all the reason for exultation which the friends of the administration display, and which all Americans may be allowed to feel.

As to the pecuniary value of the bargain, we know not enough of the particulars to pronounce upon it. It is understood generally, that we are to assume *debts* of France to our own citizens not exceeding four millions of dollars; and that for the remainder, being a very large sum, 6 per cent stock to be created, and payment made in that.[17] But should it contain no conditions or stipulations on our part, no "tangling alliances" of all things to be dreaded, we shall be very much inclined to regard it in a favorable point of view though it should turn out to be what may be called a costly purchase. By the way a question here presents itself of some little moment: Mr. Jefferson in that part of his famous electioneering message, where he took so much pains to present a flattering state of the Treasury in so few words that every man could carry it in his noddle and repeat it at the poll, tells us, that "experience too so far authorises us to believe, *if no extraordinary event supervenes, and the expences which will be actually incurred shall not be greater than was contemplated* by Congress at their last session, that we shall not be disappointed in the expectations formed" that the debt would soon be paid, &c. &c.[18] But the first and only measure of the administration that has really been of any material service to the country (for they have hitherto gone on the strength of the provisions made by their predecessors) is really "*an extraordinary event*," and calls for more money than they have got. According to Mr. Gallatin's report, they had about 40.000 to spare for contingencies,[19] and now the first "*extraordinary event*" that "*supervenes*" calls upon them for several millions. What a poor starvling system of administering a govern-

17. See Articles 1 and 2 of the Convention for the Payment of Sixty Million Francs ($11,250,000) by the United States, signed at Paris on April 30, 1803 (Miller, *Treaties*, II, 513–14), and Articles 1, 2, and 3 of the Convention for the Payment of Sums Due by France to Citizens of the United States, signed at Paris on April 30, 1803 (Miller, *Treaties*, II, 517–18).

18. See Thomas Jefferson's second annual message, which he sent to Congress on December 15, 1802 (*Annals of Congress*, XII, 12–15).

19. See "State of Finances," which Albert Gallatin wrote on December 17, 1802, and submitted to Congress on December 20 (*ASP, Finance*, II, 5–9).

ment! *But how is the money to be had? Not by taxing luxury and wealth and whiskey, but by increasing the taxes on the necessaries of life.* Let this be remembered.

But we are exceeding our allowable limits. It may be satisfactory to our readers, that we should finish with a concise account of New-Orleans itself.

The Island of New-Orleans is in length about 150 miles; its breadth varies from 10 to 30 miles. Most of it is a marshy swamp, periodically inundated by the river. The town of New-Orleans, situated about 105 miles from the mouth of the river, contains near 1300 houses, and about 8000 inhabitants, chiefly Spanish and French. It is defended from the overflowings of the river, by an embankment, or *leveé*, which extends near 50 miles.

The rights of the present proprietors of real estate in New-Orleans and Louisiana, whether acquired by descent or by purchase, will, of course, remain undisturbed.[20] How they are to be governed is another question; whether as a colony, or to be formed into an integral part of the United States, is a subject which will claim consideration hereafter. The probable consequences of this cession, and the ultimate effect it is likely to produce on the political state of our country, will furnish abundant matter of speculation to the American statesman.

If reliance can be placed on the history given of the negociation of *Louisiana* in private letters, from persons of respectability residing at Paris, and who speak with confidence, the merit of it, after making due allowance for the great events which have borne it along with them, is due to our ambassador, Chancellor Livingston, and not to the Envoy Extraordinary. "The cession was voted in the Council of State on the 8th of April, and Mr. Munro did not even arrive till the 12th." [21] Judging from Mr. Munro's former communications

20. See Article III of the Treaty of the Cession of Louisiana, signed at Paris April 30, 1803 (Miller, *Treaties*, II, 501).

21. H presumably obtained this information from an unsigned letter which was printed in the *New-York Evening Post* on July 1, 1803, and which also appeared in other newspapers during the first half of July ([Boston] *New-England Palladium*, July 1, 1803; [New York] *American Citizen*, July 7, 1803; *National Intelligencer and Washington Advertiser*, July 8, 1803). The letter, which was written from Paris on May 13, 1803, reads in part: "I inclose you a memorial, which Mr. Livingston, our minister here, presented to the French

to the French Government on this subject,[22] we really cannot but regard it as fortunate, that the thing was concluded before he reached St. Cloud.

Government, which was really the primary cause of the cession of LOUISIANA to the UNITED STATES. I beg you to have it translated and published, that the tribute due to the exertions of that able negotiator be rendered by every citizen, who is capable of appreciating the inestimable benefit he has obtained. The cession was voted in the Council of State the 8th of April. I was at *St. Cloud* that day. The 9th, propositions were made to Mr. LIVINGSTON to fix on a price. The 10th, the thing was talked over, and the principles agreed upon, when news of Mr. MUNRO's arrival at *Havre* got to town. The 12th, in the evening Mr. M. did arrive at *Paris*. The previous negociations of Mr. L. were communicated to him and every thing was closed and signed the 30th— even before Mr. MUNRO was presented at Court" (*New-York Evening Post,* July 1, 1803).
The memorial, entitled "A Memorial on this question—whether it be advantageous for France to take possession of Louisiana?," was printed in the *New-York Evening Post,* July 19, 20, 1803. See also *ASP, Foreign Relations,* II, 520–24.
22. This is a reference to Monroe's mission to France from 1794 to 1796.

From Josiah Parker [1]

Macclesfield [2] Virga July 9th. 1803

Dear Sir.

I trespass on your hospitality & former acquaintance to recommend to your civility in New York my friend M. M. Robinson esq. a neighbour of mine whose late bad health has determined him on a trip to the Eastward to endeavour to renevate himself; he is not a modern politician but an admirer of those men & measures that has brought our Country to its present State of affluence & respectability: all that I shall expect from you in respect to him is that you will be good enough to shew him a favourable countenance whilst in New york; he will not like most of my Country men who go abroad require any pecuniary aid—accept by best wishes for your health & prosperity.

Josiah Parker

ALS, MS Division, New York Public Library.
1. Parker, who was a colonel in the Fifth Virginia Regiment during the American Revolution, was a member of the Virginia House of Delegates in 1780 and 1781 and of the House of Representatives from 1789 to 1801.

2. Macclesfield was the name of Parker's estate in Isle of Wight County, Virginia.

From John Murray [1]

Baltimore, July 13, 1803. Requests Hamilton's opinion concerning his father's [2] claim to lands in New York State.

ALS, Hamilton Papers, Library of Congress.
  1. This letter is printed in full in Goebel, *Law Practice*, I, 263–64.
  2. John Murray, fourth Earl of Dunmore. See John Hamilton to H, April 16, 1803.

From William R. Putnam

[*Marietta, Ohio, August 1, 1803.* In October, 1803, Hamilton wrote to Putnam: "I have to thank you for your letter of the 1st of August." *Letter not found.*]

From Philip Schuyler

Albany Wednesday 3rd
Augt 1803.

My Dear Sir

How greatly have you Obliged And my Beloved Eliza relieved me of anxiety, by drawing from the unhappy seat of Contagion [1] Mr Morton and his family.[2] How much Am I pleased to Learn that you are to make an excursion into the country. I shall now no longer labour under those apprehensions which have so greatly distressed me least some Calamity Should befal my family.

My fine Grandson Alexander [3] Accompanies his Aunt Church [4] tomorrow on a vist to my Sister [5] they will proceed to Utica and visit the canal Companys works [6] at the falls.[7] I have directed him to examine those works and to bring me a report of the progress of the works prosceeding there. My James [8] will on Monday go to Eastown [9] to pass some days with his Uncle [10] and Couzin Phill.[11] I will not part with those Children until the disorder has so far abated as that they may with safety return to their Studys in NYork.[12]

I have by the advice of Mr Stringer [13] confined myself to my bed, as a mean the more speedily of healing the Ulcers on my foot, and have already experienced a good Effect, probably a week more will restore me to the ⟨use⟩ of my legs.

Angelica [14] & Catherine [15] unite in love to you, to their Sisters, & the Children, and all with you.

It would amuse my Dear Angelica [16] to take a tour to this place, and be greatly pleasing to me, cannot you find a conveyance for her.

Adieu My very Dear Sir   I am Ever most affectionately   Yours

Ph. Schuyler

Gen Hamilton

ALS, Hamilton Papers, Library of Congress.

1. On August 20, 1803, Rufus King wrote to Christopher Gore, United States chargé d'affaires at London: "Our City continues to be scourged with the yellow fever: it is probable that upwards of 20.000 of the Inhabitants have retired to the country & the quarters of the city, where the influence is supposed to have most prevailed, are evacuated, and in consequence of their Removal, fewer cases happen than otherwise wd. take place—hitherto not more than 18 new cases, nor more than 9 deaths have taken place any one day; but from the severity of the attack in a plurality of cases, the Effects of the Disease are more and more alarming than formerly. Men in perfect health to all appearance, and who are engaged in their business as usual, are seized and die in the course of 40 hours" (King, The Life and Correspondence of Rufus King, IV, 294).
    See also I. N. Phelps Stokes, The Iconography of Manhattan Island, V (New York, 1926), 1412–13.
    2. Washington Morton, a New York City lawyer, was the husband of Cornelia Schuyler Morton, one of Schuyler's daughters. The Mortons had a three-year-old son named Alexander Hamilton Morton (Schuyler to H, August 25, 1800).
    3. Alexander Hamilton, H's oldest surviving son, was seventeen years old.
    4. Angelica Church was Elizabeth Hamilton's oldest sister and the wife of John B. Church.
    5. Gertrude Schuyler Cochran, Schuyler's older sister, lived in Palatine, New York.
    6. The Western Inland Lock Navigation Company. See Théophile Cazenove to Egbert Benson and H, May 29, 1797; Schuyler to H, April 5, August 19, 1802.
    7. The falls of the Mohawk River located at Little Falls, Herkimer County, New York, eighteen miles southeast of Utica.
    8. James Alexander Hamilton, one of H's sons, was fifteen years old.
    9. Eastown is in Washington County, New York, approximately thirty miles northeast of Albany.

10. Rensselaer Schuyler, one of Philip Schuyler's sons, was married to Elizabeth Ten Broeck.

11. Schuyler had three grandsons who were named Philip: Philip P. Schuyler, oldest son of Philip Jeremiah Schuyler; Philip Schuyler, oldest son of John Bradstreet Schuyler; Philip Church, oldest son of Angelica Church.

12. Both Alexander and James Hamilton were students at Columbia College in 1803. Alexander was graduated in 1804, and James was graduated in 1805.

13. Dr. Samuel Stringer, a native of Maryland, received his medical education in Philadelphia and served as director general of hospitals in the northern department during the American Revolution. After the war he settled in Albany and continued to practice medicine. He was the Hamilton family's doctor in Albany. See H to Elizabeth Hamilton, August 2, 1791; August 8, 1794.

14. Angelica Church.

15. Catherine Schuyler, Schuyler's youngest daughter.

16. Angelica Hamilton, H's older daughter.

From John Nicholas [1]

Richmond August 4th 1803

Dear Sir

Although we have no personal acquaintance with each other; yet, as we have long had the same principles & cause, I believe, equally at heart, I take the liberty to address you on what ought to be dear to every virtuous and honest man—to every real and hearty well-wisher to the true interests & prosperity of this country. Sir, it is a melancholy & undeniable truth, that the principles, the conduct & examples of men high in influence & power are leading us rapidly to a state that must in a little time prove our inevitable ruin; while the fact is also, the talents, the virtue, the wealth—in fact, all the most ample means of counteraction lie expressly against them. And why is it, that those mere chimerical, *whimsical* and *theoretical* visionaries, who are only as *cunning* in intrigue, as they are vicious in practice & unprincipled in character, should sway the public opinion & hold the rod of popular despotism, in despite of all those better qualifications & more useful powers! Certainly because of their incessant industry & application to those objects, & our supineness & want of exertion. One of their main plans has ever been, to support with all their best *energies*, both Mentally and pecuniarily, their best printers; & with the utmost industry, care & activity, to disseminate their papers & pamphlets: While the Federalists on their part leave their printers to scuffle on the support of their *subscribers*, I believe a very *flimsy & uncertain daily sustenance,* and to scribble

out their *own way* to conquest! On their part they are deficient too
in one particular. They seldom republish from each other; while on
the other hand, their antagonists never get hold of any thing, however trivial in reality, but they make it ring thro' *all their papers*
from one end of the Continent to the other. For heaven sake, sir, let
us endeavour to rouse from this state of indifference & absolute
submission to our actual inferiors, unless we mean to be their bond-
slaves & our children after us forever. We look up to you with some
degree of confidence & hope, for some general & effectual plan in
which we may unite our powers and make at least one Manly &
vigorous effort. Let us in the first place fall upon some method to
support our papers, without leaving them to the precarious dependence of *scattered subscriptions*. At least one in N. Y. one in Phida.
one in Baltre. one in Washington, one in this place & one in Charleston. This done, then let us, or such of us as can furnish information
either as to arguments or facts, come forward and assist them. I have
suggested these things to some of our best and strongest friends
here; viz Marshal,[2] Carrington [3] &c. &c and will write to Rutledge [4]
& some other gentlemen to the south with whom I have the honor
of a correspondence, if you approve of & determine to do any thing
in this way for your country, yourself & your posterity. Be so good
as to write me & direct to Charlottesville, Albemarle, Virga. & if any
general plan like the above, or any other you may suggest, is fallen
on, which I imagine had better be by a meeting at Washington during the next Session of Congress, I shall be happy in attending &
rendering my little aid in any way I am capable. Living immediately
at *Headquarters* & being long intimately & personally acquainted
with certain characters & their secret Movements, I trust I can render
my share of service. With sentiments of sincere respect & esteem,
I am, Dear Sir,

Your most obedient & very humble servant   John Nicholas

Excuse the badness of the paper & the Letter. I have written in a
crowd of private business at this place.

☞ The unpleasant affair between W, J, & L,[5] which you have
heard & seen much of, will certainly come out at full length now, in
consequence of the late infamous & foolish publications in the "Examiner." I have just been with my friend W—— who I have always
before advised to silence on the subject. But what are men to do?

They cannot always submit to injuries of the most offensive nature, & to be abused for them too! In fact, you may be assured that W & L are now holding the *great man* in a very unpleasant situation. They have both written to him & demanded certain things; which, I suppose, he will not comply with—and of course you may guess the rest. But this flagrant breach of *pretended* private friendship, you may depend forms but a small link in the great chain of deformity & vice, well known to many in the particular quarter I reside in, & shall be known generally, if the exertions I propose are attempted & I live.

I have just heard from my friend Carrington that Rutledge is to the North: You will probly. therefore have an opportunity of communicating with *him personally* on the topics of this letter—he knows my handwriting.

J. N.

ALS, Hamilton Papers, Library of Congress.

1. Nicholas, a veteran of the American Revolution, was a Republican member of the House of Representatives from Albemarle, Virginia, from 1793 to 1801. In 1797 he accused Jefferson of establishing correspondence with George Washington under an assumed name in order to embarrass the President. Nicholas subsequently became a Federalist. In 1803, after he had written this letter, he moved to Ontario County, New York.

2. John Marshall, Chief Justice of the United States, was one of three representatives to France in 1797 in the mission which culminated in the XYZ affair. He was a member of the House of Representatives from Virginia from 1799 to May 12, 1800, when John Adams nominated him to be Secretary of State. The Senate confirmed the nomination on May 13 (*Executive Journal*, I 353, 354). On January 20, 1801, Adams nominated him Chief Justice, and the Senate confirmed the nomination on January 27 (*Executive Journal*, I, 371, 374).

3. Edward Carrington, a veteran of the American Revolution and a member of the Continental Congress from Virginia in 1785 and 1786, was United States marshal in Virginia from 1789 to 1791 and supervisor of the revenue for the District of Virginia from 1791 until the office was abolished under the terms of "An Act to repeal the Internal Taxes" (2 *Stat.* 148–50 [April 6, 1802]).

4. John Rutledge, Jr., a South Carolina lawyer, planter, and Federalist, was a member of the state House of Representatives from 1778 to 1794 and the United States House of Representatives from 1797 to 1803.

5. John Walker, Thomas Jefferson, and Henry Lee. This is a reference to an episode known as the "Walker Affair" which occurred in the late seventeen-sixties when Jefferson, who was not yet married, made what must have been a tentative sexual advance to Betsy Moore Walker, the wife of John Walker, Jefferson's boyhood friend, college classmate, and neighbor. Lee, a Federalist who supported Burr for President in the House of Representatives in 1801, was married to a niece of Betsy Walker. For a detailed discussion of this "affair," see Dumas Malone, *Jefferson the Virginian* (Boston, 1948), 153–55, and Appendix III; *Jefferson the President: First Term 1801–1805* (Boston, 1970), 216–23.

The "Walker Affair," became public knowledge when James Callender, editor of the [Richmond] *Recorder* and a former admirer of Jefferson, turned critic and published one version of the story in his newspaper in the fall of 1802. On

June 22, 1803, an article concerning the "Walker Affair," which appeared in another Richmond paper, the *Examiner*, published by Meriwether Jones, stated that Lee has recently presented Jefferson with a challenge to a duel from Walker. See also the *Examiner*, June 25, 1803. No other evidence of this challenge or its aftermath has been found. The Federalists attempted to use the "Walker Affair" to embarrass Jefferson throughout the remainder of his administration.

From Henry William De Saussure

Charleston [*South Carolina*], *August 6, 1803.* Replies to Hamilton's letter of June 9, 1803.[1] States his opinion on Isaac Clason's[2] attachments on the property of Bird, Savage, and Bird and on the property of Robert Bird and Company and on the validity of an assignment of property which the partners had made to Richard Harison.[3]

ALS, Hamilton Papers, Library of Congress.
1. Letter not found.
2. Clason was a New York City merchant.
3. Bird, Savage, and Bird was a South Carolina firm of merchants and bankers operating in London. The partners were Benjamin Savage and Robert and Henry Bird, who were brothers. Savage and Henry Bird lived in England and Robert Bird in the United States, where the firm was known as Robert Bird and Company. On December 3, 1802, shortly before the three partners were declared bankrupts, they made a secret assignment of part of their property to Richard Harison, a New York City attorney, "in trust for certain of their creditors" (William Johnson, *Reports of Cases Argued and Determined in the Supreme Court of Judicature, and in the Court for the Trial of Impeachments and the Correction of Errors in the State of New-York*, I [New York, 1807], 118).

To Jonas Platt [1]

New York, August 16, 1803. "The enclosed[2] is pursuant to an arrangement between Judge Thompson & Mr. Troupe. The *parties* trust and hope, that you will by all means have the goodness to attend. . . ."

ALS, Hamilton Papers, Library of Congress.
1. Platt, Smith Thompson, and Robert Troup had been appointed arbitrators and commissioners to settle the dispute over lands in Claverack, Columbia County, New York, between the heirs of John Van Rensselaer and those individuals who were charged with occupying his lands without acknowledging themselves as tenants and without accepting leases. For a discussion of this controversy and for the full text of the letter printed above, see Goebel, *Law*

Practice, forthcoming volumes. See also Philip Schuyler to H, July 17, 1800, note 22; September 29, October 9, 1800; April 16, 1803.

Platt, a New York Federalist, was admitted to the bar in 1790 and began to practice law in Poughkeepsie. He was county clerk of Herkimer County from 1791 to 1798 and a member of the Assembly from Herkimer County in 1796. From 1798 to 1802 he was county clerk of Oneida County, and from 1799 to 1801 he was a member of the House of Representatives. In 1801 he resumed the practice of law.

Thompson, a Republican lawyer from Dutchess County, New York, was a delegate to the New York State convention of 1801 and a member of the Assembly in 1800 and 1801. He was attorney of the Second District of New York from August to October, 1801, and a puisne justice of the New York Supreme Court from 1802 to 1814.

2. The "enclosed" was presumably an undated, unaddressed letter, drafted by H, which requests the commissioners to attend a meeting in Claverack on October 17, 1803, "to hear examine settle and determine" the dispute over the Claverack lands (ADfS, Columbia University Libraries). This letter is printed in full in Goebel, *Law Practice,* forthcoming volumes.

From Elisha Williams [1]

[*Hudson, New York, August 20, 1803.* On September 11, 1803, Williams wrote to Hamilton: "I took the liberty of Stating a Case & inclosing it to you about the 20th of August for your opinion." *Letter not found.*]

1. A Federalist and a member of the New York bar, Williams practiced law in Spencertown, New York, from 1793 to 1800, when he moved to Hudson. He was a member of the New York Assembly from Columbia County in 1800 and 1801.

From Benjamin Walker [1]

Utica [New York], September 3, 1803. "It unfortunately falls to my Lot to have the principal charge of the Estate of the late Mrs. Francis Bainbridge who in right of her Mother, Agatha Evans, was entitled to ⅔ of the Bradstreet Estate. From some of the papers and from some information I have reced it would appear that you have in your hands some Deeds or property belonging to this Estate.[2] If I rightly comprehend the matter Genl Schuyler Conveyed some Lands to you for the Heirs & you have to convey it to them on their paying their proportion of the cost of obtaining them. . . ."

ALS, Hamilton Papers, Library of Congress.

1. Walker, a native of London, had emigrated to America before the Amer-

ican Revolution and settled in New York City. During the war he was an aide-de-camp to Baron von Steuben. In 1786 he was appointed commissioner to settle the accounts of the hospital, marine, and clothing departments. He was a director of the Society for Establishing Useful Manufactures and from 1789 to 1797 was naval officer for New York. In May, 1795, he became a representative of the Pulteney Associates, an organization which speculated in lands in the Genesee country in western New York. See Walker to H, September 15, 1793. In 1797 he moved to Utica, and in 1801 he was elected to the House of Representatives as a Republican.

This letter concerns the case of *Matthew Codd and Martha his wife* v *Edward Goold and Samuel Bradstreet,* which involved a dispute over shares of land in Cosby Manor between the heirs of General John Bradstreet and his wife, Mary Aldrich, and her descendants by her first marriage to Colonel John Bradstreet (no relation to General John Bradstreet).

(first marriage)

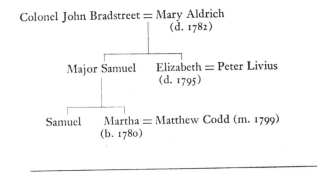

(second marriage)

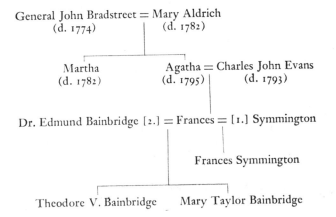

Before the American Revolution General John Bradstreet was the deputy quartermaster general of the British forces in New York. In the winter of 1755–1756 Philip Schuyler became Bradstreet's deputy, a position he held until Bradstreet's death in 1774. Schuyler's responsibilities and activities were extensive, for he not only purchased supplies for the British army in New York in Bradstreet's name, but he also bought land jointly with Bradstreet, looked after Bradstreet's personal and official accounts, and dealt with his debtors and creditors. A measure of Bradstreet's confidence in his deputy is revealed by the fact that in 1761 he sent Schuyler to England to settle his accounts in that country. In addition, Schuyler was named an executor in Bradstreet's final will in 1774.

In his will, Bradstreet divided his Cosby Manor lands equally between his daughters Martha and Agatha. When Martha died in 1782, she left one-third of her share to her sister Agatha, one-third to her stepsister, Elizabeth Livius, who was the daughter of Mary Aldrich Bradstreet and Colonel John Bradstreet, and divided the remaining one-third equally between Samuel and Martha Bradstreet, the children of Major Samuel Bradstreet and grandchildren of Mary Aldrich Bradstreet and Colonel John Bradstreet. Agatha Bradstreet married Charles John Evans, and on May 3, 1788, they filed a bill in Chancery calling for an accounting from Schuyler of General John Bradstreet's estate and a conveyance of her lands to them (Bill, New York Chancery Decrees Before 1800, E-29C [Historical Documents Collection, on deposit at Queens College, City University of New York]). The land in question consisted of 21,900 acres in Cosby Manor, which was located in the present Oneida and Herkimer counties and which Schuyler and Bradstreet had purchased in 1772. Schuyler's answer to the bill, which was sworn to on March 3, 1789, states that he had already paid some amounts of money to Agatha Evans, that the estate was well on its way toward settlement, and that he would deliver the remainder owed, including her share of the land, in the near future (Answer, filed March 10, 1789, New York Chancery Decrees Before 1800, E-29G [Historical Documents Collection, on deposit at Queens College, City University of New York]). A draft of Schuyler's answer, entitled "The answer of Philip Schuyler of the city of Albany in the County of Albany Defendant to the bill of Complaint of John Evans of the City & state of New York Gentleman and Agatha his wife" is in the handwriting of H and is located in the MS Division, New York Public Library. Schuyler's counsel were H and Robert Troup. Richard Harison was counsel for Charles and Agatha Evans. No decree in this case has been found. See Philip Schuyler to H, September 2, 1788, a letter which became available after the publication of *PAH*, III, and is printed in this volume.

In 1794, after Charles John Evans had died, Schuyler, by deed, transferred two-thirds of General John Bradstreet's estate to Agatha Evans and the remaining one-third to Edward Goold, a New York City merchant who held the land in trust for the heirs of Martha Bradstreet, Agatha Evans's sister. Goold was acting under a power of attorney from his father, Charles Goold, an Englishman who was the executor of Martha Bradstreet's estate.

Charles and Agatha Evans left their two-thirds of General John Bradstreet's holdings in Cosby Manor to their daughter Frances, whose second husband was Dr. Edmund Bainbridge of Utica. The Bainbridges brought suit against Richard Harison, Charles Wilkes, and Edward Goold, who were executors of Agatha Evans's estate, to have Frances Bainbridge's share of her mother's estate transferred to her. Both Bainbridges had died by 1803. See MS Minutes of the New York Court of Chancery under the date of April 4, 1801, 1801–1804 (Hall of Records, New York City), and Bill, filed June 23, 1800, Chancery Papers, BM-1582-B (Hall of Records, New York City).

In 1801 Martha Bradstreet Codd, who was Mary Aldrich Bradstreet's granddaughter, became twenty-one, and with her husband, Matthew Codd, she brought suit against Edward Goold and Samuel Bradstreet, her brother, to receive the lands Goold was holding in trust for her (MS Minutes, New York Court of Chancery, under the dates of November 24, 1801, January 12, 1802, March 1, May 17, 1803, 1801–1804 [Hall of Records, New York City]). After the deaths of Frances and Edmund Bainbridge, the Codds also brought suit against Harison, Goold, and Wilkes, the executors of Agatha Evans's estate, and against Benjamin Walker, Nathan Williams, Jonas Platt, and Samuel Bradstreet, the executors of Frances Bainbridge and the guardians of her children (MS Minutes of the New York Supreme Court, under the dates of May 6, 1805, May 5, 1806, 1801–1805, 1806–1810 [Hall of Records, New York City]; MS Minutes of the New York Court of Chancery, under the date of August 5, 1805 [Historical Documents Collection, on deposit at Queens College, City University of New York]).

For additional information on these cases, see Don R. Gerlach, *Philip Schuyler and the American Revolution in New York, 1733–1777* (Lincoln, Nebraska, 1964), 21–33; Daniel E. Wager, ed., *Our Country and Its People: A Descriptive Work on Oneida County, New York* (Boston, 1896), 100–03; Pomroy Jones, *Annals and Recollections of Oneida County* (Rome, New York, 1851), 528–38; Samuel W. Durant, ed., *History of Oneida County . . .* (Philadelphia, 1878), 55–59.

H made the following entry in his Law Register, 1795–1804:
"Codd
    v   Evertson decree for Comp.
Bradstreet" (D, partially in H's handwriting, New York Law Institute, New York City). Nicholas Evertson was a New York City attorney. For additional information on this case, see Goebel, *Law Practice*, forthcoming volumes.

2. When Schuyler died on November 18, 1804, he left part of his lands in Cosby Manor to Elizabeth Hamilton.

Receipt from Louis Le Guen [1]

[Morrisville, Pennsylvania, September 5, 1803]

J'ai Ce Jour 5. Sepbre. 1803 recu du General Hamilton, *trois Cents Cinquante* d'ollars, Pour Linterest d'un ân, Sur la Somme de Cinq milles d'ollars mentionnée au dit Bond. Morris Ville 5. Septembre 1803.

L. Le Guen

ADS, Yale University Library.
1. For an explanation of the contents of this document, see "Indenture between Alexander Hamilton of the First Part and Richard Harison and Aaron Ogden of the Second Part," July 1, 1801; "Bond to Richard Harison and Aaron Ogden," July 1, 1801; "Description of Account with Louis Le Guen," June 8, 1802.

From Elisha Williams

Hudson [New York], September 11, 1803. "I took the liberty of Stating a Case & inclosing it to you about the 20th of August [1] for your opinion. Not hearing from you I fear the Letter has been intercepted. You will oblige me by informing whether you received that Letter and if you have by forwarding your Answer. . . ."

ALS, Hamilton Papers, Library of Congress.
  1. Letter not found.

To Louis Le Guen

[*New York, September 12, 1803.* On September 30, 1803, Le Guen wrote to Hamilton: "Votre Lettre du 12, timbré du 19, ne m'est Parvenue que Le 29." *Letter not found.*]

To Timothy Pickering

New York September 16
1803 [1]

My Dear Sir

I will make no apology for my delay in answering your inquiry [2] some time since made, because I could offer none which would satisfy myself. I pray you only to believe that it proceeded from any thing rather than want of respect or regard. I shall now comply with your request.

The highest toned propositions, which I made in the Convention, were for a President, Senate and Judges during good behaviour—a house of representatives for three years. [3] Though I would have enlarged the Legislative power of the General Government, yet I never contemplated the abolition of the State Governments; but on the contrary, they were, in some particulars, constituent parts of my plan.

This plan was in my conception comfortable with the strict theory of a Government purely republican; the essential criteria of which are that the principal organs of the Executive and Legislative departments be elected by the people and hold their offices by a *responsible* and temporary or *defeasible* tenure.

A vote was taken on the proposition respecting the Executive. Five states were in favour of it; among those Virginia; [4] and though from the manner of voting, by delegations, individuals were not distinguished, it was morally certain, from the known situation of the Virginia members (six in number, two of them *Mason* and *Randolph* [5] possessing popular doctrines) that *Madison* [6] must have concurred in the vote of Virginia. Thus, if I sinned against Republicanism, Mr. Madison was not less guilty.

I may truly then say, that I never proposed either a President, or Senate for life, and that I neither recommended nor meditated the annihilation of the State Governments.

And I may add, that in the course of the discussions in the Convention, neither the propositions thrown out for debate, nor even those voted in the earlier stages of deliberation were considered as evidences of a definitive opinion, in the proposer or voter. It appeared to me to be in some sort understood, that with a view to free investigation, experimental propositions might be made, which were to be received merely as suggestions for consideration.

Accordingly, it is a fact, that my final opinion was against an Executive during good behaviour, on account of the increased danger to the public tranquil[i]ty incident to the election of a Magistrate of this degree of permanency. In the plan of a Constitution, which I drew up, while the convention was sitting & which I communicated to Mr. Madison about the close of it, perhaps a day or two after, the Office of President has no greater duration than for three years.[7]

This plan was predicated upon these bases—1 That the political principles of the people of this country would endure nothing but republican Government. 2 That in the actual situation of the Country, it was in itself right and proper that the republican theory should have a fair and full trial—3 That to such a trial it was essential that the Government should be so constructed as to give it all the energy and stability reconciliable with the principles of that theory. These were the genuine sentiments of my heart, and upon them I acted.

I sincerely hope, that it may not hereafter be discovered, that through want of sufficient attention to the last idea, the experiment of Republican Government, even in this Country, has not been as complete, as satisfactory and as decisive as could be wished.

Very truly   Dear Sir   Yr friend & servt   A Hamilton

Timothy Pickering Esqr.

ALS, Massachusetts Historical Society, Boston; two copies, Hamilton Papers, Library of Congress; copy, in Pickering's handwriting, Massachusetts Historical Society, Boston.

1. In *JCHW*, VI, 551, and *HCLW*, X, 446, this letter is dated "September 18, 1803."

2. Pickering to H, April 5, 1803.

3. See "Constitutional Convention. Plan of Government," June 18, 1787.

4. If H is referring to the vote on the proposal that the President serve during good behavior, he was mistaken, for on July 17, 1787, four, not five, states voted in the affirmative. He was correct, however, in stating that Virginia was one of the states voting in the affirmative. See Max Farrand, ed., *The Records of the Federal Convention of 1787* (rev. ed., New Haven, 1966), II, 36. It should, nevertheless, be kept in mind that the "statement of questions [before the convention] is probably accurate in most cases, but the determination of those questions and in particular votes upon them should be accepted somewhat tentatively" (Farrand, *Records*, I, xiii–xiv).

5. Neither George Mason nor Edmund Randolph signed the Constitution.

6. James Madison.

7. H is mistaken, for in Article IV, Section 9, of his "Draft of a Constitution," September 17, 1787, he proposed that the President "hold his office during good behaviour."

To William R. Putnam

[New York, September 19, 1803]

Dr. Sir

I have to thank you for your letter of the 1st of August [1] stating the amount of taxes on my lands [2] payable the present year being Dollars 21 & 97 Cents.

Inclosed you will find thirty Dollars to enable you to pay them. [3]

You will oblige me by a line informing me of the Receipt of this letter.

With great esteem & regard   Yr Obed ser   A Hamilton

Wm. R Putnam Esq

ALS, Dawes Memorial Library, Marietta College, Marietta, Ohio.
    1. Letter not found.
    2. See H to Oliver Wolcott, Jr., October 3, 1802.
    3. An entry in H's Cash Book, 1795–1804, in his account of receipts and expenditures under the date of September 19, 1803, reads: "(Lands Tax) 30" (AD, Hamilton Papers, Library of Congress).

From Pierre Jean François Turpin [1]

philadelphia 22 Septembre 1803.

Turpin A monsieur hamilton,
Profitant, monsieur, de la permission que vous m'avez donnée, et encouragé par vos bontés, je vais vous instruire de ce qui s'est passé depuis mon arrivée. j'ai vu monsieur Stevens à la quarantaine, il m'a parlé du désir qu'avait monsieur william hamilton [2] de m'employer d'abord à faire la flore de Son jardin Celle des environs de philadelphie, et Successivement celle des états-unis en Générale ayant voulu m'y presenter lui mëme il n'a put le faire jusqu'à présent, des affaires de premiere nécessite ayant applé le dernier à lancaste pour quelques jours. monsieur Stevens dans les différens entretiens que nous avons eu ensemble m'a beaucoup parlé d'un projet Semblable à celui dont vous m'avez fait part à newyorc, il désire Comme vous de réunir une Société d'hommes instruits qui par leur zèle et leur amour pour la Science fourniraient à leur nation un ouvrage renfermant les Connaissances utiles de règne végétale.

Le Congrès devant avoir lieu incessament et etant au point de réunion Général,[3] il Compte vous en parler ainsi qu'a quelques autres de Ses amis et il espere que vous approuverez Ce projèt.[4]

Veuillez monsieur agreez mes plus humbles respects   Votre devoué
serviteur   Turpin

je vous prie de vouloir bien presenter de ma part, à madame hamilton ainsi qu'à vous enfin mes hommages les plus respectueux.

ALS, Hamilton Papers, Library of Congress.

1. Turpin was a French botanist and horticulturalist. Between 1794 and 1800 he made two trips to Santo Domingo where he met Edward Stevens, United States consul at Santo Domingo. In 1800 Turpin designed and built gardens for Stevens on Tortuga Island off the coast near Port-de-Paix. In 1802 Turpin made his first trip to the United States, and at the end of that year he returned briefly to France.

2. Hamilton, a former Loyalist and a member of a prominent and wealthy Pennsylvania family, was a landowner with estates at Bush Hill and "The Woodlands" in Philadelphia County.

3. Congress convened in Washington on October 17, 1803 (*Annals of Congress*, XIII, 9).

4. Although Turpin addressed this letter to H at Robinson Street in New York City, there is no record that H had a residence or office at that address. In 1803 H's permanent residence was the Grange, his country house in upper Manhattan (Hamilton, *Intimate Life*, 207). However, Thomas L. Ogden, an attorney with whom H shared offices at 12 Garden Street, lived on Robinson Street in 1803.

From Louis Le Guen

Morrisville [Pennsylvania] 30. Sepbre. 1803

Cher Géneral

Votre Lettre du 12, timbré du 19,[1] ne m'est Parvenue que Le 29, alors Je penssaie inutille de vous Ecrire, vous attendant Le 28; maie désapointée de ne vous Voir point arriver, Je vais vous Prier de me mander En reponse, Sy nous pouvons nous flater du Plaisir de Vous Voir en Peu. Mme. Le Guen Et Moy nous flatonts que vous nous favoriserée de Votre Visite, Et Bien fachée que Madame Et Mlle. Hamilton [2] ne Puissent vous accompagner, Veuillée bien Je vous Prie Leurs En témoinger tous nos Regrets, Et Leurs faire agréer nos Compliments, ainsy qu'á Monr. et Madme. Washington Morton.[3]

J'ai vue par votre Lettre que Le Cel. Burr, a Encorre Renvoyés Le Payement jusqu'a En Aoust Prochain, dieu Veuillent qu'aprés tous Ses Delais il Saquitte Envers Moy.[4]

Je Suis Bien Reconnoissant a La remise que vous mavès fait faire Par Mr. Ogdon des 500 dollars.[5] J'ai depuis recu de Mr. Prime 1900 dollars en deduction des 7000. donc qu'il ne restera me devoir que 5500 d'ollars avec quelques interest.[6]

Sy Par hazard Vous alliés ou Envoyés a Newyork, Je Vous Serrai Obligée d'envoyer recevoir Les interests que depuis Le 1er. avril au 1er. octobre Sur Les 10244. dollars 30 Cts. dans Les 6 ⅌ %. Stocks,

Et aussy, Sil Est agréable à Mr. harrison L'Interest due, d'un ân Sur Les 5000 dollars,[7] Le tout à recevoir En Votre qualitée de trustis de conformitée au Contrat de mariage.

Je desire que la Calamitée dont Est Afligée Votre Ville [8] disparoissent. Mme. Le Guen à Ettée Constament Malade depuis près de 3 mois, Et qu'oy q'un peu miuy Son Ettat minquiètte Et m'aflige, Et aussy tôt après Vous avoir Vue à Notre Retraite, Je me propose de Lui faire faire un Petit Voyage a Elizabethown et Parterson. Nos trois Petits Enfants [9] Sont Bien Et notament Votre Petite Fïeulle.

Agrée, her Géneral, Le Nouvel Assurance de Lattachement Bien Sincere qui Vous a devoue Pour La Vie

Votre bien Obéiss Et Affectionnée Serviteur   L. Le Guen

Géneral Hamilton

ALS, Yale University Library.
    1. Letter not found.
    2. Le Guen is referring either to Angelica Hamilton, who was born on September 25, 1784, or to Eliza Hamilton, who was born on November 20, 1799.
    3. Elizabeth Hamilton's sister, Cornelia, was married to Washington Morton, a New York City lawyer.
    4. Aaron Burr had not paid Le Guen all of the $6,730.13, which had been due on June 1, 1801, and for which Burr had signed a bond dated January 13, 1801. (H to Ezra L'Hommedieu, April 4, 1799; Le Guen to H, May 1, May, December 27, 1800; "Receipt to Louis Le Guen," January 15, 1801; "Description of Account with Louis Le Guen," June 8, 1802). At the beginning of 1804 Burr maintained that he owed Le Guen $2,717.37, but Le Guen put Burr's debt at $2,920.53. For an explanation of Burr's and Le Guen's disagreements over the amount of Burr's debts, see the following letters and document in The Huntington Library, San Marino, California: Le Guen to Thomas L. Ogden, his New York City lawyer, January 18, 1804 (ALS); Ogden to Le Guen, January 12, 1805 (ALS); Burr to Le Guen, July 21 (AL), November 20 (ALS), 1804; Burr's statement of his account with Le Guen, January 1, 1805 (AD).
    Burr repaid part of his debt to Le Guen in three installments, which are cited as follows in the endorsement to Burr's bond to Le Guen, January 13, 1801 (copy, The Huntington Library, San Marino, California): "July 23, 1801. Received on Account of the within Bond Two thousand Dollars.

for Louis Le Guen

2000Ds.   A. Hamilton

December 28. 1802. Received of A Burr Esquire Twelve hundred and fifty dollars on account.   For Louis Le Guen
                                             A. Hamilton
November 14. 1802. Received of A Burr Esqr. One thousand Seven hundred and fifty Dollars for the Appropriation of General Hamilton, the Employed of Louis Le Guen.
$1750.   Daniel D. Thompson."

For information on Thompson, see Thompson to H, October 7, 1801.

An entry in H's Cash Book, 1795–1804, under the heading "Louis Le Guen" and dated March 5, 1803, reads: "This sum paid being ballance of 1250 Ds. received of A Burr   250" (AD, Hamilton Papers, Library of Congress).

5. In this and the following paragraph Le Guen is discussing the disposal of funds in the trust established by his antenuptial contract in February, 1799. See Le Guen to H, December 27, 1800, note 7, January 15, 1801; "Receipt to Louis Le Guen," January 15, 1801; Aaron Ogden to H, January 15, 1801; "Indenture between Alexander Hamilton of the First Part and Richard Harison and Aaron Ogden of the Second Part," July 1, 1801; "Bond to Richard Harison and Aaron Ogden," July 1, 1801; "Account with Louis Le Guen," June 6, 1802; "Description of Account with Louis Le Guen," June 8, 1802; "Receipt from Louis Le Guen," September 10, 1802; "Account of Louis Le Guen," April 1, 1803; "Receipt from Louis Le Guen," September 5, 1803.

6. See Le Guen to H, January 15, 1801; "Account with Louis Le Guen," June 6, 1802; "Description of Account with Louis Le Guen," June 8, 1802.

7. See "Description of Account with Louis Le Guen," June 8, 1802.

8. See Philip Schuyler to H, August 3, 1803, note 1.

9. Louisa, Emily, and Josephine Le Guen.

To Oliver Wolcott, Junior

New York [September] 1803

Dear Sir

The necessity of purchasing a quantity of land,[1] which I did not intend, in consequence of a mortgage that comprehended a tract I had before purchased, has so far disconcerted my pecuniary arrangements as to require that I should obtain some further Bank accommodations, instead of gradually extinguishing those I had already procured. It is therefore my wish to obtain from the Merchants Bank[2] a durable loan (by discounts and renewals in the ordinary mode) of 5000 Dollars including the 1000 already had.

This will place my affairs in a situation that from the average gains of my profession, I can discharge floating demands and pay off, by small but regular installments, the sum I owe to each Bank.[3] As my lands are beginning to settle, the proceeds as received will be applied in the same way and will accelerate the reimbursement.[4]

I will be obliged to you for your opinion whether I may venture to count upon the accommodation I have mentioned, as I should be unwilling that my paper should be presented, if there was even a prospect of hesitation. I shall not stand in need of the sum mentioned immediately, but shall call for it by parcels in the course of four or five months. With true esteem & regard.

Yrs. always   A Hamilton

Ol Wolcott Esq

ALS, Connecticut Historical Society, Hartford.
1. This is a reference to the purchase from Jacob Mark of additional land in Scriba's Patent that H, John Laurance, and John B. Church made in August, 1802. See "Mortgage by Laurance, Church, and H to Robert Gilchrist," August 21, 1802.
2. See "Articles of Association of the Merchants' Bank," April 7, 1803.
3. For H's transactions with the Bank of New York and the New York branch of the Bank of the United States, see his Cash Book, 1795–1804 (AD, Hamilton Papers, Library of Congress).
4. For the sale of H's lands, see H to John V. Henry, March 20, 1803; H to John B. Graves, June 9, 1803.

From Charles Cotesworth Pinckney

Newton near Boston Octr: 4th: 1803

Dear Sr:

The salubrious air of this place has so well succeeded in restoring Mrs: Pinckney's health that we shall set out for the Southward tomorrow.[1] I shall endeavour to shake you by the hand in passing through the State of New York.

This will be handed to you by my young Countryman Mr: Wm: Hayward who is ambitious of paying his respects to you, & I am sure your good nature will indulge him. He is a young gentleman of merit & a federalist. His father[2] was an officer in my regiment in the revolutionary war.

Mrs: Pinckney & my Daughter Eliza[3] unite with me in respects to Mrs: & Miss Hamilton[4] & I always am

Your sincere friend   Charles Cotesworth Pinckney

Honble
Genl: Hamilton

ALS, Hamilton Papers, Library of Congress.
1. From May to November, 1803, Pinckney and his wife, Mary Stead Pinckney, made a tour of New England.
2. Thomas Heyward, William Heyward's father, was known as Thomas

Heyward, Jr., to distinguish him from other members of his family who had the same name. A veteran of the American Revolution, Heyward was a member of the South Carolina legislature from 1782 to 1784 and a Circuit Court judge from 1778 to 1779 and from 1784 to 1789.

3. Eliza Pinckney was the daughter of Pinckney and his first wife, Sarah Middleton Pinckney, who had died on May 8, 1784.

4. Angelica Hamilton.

From Barent Gardenier [1]

Kingston [*New York*], *October 6, 1803.* "In the course of our political wr⟨angling⟩ I have engaged in a Controversy with Gen. Ar⟨mstrong.⟩[2] Perhaps I have touched a little too hard on ⟨the judge⟩ who presided at Lt. Croswells Trial. . . .[3] I enclose 'a View of the whole ground', confident that in a Case of this Kind you will give us all Aid in your power. . . ."

ALS, Hamilton Papers, Library of Congress.

1. Gardenier was a Federalist and a lawyer in Kingston, New York.

This letter concerns the case of *The People of the State of New York* v *Samuel S. Freer*, in which H served as counsel for the defendant. On August 6, 1803, during Harry Croswell's trial for libel in the New York Circuit Court, Freer, who was the publisher of the [Kingston] *Ulster Gazette*, printed an article concerning the trial. On November 22, 1803, after two hearings in the Supreme Court of New York, the state issued an attachment against Freer for contempt of court on the basis that Freer's article was printed "to prejudice and Influence the Public mind, and to Intimidate and Influence this Court. . . ." On February 14, 1804, the court ordered Freer to pay a ten dollar fine (MS Minutes of the New York Supreme Court, 1803–1807 [Historical Documents Collection, on deposit at Queens College, City University of New York]; MS Minutes of the New York Supreme Court, 1801–1805. [Hall of Records, New York City]). See also Goebel, *Law Practice*, I, 800.

2. John Armstrong, a veteran of the American Revolution and a resident of Dutchess County, New York, was formerly a Federalist who had become a Republican as a result of his opposition to the Alien and Sedition Acts. He was a member of the United States Senate from 1800 to 1802.

3. Morgan Lewis, chief justice of the New York Supreme Court, presided at Harry Croswell's trial for libel when the Circuit Court held for Columbia County convened at Claverack in July, 1803. For information concerning Croswell's trial, see Goebel, *Law Practice*, I, 775–848. See also H to William Rawle, June 26, 1803.

To Harrison Gray Otis [1]

Grange, New York, October 8, 1803. States: "A slight indisposition has prevented an earlier acknowlegement of your favour of   ."[2] Gives his opinion concerning the admissibility of evidence in a case in which Otis was acting as counsel for John B. Church.[3]

ALS, anonymous donor.
  1. Otis, a Boston Federalist and lawyer, was United States attorney for the District of Massachusetts from 1796 to 1797 and a member of the House of Representatives from 1797 to 1801. From 1802 to 1805 he was a member of the Massachusetts House of Representatives.
  2. Space left blank in MS. Letter not found.
  3. This letter concerns the case of *John B. Church, Jr.* v *Tuthill Hubbart.* For information on this case, see H to Theophilus Parsons, December 31, 1801.

To Aaron Burr [1]

Grange [New York] October 10th. 1803

Dear Sir

I distinctly recollect (as was once before verbally explained between us) that just before you made a payment of Two thousand Dollars on your Bond,[2] Winships Mortgage [3] was returned to you, as the mean by which the money was to be procured. I think it was sent to you by Le Guen himself.

It is to be presumed, that Winship has had since some intimation from the possessor of his mortgage, and that his information will assist your memory in retracing the circumstances of the negotiation. The mortgage is certainly not now in my possession—nor has a cent been received by me on account of it.

Respectfully   Yr. obedient servt   A Hamilton

Greenwich [4]

I observe in your warrant of Attorney a new error. You add the Shillings & pence to the penalty whereas they belong to the condition. The penalty is simply ⟨–⟩.

Col Burr

ALS, Princeton University Library.
  1. For background to this letter, see H to Ezra L'Hommedieu, April 4, 1799; Louis Le Guen to H, May 1, May, December 27, 1800, September 30, 1803;

"Receipt to Louis Le Guen," January 15, 1801; "Description of Account with Louis Le Guen," June 8, 1802.

2. Burr paid Le Guen two thousand dollars on July 23, 1801. See Le Guen to H, September 30, 1803, note 4. See also Burr's statement of his account with Le Guen, January 1, 1805 (AD, The Huntington Library, San Marino, California; copy, dated November 20, 1812, in Le Guen's handwriting, The Huntington Library, San Marino, California).

3. Daniel, Ebenezer, John, Samuel, and Thomas Winship were New York City butchers.

4. Burr's country estate, Richmond Hill, was in the section of lower Manhattan known as Greenwich.

From Abraham Ellery [1]

Dear Park,[2] *near Natchez* [*Mississippi Territory*], *October 10, 1803.* Requests Hamilton's assistance in securing a clear title to lands in upstate New York which his wife, Charlotte Weissenfels Ellery, had inherited from her father, Charles F. Weissenfels.[3]

ALS, Hamilton Papers, Library of Congress.

1. Ellery, a native of Newport, Rhode Island, and a lawyer, had been a captain in the Sixteenth Regiment of Infantry during the undeclared war with France and was honorably discharged when the Additional Army was disbanded on June 14, 1800. Ellery and his wife left New York in May, 1803, and arrived in New Orleans in August.

2. Deer Park, Louisiana, is on the Mississippi River approximately fifteen miles south of Natchez, Mississippi.

3. Weissenfels was a veteran of the American Revolution. On July 9, 1790, for his service during the war ("An Act for granting certain Lands promised to be given as Bounty Lands by Laws of this State, and for other Purposes therein mentioned" [*New York Laws*, 7th Sess., Ch. XLIII (May 11, 1784)]), Weissenfels was granted six hundred acres of land in Lot No. 77 in Locke, the eighteenth township in the military tract, and six hundred acres in Lot No. 90 in Romulus, the eleventh township in the military tract (*The Balloting Book and Other Documents relating to Military Bounty Lands in the State of New York* [Albany, 1825], 66, 125, 132).

Weissenfels, a resident of New York City, held the lease on the ferry from New York City to Hoboken from 1787 to 1788. In 1792 and 1793 he was a collector of the revenue in New York City. At the time of his death in 1795 he was a major in the Fifth Regiment of the Brigade of the City and County of New York.

From Stephen Higginson [1]

Boston, October 10, 1803. "I wrote to you several months since,[2] & inclosed to you a State of facts &c relative to the seizure of the

Diana at Lima, & requested your Opinion as to the validity of our Insurance.[3] to that letter I have no answer, & am now apprehensive it never reached you; but if you have received it, & have had leisure to form a deliberate opinion on this Subject, I wish to have it as soon as may be convenient. . . . having obtained a copy of a regular condemnation, in Mr. Church's case,[4] by which they expect to avoid his demand, our Insurers are encouraged to hope They may in the same way get rid of Ours. But we believe that no condemnation ever has or will take place in the Diana's case, to conclude against us. the property will remain in the hands of the Govr. at Lima, & those concerned with him in the seizure, an Appeal or reference of the case to the Spanish Govt in Madrid would deprive them of their plunder. . . ."

ALS, Hamilton Papers, Library of Congress.

1. This letter concerns the seizure in 1800 of the cargo of the ship *Diana*, which was jointly owned by Stephen Higginson and Company and James and Thomas H. Perkins, merchants in Boston. The *Diana* left Boston in July, 1800, with a cargo consigned to a merchant in Guatemala who wished the cargo sold in either Lima, Peru, or Sonsonate, El Salvador. At Callao, the outpost of Lima, the *Diana*'s cargo was seized and sold. The money from the sale was "deposited in the Royal Chest subject to the order of his majesty." The government of Peru allowed the *Diana* to depart, and she proceeded to El Salvador where the captain and crew were imprisoned. Samuel Burling, who was supercargo and who subsequently used the name Samuel Curson, then sailed the *Diana* "to China and thence to the Isle of France where she was sold" ("Memorial of James Perkins and others," May 23, 1822 [DS, RG 76, Allowed Claims, 1821–1824, National Archives]). In 1802 Higginson and his associates appealed to Secretary of State James Madison for aid in obtaining restitution from the Spanish government (Madison to Charles Pinckney, March 27, 1802 [copy, RG 59, Diplomatic Instructions of the Department of State, 1801–1906, All Countries, October 2, 1801–December 21, 1814, National Archives]), and in 1806 Burling (now Curson) was able through the intervention of the United States to obtain $20,000. He insisted, however, that he was owed an additional $53,798. which the Spanish government refused to pay on the ground that such money should be used as compensation for injuries sustained by Francisco de Miranda's abortive expedition, which sailed from New York in 1806. The matter dragged on until 1819, when Spain and the United States concluded the Treaty of Amity, Settlement and Limits (Miller, *Treaties*, III, 3–18). Article 9 of that treaty provided that Spain would renounce "all injuries caused by the expedition of Miranda that was fitted out and equipped at New York," and Article 11 stated: "The United States, exonerating Spain from all demands in future, on account of the claims of their Citizens, to which the renunciations herein contained extend, and considering them entirely cancelled, undertake to make satisfaction for the same, to an amount not exceeding Five Millions of Dollars." Acting under the provisions of this treaty, which went into effect in 1821, a joint commission allowed Claim No. 1315, which had been submitted by the owners of the *Diana*, and the United States paid them $43,619.11. For the records on which this summary is based, see RG 76, Records Relating to International Claims; Spain, Treaty of 1819 (Article XI) Spoliation, National Archives.

2. Letter not found.

3. Peter C. Brooks was underwriter for the cargo with the Boston Marine Insurance Company and the Massachusetts Fire and Insurance Company. Documents concerning the suit brought in the Massachusetts Court of Common Pleas by the owners of the *Diana* against the underwriters may be found in the Suffolk County Court House, Boston.

4. *John B. Church, Jr.* v *Tuthill Hubbart.* See H to Theophilus Parsons, December 31, 1801.

To Elizabeth Hamilton

Claverack [1] [New York] Oct 14. 1803

My Dear Eliza

I arrived here this day, in about as good health as I left home though somewhat fatigued.

There are some things necessary to be done which I omitted mentioning to you.[2] I wish the Carpenters to make and insert two Chimnies for ventilating the Ice-House, each about two feet Square & four feet long half above and half below the ground—to have a cap on the top sloping downwards so that the rain may not easily enter—the aperture for letting in and out the air to be about a foot and a half square in the side immediately below the cap (see *figure* on the other side).

Let a separate compost bed be formed near the present one; to consist of 3 barrels full of the *clay* which I bought[3] 6 barrels of *black mould* 2 waggon loads of the best clay on the Hill opposite the *Quakers* [4] *place* this side of Mrs. Verplanks[5] (the Gardener must go for it himself) and one waggon load of pure cow-dung. Let these be well and repeatedly mixed and pounded together to be made use of hereafter for the Vines.

I hope the apple trees will have been planted so as to profit by this moderate and wet weather. If not done—Let *Tough* [6] be reminded that a temporary fence is to be put up along the declivity of the Hill from the Kings bridge road to the opposite wood so as to prevent the cattle injuring the young trees—the fence near the entrance to the *Helicon spring* ought for the same reason to be attended to. The materials of the fence taken down in making the Kitchen Garden & some rubbish which may be picked up will answer.

Remember that the piazzas are also to be caulked & that additional accommodations for the pidgeons are to be made.

You see I do not forget the Grange.[7] No that I do not; nor any one that inhabits it. Accept yourself my tenderest affection. Give my love to your Children & remember me to Cornelia.[8] Adieu my darling   A H

Mrs. H

ALS, MS Division, New York Public Library.

1. H was in Claverack in his capacity as counsel for the heirs of John Van Rensselaer, who had brought actions against those individuals who were charged with occupying his lands in Claverack without acknowledging themselves as tenants and without accepting leases. For a discussion of the controversy involving the Claverack lands, see Goebel, *Law Practice*, forthcoming volumes.

2. The remainder of H's letter concerns the Grange, his country house in upper Manhattan. See the introductory note to Philip Schuyler to H, July 17, 1800.

3. An entry in H's Cash Book, 1795–1804, under the date of October 8, 1803, reads: "Grange (Clay)   10" (AD, Hamilton Papers, Library of Congress).

4. Joseph Mott.

5. Cornelia Verplanck, the widow of Gulian Verplanck, president of the Bank of New York from 1791 until his death in 1799, owned property from 121st Street to 127th Street on the west side of Bloomingdale Road.

6. For H's payments to William Tuff for his services, see Tuff's account in H's Cash Book, 1795–1804 (AD, Hamilton Papers, Library of Congress).

7. On November 20, 1803, Rufus King, who had returned to New York City from London in July, 1803, wrote to Christopher Gore: "Hamilton is at the head of his profession, and in the annual rect. of a handsome income. He lives wholly at his house 9. miles from town so that on an average he must spend three hours a day on the road going and returning between his house and town, which he performs four or five days each week. I don't perceive that he meddles or feels much concerning Politics. He has formed very decided opinions of our System as well as of our administration, and as the one and the other has the voice of the country, he has nothing to do but to prophecy!" (King, *The Life and Correspondence of Rufus King*, IV, 326).

8. Cornelia Morton, Elizabeth Hamilton's youngest sister and the wife of Washington Morton.

From Timothy Pickering

City of Washington Oct. 18. 1803.

Dear Sir,

I hoped to have seen you on my way hither; but the distance at which you were from the place of crossing the Hudson, & my engagements with my travelling companions, prevented.[1]

I duly received your letter of Septr. 16th. relative to the proposition you made in the General Convention. It was obvious, that those, with the propositions of others, were presented for consideration and discussion, to be adopted or rejected, as a sense of the public safety should require; and by no means as the definitive opinions of the movers.

Dining in company with General Pinckney, as he passed thro' Salem, in September,[2] I was asked, by one of the guests, some question concerning the nature of the propositions you made in the General Convention. I referred the enquirer to the General, who was a member. He answered, that you proposed, That the Governors of the several states should be appointed by the President of the U States.[3] But that Mr. Madison [4] moved, and was seconded by his cousin Charles Pinckney,[5] That all the laws of the individual states should be subject to the negative of the Chief Executive of the U. States.[6] The General added, that he did not know which would be deemed the strangest measure.

You will see in the news-papers the Presidents' message: [7] but perhaps you may wish to have it in a more convenient form; & I enclose it. If you desire to possess similar documents which shall be published in the course of the session, have the goodness to let me know it. And as any correspondence between us will be liable to suspicions, be pleased to inform me how I shall make my communications to you.

I am very truly & respectfully yours   Timothy Pickering

General Hamilton.

ALS, Hamilton Papers, Library of Congress.
    1. Pickering traveled from his home in Essex County, Massachusetts, to Washington to attend the Senate, which convened on October 17, 1803 (*Annals of Congress*, XIII, 9).
    2. See Charles Cotesworth Pinckney to H, October 4, 1803.
    3. See Article X of H's "Plan of Government," June 18, 1787; Article VIII of H's "Draft of a Constitution," September 17, 1787.
    4. James Madison.
    5. Charles Pinckney, a delegate to the Constitutional Convention from South Carolina, was a second cousin of Charles Cotesworth Pinckney, who was also a delegate from South Carolina.
    6. No such vote has been found in Max Farrand, ed., *The Records of the Federal Convention of 1787* (rev. ed., New Haven, 1966).
    7. Thomas Jefferson sent his third annual message to Congress on October 17,

1803 (*Annals of Congress*, XIII, 11–15). The message was printed in the *New-York Evening Post*, October 20, 1803.

From Samuel Jones, Junior [1]

[*New York*] *October 19, 1803.* "Mr S. Jones Junior begs leave to remind Gen Hamilton of the case of Mr Remsen [2] *adm* the corporation of the City of New york respecting the water lots at Burling Slip, which the Gen. has under his consideration. . . ." [3]

AL, Hamilton Papers, Library of Congress.
  1. Jones was a New York City lawyer and the second son of Samuel Jones, first comptroller of New York State.
  2. This is a reference to either Simon or Rem Remsen, sons of Peter Remsen, a New York City merchant. Simon and Rem Remsen were also merchants.
  3. For the full text of this letter and information concerning it, see Goebel, *Law Practice*, forthcoming volumes.

To Elizabeth Hamilton

Kinderhook [New York] Oct 22
1803 Saturday

I am here, my beloved Eliza, on my way to Albany [1]—in much better health than I have been since my first attack at home. To avoid the risk of bringing on a relapse by too much exercise, it is my intention to continue here 'till tomorrow morning. Judge Benson [2] is with me.

The Arbitrators [3] are gone to view the land in which business they will be engaged till Wednesday. On that day I must be back at Claverack, if my health proceeds in mending—otherwise I shall embark in an Albany Sloop for Greenwich. But there is every present appearance of progressive amendment.

Affecty Yrs.   A H

ALS, Albany Institute of History and Art, Albany, New York.
  1. H was on his way to Albany from Claverack, New York, where he had arrived on October 14 to act as counsel for the heirs of John Van Rensselaer in

a suit involving the disposition of his property in Claverack. See H to Elizabeth Hamilton, October 14, 1803.

2. Egbert Benson.

3. Jonas Platt, Smith Thompson, and Robert Troup. See H to Platt, August 16, 1803, note 1.

From Abraham Ellery

Deer Park, near Natchez
[Mississippi Territory] Octr. 25th. 1803

Dear Sir,

I snatch the few moments allowed me by a Gentleman, who is going directly to New York, to transmit one of the charts I promised you. The others are not yet completed, as Mr. E who is my Hydrographer Genl. has been obliged to suspend his employment in that line. My intention is, to collect & copy the different charts of the river, that have any character for correctness, to check one by another, and after having reduced them to one uniform scale, to concentre them all in one large chart, which will be more worthy of your acceptance. The one accompanying this, was taken by a Capt. McGrudar, last fall whose passage of nearly four months, from N. Orleans to Natchez, allowed him full time to complete his chart; & I am told, his abilities are competent to the correct formation of one. It is unnecessary to dwell upon the sinuosities of the river, or how easily, & at what little expense, its course might be rectified, & its navigation abridged. Hutchins [1] mentions, that at point Coupée,[2]

ALS, Hamilton Papers, Library of Congress.

1. Thomas Hutchins, a native of New Jersey and a military engineer in the British service until 1780, was appointed Geographer of the United States of America in 1781 (*JCC,* XX, 475, 738). In 1785 he was placed in charge of the survey of western lands which had been ceded to the Federal Government by the states. He died in 1789 before completing the project.

Ellery obtained the information in this sentence from Hutchins's *An Historical Narrative and Topographical Description of Louisiana, and West Florida, Comprehending the River Mississippi And Its Principal Branches and Settlements, and the Rivers Pearl, Passagoula, Mobille, Perdido, Escambra, Chacta-Hatcha, &c. The Climate, Soil, and Produce Whether Animal, Vegetable, or Mineral; with Directions for Sailing into all the Bays, Lakes, Harbours and Rivers on the North Side of the Gulf of Mexico, and for Navigating between the Islands situated along that Coast, and ascending the Mississippi River. By Thomas Hutchins, Geographer to the United States* (Philadelphia: Printed for the Author, and Sold by Robert Aitken, near the Coffee-House, in Market-Street. MDCC. LXXXIV), 24.

2. Pointe Coupee, Louisiana, is on the western bank of the Mississippi just north of Baton Rouge.

about eighty years since, some Canadians, by deepening the channel of a small brook, diverted into it the course of the river & thus curtailed the passage by 14 leagues. Major Wadsworth [3] also tells me, that in his passage up the river, last summer, he landed by the bend of the river, to the westward of the Baya Tunica,[4] & went across by land to the Heights, a distance only of 12 miles, while the course of the river makes it above 60. There are a number of other points that might easily be cut through, & the loose texture of the soil, aided by the rapidity of the river, would soon excavate a channel of sufficient depth for navigation. How far straightening the river may augment the force of the main current, & by lessening the operation of the eddy or counter currents, increase the difficulties of ascending the river, I cannot pretend to say: I must confess, however, I have less fears on this score, than many gentlemen, with whom I have conversed upon this subject; neither do I think, that the difficulties of ascending it, should be put in competition with the facilities of descending it, as the latter is by so much more the important point in its navigation.

As I hardly know in what manner my letters may be recd., having as yet not been honored with an answer, I feel rather diffident in throwing out my sentiments too freely: I may however, observe, that the sale of Louisiana to the U. States [5] has awakened in this quarter, no small spirit of speculation, & excited no little degree of interest: more particularly, as the time speedily approaches, when the Province will formally be received, & its government organized. Govr. C——[6] it appears, will be the person appointed to receive its surren-

3. Decius Wadsworth of Connecticut was a captain in the Corps of Artillerists and Engineers from 1794 to 1796, when he resigned. He was a captain in the Second Corps of Artillerists and Engineers from 1798 to 1800, when he was promoted to major. When the United States Army was reorganized in 1802 ("An Act fixing the military peace establishment of the United States" [2 *Stat.* 132–37 (March 16, 1802)]), Wadsworth was retained as a major both in the Corps of Engineers and in the regiment of Artillerists.

4. Ellery is referring to land on the eastern bank of the Mississippi River about thirty miles south of Memphis, Tennessee, which is part of present-day Tunica County, Mississippi.

5. See "Purchase of Louisiana," July 5, 1803, note 2.

6. William C. C. Claiborne, a Republican and an attorney in Nashville, Tennessee, helped to frame a constitution for Tennessee in 1796 and was appointed a judge of the state Supreme Court under the new government. He served in the House of Representatives from Tennessee from 1797 to 1801, when Thomas Jefferson appointed him **governor** of the Mississippi Territory. On

der: having recently applied for leave of absence from this Territory, on a visit to Tennessee, where his wifes[7] relations reside, it was granted him, but he was directed to hold himself in readiness at Nashville in November to receive orders from Government, & to make preparations for his departure.[8] This added to other circumstances, leaves little doubt of the fact; it is also strongly conjectured, that he will also be appointed Governor of Louisiana, or that part of it including New Orleans, either as incorporated with this government, or as a distinct Territory. These events are contemplated with regret: neither his manners, disposition, or talents qualify him for either of these situations; the simple circumstance of his ignorance of the French language & manners is no small objection—Whereas Genl. W—— [9] who is the person anxiously desired on the part of the Inhabitants, appears peculiarly qualified for them. I say nothing of his merits as an old Officer, or the late labors in wh. he has been engaged in making an advantageous treaty, of considerable importance to the U. States,[10] or his present ones in running lines through a rude

---

October 31, 1803, Claiborne was appointed a commissioner to receive Louisiana from the French. In 1804, during the Congressional recess, Jefferson appointed him governor of the Territory of Orleans, and the Senate approved the appointment on December 12, 1804 (*Executive Journal,* I, 476, 477).

7. In 1801 Claiborne married Eliza W. Lewis of Nashville, who died in 1804.

8. See Claiborne to Jefferson, June 23, 1803 (ALS, Thomas Jefferson Papers, Library of Congress); Jefferson to Claiborne, July 18, 1803 (ALS, letterpress copy, Thomas Jefferson Papers, Library of Congress).

9. James Wilkinson, who had served as deputy adjutant general in the Army during the American Revolution, later became involved in questionable land speculation and commercial ventures with the Spanish in Kentucky and the old Southwest. In 1791 he re-entered the army as a lieutenant colonel, and on April 16, 1792, the Senate approved his appointment as brigadier general (*Executive Journal,* I, 117, 119, 120). After June 14, 1800, when H and other officers who outranked Wilkinson were discharged, Wilkinson became the senior officer in the United States Army. On January 6, 1802, Jefferson nominated him as a commissioner to treat with the Cherokees, Chickasaws, Choctaws, and Creeks, and the Senate approved the nomination on January 26, 1802 (*Executive Journal,* I, 401, 405). In 1803 Wilkinson was appointed, along with Claiborne, as a commissioner to receive Louisiana from the French.

10. For the treaties which Wilkinson negotiated with various Indian tribes, including the Choctaws, Chickasaws, and Creeks in 1802 and 1803, see *Indian Treaties, and Laws and Regulations Relating to Indian Affairs: To Which is Added an Appendix, Containing the Proceedings of the Old Congress, and Other Important State Papers, in Relation to Indian Affairs. Compiled and Published Under Orders of the Department of War of the 9th February and 6th October, 1825* (Washington City: Way & Gideon, Printers, 1826), 155–61, 177–79, 202–05; *ASP, Indian Affairs,* I, 668–69, 681–82, 688–89.

country, in an unwholesome climate, & among barbarous tribes.[11] I give up all his claims arising from former services—but take him upon the ground of his present qualifications. In the first place he is a military man—as have been all the spanish governors of La.—it is what they expect, & what, in the first outset, appears to be almost absolutely necessary, in their change from one government to another; His deportment is also military, I will not say, pompous: that also suits the Inhabitants: His acquaintance too, in that quarter, is extensive, & his connections influential, & his knowledge of the language sufficiently correct: He also possesses a knowledge of the world, & his talents I presume, in other respects, are competent to the duties of the civil administration. With respect to the other, every thing is nearly *tout au contraire*. As it regards the manner of receiving the province, I feel likewise a little ashamed for my Countrymen. Govr. C—— thinks one or two companies sufficient for that purpose [12] & is calculating how expenses may be avoided or lessened. What an unfavorable impression this is calculated to make upon the minds of the Inhabitants! More particularly, as they expect something handsome in the style of doing it, & as it is the interest of government, in the first outsets to make itself respected if not feared—& when it will be delivered to us,[13] with probably some 7 or 800 Spanish soldiers under arms, well cloathed, well armed, & well disciplined. New Orleans too, it appears is to have little or no garrison kept up in it. A place inhabited by a Mixture of Americans, English, Spanish & French & crouded every year, (independent of those from other quarters) with two or three thousand boatmen from the back country, remarked for their dissipated habits, unruly tempers, & lawless conduct, in a frontier province too, where there is above 15,000 militia, all foreigners & frenchmen—& where the white population bears so small a proportion to the black, & where the Blacks have already been guilty of two or three insurrections

11. In 1802 and 1803 Wilkinson surveyed the boundaries between the United States and the Choctaws and the Creeks in the Mississippi Territory. See Carter, *Territorial Papers*, V, 236, 330.

12. On September 29, 1803, Claiborne wrote to Jefferson: "I do suppose that three or four companies of regular Troops, will be sufficient to take care of the *fortifications* &c at New Orleans and *between* that City and the Mouth of the Mississippi" (Carter, *Territorial Papers*, IX, 59).

13. On November 30, 1803, Spain formally ceded Louisiana to France, and on December 20, 1803, the United States took possession of the territory.

within a few years back,[14] and in a place too, where the inhabitants do not regard a military force, as a despotic arm to awe or crush them, but look up to it, as a necessary safeguard & protecting power. It must indeed be acknowledged, that our military, is rather scant in point of numbers, our whole force not intended to exceed 2500, & actually falling short of 1500:[15] yet, for a Country, whose acquisition is to atone for past errors, & to furnish a fund for future merit, a little additional force, for its security & tranquillity, might be allowed.

We are extremely anxious, in this quarter, to know, in what manner, our new acquisition is to be divided, & what form of government it will receive: how far W. Florida is comprised in the purchase, or whether the Western Bank will be bartered for it. The Fr. Inhabitants, tho mortified at being put up, in ye. Manner, at auction, are yet well pleased with being transferred to the Americans. Some of them have been calculating at what rate they were actually sold, & make it amount to about eleven sous per head, including negroes & cattle. But I have already transgressed too far upon your time. I have the honor to be with great respect & friendship.

yr. most obedt. serv.   Abr. R. Ellery

14. In 1795 three slave rebellions occurred in the territory of Louisiana, one in New Orleans, one in Natchitoches, and one in Pointe Coupee Parish.
15. See H to Rufus King, June 3, 1802, note 9.

From John Wilkes [1]

New-York, 26th October 1803

Sir,

I am desired to inform you, That Aa. Giles [2] Note for One thousand Dollars endorsed by you was protested yesterday Evening for non-payment, and that the Holder looks to you for payment of it.

I am, Sir,   Your most obedient Servant,   John Wilkes.

A. Hamilton Esqe

LS, Hamilton Papers, Library of Congress.
1. Wilkes was a notary public at 27 William Street in New York City.

2. Aquila Giles, a resident of Kings County, served in the New York Assembly from 1788 to 1793. From May, 1792, to March, 1801, he was United States marshal for the District of New York.

To Elizabeth Hamilton [1]

[October 27, 1803]

It is with great pleasure, I am able to inform my beloved Eliza that I continue to progress in convalescence; so that I propose to go to day from your Uncles [2] where I have been to claverack where the Arbitrators are. But I do not mean to take any other part than that of Chamber Counsel in the business, till I am quite strong, for it will be my careful endeavour not to hazard another relapse. I trust in five or six days the Arbitration will be in train to permit my return to you. Adieu my love.

A H

Thursday Morning

ALS, Hamilton Papers, Library of Congress.
1. For background to this letter, see H to Elizabeth Hamilton, October 14, 22, 1803.
2. This is presumably a reference to James Van Rensselaer, Catherine Van Rensselaer Schuyler's brother, who lived at Crystal Hill Farm on the outskirts of Albany.

From John Foncin [1]

New-york 28th. October 1803.

Sir

Having been favored by General Lafayette with a letter for you,[2] I greatly desired to present you my respects; and indeed I was very much disapointed, when I did hear at your country house that you were absent.[3] however as I come again in this country, with a firm resolution never to return to Europa,[4] I hope that I Shall have the honor to be once introduced to you; and as I have Served with zeal the united States, while I have built the forts of Baltimore and Boston, under the qualification of a Colonel, I hope that the hon. Secretary of war will again give me Some employment; especially my desire of being useful having induced me to carry from France the whole instruction which belongs to the line of an Engineer. But I want recommendations; and as not one in the military Business may have So great an influence as yours, Sir, I instantly beg this distinguished favor. if you be So Kind as to grant it to me, I Shall be very Happy to receive your letter at Mr. *Francis Breuil's at Philadelphia.*[5] This Gentleman will know my direction at washington, where I design to go on next week.

I am with great respect Sir your most humble and obedient Servant   John Foncin

ALS, Hamilton Papers, Library of Congress.

1. On December 9, 1800, Foncin, a French engineer who was working on the batteries at Fort Independence on Castle Island in Boston Harbor, submitted a plan to the War Department for the completion of the fortifications on the island. On May 1, 1801, Secretary of War Henry Dearborn gave permission to Foncin to proceed with his plan. On June 24 Foncin reported to Dearborn on the progress of the work on Castle Island and stated that because of difficulties in his work arising from his lack of rank, he wished to be appointed a colonel in the Army. Although no record of Foncin's commission has been found, he appears as a colonel in subsequent correspondence with the War Department. On January 18, 1802, he requested a transfer to Washington and a position "in arranging and keeping order Mily Archives," and on December 22 Dearborn instructed Foncin "to suspend any further expense at Fort Independence." Although Dearborn offered him a position in North Carolina working on a fortification near Wilmington, Foncin declined the appointment unless he could receive a permanent appointment (RG 107, Records of the Office of Secretary of War, Registers of Letters Received, Main Series, 1800–1870, Vol. 1, 1800, 1802, Nos. 4, 37, 94, 101, 102, 103, 133, Vol. 2, 1803–1806, No. 10, National Archives; Dearborn to Foncin, January 23, March 26, April 21, 22, 23, May 1, December 11, 1801, February 2, 23, June 14, July 5, 27, October 18, December 22, 1802, March 16, 1803 [LC, RG 107, Records of the Office of the Secretary of War, Miscellaneous Letters Sent by the Secretary of War, 1800–1809, Vol. 1A, 1800–1803, National Archives]).

2. Letter not found.

3. See H to Elizabeth Hamilton, October 14, 22, 27, 1803.

4. Some time after April 1, 1803, Foncin had returned to France (Foncin to Dearborn, April 1, 1803 [RG 107, Records of the Office of Secretary of War, Registers of Letters Received, Main Series, 1800–1870, Vol. 2, 1803–1806, No. 14, National Archives]), and he returned to the United States during October of the same year (Marquis de Lafayette to Thomas Jefferson, September 1, 1803 [ALS, Thomas Jefferson Papers, Library of Congress]).

5. Breuil was a Philadelphia merchant and shipowner.

To Elizabeth Hamilton [1]

[Albany] Friday October [1803]

This morning my b⟨e⟩loved Eliza I leave Albany for C⟨lav⟩erack, my health greatly mended ⟨a⟩nd I hope to make but a short stay there. My plan is to go to Poughkepsie and there embark.

I shall be glad to find that my dear little Philip [2] is weaned, if circumstances have rendered it prudent. It is of importance to me to rest quietly in your bosom. Adieu my beloved.

A H

Kiss all the Children for me. Love to Cornelia. [3]

ALS, Columbia University Libraries.
  1. For background to this letter, see H to Elizabeth Hamilton, October 14, 22, 27, 1803.
  This letter was addressed to Elizabeth Hamilton "to the care of David A Ogden Esq Greenwich New York." Ogden was a New York City lawyer who shared offices with H at 12 Garden Street, the present-day Exchange Place.
  2. Philip Hamilton, H's youngest child, was born on June 1, 1802.
  3. Cornelia Schuyler Morton, Elizabeth Hamilton's younger sister and the wife of Washington Morton.

From John Wilkes

New-York, 4th November 1803

Sir,

I am desired to inform you, That Jacob Morton's [1] Note for One thousand Dollars endorsed by you was protested yesterday Evening, for non-payment, and that the Holder looks to you for payment of it.

I am, Sir,   Your most obedient Servant,   John Wilkes.

Alexander Hamilton Esqr.

LS, Hamilton Papers, Library of Congress.
1. Morton, who was trained as a lawyer, held several appointive offices in New York City and was a member of the New York Assembly in 1796 and 1797. He was a brother of Washington Morton, the husband of Elizabeth Hamilton's sister, Cornelia.

To Harrison Gray Otis

New York, November 12, 1803. Urges "the utmost caution and care" in preparing John B. Church's case for hearing before the Supreme Court.[1]

ALS, Hamilton Papers, Library of Congress.
1. This letter concerns the case of *John B. Church, Jr.* v *Tuthill Hubbart.* See H to Theophilus Parsons, December 31, 1801; H to Otis, October 8, 1803.

From Aaron Burr [1]

[New York] 15 Nov. 1803

Dr Sir

I have paid to Mr Thompson Seventeen hundred and fifty dollars,[2] taken up the Leases of Ross & Duzenbury [3] and left the Titles to the house in Chapel & Murray St. It was my intention *now* to have paid the Whole—But having ordered this house (cor. of Chap. & Murray) to be sold which has not been effected the balance of about 2000 Ds. is left to be discharged by Sale of the house. James Clapp who is my agent for this purpose has orders to pay you the money arising from this Sale which will be made without delay.[4] Should any balance then remain, it will be forthwith paid.[5]

My bond to Hare [6] was to have been without Interest. He writes me that it bears interest. Have you no recollection on this subject.

Yrs

A Burr

Genl. Hamilton

My Warrant of atty to you may now I suppose be delivered up.[7]

ALS, The Huntington Library, San Marino, California.
1. For background to this letter, see H to Ezra L'Hommedieu, April 4, 1799;

Louis Le Guen to H, May 1, May, December 27, 1800; "Receipt to Louis Le Guen," January 15, 1801; "Description of Account with Louis Le Guen," June 8, 1802; H to Burr, October 10, 1803.

2. On November 15, 1803, Burr paid Daniel D. Thompson $1,750. See Le Guen to H, September 30, 1803, note 4. See also Burr's statement of his account with Le Guen, January 1, 1805 (AD, The Huntington Library, San Marino, California; copy, dated November 20, 1812, in Le Guen's handwriting, The Huntington Library, San Marino, California). For information on Thompson, see Thompson to H, October 7, 1801.

3. Richard Dusenbury was a lumber merchant on Chapel Street, New York City.

4. On September 3, 1804, Le Guen wrote to an unnamed correspondent: ". . . [Je] Vois que Mr. Burr a due recevoir Le montant de la vente de la maison qui etoit Entendue devoir Estre Affectée au Payement de Ce quil restait me devoir. Et Pour qu'oy dónc m'indiquer dernierement de m'adresser à Mr. Clapp, S'il en avoit touchée L'argent, et qui Diable pouroit rien Comprandre à une telle Conduitte" (ALS, The Huntington Library, San Marino, California).

James Clapp was a New York City grocer.

5. Burr's account with Le Guen remained unsettled until as late as 1824. On October 9, 1817, the Supreme Court of New York heard the case of *Louis Le Guen* v *Aaron Burr* and ruled "that the said Louis Le Guen recover against the said Aaron Burr his Debt . . ." (Judgment Roll, filed October 9, 1817, Law Judgments 1817, B-177 [Hall of Records, New York City]). See also Burr to Thomas L. Ogden, June 12, 1817 (ALS, The Huntington Library, San Marino, California). By 1820 Burr's debt amounted to $5,032.72 because of interest, and Le Guen agreed to accept land as security for the debt (Ogden and Cadwallader R. Colden, who held the title to the land, to Barent Van Benthuysen, Charles Leggett, and Gerrit Quackenboss, who were to appraise the land, May 20, 1820 [two copies, The Huntington Library, San Marino, California]). Burr, however, failed to pay Le Guen, and on January 7, 1824, Ogden wrote to Ambrose Spencer, the former chief justice of the New York Supreme Court: "I am directed by Mrs. Le Guen to proceed on the Judgment against Colo. Burr or to enforce the Covenant against Mr. Colden as I may think most expedient unless some satisfactory Arrangement shall be immediately made. She declines accepting other Lands by way of substitute for those which were to have been conveyed and therefore this part of the Negotiation is to be considered as at an End" (ALS, The Huntington Library, San Marino, California). Mary Le Guen, who had been in France, was in the United States in 1824 to settle the family's financial affairs. See Le Guen to Ogden, April 18, 1823 (ALS, The Huntington Library, San Marino, California).

6. Charles Willing Hare, the nephew of the late Mrs. William Bingham of Philadelphia, became William Bingham's agent in the summer of 1801 when Bingham left the United States for London. See Bingham to H, July 21, 1801. For Burr's involvement with Hare and John J. Angerstein, see Alexander Baring to H, November 16, 1797; the enclosure to H to John Rutledge, Jr., January 4, 1801; Hare to H, January 14, 1802. See also Goebel, *Law Practice*, forthcoming volumes.

7. See H to Burr, October 10, 1803.

From James Wilkinson

Mobile [Mississippi Territory] Novr 15th. 1803

Dear Sir

Although you can have no motive for desiring to extend the circle of your acquaintance, yet I am persuaded your Hand & your Heart will ever be free, to the Honourable, the amiable & the erudite of whatever clime or Country; under this impression I have presumed to introduce to you Mr John Forbes of Pensacola, principal Copartner in America, of the opulent & respectable House of Paton & Leslie,[1] in whom you will find sound Intelligence & sterling worth, and therefore I beg leave to recommend Him to your attentions.

Flattering myself that you take Interest in what concerns me, I will briefly relate to you, that my Life, for more than two years, has been an almost incessant itinerary, between the Mississippi River & the frontier of Georgia, during which period I have rendered some services to the State,[2] and with military Eyes I have explored every critical pass, every direct route, & every devious way between the Mexican Gulph & the Tenessee River; I have extended my capacities for utility, but not my sphere of Action, & in the present moment my destination is extremely precarious. To divorce my Sword is to rend a strong Ligament of my affections & to wear it without active service is becoming disreputable. I have revolved the question in my Mind. I have paused for a resolution, & am still waiting Events. Should I retire my permanent abode will be fixed in this Quarter, because, after seeing & examining our whole Country, I find this to be the most desirable part for a Man of small Capital, as it contains more Interests & advantages in the important Articles of Health, accommodation & products, than any other which has attracted my observation.

I have been drawn to the vicinity of Pensacola, by the termination of a Line of demarcation, between our settlements & the Creek Indians,[3] and availed myself of the occasion, to pay my respects to the Spanish Governor [4] there, not from mere motives of Courtesy & personal accommodation. The site is a good one & the Harbour divine. I have examined its practicable defences, & have ascertained that 26 feet Water may be carried into it at ordinary Tides, which seldom rise more than 2½ feet. It is capacious & is abundantly supplied with fine Spring Water.

This Spot may be considered the Montpelier [5] of the United States —being exempt from the Chronic, acute & inflammatory diseases of the North, from the Endemical complaints of Southern Climes, and Epedemicks which have ravaged our Seaports: The Geographical relation of this place, to the Indian & American Estates of the European Powers, renders it in my conception immeasureably valuable; and the Acquisition of the Floridas, is rendered additionally important, by the luxuriant soil with which its Water courses are bordered, by the Iron ore with which the interior abounds, and by the Live Oak & Cedar to be found, I am well assured, in great quantities on the Inlets, Bays, & Rivers of the Gulph.

Your own discretion will suggest to you, the expediency of treating this communication with reserve, while I remain with strict sincerity & undiminished attachment

Dear General   Your obliged faithful & affectionate   Ja: Wilkinson

General Hamilton

ALS, Hamilton Papers, Library of Congress.

1. In 1784 the British firm of Panton, Leslie, and Company received permission from the Spanish government to trade in Indian goods in East Florida, a territory which Spain had acquired from Great Britain in 1783. By 1795 the company controlled a large portion of the southern Indian trade in East and West Florida and Louisiana (James McHenry to H, May 21, 1799). After William Panton died in 1802, the company continued to operate under the name of John Forbes and Company.

2. See Abraham Ellery to H, October 25, 1803, notes 9, 10, and 11.

3. See Ellery to H, October 25, 1803, note 11.

4. Vincente Folch y Juan was the Spanish commandant of Pensacola from 1795 to 1811. He exercised the civil and military powers of the office of governor although he was never formally commissioned. His contemporaries referred to him as "governor."

5. Montpellier, a city located in Hérault Department in southern France seventy-five miles northwest of Marseilles, was a popular resort for English invalids.

From Richard Soderstrom [1]

Washington, November 16, 1803. "Mr: J: Sands of New York and at Present here as member of Congress, . . . informed me that Judgement was against him for damages sustained by the arrest of the Brig Jennet, owned by Mr: Haylegas of St. Croix. . . . I have brought payments forward in Similare cases, and I have good reason to believe that the present Secretary of the Treasury [2] will not put any obstacles in the way. . . ."

ALS, Hamilton Papers, Library of Congress.

1. Soderstrom, a resident of Philadelphia, was the Swedish consul general.

This letter concerns the cases of *John W. Leonard, master of the United States Revenue Cutter, the Governor Jay, qui tam &c Libellant v The Schooner or Vessel called the Juno of Middletown in Connecticut otherwise the Jennet her Tackle, Apparel, Furniture and Cargo* and *Thomas Knox v Joshua Sands.* Knox, a New York City merchant, was the administrator of the estate of Raapzat Heyleger, the owner of the *Juno,* also called the *Jennet.* Sands, as collector of the customs at New York, had had the *Jennet* seized for a violation of "An Act to suspend the commercial intercourse between the United States and France, and the dependencies thereof" (1 *Stat.* 565–66 [June 13, 1798]). The case was heard before the United States District Court for New York on July 30, August 8, November 22, 1799, February 4, March 5, 1800 (RG 21, Minutes of the United States District Court for New York, 1790–1808, Records of the United States District Court for the Southern District of New York, National Archives), before the New York Supreme Court on September 21, 1802 (MS Common Rule Book of the New York Supreme Court, 1801–1805 [Historical Documents Collection, on deposit at Queens College, City University of New York]), and before the New York Circuit Court on June 23, 25, 1803, November 20, 1804, when the Court decided in favor of the plaintiff (MS Minutes of the New York Circuit Court, 1801–1805 [Hall of Records, New York City]). See also Judgment Roll, filed December 29, 1804, and the Satisfaction Piece, September 11, 1804, which is attached to the Judgment Roll (Law Judgments, 1804, S-82 [Hall of Records, New York City]).

On February 27, 1815, Congress passed an act entitled "An Act for the relief of Joshua Sands," which reads: "*Be it enacted, &c.,* That the proper accounting officers of the treasury be, and hereby are, authorized and directed to liquidate and adjust with Joshua Sands, late collector of the port of New York, the account of damages, interest and charges, in the cases of the brig Harriet, otherwise called the John, and cargo, and the Jennet, and cargo, seized by him whilst he was collector of the port of New York, for a violation of the act to suspend commercial intercourse between the United States and France, for which seizures suits were brought, and damages and costs recovered, against the said collector; and to satisfy and discharge the same, a sum sufficient is hereby appropriated, to be paid out of any moneys in the treasury not otherwise appropriated" (6 *Stat.* 150–51).

For the brig *Harriet,* see *John Imlay* v *Joshua Sands* in George Caines, *New-York Term Reports of Cases Argued and Determined in the Supreme Court of That State* (New York, 1804), I, 566–73.

An entry in H's Cash Book, 1795–1804, under the date of "June Circuit 180-," reads: "Knox adn ⎫

         v   ⎬   verdict for Plaintiff

    Sands"   ⎭

(AD, Hamilton Papers, Library of Congress).

2. Albert Gallatin.

From Louis Le Guen

[New York, November 22, 1803]

Je Vous Prie Cher General de transferer à Mr. Prime Les Shares Colombia insurance Compe. qui etoient en vos mains Pour Securité des Sept milles d'ollars Laquelle Somme Jai recu dudit Mr Prime.[1]

    Votre Obnt Serviteur   L. Le Guen

Newyork 22. Nbre 1803.

ALS, Yale University Library.

1. See Le Guen to H, January 15, 1801; "Account with Louis Le Guen," June 6, 1802; "Description of Account with Louis Le Guen," June 8, 1802.

From Israel Loring [1]

New York, November 24, 1803. "By a variety of unavoidable Circumstance I am reduced to a State of dependance upon the bounty of my friends. I am in consequence of the injury received in my hip rendered incapable of very Active employment. I have solicited in vain for a situation in one of the Banks as yet there is no vacancy; and now have taken the liberty of addressing you soliciting the favor of some employment as engrossing Clerk for you or some of your friends. . . . under the present order of things an application for public employment would be in vain, as I was the first victim of democratic extermination having been dismissed on the 14th. March 1801 by Henry Dearborn the Secretary of War, from his

Office (where I was placed by Mr. Dexter) [2] for the Sin of Federalism."

ALS, Hamilton Papers, Library of Congress.

1. Loring, a native of New York City, served as a second lieutenant in the Twelfth Regiment of Infantry from September 12, 1799, to June 14, 1800, when he was honorably discharged.

2. Loring was a clerk in the office of Samuel Dexter, Secretary of War, from July, 1800, until his dismissal (DS, RG 217, Miscellaneous Treasury Accounts, 1790–1894, Account No. 11,730, National Archives).

Dexter was Secretary of War from July 12, 1800, to December 31, 1800, when he became Secretary of the Treasury.

To Samuel Gouverneur [1]

New York, December 9, 1803. Gives opinion concerning the effect of the French *arrêt* of June 20, 1803, on neutral shipping.[2]

ALS, The Huntington Library, San Marino, California.

1. Gouverneur was a New York City merchant.

For the full text of this letter and a discussion of its contents, see Goebel, *Law Practice,* II, 608–10.

2. "Arrété qui prohibe l'introduction dans les ports de France, de toute denrée et marchandise provenant de colonie ou de fabrique anglaise" (J. B. Duvergier, *Collection Complète des Lois, Décrets, Ordonnances, Réglemens, et Avis du Conseil-d'Etat, Publiée sur les Editions Officielles du Louvre; de L'Imprimerie Nationale, Par Baudouin; et Du Bulletin des Lois* [Paris, 1824–1825], XIV, 335).

From Philip Jeremiah Schuyler [1]

Rhinebeck [New York], December 10, 1803. Discusses a suit involving ownership of lots in New York City claimed by his wife and sister-in-law.[2] Sends information on the progress of a survey of the Claverack lands being made by Judge David Brooks.[3]

ALS, Yale University Library.

1. Schuyler was one of Philip Schuyler's sons and a younger brother of Elizabeth Hamilton.

2. Schuyler is referring to the case of *Philip J. Schuyler and Sarah his wife, and George Suckley and Catherine his wife* v *John R. Cozine et al.,* which was a writ of right cause involving the ownership of land in the Third Ward of New York City. Sarah Rutsen Schuyler and Catherine Rutsen Suckley were

sisters, and they claimed possession of the land through an inheritance. Suckley was a merchant living in Greenwich whose countinghouse was at 17 Beekman Street in New York City. Cozine and twenty other defendants named in the other causes accompanying this suit were the tenants of the land in question. The suit was commenced in the New York State Supreme Court on January 31, 1800, and writs of right were issued on August 6, 1804 (MS Minutes of the New York Supreme Court, 1797–1802, 1803–1807 [Historical Documents Collection, on deposit at Queens College, City University of New York]).

3. A veteran of the American Revolution, Brooks was a member of the New York Assembly in 1787 and 1788 and from 1794 to 1796 and a member of the House of Representatives from 1797 to 1799. He was the first judge of the Dutchess County Court of Common Pleas from 1795 to 1807. He was one of the surveyors appointed by the commissioners assigned to settle the dispute over lands in Claverack, Columbia County, New York, between the heirs of John Van Rensselaer and those individuals who were charged with occupying his lands without acknowledging themselves as tenants and without accepting leases. For a discussion of this controversy, see Goebel, *Law Practice*, forthcoming volumes. See also Philip Schuyler to H, July 17, 1800, note 22, September 29, October 9, 1800, April 16, 1803; H to Jonas Platt, August 16, 1803; H to Elizabeth Hamilton, October 22, 27, 1803.

To Herman LeRoy [1]

New York, December 12, 1803. Discusses the contents of a letter "this morning received from Mr. Pendleton" [2] concerning an agreement made between Henry Sands and the Bank of New York which provided for the sale of mortgaged property owned by Sands in order to pay Sands's creditors.

AL[S], Bank of New York, New York City.
1. For background to this letter, see H to LeRoy, September 19, 1802.
2. The letter from Nathaniel Pendleton has not been found.

From William R. Putnam

Marietta [Ohio] Decemr 12th 1803

Dear Sir

your last [1] inclosing thirty dollars has been receiv'd & your taxes paid—and your acct stands thus

1803	Viz	Dr	to ballance of old account	$ 3.57 [2]
	Oct		to postage of a letter	.50 [3]

29   to taxes paid (see bill)   13.39 [4]
     to commissions   5.00
                                       ‾‾‾‾‾‾
                                       22.46

Cr   By cash per mail   30
                                       ‾‾‾‾‾
                    Ballance   Cr $ 7.54 for 1804.

I am Sir your Obedient Sert   Wm Rufus Putnum

The Hbl. A Hamilton Esqr

ALS, Yale University Library.
    1. H to Putnam, September 19, 1803.
    2. See Putnam to H, January 17, 1803.
    3. Letter not found.
    4. In the Yale University Library there is a receipt which reads: "Recie'd of Wm Rufus Putnam thirteen dols and thirty nine Cents, being the amount of taxes upon Alexander Hamiltons lands for the present year. Duplicates signed Marietta Oct 29th
        1803   Wm Skinner Sheriff
                                                 & Collector."

From Thomas Truxtun

Perth amboy [New Jersey] 15th December 1803.

Dear General

In a conversation we had at new York on the Subject of the threatened invasion of England by Bonaparte—you expressed a wish that oppertunity had offered So that you could have had the map of England and France &c before you. I now do myself the honor of transmitting my opinion as then Stated to you in a letter to Mr Pickering [1] and after you have examined it with the map, I shall be greatly obliged by your Sealing the letter and causeing it to be put in the post office as soon as may be as he should in Strictness have had it before now, but my Absence from home prevented usual punctuality.

My Opinion is Stated Simply and unadorned with embellishments which are foreign to my profession and habits and ought Not to be expected from me. time and a Short time will make manifest Whether I have Judged correctly of the Subject in question—for the happiness of Nations I hope I have. I find the Senate of the U S have agreed to an important alteration of the Constitution[2] & thus that instrument is kicked about to answer the purposes of the ruleing faction And as it is to be mutilated at their will and pleasure, it is to be hoped we shall in time have our turn in having Something to Say in such important measures, and that then an Instrument will be So Contrived as to prevent such an abomniable Set from exclusively governing us a Second time or of governing us at all.

I have the honor to be sir with great respect your very obedient humble servt,   Thomas Truxtun.

Honorable General Alexander Hamilton
New York.

ALS, Hamilton Papers, Library of Congress.
1. Truxtun to Pickering, December 15, 1803 (ALS, Massachusetts Historical Society, Boston).
In this letter Truxtun discusses in detail various locations in England suitable for invasion and the advantages and disadvantages to France of such an invasion.
2. See "Draft of a Resolution for the Legislature of New York for the Amendment of the Constitution of the United States," January 29, 1802, note 1.

From John V. Henry[1]

[Albany, December 17, 1803]

Dear Sir

I have paid the taxes & charges upon ⟨the⟩ lands in which you are interested described in the Comps certificate which you lately enclosed to me. As the tax of 1802 was unpaid I thought it best to discharge it also. The necessary voucher of these payments is herewith transmitted.

After crediting the Bank dft. of $950 I am according to the preceding statement in advance for you $174.69 for which sum I shall draw upon you whenever I shall have occasion to remit money to N York.

I am with great respect & esteem   Your ob serv   John V. Henry
                                                                16th Decr 1803
Alexander Hamilton Esqr

ALS, Hamilton Papers, Library of Congress.
1. For background to this letter, see H to Henry, March 20, 1803.

To Elizabeth Hamilton

Fish Kill [New York] Sunday
Evening [1803] [1]

I arrived here, my beloved, about five this afternoon. According to my first day's journey, I ought now to be much further advanced. But some how *Riddle* sprained the ancle of one of his hind legs, which very much retarded my progress to day. By care and indulgence, he is much better this Evening; so that I count upon being able to reach Albany with him early on Wednesday morning. I have travelled comfortably & my health is improved.

Wife Children and *hobby* [2] are the only things upon which I have permitted my thoughts to run. As often as I write, you may expect to hear something about the *latter.*

Don't lose any opportunity which may offer of ploughing up the new garden spot and let the waggon make a tour of the ground lately purchased [3] to collect the dung upon it to be scattered over that spot.

When it is too cold to go on with grubbing, our men may be employed in cutting and clearing away the underbrush in the Grove and the other woods; only let the *center* of the principal wood in the line of the different rocks remain rough and wild.

The Country people all agree that to fat fowls, it is essential to keep them well supplied with gravel. One, of whom I inquired, informed me, that sea shore gravel, not too large, is particularly good. They also say the coops must be cleaned out every two or three days. After the Fowls have had a sufficient opportunity of drinking, the remaining water must be removed.

Adieu My Betsey. Kiss my little ones for me & accept many kisses for yourself from Yrs ever   AH

ALS, Hamilton Papers, Library of Congress.
1. In *HCLW*, X, 421-22, this letter is dated "February 19, 1801," and the second paragraph of H to Elizabeth Hamilton, 1801-1802, is included as part of this letter.

2. The Grange. See the introductory note to Philip Schuyler to H, July 17, 1800.

3. See the introductory note to Schuyler to H, July 17, 1800, note 7.

Plan for a Garden [1]

[1803]

1. Transplant fruit trees from the other side of the stable.

2. Fences repaired.   [2] repaired behind stable. The cross fence at the foot of the hill? Potatoes Bradhursts? [3] Ground may be removed and used for this purpose. Cows no longer to be permitted to range.

3. The Sod and earth which were removed in making the walks *where it is good* may be thrown upon the grounds in front of the House, and a few waggon loads of the compost.

4. A *Ditch* to be dug along the fruit garden and grove about four feet wide, and the earth taken and thrown upon the sand hill in the rear.[4]

2. The Gardener, after marking these out and making a beginning by way of example, will apply himself to the planting of Raspberries in the orchard. He will go to Mr. Delafield [5] for a supply of the English sort and if not sufficient will add from our own and some to be got from our neighbors.

3. If it can be done in time I should be glad if space could be prepared in the *center* of the flower garden for planting a few tulips, lilies, hyacinths, and   . The space should be a circle of which the diameter is Eighteen feet: and there should be nine of each sort of flowers; but the gardener will do well to consult as to the season.

They may be arranged thus: [6] Wild roses around the outside of the flower garden with laurel at foot.

If practicable in time I should be glad some laurel should be planted along the edge of the shrubbery and round the clump of trees near the house; also sweet briars and   .

A few dogwood trees not large, scattered along the margin of the grove would be very pleasant, but the fruit trees there must be first removed and advanced in front.

These labours, however, must not interfere with the hot bed.

Hamilton, *Intimate Life,* 347–49.

1. This document concerns the Grange. See the introductory note to Philip Schuyler to H, July 17, 1800.

2. This and other spaces left blank in the document.

3. Samuel Bradhurst, a New York City physician, and his wife owned land in Harlem adjoining the northern boundary of H's property.

4. Part of the document is missing at this point. Allan McLane Hamilton, *Intimate Life,* 348, wrote at this point: "After referring to the arrangement of flower beds and the laying out of a vegetable garden he [H] proceeded."

5. John Delafield, who came to America from England in 1783, was a merchant and marine underwriter in New York City. He was a founder of the Mutual Insurance Company and the United Insurance Company, and in 1793 was a director of the New York branch of the Bank of the United States. His country house, "Sunswick," was on Long Island on the East River opposite Blackwell's Island.

6. At this point in the document H drew a circle and indicated in a diagram the arrangement of flowers he wished to have planted.

1804

From Abraham Ellery

Deer Park, near Natchez [1] [*Mississippi Territory*], *January 7,
1804.* "Having it in contemplation to establish myself in the law line
at New Orleans, I conceive that it would very much assist me in
my debut to be made known to the Governor of that province.[2] I
have already written for letters of recommendation to him to . . .
some others of my friends in the Atlantic States—will you suffer me,
Sir, to include you in that number. . . ?"

ALS, Hamilton Papers, Library of Congress.
  1. For Ellery's activities at Natchez, see Ellery to H, October 10, 25, 1803.
  2. William C. C. Claiborne.

From Louis Le Guen

[*Philadelphia, January 10, 1804.* On January 18, 1804, Le Guen
wrote to Hamilton and referred to "La Lettre . . . que jai la
Lhonneur de vous Ecrire Le 10." *Letter not found.*]

To Louis Le Guen

[*New York, January 11, 1804.* On January 18, 1804, Le Guen
wrote to Hamilton: "Je n'ai recu que Ce matin, La Lettre dont Vous
mavés favorisé Le 11." *Letter not found.*]

From Louis Le Guen [1]

Philadelphia 18. Janvier 1804.

Cher General
    Je n'ai recu que Ce matin, La Lettre dont Vous mavés favorisé
Le 11.[2] maie timbre du 13, Ce qui me fait Croire, que Cette premiere

Epoque vous N'aviée pas recu celle que jai Eu Lhonneur de vous Ecrire Le 10.[3] Par la quelle je vous Prie d'avoir la bontée d'envoyer toucher Le devidend de 10. ₱ %. annoncée Par la Compe. d'assurance de Newyork, et men faire La remise.[4]

Maintenant, cher Gènéral, en vous Accusant reception de votre check de $300.—permittée moy de Vous Observer que j'ai ettée bien peinnée en remarquent ce que vous me dite au Sujet des 3000 d'ollars Montant de votre billet En ma faveur, et des interets due a Compte desquels vous me remettée Cent dollars,[5] Enconcequ'ence Je Vais de nouveaux Vous Suplier, de me traiter avec Plus d'amittiée, Et pour m'en donner de nouvelles Preuves, Ne vous Occupée plus de Ce Petit Capital ny des interests, qui Lors quil Vous Serra parfaitemt. Convenable de men faire La remise, et Sy Vous En agissiée differament je Craindraie A Lors, de N'avoir Plus La Meme part à Votre amittiée au quel Je met tant de Prix.

Agré Lassurance de Mon Entiere devouement   Votre Affnée.
Serviteur   L. Le Guen

ALS, Hamilton Papers, Library of Congress.
    1. This letter concerns the disposition of the funds assigned by Le Guen in his antenuptial contract of February, 1799. See Le Guen to H, December 27, 1800, note 7, January 15, 1801, September 30, 1803; "Receipt to Louis Le Guen," January 15, 1801; Aaron Ogden to H, January 15, 1801; "Indenture between Alexander Hamilton of the First Part and Richard Harison and Aaron Ogden of the Second Part," July 1, 1801; "Bond to Richard Harison and Aaron Ogden," July 1, 1801; "Account with Louis Le Guen," June 6, 1802; "Description of Account with Louis Le Guen," June 8, 1802; "Receipt from Louis Le Guen," September 10, 1802; "Account of Louis Le Guen," April 1, 1803; "Receipt from Louis Le Guen," September 5, 1803.
    2. Letter not found.
    3. Letter not found.
    4. See "Account with Louis Le Guen," June 6, 1802; "Description of Account with Louis Le Guen," June 8, 1802.
    5. See "Indenture between Alexander Hamilton of the First Part and Richard Harison and Aaron Ogden of the Second Part," July 1, 1800; "Bond to Richard Harison and Aaron Ogden," July 1, 1800; "Description of Account with Louis Le Guen," June 8, 1802; "Receipt from Louis Le Guen," September 10, 1802, September 5, 1803.

To Louis Le Guen

[*New York, January 24, 1804.* On July 12, 1804, Le Guen wrote to Hamilton: "Le 24 Janvier aussy dernier, Vous maves fait la remise." *Letter not found.*]

To Victor Marie Du Pont de Nemours [1]

[New York, January 30, 1804]

Dr. Sir

I send you three Notes on account of my bond each for 800 Ds [2] as agreed.

On Saturday I took the bond in the Country & forgot to bring it to Town with the calculation; so that ⟨I m⟩ust defer the completion of the arrange⟨ment⟩ to my return from Albany.[3] But you may consider it as done & in⟨form⟩ your correspondents accordingly. Yrs. with gre⟨at⟩ regard

A H

ALS, Mr. Henry Francis du Pont, Winterthur, Delaware.

1. Du Pont served as attaché to the French legation in the United States from 1787 to 1789, as second secretary from 1791 to 1792, and as first secretary from 1795 to 1796. In 1796 he became the acting French consul in Charleston, South Carolina, and a year later he was named consul. Because of the undeclared war with France, John Adams refused to issue Du Pont's exequatur as consul general in 1798, and Du Pont returned to France. He made another voyage to the United States in 1799 with his family and joined the New York City commission firm of Du Pont de Nemours, Fils & Cie., which had been established by his father, Pierre Samuel Du Pont de Nemours.

In the letter printed above, Du Pont was representing the heirs of Gaspard Joseph Amand Ducher in their efforts to collect a debt H owed to Ducher. For this debt, see H's "Cash Book," March 1, 1782–1791; H to Robert Troup, July 25, 1795; Ducher to H, July 4, 1798.

In 1786 Ducher was appointed vice consul *ad interim* at Portsmouth, New Hampshire, and in 1788 was transferred to Wilmington, North Carolina. He returned to Paris in 1790 and for the next three years sought to induce the French government to adopt a policy of encouraging trade through navigation laws (Frederick L. Nussbaum, *Commercial Policy in the French Revolution* [Washington, 1923], 14, 17, 35, 271–304).

2. See "Statement of my property and Debts July 1, 1804."

3. H went to Albany in February as one of the defense attorneys in the *People* v *Croswell*. For H's role in this case, see Goebel, *Law Practice*, I, 775–848.

An entry in H's Cash Book, 1795–1804, under the date of February 1, 1804, reads: "Expence including journey 110." A second entry under the date of March, 1804, reads: "Expence (journey down included) 250" (AD, Hamilton Papers, Library of Congress).

Speech at a Meeting of Federalists in Albany [1]

[Albany, February 10, 1804]

Reasons why it is desirable that Mr. Lansing rather than Col. Burr should succeed.

1. Col Burr has steadily pursued the ⟨track⟩ [2] of democratic policies. This he has done either from *principle* or from *calculation*. If

AD, Hamilton Papers, Library of Congress.

1. This speech concerns the New York gubernatorial election of 1804. In describing this document, John Church Hamilton wrote: "On the fifteenth of February, five days prior to the nomination of Burr in the city of New York, [John] Lansing[, Jr.] was nominated by a large vote of the Democratic members of the State legislature, as successor to Clinton; by whom he had recently been appointed Chancellor. What course the Federalists should pursue at this election, for though too weak to elect a member of their own party, it was in their power to decide the result, was the important question. Five days previous to Lansing's nomination, a few leading Federalists held an informal conference at Albany to consider the expediency of nominating a Federal candidate; if deemed not expedient, whether, as a party, they ought to support either candidate of their opponents.

"Hamilton viewing it as a question far beyond the politics of New York, but as, in fact, a question of the preservation or dissolution of the Union, was present at this conference. He avoided taking any part in the conference until the moment when the interview was about to end. Then he arose and read a paper, which, in order to guard against any misconception, he had prepared, assigning the reasons for a preference of Lansing. That this preference was solely on public grounds is shown by the fact, that the personal ill feeling of Lansing towards him, seen in the Convention of New York, which adopted the Constitution, had manifested itself recently during an important trial." (Hamilton, *History*, VII, 769–70.)

For lieutenant governor, the Republicans nominated John Broome. Broome, a New York City merchant, had been a member of the New York Committee of One Hundred in 1775, the Provincial Congress in New York City in 1776 and 1777, and the committee which drew up the New York Constitution of 1777. In 1804 he served in the state Senate.

Dissenting Republicans met in Albany on February 18 ("Nomination At a respectable Meeting of REPUBLICAN CITIZENS, . . . on . . . the 18th day of February, 1804 . . ." [Broadside Collection, New York Public Library]) and in New York on February 20 (*New-York Evening Post*, February 21, 1804) and nominated Aaron Burr for governor. Oliver Phelps, a land speculator who at this time lived in Ontario County, was nominated for lieutenant governor.

For Lansing's opposition to H in the New York Ratifying Convention, see *PAH*, V, *passim*. For the "important trial" in the case of the *People v Levi Weeks*, see Goebel, *Law Practice*, I, 693–774.

2. Words within broken brackets in this document have been taken from Hamilton, *History*, VII, 770–72.

the former he is not likely now to change his plan, when the fœderalists are prostrate and their enemies predominent. If the latter, he will certainly not at this time relinquish the ladder of his ambition and espouse the cause or views of the weaker party.

2   Though detested by some of the leading Clintonians,[3] he is certainly not personally disagreeable to the great body of them, and it will be no difficult task for a man of talents intrigue and address possessing this chair of Government to rally the great body of them under his standard and thereby to consolidate for personal purposes the mass of Clintonians, his own adherents among the democrats and such fœderalists as from personal good will or interested motives may give him support.

3   The effect of his elevation will be to reunite under a more adroit able and daring chief the now scattered fragments of the democratic party and to reinforce it by a strong detachment from the fœderalists. For though virtuous fœderalists who from miscalculation may support him, would afterwards relinquish his standard a large number from various motives would continue attached to it.

4   A further effect of his elevation by the aid of fœderalists will be to present to the confidence of New England a man already the man of the democratic leaders of that Country, and towards whom the mass of the people have no weak predilection as their countryman, as the Grandson of President Edwards, and the son of President Burr.[4] In vain will certain men resist this predilection when it can

3. The conflict between the Clintonians and the Burrites began after George Clinton's election as governor in 1801. Clinton's supporters, including his nephew, DeWitt Clinton, and Ambrose Spencer, refused to give any appointments to Burr's followers. During 1802 and 1803 both factions attacked each other in a series of political pamphlets. By 1804 Burr knew that he would not be renominated for the Vice Presidency. He hoped to win office in New York, but the Clinton-Livingston group controlled the state's Republican party. For the standard accounts of the struggle between the Clintonians and the Burrites, see Dixon Ryan Fox, *The Decline of Aristocracy in the Politics of New York* (New York, 1919), 57–69; Jabez D. Hammond, *The History of Political Parties in the State of New York from the Ratification of the Federal Constitution to December, 1840* (Albany, 1842), I, 164–209; Samuel H. Wandell and Meade Minnigerode, *Aaron Burr* (New York and London, 1927), I, 239–73.

DeWitt Clinton, a New York City lawyer, was a member of the New York Assembly in 1798 and the state Senate from 1798 to 1802. In 1802 he was elected to the United States Senate to fill the vacancy caused by the resignation of John Armstrong. In 1803 he resigned from the Senate to become mayor of New York City.

4. Burr's father, Aaron Burr, was the president of the College of New Jersey (now Princeton) from 1748 until his death in 1757, when Jonathan Edwards,

be said that he was chosen Governor of this state, in which he was best known principally or in a great degree by the aid of fœderalists.

5. This will give him fair play to disorganize New England if so disposed; a thing not very difficult when the strength of the democratic party in each of the N E states in considered and the natural tendency of our civil institutions is duly weighed.

6. The ill opinion of Jefferson and jealousy of the ambition of Virginia is no inconsiderable prop of good principles in that Country. But these causes are leading to an opinion that a dismemberment of the Union is expedient. It would probably suit Mr. Burrs views to promote this result to be the chief of the Northern portion —And placed at the head of the state of New York no man would be more likely to succeed.

7 If he be truly, as the fœderalists have believed, a man of irregular and insatiable ambition; if his plan has been to rise to power on the ladder of Jacobinic principles, it is natural to conclude that he will endeavor to fix himself in power by the same instrument, that he will not lean on a fallen ⟨and⟩ falling party, generally speaking of a character not to favour usurpation and the ascendancy of a despotic chief. Every day shews more and more the much to be regretted tendency of Governments intirely popular to dissolution and disorder. Is it rational to expect, that a man who had the sagacity to foresee this tendency, and whose temper would permit him to bottom his aggrandisement on popular prejudices and vices would desert this system at a time, when more than ever the state of things invites him to adhere to it?

8 If Lansing is Governor his personal character affords some security against pernicious extremes, and at the same time renders it morally certain, that the democratic party already much divided and weakened will moulder and break asunder more and more. This is certainly a state of things favorable to the future ascendancy of the wise and good. May it not lead to a recasting of parties by which the fœderalists will gain a great accession of force from former opponents? At any rate, is it not wiser in them to promote a course of things by which scism among the democrats will be fostered and increased, ⟨than one likely, upon a⟩ fair calculation to give them a

the most renowned American clergyman of his day, succeeded him. Edwards was the father-in-law of Aaron Burr, Senior.

chief better able than any they have yet had to unite and direct them and in a situation to infuse rottenness in the only part of our Country which still ⟨remains⟩ sound—the fœderal states of New England.[5]

5. On February 23, 1804, the *New-York Evening Post* printed a letter concerning H's speech, dated "Albany, February 18." This letter reads in part: "This celebrated speech, it is said, opens the eyes of the Republicans, to the falsity of those charges which declared that Col. Burr, was acting in concert with Gen. Hamilton. It is one of the most fortunate occurrences that could have taken place, to elevate Mr. Burr in the esteem of the republicans. On the other hand, Gen. Hamilton's harrangue has soured his own party. The spirit of disappointed rivalship it bespeaks, is censured by all. It is generally presumed, that he has spoken without previous consultation, and that he rather over rates his controuling influence. The Clintonians are delighted. They laugh in their sleeves, pronounce the General's opinion binding on his party, and boast of the federal interest as certainly with them."

An editorial, which follows this letter, reads in part: "The above is given to our readers merely for the purpose of observing that, without departing from that neutrality which we yesterday recommended, the federalists in this city cannot be too much on their guard against the practices that, we are well assured, are at this time resorted to, for the purpose of dividing, weakening, and finally destroying them as a party.

"The following is all the foundation for the above letter. Some gentlemen in Albany one evening desired that there might be a few of the leading federalists collected for the purpose of interchanging sentiments on two questions: First, whether it would be expedient to set up a federal candidate at all; 2d, whether the federalists ought as a party to side with either of the candidates proposed by our political opponents? At this meeting, not a formal one, and at which no vote was taken nor designed to be taken, several gentlemen expressed their opinions on both questions. General Hamilton so far from taking a lead, did not offer his sentiments till just before it broke up, when he said that he could not think it adviseable for the federal party, as a party, to lend themselves to either, but to remain neuter between them; that every gentleman might be left to act for himself; that for his part, speaking as an individual, if it became necessary for him to act at all, he should vote for Mr. Lansing in preference to Mr. Burr. But it is not true that he made a formal speech of 'two hours, inculcating the necessity and propriety of supporting Mr. Lansing in preference to Mr. Burr.' "

To Robert G. Harper [1]

Albany February 19th 1804

Dr Sir

Since the receipt of your letter [2] on the subject of the impeachment of the Judges,[3] this is perhaps the first moment, that indifferent health and excessive occupation have permitted a reply.

I view the attempts which are making completely in the light you do; and have very little doubt that they are in prosecution of a deliberate plan to prostrate the independence of the Judicial Department, and substitute to the present judges creatures of the reigning party, who will be the supple instruments of oppression and usurpation, under the forms of the Constitution. This being my apprehension of the matter, I shall not be backward to give the scheme all practicable resistance; and certainly, if an impeachment shall be instituted and other prior and indispensable duties will permit, I shall chearfully aid in the defence of the accused, as a very high obligation. It is not however in my power to promise absolutely attendance; because the possibility of it must depend on the time of Trial. There is hardly a sitting of our Circuit or Supreme Court, at which there are not causes depending, which involve the whole fortunes of Individuals who place a material reliance on my efforts. Propriety or good faith would not permit me to be absent during these periods; and though the public cause might call me elsewhere I should be convin⟨ced⟩ that it would be in hands (exclusive of mine) in which it would have every possible advantage.

But nothwithstanding the opinion I have expressed, it will not surprise me if the execution of the plan is suspended. It is certain that in this state leading me⟨n⟩ of the popular party either disapprove the attempt or are fearful of its influence upon the affairs of the party. Hints will probably go to the prompters at Washington which may induce, if not a relinquishment, a postponement.[4]

The republican party (soi disant) are greatly distracted in this state.[5] The violence of their measures added to the disappointments of partisans who have been candidates for office, has produced a mass of discontent which threatens their power. Col Burr intends to profit by it, if he can, and has no bad chance of being lifted to the chair of Government by the united efforts of personal adherents among the democrats, malcontents of the same party and fœderalists too angry to reason.

One consequence of the distraction of the party is the declining of Governor Clinton [6] to be candidate at the next election. A very respectable man as to private character, Chancellor Lansing, is the substitute.[7] He had secretly many competitors and is far from being a general favourite of the party. From this moment, it is destined to be split into fragments, unless hereafter reunited under the more skilful adroit and able lead of Col Burr.

You will conclude from this that I do not look forward to his success with pleasure. The conclusion will be true. It is an axiom with me that he will be the most dangerous chief that *Jacobinism* can have; and, in relation to the present question, a full persuasion, that he will reunite under him the popular party and give it new force for personal purposes—that a dismemberment of the Union is likely to be one of the first fruits of his elevation, and the overthrow of good principles in our only sound quarter, the North, a result not very remote.

I had rather see Lansing Governor & the party broken to pieces. This will be no bad state of things for those who really love their country & understand its true interest.

Yrs. with sincere regard   A Hamilton

PS Since writing the foregoing Chancellor Lansing has declined,[8] and chief Justice Lewis[9] is the substitute. Burr's prospect has extremely brightened.

ALS, Mrs. Otto Madlener, Hubbard Woods, Illinois.
    1. Harper, who had been a Federalist member of the House of Representatives from South Carolina from 1795 to 1801, practiced law in Baltimore, Maryland. In 1801 he married Catherine Carroll, the daughter of Charles Carroll of Carrollton.
    2. Letter not found.
    3. This is a reference to the impeachments of Samuel Chase, an associate justice of the Supreme Court since January, 1796, and John Pickering, United States judge for the District of New Hampshire since January, 1795.
    On March 12, 1804, the House of Representatives impeached Chase for his conduct during the trials of John Fries and James T. Callender and for an intemperate and allegedly partisan charge to a Baltimore grand jury on May 2, 1803. On March 1, 1805, the Senate acquitted Chase. For the articles of impeachment and proceedings of Chase's trial, at which Harper served as one of his counsel, see *Annals of Congress*, XIV, 81–676. For Fries's second trial in 1800, see William Lewis to H, October 11, 1800. For Callender's trial, see Philip Schuyler to H, August 19, 1802, note 5.
    Pickering had suffered a mental breakdown and used offensive language, while intoxicated, during his handling of the case of the ship *Eliza*. In accordance with the provisions of Article 25 of "An Act to provide for the more convenient organization of the Courts of the United States" (2 *Stat.* 97 [February 13, 1801]), a Circuit Court judge assumed Pickering's District Court duties while Pickering was incapacitated. When the Judiciary Act of 1801 was repealed ("An Act to repeal certain acts respecting the organization of the Courts of the United States; and for other purposes" [2 *Stat.* 132 (March 8, 1802)]), Pickering refused to resign, and the only way to remove him from office was by impeachment. On March 2, 1803, the House of Representatives impeached Pickering (*Annals of Congress*, XII, 641–42), and on March 12, 1804,

the Senate voted to remove him from office (*Annals of Congress*, XIII, 367). For the proceedings against Pickering, at which Harper appeared for the defense, but was not formally entered as counsel, see *Annals of Congress*, XIII, 318–68.

4. On May 13, 1803, Thomas Jefferson wrote to Joseph H. Nicholson, a Republican Representative from Maryland: "you must have heard of the extraordinary charge of Chace to the grand jury at Baltimore. ought this seditious & official attack on the principles of our constitution, and on the proceedings of a State, to go unpunished? and to whom so pointedly as yourself will the public look for the necessary measures? I ask these questions for your consideration. for myself, it is better that I should not interfere" (ALS, letter-press copy, Thomas Jefferson Papers, Library of Congress). Nicholson consulted Speaker of the House Nathaniel Macon, a Republican from North Carolina, who discouraged Nicholson by questioning the validity of impeachment proceedings in a case of a grand jury charge (A. B. Lacy, "Jefferson and Congress, 1801–1809" [unpublished Ph.D. dissertation, University of Virginia, 1963]). On January 5, 1804, John Randolph, a member of the House of Representatives from Virginia, introduced the resolution in the House calling for a committee of inquiry concerning Chase's conduct (*Annals of Congress*, XIV, 81–82).

5. For the split in the Republican party in New York, see "Speech at a Meeting of Federalists in Albany," February 10, 1804, note 3.

6. George Clinton had been governor of New York from 1777 to 1795 and from 1801 to 1804, when he declined renomination ostensibly on the grounds of age and ill health (Clinton to Jefferson, January 20, 1804 [ALS, Thomas Jefferson Papers, Library of Congress]). At a caucus of Republican congressmen on February 25, 1804, Jefferson was unanimously nominated for President and Clinton was nominated by the majority for Vice President (*National Intelligencer and Washington Advertiser*, February 29, 1804).

7. For the nomination of John Lansing, Jr., for governor of New York, see "Speech at a Meeting of Federalists in Albany," February 10, 1804, note 1.

8. On February 18, 1804, Lansing wrote to Ebenezer Purdy, a state senator who was chairman of the caucus of Republican legislators that had nominated Lansing, reversing his earlier decision and declining the nomination (*New-York Spectator*, February 23, 29, 1804).

9. Morgan Lewis, a lawyer, had been deputy quartermaster general of the New York department during the American Revolution. He was a member of the New York Assembly from 1789 to 1790 and again in 1792. From 1791 to 1792 he was attorney general of New York. He became third justice of the state Supreme Court in 1792, and in 1801 he became chief justice. Lewis was married to Gertrude Livingston, the sister of Robert R. Livingston, the former Chancellor. For Lewis's nomination for governor, see the *New-York Spectator*, February 23, 1804.

From Rufus King

[New York] feb. 24 1804

Dr sir

Mr. D. Ogdon [1] called upon me a few minutes past, and as I understood from him that he purposes writing to you by the mail of this Evening,[2] I think it proper, in order to avoid any misconception of the tenour of our conversation to repeat to you the purport of what I said to him. viz.

"Whether it will be expedient to offer a federal candidate for the Govr.[3] is a point upon wh, from the want of information concerning the relative strength and disposition of parties, and the consequent probability of success, I proposed myself (to Mr. O) quite unable to judge.

With respect to my being the fedl. Candidate [4] althoh. I wd. not say, that my mind was absolutely decided, as I had never considered the subject, the Objections to my consenting appeared to me to be insurmountable."

faithfully &c   RK.

Genl. Hamilton. Albany

P.S. On the subject of our last interview, I have conversed with Wolcott,[5] who agrees with you in Opinion, wh. I ought before to have told you.

Copy, in King's handwriting, New-York Historical Society, New York City.
1. David A. Ogden was a New York City lawyer.
2. Letter not found.
3. For the gubernatorial election in New York, see "Speech at a Meeting of Federalists in Albany," February 10, 1804; H to Robert G. Harper, February 19, 1804.
4. See H to King, February 24, 1804.
Most leading Federalists hoped that King would be the party's candidate for President or Vice President in 1804. See Theodore Sedgwick to H, January 27, 1803, note 9.
5. Oliver Wolcott, Jr.

To Rufus King [1]

Albany February 24. 1804

My Dear Sir

You will have heared, before this reaches you, of the fluctuations and changes which have taken place in the measures of the reigning party, as to a candidate for Governor; and you will probably have also been informed that pursuant to the opinions professed by our friends, before I left New York, I had taken an open part in favour of Mr. Lansing.

It is a fact to be regretted, though anticipated, that the fœderalists, very extensively, had embarked with zeal in the support of Mr. Burr; yet an impression to the contrary and in favour of Mr. Lansing had been made, and there was good ground to hope that a proper direction, in the main, might have been given to the current of fœderalism. The substitution of Mr. Lewis has essentially varied the prospect; and the best informed among us here agree that the Fœderalists, as a body, could not be diverted from Mr. Burr to Mr. Lewis, by any efforts of leading characters, if they should even deem the support of the latter expedient.

Though I have no reason to think, that my original calculation was wrong, while the competition was between *Clinton* and *Burr*; yet from the moment the former declined, I began to consider the latter as having a chance of success. It was still however my reliance that *Lansing* would outrun him, but now that Chief Justice Lewis is the competitor, the probability of success in my judgment inclines to Mr. Burr.

Thus situated two questions have arisen 1 whether a fœderal candidate ought not to be run as a mean of defeating Mr Burr and of keeping the fœderalists from becoming a personal faction allied to him. 2 whether in the conflict of parties ⟨as⟩ they now stand, the strongest of them discon⟨nected⟩ and disjointed, there would not be a considerable hope of success for a Fœderal candidate.

These questions have received no solution in scarcely any one's mind; but it is agreed that if an attempt is to be made, You must be the candidate. There is no other man among us, under whose standard either fragment of the democratic party could as easily rally. It is enough to say, you have been absent during the time in which party animosities have become matured and fixed, and therefore are much less than any other distinguished fœderalist an object of them.

To detach the fœderalists from Burr, they must believe two things: *one* that we are in earnest, as to our Candidate, & that it is not a mere diversion—the other that there is some chance of success. All believe, and some leading democrats admit, that if either of the two democratic rival parties should come to expect a defeat, they would arrange themselves under your banners.

Reflect well on all these things and make up your mind in case you should be invited to consen⟨t. I⟩ have not time to enlarge.

Yrs. very truly   A H

Rufus King Esq

ALS, New-York Historical Society, New York City.
    1. For background to this letter, see "Speech at a Meeting of Federalists in Albany," February 10, 1804; H to Robert G. Harper, February 19, 1804; King to H, February 24, 1804.

Nathaniel Pendleton's Memorandum on a Conversation between Alexander Hamilton and Ebenezer Purdy [1]

[Albany, February 25, 1804]

On Saturday the 25th of february 1804 I went with General Hamilton to the lodgings of Judge Purdy in Albany who was at home.

General H. said that he had called on Mr. Purdy, supposing he had had sufficient time for reflection, to know who was the person alluded to [2] in the conversation he had had with him a day or two before when Mr. Kane [3] was present.

Mr. Purdy said he had thought of it, but had not seen the gentleman alluded to, and as he had desired his name might not be mentioned he did not wish to do it without his consent, but that the same person had mentioned it to several others, and therefore he presumed he would have no objection.

Genl. H. asked if the Gentleman was in Albany. Mr. P. said No. He lived in Westchester.

Gen H said he did not wish to be thought too pressing. He was willing to allow a reasonable time, but wished to have an answer as soon as it could be obtained.

Gen H. asked Mr. Purdy to repeat what he had before told him, that there might [be] no misapprehension.

Purdy said that in conversation with several republican members of the Legislature several years ago it was mentioned that some of the leading men among the federal party were in favor of a *monarchal* Gouvernment and the person to whom he alluded said that a letter had been written from the Eastward which was seen in General Hamilton's Office and that several Copies had been given out from thence. That this letter proposed to Establish a monarchy in the United States, and that one of the Sons of George the third was to be King. He said he understood the proposal to have come from England; he did not know who wrote the letter nor to whom it was written, but it was from Some person to the Eastward.

Genl. H asked if he had understood that the Copies alluded to, were made by him or with his privity? He said no. Genl. H. told him he had understood him otherwise a day or two before. Mr. P—— said he had misunderstood him or he Purdy had not clearly expressed himself. He said he had not said so, but he supposed it would be understood he knew of it as they came from his Office. He also said Gouvernor Clinton had also mentioned to him the letter, and that he had one of the Copies. He said it was talked of Publickly about the time he heard it.

Genl H. told him it was a Slander he was determined to trace. That he should write to Gouvernor Clinton on the subject, and Should expect an answer from Mr Purdy, as soon as possible. We then came away.

There were three other persons present whom I did not know.

On the Monday following I asked Mr Purdy if he meant that the person he alluded to lived in Westchester and he said Westchester County.[4]   Nathl: Pendleton

ADS, New-York Historical Society, New York City.

1. Pendleton, a native of Virginia and a veteran of the American Revolution, was a lawyer in Georgia from 1785 to 1789, when he became United States judge for the District of Georgia. He moved to New York in 1796 and during that year was admitted to practice in the New York Supreme Court and the United States District Court of New York. Pendleton, who was one of the executors of H's estate, was also one of H's seconds in the duel with Aaron Burr.

Purdy, who had served in the New York Assembly at various times between 1779 and 1795, was a member of the state Senate from 1800 to 1806. He was also judge of Westchester County from 1797 to 1798 and a member of the Council of Appointment from February, 1803, to February, 1804.

2. This is a reference to Pierre Van Cortlandt, Jr., a Westchester County lawyer and a member of the New York Assembly in 1792, 1794, and 1795. Van Cortlandt had been a law clerk in H's office from 1784 to 1786. See the first entry in H's "Cash Book," March 1, 1782–1791.

3. James Kane was a prominent Albany merchant. H, Kane, and Purdy had met on February 23, 1804.

4. Purdy reported this conversation to George Clinton, who wrote to Van Cortlandt on February 24, 1804: "It seems you had mentioned to Purdy the Circumstance of these Letters having been copied in Hamiltons Office but Purdy as he tells me refused to give his Author to Hamilton but referred him to me and asked him why he did not call on me—he replied he intended to write me on the subject. He appeared to be very desirous to know whether it was said that the Letters were copied in his Office by his Order or coment to this Purdy answered in the Negative but said It was the natural presumption.

"I presume I shall be honored with a Letter from the General on this subject and I have thought proper to apprize you of it that you may be on your guard. It will be prudent not to utter a sylable on the subject to any person whatever till you hear further from me. Coud not Strong through the Medium of P Van Wyck or some of your Friends in New York be brought to acknowledge his Agency in the Business. For Reasons that will naturaly occur to you such Confession would be very desireable." (ALS, MS Division, New York Public Library.) See also Purdy to Van Cortlandt, February 25, 1804 (ALS, Sleepy Hollow Restorations, Inc., Tarrytown, New York).

Joseph Strong, an Albany lawyer, had been a clerk in H's law office from 1786 to 1789. See "Certificate of Clerkship for Joseph Strong," January 20, 1789, printed in this volume. Pierre C. Van Wyck was a New York City merchant.

On February 27, 1804, Van Cortlandt wrote to an unnamed correspondent: "Sometime in the Spring or Summer of the year 1787 I accidently went into the Office of Alexander Hamilton, where I found Joseph Strong (his then Clerk) alone in the Office above stairs making Copies of a Letter, which upon my coming into the Office He endeavoured to keep from my Sight by covering them; This Design of Secrecy Strongly excited my Curiosity to see it and after expostulating with him he at length shewed me One of his Copies but without a Signature. The Letter was written by a gentleman then in London & Strong told me it was from our Embassador at that place [John Adams], to a gentleman at Boston. The Substance of the Letter was that Overtures had been made either by Some of the Ministry or Gentlemen high in Confidence Of Ministers (which I do not rightly recollect) to the Letter Writer in Order to Strengthen the Bonds of friendship between G. Britain & the United States more firmly, G. Britain would cede over to the United States her Canadas Nova Scotia and all other of her Possessions & Territory in North America Upon the Express Condition that One of the Sons of the King of England (I think it mentioned the Bishop of Oznaburgh the present Duke of York) should be acknowledged the King; as it would then be of the whole of North America; The Letter Writer thought it an Eligible thing and wished the Leading men in the United States attached to the then prevaling Federal Politicks might be consulted. The Copies I understood from Strong were to be forwarded on to particular Gentlemen in the Southern States: as this Copy was shewn to me by Strong in confidence, and as I had myself studied with Mr Hamilton & had shortly before this taken license and from my personal friendship to Mr Hamilton at that time I forebore mentioning the Secret with which I had been entrusted, nor did I do this until long afterwards (except to One Person) when it became notorious that Mr Hamilton had proposed in the Convention in 1787 (a few weeks after I saw the Copy of the Letter in question) a Constitution for the United States, the features of which was to have a King &c. I then was convinced that I had done wrong in not making public the Copy of the Letter I had seen in his Office. I then mentioned it to some Gentlemen in Confidence, fearing as Strong was a warm federalist and under the Influence of Hamilton that he would deny it & Mr Hamilton certainly would, for the truth of that thing being generally known would ruin his popularity & damn his future prospects. And I not being able to substantiate it without stronger testimony would be viewed as the Calumniator of the Tool of the Federal Party—among those to whom I mentioned this thing to was the Govenor as Early as 1793. I have since it seems mentioned it to Judge Purdy who a few Days since in Company where James Kane was mentioned that Hamilton was in favor of monarchy & that the Govenor had seen a Letter which was copied in Hamilton's Office to that Effect, Kane immediately detailed this Conversation with much exagerations to Hamilton who called upon Purdy for an Explanation who referred him to the Govenor, so the business now is . . ." (AL [incomplete], Sleepy Hollow Restorations Inc., Tarrytown, New York).

No such letter from John Adams has been found. On July 29, 1791, Adams wrote to Thomas Jefferson: ". . . If you Suppose that I have or ever had a design or desire of attempting to introduce a Government of Kings, Lords and Commons or in other Words an hereditary Executive or an hereditary Senate, either into the Government of the United States, or that of any Individual State in this Country, you are wholly mistaken. There is not Such a Thought expressed or intimated in any public writing or private Letter of mine, and I may Safely challenge all Mankind to produce Such a passage and quote the Chapter and Verse" (ALS, Thomas Jefferson Papers, Library of Congress).

For H's plan of government in the Constitutional Convention, see "Constitutional Convention. Plan of Government," June 18, 1787.

To George Clinton [1]

Albany Feby. 27. 1804

Sir

It is now a long time since a very ⟨odious⟩ [2] slander has been in circulation to the prejudice of my character. It has come to my ears in more than one way, but always 'till lately without the disclosure ⟨of⟩ any source to which I could resort for explanation or detection. Within a few days, Mr. Kane of this City related to me a story as coming from Judge Purdy, in substance very similar to the calumny to which I have alluded. The amount of his information and the result of an interview with Judge Purdy are contained in the inclosed paper. [3] You will observe, Sir, that your name is implicated in the transaction, with what warrant it would be improper for me to prejudge. But the very mention of your name adds importance to the affair and increases the motives to investigation.

The charge, even in the mitigated f⟨orm⟩ to which it is reduced by Judge Purdy's admission, is ⟨of⟩ a nature too derogatory to permit me to pass it lightly over. It is essential that its origin and progress should be traced as fully as may be practicable, in order to the thorough exposure of its falshood and malignity.

The assertions of Judge Purdy ⟨au⟩thorise me to appeal to you for a frank and candid explanation of so much of the matter as relates to yourself. This explanation I request as speedily as may be.

I have the honor to be   Sir   Your obed ser

His Excelly ⟨Governor Clinton⟩

ADf, Hamilton Papers, Library of Congress.
  1. For background to this letter, see "Nathaniel Pendleton's Memorandum on a Conversation between Alexander Hamilton and Ebenezer Purdy," February 25, 1804.
  2. Material within broken brackets in this letter has been taken from *JCHW*, VI, 561.
  3. Enclosure not found.

From James Kane [1]

[Albany, February 28, 1804]

Genl Hamilton

Dr Sir

Attach'd to this You have the *Purdy* Statement, which I am *very Clear* is in substance Correct. If you deem it very important that I should make affidavit of what is Here related—I will do it. At the same time I must acknowledge I shall have some difficulty in bringing my mind to it. My *pride* & *Delicacy* being in Opposition &c.

With much respect & Esteem   I remain Dr Sir &c   James Kane

[ENCLOSURE] [2]

[Albany, February 28, 1804]

Some time in the month of January last, I call'd on Jacob Snell,[3] a member of the Council of appointment, where I found Ebenezer Purdy Esqr together with a Mr. Hughes and one or two other Gentlemen whose names I do not recollect (being Strangers to me).

Mr Purdy immediately ask'd me if I had any objection to hear an oration read, that was delivered on the 4th. July, by a young irishman who, if I mistake not, then resided in His family. I replied,

certainly not,—it was a violent *phillippic* against the federal Administration, the Stamp act,[4] Sedition law,[5] Standing Army [6] &c were
represented as the leading features of the federal faction. After some
Considerable conversation on the merits of the oration between Mr
Purdy and myself, he remark'd, he fully believed *monarchy* was
the object of the federalists, that there was a Person, who did not
wish to have his name mention'd, who Cou'd prove the fact & stood
ready to make affidavit of it, That some time in the Year '98 a negociation was opened between Genl Hamilton, Mr. Adams and the
King of England, for the purpose of introducing monarchy into this
Country, at the Head of which was to be placed one of the Royal
Family and that Canada was to be ceded to the States, for the truth
of the above Mr P—— refered me to Governor Clinton, who He
said wou'd not deny it, altho' He did not wish to say any thing
about it.

On the 23d Feby 1804 Genl Hamilton & myself call'd on Mr
Purdy for the purpose of investigating the affair. Genl H introduced
the Subject to Mr Purdy, by telling Him, He had received information from Mr K of a certain declaration of His of a nature very interesting to His Character, which He was determined to have explained and investigated. I then related to Mr Purdy the Conversation
He had with me, as above stated. Mr Purdy replied what you have
said Mr K is pretty nearly Correct (or words to that effect) but
with this difference. I did not mention Mr Adams' name, and that
affair which I spoke of to you did not happen in '98 but some time
previous to the Convention which form'd the present Constitution
of the United States. What I told you was nearly this, that Some
body in England had made proposals to Some body to the Eastward,
for establishing a Monarchy in this Country and for placing at the
head of it a Son of the King of Great Britain, that some letters, or
papers Containing these proposals was sent to Genl. Hamilton, Copies of which were made in His office to be distributed among certain Persons. Mr Purdy then ask'd me if this was not the Substance
of what he had told me. I replied that the difference was between
that & what I had before stated and recapitulated what I had before
said. I also pressed upon Mr P what I had before Stated, respecting
Governor Clinton and Question'd Him whether He had not made
such an appeal to Govr Clinton and also whether He had not affirm'd that there was a Person who cou'd attest the truth of the

story. Mr Purdy persisted in the statement which He had just made. As to Gov Clinton He admitted, that He had mention'd to the Govr. the Story He had hear'd, and that the Governor had replied that He had had One of the letters. On being interrogated by Genl Hamilton whether He had mention'd His name to Governer Clinton, He answered He was not Sure whether He had done it or not. On being farther interrogated as to his having said there was a person ready to prove the transaction He had Stated, He answered there was a person who had assured Him of His knowledge of the transaction, as it was now related by Him. A variety of other Conversation pass'd but the above Comprises the Most Material particulars.

James Kane

Albany Feb. 28th. 1804

ALS, New-York Historical Society, New York City.
    1. For background to this letter, see "Nathaniel Pendleton's Memorandum on a Conversation between Alexander Hamilton and Ebenezer Purdy," February 25, 1804; H to George Clinton, February 27, 1804.
    2. ADS, New-York Historical Society, New York City.
    3. Snell, a resident of Montgomery County, was a member of the New York Assembly from 1798 to 1802 and of the state Senate from 1803 to 1804. He served on the Council of Appointment from February, 1803, to February, 1804.
    4. See "An Act laying Duties on stamped Vellum, Parchment and Paper" (1 Stat. 527–32 [July 6, 1797]); "An Act to amend the act intituled 'An Act laying duties on stamped vellum, parchment and paper'" (1 Stat. 545–46 [March 19, 1798]); "An Act to alter the Stamp Duties imposed upon Foreign Bills of Exchange and Bills of Lading, by an act intituled 'An Act laying duties on stamped vellum, parchment and paper'; and further to amend the same" (1 Stat. 622–24 [February 28, 1799]).
    5. "An Act in addition to the act, entitled 'An act for the punishment of certain crimes against the United States'" (1 Stat. 596–97 [July 14, 1798]).
    6. See the introductory note to H to James Gunn, December 22, 1798; H to Rufus King, June 3, 1802, note 9.

From George Clinton [1]

Albany 29th February 1804

Sir

This is the first moments leisure I have had to answer your Letter of the 27th Instant which was handed to me yesterday. I have carefully perused the Papers it inclosed under the signature of Mr. James

Kane and find the statement of the transaction aluded to as admitted by Judge Purdy to be correct as far as my Name is implicated, and I believe it contains as reduced by Judge Purdy the substance of all the Conversation that passed between him and me on that Subject. I recollect to have mentioned to him that I had seen the Copy of a Letter similar to the one mentioned in the Statement on or about the Time the Convention which formed our Federal Constitution was sitting. This Copy was put into my Hands by the late General Malcom [2] who informed me he had received it from Connecticut. It was without signature or direction.

I have the Honor to be   Your most Obedient Servant

Geo Clinton

General Hamilton

ALS, Hamilton Papers, Library of Congress.

1. For background to this letter, see "Nathaniel Pendleton's Memorandum on a Conversation between Alexander Hamilton and Ebenezer Purdy," February 25, 1804; H to Clinton, February 27, 1804, James Kane to H, February 28, 1804.

2. William Malcolm, a veteran of the American Revolution, was a New York City merchant and a member of the New York Assembly in 1784, 1786, and 1787.

From Oliver Wolcott Junior [1]

(Private)   New York February 1804

My Dear Sir.

By Letters lately recd. from Albany, by Gentlemen interested in the Merchants Bank, we are informed, that a meeting of political

ALS, Connecticut Historical Society, Hartford.

1. This letter, which Wolcott wrote in his capacity as president of the Merchants' Bank, concerns his and his fellow-directors' efforts to secure a charter for that bank from the New York legislature. See "Articles of Association of the Merchants' Bank," April 7, 1803.

As soon as the bank's articles of association had been printed in the New-York Evening Post on April 11, 1803, the bank became an issue between New York Federalists and Republicans. In this connection it should be kept in mind that the Merchants' Bank was essentially a Federalist institution, and that as such it was in a position to threaten the interests of the Manhattan Bank, which was dominated by Republican financial and political leaders (see the introductory note to Philip Schuyler to H, January 31, 1799). In addition, the Republicans were understandably disturbed by the fact that the Merchants' Bank was permitted to perform banking operations without first being authorized to do so by the state legislature. An article in the [New York] *American Citizen*, a Republican newspaper edited by James Cheetham, reads: "A similar association was never before palmed upon the community. With a power to issue notes to any extent, the projectors take care that they shall not be liable for any abuse of trust . . . . we will only say that the greatest injustice may be committed if such associations be legal. With one share a person may continue director. What interest can such a director feel in the welfare of the institution or of the community? . . . What right had the directors to more shares than the other parties to the association? What right had they to choose themselves directors? . . . The whole of the transaction is one of ignorance and folly . . ." ([New York] *American Citizen*, April 19, 1803; see also *American Citizen*, April 16, 1803). Editorials in the *New-York Evening Post* defended the Merchants' Bank and charged that the Republicans through the Manhattan Bank were attempting to secure a monopoly on banking in the city (*New-York Evening Post*, April 16, 18, 1803).

When in the first months of 1804 the Merchants' Bank sought to obtain a charter from the legislature, the struggle was resumed in Albany with the Federalists and Republicans using much the same arguments that had appeared in the city's partisan press in 1803 (Philip G. Hubert, Jr., *The Merchants' National Bank of the City of New York* [New York, 1903], 52–54).

Opponents and supporters of the bank submitted several petitions to the Assembly in February and March, 1804, all of which were referred to a select committee appointed on February 24 consisting of one member of the Assembly from each county. On February 24 a memorial of Daniel Ludlow and others from New York City was presented to the Assembly opposing the charter, and the next day a petition by Willet Seaman, signed by six hundred and fourteen supporters of the bank, was also submitted (*Journal of the Assembly of the State of New-York. At Their Twenty-seventh Session, Begun and Held at the City of Albany, the Thirty-first Day of January, 1804* [Albany: Printed by John Barber, Printer to the State, n.d.], 103, 106, 113, 114, 127, 207, 214). On March 14, 1804, the select committee submitted a report recommending that the Merchants' Bank not be granted a charter of incorporation (D, New York Assembly Miscellaneous Documents, VI, 95 [New York State Library, Albany]).

"An Act to restrain unincorporated banking associations," which passed the Assembly on March 24 and the Senate on March 31, became law on April 11, 1804. According to its provisions, no person or association unauthorized by law was permitted to perform banking operations with the exception of "the association in the city of Albany, known by the name of the Mercantile Company, nor the association in the city of New-York, known by the name of the Merchants' Bank, until the first Tuesday in May one thousand eight hundred and five" (*New York Laws*, 27th Sess., Ch. CXVII). This provision represented a compromise between Republicans and Federalists in the legislature, for the Mercantile Company of Albany was dominated by Republicans, and, like the Merchants' Bank, it had applied to the Assembly for an act of incorporation in February, 1804 (*Journal of the Assembly. 27th Sess.*, 67).

Despite continued opposition, the Merchants' Bank did obtain a charter at the 1805 session of the state legislature ("An Act to incorporate the stockholders of the Merchants' Bank, in the city of New-York" [*New York Laws*, Ch. XLIII, March 26, 1805]).

characters connected with the Legislature, has been held, and that it has been resolved at all events to suppress this Company.[2] This violent decision was altogether unexpected, as from prior intelligence, it appeared that several influential characters of the ruling party had expressed opinions in favour of an act of incorporation. The report here is, that since Chancellor Lansing declined a nomination,[3] serious apprehensions have been entertained of the Success of Colo. Burrs party,[4] unless the Federalists can by some means be divided, and that this division is expected to be effected, by complying with the prayer of a Memorial for our suppression which has been signed by a number of respectable men, chiefly connected with the other Banks in this city.[5]

That a Memorial of some kind has been forwarded is certain. Some time since at the request of a number of our Board, I made inquiry of D. Ludlow [6] Esqr. in respect to the fact and he admitted it; but declined shewing me the Copy. All that we know is, that it is substantially like that which appeared in Cheetham's paper,[7] though it is presumed that some of the most offensive passages were omitted. There is no doubt, that most of the Directors of the three Banks, have petitioned not only *that a charter may be refused*, but that our Bank may be *restrained from transacting business in future*.

2. The *New-York Evening Post*, February 27, 1804, carried the following item: "Accounts received by this day's mail from Albany, state, that on Thursday evening a Legislative caucus was held, in which a hostile proceeding towards the Merchants' Bank . . . was determined on. . . . The new line of conduct which the Clintonian faction have adopted . . . arises, it is understood, from a belief that they can create a division in the federal party at the coming election by urging a suppression of the Merchant's Bank, & that more federalists will support them in consequence of this measure than if they suffered that institution to remain unmolested. The petition from the Directors of the three other banks, it is said was signed by several federal gentlemen whose influence they believe to be very great."

3. See "Speech at a Meeting of Federalists in Albany," February 10, 1804, note 1; H to Robert G. Harper, February 19, 1804, note 8.

4. See "Speech at a Meeting of Federalists in Albany," February 10, 1804, note 1.

5. See *Journal of the Assembly. 27th Sess.*, 103.

6. Daniel Ludlow, a New York City merchant, was the first president of the Bank of the Manhattan Company.

7. James Cheetham, a Republican journalist, edited the [New York] *American Citizen*. On February 21, 1804, an article "By the Editor" entitled "Remarks on the Merchants' Bank, Respectfully submitted to the Legislature of the State of New-York" appeared in the *American Citizen*. The article was continued in subsequent issues (*American Citizen*, March 2, 7, 1804).

It is said, that Mr. Murray, Mr. Schermerhorn, Mr. Glover, Genl Stevens, & Mr. Townsend of the Branch Bank [8]—an equal number of the Directors of the Bank of New York and Mr. Coles & Mr. Fairly [9] of the Manhattan Company have refused to lend their names to this instrument. These exceptions however, cannot compensate the injury which has been done to my feeling from the information, that men of such standing in society as Mr. Ray,[10] Mr. Le Roy [11] and Mr Lenox,[12] Mr. Buchannan [13] &c &c. have placed their names to a paper, representing an association of which I happen to be a conspicuous member as dangerous to the community and a violation of the rights of Property. A few years since, I should not have been easily persuaded that *such an imputation* upon my conduct would ever have recd. the sanction of *such characters;* blunted as my sensibility is, by several disappointments and new views of human nature, during a few of the last years, I am not yet prepared to meet with patience an accusation the most unreasonable & unjust that could possibly be preferred against me.

There is one fact however, that the Politicians in Albany, appear to have taken for granted in which they are totally mistaken; no diversion from the federal party in favour of Judge Lewis,[14] can possibly be made by adopting violent measures against the Merchants Bank. Some gentlemen who signed the adversary petition, seriously regret the step they have taken, and reflecting men of all Parties, are impressed with a decided conviction that the Bank cannot be suppressed without producing incalculable mischief and disorder in the city. Indeed so decided is the opinion, that an attack on this Institution, would promote Colo. Burrs views, that surmises have not unfrequently been made that his partizans, might secretly stimulate violent measures, with a view to this consequence. I know

8. John Murray, Peter Schermerhorn, John J. Glover, Ebenezer Stevens, and John Townsend were directors of the New York branch of the Bank of the United States.

9. John B. Coles and James Fairlie were New York City merchants.

10. Cornelius Ray was president of the New York branch of the Bank of the United States.

11. Herman LeRoy was a director of the Bank of New York.

12. Robert Lenox was a director of the New York branch of the Bank of the United States.

13. Thomas Buchanan was a director of the New York branch of the Bank of the United States.

14. See H to Harper, February 19, 1804, note 9.

of no fact, which can justify the slightest suspicion of this nature, but the suggestion proves, the course which the public passions would take, and it is an ascertained fact, that a great proportion of the active spirits, of almost every description of men, & especially among the Federalists, would be brought into action with a degree of energy of which there has been no recent example. Indeed the circumstances will justify vigour, for after knowing, that the Leaders of the present party, and among others Judge Lewis himself, have publickly expressed themselves in favour of the Bank; its distruction, with the view of promoting his election, by conciliating the support of a few Directors of rival Banks, would be such an outrage upon Justice, as the Community would not, and ought not to tolerate.

I am inclined to believe, that when the state of public opinion here is known at Albany, and when it is seen, that the Memorial in our favour, has been signed by about One thousand Merchants & Traders comprizing the great Body of those in active business of all political denominations, that the decision of which we have heard, will be rescinded. Hitherto we have pursued a conduct strictly neutral and conciliatory: We shall not deviate from this system at present, nor at any future time without urgent motives; if however, our rights & property are disposed of, to promote an election, we mean to render the bargain as unprofitable as possible.

In case the attack which has been threatened should be persisted in, it is proposed to apply to the Legislature to be heard by Council, in which case the Board wish your assistance. The agents at Albany will apply to you on this subject, and I sincerely hope, that your aid will not be refused. In many respects, and with reference to more Interests than are immediately affected by the question in issue, would a public discussion by you, be useful.

Reports from Washington announce serious and increasing divisions among the ruling Party: and here the Clintonians, are said to be endeavouring to encourage the Federalists to offer a Candidate of their own Party for the office of Governor. If the design was any other than to promote the election of Judge Lewis, the suggestion would be worthy of Notice; but to make use of the name of a respectable man, to exhibit the inferiority of the Federalists, and *indirectly to oppose Colo Burr*, will not I presume be thought proper. If the Clintonians as they say is the case, prefer a Federalist to Colo. Burr, and are apprehensive of his success, in consequence of divisions among themselves, let them publickly renounce their pretensions & then I presume, their preference can ⟨be⟩ realised.

I remain Dear Sir, truly & affectionately yours.   Oliv: Wolcott

Alexander Hamilton Esqr.

From Rufus King

N Yk Mar 1. 1804

Dr sir

Since my letter of the 24th. I have recd. yrs. of the same date; and after maturely reflecting upon the subject, and consulting one or two of our friends here I am confirmed in the Sentiment that I ought not to consent to be a candidate for the Govr. shd. the federalists think of offering me.

This being my determination, it is right that I shd apprize you of it, in order that our friends may not make an offer which I shd. be obliged to decline.

If you consider to what the office of Govr. has been curtailed, and what in the actual State of Parties must be his condition, if a man of virtue & independence, I can't but persuade myself that you will see insuperable objections to my consenting to be thus disposed of.

with sentiments of Regard   I am always yr ob & faithl. Ser   R K

ADfS, New-York Historical Society, New York City.

To George Clinton [1]

Albany March 2. 1804

Sir

If our correspondence does not terminate with your letter of the 29th. of February, received yesterday, I wish it to be understood that it proceeds merely from the desire of removing all ambiguity from a transaction, in which my character may be materially interested.

It is perhaps the natural inference from what you have stated, that nothing took place on your part, to sanction or corroborate the story related to you by Judge Purdy, in reference to any agency or co-operation of mine in the supposed project. Yet some of the circumstances are such, that a different inference might possibly be drawn.

I therefore trust, that you will be sensible of the propriety of dissipating all obscurity on this point.

If the letter, which you mention to have been put into your hands by General Malcom, was not withdrawn by him, or if any copy was retained by you, it would be satisfactory to me to have an inspection of the one or the other, with leave to take a copy; in order that I may have an additional clue to the source of a story, which I verily believe originated intirely in fabrication.

I have the honor to be   Your Excellency's Obed servt

A Hamilton

His Excellency Governor Clinton.

ALS, Columbia University Libraries; ADf, Hamilton Papers, Library of Congress; copy, MS Division, New York Public Library.

1. For background to this letter, see "Nathaniel Pendleton's Memorandum on a Conversation between Alexander Hamilton and Ebenezer Purdy," February 25, 1804; H to Clinton, February 27, 1804; Clinton to H, February 29, 1804; James Kane to H, February 28, 1804.

From George Clinton [1]

Albany March 6th. 1804.

Sir

I have had the honor to receive your Letter of the 2d. Instant. I cannot conceive it possible that Inferences can be drawn from any Circumstance attending the transaction alluded to repugnant to the explicit declaration contained in my Letter to you of the 29th. of last Month without calling in question the truth of them, and this I trust will not be attempted. It was not to be expected that I could recollect so as to repeat the precise Words used in the conversation which Judge Purdy had with me, nor is it essential to your Inquiries as they wou'd throw no new Light on the Subject.

With respect to the Copy of the Letter put into my Hands by General Malcomb it is a circumstance of so old a date that I dare not venture positively to assert that I returned it to him; but I believe I did and what serves to confirm me in this Opinion is my not being able to find it amongst my papers. The Contents of it however were so interesting as to make a strong and durable impression on my Mind. It recommended a Government for the United States similar to that of Great-Britain, and to obviate the difficulties which might attend fixing on a suitable Character for a King and to form an intimate connection with that Country The Prince Bishop of Oznaburgh was proposed. The House of Lords was to be composed partly of the British hereditary Nobility and partly of such of our own Citizens as should have most Merit in bringing about the Measure. The house of Commons to be elected by the People. In consideration of this provision for one of the British royal Family, Canada was to be ceded to the United States with a certain portion of the British Navy, and a perpetual Treaty of alliance Offensive and defensive entered into between the two Countries. The Letter was well written, and interspersed with much plausible reasoning, which I do not fully recollect, calculated to obviate any objections that might be raised against the Measures it proposed, & to shew the Advantages which would result from them.

The charge of having countenanced an Attempt to establish a monarchical Government, however modified, in the United States I consider odious and disreputable and I am pleased to find that however much we may differ on other political Subjects we agree in Sentiment as to this, and you may rest assured that should the Copy of the Letter alluded to be found amongst my papers or otherwise acquired by me you shall have a Copy of it with an Opportunity of examining the original.[2]

　　I am your most Obedt Servant　　　　　　　　　　Geo: Clinton

General Hamilton

ALS, Hamilton Papers, Library of Congress; copy, MS Division, New York Public Library; copy, Columbia University Libraries.
　　1. For background to this letter, see "Nathaniel Pendleton's Memorandum on a Conversation between Alexander Hamilton and Ebenezer Purdy," Feb-

ruary 25, 1804; H to Clinton, February 27, March 2, 1804; Clinton to H, February 29, 1804; James Kane to H, February 28, 1804.

2. On March 7, 1804, Clinton wrote to Pierre Van Cortlandt, Jr.: "I wrote you some days ago inclosing the Copies of Letters which Had passed between me and Genl. Hamilton. I was in hopes these woud have terminated our Correspondence, but in this I was mistaken. I now annex the Copy of a second Letter from him and my answer. You will perceive the object of his second Epistle is obviously to ascertain whether the Copy of the Letter alluded to was returned to Malcom or in my Possession being apprehensive if the latter shoud be the case it might lead to discovery by being in Strong's hand writing. For he is not apprized that it was a Copy of the original Copy only. I have thought it prudent to leave him in Doubt on this Subject at the same Time to apprize you of these particulars" (ALS, MS Division, New York Public Library).

To Louis Le Guen

[*Albany, March 6, 1804.* On March 22, 1804, Le Guen wrote to Hamilton: "Je nai recu que hier, Votre Lettre du 6." *Letter not found.*]

To George Clinton

Albany March 7. 1804

Sir

On Saturday last I sent you a letter of which the foregoing is a copy,[1] to which I have as yet received no reply.

Intending to leave this place for New York on Saturday next, it is important that I should receive an answer before that day.

I have the honor to be   Your Excelly's Obed servt

His Ex G C

ADf, Hamilton Papers, Library of Congress.
1. H to Clinton, March 2, 1804.

To George Clinton

Albany March 9. 1804

Sir

I had the honor of receiving, yesterday, your Excellency's letter of the 6th instant. It is agreeable to me to find in it a confirmation of the inference, that you had given no countenance to the supposition of my agency or cooperation in the project, to which the story of Judge Purdy relates; and it only remains for me to regret that it is not in your power to furnish the additional clue, of which I was desirous, to aid me in tracing the fabrication to its source.

I shall not only rely on the assurance which you give, as to the future communication of the copy of the letter in question, should it hereafter come to your hands; but I will take the liberty to add a request, that you will be pleased to make known to me any other circumstance, if any should reach you, which may serve to throw light upon the affair. I feel an anxiety, that it should be thoroughly sifted, not merely on my own account, but from a conviction that the pretended existence of such a project, long travelling about in whispers, has had no inconsiderable influence in exciting false alarms and unjust suspicions, to the prejudice of a number of Individuals every way worthy of public confidence; men who have always faithfully supported the existing institutions of the Country and who would disdain to be concerned in any intrigue with any foreign power or its agents, either for introducing monarchy, or for promoting or upholding any other scheme of Government within the UStates.

I have the honor to be   Your Excellency's most obedient servt.

A Hamilton

His Excellency Governor Clinton

ADfS, Hamilton Papers, Library of Congress.

Indenture: Alexander Hamilton and Elizabeth Hamilton to Catherine Bleecker, John R. Bleecker, Elizabeth Brinckerhoff, Maria Bleecker, and Blandina Bleecker

Albany, March 10, 1804. Convey to the heirs of Rutger Bleecker [1] the land in Cosby Manor which Hamilton had purchased in trust for them in 1797.[2]

DS, Oneida County Clerk's Office, Utica, New York.
1. Bleecker had been an Albany merchant.
2. See "Deed from Peter Goelet, Robert Morris, and William Popham," April 4, 1797. See also the introductory note to Philip Schuyler to H, August 31, 1795, and Goebel, *Law Practice*, forthcoming volumes.

From Louis Le Guen [1]

philadelphia 22. Mars 1804.

Cher General

Je Profitte de L'occasion du Cel. Williamson [2] qui Part Pour Newyork Par Le Mail, Pour Vous Aviser, que depuis 10. Jours absent de chés Moy, je nai recu que hier, Votre Lettre du 6.[3] Je ne Sai a quoy devoir Latribuer, Sy Ce nest à la Négligence du directeur de La Poste Office a trenton, il n'en Est pas moins Vraie, que Cella ma Empeschée de Proffiter des Avantages, que Votre attention Génereuse me metoit a mesme. Et comme Je Croie qu'il Est trop tard En Ce moment, et que Laffaire du Merchant Banke [4] Est decidée, Je ne Crois pas nècessaire de me rendre a Newyork, a moins que, Sy apres La reception de Cette Lettre, Vous Croyés qu'il Est Encorre temps, et que Par deux Mots Vous Vouliée bien m'en donner avis, en Ce Cas, me rendrais imediatement á Newyork. Je dois Cependant Vous Observer, que Pour me procurer les fonds necessaires, Je Serrais obligée de Vendre des Shares que Jai dans Les Compagnies d'assurances des Etats unies, et du Newyork [5] Laquelles En Ce Moment, Sonts tres Basse, et à 10. a 15. pour Cents audessous du Prix ou Jai Les ai Achettés il y a Plus dun Ân, Sans Avoir depuis Ce temps recu des premieres un Shiling de dèvident.

Je Vous ai accusée, dans Le temps, reception des 500 d'ollars du devident des Cents Shares dans la Compagnie d'Assurance de New-york, et ne Puis Concevoir Comment ma Lettre [6] ne Vous Est Pas Parvenue.

Je me rend aujoudhuy à Morrisville, ou Je attendrai de Vous nouvelles. En attendant Veuillés recevoir Le Nouvel Assurance du respectueux Attachement Avec Le quel J'ay L'honneur D'Estre

Votre Affectionnée Et Devouée Serviteur   L. Le Guen

ALS, Hamilton Papers, Library of Congress.
1. For background to this letter, see Le Guen to H, December 27, 1800, note 7, January 15, 1801, September 30, 1803, January 18, 1804; "Receipt to Louis Le

Guen," January 15, 1801; Aaron Ogden to H, January 15, 1801; "Indenture between Alexander Hamilton of the First Part and Richard Harison and Aaron Ogden of the Second Part," July 1, 1801; "Bond to Richard Harison and Aaron Ogden," July 1, 1801; "Account with Louis Le Guen," June 6, 1802; "Description of Account with Louis Le Guen," June 8, 1802; "Receipt from Louis Le Guen," September 10, 1802; "Account of Louis Le Guen," April 1, 1803; "Receipt from Louis Le Guen," September 5, 1803.

2. This is presumably a reference to Hugh Williamson, who had been a merchant in Edenton, North Carolina, and a Philadelphia physician before the American Revolution. From 1779 to 1782 he was surgeon general of the North Carolina troops. He was a member of the Continental Congress from 1782 to 1785 and in 1787 and 1788. After serving as a delegate to the Constitutional Convention in 1787, Williamson became a member of the North Carolina Ratifying Convention in 1789. From 1789 to 1793 he was a Federalist member of the House of Representatives from North Carolina. In 1793 he moved to New York City.

3. Letter not found.

4. See "Articles of Association of the Merchants' Bank," April 7, 1803.

5. See "Account with Louis Le Guen," June 6, 1802; "Description of Account with Louis Le Guen," June 8, 1802.

6. Letter not found.

From Archibald Gracie [1]

[New York, March 23, 1804]

Dear Sir

I enclose a newspaper in which you will find a Copy of the Bill before the Legislature for restraining unincorporated Institutions from Banking.[2]

It has occured to me & several Gentlemen with whom I have conversed upon the subject of this bill that it goes much farther than probably the Committee intended it should, and if pass'd into a Law, will prevent Individuals or Partnerships receiving deposits of Goods or money, or discounting at legal Interest or Bank discount, business notes which may be offer'd to them, which will certainly be a restriction unknown in this or any other commercial Country. Will you have the goodness to peruse the bill and favor me with your opinion whether or not it can be so construed.

I am with much respect   Dear sir   Yours truly
Arch: Gracie
New york 23rd March 1804

General Hamilton

ALS, Columbia University Libraries.
1. Gracie, a native of Scotland, emigrated to Virginia and then moved to New York City, where he was a prominent merchant and banker. He was a director of the New York branch of the Bank of the United States.

For an explanation of the contents of this letter, see "Articles of Association of the Merchants' Bank," April 7, 1803; Oliver Wolcott, Jr., to H, February, 1804.

2. "An Act to restrain unincorporated Banking Associations," March 15, 1804 (*New-York Evening Post*, March 20, 1804).

To Archibald Gracie [1]

[New York, March 23, 1804]

Dr. Sir

I have perused the Bill & am of opinion that the prohibition will extend only to Associations or Companies of which the *primary* and *essential purpose* or *end* is, to *issue notes make discounts* &c, in other words, to operate as a Bank, and not to Commercial companies which may incidentally transact such business. Yet there is some degree of Ambiguity on the subject and questions may arise. The Bill therefore may be considered in this view as dangerous to the Mercantile interest.

Dr Sir   Yrs. truly   A Hamilton

ADfS, Columbia University Libraries.
1. H wrote this draft at the bottom of the letter which Gracie had written to him on March 23, 1804.

To Charles Maurice de Talleyrand-Périgord [1]

[New York, March 25, 1804]

Sir

Presuming on the acquaintance, from which I derived so much pleasure during your stay in this Country, I am going to take a very great liberty. It concerns a near relation of mine, Mr. Alexander Hamilton,[2] now a prisoner of war on parol, at Paris.

His brother, from whom I have just received a letter [3] informs me, that being upon a visit to the Continent as a Traveller, he was overtaken by the war between France & G Britain, and has been since that time in the situation which I have mentioned. He is a Scotch Gentleman of Education and literary acquirement, who having amassed a pretty handsome fortune in the East Indies, had returned to his own country to devote himself to the pursuits of knowlege; and was induced to pass over to the Continent to indulge his curiosity, with a particular eye to the very interesting monuments of the arts of which Paris is now the Depository.

I will ask nothing specific for him because I know not what could with propriety be done; contenting myself with merely saying, that if your interposition can procure for him any facility, indulgence, or favour, it will confer a personal obligation on one, who has the honor to remain with great respect and regard

Your very obedt servt   A Hamilton

New York March 25. 1804

ADfS, Hamilton Papers, Library of Congress.

1. In September, 1792, Talleyrand fled from Paris to England. Expelled from England in the spring of 1794, he sailed for the United States, where he and H became friends. He remained in the United States until June, 1796. In 1797 he became the French Minister for Foreign Affairs.

For two reports on Talleyrand's admiration of H, see Hamilton, *Reminiscences*, 7 and note. For Talleyrand's recollection of a conversation he had with H on the probable direction of economic growth in the United States, see Talleyrand, *Memoires 1754–1807* (Paris: Librairie Plon, 1957), 232–33.

2. See Alexander Hamilton to H, August 4, 1797.

3. Robert Hamilton's letter has not been found. See H to William Hamilton, May 2, 1797.

From Jacob Rutsen Van Rensselaer [1]

[*March 25, 1804.* The calendar description of this letter reads: "presenting a pair of horses." *Letter not found.*]

Philip Hamilton's calendar of letters "taken by my brother Alexr Hamilton from the House of my sister E[liza] H Holly immediately after her death without any colour of right or authority," December 30, 1859 (AD, Hamilton Papers, Library of Congress).

1. Van Rensselaer, a resident of Claverack, New York, was a member of the New York Assembly in 1800 and clerk of Columbia County in 1801.

From James Wilkinson

New Orleans [Territory of Orleans]
March 26th. 1804

Mon cher General & ami

I have received your Testimonials in favor of Mr. Ellery [1] &
Mr. Alexander,[2] which flatter my pride & gratify my affections, because they bring me Evidence of your remembrance, & inform me
that you repose some confidence in the assurance, by which I am
bound to receive your Commands, & to Honor your recommendation.

The merited repute of this Interesting portal, to worlds known &
unexplored, is attracting to it men of all nations, ages, professions,
Characters & Complexions, and *women* too; The Market (permit me
the expression) will at first be overstocked in all *things*, but the increasing population & expanding improvements, of the boundless
Regions which must pay tribute here, will soon supply every defect
& give full exployment to all—in the mean time the young Gentlemen, whom you Honor with your good wishes, may find employ
in studying the Language, manners, Characters, & Interests of the
Country. I shall endeavour to secure to them the ablest patronage,
before I embark for the atlantic, which I calculate for the 15th
proximo.[3]

This Letter will be handed to you by Mr. W. Burling,[4] whose
sensibilities proved too acute for the Health of poor Cushon.[5] I hold
Him to be a man of strong Intellect, good Manners, & decisive worth,
and therefore I beg to name Him for your Civilities.

My best wishes & respectful attachment are for Mrs. Hamilton.

believe me ever your obliged & affectionate   Ja Wilkinson

General Hamilton

Mr. Burling will give you the details of this Country—which I
dare not enter upon.

confidential

Mr. Burling is among the warmest of your admirers. I would give a
Spanish Province for an Interview with you. My Topographical

information of the So. West is now compleat. The infernal designs of France are obvious to me, & the destinies of Spain are in the Hands of the U.S. Name me if you please with grateful & affectionate respect to Mr. G. Morris.[6]

ALS, Hamilton Papers, Library of Congress.
1. H's letter has not been found, but see Abraham Ellery to H, January 7, 1804.
2. H's letter has not been found. James Alexander was a lawyer. In 1806 Wilkinson arrested him at New Orleans as an agent of Aaron Burr.
3. On April 25, 1804, Wilkinson sailed for Washington on the ship *Louisiana* (Carter, *Territorial Papers*, IX, 234).
4. In the spring of 1802 William C. C. Claiborne appointed Walter Burling a justice of the Adams County Court in the Territory of Mississippi (Dunbar Rowland, ed., *Official Letter Books of W. C. C. Claiborne, 1801–1816* [Jackson, Mississippi, 1917], I, 141). During the Burr conspiracy, Burling became a military aide to Wilkinson.
5. Wilkinson used this pseudonym for Thomas H. Cushing, lieutenant colonel of the Second Infantry Regiment and adjutant and inspector of the Army (Royal O. Shreve, *The Finished Scoundrel: General James Wilkinson* [Indianapolis, 1933], 149).
6. Gouverneur Morris.

To Louis Le Guen

[*New York, April 10, 1804.* On July 12, 1804, Le Guen wrote to Hamilton: "Vous m'aves fait La remise Le 10. avril dernier." *Letter not found.*]

To Robert R. Livingston [1]

[New York, April 10, 1804]

Dear Sir

You were probably acquainted in this Country with Colonel Toussard [2] who will have the honor of delivering you this letter. He has filled several stations in our Military service at different periods and always with much credit to himself and advantage to the service. During our revolutionary war he lost an arm in an action in which he displayed much zeal and bravery, and to my knowlege was regarded by General Washington as a good officer and an estimable man. If after this it can be any title to him to say that he possesses in a high degree my esteem and friendship, it is a title which he may freely claim. Permit me to recommend him to your good offices.

Very respectfully & with great personal regard   I have the honor to be   Sir   Your obed ser   A Hamilton

New York April 10. 1804

Colonel Toussard is, as I understand, a citizen of the *U States.*

His Exy R R Livingston Esq

ALS, New-York Historical Society, New York City.
1. Livingston was United States Minister to the Republic of France.
2. Lewis Tousard.

To ——————[1]

New York, April 13, 1804.[2]

Dear Sir,

The post of to day brought me a letter from you,[3] and another from Mr. ——.[4] I have no doubt but the latter would serve you if he could; but he cannot at this time.

On the whole I would advise you to return to New-York, and accept any respectable employment in your way, 'till an opportunity of something better shall occur. 'Tis by patience and perseverance that we can expect to vanquish difficulties, and better an unpleasant condition.

Arraign not the dispensations of Providence—they must be founded in wisdom and goodness; and when they do not suit us, it must be because there is some fault in ourselves, which deserves chastisement, or because there is a kind intent to correct in us some vice or failing, of which, perhaps, we may not be conscious; or because the general plan requires that we should suffer partial ill.

In this situation it is our duty to cultivate resignation, and even humility, bearing in mind, in the language of the Poet, that it was *"Pride which lost the blest abodes."* [5]

With esteem and regard, &c.   A. Hamilton.

New-York Evening Post, October 30, 1804; copy, Hamilton Papers, Library of Congress.

1. This letter is preceded in the *New-York Evening Post* by the following statement: "In giving publicity to the following letter we perform an office, not less grateful to our own feelings, than honorable to the fame of him, whose loss we can never think of but with the deepest sorrow. It was inclosed to us, from an unknown hand, in a note thus happily expressed: 'The High and deserved veneration in which the character of the late illustrious Hamilton is held, by every admirer of worth and talents, has induced me to forward for insertion in your paper, the subjoined letter to a young friend. It will add another brilliant, and decisive evidence, to the many already adduced, of the religious sentiments of that great and most excellent man: and cannot, I think, fail of being acceptable to every admirer of his virtues.' "

2. In *HCLW*, X, 456, this letter is dated "April 12, 1804."

3. Letter not found.

4. Letter not found.

5. The exact quotation reads:
"In pride, in reas'ning pride, our error lies;
   All quit their sphere, and rush into the skies!
   Pride is still aiming at the bless'd abodes,
  Men would be angels, angels would be gods" (Alexander Pope, *Essay on Man. Epistles to a Friend* [London: Printed for J. Wilford, 1733–1734], Epistle 1, lines 123–27).

Receipt from John Laurance [1]

[April 16, 1804]

Recd april 16 1804 from A Hamilton Esqr Eighty Eight Dollars and Eighty Eight Cents two third parts of Mr Bogerts [2] Bill in the Chancery Cause for the Lands of Mark.

$$\frac{88}{88\ 100}\ Ds$$ John Laurance

ADS, Yale University Library.

1. This document is a receipt for John B. Church's and H's share of the complainant's costs in the Chancery suit of *Robert Gilchrist v Jacob Mark, John Laurance, and others*. For information concerning this suit, see "Mortgage by John Laurance, John B. Church, and Alexander Hamilton to Robert Gilchrist," August 21, 1802.

2. Cornelius I. Bogert, a New York City lawyer, was Gilchrist's solicitor and counsel.

Associates of the Jersey Company to Alexander Hamilton and Josiah Ogden Hoffman [1]

[*April 19, 1804.* "Sometime since Powles Hook was purchased for our mutual benefit from Mr. Van Vorst at a rent charge upon the whole of $6000 per annum forever.[2] We have agreed to lay it out into town lots and dispose of it to purchasers, receiving a rent charge upon each lot. We are desirous to give to each purchaser a good and sufficient deed of conveyance, and also to provide for the payment of the annuity to Mr. Van Vorst in such way as will appear best calculated to give security to the purchasers.[3] We enclose you a draft of the covenant [4] we propose to make with all the purchasers and to have it recorded in the office of the Clerk of the County of Bergen for their general benefit. An opinion is entertained by some persons that the proprietors of Powles Hook have no right to the ground under water below low water mark on their shore, some imagine that the Mayor, Aldermen and Commonalty of the City of New York have the right of property, and others contend that the State of New York has the right of jurisdiction to low water mark: [5] we submit the following queries to you and request your answer thereto: 1. Whether the Corporation of the City of New York have any right of property to the land under water opposite Powles Hook? 2. Admitting the State of New York has the right of jurisdiction to low water mark at the Jersey shore (which New Jersey will not admit), would wharves and docks into the water below low water mark thereby become subject to the jurisdiction of New York, or would it by accession belong to New Jersey?" *Letter not found.*]

Winfield, *Jersey City,* 39, 41–42.
    1. Although this letter is printed in two different parts and in two different places in Winfield, *Jersey City,* H and Ogden's response, dated May 3, 1804, indicates that it is actually one letter. It has not been possible to determine if the text of the letter printed above is complete.
    The Associates of the Jersey Company were Richard Varick, Jacob Radcliff, and Anthony Dey. Varick had been mayor of New York City from 1789 to 1801. Radcliff, a New York lawyer, represented Dutchess County in the New York Assembly from 1794 to 1795 and was a justice of the state Supreme Court

from 1798 until his resignation in February, 1804. Dey was a New Jersey lawyer.

Hoffman, who had been attorney general of New York from 1795 to 1802, was a New York lawyer.

2. The Associates purchased Powles Hook, New Jersey, from Cornelius Van Vorst of Bergen County on February 22, 1804 (Winfield, *Jersey City*, 23).

3. An article in *The* [Newark] *Centinel of Freedom* on March 13, 1804, described the proposed development of Powles Hook as follows: ". . . It is contemplated to level the place, and lay out a regular planned city. It will be divided into 1000 lots, valued at 100 dollars each, requiring of every original adventurer 6 per cent, which amounts to 6000 dollars, equal to the sum agreed to be paid to Mr. Van Vorst annually."

The proprietors first advertised the sale of lots, which was scheduled for May 15, 1804, in the *New-York Evening Post* on April 12, 1804. See also the *New-York Evening Post*, May 14, 1804.

4. For this covenant, dated April 12, 1804, see Winfield, *Jersey City*, 39.

5. For the rights claimed by New York City and the opinions of the city's lawyers, Richard Harison and Robert Troup, see *Minutes of the Common Council*, III, 520–23.

Associates of the Jersey Company to Alexander Hamilton and Josiah Ogden Hoffman [1]

[*April 20, 1804*. "Probably it will be wholly out of our power to induce Mr. Van Vorst, from whom we purchased, to accept to any other property instead of a mortgage of the premises to secure his annuity, and he will certainly not allow it to be extinguished by accepting any equivalent. We are therefore obliged to provide the best security to purchasers which the case will admit, and we are inclined to believe the deed and covenants we offer will be sufficient." *Letter not found.*]

Winfield, *Jersey City*, 39–40.
1. For background to this letter, see the Associates of the Jersey Company to H and Hoffman, April 19, 1804.

From William Jackson [1]

Philadelphia April 20th. 1804

My dear General,

Having been induced to undertake the publication of a daily gazette in this city,[2] I have not hesitated to number you among its

Patrons—and under this impression, I now presume to enclose to you a copy of the prospectus, and to request, as far as may consist with convenience, your aid in promoting the subscription in New-York.

The objects of the paper are generally detailed in the prospectus. To yourself I have no reserve in saying that it will be steadily directed to assist in restoring the tone of the Constitution, and the principles of General Washington's policy; to detect and expose the errors and incapacity of a weak and unworthy administration, and to remove the vail of hypocrisy, which the present Chief Magistrate has placed between himself and the public observation.

The Register will receive the decided support of the constitutional interest in this State; but, as it will be conducted on an extensive plan, it will require the best assistance which our friends in the other States can furnish.

In literary contribution it would flatter me exceedingly to receive the occasional support of your opinions.

I am, most sincerely,   My dear General,   Your faithful affectionate Servant   W Jackson

General Hamilton
New York

P.S When the list of Subscribers is completed to the number within your convenience, you will greatly oblige me by enclosing to me a copy of it with the places of residence, retaining the original to guard against any accident in the transmission

W. J.

ALS, Hamilton Papers, Library of Congress.

1. Jackson served as an aide to Major General Benjamin Lincoln during the American Revolution, and in 1781 he was named secretary to the French mission headed by John Laurens. H nominated Jackson to be secretary of the Constitutional Convention, and he was elected on May 25, 1787. Jackson became one of George Washington's secretaries, serving until his resignation in December, 1791. He subsequently formed a partnership with William Bingham and in 1795 married Elizabeth Willing, who was the daughter of Thomas Willing, president of the Bank of the United States. In 1796, Jackson was appointed surveyor and inspector of the revenue for Philadelphia. For Jackson's role in the "Reynolds Affair," see the introductory note to Oliver Wolcott, Jr., to H, July 3, 1797.

2. The first issue of *The* [Philadelphia] *Political and Commercial Register* was published on July 2, 1804.

Jacob Radcliff to Alexander Hamilton and Josiah Ogden Hoffman [1]

[*April 20, 1804.* "As to any right of property claimed by the corporation of this City to the land under water we have ourselves no doubt that it is wholly unfounded, and if you should be of the same opinion we wish it to be expressed. This will in the first instance depend on the Charter of this City. With respect to the claim of jurisdiction by this State we at present wish your opinion only on the proposition that it extends to low water mark on the Jersey Shore. It is thus far claimed by this State but resisted by New Jersey, and we are informed that on the water an interfering Jurisdiction has in fact been exercised in the few cases that have occurred. The question on the hypothesis we make is whether the increase of territory by wharfing or any extension of the western Bank of the Hudson would not of course belong to the Jurisdiction of New Jersey, whatever may be the present claim of this State upon the water? If it would belong to New Jersey, within the Jurisdiction of which of the States would vessels lying at wharves constructed there be deemed to be?" *Letter not found.*]

Winfield, *Jersey City,* 42–43.
1. For background to this letter, see the Associates of the Jersey Company to H and Hoffman, April 19, 20, 1804.

To Philip Jeremiah Schuyler [1]

[New York] April 20, 1804.

My Dear Sir:

I did not write to you on the subject of the awards, because I was in correspondence with Mr. Jacob Van Rensselaer [2] respecting the matter.

He has sent me the draughts of deeds which I shall in a few days inspect, and return with such suggestions as may be requisite.

The things most urgent are   1. The completion of the survey, which Mr. R. writes me is in train.   2. The appointment of a guardian for Mr. Kane's daughter[3] at Schenectady. On both objects, I have written particularly to Mr. J. Van Rensselaer.

I say nothing on politics, with the course of which I am too much disgusted to give myself any future concern about them.

HCLW, X, 457.

1. For background to this letter, see H to Jonas Platt, August 16, 1803. For a discussion of the dispute over the lands in Claverack, New York, see Goebel, *Law Practice*, forthcoming volumes.

On July 1, 1799, Philip and Catherine Schuyler executed a power of attorney appointing their son, Philip Jeremiah Schuyler, as their agent in the management of Catherine Schuyler's Claverack lands (DS, MS Division, New York Public Library).

2. H's correspondence with Jacob Rutsen Van Rensselaer has not been found.

3. Alida Van Rensselaer Kane. Her father, Elisha Kane, was the son-in-law of Robert Van Rensselaer, who was Catherine Schuyler's brother.

To Charles Wilkes [1]

[*Grange, New York, April 26, 1804.* "I would not pronounce against the power of the Directors to go into the operation you mention;[2] but I think it liable to so much question as hardly to be advisable without the sanction of the stock holders at a general meeting. I should perceive no difficulty in their giving a gross sum out of their profits for the renewal or extention of their charter. The difference in the two cases is that the former operation affects the basis of the institution. The association of the stock holders is predicated upon a given capital."[3] *Letter not found.*]

1. ALS, sold by Kenneth W. Rendell, Inc., Catalogue 64, Item 71. Wilkes was cashier of the Bank of New York.

2. The minutes of the board of directors of the Bank of New York do not contain any reference to the subject discussed in this letter (MS Minutes of the Board of Directors, Bank of New York, New York City). Although it cannot be stated with certainty, it seems likely that this letter concerns the repeated efforts of the bank to have certain limitations removed from its charter. See Henry W. Domett, *A History of the Bank of New York, 1784–1884* (New York, 1884), 60, 61, 62.

3. Text taken from the dealer's catalogue.

From Vincent Gray

General Alexr. Hamilton   [Havana, April 28, 1804]
New York

Sir,

Baron Humboldt [1] Supreme counseller of Mines in the service of
His Prussian Majesty and Member of the Royal Academy of Science at Berlin, Travelling for the purpose of Advancing the progress
of Natural History, being on his return from South America and
New Spain, to the Dominions of his Prussian Majesty, by way of
the United States, I take leave to recommend him to your particular friendship and protection while he remains in your city; from a
belief that you will from his character and pursuits, be highly gratified by being personally acquainted with him.

I have the Honor to be,   Sir   Very respectfully   Your most ob.
Servt.   Vincent Gray

Havana 28th. April 1804

ALS, Hamilton Papers, Library of Congress.
   1. Baron Friedrich Wilhelm Heinrich Alexander von Humboldt was a naturalist and explorer. In 1799 he began an expedition of Central and South
America with Aimé Jacques Alexandre Bonpland, a French naturalist. During
his trip to the United States he met with Thomas Jefferson and members of
the cabinet.
   This letter was enclosed in Humboldt to H, June 27, 1804.

From Abraham Van Vechten [1]

[Albany, April 30, 1804]

Dear Sir,

In Consequence of a Letter from Mr. Jac. R. Van Rensselaer I
have been with the Chancellor [2] in order to have a guardian appointed for ⟨Mr.⟩ Kane's Daughter, but on acct. of Mr. Kanes absence nothing can be done. The Chancellor requires a Petition from
himself or an Atty in fact regularly constituted by him. He how-

ever suggests that as there are two Children[3] you may procure a petition including both & send it up, in which Case the Examination as to property may be here made at once. You can also send up a Certificate from a master of the Inspection of the Law & a bond in an adequate Sum. This done the Chancellor says he'll give every possible facility in the business.

Yours &c.   Ab Van Vechten

April 30. 1804.

ALS, Hamilton Papers, Library of Congress.
  1. For background to this letter, see H to Jonas Platt, August 16, 1803; H to Philip Jeremiah Schuyler, April 20, 1804. For a discussion of the dispute over the lands at Claverack, New York, see Goebel, *Law Practice*, forthcoming volumes.
  2. John Lansing, Jr.
  3. Alida Van Rensselaer Kane and John Kintzing Kane.

Jacob Radcliff to Alexander Hamilton and Josiah Ogden Hoffman[1]

New York, May 1st, 1804.

Gent'n,

It being deemed important to obtain an early opinion on some of the points submitted to you, the gent'n associated with me will thank you for an answer, at present to the questions stated on the enclosed paper. The other points concerning the claim of *property* or *Jurisdiction* of this state to the land under water require perhaps too much investigation to be immediately disposed of, and are therefore proposed to be deferred. At the same time if you have not definitively formed your opinions on the question of *Jurisdiction* as *first stated*, I wish you once more to think of it in that light. On the general question it may be useful to mention that I find by Smith's History of New Jersey, page 156–7, that the Duke of York, of the 14th March, 1682, made a new grant to the twenty-four proprietors of east Jersey, which is there mentioned in a note to be "more full and express than any that went before."[2] The grant itself is not given but it is stated to be published in A. Leaming, and

J. Spicer's grants, concesions &c.[3] These books I have not seen and do not know at present where to find them.

I also observe by Smith's History of New Jersey, page 211, &c., that in 1702 the proprietors of both East and West Jersey surrendered their pretensions to the Govt. of that Country to Queen Anne, and she thereupon appointed Lord Cornbury[4] Gov'r and instituted one regular Provincial Govt. over the whole but the extent or boundaries of the province are not defined. About this period too the laws of New Jersey as published in their present code appear to have commenced.[5]

I also take the liberty to refer you to Vatt. 6, 1 ch. 22s. 269,[6] as to the general rule where Countries are divided by navigable rivers, and to Harg. law tracts 22, 36,[7] as to the right of navigation which remains in the *Public* notwithstanding the grant of a river, &c., to a subject. If the position be correct that a *right of passage* to and from the adjoining territory remains in the public and cannot be granted by the Crown, will it not follow that every thing necessary to the full enjoyment of that right (as by wharfing, &c.,) equally remains? Is not this case the right of navigation in the public, the principal right to which all others must yield?

I have looked at the constitution of the United States and find nothing there that appears to me to deny the power of Congress to make Powles Hook a Port of Entry.

An additional question is stated within as to Dower respecting which I presume you will have no trouble. It is desired to be mentioned merely for the satisfaction of purchasers.

[E N C L O S U R E]

Questions submitted to Mr. Hamilton and Mr. Hoffman, in the foregoing letter:

1. Have the Corporation of New York any title to the land under the water of Hudson River opposite to and adjoining Powles Hook?

2. Have not Congress the power to make Powles Hook a Port of Entry?

3. Are the covenants contained in the draft submitted and marked No. 1 proper on the part of the proprietors and valid in law?

4. Will not Deeds according to the draft No. 2 be also proper and valid?

5. Will not the execution of the plan proposed by the covenants and Deeds above mentioned afford an adequate security to purchasers?

6. The proprietors holding their estate in the premises in joint tenancy, can their wives have any though they do not execute the Deeds?

Winfield, *Jersey City,* 43–44.
1. For background to this letter, see the Associates of the Jersey Company to H and Hoffman, April 19, 20, 1804; Jacob Radcliff to H and Hoffman, April 20, 1804.
2. Samuel Smith, *History of the Colony of Nova-Caesaria, or New Jersey* (Burlington, 1765).
3. Aaron Leaming and Jacob Spicer, *Grants, Concessions, and Original Constitutions of the Province of New Jersey (1664–1682)* (Philadelphia, 1752).
4. Edward Hyde, Lord Cornbury, was governor of New York from 1701 to 1708 and governor of New Jersey from 1702 to 1708.
5. Samuel Allinson, ed., *Acts of the General Assembly of the Province of New Jersey, 1702–1776* (Burlington, 1776).
6. Emeric de Vattel, *Law of Nations, or Principles of the Law of Nature: Applied to the Conduct and Affairs of Nations and Sovereigns* (London, 1759–1760).
7. Francis Hargrave, ed., *Collectania Juridica consisting of Tracts Relative to the Law and Constitution of England.* 2 vols. (London, 1791–1792).

From Louis Le Guen

[*Morrisville, Pennsylvania, May 2, 1804.* On July 12, 1804, Le Guen wrote to Hamilton: "J'ai hier recu Votre Lettre du 6. mai . . . La quelle m'accuse reception de la Mienne du 2." *Letter not found.*]

Alexander Hamilton and Josiah Ogden Hoffman to Richard Varick, Jacob Radcliff, and Anthony Dey [1]

New York, May 3, 1804.

Gentlemen:

Having attentively considered the subject of your letter of the 19th April last, and the questions submitted to us, we shall now communicate the result of our reflections on the several questions in the order they are stated.

Question 1. Have the Corporation of New York any title to the land under the water of Hudson's River opposite to and adjoining Powles Hook?

Answer.

Comparing the provisions in the different parts of the Charter of New York, with each other, we are of opinion that the Corporation of this City have no right of Soil in or title to the land, under the water to and adjoining Powles Hook.

2. Are not the covenants contained in the drafts submitted and marked No. 1, proper on the part of the proprietors and valid in law?

3. Will not deeds according to the draft No. 2 be also proper and valid?

Answer.

We judge it proper to answer these questions together as the proposed draft of a deed No. 1, and considering them in connection with our opinion, they are proper and valid in law.

4. Will not the execution of the plan, proposed by the agreement and Deed above mentioned, afford an adequate security to purchasers?

Answer.

Confiding in the faithful executions of the plan, proposed by the proprietors, we think there will result an adequate security to purchasers. We are Gentlemen,

Yr. Obt. Svts.   A. Hamilton,
                                                Jos. Ogden Hoffman.

Richard Varick,
Jacob Radcliff,
Anthony Dey.

Winfield, *Jersey City*, 44–45.
    1. For background to this letter, see the Associates of the Jersey Company

to H and Hoffman, April 19, 20, 1804; Radcliff to H and Hoffman, April 20, May 1, 1804.

To Louis Le Guen

[*New York, May 6, 1804.* On July 12, 1804, Le Guen wrote to Hamilton: "J'ai hier recu Votre Lettre du 6. mai." *Letter not found.*]

To Elizabeth Hamilton [1]

[New York, May 7–11, 1804] [2]

My Dear Eliza

On Sunday Bonaparte & wife [3] with the Judges will dine with you. We shall be 16 in number if Morris [4] will come. Send him the enclosed note [5] on horseback, this Evening, that James [6] may bring me an answer in the morning. He is promised the little horse to return.

If not prevented by the cleaning of your house I hope the pleasure of seeing you tomorrow.

Let the waggon as well as the Coachee come in on Saturday. I mention this now, lest you should not come to Town yourself. I have particular reasons for this request.

It is my intention to get out *Gentis* [7] & perhaps Contoix.[8]

Yrs. Affecty   A H

ALS, Hamilton Papers, Library of Congress.

1. When H wrote this letter, he was at 54 Cedar Street, his rented house in New York City, while Elizabeth Hamilton was at the Grange in upper Manhattan.

2. For the dating of this letter, see H to Victor Marie Du Pont de Nemours, May 12, 1804.

3. Jérôme Bonaparte was Napoleon's youngest brother. On Christmas Eve, 1803, when he was nineteen and was visiting Baltimore, he married Elizabeth Patterson of that city. In 1805 he returned to France, where Napoleon had their marriage annulled. He subsequently married Princess Catherine of Württemberg and was made king of Westphalia by Napoleon.

4. On May 13, 1804, Gouverneur Morris entered the following in his diary: "Dine at Genl. Hamiltons with the Bonaparte Party" (AD, Gouverneur Morris Papers, Library of Congress).

5. Letter not found.

6. H's son was sixteen years old.

7. Genti was a cook. See H to Aaron Ogden, May 19, 1800.

8. Contoix worked for H's family on other occasions. See Angelica Church to her son, Philip, June 14, 1804 (ALS, New-York Historical Society, New York City).

To Gouverneur Morris

[*New York, May 7–11, 1804.* On May 7–11, 1804, H wrote to Elizabeth Hamilton: ". . . if Morris will come. Send him the enclosed note." *Letter not found.*]

To Victor Marie Du Pont de Nemours [1]

New York May 12. 1804

Dr. Sir

I now send you my bond with condition for the payment of One thousand & Twenty seven Dollars & seventy Eight Cents; which sum is thus composed—

Ballance of principal and interest beyond my notes	Ds. 60.23
Difference between simple & compound Interest	967.55
	Ds 1027.78

The statement delivered to you some time since will explain this result. The Bond bears interest only from the first of August next, because the calculation of interest has already been extended to that term.

The payment of principal is deferred to a remote period; but I trust it will be in my power to anticipate that period. The allowance of compound interest being as you know a matter intirely volu[n]tary and not usual, I have supposed that I might without impropriety consult my convenience as to the time of payment.

The multiplicity of my affairs will excuse my delay in completing this business.

With great regard   Your Obedient serv   A Hamilton

P. S. I sent you some days since a note [2] requesting you to meet Mr. Bonaparte at my house on Sunday three oClock to dine.[3] I hope to have the pleasure of seeing you.

V D P. Esq

ALS, Mr. Henry Francis du Pont, Winterthur, **Delaware.**
 1. For background to this letter, see H to Du Pont, January 30, 1804.
 2. Letter not found.
 3. See H to Elizabeth Hamilton, May 7–11, 1804.

From Samuel Jones [1]

[*New York*] *May 21, 1804.* Asks Hamilton to answer questions concerning David Lydig's "rights to the Bronx River, and how far those rights are affected by the Lease to Doctor J. Brown. . . ." [2]

ALS, anonymous donor; LS, New York State Library, Albany.
 1. Jones, who lived in Oyster Bay, New York, was comptroller of New York State from 1797 to 1800. He had been a member of the Continental Congress, the New York Ratifying Convention, and the New York Assembly from 1786 to 1790. From 1791 to 1797 he was a member of the New York Senate from the Southern District.
 2. For the rights of Lydig and Joseph Browne to use the waters of the Bronx River, see H's Law Register, 1795–1804 (D, partially in H's handwriting, New York Law Institute, New York City), in Goebel, *Law Practice,* forthcoming volumes. See also the introductory note to Philip Schuyler to H, January 31, 1799.

From Abraham Du Buc de Marentille [1]

Elizabeth town [New Jersey] Ce. 23. mai. 1804.

Mousieur,

Si, comme je l'espère, vous avez trouvé mon manuscrit, Je vous Serai obligé de vouloir bien le remettre à la personne qui vous délivrera cette lettre Sous mon couvert.[2]

J'ai l'honneur d'être avec les Sentimens les plus distingués, Monsieur, Votre très humble et très obeissant serviteur

Du Buc de Marentille

ALS, Hamilton Papers, Library of Congress.

1. Du Buc de Marentille had served in the French army during the reign of
Louis XVI. He owned property in the West Indies, and after the outbreak of
the French Revolution, he emigrated to the United States, where he settled
in Elizabethtown, New Jersey (Jonathan Williams to Timothy Pickering,
December 6, 1807 [ALS, Massachusetts Historical Society, Boston]; Aaron
Ogden to Henry Dearborn, July 23, 1807 [copy, Massachusetts Historical Society, Boston]).

2. At the bottom of this letter H wrote a receipt for the manuscript, dated
May 24, 1804, which is signed "Delagroüe ⟨----⟩."

From Theodore Sedgwick

[*Stockbridge, Massachusetts, May 24, 1804.* On July 10, 1804,
Hamilton wrote to Sedgwick: "I have received two letters from
you . . . that of the latest date being the 24 of May." *Letter not
found.*]

[Draft of "An Act to incorporate 'the Associates of the Jersey Company' "] [1]

[May–June, 1804]

1. Although William H. Richardson, *Jersey City: A Study of Its Beginning,
Its Growth, and Its Destiny* (Jersey City, New Jersey, 1927), 26, and Winfield,
Jersey City, 59, attribute the draft of the bill of this act to H, no evidence has
been found that H wrote it.

For the text of the act, see *New Jersey Laws,* 29th Sess., Ch. CXXXIV (November 10, 1804).

From John Johnston

June 1, 1804. "You may recollect that previous to Mr Caines marriage with my sister Mrs Verplanck,[1] I applied to you and Mr Charles
Wilkes [2] to become trustees together with Mr Keese [3] in a marriage
settlement. . . . I am induced to request you to take such steps as
you may think necessary to secure the property vested in you by
the settlement." [4]

ALS, Hamilton Papers, Library of Congress.

1. George Caines, who had been a lawyer in Bermuda before he came to New York City, where he also practiced law, was the author of *Lex Mercatoria Americana* (New York, 1802). On May 27, 1802, he married Cornelia Johnston Verplanck, widow of Gulian Verplanck, who had been president of the Bank of New York from 1791 to 1799 (*New-York Evening Post*, June 7, 1802).

2. Wilkes was cashier of the Bank of New York.

3. John Keese was a New York City notary.

4. Gulian Verplanck died in 1799, and in his will left all his real and personal estate to his wife for life and after her death to his children. The executors, one of whom was Johnston, and Cornelia Verplanck, who was the executrix, in accordance with the authority under the will sold parts of the real estate and accepted bonds and mortgages as security for the purchase money. When Caines married Cornelia Verplanck, he came into possession or controlled some of the money in question, and he refused to give any account of such funds to Verplanck's children, who were the eventual heirs. In 1814 the heirs in a bill in Chancery asked for an account of the principal and interest which had been received and requested that "all the said bonds and mortgages . . . be assigned to *John Johnston,* with power to receive the moneys, and to pay the interest thereon, annually, to the defendants, during the life of the wife, or that some other fit person be appointed *receiver* of the moneys, &c." The defendants "*demurred* to so much of the bill as sought a discovery of the sums received by the defendants for interest, and to that part which prayed for the appointment of a receiver, &c." The chancellor ruled that the "defendants are not bound to account for, or, perhaps, to disclose the amount of interest which has been received by them," for the "interest belongs exclusively to the defendants. . . . But . . . they are accountable" for the principal due on the sales of the real estate. The chancellor, however, ruled against the demurrer by the defendants (William Johnson, *Reports of Cases Adjudged in the Count of Chancery of New-York* [Philadelphia, 1836], I, 57–59).

The Duel Between Aaron Burr and Alexander Hamilton

[June 18–October 23, 1804]

Introductory Note

The document printed below contains the first mention in this volume of the events relating to the duel between Alexander Hamilton and Aaron Burr. Each aspect of the encounter, undoubtedly the most famous duel in American history, intrigued contemporaries of every political persuasion and has fascinated generations of historians.

Both before and after Hamilton's death, dueling, which was at least as old as the age of chivalry, was probably the most publicized method for settling questions of "honor" among some individuals in certain classes and in certain areas of the United States. On the other hand, its popularity should not be exaggerated, for even in Hamilton's day, it was the exceptional rather than the common response to real or imagined wrongs, and it was condemned by many of Hamilton's most prominent contemporaries.[1]

On four different occasions before his encounter with Aaron Burr in 1804 Hamilton was involved in duels as either a second or challenger.[2] He first appeared on the field of honor on December 23, 1778, when he served as a second to Lieutenant Colonel John Laurens in Laurens's duel with Major General Charles Lee. Laurens charged that Lee had cast aspersions on the character of George Washington. After Laurens had wounded Lee, Hamilton and Major Evan Edwards, a member of the Eleventh Pennsylvania Regiment who was Lee's second, stopped the duel.[3] The following year Hamilton challenged Dr. William Gordon, a Congregational clergyman in Jamaica Plains, Massachusetts, on the ground that Gordon had made insulting remarks about Hamilton's political views to Francis Dana, a Massachusetts congressman. The duel was never fought because Gordon refused to accept the challenge.[4] Hamilton issued no further challenges until July, 1795, when he interposed in an altercation between Commodore James Nicholson and Josiah Ogden Hoffman. When Nicholson accused Hamilton of being an "Abettor of

1. See, for example, the statements by Charles Cotesworth Pinckney and others in Lorenzo Sabine, *Notes on Duels and Dueling, Alphabetically Arranged with a Preliminary Historical Essay* (Boston, 1855), 322–26.

2. It should be kept in mind, however, that H's interest in dueling has frequently been exaggerated. An example of such exaggeration is the following apochryphal story which was printed under the heading, "Anecdote of Gen. Hamilton," in the [Philadelphia] *Gazette of the United States & Daily Advertiser,* June 28, 1800: "When a youth of seventeen he was Chief Clerk to an eminent merchant of St. Eustatia, who being absent, the business of the Compting Room, of course, devolved on young Hamilton. He had handed to him a letter, directed to his master, which, supposing it related to mercantile concerns, he opened; but his surprize was great when he found that it contained a *Challenge* to his master, whose proxy he was. The young hero answered the Challenge in the name of his master and the time and place was mentioned in the reply. Hamilton appeared to the antagonist of his master on the field; and, to use his own words, 'did his *business* in his absence,' and would not agree to any compromise, except on the express condition that the *Challenger* should acknowledge, in writing, that he had received suitable satisfaction from Mr. ——, that he was a gentleman of honour, &c. and further, that he (Hamilton) should never be known in the business—which terms the Challenger was obliged to accede to, or fight young Hamilton; he chose the former, and the parties separated. In a few months, however, it came to his master's ear, who was so struck with the magnanimity of such conduct, that he gave him liberty to come to the Continent, choose what profession he pleased, and draw on him to any amount! Perhaps to this anecdote, we are indebted for the services and abilities of a man who has not his superior, as a Soldier, a Financier, and a Statesman."

3. See "Account of a Duel between Major General Charles Lee and Lieutenant Colonel John Laurens," December 24, 1778.

4. See H to John Brooks, August 6, September 10, 1779; Brooks to H, July 4, August 8, 1779; H to David Henley, July 12, 1779; Henley to H, September 1, 22, 1779; H to Francis Dana, July 11, August 10, 1779; Dana to H, July 25, August 25, 1779; H to William Gordon, August 10, September 5, December 10, 1779; Gordon to H, August 25, September 23, November 15, 1779; H to George Washington, May 2, 1780; Washington to H, May 2, 1780.

Tories," who had declined an interview on an earlier occasion, Hamilton challenged him to a duel. The dispute, however, was settled without an encounter.[5] Hamilton issued his next challenge following the publicity concerning his relationship with Maria Reynolds. In the summer of 1797 James Thomson Callender published his accusation that Hamilton, as Secretary of the Treasury, had engaged in improper speculations with James Reynolds. Hamilton asked James Monroe, to whom he had explained his relationship with Maria and James Reynolds as early as 1792, to affirm unequivocally his belief in Hamilton's version of the "Reynolds Affair." When Monroe refused, Hamilton replied with an equivocal challenge to a duel. Monroe remained adamant and selected Burr as his second. Although the duel was averted, no evidence has been found concerning the settlement of the dispute.[6]

In addition to these four episodes, Hamilton was personally affected by two other duels in which members of his family were participants. In September, 1799, Burr challenged John B. Church, Elizabeth Hamilton's brother-in-law, on the ground that Church had stated that Burr had accepted a bribe from the Holland Land Company. After the first shots had missed, Church apologized.[7] In horrifying contrast to this bloodless encounter was the death of Philip Hamilton, Hamilton's eldest child, in a duel with Captain George I. Eacker in 1801.[8] Few, if any, other events had an emotional impact on Hamilton equal to that of his son's violent death, but needless to say, this tragedy did not lead him to the conclusion that he should refuse Burr's challenge.

In an age in which everyone is either his own or somebody else's psychiatrist, it may be plausible to conclude that Hamilton, having risen from insular obscurity and bastardy to the upper reaches of society in Federal America, was more likely than other more socially secure individuals to abide by the code duello. This may well have been the case, but it should not obscure a curious feature of his apparent addiction to dueling. Until his meeting with Burr, none of the disputes in which Hamilton was a principal ever reached the stage where he exchanged shots with his opponent. Under the circumstances, one might even conclude that until the summer of 1804 he was obsessed with dueling in the abstract, but not with duels in fact.

But the fact remains that Hamilton did fight a duel with Burr, and this fact, as well as the outcome, necessitates a brief review of the long and somewhat unusual relationship between the two men before their final meeting at Weehawken. Although they became political opponents in the years following the Constitutional Convention, their early careers reveal striking similarities. Both received at least part of their education in New Jersey, served in the Army during the American Revolution,

5. See H to James Nicholson, two letters of July 20, July 22, 1795; Nicholson to H, July 20, 21, two letters of July 22, 1795; "Drafts of Apology Required of James Nicholson," July 25–26, 1795.
6. See the introductory note to Oliver Wolcott, Jr., to H, July 3, 1797.
7. See Samuel H. Wandell and Meade Minnigerode, *Aaron Burr* (New York and London, 1927), I, 180–81.
8. See Benjamin Rush to H, November 28, 1801, note 1.

and practiced law in New York City after the war. As lawyers, they were two of the most respected members of the New York bar, and, as in the cases of Levi Weeks and Louis Le Guen, they sometimes represented the same client.[9]

In politics their differences can be traced back to the New York gubernatorial election of 1789. Burr agreed to support Robert Yates, who was Hamilton's candidate, over George Clinton. When Clinton won, he decided to secure Burr's future loyalty by offering him the position of state attorney general, which Burr accepted.[10] Burr held this office until 1791, when a combination of the Livingston and Clinton factions elected him to the United States Senate upon the expiration of Philip Schuyler's term.[11]

During his term in the Senate, Burr clashed repeatedly with Hamilton on both state and national levels. In 1792, for example, some Federalists as well as a group of dissatisfied Republicans had hoped that Burr would run against Clinton for governor, but Hamilton and his supporters succeeded in nominating John Jay. The results of the Clinton-Jay election were disputed because of voting irregularities in three counties. In order to decide the election, the legislature asked New York's two senators, Burr and Rufus King, for legal opinions concerning the validity of the voting. The two senators disagreed, and the legislature accepted Burr's opinion. As a result, Clinton was reelected.[12] Later that same year, Republicans were unsuccessful in their efforts to replace Vice President John Adams with Burr, Clinton, or Thomas Jefferson.[13] Then, in 1794, Republicans became convinced that Hamilton had influenced Washington not to appoint Burr as Gouverneur Morris's successor as United States Minister to France.[14] Finally, in 1797, the New York legislature re-elected Schuyler to Burr's Senate seat.[15] Burr in turn was elected to the New York Assembly.[16]

Although Burr and Hamilton were political opponents, they continued

9. For the Weeks and Le Guen cases, see Goebel, *Law Practice*, I 693–774; II, 48–164. For examples of Burr and H appearing in the other cases as colleagues or opponents, see Goebel, *Law Practice*, I, 266, 478, 508, 510–11, 512, 514, 516; II, 524, 546, 572, 616, 646n, 647, 648, 754, 858, 916.

10. See "Appointment as Member of Committee of Correspondence," February 11, 1789; H to Pierre Van Cortlandt, February 16, 1789; H to the Supervisors of the City of Albany, February 18, 1789; "H. G. Letter IV," February 24, 1789; H to the Electors of the State of New York, April 1, 7, 1789; Morgan Lewis to H, June 24, 1789.

11. William Duer to H, January 19, 1791; Robert Troup to H, January 19, 1791; James Tillary to H, January, 1791.

12. Isaac Ledyard to H, February 17, 1792; Tillary to H, March 6, 1792; Troup to H, March 19, 1792; Philip Schuyler to H, May 9, 1792; H to John Adams, June 25, 1792.

13. H to Adams, August 16, September 9, 1792; Rufus King to H, September 17, 1792; H to Charles Cotesworth Pinckney, October 10, 1792; H to John Steele, October 15, 1792.

14. See "List of Names From Whence to Take a Minister for France," May 19, 1794.

15. See Schuyler to H, March 19, 1797.

16. See the introductory note to Schuyler to H, January 31, 1799.

to maintain, at least until 1800, those contacts required in the course of their professional and official lives. As has been mentioned, they saw each other more or less regularly as lawyers. They were both members of the Military Committee to prepare New York against attack during the war scare in the summer of 1798.[17] Hamilton, despite the fact that he was duped, also cooperated with Burr in a variety of ways to secure the establishment of the Manhattan Company in 1799.[18] According to the recollection of James Wilkinson, an admittedly unreliable witness, Hamilton in 1800 said of his relationship with Burr: ". . . we have always been opposed in politics but always on good terms, we sat out in the practice of the law at the same time, and took opposite political directions, Burr beckoned me to follow him, and I advised him to come with me; we could not agree, but I fancy he now begins to think he was wrong and I was right." [19]

It was not, however, quite that simple. They were outwardly polite to one another, and no evidence has been found to suggest that before 1800 Burr viewed Hamilton as other than a political opponent and a respected colleague at the bar. On the other hand, Hamilton looked with deep distrust, and even distaste, on Burr. In 1792, when Burr was being considered as a possible candidate for the Vice Presidency, Hamilton wrote privately that Burr was "unprincipaled, both as a public and private man," that "his integrity as an Individual is not unimpeached . . . , as a public man he is of the worst sort," and that "he is a man whose only political principle is, to *mount at all events* to the highest political honours of the Nation, and as much further as circumstances will carry him." [20]

During the final stages of the protracted process which culminated in Jefferson's election to the Presidency in 1801, Hamilton became even more outspoken in his opposition to Burr. By 1800 Burr's state organization was strong enough to achieve a Republican victory in the New York legislative elections and thus assure Jefferson of all New York's electoral votes.[21] When Hamilton, who supported Charles Cotesworth Pinckney, prepared, supposedly for private circulation, his *Letter . . . Concerning the Public Conduct and Character of John Adams*, it was Burr and his followers who obtained a copy and had excerpts published in the newspaper.[22] But Hamilton evened the score in the winter of 1800–1801. In an effort to win over those Federalists in the House who favored Burr over Jefferson, he wrote a series of letters in which his attacks on Burr were

---

17. See the introductory note to H to James McHenry, June 1, 1798.

18. See the introductory note to Schuyler to H, January 31, 1799.

19. Wilkinson, *Memoirs of My Own Times* (Philadelphia, 1816), I, 439. See also Wilkinson to H, August, 1799, note 3.

20. All these quotations are from Willard M. Wallace's introduction to Syrett and Cooke, *Interview in Weehawken*, 16–17. For the full texts of the letters from which the quotations have been taken, see H to ——, September 21, 26, 1792; H to Steele, October 15, 1792.

21. See H to Theodore Sedgwick, May 4, 1800, note 48.

22. See the introductory note to the "Letter from Alexander Hamilton, Concerning the Public Conduct and Character of John Adams, Esq. President of the United States," October 24, 1800.

both more numerous and vituperative than those he had made in 1792.[23]

The final political confrontation between Burr and Hamilton occurred during the New York gubernatorial election of 1804. Once again there was considerable Federalist sentiment for Burr, but Hamilton supported Republican John Lansing, Jr., who accepted and then declined the nomination. Hamilton then urged Federalists to vote for Lansing's replacement, Morgan Lewis.[24] Lewis defeated Burr, and it was apparently after this election that Hamilton made the alleged statement that led to the duel. On July 18, 1804, Burr wrote to his close friend Charles Biddle: "It is too well known that Genl. H. had long indulged himself in illiberal freedoms with my character. He had a peculiar talent of saying things improper and offensive in such a manner as could not well be taken hold of. On two different occasions however having reason to apprehend that he had gone so far as to afford me fair occasion for calling on him, he anticipated me by coming forward voluntarily and making apologies and concessions. From delicacy to him and from a sincere desire for peace, I have never mentioned these circumstances, always hoping that the generosity of my conduct would have some influence on his. In this I have been constantly deceived, and it became impossible that I could consistently with self-respect again forbear." [25]

Although the events leading to the duel are well known, and most of the relevant documents and letters have at one time or another been printed,[26] many mysteries surrounding the event have remained unresolved. For example, no one still knows just what Hamilton said that prompted Burr to challenge him. But there are many other questions to which the correspondence in this volume cannot—and does not purport to—provide definitive answers. Why did Hamilton appear to go out of his way to accept Burr's challenge when he could have simply stated that he did not recall having made the statement attributed to him? [27] Did he, indeed, have a death wish? And if the answer to that question is in the affirmative, why did he take such a peculiar—if not roundabout—way to fulfill it? What were Burr's motives for enlarging or expanding the original demands made on Hamilton? [28] Did Hamilton actually delay his fire? [29] Have the dueling pistols survived, and if so, which of the many

23. For a list of these letters, see H to Wolcott, December 16, 1800, note 1.

24. See "Speech at a Meeting of Federalists in Albany," February 10, 1804; H to Robert G. Harper, February 19, 1804; King to H, February 24, March 1, 1804; H to King, February 24, 1804.

25. Copy, Columbia University Libraries.

26. See especially [William Coleman] *A Collection of the Facts and Documents, Relative to the Death of Major-General Alexander Hamilton; with Comments: Together with the Various Orations, Sermons, and Eulogies, That Have Been Published or Written on His Life and Character* (New-York: Printed by Hopkins and Seymour, For I. Riley & Co. Booksellers, No. 1, City-Hotel, Broadway, 1804); Syrett and Cooke, *Interview in Weehawken.*

27. See H to Burr, June 20, 1804; "William P. Van Ness's Narrative of the Events of June 22, 1804."

28. See Burr to Van Ness, June 26, 1804; Van Ness to Nathaniel Pendleton, June 26, 1804; Pendleton to Van Ness, June 26, 1804; Van Ness to Pendleton, June 27, 1804.

29. See "Statement on Impending Duel with Aaron Burr," June 28–July 10, 1804; H to Elizabeth Hamilton, July 10, 1804; Benjamin Moore to William

pairs which iconographers and antiquarians have described were those actually used? [30] Finally, did Hamilton's pistol have a hair trigger which gave him an unfair advantage over Burr? [31] Those interested in such questions must for the most part look elsewhere for answers, for this volume presents only the written record of the events preceding, during, and following what the Reverend Eliphalet Nott called "MURDER—*deliberate, aggravated* MURDER." [32]

Coleman, July 12, 1804; "Nathaniel Pendleton's Amendments to the Joint Statement Made by William P. Van Ness and Him on the Duel between Alexander Hamilton and Aaron Burr," July 19, 1804.

30. It seems likely that the Hamilton-Burr duel pistols are now in the possession of the Chase Manhattan Bank, New York City. They had been owned by John B. Church and were probably used in his duel with Burr and in Philip Hamilton's duel with Eacker (Merrill Lindsay, "Pistols Shed Light on Famed Duel," *Smithsonian*, VI [November, 1976], 94–98). A second pair of pistols, which some have suggested were the weapons used at Weehawken in 1804, were stolen in 1976 from the Van Cortlandt Park Museum in New York City (*New York Times*, November 10, 1976), but no evidence has been found that these were the ones used by H and Burr. Finally, a third pair, stolen from the Grange some years ago, were not those fired in the duel, but they may have been the extra set required by the dueling code (Eric Sloane and Edward Anthony, *Mr. Daniels and the Grange* [New York, 1968], 105).

31. For the controversy concerning the hair-trigger controversy, see Lindsay, "Pistols Shed Light on Famed Duel," and Virginius Dabney, "The Mystery of the Hamilton-Burr Duel" (*New York*, 9 [March 29, 1976], 37–41).

32. Sabine, *Notes on Duels*, 334.

William P. Van Ness's Narrative of the Events of June 18, 1804 [1]

On the afternoon of the 17th June last I received a Note from Col: Burr requesting me to call on him the following morning which I did. Upon my arrival he observed that it had of late been frequently stated to him that Genl Hamilton had at different times and upon various occasions used language and expressed opinions highly injurious to his reputation—that he had for some time felt the necessity of calling on Genl Hamilton for some explanation of his conduct, but that the statements which had been made to him, did not appear sufficiently authentic to justify the measure. That a Newspaper had however very recently been put into his hands in which he perceived a letter signed Ch: D. Cooper [2] containing information, which he thought demanded immediate investigation. Urged by these circumstances and justified by the opinion of his friends, he said, that he had determined to write Genl Hamilton a Note upon the subject which he requested me to deliver. I assented to his request, and on my return to the City which was at 11 o clock the same morning, I delivered to Genl Hamilton the Note [3] which I received from Col: Burr for that purpose & of which the following is a Copy.

"Van Ness's Narrative," AD, New York State Historical Association, Cooperstown, New York; ADf, New York State Historical Association, Cooperstown, New York.

1. The excerpt printed above is part of Van Ness's complete narrative of the events and correspondence leading up to the duel.

Van Ness was a New York City lawyer and one of Aaron Burr's most loyal supporters. Burr chose Van Ness to act as his representative in the negotiations preceding the duel and to be his second in the duel.

Van Ness's narrative was printed with minor changes on July 17, 1804, in the [New York] *Morning Chronicle*, a Republican newspaper. In the newspaper the following statement preceded the narrative: "The gentleman who accompanied Col. Burr to the field in the late unfortunate contest, comes forward reluctantly with a statement on the subject, at a moment when any publication of the kind may expose his principal to judicial embarrassment, perhaps to very serious hazard.

"In the following narrative, he disclaims the most distant idea of injuring the memory of the deceased, for whom, while living, he entertained sentiments of high respect, and for whose melancholy exit he, as also his principal, feels particular regret. The task devolved on him by the duties of his situation shall be discharged with fidelity, but with every delicacy the circumstances of the case can claim."

2. The letter from Dr. Charles D. Cooper to Philip Schuyler, dated April 23, 1804, was printed in *The Albany Register*, April 24, 1804, and was enclosed in Burr to H, June 18, 1804.

Cooper was the son-in-law of John Tayler of Albany, who had been judge of Albany County.

3. Burr to H, June 18, 1804.

From Aaron Burr

Nyork 18 June 1804

Sir,

I send for your perusal a letter signed Ch. D. Cooper which, though apparently published some time ago, has but very recently come to my knowledge. Mr Van Ness who does me the favor to deliver this, will point out to you that Clause [1] of the letter to which I particularly request your attention.

ALS, New-York Historical Society, New York City; copy, in the handwriting of William P. Van Ness, New York State Historical Association, Cooperstown, New York; copy, Columbia University Libraries.

1. The clause to which Burr is referring reads: ". . . I could detail to you a still more despicable opinion which General HAMILTON has expressed of Mr. BURR."

You might perceive, Sir, the necessity of a prompt and unqualified acknowledgment or denial of the use of any expressions which could warrant the assertions of Dr Cooper.

I have the honor to be   Your Obt Svt   A. Burr

Genl. Hamilton

[E N C L O S U R E]

Charles D. Cooper to Philip Schuyler [2]

[Albany, April 23, 1804]

SIR,

The malignant attack which my character has sustained in an anonymous hand-bill, to which your letter of the 21st inst. directed to the chairman of the Federal electioneering committee of this city [3]

2. *The Albany Register*, April 24, 1804.

3. Schuyler's letter to Dr. Samuel Stringer, chairman of the Albany Federal Republican Committee, reads: "Having seen a letter subscribed with the name of Charles D. Cooper, dated on the 12th instant addressed to Andrew Brown, Esq. Bern, making sundry assertions relative to the part that General Hamilton, Mr. S. Van Rensselaer, Judge [James] Kent and others would act in the approaching election: I think it proper to mention, that while Chancellor [John] Lansing[, Jr.] was considered as the candidate, General Hamilton was in favour of supporting him; but that after the nomination of Chief Justice [Morgan] Lewis, he declared to me that he would not interfere. And I can further inform you, that Stephen Van Rensselaer, Esq. who has lately left this city for New-York, declared his decided opinion in favour of the election of Colonel Burr, and that he has uniformly declared that opinion since Mr. Lewis was first nominated. That in a late conversation with John Tayler, Esq. in whose house the above mentioned Charles D. Cooper resides, and whose near connexion he is, I observed to Judge Tayler, that I had been informed that it was reported that Mr. Van Rensselaer and myself were in favour of Judge Lewis, and that Judge Tayler answered, that he had never heard that such a report was circulated respecting Mr. Van Rensselaer or myself; but that on the contrary, Mr. Van Rensselaer had declared to him, that he should vote for Colonel Burr.

"I further declare, that on or about the 3d of April instant, Judge Kent declared to me, that in a late conversation with Judge Lewis, he informed the judge himself, that he was in favour of the election of Colonel Burr:—and Also that Judge Kent did, at a prior day, make a declaration to me in favour of Colonel Burr, in preference to Judge Lewis; and I have understood that he, Judge Kent, has been uniformly of this mind since the nomination of the Chief Justice."

For information concerning the New York gubernatorial election, see "Speech at a Meeting of Federalists in Albany," February 10, 1804; H to Robert G. Harper, February 19, 1804; Rufus King to H, February 24, March 1, 1804; H to King, February 24, 1804.

is annexed; and in which you contradict certain facts contained in a letter, said to have been written by me to ANDREW BROWN, Esq. of Bern, will be my apology for repelling the unfounded aspersions which have been thus dishonorably obtruded on the public. My letter to Mr. BROWN [4] was committed to the care of JOHAN J. DEITZ, Esq. of Bern; but to this gentleman, I hope, cannot be imputed the embezzling and breaking open of a letter, a crime which in England has met with the most ignominious punishment.

Admitting the letter published to be an exact transcript of the one intended for Mr. BROWN, and which, it seems, instead of being delivered according to promise, was EMBEZZLED and BROKEN OPEN; I aver, that the assertions therein contained are substantially true, and that I can prove them by the most unquestionable testimony. I assert that Gen. HAMILTON and Judge KENT [5] have declared, in substance, that they looked upon Mr. BURR to be a dangerous man, and one who ought not to be trusted with the reins of government. If, Sir, you attended a meeting of federalists, at the city tavern, where Gen. HAMILTON made a speech on the pending election,[6] I might appeal to you for the truth of so much of this assertion as relates to him. I have, however, other evidence to substantiate the fact. With respect to Judge KENT's declaration, I have only to refer to THEODORUS V. W. GRAHAM, Esq.[7] and Mr. JAMES KANE,[8] of this

4. Cooper's letter to Brown, dated April 12, 1804, reads: "You will receive some election papers, and some of them in the German language. I presume you will make use of them to the best advantage: have them dispersed and scattered as much as possible. The friends of Col. Burr are extremely active, and will require all our exertion to put them down. It is believed that most of the reflecting Federalists will vote for Lewis. Gen. *Hamilton*, the patroon's brother-in-law, it is said, has come out decidedly against Burr; indeed when *'he was here he spoke of him as a dangerous man, and who ought not to be trusted.'* Judge Kent also expressed the same sentiment. The patroon was quite indifferent about it when he went to New-York. It is thought when he sees Gen. Hamilton and his brother-in-law Mr. [John B.] Church (who Burr some time ago fought a duel with, and of course, must bear Burr much hatred) I say many feel persuaded that Mr. Renselaer will be decidedly opposed to Mr. Burr. If you think any of us can aid you in the election in your town let us know and we will give you what assistance is in our power; can you send me word what you think will be the result of the election in your town?

"Yours sincerely,   Charles D. Cooper

"Perhaps it will be of use to shew the part of this letter that relates to the Patroon, Hamilton and Church, to some of the patroons tenants. I leave it to your discretion. In haste." (*New-York Evening Post*, July 23, 1804.)

5. James Kent, a Federalist, was a judge of the New York Supreme Court.

6. See "Speech at a Meeting of Federalists in Albany," February 10, 1804.

7. Graham was an Albany lawyer.

8. Kane was an Albany merchant.

city, whose veracity, I trust, will not be impeached; but should the fact have escaped their recollection, I am not in want of other evidence, equally respectable, to support it. Mr. VAN RENSSELAER,[9] a few days before he left town for New-York, in a conversation with me, declared in substance what I communicated in the letter to Mr. BROWN, as coming from him; and I am perfectly willing to repose myself on his well-known candour for the truth of this declaration.

I asserted, in the letter which has been so disgracefully EMBEZZLED, and the BREAKING OPEN of which must be ranked with the lowest species of villainy, that many of the reflecting federalists would support Judge LEWIS. Will this be considered a rash assertion, when it is known, that two federal gentlemen, high in office in this city, have declared they would vote for him? Judge PENDLETON,[10] of New-York, made the same declaration in this city, under the impression, however, that no federal candidate was to be offered. OLIVER PHELPS,[11] when in this city, on his way to Canandaigua, stated, that Gen. HAMILTON, and about one hundred federalists in New-York, would not vote for Mr. BURR.

It is true, that Judge TAYLER intimated to me, the conversation Mr. VAN RENSSELAER had with him, to which you allude, but it was subsequent to my having written and dispatched the letter for Mr. BROWN.

I beg leave to remark, sir, that the anxiety you discovered, when his Honor the Chancellor was about to be nominated, induced me to believe, that you entertained a bad opinion of Mr. BURR, especially when taken in connection with General HAMILTON's harangue at the city tavern; and although I have never suggested that you would act on the one side or the other in this election—yet, presuming on the correctness of your mind, and the reputation you sustain of an upright and exemplary character, I could not suppose you would support a man whom I had reason to believe, you held in the lowest estimation.

It is sufficient for me, on this occasion, to substantiate what I have asserted. I have made it an invariable rule of my life, to be circum-

9. Stephen Van Rensselaer, the eighth patroon, had been married to Elizabeth Hamilton's sister, Margarita Schuyler Van Rensselaer, who died on March 14, 1801.

10. Nathaniel Pendleton.

11. Phelps, a large landowner in Ontario County, had been nominated for lieutenant governor on Burr's ticket.

spect in relating what I may have heard from others; and in this affair, I feel happy to think, that I have been unusually cautious—for
really sir, I could detail to you a still more despicable opinion which
General HAMILTON has expressed of Mr. BURR.

I cannot conclude, without paying some attention to your friend,
Dr. STRINGER; I have to regret that this gentleman, so renowned for
the Christian virtues, should have consented to dishonour your name,
by connecting your letter with an anonymous production, replete
with the vilest falsehood and the foulest calumny.

I am, Sir, with due respect,   Your humble servant,

CHARLES D. COOPER.

April 23, 1804.

William P. Van Ness's Narrative of the Events of June 18–21, 1804 [1]

Genl Hamilton read the Note of Mr Burr [2] and the printed letter of
Mr Cooper to which it refers, and remarked that they required some
consideration, and that in the course of the day he would send a
answer to my office. At ½ past 1 O clock Genl Hamilton called at
my house and said that a variety of engagements would demand his
attention during the whole of that day and the next—but that on
wednesday the 20th Inst: he would furnish me with such answer to
Col: Burr's letter as he should deem most suitable and compatible
with his feelings.

In the evening of wednesday the 20th while I was from home, the
following letter addressed to Col: Burr [3] was left at my house under
cover to me. On the morning of Thursday the 21st I delivered to
Col: Burr the above letter. . . .

"Van Ness's Narrative," AD, New York State Historical Association, Cooperstown, New York; ADf, New York State Historical Association, Cooperstown,
New York.

1. In the draft of his narrative Van Ness described these events as follows:
"1804 June 18, Delivered a copy of the letter on the other side written to
Genl Hamilton at 11 oclock A.M.

"Genl Hamilton upon examining the letter alluded to by Col. Burr, & signed
C. D. Cooper observed, that he did not think that the publication in question
authorised Col. Burr to call upon him in the way he had—that its language and

its references were so general and undefined that he did not perceive how he could with propriety return a specific answer to Col Burr's letter. That if Mr. Burr would refer to any *particular expressions* he would recognize or disavow them. I remarked that I did not think Mr Burr was prepared to point out any specific & exceptionable language that had been used by him Mr Hamilton—but that the publication of Mr Cooper evidently alluded to expressions made by Mr Hamilton derogatory to the character and reputation of Mr Burr—and that the laws of honor would justify Mr Burr in enquiring of any gentleman whether he had uttered expressions that imparted dishonor. Mr Hamilton said that he did not think my position correct, that he would examine the publication in question—and return me an answer in the course of the day.

"P.M. At half past one oclock Genl Hamilton called at my house in person, and said that a variety of engagements would demand his attention through this day and tomorrow, but that on wednesday he would return such answer to Mr Burr's letter as he should deem most suitable and compatible with his feelings. That he was sorry Mr Burr had adopted the present course, that it was a subject that required some deliberation, and that he wished to proceed with justifiable caution and circumspection.

"On Wednesday morning I saw Genl Hamilton in Court; He told me that I should be furnished with an answer to Col Burr's letter in the course of the afternoon. I assented very readily to the delay. I remained at home most of the afternoon, at 8 o clock I went out and during my absence the letter of which No. 2 [H to Burr, June 20, 1804] is a copy was left at my house.

"I delivered the same to Col Burr on the morning of thursday the 21. Instant."

2. Burr to H, June 18, 1804.
3. H to Burr, June 20, 1804.

To Aaron Burr

New York June 20. 1804

Sir

I have maturely reflected on the subject of your letter of the 18th instant; and the more I have reflected the more I have become convinced, that I could not, without manifest impropriety, make the avowal or disavowal which you seem to think necessary.

The clause pointed out by Mr. Van Ness is in these terms "I could detail to you a *still more despicable opinion,* which General Hamilton has expressed of Mr. Burr." To endeavour to discover the meaning of this declaration, I was obliged to seek in the antecedent part of the letter, for the opinion to which it referred, as having been already disclosed. I found it in these words "General Hamilton and Judge Kent have declared, *in substance,* that they looked upon Mr. Burr to be *a dangerous man,* and one *who ought not to be trusted with the reins of Government*". The language of Doctor Cooper plainly implies, that he considered this opinion of you, which he attributes to me, as a *despicable* one; but he affirms that I have expressed some other *still more despicable;* without however mentioning to whom, when, or where. 'Tis evident, that the phrase "still more dispicable" admits of infinite shades, from very light to very dark. How am I to judge of the degree intended? Or how shall I annex any precise idea to language so indefinite?

Between Gentlemen, *despicable* and *more despicable* are not worth the pains of a distinction. When therefore you do not interrogate me, as to the opinion which is specifically ascribed to me, I must conclude, that you view it as within the limits, to which the animadversions of political opponents, upon each other, may justifiably extend; and consequently as not warranting the idea of it, which Doctor Cooper appears to entertain. If so, what precise inference could you draw as a guide for your future conduct, were I to acknowlege, that I had expressed an opinion of you, *still more despicable*, than the one which is particularised? How could you be sure, that even this opinion had exceeded the bounds which you would yourself deem admissible between political opponents?

But I forbear further comment on the embarrassment to which the requisition you have made naturally leads. The occasion forbids a more ample illustration, though nothing would be more easy than to pursue it.

Repeating, that I cannot reconcile it with propriety to make the acknowlegement, or denial, you desire—I will add, that I deem it inadmissible, on principle, to consent to be interrogated as to the justness of the *inferences*, which may be drawn by *others*, from whatever I may have said of a political opponent in the course of a fifteen years competition. If there were no other objection to it, this is sufficient, that it would tend to expose my sincerity and delicacy to injurious imputations from every person, who may at any time have conceived the import of my expressions differently from what I may then have intended, or may afterwards recollect.

I stand ready to avow or disavow promptly and explicitly any precise or definite opinion, which I may be charged with having declared of any Gentleman. More than this cannot fitly be expected from me; and especially it cannot reasonably be expected, that I shall enter into an explanation upon a basis so vague as that which you have adopted. I trust, on more reflection, you will see the matter in the same light with me. If not, I can only regret the circumstance, and must abide the consequences.

The publication of Doctor Cooper was never seen by me 'till after the receipt of your letter.

I have the honor to be   Sir   Your obed. servt   A Hamilton

Aaron Burr Esqr

ALS, New York State Historical Association, Cooperstown, New York; ADf, New-York Historical Society, New York City; copy, in the handwriting of William P. Van Ness, New York State Historical Association, Cooperstown, New York.

William P. Van Ness's Narrative of the Events of June 21–22, 1804

On the morning of Thursday the 21st I delivered to Col: Burr the above letter [1] and in the evening was furnished with the following letter for Genl Hamilton which I delivered to him at 12 o clock on friday the 22d Inst, (Mr B's letter 21 June) of which No. 3 [2] is a copy.

"Van Ness's Narrative," AD, New York State Historical Association, Cooperstown, New York.
  1. H to Aaron Burr, June 20, 1804.
  2. Burr to H, June 21, 1804.

From Aaron Burr [1]

Nyork 21 June 1804

Sir

Your letter of the 20th. inst. has been this day received. Having Considered it attentively I regret to find in it nothing of that sincerity and delicacy which you profess to Value.

Political opposition can never absolve Gentlemen from the necessity of a rigid adherence to the laws of honor and the rules of decorum: I neither claim such priviledge nor indulge it in others.

The Common sense of Mankind affixes to the epithet adopted by Dr Cooper the idea of dishonor: it has been publicly applied to me under the Sanction of your name. The question is not whether he has understood the meaning of the word or has used it according to Syntax and with grammatical accuracy, but whether you have authorised this application either directly or by uttering expressions or opinions derogatory to my honor. The time "when" is in your own knowledge, but no way material to me, as the calumny has now first been disclosed so as to become the Subject of my Notice, and as the effect is present and palpable.

Your letter has furnished me with new reasons for requiring a definite reply.

I have the honor to be   sir   your obt st   A. Burr

Genl Hamilton

ALS, New-York Historical Society, New York City; ADfS, New York State Historical Association, Cooperstown, New York; Df, in the handwriting of William P. Van Ness, New York State Historical Association, Cooperstown, New York.

1. The draft in Van Ness's handwriting, which differs from the letter printed above, reads: "I have this day received your letter of the 20th: Political opposition can never absolve gentlemen from a rigid adherence to the laws of honor or the rules of decorum. I neither claim such privilege myself nor indulge it in others.

"You appear sensible that from the style of your conversations inferences injurious to my character may have been drawn. I also feel a conviction that they have. Ordinary attention to the transactions of Society and the language of the world would evince that opinions highly desreputable to me have been expressed by you. Justified by these circumstances and peculiarly urged by the formal declaration of Mr Cooper respect for my own character & the opinion of the public demand the enquiry I have made. I cannot conceive it incumbent on me to trace reports publicly and extensively delivered to their source. They exist and can only be contradicted by a direct application to you. They are either well or ill founded which you alone can know, and a refusal to disavow them is not only a confirmation of their truth but an adoption of the sentiments ascribed to you.

"If you have used language of a dubious import without intending to convey injurious impressions, it behoves you as a man 'of sincerity and delicacy,' by a general disavowal of such intention to correct the hasty opinions of others and remove imputations which have thus been improperly connected with my reputation.

"To the word: 'despicable' the common sense of mankind, unaided by either

Syntax or Grammar affixes the idea of *dishonor*, every shade of which demands investigation. The application of this term has been made under the sanction of your name. To ascertain how far it has been authorized by you is my object. Permit me therefore to solicit again your attention to the enquiry which I deemed before sufficiently intelligible, whether, you have indulged in the use of language derogatory to my honor as a gentleman or which in this same sense could warrant the expressions of Dr Cooper. To this I expect a definite reply, which must (lead) to an accomodation or to the only alternative which the circumstances of the case will justify."

William P. Van Ness's Narrative of the Events of June 22, 1804

General Hamilton perused it,[1] & said it was such a letter as he had hoped not to have received—that it contained several offensive expressions & seemed to close the door to all further reply—that he had hoped the answer he had returned to Col Burr's first letter would have given a different direction to the controversy—that he thought Mr Burr would have perceived that there was a difficulty in his making a more specific reply, & would have desired him to state what had fallen from him that might have given rise to the inference of Doctor Cooper. He would have done this frankly—& he believed it would not have been found to exceed the limits justifiable among political opponents. If Mr Burr should upon the suggestion of these ideas be disposed to give a different complexion to the discussion, he was willing to consider the last letter not delivered; but if that communication was not withdrawn he could make no reply and Mr Burr must pursue such course as he should deem most proper.

At the request of General Hamilton, I replied that I would detail these ideas to Col Burr; but added that if in his first letter he had introduced the idea (if it was a correct one) that he could recollect the use of no terms that would justify the construction made by Dr Cooper it would in my opinion have opened a door for accomodation. General Hamilton then repeated the same objections to this measure which were stated in substance in his first letter to Col Burr.

When I was about leaving him he observed that if I preferred it, he would commit his refusal to writing. I replied that if he had resolved not to answer Col. Burr's letter, that I could report that to him verbally, without giving him the trouble to writing it—when he again repeated his determination not to answer—and that Col: Burr must pursue such course as he should deem most proper.

In the afternoon of this day I reported to Col: Burr at his house out of town [2] the above answer and determination of General Hamilton. . . .

"Van Ness's Narrative," AD, New York State Historical Association, Cooperstown, New York; ADf, New York State Historical Association, Cooperstown, New York.
  1. Aaron Burr to H, June 21, 1804.
  2. Burr's house, Richmond Hill, was in Greenwich in lower Manhattan.

Nathaniel Pendleton's Narrative of the Events of June 22, 1804 [1]

On Saturday the 22d of June, General Hamilton, for the first time, called on Mr. P. and communicated to him the preceeding correspondence.[2] He informed him that in a conversation with Mr. V. N. at the time of receiving the last letter,[3] he told Mr. V. N. that he considered that letter as rude and offensive, and that it was not possible for him to give it any other answer than that Mr. Burr must take such steps as he might think proper. He said farther, that Mr. V. N. requested him to take time to deliberate, and then return an answer, when he might possibly entertain a different opinion, and that he would call on him to receive it. That his reply to Mr. V. N. was, that he did not perceive it possible for him to give any other answer than that he had mentioned, unless Mr. Burr would take back his last letter and write one which would admit of a different reply. He then gave Mr. P. the letter hereafter mentioned of the 22d of June, to be delivered to Mr. V. N. when he should call on Mr. P. for an answer, and went to his country house.[4]

The next day General Hamilton received, while there, the following letter.[5]

New-York Evening Post, July 16, 1804.
  1. On July 26, 1804, in a letter to William Bard, a New York City businessman, Pendleton explained why he became H's representative in the negotiations leading up to the duel between H and Aaron Burr and H's second when the duel took place. Pendleton wrote: ". . . altho I know I suffered a more keen

anguish from the agency I had in the causes that preceded it, yet I feel now that it was impossible for me to have declined, or even to have hesitated for a moment whether I would decline it. You know that besides the love, the admiration and respect I always had for the amiable qualities, the Sublime talents the generous spirit of that man, I was under particular obligations to him for particular acts of kindness, and of late also much more in the habits of confidence with him than any other man in New York" (ALS, Bard College, Annandale-on-Hudson, New York).

The excerpt printed above is part of Pendleton's complete narrative of the events and correspondence leading up to the duel, which was printed in the *New-York Evening Post* on July 16, 1804. In the newspaper the following statement preceded the narrative: "The shocking catastrophe which has recently occurred, terminating the life of ALEXANDER HAMILTON, and which has spread a gloom over our city that will not be speedily dissipated, demands that the circumstances which led to it, or were intimately connected with it, should not be concealed from the world. When they shall be truly and fairly disclosed, however some may question the soundness of his judgment on this occasion, all must be ready to do justice to the purity of his views, and the nobleness of his nature. It will only here be added, that the authenticity of the documents and the accuracy of the information which we have at last obtained, are beyond any question; and must put an end to all mistake or misrepresentation.

"The following is the correspondence that passed between General Hamilton, and Colonel Burr, together with an explanation of the conduct, motives and views of General Hamilton, written with his own hand the evening before the meeting took place and only to have been seen in the deplorable event that followed."

2. Burr to H, June 18, 21, 1804; H to Burr, June 20, 1804.
3. Burr to H, June 21, 1804.
4. The Grange, in upper Manhattan.
5. William P. Van Ness to H, June 23, 1804.

To Aaron Burr

New York June 22d. 1804

Sir

Your first letter,[1] in a style too peremptory, made a demand, in my opinion, unprecedented and unwarrantable. My answer,[2] pointing out the embarrassment, gave you an opportunity to take a less exceptionable course. You have not chosen to do it, but by your last letter,[3] received this day, containing expressions indecorous[4] and improper, you have increased the difficulties to explanation, intrinsically incident to the nature of your application.

If by a "definite reply" you mean the direct avowal or disavowal required in your first letter, I have no other answer to give than that which has already been given. If you mean any thing different admitting of greater latitude, it is requisite you should explain.[5]

I have the honor to be Sir Your obed servt. A Hamilton

Aaron Burr Esqr

ALS, New York State Historical Association, Cooperstown, New York; ADfS, New-York Historical Society, New York City.
1. Burr to H, June 18, 1804.
2. H to Burr, June 20, 1804.
3. Burr to H, June 21, 1804.
4. In the draft H first wrote and then crossed out the word "rude."
5. Instead of this paragraph, H first wrote in the draft and then crossed out: "I have no other reply to make than it remains for you to take such measures as shall appear to you expedient" and added the following note: "This clause and word indecorous substituted with the advice of Mr P——."

William P. Van Ness's Narrative of the Events of June 22–23, 1804 [1]

In the afternoon of this day I reported to Col: Burr at his house out of town the above answer [2] and determination of General Hamilton and promised to call on him again in the evening to learn his further wishes. I was detained in Town however this evening by some private business and did not call on Col: Burr untill the following morning Saturday the 23d Inst; I then received from him a letter for Genl Hamilton which is numbered 4,[3] but as will presently be explained never was delivered. The substance of it will be found in No 12.[4]

"Van Ness's Narrative," AD, New York State Historical Association, Cooperstown, New York; ADf, New York State Historical Association, Cooperstown, New York.
1. In the draft of his narrative, Van Ness gave the following account of these events: "In the afternoon of this day I reported to Col B at his house out of town the above conversation, and promised to call on him again in the evening for his further instructions. I was detained in town this evening by some private business, and did not call on Col: Burr according to appointment.
"On Saturday morning the 23d. I went out to his house, and received from him for Genl Hamilton, a letter of which No 4 [Burr to H, June 22, 1804] is a Copy with some instructions for a verbal communication of which No 5 ["Aaron Burr's Instructions to William P. Van Ness," June 22–23, 1804] is a copy."

2. See "William P. Van Ness's Narrative of the Events of June 22, 1804."
3. Burr to H, June 22, 1804.
4. Van Ness to Nathaniel Pendleton, June 27, 1804.

From Aaron Burr [1]

Nyork June 22d. 1804

Sir

Mr. V Ness has this evening reported to me Verbally that you refuse to answer my last letter,[2] that you consider the course I have taken as intemperate and unnecessary and some other conversation which it is improper that I should notice.

My request to you was in the first instance proposed in a form the most simple in order that you might give to the affair that course to which you might be induced by your temper and your knowledge of facts. I relied with unsuspecting faith that from the frankness of a Soldier and the Candor of a gentleman I might expect an ingenuous declaration; that if, as I had reason to believe, you had used expressions derogatory to my honor, you would have had the Spirit to Maintain or the Magnanimity to retract them, and, that if from your language injurious inferences had been improperly drawn, Sincerity and delicacy would have pointed out to you the propriety of correcting errors which might thus have been widely diffused.

With these impressions, I was greatly disappointed in receiving from you a letter [3] which I could only consider as evasive and which in manner, is not altogether decorus. In one expectation however, I was not wholly deceived, for at the close of your letter I find an intimation, that if I should dislike your refusal to acknowledge or deny the charge, you were ready to meet the consequences. This I deemed a sort of defiance, and I should have been justified if I had chosen to make it the basis of an immediate message: Yet, as you had also said something (though in my opinion unfounded) of the indefiniteness of my request; as I believed that your communication was the offspring, rather of false pride than of reflection, and, as I felt the utmost reluctance to proceed to extremities while any other hope remained, my request was repeated in terms more definite. To this you refuse all reply, reposing, as I am bound to presume on the tender of an alternative insinuated in your letter.

Thus, Sir, you have invited the course I am about to pursue, and now by your silence impose it upon me. If therefore your determinations are final, of which I am not permitted to doubt, Mr. Van Ness is authorised to communicate my further expectations either to yourself or to such friend as you may be pleased to indicate.

I have the honor to be   Your Ob st   A. Burr

ALS (photostat), Hamilton Papers, Library of Congress.

1. William P. Van Ness never delivered the letter printed above. On June 25, 1804, he visited H to deliver it, but H stated that he had written a reply to Burr's letter of June 21 and had given it to Nathaniel Pendleton to deliver to Van Ness. Van Ness thought that Burr should read H's reply before he delivered Burr's letter of June 22 to H. See "William P. Van Ness's Narrative of the Events of June 22–23, 1804," ". . . of June 23, 1804," ". . . of June 25, 1804."

In an undated memorandum Van Ness wrote: "After the second letter of A. B. Ham. expressed to V. N. a wish that A. B. would take back that letter which V. N. declined to report to A. B.

"Insert A. B's letter No. 4 verbatim. By the letter No. 4 is meant that letter which was not delivered, but which was *substantially* contained in the subsequent one of V. N. Relate the manner in which Ham. evaded the reception of that letter, being aware of it's import. How he met you and without salutation begged you not to deliver it.

"Relate minutely all the various propositions made by B. for accomodation; and insert particularly those circumstances which shew the evasion, hesitation and tergiversation of H." (AD, New-York Historical Society, New York City.)

2. Burr to H, June 21, 1804.
3. H to Burr, June 20, 1804.

Aaron Burr's Instructions to William P. Van Ness [1]

[New York, June 22–23, 1804]

⟨–⟩ of withdrawing the Letter.

Impossible unless in lieu of it I should send a Challenge
            vid. *the* Hypothesis
                the defiance

a. b. so uncommunicative that p. s. did not till now know his impressions of a H. letter, except by Conjecture.   No 7 [2]

    a. b. far from conceiving that rivalship authorises a latitude not otherwise justifiable, always feels greater delicacy in such cases & would think it meaness to speak of a rival but in terms of respect—to do justice to his merits—to be silent of his foibles. Such has invariably been his conduct toward Jay, adams, Hamn. the only three who can be supposed to have stood in that relation to him.

That he has too much reason to believe that in regard of Mr H. there has been no reciprocity—for several years his name has been lent to the support of base Slanders—He has never had the generosity the magnanimity or the Candor to contradict or disavow. B. forbears to particularize as it could only tend to produce new irritations; but having made great sacrifices for the Sake of harmony—having exercised forbearance till it approached to humiliation, he has seen no effect produced by such Conduct, but a repetition of injury & is obliged to conclude that there is on the part of Mr H. a setled & implacable malevolence, that he will never cease in his Conduct toward Mr B. to violate those courtesies of life & that hence he has no alternative but to announce these things to the world which consistently with Mr Bs ideas of propriety can be done in no way but that which he has adopted. He is incapable of revenge, still less is he capable of imitating the Conduct of Mr H. by committing secret depredations on his fame & character—but these things must have an end.

ADf, New-York Historical Society, New York City; [New York] *Morning Chronicle*, July 17, 1804.

1. In the draft of his narrative Van Ness wrote: "On Saturday morning the 23d. I went out to his house, and received from him for Genl Hamilton a letter of which No 4 [Burr to H, June 22, 1804] is a Copy with some instructions for a verbal communication" (ADf, New York State Historical Association, Cooperstown, New York). See also "William P. Van Ness's Narrative of the Events of June 25, 1804," note 1.

2. The remainder of this document appeared in the [New York] *Morning Chronicle*, July 17, 1804.

From William P. Van Ness

[*New York, June 23, 1804.* In describing the events of this day in his narrative,[1] Van Ness wrote: "I sent a Note to Genl Hamilton's Office and also to his house." *Notes not found.*]

1. "Van Ness's Narrative," AD, New York State Historical Association, Cooperstown, New York; ADf, New York State Historical Association, Cooperstown, New York.

William P. Van Ness's Narrative of the Events of June 23, 1804

When I returned with this letter [1] to the City which was about 2 o clock in the afternoon of the same day, I sent a Note to Genl Hamilton's Office and also to his house [2] desiring to know when it would be convenient for him to receive a communication. The Servant as he informed me received for answer at both places that Genl Hamilton had left the City and was gone to his Country residence. I then wrote a Note to Genl Hamilton of which No 5 [3] is a Copy & sent it out to him in the Country.

"Van Ness's Narrative," AD, New York State Historical Associaion, Cooperstown, New York; ADf, New York State Historical Association, Cooperstown, New York.

1. Aaron Burr to H, June 22, 1804.
2. Notes not found. H's office was at 12 Garden Street and his house in New York City was at 54 Cedar Street.
3. Van Ness to H, June 23, 1804.

From William P. Van Ness

[New York] June 23, 1804

Sir

In the afternoon of yesterday I reported to Col. Burr the result of my last interveiw with you, and appointed the evening to receive his further instructions. Some private engagements however prevented me from calling on him 'till this morning. On my return to the City I found upon enquiry both at your office and house, that you had returned to your residence in the Country. Least an interveiw there might be less agreeable to you than elsewhere, I have taken the liberty of addressing you this Note, to enquire when and where it will be most convenient to you to receive a communication.

Your most & very hum Sert   W: P: Van Ness

Genl Hamilton

ALS, New-York Historical Society, New York City; ADfS, New York State Historical Association, Cooperstown, New York.

Nathaniel Pendleton's Narrative of the Events of June 23, 1804

Mr. P—— understood from General Hamilton that he immediately answered,[1] that if the communication was pressing he would receive it at his Country House that day, if not, he would be at his house in town the next morning at nine o'clock. But he did not give Mr. P. any copy of this note.

New-York Evening Post, July 16, 1804.
   1. H to William P. Van Ness, June 23, 1804.

To William P. Van Ness

Grange [New York] June 23. 1804

Sir

I was in Town to day till half past one. I thank you for the delicacy which dictated your note to me.[1] If it is indispensable the communication should be made before Monday Morning, I must receive it here. But I should think this cannot be important. On monday by Nine I shall be in Town at my house in Cæder Street No 52,[2] where I should be glad to see you. An additional reason for preferring that is, that I am unwilling to occasion to you trouble.

   With esteem I am Sir   Your Obed ser   A H

Wm. P. Van Ness Esq

ALS, New York State Historical Association, Cooperstown, New York.
   1. Van Ness to H, June 23, 1804.
   2. H is mistaken, for his rented house in New York City in 1804 was at 54 Cedar Street. See Longworth's American Almanac, New-York Register, and City Director, for the Twenty-ninth Year of American Independence (New-York: Printed . . . by D. Longworth, 1804), 156; Receipt for the sub-lease of H's house from Labiche de Reigenefort, September 15, 1804 (ADS, Pendleton Papers, New-York Historical Society, New York City).

Nathaniel Pendleton's Narrative of the Events of June 23–25, 1804

This letter, although dated on the 23d June,[1] remained in Mr. P.'s possession until the 25th, within which period he had several conversations with Mr. V. N. In these conversations Mr. P. endeavored to illustrate and enforce the propriety of the ground which General Hamilton had taken. Mr. P. mentioned to Mr. V. N. as the result, that if Col. Burr would write a letter, requesting to know in substance whether in the conversation to which Dr. Cooper alluded, any particular instance of dishonorable conduct was imputed to Col. Burr, or whether there was any impeachment of his private character, G. Hamilton would declare to the best of his recollection what passed in that conversation; and Mr. P. read to Mr. V. N. a paper containing the substance of what Gen. H. would say on that subject, which is as follows. . . .[2]

New-York Evening Post, July 16, 1804.
   1. Pendleton is mistaken. H's letter to Aaron Burr is dated June 22, 1804.
   2. See "Nathaniel Pendleton's First Account of Alexander Hamilton's Conversation at John Tayler's House," June 25, 1804.

Nathaniel Pendleton's First Account of Alexander Hamilton's Conversation at John Tayler's House

[New York, June 25, 1804]

General Hamilton says he cannot imagine to what Doctr. Cooper may have alluded unless it were to a conversation at Mr. Taylors in Albany last winter, (at which Mr. Taylor he & General H—— were present).[1] Genl H—— cannot recollect distinctly the particulars of that conversation so as to undertake to repeat them, without runing the risk of varying or omitting what might be deemed important circumstances. The expressions are intirely forgotten, and the

Specific ideas imperfectly remembered; but to the best of his recollection it consisted of comments on the political principles and views of Col. Burr, and the results that might be expected from them in the event of his Election as Governor, without referrence to any particular instance of past conduct, or to private character.

AD, New-York Historical Society, New York City.
  1. See the enclosure to Aaron Burr to H, June 18, 1804.

William P. Van Ness's Narrative of the Events of June 25, 1804 [1]

At nine O clock on Monday the 25th Inst: I called on Genl Hamilton at his house in Cedar Street to present the letter No 4 [2] already alluded to, and with instructions for a verbal communication of which the following Notes No 7 [3] handed me by Mr Burr were to be the basis. The substance of which though in terms as much softened as my instructions would permit, was accordingly communicated to Genl Hamilton.

Before I delivered the written communication with which I was charged [4] Genl Hamilton said that he had prepared a written reply [5] to Col: Burr's letter of the 21st which he had left with Mr xxx [6] and wished me to receive. I answered that the communication I had to make to him was predicated upon the idea that he would make no reply to Mr Burrs letter of the 21st Inst: and that I had so understood him in our conversation of the 22d. Genl H said that he believed before I left him, he had offered to give a written reply. I observed that when he answered verbally he had offered to put that refusal in writing but that if he had now prepared a written reply I would receive it with pleasure. I accordingly called on Mr xxx on the same day Monday June 25 between 1 & 2 O clock P M—and stated to him the result of my recent interview with Genl Hamilton, and the reference he had made to him.

I then received from Mr xxx the letter No 8. . . .[7]

This letter was unsealed, but I did not read it in his presence. After some conversation relative to what Genl Hamilton would say on the subject of the present controversy, during which Mr xxx

read from a paper [8] his ideas on the subject, he left me for the purpose of seeing and consulting Mr Hamilton taking the paper with
him.

"Van Ness's Narrative," AD, New York State Historical Association, Cooperstown, New York; ADf, New York State Historical Association, Cooperstown,
New York.

1. In his draft of his narrative Van Ness wrote: "At nine Oclock on monday the 24 Inst: I called on Genl Hamilton at his House in Cedar Street to
deliver the letter No 4 [Burr to H, June 22, 1804], and make the remarks I
was instructed to do. When I entered he said before I delivered any communication he wished to state, that he had prepared a written reply [H to
Burr, June 22, 1804] to Mr Burr's last letter, which was in the hands of Mr Pendleton who would deliver it to me. I answered that the communication I had
to make to him was predicated upon the idea that he would make no reply to
Mr Burr's letter of the 21st Instant—And that I had so understood him in our
conversation of the 22d Inst: Genl. Hamilton said that he believed he had
offered to give a written reply which was however omitted, I said I recollected
when he answered verbally that he could not answer Mr Burr's letter that he
offered to put that in writing—and I concluded by observing that if he wished
to reply that I would receive it. In our conversation I repeated to him as
nearly as I could recollect the observations contained in No. 5 ["Aaron Burr's
Instructions to William P. Van Ness," June 22, 1804]. Genl Hamilton said that
he disclaimed every idea of personal enmity—that to be sure he had been a
uniform political opponent of Col. Burr, but in that opposition he had been
governed by public principles. Between 1 & 2 O clock on the same day Monday 25 June I called on Mr Pendleton and stated that after my interview with
Genl H. on friday, I had reported to Col B that Genl H. would make no reply
to his letter of the 21. that I then received from Col B. a communication for
Genl H, predicated upon that reply—that agreeable to appt I had seen Genl H.
at 9 o clock, & that he supposed I had somewhat misunderstood him, and
wished me to call on him Mr P. for a written reply which had been left with
him. I then received from Mr Pendleton the letter No 8, but first premised
that we were averse to continuing this correspondence any longer and that we
should only return a verbal answer whether it was satisfactory or not. It was
unsealed but I did not read it in his presence. After some little conversation
concerning what Genl: Hamilton would say upon the subject of the present
controversy, Mr Pendleton left me for the purpose of seeing and consulting
Mr Hamilton."
   2. Burr to H, June 22, 1804.
   3. See "Aaron Burr's Instructions to William P. Van Ness," June 22, 1804.
   4. Burr to H, June 22, 1804.
   5. H to Burr, June 22, 1804.
   6. Nathaniel Pendleton.
   7. H to Burr, June 22, 1804.
   8. See "Nathaniel Pendleton's First Account of Alexander Hamilton's Conversation at John Tayler's House," June 25, 1804.

Nathaniel Pendleton's Narrative of the Events of June 25, 1804

After the delivery of the Letter of the 22d,[1] as above mentioned: in another interview with Mr. V. N. he desired Mr. P. to give him *in writing* the substance of what he had proposed on the part of General Hamilton, which Mr. P. did in the words following.[2]

New-York Evening Post, July 16, 1804.
 1. H to Aaron Burr, June 22, 1804.
 2. See "Nathaniel Pendleton's Second Account of Alexander Hamilton's Conversation at John Tayler's House," June 25, 1804.

Nathaniel Pendleton's Second Account of Alexander Hamilton's Conversation at John Tayler's House

[New York, June 25, 1804]

In answer to a letter properly adapted to obtain from General Hamilton a declaration whether he had charged Colo Burr with any particular instance of dishonorable conduct, or had impeached his private character, either in the conversation alluded to by Doctr. Cooper, or any other particular instance to be specified.[1]

He would be able to answer consistantly with his Honor, and the truth, in substance That the conversation to which Doctr Cooper alluded turned wholly on political topics and did not attribute to Colo Burr, any instance of dishonorable conduct, nor relate to his private character; and in relation to any other language or conversation of General H, which Col B. will specify, a prompt and frank avowal or denial will be given.

AD, New-York Historical Society, New York City; AD, New York State Historical Association, Cooperstown, New York.
 1. For this proposed letter, which Aaron Burr never wrote, see "Nathaniel Pendleton's Narrative of the Events of June 23–25, 1804."

William P. Van Ness's Narrative of Later Events of June 25, 1804 [1]

In about an hour he [2] called at my house. I informed him, that I had shewn to Col Burr the letter [3] he had given me from Genl Hamilton that in his opinion it amounted to nothing more than the verbal reply I had already reported—that it left the business precisely w[h]ere it then was—that Mr Burr had very explicitly stated the injuries he had received, and the reparation he demanded, and that he did not think it proper to be asked now for further explanation. Toward the conclusion of our conversation I informed him that Col: Burr required a General disavowal of any intention on the part of Genl Hamilton in his various conversations to convey impressions derogatory to the honor of Mr Burr. Mr. Pxxx replied that he believed Genl Hamilton would have no objection to make such declaration and left me for the purpose of consulting him requesting me to call in the course of the afternoon for an answer. I called on him accordingly about 6. O clock. He then observed that Genl Hamilton declined making such a disavowal as I had stated in our last conversation, that he Mr xxx did not then perceive the whole force and extent of it—and presented me with the following paper No 9 [4] which I transmitted in the evening to Mr. Burr.

"Van Ness's Narrative," AD, New York State Historical Association, Cooperstown, New York; ADf, New York State Historical Association, Cooperstown, New York.

1. In the draft of his narrative Van Ness wrote: "At ½ past 2 oclock Mr Pendleton called at my house. I told him that I had perused the letter [H to Burr, June 22, 1804] which he had given me a short time before and shewn it also to Col: Burr—That it appeared to Col Burr to be nothing more than the verbal reply which I had already reported to him—That it left the business precisely w[h]ere it was then—That I did not think it proper or necessary to ask now for further explanation from us—That Mr Burr had very explicitly stated the injuries he had received and the satisfaction he required. He then presented me with a paper ["Nathaniel Pendleton's First Account of Alexander Hamilton's Conversation at John Tayler's House," June 25, 1804] to which I objected as being confined to a particular occasion, that we required a Genl disavowal of any intention on the part of Mr Hamilton in his various conversations to convey impressions derogatory to the honor of Mr Burr. Mr Pendleton replied that he believed Genl Hamilton would have no objection to say that much and left me for the purpose of consulting Genl. H—and wished me to call on him in the course of the afternoon for an answer."

2. Nathaniel Pendleton.
3. H to Burr, June 22, 1804.
4. See "Nathaniel Pendleton's Second Account of Alexander Hamilton's Conversation at John Tayler's House," June 25, 1804.

Aaron Burr to William P. Van Ness

[New York, June 25, 1804]

I am disappointed of my ride.

If xxx [1] should propose to charge you with any verbal message, you may reply, that being authorised for a particular purpose, you cannot so far exceed your power and assume upon your self as to present to your principal an overture for negociation on a new basis —that you consider the negociation in which you engaged, as concluded and that it would be highly improper in you to propose one anew as *his agent*—that if he should think proper to attempt any thing of the kind, it must be through some other channel.

If it should be asked whether there is no alternative, most certainly there is; but more will now be required than would have been asked at first.

These hints are only intended to attract your attention to the Various Shapes which the thing may assume so that you may be at all points prepared.

25 June

AL, New York State Historical Association, Cooperstown, New York.
1. Nathaniel Pendleton.

Disclaimer for Alexander Hamilton Prepared by William P. Van Ness [1]

[New York, June 25, 1804]

Being apprised that expressions are ascribed to me impeaching the honor and affecting the private reputation of Col. Burr, and perceiving that reports to this effect have been widely disseminated, I feel it due to my own honor, as also to that of a gentleman thus traduced under the sanction of my name, to remove such injurious impressions.

I therefore frankly and explicitly disclaim and disavow, the use of any expressions tending to impeach the honor of Col. Burr. My own sincerity and candor require this declaration; and, while I regret that my expressions have been misrepresented or misconstrued, I can only account for the inferences which have been drawn, from them, by supposing that language I may have employed in the warmth of political discourse has been represented in a latitude entirely foreign from my sentiments or my wishes.

D, in the handwriting of William P. Van Ness, New York State Historical Association, Cooperstown, New York; Df, in the handwriting of William P. Van Ness, New York State Historical Association, Cooperstown, New York.
    1. The draft, which is written in the third person, is incorrectly printed in Syrett and Cooke, *Interview in Weehawken*, 86, as a separate document written by Burr.
    The last paragraph of the draft, which was omitted from the final document printed above, reads: "If G H has on any occasions uttered such expressions he feels a propriety in fully & explicitly with drawing them as the ebulitions of party feelings which may have escaped him in the heat of political discourse but which he is conscious are unmerited & regrets having employed."

Aaron Burr to William P. Van Ness

[New York, June 26, 1804]

The last propn. of gen H. is a worse libel than even the letter of Dr C & throughout manifests a disposition to evade.[1]

A "letter properly adapted"—Who is to judge of this—Mr B. will judge for himself & thinks his two letters very properly adapted & having expressed himself definitively on that point he is surprized to find it again brought in question.

"any particular instance of dishonorable Conduct." This seems intended to leave ample room for the inference that there have been general opinions and general charges.

"in relation to any other language &c" which "Col. B shall *specify*." Col. B. is ignorant of the particular Conversations & ex-

pressions which Genl. H. may have had or used & he will only inquire from Genl. H. himself. That he has said things derogatory to
Mr B's honor is to be presumed from the letter of Dr C. until it
shall be contradicted by Genl. H.

If Mr B. should specify & Genl. H. should deny as to one particular Conversation—Dr C & the world may say "true, but the day
anterior or the day subsequent such things were said by Genl. H."
and this would indeed be a fair inference from such partial negation.
These things must be perfectly obvious to the perspicatious mind of
Genl H. Propositions therefore fraught with such ambiguity and
liable to such injurious Construction must be considered as insidious
and insulting and they call imperiously for the last appeal.

I was writing the preceeding by way of notes for you when your
boy arrived. They are sent to you unfinished. It seems that our sentiments are pretty much in harmony. Interweave into your's what you
think proper of the preceeding. I will be at your house before noon
& will dine with you.

[June] 26

ALS, New York State Historical Association, Cooperstown, New York.
   1. See "Nathaniel Pendleton's Second Account of Alexander Hamilton's
Conversation at John Tayler's House," June 25, 1804.

William P. Van Ness's Narrative of the Events of June 26, 1804

The following day (tuesday 26. June) as early as was convenient
I had an interview with Col: Burr, who informed me that he considered Genl Hamiltons proposition a mere evasion, which evinced
a desire to leave the injurious impressions which had arisen from the
conversations of Genl Hamilton in full force. That when he had undertaken to investigate an injury his honor had sustained it would
be unworthy of him not to make that investigation complete. He
gave me further instructions which are substantially contained in
the following letter to Mr. xxx No 10.[1]

"Van Ness's Narrative," AD, New York State Historical Association, Cooperstown, New York; ADf, New York State Historical Association, Cooperstown, New York.
1. Van Ness to Nathaniel Pendleton, June 26, 1804.

William P. Van Ness to Nathaniel Pendleton [1]

[New York, June 26, 1804]

Sir

The letter [2] which you yesterday delivered me and your subsequent communications,[3] in Col Burrs opinion evince no disposition on the part of Genl Hamilton to come to a satisfactory accomodation. The injury complained of and the reparation expected are so definitely expressed in Col: Burr's letter of the 21st Instant, that there is not perceived a necessity for further explanation on his part. The difficulty that would result from confining the enquiry to any particular times and occasions must be manifest. The denial of a specified conversation only, would leave strong implications that on other occasions improper language had been used. When and where injurious opinions and expressions have been uttered by Genl Hamilton must be best known to him and of him only will Col: Burr enquire. No denial or declaration will be satisfactory unless it be general, so as wholly to exclude the idea that rumors derogatory to Col: Burr's honor have originated with Genl Hamilton as have been *fairly* inferred from any thing he has said. A definite reply to a requisition of this nature was demanded by Col: Burrs letter of the 21 Inst. This being refused invites the alternative alluded to in Genl Hamilton's letter of the 20th. It was required by the position in which the controversy was placed by Genl Hamilton on friday last and I was immediately furnished with a communication demanding a personal interview. The necessity of this measure has not in the opinion of Col. Burr been diminished by the General's last letter or any communication which has since been received.

I am consequently again instructed to deliver you a message as soon as it may be convenient for you to receive it. I beg therefore

you will be so good as to inform me at what hour I can have the
pleasure of seeing you.

Your Most obt & very hm Sert   W: P: Van N⟨ess⟩

June 26, 1804
Nathaniel Pendleton Esqr

ALS, New-York Historical Society, New York City; ADfS, New York State
Historical Association, Cooperstown, New York; ADf, New York State Historical Association, Cooperstown, New York.
  1. The unsigned draft, which differs from the letter printed above, reads:
"The letter which you yesterday delivered me from Genl Hamilton in Col.
Burr's opinion evinces as little disposition on the part of Genl Hamilton to
come to a satisfactory accomodation [as any of his former communications &
least it may not be accurately understood however what Col. Burr conceives
to be the injury he has sustained, and the reparation which he deems necessary,
permit me again to solicit your attention to his letter of the 21 Instant. You
will there find his complaint specified in language so definite and precise as to
preclude in his opinion the necessity of all further explanation on his part. It
is impossible for Col. Burr to point out the various objectionable conversations
and expressions which at different times may have been indulged in by Genl
Hamilton, and from him alone he can make the enquiry. It is too evident to
be denied, that reports injurious to the character of Col. Burr have been extensively circulated under the sanction of Genl Hamilton's name, and that
language derogatory to his honor has been used by Genl Hamilton he has sufficient reason to presume. The time when is not material, and you must perceive
the difficulty that would result from a specification. Should Genl Hamilton
deny having used exceptionable language on any specified occasion—this though
true would not remedy the evil which is complained of, for the preceeding or
subsequent day might be referred to as that on which the injury had been done
and the controversy would thus become endless. A retraction or *denial* therefore of all such declarations or *a disavowal of any intention to impeach the
character of Col Burr without reference* to time or place is the only reparation
that can be made,] and a definite reply to a requisition of this nature is demanded in Col: Burr's letter of the 21st Inst. This being refused, invites the
alternative alluded to, in Genl Hamiltons letter of the   inst. [H to Burr,
June 20, 1804]. It was demanded by the position in which the controversy was
placed by Genl Hamilton on the 22d Inst. and I was immediately furnished
with a communication demanding *the usual* interview. The necessity of resort-
ing to this measure has not in the opinion of Col: Burr been diminished by
Genl Hamiltons last letter or any subsequent communications which have been
received and I am again instructed to deliver you a Message as soon as it may
be convenient for you to receive it. If therefore you will have the politeness to
inform me at what hour I shall wait on you, I shall be greatly obliged."
  Van Ness endorsed this unsigned draft: "Drt letter 1st to Mr Pendleton
which was altered by Col B & not sent—this be substituted." Burr's alteration,
which was to be used as a substitute for the bracketed material in Van Ness's
unsigned draft, reads: "The injury complained of and the reparation expected,
are so definitely expressed in his letter of the 21 that there is not perceived a
necessity for further explanation on his part—to ask of him to specify par-

ticular times & occasions is *absurd*. The denial of a specified conversation only,
would have strong implications that on other occasions language   had been
used.

"When and where injurious expressions and opinions have been   is best
known to genl H & of him only will Col. B. inquire. No denial or declaration
will be satisfactory unless it be general so as perfectly to exclude the idea
that rumors derogatory to Col. B.' honor can have originated with Genl H
or have been fairly inferred from any thing he had said." (ADf, New York
State Historical Association, Cooperstown, New York.)

2. H to Burr, June 22, 1804.

3. See Pendleton's first and second accounts of "Alexander Hamilton's Conversation at John Taylor's House," June 25, 1804.

Nathaniel Pendleton to William P. Van Ness [1]

[New York] 26 june 1804.

Sir.

I have communicated to General Hamilton the letter you did me
the honor to write me of this date. The expectations now disclosed
as on the part of Colo. Burr, appear to him to have greatly changed
and extended the original ground of inquiry, and instead of presenting a particular and definite case for explanation, seem to aim at
nothing less than an inquisition into his most confidential, as well as
other conversations, through the whole period of his acquaintance
with Col Burr. While he was prepared to meet the particular case
fully and fairly he thinks it inadmissible that he should be expected
to answer at large as to any thing that he may possibly have said in
relation to the character of Colo. Burr, at any time or upon any occasion. Though he is not conscious that any charges that are in
circulation to the prejudice of Col. Burr have Originated with him,
except one which may have been so considered, and which has been
long since explained between Col. Burr and himself; yet he cannot
consent to be questioned generally as to any *rumours* which may be
afloat derogatory to the character of Colo. Burr without specification of the particular rumours, many of them probably unknown to
him. He does not however mean to authorise any conclusion as to
the real nature of his Conduct in relation to Col. Burr, by his declining so loose and vague a basis of explanation; and he disavows an
unwillingness to come to a satisfactory, provided it be an honorable

accommodation. His objection is to the very indefinite ground which Col. Burr has assumed, in which he is sorry to be able to discover nothing short of predetermined hos[t]ility.

Presuming therefore that it will be adhered to he has instructed me to receive the message which you have it [in] charge to deliver. For this purpose I shall be at home and at your command tomorrow morning from eight to ten oClock.

I have the honor [to] be respectfully   Your Obedient Servt.

Nathl: Pendleton

William P. Van Ness Esqr.

ALS, New York State Historical Association, Cooperstown, New York; DfS, in the handwriting of H and signed by Pendleton, New-York Historical Society, New York City.

1. In his narrative Van Ness wrote that he had received this letter on the evening of June 26 and delivered it to Burr that evening (AD, New York State Historical Association, Cooperstown, New York; ADf, New York State Historical Association, Cooperstown, New York).

To Peter Gerard Stuyvesant [1]

[New York, June 26, 1804]

Dr Sir

I should like to see you on the subject of a poor fellow Peter Dunken who says, you have been employed for him & appears unfortunate which is his title to my attention.[2]

Yrs. truly

A Hamilton

June 26. 1804

ALS, The Rutherford B. Hayes Library, Fremont, Ohio; copy, Columbia University Libraries.

1. Stuyvesant was a New York City landowner.

2. On February 17, 1841, Stuyvesant wrote to John Church Hamilton: "Near forty years ago I had charge of some trifling business for an illiterate man in the humble walks of life. In the simplicity of his nature, however, he called on your father & related his grievances, which occasioned the penning of the enclosed note. When it was delivered to me, I reproved the man for the freedom in which he had indulged, & undertook to convince him of the impropriety of troubling Genl. Hamilton with his concerns; his reply to me was, O no Sir he treated me very kindly" (ALS, Columbia University Libraries).

William P. Van Ness to Nathaniel Pendleton [1]

[New York, June 27, 1804]

Sir

The letter which I had the honor to receive from you under date of yesterday, states among other things, that in Genl Hamilton's opinion, Col: Burr has taken a very indefinite ground, in which he evinces nothing short of predetermined hostility; and that Genl Hamilton thinks it inadmissable that the enquiry should extend to his confidential as well as other conversations. To this Col. Burr can only reply that secret whispers traducing his fame and empeaching his honor, are at least equally injurious, with slanders publickly uttered; That Genl H. had at no time and in no place a right to use any such injurious expressions; and that the partial negative he is desposed to give with the reservations he wishes to make, are proofs that he has done the injury specified.

Col: Burr's request was in the first instance proposed in a form the most simple, in order that Genl Hamilton might give to the affair that course to which he might be induced by his temper and his knowledge of facts. Col. B. trusted with confidence that from the frankness of a soldier and the candor of a gentleman he might expect an ingenuous declaration; that if, as he had reason to believe Genl H. had used expressions derogatory to his honor, he would have had the magnanimity to retract them; and that if, from his language injurious inferences had been improperly drawn he would have perceived the propriety of correcting errors, which might thus have been widely diffused. With these impressions Col. Burr was greatly surprised at receiving a letter which he considered as evasive and which in manner he deemed not altogether decorous. In one expectation however, he was not wholly deceived, for the close of Genl Hamilton's letter contained an intimation that if Col. Burr should dislike his refusal to acknowledge or deny, he was ready to meet the consequences. This Col. B. deemed a sort of defiance, and would have felt justified in making it the basis of an immediate message. But as the communication contained something concerning the indefiniteness of his request: As he believed it rather the off-spring of false pride than of reflection, and as he felt the utmost reluctance to proceed to extremities, while any other hope remained, his request was repeated in terms more explicit. The replies and propositions on the part of Genl H. have in Col. B's opinion been constantly in substance the same.

Col: Burr disavows all motives of predetermined hostility. A charge by which he thinks insult is added to injury, he feels as a gentleman should feel, when his honor is impeached or assailed, and without sensations of hostility or wishes of revenge, he is determined to vindicate that honor at such hazard as the nature of the case demands.

The length to which this correspondence has extended only tending to prove that the satisfactory redress, earnestly desired cannot be obtained, he deems it useless to offer any proposition except the simple Message which I shall now have the honor to deliver.

I have the honor to be with great respt. Your Obt & very hum Servt

W: P. Van Ness

Wednesday morning June 27, 1804

ALS, New-York Historical Society, New York City; ADf, New York State Historical Association, Cooperstown, New York.

1. In his narrative Van Ness introduced the letter printed above with the following statement: "I transmitted this [Pendleton to Van Ness, June 26, 1804] to Col: Burr and after a conference with him in which I received his further instructions and that no misunderstanding might arise from verbal communications I committed to writing the remarks contained in No 12 which follows" (AD, New York State Historical Association, Cooperstown, New York; ADf, New York State Historical Association, Cooperstown, New York).

From Baron von Humboldt [1]

[Philadelphia, June 27, 1804]

Monsieur,

Il aurait été un moment bien interessant pour moi que celui de Vous être présenté personnellement, et de Vous offrir le temoignage respectueux de mon devouement. Une reunion de circonstances et l'obligation que j'ai de ne pas retarder la Publication de mes travaux litteraires me font partir pour Paris sans jouir du plaisir de Vous admirer de près et de voir le Cercle interessant dans lequel Vous vivez. Je me hate par consequent d'inclure la lettre que mon ami Mr. Gray avait bien voulu me communiquer et de Vous prier d'agreer les sentimens du plus profond respect avec lequel j'ai l'honneur d'etre.

Monsieur   Votre tres humble et tres obeissant serviteur

Le Bn de Humboldt

à Philadelphie
ce 27 Juin
1804

ALS, Hamilton Papers, Library of Congress.
   1. For background to this letter, see H to Vincent Gray, April 28, 1804.

William P. Van Ness's Narrative of the Events of June 27–28, 1804

I handed this[1] to him[2] at 12 Oclock on Wednesday the 27th Instant. After he had perused it agreeable to my instructions I delivered the Message which it is unnecessary to repeat. The request it contained, was acceded to—after which Mr xxx remarked that a Court was then sitting in which Genl Hamilton had much business to transact, and had also some private arrangements to make which would render some delay unavoidable. I acceded to his wish—and Mr xxx said he would call on me again in the course of the day or the following morning to confer farther relative to time & place.

Thursday June 28th 10 clock P. M. Mr. xxx called on me with a paper[3] he said contained some remarks on the letter I had yesterday delivered him. I replied that if the paper he offered contained a definite and specific proposition for an accomodation, I would with pleasure receive it and submit it to the consideration of my Principal. If not that I must decline taking it, Mr Burr viewed the correspondence completely terminated by the acceptance of the invitation contained in the Message I had yesterday delivered. Mr xxx replied that it did not contain any proposition of the kind I alluded to, but was a reply to my last letter. I of course declined receiving it. Mr xxx then took leave and said that he would call again in a day or two to arrange time and place.

"Van Ness's Narrative," AD, New York State Historical Association, Cooperstown, New York; ADf, New York State Historical Association, Cooperstown, New York.
1. Van Ness to Nathaniel Pendleton, June 27, 1804.
2. Nathaniel Pendleton.
3. "Remarks on the letter of June 27. 1804," June 28, 1804.

Nathaniel Pendleton's Narrative of the Events of June 27–28, 1804

With this letter [1] a message was received, such as was to be expected, containing an invitation, which was accepted, and Mr. P. informed Mr. V. N. he should hear from him the next day as to further particulars.

This letter was delivered to Gen. H. on the same evening, and a very short conversation ensued between him and Mr. P. who was to call on him early the next morning for a further conference. When he did so, Gen. Hamilton said he had not understood whether the message and answer was definitely concluded, or whether another meeting was to take place for that purpose between Mr. P. and Mr. V. N. Under the latter impression, and as the last letter contained matter that naturally led to animadversion, he gave Mr. P. a paper of remarks in his own hand writing,[2] to be communicated to Mr. V. N. if the state of the affair rendered it proper.

In the farther interview with Mr. V. N. that day, after explaining the causes which had induced Gen. Hamilton to suppose that the state of the affair did not render it improper, he offered this paper to Mr. V. N.—but declined receiving it, alledging, that he considered the correspondence as closed by the acceptance of the message that he had delivered.

Mr. P. informed Mr. V. N. of the inducements mentioned by General Hamilton in those remarks, for the postponing of the meeting until the close of the Circuit; and as this was uncertain Mr. P. was to let him know when it would be convenient.

New-York Evening Post, July 16, 1804.
    1. William P. Van Ness to Pendleton, June 27, 1804.
    2. "Remarks on the letter of June 27. 1804," June 28, 1804.

To John B. Church

[*New York, June 28–July 10, 1804.* Nathaniel Pendleton described the seventh item on a list of ten,[1] which were given to him after Hamilton's death, as a "Letter to John B Church inclosing an assignment of some debts." [2] *Letter not found.*]

    1. See "List of Papers Given to Nathaniel Pendleton," July 19, 1804.
    2. See "Assignment of Debts and Grant of Power of Attorney to John B. Church," July 9, 1804.

Partition Deed among John Laurance, John B. Church, and Alexander Hamilton [1]

New York, June 28, 1804. Describes the lots in the townships in Scriba's Patent which Hamilton, Church, and Laurance had drawn by lot from land which they had purchased from Jacob Mark and Company in 1796 and from Robert Gilchrist and Theodosius Fowler in 1802.

Copy, Oneida County Clerk's Office, Deeds, Vol. X, 499–502, Utica, New York.
    1. For background to this document, see "Mortgage by John Laurance, John B. Church, and Alexander Hamilton to Robert Gilchrist," August 21, 1802. See also "Promissory Note to Theodosius Fowler," August 21, 1802.

To Ann Mitchell [1]

[*New York, June 28–July 10, 1804.* Nathaniel Pendleton described the eighth item on a list of ten,[2] which were given to him after Hamilton's death, as a "Letter to Mrs. Mitchell inclosing 400 dollars as was mentioned on the outside. Sealed." *Letter not found.*]

1. Ann Mitchell, the daughter of James and Ann Lytton, was H's cousin. Her mother was the sister of H's mother, Rachel Lavien. In 1759, when Ann Mitchell was sixteen years old, she married John Kirwan Venton. They had one child, a daughter named Ann Lytton Venton. John Venton died in 1776, and in 1780 his widow married George Mitchell, a native of Scotland who had emigrated first to Virginia and then to St. Croix. Ann Mitchell died in Christiansted in 1827. See Ann Mitchell to H, 1796.

2. See "List of Papers Given to Nathaniel Pendleton," July 19, 1804.

To George Mitchell [1]

[*New York, June 28–July 10, 1804.* Nathaniel Pendleton described the ninth item on a list of ten,[2] which were given to him after Hamilton's death, as a "Letter to Geo: Mitchell inclosing a lottery ticket, as mentioned on the outside. Sealed." *Letter not found.*]

1. Mitchell, the husband of Ann Mitchell, H's cousin, had died in the spring of 1797.

2. See "List of Papers Given to Nathaniel Pendleton," July 19, 1804.

Remarks on the letter of June 27. 1804 [1]

[New York, June 28, 1804]

Whether the observations in this letter are designed merely to justify the result, which is indicated in the close of the letter, or may be intended to give an opening for rendering any thing explicit which may have been deemed vague heretofore can only be judged of by the sequel. At any rate it appears to me necessary not to be misunderstood. Mr. Pendleton is therefore authorised to say that in the course of the present discussion, whether written or verbal, there has been no intention to evade defy or insult, but a sincere disposition to avoid extremities, if it could be done with propriety. With this view G H—— has been ready to enter into a frank and free explanation on any and every object of a specific nature; but not to answer a general and abstract enquiry, embracing a period too long for any accurate recollection, and exposing him to unpleasant criticisms from or unpleasant discussions with any and every person, who may have understood him in an unfavourable sense. This (admitting that he could answer in a manner the most satisfactory to Col Burr) he should deem inadmissible, in principle and precedent, and humiliating in practice. To this therefore he can never submit. Frequent allusion has been made to slanders said to be in circulation. Whether this be openly or in whispers they have a form and shape and might be specified.

If the alternative alluded to in the close of the letter is definitively tendered, it must be accepted, the time place and manner to be afterwards regulated. I should not think it right in the midst of a circuit Court to withdraw my services from those who may have confided important interests to me and expose them to the embarrassment of seeking other counsel who may not have time to be sufficiently instructed in their causes. I shall also want a little time to make some arrangements respecting my own affairs.

AD, New-York Historical Society, New York City.
    1. In this document H is commenting on the contents of William P. Van Ness to Nathaniel Pendleton, June 27, 1804.
    Van Ness refused to accept this document. See "William P. Van Ness's Narrative of the Events of June 27–28, 1804" and "Nathaniel Pendleton's Narrative of the Events of June 27–28, 1804."

Statement on Impending Duel with Aaron Burr [1]

[New York, June 28–July 10, 1804]

On my expected interview with Col Burr, I think it proper to make some remarks explanatory of my conduct, motives and views.

I am certainly desirous of avoiding this interview, for the most cogent reasons.

1   My religious and moral principles are strongly opposed to the practice of Duelling, and it would even give me pain to be obliged to shed the blood of a fellow creature in a private combat forbidden by the laws.

2   My wife and Children are extremely dear to me, and my life is of the utmost importance to them, in various views.

3   I feel a sense of obligation towards my creditors; who in case of accident to me, by the forced sale of my property, may be in some degree sufferers. I did not think my self at liberty, as a man of probity, lightly to expose them to this hazard.

4   I am conscious of no *ill-will* to Col Burr, distinct from political opposition, which, as I trust, has proceeded from pure and upright motives.

Lastly, I shall hazard much, and can possibly gain nothing by the issue of the interview.

But it was, as I conceive, impossible for me to avoid it. There were *intrinsick* difficulties in the thing, and *artificial* embarrassments, from the manner of proceeding on the part of Col Burr.

Intrinsick—because it is not to be denied, that my animadversions on the political principles character and views of Col Burr have been extremely severe, and on different occasions, I, in common with many others, have made very unfavourable criticisms on particular instances of the private conduct of this Gentleman.

In proportion as these impressions were entertained with sincerity and uttered with motives and for purposes, which might appear to me commendable, would be the difficulty (until they could be removed by evidence of their being erroneous), of explanation or apology. The disavowal required of me by Col Burr, in a general and indefinite form, was out of my power, if it had really been proper for me to submit to be so questionned; but I was sincerely of opinion, that this could not be, and in this opinion, I was confirmed by that of a very moderate and judicious friend whom I consulted. Besides that Col Burr appeared to me to assume, in the first instance, a tone unnecessarily peremptory and menacing, and in the second, positively offensive. Yet I wished, as far as might be practicable, to leave a door open to accommodation. This, I think, will be inferred from the written communications made by me and by my direction, and would be confirmed by the conversations between Mr van Ness and myself, which arose out of the subject.

I am not sure, whether under all the circumstances I did not go further in the attempt to accommodate, than a pun[c]tilious delicacy will justify. If so, I hope the motives I have stated will excuse me.

It is not my design, by what I have said to affix any odium on the conduct of Col Burr, in this case. He doubtless has heared of animadversions of mine which bore very hard upon him; and it is probable that as usual they were accompanied with some falshoods. He may have supposed himself under a necessity of acting as he has done. I hope the grounds of his proceeding have been such as ought to satisfy his own conscience.

I trust, at the same time, that the world will do me the Justice to believe, that I have not censured him on light grounds, or from unworthy inducements. I certainly have had strong reasons for what I may have said, though it is possible that in some particulars, I may have been influenced by misconstruction or misinformation. It is also my ardent wish that I may have been more mistaken than I think I have been, and that he by his future conduct may shew himself worthy of all confidence and esteem, and prove an ornament and blessing to his Country.

As well because it is possible that I may have injured Col Burr, however convinced myself that my opinions and declarations have been well founded, as from my general principles and temper in relation to similar affairs—I have resolved, if our interview is conducted in the usual manner, and it pleases God to give me the opportunity, to *reserve* and *throw away* my first fire, and I *have thoughts* even of *reserving* my second fire—and thus giving a double opportunity to Col Burr to pause and to reflect.

It is not however my intention to enter into any explanations on the ground. Apology, from principle I hope, rather than Pride, is out of the question.

To those, who with me abhorring the practice of Duelling may think that I ought on no account to have added to the number of bad examples—I answer that my *relative* situation, as well in public as private aspects, enforcing all the considerations which constitute what men of the world denominate honor, impressed on me (as I thought) a peculiar necessity not to decline the call. The ability to be in future useful, whether in resisting mischief or effecting good, in those crises of our public affairs, which seem likely to happen, would probably be inseparable from a conformity with public prejudice in this particular.

AH

ADS, New-York Historical Society, New York City.

1. This document, which is printed at the end of Nathaniel Pendleton's account in the *New-York Evening Post* of events leading to the duel with Aaron Burr, was preceded by the following statement: "The following paper, in the hand writing of Gen Hamilton, was inclosed with his will and some other papers in a packet addressed to one of his executors which was of course not to have been delivered but in case of the melancholy event that has happened. As it contains his motives and reflections on the causes that have led to this fatal catastrophe it is deemed proper to communicate it to the public" (*New-York Evening Post,* July 16, 1804).

The document printed above was the fourth of ten items delivered to Pendleton after H's death. See "List of Papers Given to Nathaniel Pendleton," July 19, 1804.

To James A. Hamilton [1]

[New York, June, 1804]

My Dear James

I have prepared for you a Thesis on Discretion. *You may need it.* God bless you.

Your affectionate father.

A. H.

[E N C L O S U R E] [2]

The celebrated DEAN SWIFT calls discretion an Aldermanly virtue.[3] With all his great and estimable qualities he possessed very little of it himself; and thus was disposed to turn it into derision. But his own experience should have taught him, that if not a splendid it is at least a very useful virtue, and ought on that account to be cultivated and cherished.

Sayings of ⟨this⟩ kind by distinguished men are extremely dangerous. They ought not to be hazarded even in jest, from their tendency to mislead the young and inexperienced. A youthful mind, especially if generous and ardent, finding a character [4]

the most useful qualities a man can possess. It will dispose him to conduct himself with circumspection and enable him to avoid many errors. ⟨It⟩ will assist him in making the most ⟨of⟩ whatever talents and qualifications he may have, and often will cause him to pass for a great deal more than he is worth. A prudent silence will frequently be taken for wisdom, and a sentence or two cautiously thrown in will sometimes gain the palm of knowlege—while a man well informed but indiscreet and unreserved will not uncommonly talk himself out of all consideration and weight.

The want of discretion is apt to be considered as an indication of folly. The greatest abilities are sometimes thrown into the shade by this defect or are prevented from obtaining the success to which they are intitled. The person on whom it is chargeable ⟨is⟩ also apt to make and have numerous enemies and is occasionally involved by it, in the most ⟨– – difficu⟩lties and dangers.

⟨–⟩ with moderate talents have arrived [5]

⟨Instead⟩ therefore of adopting the sentiment of the celebrated Wit to whom I have alluded—let us rather establish it as a general rule, that *Discretion* is the MENTOR which ought to accompany every Young *Telemachus* [6] in his journey through life; And taking care not to assume a character artificial disguised and covert, let us study ⟨in⟩ all our discourses and actions to be circumspect and discreet.

Hamilton, *Reminiscences,* 40.

1. In describing this letter and its enclosure, James A. Hamilton wrote: "In 1804 a student in Columbia College being required to deliver a speech at one of the exhibitions, I asked my father to prepare one for me. With his usual kindness he complied, and a few days before the fatal duel handed me a manuscript with a note. . . .

"The first impression as to the words underscored was, that I might need the Thesis as an exercise. Immediate subsequent events of the most painful character induced the belief that it was intended as an admonition that I wanted that '*homely virtue*,' discretion, of which the thesis treated. How far I have profited by the admonition this relation of the errors of my life may prove. The reader may perhaps say that in attempting to write these reminiscences I have shown that the admonition was thrown away." (*Reminiscences,* 40.)

2. AD, MS Division, New York Public Library.

3. H is apparently referring to the following passage in Jonathan Swift's "The Intelligencer," Numbers V and VII: "There is no *Talent* so useful towards rising in the World, or which puts Men more out of the Reach of Fortune, than that Quality generally possessed by the dullest Sort of People, in common Speech called *Discretion;* a Species of lower Prudence, by the Assistance of which, People of the meanest Intellectuals, without any other Qualification, pass through the World in great Tranquility, and with universal good Treatment, neither giving nor taking Offence. . . .

"Men of eminent Parts and Abilities, as well as Virtues, do sometimes rise

in *Courts,* sometimes in the *Law,* and sometimes even in the *Church.* . . . But
. . . many more, under different Princes, and in different Kingdoms, were *disgraced,* or *banished,* or *suffered Death,* merely in Envy to their Virtues and
superior Genius, which emboldened them to great Exigencies and Distresses of
State, (wanting a reasonable Infusion of this Aldermanly Discretion) to attempt the Service of their Prince and Country, out of the common Forms."
(Herbert Davis, ed., *The Prose Works of Jonathan Swift: Irish Tracts 1728–
1733* [Oxford, 1955], XII, 38–39.)

4. At this point the center of the MS containing ten lines that H wrote is
badly damaged and illegible.

5. At this point in the MS the center of five lines that H wrote is illegible.

6. Telemachus, the son of Odysseus and Penelope, protected his mother during his father's extended absence. When Odysseus returned, Telemachus helped
him to kill Penelope's suitors.

Statement of my property and Debts July 1. 1804 [1]

Real Estate

My share of Townships No. 9. 10. 15. 17 and 21 in
Scribas Patent in connection with J B Church and
John Lawrance viz

⅙ of the first purchase the whole being
31528 acres & ¼ of an acre & one third of the
residuary purchase upon the suit in chancery ⎬   33000
being together nearly 20000 acres which now
stand me in about [2]

My ¼ of purchase in Nobleborough together with
J Laurance Robert Troupe & N Fish being 5450 ⎬   9000
acres computed now to stand me in abt. [3]

Five shares of lands in the Ohio Company [4] being
about 6000 acres purchased chiefly with a certificate for my own services & estimated to now   6000
stand me in

AD, New-York Historical Society, New York City.

1. This document was part of the third item on the "List of Papers Given
to Nathaniel Pendleton," July 19, 1804.

2. See "Mortgage by John Laurance, John B. Church, and Alexander Hamilton to Robert Gilchrist," August 21, 1802; "Promissory Note to Theodosius
Fowler," August 21, 1802; "Partition Deed among John Laurance, John B.
Church, and Alexander Hamilton," June 28, 1804. See also Jacob Mark and
Company to Church, H, and Laurance, May 30, 1797.

3. See H to Robert Troup, July 25, 1795; H to John V. Henry, March 20,
1803.

4. See H to Oliver Wolcott, Jr., October 3, 1802, note 7.

4 lots in the City of New York [5] being the moiety
of 8 lots purchased of I Riley the other moiety
for J B Church now stand me in about   1800

    deduct a subsisting morgage there-
    upon not precisely recollected
    suppose   650   1150

My establishment in the Country [6] *at Hærlem*
estimated to now stand me in about   25000

        Dollars   74150

Personal Estate

Furniture and Library   3000
Horses and Carriages   600

Good Debts

Due me from W Greene on account of a
Purchase of Trustees of Ringwood Company [7] on the Guaranty of P Schuyler &
others say principal & interest abt   500

    deduct this sum still unpaid
    to Trustees ab.   250

        250

      Ds 3850

Estimated cost of real Estate   Ds.   74150
Personal Estate   3850
Due me for professional services say   2500   6350

        Dollars 80500

Debts which I owe

1   To the several Banks in the City
   of New York [8]   **20000**

5. See "Conveyance from Isaac and Hannah Riley," July 7, 1796; "Account with John Barker Church," June 15, 1797.

6. See the introductory note to Philip Schuyler to H, July 17, 1800.

7. See the introductory note to Schuyler to H, August 31, 1795.

8. For H's transactions with the Bank of New York and the New York branch of the Bank of the United States, see his Cash Book, 1795–1804 (AD, Hamilton Papers, Library of Congress).

Under this item at this point H wrote and then crossed out: "Further sum

2	To Gilchrist & Fowler [9] (suppose)		10000
3	To Richard Harrison and Aaron Ogden as Trustees for Louis Le Guen & his wife secured by Mortgage on my house 5000 Ds. with one years interest [10]		5350
4	To the same for this sum passed to my Credit on Bank of UStates [11] on account of 6 ₱ Ct Stock		269.57
5	To Louis Le Guen, this sum borrowed of him ₱ my Note (a years interest being paid)		3000
6	To Herman Le Roy Mortgage to Schiefflin [12] assigned to him years interest nearly due	4000 280	4280
7	To J B Church per account June 23. 1803 Interest for a year	3000.60 210 3210.60	
	Due me per my Book suppose	600	2610
8	To Nicholas Fish suppose		1500

which I expect to borrow 600." Next to this entry he wrote: "(not done.)"
See H to Wolcott, September, 1803.

9. See "Mortgage by John Laurance, John B. Church, and Alexander Hamilton to Robert Gilchrist," August 21, 1802.

10. See Le Guen to H, December 27, 1800, note 7, January 15, 1801, September 30, 1803; "Receipt to Louis Le Guen," January 15, 1801; Aaron Ogden to H, January 15, 1801; "Indenture between Alexander Hamilton of the First Part and Richard Harison and Aaron Ogden of the Second Part," July 1, 1801; "Bond to Richard Harison and Aaron Ogden," July 1, 1800; "Account with Louis Le Guen," June 8, 1802; "Receipt from Louis Le Guen," September 10, 1802, September 5, 1803; "Account of Louis Le Guen," April 1, 1803.

11. On July 16, 1804, Church, Nicholas Fish, and Pendleton, H's executors, wrote to the president and directors of the New York branch of the Bank of the United States asking that H's "notes in your Bank when they fall due may remain with their present endorsements . . . until a favorable time and opportunity may offer for disposing advantageously of such part of his property as it may become necessary to see for the purpose of discharging his debts . . ." (LS, Mr. Hall Park McCullough, Bennington, Vermont).

12. Jacob Schiefflin. See the introductory note to Schuyler to H, July 17, 1800.

9	To Victor Du Pont per my bond abt	1000	
	My Note to him payable 1 Aug [13]	800	
		48809.57	
10	To S Bradhurst [14] for part of my Country seat purchased of him principal & half a years interest say	3110	
11	To Jacob Sherrid [15] probably	1000	
12	To John Laurance for two thirds of an accommodation Note discounted at the Mercts. Bank (say) 600	490	
	Deduct what he owes me ⅌ act. 100		
13	To J B Dash Junr.[16] ⅌ Note	512.32	
	Miscellany	800	54722
	Ballance in my favour Dollars		25778

Remarks

No. 2   The sum due to Fowler & Gilchrist is on account of a purchase under a mortgage which they had upon a tract of land including that which was bought by Church Laurance & myself. By agreement this money was payable by installments. For the first I gave them my notes which have been paid, though they retain the bond for that installment, which ought to be delivered up. The remaining installments are to be paid—the first is now due.

No. 7   Sometime last fall, I authorised J B Church to sell my four lots if they would bring each 200 pounds & apply the proceeds to my credit. Since that I have verbally told him that he might sell them at whatever he should be willing to sell his own for. I consider what has been done as amounting to an appropriation of these lots

13. See H to Victor Marie Du Pont de Nemours, January 30, May 12, 1804.

14. Samuel Bradhurst. See the introductory note to Schuyler to H, July 17, 1800, note 7.

15. Jacob Sherrid, a New York City painter and glazier. See H's Cash Book, 1795–1804, under the date of June 2, 1803 (AD, Hamilton Papers, Library of Congress).

16. John B. Dash, Jr., a New York City ironmonger. See H's Cash Book, 1795–1804 (AD, Hamilton Papers, Library of Congress).

towards the payment of his Debt and so has been my intention. I have hesitated indeed whether I ought not now to do a definitive act to effect this object. But on reflection I thought it adviseable to leave things in *statu quo* with this explanation.

As to Item No. 4 of my debts, I have thought it right to put it on the same foot with my bank accommodations because it is part of a Trust fund being the 2 per cent which was paid on account of the *principal* of the Stock, for which reason it was not paid over to Mr Le Guen. But I think I have made a mistake in paying the full interest as received, since from the Constitution of the public debt a part of this must represent the remaining principal. If there be any error Mr. Le Guen will readily replace it or it can be retained out of the sum I owe him individually. I have been rather negligent as to the entry of my remittances but except fragments amounting to a few dollars he has had as I believe all I have received for him on account of the trust fund or otherwise not noted in this paper. This he will himself put right & indeed may be collected from his letters.

I have thought it right to do the like as to Item No 12 because in fact this is a joint accommodation note. So also as to 11 & 13 because the labour & supplies of these parties have contributed to form this the fund—being for the purpose of my house &c at Haerlem.

Alexander Hamilton's Explanation of His Financial Situation [1]

[New York, July 1, 1804]

Herewith is a general statement of my pecuniary affairs; in which there can be no material error. The result is that calculating my

ADS, RG 233, Records of the Committee on Pensions and Claims, National Archives; copy, New-York Historical Society, New York City; copy, Connecticut Historical Society, Hartford; copy, Columbia University Libraries.
    1. This document was part of the third item on the "List of Papers Given to Nathaniel Pendleton," July 19, 1804.
    This document was enclosed in a petition for a claim based on H's military service which Elizabeth Hamilton submitted to Congress on January 10, 1816 (ADS, RG 233, Records of the Committee on Pensions and Claims, National Archives). In support of this petition Nathaniel Pendleton prepared a report,

property at what it stands me in, I am now worth about Ten thousand pounds, and that estimating according to what my lands are now selling for and are likely to fetch, the surplus beyond my debts may fairly be stated at nearly double that sum. Yet I am pained to be obliged to entertain doubts whether, if an accident should happen to me, by which the sales of my property should come to be forced, it would be even sufficient to pay my debts.

In a situation like this, it is perhaps due to my reputation to explain why I have made so considerable an establishment in the country. This explanation shall be submitted.

To men, who have been so much harassed in the busy world as myself, it is natural to look forward to a comfortable retirement, in the sequel of life, as a principal desideratum. This desire I have felt in the strongest manner; and to prepare for it has latterly been a favourite object. I thought that I might not only expect to accom-

---

which is undated and which reads in part: "Shortly after the death of General Hamilton I received a packet, Sealed and addressed to me, which inclosed a note from him, in substance among other things importing that that packet would only be delivered to me in the event of his death.

"It inclosed also his will, and three other papers, in his own hand writing. In one of them, containing some observations upon his pecuniary affairs, he declared among other circumstances that he had never received the half pay for life, nor the equivalent for it, which other officers, who had served in the Army, in the Revolutionary War had received." (ADS, RG 233, Records of the Committee on Pensions and Claims, National Archives.) H's note to Pendleton has not been found.

Also accompanying Elizabeth Hamilton's petition is a second report written by Pendleton, dated February 18, 1801, in which Pendleton quotes the last two paragraphs of H's document printed above (ADS, RG 233, Records of the Committee on Pensions and Claims, National Archives).

In RG 233, Records of the Committee on Pensions and Claims, National Archives, there is a printed copy of the committee report, dated February 24, 1816, approving the claim.

On April 29, 1816, Congress enacted "An Act for the relief of Elizabeth Hamilton," which allowed her "five years' full pay for the services of her deceased husband, as a lieutenant-colonel in the revolutionary war, which five years' full pay is the commutation of his half pay for life . . ." (6 *Stat.* 173). On March 3, 1839, under the provisions of "An Act for the relief of the widow and other heirs at law of Alexander Hamilton, deceased," the Secretary of War, Joel E. Poinsett, issued to Elizabeth Hamilton and H's other heirs "a bounty land warrant for four hundred and fifty acres of land, in lieu of a warrant for a like quantity issued in the name of the said widow and heirs the thirtieth day of July, eighteen hundred and thirteen, and numbered six hundred and twenty-two; and which said last-mentioned warrant never has been surrendered to the General Land Office for the purpose of being satisfied, but is represented to have been lost or mislaid" (6 *Stat.* 772).

plish the object, but might reasonably aim at it and pursue the preparatory measures, from the following considerations.

It has been for some time past pretty well ascertained to my mind, that the emoluments of my profession would prove equal to the maintenance of my family and the gradual discharge of my debts, within a period to the end of which my faculties, for business might be expected to extend, in full energy. I think myself warranted to estimate the annual product of those emoluments at Twelve * Dollars at the least. My expences while the first improvements of my country establishment were going on have been great; but they would this summer and fall reach the point, at which it is my intention they should stop, at least 'till I should be better able than at present to add to them; and after a fair examination founded upon an actual account of my expenditures, I am persuaded that a plan I have contemplated for the next and succeeding years would bring my expences of every kind within the compass of four thousand Dollars yearly, exclusive of the interest of my country establishment. To this limit, I have been resolved to reduce them, even though it should be necessary to lease that establishment for a few years.

In the mean time, my lands now in a course of sale & settlement would accelerate the extinguishment of my debt, and in the end leave me a handsome clear property. It was also allowable for me to take into view, collaterally, the expectations of my wife; which have been of late partly realised. She is now intitled to a property of between two and three thousand pounds (as I compute) by descent from her mother; [3] and her father is understood to possess a large estate. I feel all the delicacy of this allusion; but the occasion I trust will plead my excuse. And that venerable father, I am sure, will pardon. He knows well all the nicety of my past conduct.

Viewing the matter in these different aspects, I trust the opinion of candid men will be, that there has been no impropriety in my conduct; especially when it is taken into the calculation that my Country establishment, though costly, promises, by the progressive rise of property on this Island, and the felicity of its situation to become more and more valuable.

* thousand must have been omitted [2] through inadvertence.
2. At this point H wrote and crossed out "by me."
3. See the discussion on the Claverack lands in Goebel, *Law Practice*, forthcoming volumes.

My chief apology is due to those friends, who have from mere kindness, indorsed my paper discounted at the Banks. On mature reflection I have thought it jus[ti]fiable to secure them in preference to other Creditors, lest perchance there should be *a deficit*. Yet while this may save them from eventual loss, it will not exemp⟨t⟩ [4] them from some present inconvenience. As to this I can only throw myself upon their kindn⟨ess,⟩ and entreat the indulgence of the Banks for them. Perhaps this request may be supposed intitled to some regard.

In the event, which would bring this paper to the public eye, one thing at least would be put beyond a doubt. This is, that my public labours have amounted to an absolute sacrifice of the interests of my family—and that in all pecuniary concerns the delicacy, no less than the probity of my conduct in public stations, has been such as to defy even the shadow of a question.

Indeed, I have not enjoyed the ordinary advantages incident to my military services. Being a member of Congress, while the question of the commutation of the half pay of the army in a sum in gross was in debate,[5] delicacy and a desire to be useful to the army, by removing the idea of my having an interest in the question, induced me to write to the Secretary of War and relinquish my claim to half pay;[6] which, or the equivalent, I have accordingly never received. Neither have I ever applied for the lands allowed by the United States to Officers of my rank. Nor did I ever obtain from this state the allowan⟨ce⟩ of lands made to officers of similar rank.[7] It is true that having served through the latter period of the War on the general staff of the UStates and not in the line of this State. I could not claim that allowance as a matter of course. But having before the War resided in this State and having entered the military career at the head of a company of Artillery [8] raised for the particular defence of this State, I had better pretensions to the allowance

---

4. The material within broken brackets has been taken from the copy in the Connecticut Historical Society.

5. The debate occurred in 1782–1783.

6. See the two letters that H wrote to George Washington, March 1, 1782, one of which was forwarded to Benjamin Lincoln, Secretary at War.

7. See "An Act for granting certain Lands promised to be given as Bounty Lands by Laws of this State, and for other purposes therein mentioned" (*New York Laws*, 7th Sess. Ch. XLIII [May 11, 1784]).

8. See H to Colonel Alexander McDougall, March 17, 1776, note 2.

than others to whom it was actually made—Yet has it not been extended to me.

A H

From John C. Kunze [1]

Chatham str. [New York] July 3d 1804

Dear Sir

In a conversation, my esteemed friend Dr. Livingston [2] had with Judge Benson,[3] this gentleman received an information of the injustice, the Lutheran church-trustees in Albany intend to do to me and the Lutheran church in general in America. As he intends to go up to Albany, where he is to Stay a considerable time, he generously promised Dr. Livingston, to look into this matter & endeavour to bring it to rights. Dr. Livingston desires me to make a statement of the case, for which I Should have the documents, now in Your hands.[4] Be so kind, Sir, & intrust the bearer of this with them. They consist of our minute-book & some loose papers. I have the honor to be

Dear Sir   Your most obedient humble Servant   John C. Kunze

ALS, Hamilton Papers, Library of Congress.
    1. The Reverend John C. Kunze was the pastor of the German Lutheran Church in New York City and professor of Oriental languages at Columbia College.
    2. The Reverend John Henry Livingston was a Dutch Reformed clergyman in New York City and the grandson of Gilbert Livingston, the youngest son of the first lord of Livingston Manor.
    3. Egbert Benson.
    4. In the Hamilton Papers, Library of Congress, is a list of the papers "Doctor J. C. Kunze left in the hands of General Hamilton." A statement at the bottom of this document reads: "Delivered the above to Graham Newall Clerk to D. A Ogden 26 July 1804."

To William Short [1]

[New York, July 3, 1804]

General Hamilton waited on Mr. Short to pay his respects & to request the pleasure of his Company at a Family Dinner [2] in the Country on Saturday next three oClock.[3]

July 3. 1804

ALS, Historical Society of Pennsylvania, Philadelphia.

1. Short, who had been Thomas Jefferson's secretary when Jefferson was Minister to France during the Confederation period, became chargé d'affaires at Paris in 1789. In 1792 he was appointed United States Minister at The Hague, and the following year he went to Madrid to assist in negotiating a treaty between the United States and Spain. Short was responsible for negotiating the Dutch loans to the United States. In 1802 he returned to the United States.

2. H's other guests were William S. and Abigail Smith, John Adams's son-in-law and daughter, and John Trumbull, the painter (Hamilton, *History*, VII, 822).

3. An undated memorandum in the handwriting of James Wilkinson reads: "Gen. James Ross of Lancaster dined with Genl. Hamilton in NYork July 3d. 1804. and was told by Gl. H. that He expected an affair with Col. B. & that he should avoid it by every means in his power, but if he was pressed must fight—or words to this Effect. so you see Gl. H. had confidants as well as Col. B. but I suppose that what is sinful in one may be honorable in the other" (AD, James Biddle Collection of the Biddle Family Papers, Andalusia, Pennsylvania).

William P. Van Ness's Narrative of the Events of July 3, 1804 [1]

Tuesday July 3d I again saw Mr Pendleton, and after a few subsequent interviews the time when the parties were to meet was ultimately fixed on for the morning of the 11th July Inst.

"Van Ness's Narrative," AD, New York State Historical Association, Cooperstown, New York; ADf, New York State Historical Association, Cooperstown, New York.

1. In the draft of his narrative Van Ness wrote: "Tuesday July 3, Mr Pendleton called and left his card upon seeing it at my office I imy waited on him

he informed that the court would rise he supposed on Saturday the 7th Inst. and that on Monday or tuesday following Mr Hamilton would be ready to meet Mr Burr, and we agreed to ride out on thursday or friday to fix upon the ground. On wednesday I wrote Mr Pend a Note of which No 15 [Van Ness to Pendleton, July 4, 1804] is a copy."

To Elizabeth Hamilton [1]

[New York, July 4, 1804]

This letter, my very dear Eliza, will not be delivered to you, unless I shall first have terminated my earthly career; to begin, as I humbly hope from redeeming grace and divine mercy, a happy immortality.

If it had been possible for me to have avoided the interview, my love for you and my precious children would have been alone a decisive motive. But it was not possible, without sacrifices which would have rendered me unworthy of your esteem. I need not tell you of the pangs I feel, from the idea of quitting you and exposing you to the anguish which I know you would feel. Nor could I dwell on the topic lest it should unman me.

The consolations of Religion, my beloved, can alone support you; and these you have a right to enjoy. Fly to the bosom of your God and be comforted. With my last idea; I shall cherish the sweet hope of meeting you in a better world.

Adieu best of wives and best of Women. Embrace all my darling Children for me.

Ever yours   A H

July 4. 1804
Mrs. Hamilton

ALS, Hamilton Papers, Library of Congress; copy, Mrs. John Church Hamilton, Elmsford, New York.
1. This letter may have been part of item six on the "List of Papers Given to Nathaniel Pendleton," July 19, 1804.

Motion Made at a Meeting of the Society of the Cincinnati

[New York, July 4, 1804]

On the 4th of July, on motion of Hamilton, the Committee were directed, in case of a favorable report upon claims for admission as a member of right (except where there may have been a previous admission in another State Society), to report specifically the ground upon which they conceive the original right of the applicant to stand, and the reason which may have prevented an earlier application for admission if any delay has been.[1]

The Institution of the Society of the Cincinnati . . . Together with Some of the Proceedings of the General Society, and the New-York Society (New York, 1851), 101.
  1. Aaron Burr also attended this meeting of the Cincinnati, at which H sang an old military song. See "What Was Hamilton's 'Favorite Song?'" *William and Mary Quarterly*, 3rd ser., XII (April, 1955), 298–307.

To Nathaniel Pendleton [1]

[New York, July 4, 1804]

I thank you My Dear Sir for your friendly offices in this last critical scene, if such it shall be. Excuse me for having inserted your name as Executor. I fear it may not be in your favor to do much good to my family. But I am sure you will do all the good you can.
  Yrs. truly   A H
                                                        July 4. 1804

My most interesting papers in regard to my pecuniary affairs will be found
1 in the upper Apartment of Escrutory or Secretary in the Country
2 In a Box with pigeon holes in the room I occupy as an office
3 In the Drawer of Press Be[d]stead in my house in Town

ALS, New-York Historical Society, New York City.
1. This letter was the fifth item on the "List of Papers Given to Nathaniel Pendleton," July 19, 1804.

Nathaniel Pendleton's First Statement of the Regulations for the Duel

[New York, July 4, 1804]

1. To leave this Island from different points in two boats precisely at five Oclock on Saturday P M and to proceed to the place proposed. The party first arriving will wait the landing of the other; each boat shall be rowed by four confidential persons only, who shall remain in their respective boats untill called for. These persons are not to be armed in any manner whatever. There will be but 7 persons in each boat. The principle, his second, one Surgeon and four oarsmen. The Surgeons may attend in Silence on the Ground.
2. The distance between the parties to be ten yards measured by the seconds, and the positions shall be directly marked.
3. The Seconds shall determine by lot the choice of positions.
4. The pistols shall not exceed 11 In. in the barrel. They are to be smooth bores, & to be loaded by the Seconds, in each others presence, shewing a smooth ball.
5. The gentlemen will stand correctly at their stations and receive their pistol. The Seconds having determined by lot who gives the words he to whom this lot falls shall take his position and shall distinctly ask the parties whether they are prepared. If they answer in the affirmative, He shall say "proceed" upon which the parties shall fire promptly—if one fires before the other, the opposite second shall say, one, two, three, fire, and he shall fire.
6. If either should be wounded before he has fired, and means to fire, he shall, if he can stand unsupported, be entitled to his shot, and not otherwise. If either has fired, is wounded and means to proceed he shall receive no assistance, his second will only exchange the pistol. If he falls forward the second will re ⟨past⟩ him.
7. At the exchange of pistols, the parties will resume their stations and the word given as in Article 5.

8. A snap or flash to be considered a fire. The Pistol not to be re-covered.

9. Neither party to quit his Station untill he is disqualified to pro-ceed.

AD, New-York Historical Society, New York City.

William P. Van Ness to Nathaniel Pendleton

[New York, July 4, 1804]

Dr Sir

I have engaged two gentlemen to dine with me tomorrow. If it be perfectly immaterial to you, I should prefer taking our ride on some subsequent day.

I have the honor to be   Your most obt & very hum Sert

W: P Van Ness

Nath. Pendleton Esqr
July 4, 1804

ALS, New York State Historical Association, Cooperstown, New York.

To Wilhelm Schuss [1]

New York July 5th 1804

Sir

During Yesterdays Fete,[2] having had occasion to discharge ⟨– –⟩ re-cently repaired; I must ⟨–⟩ the Barrel now ⟨– – –⟩ in the Opposite Di-rection. I will expect you ⟨– – –⟩ immedy upon your Return to the City.

your Servt   A Hamilton

Transcript furnished by Mr. Lincoln Diamant, Tarrytown, New York.
    1. Schuss was a New York City gunsmith.
    2. See "Motion Made at a Meeting of the Society of the Cincinnati," July 4, 1804, note 1.

Deed of Trust to John B. Church, John Laurance, and Matthew Clarkson [1]

[New York, July 6, 1804]

This Indenture made the Sixth day of July in the Year of our Lord one thousand Eight hundred and four Between Alexander Hamilton of the City of New York Counsellor at Law of the one part and John B. Church John Laurance and Matthew Clarkson of the City of New York Esquires of the other part Witnessth That the Said Alexander Hamilton for and in consideration of one Dollar to him in hand paid by the Said John B. Church John Laurance and Matthew Clarkson (the receipt whereof he doth hereby acknowledge) hath granted bargained sold conveyed released enfeoffed and confirmed and by these presents doth grant bargain Sell convey release enfeoff and confirm unto the Said John B. Church John Laurance and Matthew Clarkson and to their heirs and assigns as joint tenants and not as tenants in common all and Singular the Lands tenements and hereditaments which the Said Alexander Hamilton owns oc-

---

Certified copy, recorded under the date of January 7, 1805, Conveyances in the Office of the Register, City of New York, Liber 71, 347 (Hall of Records, New York City); copy, Oneida County Clerk's Office, Deeds, Vol. XIV, 31–32, Utica, New York.

1. This document and H's "Views of Objects for which this trust is created & the value of the fund," which presumably accompanied the deed, were item 2 on "List of Papers Given to Nathaniel Pendleton," July 19, 1804.

Church was Elizabeth Hamilton's brother-in-law.

Laurance was one of H's closest friends. See "Account with Louis Le Guen," June 6, 1802, note 7.

Clarkson, who held the rank of major at the close of the American Revolution, was a member of the New York Assembly from 1789 to 1790 and the New York Senate from 1794 to 1795. In 1794 the legislature named him to the committee in charge of fortifications in New York City. He was United States marshal of the District of New York from 1791 to 1792, and in 1795 he became commissioner of loans for New York. In 1796 he was appointed to the mixed claims commission established under Article XXI of the Treaty of Friendship, Limits, and Navigation signed at San Lorenzo el Real, October 27, 1795 (Pinckney's Treaty). In 1798 he became a director of the New York branch of the Bank of the United States.

For an explanation of the contents of this document, see "Statement of my property and Debts July 1, 1804."

cupies and possesses and to which he is or shall be intitled by virtue
of any and every purchase Conveyance Contract or agreement heretofore made between him and Jacob Scheifflin of the City of New
York Druggist or Samuel Bradhurst of Haerlem Physician Situate
lying and being at Harlem in the County of New York, including
all houses and other Buildings and elections and all commons or
right of commons and all ways water courses privileges and Ease-
ments whatsoever with the appurtenances thereupon erected and
therewith purchased agreed for used occupied or enjoyed And all
the Estate Right title property claim and demand whatsoever in
Law and Equity of the said Alexander Hamilton of in and to the
same and every part thereof Also All the Lands tenements and hereditaments of him the said Alexander Hamilton whether held in
Severalty or in common or joint tenancy with the Said John B.
Church and John Laurance or with either of them Severally, Situate
lying and in Townships Number fifteen and twenty one of Scriba's
patent in Rosevelts purchase in the County of oneida including the
benefit of all contracts for the Sale of any part or parts thereof and
the consideration money to be paid therefore And All the Estate
Right title property Claim and Demand whatsoever in Law & equity
of him the said Alexander Hamilton of in and to the Same and every
part thereof with the appurtenances. Also all the household furniture Horses Carriages and the Library (except the books of Divin-
ity) of him the Said Alexander Hamilton whatsoever and wheresoever To have and to hold all and Singular the Said Lands tenements
hereditaments goods Chattels and premises unto the Said John B.
Church John Laurance and Matthew Clarkson their heirs and assigns to and for their own proper use benefit and behoof for ever
as Joint tenants and not as tenants in common upon trust nevertheless to Sell and dispose of the said premises and every part thereof
for immediate payment or upon Credit as to them Shall Seem expedient by one or more Sales at public Auction or otherwise as
they Should think fit and to apply and pay The proceeds of such
sales towards the Satisfaction and discharge of all and every the
accommodation note and notes discounted for him the Said Alexander Hamilton by and remaining in the Bank of New York the
Manhattan Bank and the Office of Discount and Deposit of the Bank
of the United States in and for the City of New York and the

Merchants Bank (So called) in the City of New York and towards the Satisfaction and discharge of a Sum of Two hundred and Sixty nine Dollars and fifty Seven Cents remaining in his hands and belonging to the trustees for the Marriage contract of Louis Le Guen with Mary his wife and towards the Satisfaction and discharge of a certain accommodation note made by the said John Laurance and indorsed by me and Discounted in and by the Said Merchants Bank believed to be for the Sum of Nine hundred Dollars (of which two thirds are payable by the Said Alexander Hamilton) and towards the Satisfaction and discharge of the debts which the Said Alexander Hamilton owes to Jacob Sherred and John B. Dash Junior. In witness whereof the parties to these presents have hereunto Set and Subscribed their hands and Seals respectively the day and year first above written   Alexander Hamilton [2]

View of Objects for which this trust is created & the value of the fund.[3]

Objects

Bank accommodations to myself	20 000
To J Laurance—Ballance ⅌ general Statemt. being 490 say ⅔	393
Sum due to Marriage Contract of L L G	269
To *Sherrid* supposed	1 000
To *Dash*	512
	22 174
Deduct on account of an additional provision made for J B Church to bring him to a level with other principal Indorse[r]s	1 500
	20 674

2. The remainder of this part of the document lists the interlineations and erasures which H had made and states that Thomas Cooper, master in Chancery, allowed the deed to be recorded in New York City.
3. AD, New-York Historical Society, New York City.

Fund

Establist. at Haerlem which it is supposed would bring for Cash or moderate credit	25 000	
deduct incumbrances	12 000	
		13 000
9000 acres in 15 & 21 probably bring 12/ ℔ acre in same manner		13 500
other Articles (say)		3 000
		29.500

Nathaniel Pendleton's Narrative of the Events of July 6 and 9, 1804

On Friday the 6th of July, the Circuit being closed, Mr. P. gave this information, and that Gen. Hamilton would be ready at any time after the Sunday following. On Monday the particulars were arranged, and the public are but too well acquainted with the sad result.

New-York Evening Post, July 16, 1804.

Aaron Burr to William P. Van Ness

[New York, July 9, 1804]

I should with regret pass over another Day. It is left however to your discretion. If the Fort [1] is agreed on, it will [be] impossible to make an early business without fatigue. What you shall do will be satisfactory to me—except an early Morning hour. I have no predilection for time. From 7 to 12 is the least pleasant—but anything so we *but* get on.

If you go out, leave a line for me with your servant saying when I shall see, or hear from, you.

9 July

I don't see the necessity of *his* presence in order to ultimate arrangements. He has confided this Matter to P——.[2]
 H——k [3] is enough, & even that unnecessary.

AL, New York State Historical Association, Cooperstown, New York.
 1. Fort Paulus Hook at present-day Jersey City, New Jersey.
 2. Nathaniel Pendleton.
 3. Dr. David Hosack, the Hamilton family's physician.

To John B. Church

[*New York, July 9, 1804.* Nathaniel Pendleton described the seventh item on a list of ten,[1] which were given to him after Hamilton's death, as a "Letter to John B. Church inclosing an assignment of some debts." [2] *Letter not found.*]

 1. See "List of Papers Given to Nathaniel Pendleton," July 19, 1804.
 2. See "Assignment of Debts and Grant of Power of Attorney to John B. Church," July 9, 1804.

Assignment of Debts and Grant of Power of Attorney to John B. Church [1]

[New York, July 9, 1804]

Know all Men by these Presents, That I Alexander Hamilton of the City of New York Counsellor at law, in consideration of one

ADS, Hamilton Papers, Library of Congress.
 1. This document and its enclosure are part of item seven on the "List of Papers Given to Nathaniel Pendleton," July 19, 1804. H's covering letter to Church has not been found.

Dollar to me in hand paid by John B Church Esquire, (the receipt whereof is hereby acknowleged) have bargained sold assigned and conveyed and hereby do bargain sell assign & convey to the said John B Church all and singular the debts due owing and payable to me: which are specified in the schedule hereunto annexed to be by him collected and the proceeds applied first towards the payment of all and every the debt and debts which I owe to my household and other servants and labourers, and to the Woman who washes for Mrs. Hamilton—and secondly towards the satisfaction and discharge of certain accommodation notes made by me and indorsed by him and which have been or shall be discounted in and by the Manhattan Bank and the Office of Discount & Deposit of the Bank of the United States in the City of New York. And for this purpose I do hereby constitute and appoint him my Attorney to ask demand sue for recover and receive the said Debts and every of them and upon receipt thereof or any part thereof to make and give acquittances. In Witness whereof I have hereunto subscribed & set my hand and seal the Ninth day of July in the year of our lord One thousand Eight hundred & four.

Sealed & Delivered in presence
of   A. Ham⟨ilton⟩
Nathl: Pendleton

[ENCLOSURE]²

A Copy of a list of Debts assigned to John B Church Esquire per Deed Dated 9th. July 1804

paid	James & William Sterling	75
pd	Isaac Clason	160
no	William Bell—Robinson & Hartshorne	50
pd	Mess. Jenkins (Riggs)	50
pd	Pierre Van Cortland ⎫ late L. Governor ⎬	40

2. Copy, in the handwriting of Dominick T. Blake, Hamilton Papers, Library of Congress; ADS (incomplete), Hamilton Papers, Library of Congress.
For information on the accounts listed in this document, unless otherwise noted below, see Goebel, *Law Practice*, forthcoming volumes.
In the Hamilton Papers, Library of Congress, is a document in Church's

pd	P. Jay Monroe paid	40 by T L O [3]
pd no by T L O	Champlin & Smith (T L Ogden)	50
paid	Grellet & Bell credit 24–70 [4]	40
no	Out Door Underwriters ⎫ including Hallet & Bowne ⎬ adsm. Jenks (Pendleton) ⎭	200
	Assignees of Wm. L Vandervort	250
paid		
	if Successful 250 more 400 by T L O [5]	
	assignees of I Roget Furtado [6]	50
paid	De Peyster ⎫ Jones ⎭	40
paid	Abijah Hammond ⎫ D A Ogden ⎭	40
pd	Robert Cummings	75
paid	John McVickar	30
paid	Isaac Kibby	25
pd	Hubbard ⎫ Riggs ⎭	50
pd	Alexander Stewart	65
paid	Assignees of Kirkpatrick by P. A Camman T. L Ogden	40

handwriting, dated July 16, 1804, which reads: "Dominick T Blake Esqr. is authorised to collect the Amount of different Debts owed to the Deceased General Hamilton assigned to me by him by a Deed dated the 9th instant. J. B. Church."

Also in the Hamilton Papers, Library of Congress, is a document written and signed by Nathaniel Pendleton, dated October 13, 1804, which reads: "D. T. Blake esquire is authorised to collect any monies due to General Hamilton lately deceased for fees as Counsel."

Numerous receipts given to Blake by Elizabeth Hamilton, Church, and Pendleton may be found in the Hamilton Papers, Library of Congress.

3. Thomas L. Ogden, a New York City attorney.

4. On October 10, 1804, Stephen Grellet, a New York City merchant, rendered a bill for $24.70 to H's estate for shoes purchased by H (AD, Hamilton Papers, Library of Congress). On November 22, 1804, Abraham Bell, a New York City merchant, collected the money for Grellet (ADS, Hamilton Papers, Library of Congress).

5. The incomplete document begins at this entry and continues through the entry for William Byron.

6. Jacob Furtado, a New York City merchant.

paid	George Stanton	30	
paid	Louis Simond	50	
	John Hackeley	100	Pendleton paid
	Ricker		
paid	Ebenezer Stevens	50	
paid	Geo Suckly	50	
pd	Bank of N York	100	
pd	James Arden	50	
paid	Wm. Thomas	25	
paid	Wm. Cooper	75	
	Wm. Byron pd. 50	100	
paid	Wm. & Sylvester Robinson	250	
pd	Wm. Neilson	50	
pd	John B Graves	50	
pd no	James Shuter	50	
by T L O	T L Ogden		

Gouverneur including Insurance ⎫
paid cause of Beare [7] settled &c ⎬ 100
no compromised ⎭

paid	John Stewards	51.46
	note	50
	Dol	2490
	Henderson & Varick	20
	Dols	2510

Particulars will better appear by Account Book endorsed *M E M*.

A H

July 9. 1804 [8]

---

7. H represented Henry M. Beare in a suit in Chancery, commenced on February 10, 1804, against Frederick Rhinelander, *et al.*, the underwriters of Beare's ship, the *Maria Charlotte* (Chancery Papers, BM-486-R, BM 489-R, Hall of Records, New York City).

8. The last sentence, H's signature, and the date have been taken from the incomplete document.

Last Will and Testament of Alexander Hamilton [1]

[New York, July 9, 1804]

In the Name of God Amen! I Alexander Hamilton of the City of New York Counsellor at Law do make this my last Will and Testament as follows. First I appoint **John B Church Nicholas Fish** [2] and **Nathaniel Pendleton** [3] of the City aforesaid Esquires to be Executors and Trustees of this my Will and I devise to them their heirs and Assigns, as joint Tenants and not as Tenants in common, All my Estate real and personal whatsoever and wheresoever upon Trust at their discretion to sell and dispose of the same, at such time and times in such manner and upon such terms as they the Survivors and Survivor shall think fit and out of the proceeds to pay all the Debts which I shall owe at the time of my decease, in whole, if the fund shall be sufficient, proportionally, if it shall be insufficient, and the residue, if any there shall be to pay and deliver to my excellent and dear Wife Elizabeth Hamilton.

Though if it shall please God to spare my life I may look for a considerable surplus out of my present property—Yet if he should speedily call me to the eternal wor[l]d, a forced sale as is usual may possibly render it insufficient to satisfy my Debts. I pray God that something may remain for the maintenance and education of my dear Wife and Children. But should it on the contrary happen that there is not enough for the payment of my Debts, I entreat my Dear Children, if they or any of them shall ever be able, to make up the Deficiency. I without hesitation commit to their delicacy a wish which is dictated by my own. Though conscious that I have too far sacrificed the interests of my family to public avocations & on this account have the less claim to burthen my Children, yet I trust in their magnanimity to appreciate as they ought this my request. In so unfavourable an event of things, the support of their dear Mother with the most respectful and tender attention is a duty all the sacredness of which they will feel. Probably her own patrimonial resources will preserve her from Indigence. But in all situations they are charged to bear in mind that she has been to them the most devoted and best of mothers. In Testimony whereof I have hereunto subscribed my hand the Ninth day of July in the year of our lord One thousand Eight hundred & four.

Signed sealed published & declared as and for his last Will and Testament in our presence who have subscribed the same in his presence. ⠀⠀The words John B Church being above interlined.	Alexander Hamilton

Dominick T Blake
Graham Newell
Theo B Valleau [4]

ADS, Hamilton Papers, Library of Congress; copy, in the handwriting of Nathaniel Pendleton, Connecticut Historical Society, Hartford; copy, New-York Historical Society, New York City.

1. This document was the first item on the "List of Papers Given to Nathaniel Pendleton," July 19, 1804.
2. See H to Pendleton, July 4, 1804.
3. Blake was a New York City lawyer. Newell was a clerk to David A. Ogden. Valleau was a storekeeper in New York City.
4. The probate of H's will is dated July 16, 1804 (DS, signed by Silvanus Miller, New-York Historical Society, New York City).

William P. Van Ness's Regulations for the Duel

[New York, July 9, 1804]

1. The parties to leave the City at 5 O Clock A. M Wednesday morning 11th Instant.
2. The distance between the parties to be 10 yards & the Pistols not to exceed 11 Inches in the barrel. The Seconds to determine by lot the choice of Positions and the Giving of the word.
3. The parties being placed at their Stations—The Second who gives the words shall ask them whether they are ready. Being answered in the affirmative he shall say present after which the parties present & fire when they please. If one party fires before the

other, the opposite second shall say one, two, three fire and he shall fire or loose his fire.

4. A snap or flash to be considered a fire.

AD, New-York Historical Society, New York City.

Debts Owed for Services Not Rendered [1]

[New York, July 10, 1804]

These sums having been received since my *engagement* & no services rendered I consider them as forming part of my debts.

Franklin & Robinson	50
James Amory	20
D Ludlow & Co	50
Wilmerding	30
Murdock Masterson & Co	20
Steven Ray & David Dill	25
Scott & Tremaine	20

A Hamilton
July 10. 1804 [2]

ADS, New-York Historical Society, New York City.
1. This document is the tenth and final item on the "List of Papers Given to Nathaniel Pendleton," July 19, 1804.
2. At the bottom of this document Pendleton wrote: "Wrote to each of the above persons 31 July 1804. Informing them of the above. N P."

To Elizabeth Hamilton [1]

[New York, July 10, 1804]

My beloved Eliza

Mrs. Mitchel [2] is the person in the world to whom as a friend I am under the greatest Obligations. I have ⟨not⟩ [3] hitherto done my ⟨duty⟩ to her. But ⟨resolved⟩ to repair my omission as much as ⟨possible,⟩ I have encouraged her to come to ⟨this Country⟩ and intend,

if it shall be ⟨in my po⟩wer to render the Evening of her days ⟨c⟩om-
fortable. But if it shall please God to put this out of my power and
to inable you hereafter to be of ⟨s⟩ervice to her, I entreat you to d⟨o⟩
it and to treat ⟨h⟩er with the tenderness of a Sister.

    This is my second letter.[4]

The Scrup⟨les of a Christian have deter⟩mined me to expose my own
li⟨fe to any⟩ extent rather than subject my s⟨elf to the⟩ guilt of taking
the life of ⟨another.⟩ This must increase my hazards & redoubles my
pangs for you. But you had rather I should die inno⟨c⟩ent than live
guilty. Heaven can pre⟨se⟩rve me ⟨and I humbly⟩ hope will ⟨b⟩ut in
the contrary ⟨e⟩vent, I charge you to remember that you are a
Christian. God's Will be done. The will of a merciful God must be
good.

    Once more Adieu My Darling darling Wife

A H

Tuesday Evening 10 oCl⟨ock⟩

⟨Mrs Ha⟩milton

ALS, Hamilton Papers, Library of Congress; JCH Transcripts.
    1. This letter was the sixth item on the "List of Papers Given to Nathaniel
Pendleton," July 19, 1804.
    2. Ann Mitchell, H's cousin. See H to Ann Mitchell, June 28–July 10, 1804.
    3. The material within broken brackets has been taken from the JCH tran-
script.
    4. See H to Elizabeth Hamilton, July 4, 1804.

Nathaniel Pendleton's Second Statement of the Regulations for the Duel [1]

[New York, July 10, 1804] [2]

1. The parties will leave town tomorrow morning about five
o Clock, and meet at the place agreed on. The party arriving first
shall wait for the other.

2. The weapons shall be pistols not exceeding eleven inches in the
barrel. The distance ten paces.

3. The Choice of positions to be determined by lot.

4. The parties having taken their positions one of the seconds to be determined by lot (after having ascertained that both parties are ready) Shall loudly and distinctly give the word "present." If one of the parties fires, and the other hath not fired, the opposite second shall say one, two, three, fire, and he shall then fire or lose his Shot. A Snap or flash is a fire.

Monday.
11 July 1804.

AD, New-York Historical Society, New York City.
    1. Pendleton's first statement on the regulations for the duel is dated July 4, 1804. See also "William P. Van Ness's Regulations for the Duel," July 9, 1804.
    2. Pendleton dated this document "Monday. 11 July 1804." In 1804, July 11 was a Wednesday. The first sentence of this document indicates that the date should be Tuesday, July 10.

To Theodore Sedgwick

New York July 10. 1804

My Dear Sir

I have received two letters from you since we last saw each other —that of the latest date being the 24 of May.[1] I have had in hand for some time a long letter to you, explaining my view of the course and tendency of our Politics, and my intentions as to my own future conduct. But my plan embraced so large a range that owing to much avocation, some indifferent health, and a growing distaste for Politics, the letter is still considerably short of being finished. I write this now to satisfy you, that want of regard for you has not been the cause of my silence.

I will here express but one sentiment, which is, that Dismemberment of our Empire will be a clear sacrifice of great positive advantages, without any counterballancing good; administering no relief to our real Disease; which is DEMOCRACY, the poison of which by a subdivision will only be the more concentered in each part, and consequently the more virulent.[2]

King is on his way for Boston [3] where you may chance to see him, and hear from himself his sentiments.[4]

God bless you   A H

T Sedgwick Esqr

ALS, Massachusetts Historical Society, Boston.

1. Sedgwick's two letters to H have not been found.

2. This is a reference to a project of some Federalist leaders in New England to secede from the United States and form a northern confederacy. For the correspondence concerning this project, see Henry Adams, ed., *Documents Relating to New-England Federalism. 1800–1815* (Boston, 1905), 46–63, 107–330, 338–65. On December 20, 1828, William Plumer wrote to John Quincy Adams that "arrangements had been made to have, the next autumn [1804], in Boston, a select meeting of the leading Federalists in New England, to consider and recommend the measures necessary to form a system of government for the Northern States; and that Alexander Hamilton of New York had consented to attend that meeting" (Adams, *New-England Federalism*, 145). Plumer of New Hampshire and Adams were both members of the United States Senate in 1803 and 1804.

In 1829 John Quincy Adams prepared a "Reply to the Appeal of the Massachusetts Federalists," in which he wrote: "The session of Congress closed on the 4th of March, 1804, and I shortly afterwards returned to spend the summer at my father's residence at Quincy. On my way thither, I was detained several days at New York, during which I frequently visited Mr. Rufus King, who had then recently returned from his first mission to England. On the 8th day of April, I called and passed great part of the evening with him in his library. I found there, sitting with him, Mr. Timothy Pickering, who, shortly after I went in, took leave and withdrew. As he left the house, Mr. King said to me, 'Colonel Pickering has been talking to me about a project they have for a separation of the States and a Northern confederacy; and he has also been this day talking of it with General Hamilton. . . . I disapprove entirely of the project; and so, I am happy to tell you, does General Hamilton'" (Adams, *New-England Federalism*, 147–48).

John Church Hamilton described a party at the Grange on July 7 as follows: "After dinner, when they were alone, Hamilton turned to [John] Trumbull, and, looking at him with deep meaning, said: 'You are going to Boston. You will see the principal men there. Tell them from ME, at MY request, for God's sake, to cease these conversations and threatenings about a separation of the Union. It must hang together as long as it can be made to'" (Hamilton, *History*, VII, 822–23).

3. Rufus King, who opposed H's decision to fight the duel with Aaron Burr, was on his way to Boston to visit his family and friends. For King's decision to leave New York before the duel, see King, *The Life and Correspondence of Rufus King*, IV, 389–402.

4. The letter to Sedgwick printed above is the last extant letter H wrote before the duel with Burr on July 11, 1804.

John Church Hamilton described his father's final days as follows: ". . . "Sunday [July 8], before the heat of the day, he walked with his wife over all the pleasant scenes of his retreat. On his return to the house, his family being assembled, he read the morning service of the Episcopal church. The intervening hours till evening were spent in kind companionship; and at the close of the day, gathering around him his children under a near tree, he laid with them upon the grass until the stars shone down from the heavens.

"Monday he returned to the city. After disposing of the more urgent of his clients, he drew up a statement of his affairs and prepared his will." (Hamilton, *History*, VII, 823.)

On December 13, 1843, Judah Hammond, who was a clerk in H's law office in 1804, wrote to John Church Hamilton: "The last time General Hamilton was in the office was in the early part of July 1804, in the afternoon. I was the only person remaining in the office with him. The last thing he did there, in his professional business he did at my desk and by my side. Even the place seems sacred to my memory. The office was at Number twelve in Garden Street, opposite the Church Grounds. The building has been since removed. It was near sunset, the evening bright and serene. The setting sun approached the margin of the horizon, shedding his last rays on the beautiful objects illustrated by his departing splendours. At this closing of the day, when we love to linger in its pleasures, General Hamilton came to my desk, in the *tranquil* manner usual with him, and gave me a business paper with his instructions, concerning it. I saw no change in his appearance. These were his last moments in his place of business" (ALS, Columbia University Libraries).

According to John Church Hamilton, H ". . . after waiting upon his faithful friend, Oliver Wolcott, at the close of an entertainment given by him, . . . made his last visit. It was to Colonel [Robert] Troup, the companion of his early years. 'The whole tenor of his deportment manifested such composure and cheerfulness of mind, as to leave me,' Troup relates, 'without any suspicion of the rencontre that was depending; his manner having an air of peculiar earnestness and solicitude'" (Hamilton, *History*, VII, 824–25).

On July 11 Wolcott wrote to his wife: "Hamilton spent the afternoon & evening of Monday with our friends at my House. . . . He was uncommonly cheerful and gay" (Hamilton, *Intimate Life*, 407).

William P. Van Ness to Nathaniel Pendleton

[New York, July 11, 1804]

Dr Sir

If your attention to your friend will not be interrupted by it, I will be greatly obliged to you, to inform me of the situation of General Hamilton. I sincerely hope that his wound is not, as has been stated to me, pronounced mortal.

The melancholy termination of this days contest renders it expedient I think, that we should have an interview as soon as your situation & feeling will justify it. If you will please to appoint an hour for the purpose I shall have the honor of calling at your house. The propriety of withholding particular information, and answers to interrogatories at this moment has doubtless occurred to you. I only take the liberty of suggesting it here, least your present solicitude should render you less cautious than usual. No publication I presume will be made untill I have had the pleasure of seeing you.

I have the honor &c   W. P Van Ness

N. Pendleton Esqr.
July 11, 1804

ALS, New York State Historical Association, Cooperstown, New York.

Aaron Burr to David Hosack

[New York, July 12, 1804]

Mr Burr's respectful Compliments. He requests Dr. Hosack to inform him of the present state of Genl. H. and of the hopes which are entertained of his recovery.

Mr. Burr begs to know at what hours of the [day] the Dr. may most probably be found at home, that he may repeat his inquiries. He would take it very kind if the Dr. would take the trouble of calling on him as he returns from Mr. Bayard's.[1]

Thursday
12 July

AL, Mr. John Hampton Barnes, Philadelphia.
   1. William Bayard was a partner with Herman LeRoy and James McEvers in a New York City mercantile firm. H died at Bayard's house at 80–82 Jane Street.

From Louis Le Guen [1]

Morrisville [Pennsylvania] 12. Juillet 1804.

Gal. Hamilton

cher General

J'ai hier recu Votre Lettre du 6. mai [2] *timbree du 10*, La quelle m'accuse reception de la Mienne du 2.[3] ainssy que de L'Extrait de La Consultation, des deux avocats de Bordeaux, Sur mon Afaire Contre Bouchereau,[4] Et dépuis ai remis L'original avec deux autres Pieces importantes à Mr. harison,[5] Le quel ma mandé avoir obtenue Le renvois de la Cause à la Court qui doit le tenir en Octobre, Ce qui me donnera Probablement Le temps de recevoir quelqu'autre Papiers qui me Sont annoncée.

Javais, il Est Vrai, Mal Compris Ce que vous desiriés Estre informée relatif *aux remises* que Vous m'aves *fait* ou *fait faire* Par Mr. Ogden,[6] Enconcequ'ence Je vais reparer mon Erreur.

L'Interest d'un an Sur les 3000 dollars, dont jai Votre Billet en date ler. avril 1803

Vous me Laves Payée de 210. dollars, il y a trois Semaine Ettant a Newyork.

L'Interest de deux années Sur 5000. dollars, dont jai Votre *Bond Mortgage* en date du ler. Juillet 1801: Ma ette Payée Et Par moy Porte En Recu Sur Le dos dudit Bond.

Le 10 Septembre 1802 recu 350. dollars.

Le 9 Setbre 1803 recu 350 Drs.

Aussy il ny a qu'une année des interest due Le ler. de Ce mois, il En Est ainssy Sur Les 5000 dollars de Mr. harrison, dont le *Bond & Mortgage* Est En Vos Mains.[7]

L'Interest Sur Les 6 ℔ % Stocks, Vous m'aves fait La remise Le 10. avril [8] dernier de 200. dollars Pour Le dernier quartier, ainssy il y a un quartier de due, depuis Le ler. de Ce mois.

Le 24 Janvier aussy dernier,[9] Vous maves fait la remise de 500 dollars, montant du devident de 10 ℔ % Sur 5000 d'ollars. On Newyork insurance Stock: un Semblable devident Vien d'estre annoncée pour estre Payée Le 20 Courant, a Laquelle Epoque Je Vous Prierai de recevoir Ladite Somme de 500 d'ollars et men faire la remise.

Voilla Je Crois Cher General, Les détails Corrects que Vous desiriés que je vous fis Passer, aux quels je dois ajouter Mes bien Sincere remerciments, Et plus une Petite Observation Sur Le Passage de deux de Nos Lettres du 12. Septembre 1803,[10] Et 11. Janvier 1804.[11] d'ou Je Crois il resulterait une Petite Erreur, a votre desavantage de 100. ou 50. d'ollars que jaurais a Vous tenir Compte, au ler. moment que jauroit L'avantage de Vous Voir, En Vous Communiquant Ses Lettres.

Maintenant, Cher General, j'ai a rappeller à votre Memoire Le Petit Voyage que Vous avies Le Projet de faire, Le quel doit Nous Procurer le Plaisir de vous Posseder quelque temps a la Maison. Jespere qu'a Cette Epocque, Mme. Le Guen Serra Mieux de Sa Santé,

Et partagera avec moy Lagrement que Nous Procurera Votre Compagnie.

J'ay L'honneur d'Estre bien Sincerement   Votre bien Affectionne
Serviteur   L. Le Guen

ALS, Yale University Library.
  1. Le Guen wrote this letter to H before he had learned of his death.
  2. Letter not found.
  3. Letter not found.
  4. This is a reference to the case of *Louis Le Guen* adsm *Eli Bouchereau*. Bouchereau, a merchant in Bourdeaux, France, brought suit against Le Guen in the Supreme Court of New York for nonpayment of a loan secured by a bottomry bond. Le Guen maintained that he had ordered George C. Bapst, a partner in the Bordeaux commercial house of Henry Romberg, Bapst, and Company, to pay Bouchereau out of the profits of the mercantile venture. Bouchereau, however, accepted only part of the payment from Bapst and took a promissory note from Bapst as security for the balance. In 1804 Bouchereau tried to collect the balance from Le Guen, who then learned that Bouchereau was also a partner in Bapst's firm. See MS Minutes of the New York Supreme Court, 1801–1805, 1806–1810 (Hall of Records, New York City) under the dates of August 18, 1804, May 18, 1805, February 14, 1807. See also Bill, *Le Guen* adsm *Bouchereau*, filed June 19, 1804, Chancery Papers, BM-636-L (Hall of Records, New York City).
  5. Richard Harison was counsel for Le Guen in his suit against Bouchereau.
  6. See "Indenture between Alexander Hamilton of the First Part and Richard Harison and Aaron Ogden of the Second Part," July 1, 1800; "Bond to Richard Harison and Aaron Ogden," July 1, 1800; "Description of Account with Louis Le Guen," June 8, 1802; "Receipt from Louis Le Guen," September 10, 1802, September 5, 1803; Le Guen to H, September 30, 1802, January 18, 1804.
  7. See "Description of Account with Louis Le Guen," June 8, 1802; Le Guen to H, September 30, 1803.
  8. Letter not found. See Le Guen to H, September 30, 1803.
  9. Letter not found. See "Account with Louis Le Guen," June 6, 1802; "Description of Account with Louis Le Guen," June 8, 1802; Le Guen to H, March 22, 1804.
  10. Letter not found.
  11. Letter not found.

Benjamin Moore to William Coleman [1]

[New York] Thursday evening, July 12. 1804.

MR. COLEMAN,

  The public mind being extremely agitated by the melancholy fate of that great man, ALEXANDER HAMILTON, I have thought it would be grateful to my fellow-citizens, would provide against misrepresentation, and, perhaps, be conducive to the advancement of the cause of religion, were I to give a narrative of some facts which have fallen under my own observation, during the time which elapsed between the fatal duel and his departure out of this world.

Yesterday morning, immediately after he was brought from Hoboken to the house of Mr. Bayard, at Greenwich, a message was sent informing me of the sad event, accompanied by a request from General Hamilton, that I would come to him for the purpose of administering the holy communion.[2] I went; but being desirous to afford time for serious reflection, and conceiving that under existing circumstances, it would be right and proper to avoid every appearance of precipitancy in performing one of the most solemn offices of our religion, I did not then comply with his desire. At one o'clock I was again called on to visit him.[3] Upon my entering the room and approaching his bed, with the utmost calmness and composure he said, "My dear Sir, you perceive my unfortunate situation, and no doubt have been made acquainted with the circumstances which led to it. It is my desire to receive the communion at your hands. I hope you will not conceive there is any impropriety in my request." He added, "It has for some time past been the wish of my heart, and it was my intention to take an early opportunity of uniting myself to the church, by the reception of that holy ordinance." I observed to him, that he must be very sensible of the delicate and trying situation in which I was then placed; that however desirous I might be to afford consolation to a fellow mortal in distress; still, it was my duty as a minister of the gospel, to hold up the law of God as paramount to all other law; and that, therefore, under the influence of such sentiments, I must unequivocally condemn the practice which had brought him to his present unhappy condition. He acknowledged the propriety of these sentiments, and declared that he viewed the late transaction with sorrow and contrition. I then asked him, "Should it please God, to restore you to health, Sir, will you never be again engaged in a similar transaction? and will you employ all your influence in society to discountenance this barbarous custom?" His answer was, "That, Sir, is my deliberate intention."

I proceeded to converse with him on the subject of his receiving the Communion; and told him that with respect to the qualifications of those who wished to become partakers of that holy ordinance, my inquiries could not be made in language more expressive than that which was used by our Church. "Do you sincerely repent of your sins past? Have you a lively faith in God's mercy through Christ, with a thankful remembrance of the death of Christ? And are you disposed to live in love and charity with all men?" He lifted up his hands and said, "With the utmost sincerity of heart I can answer those questions in the affirmative—I have no ill will against Col. Burr. I met him with a fixed resolution to do him no harm. I forgive all that happened." I then observed to him, that the terrors of the divine law were to be announced to the obdurate and impenitent: but that the consolations of the Gospel were to be offered to the humble and contrite heart: that I had no reason to doubt his sincerity, and would proceed immediately to gratify his wishes. The Communion was then administered, which he received with great devotion, and his heart afterwards appeared to be perfectly at rest. I saw him again this morning, when with his last faltering words, he expressed a strong confidence in the mercy of God through the intercession of the Redeemer. I remained with him until 2 o'clock this afternoon, when death closed the awful scene—he expired without a struggle, and almost without a groan.

By reflecting on this melancoly event, let the humble believer be encouraged ever to hold fast that precious faith which is the only source of true consolation in the last extremity of nature. Let the Infidel be persuaded to abandon his opposition to that gospel which the strong, inquisitive, and comprehensive mind of a HAMILTON embraced, in his last moments, as the truth from heaven. Let those who are disposed to justify the practice of duelling, be induced, by this simple narrative, to view with abhorrence that custom which has occasioned in irreparable loss to a worthy and most afflicted family: which has deprived his friends of a beloved companion, his profession of one of its brightest ornaments, and his country of a great statesman and a real patriot.[4]

With great respect, I remain your friend and ser't,

BENJAMIN MOORE.

New-York Evening Post, July 13, 1804.

1. Moore was the Episcopal bishop of New York and the President of Columbia College. Coleman was the editor of the *New-York Evening Post*.

2. For H's earlier views on religion, see H to James A. Bayard, April 16, 21, 1802.

3. In the interval between the request to Bishop Moore and his actual arrival at H's bedside, H asked to see the Reverend John M. Mason, an old friend and the pastor of the Scotch Presbyterian Church on Cedar Street. Mason told H that his denomination prohibited communion being given privately, but assured him that "The Holy Communion is an exhibition and pledge of the mercies which the Son of God has purchased; that the absence of the sign does not exclude from the mercies signified; which were accessible to him by faith in their gracious author." For Mason's account, see *New-York Evening Post*, July 20, 1804.

4. On July 11, 1804, Oliver Wolcott, Jr., wrote to his wife: "I had prepared to set out to see you tomorrow morning, but an afflicting event has just occurred which renders it proper for me to postpone my journey a few days. This morning my friend Hamilton was wounded, and as is supposed *mortally* in a duel with Colo. Burr. The cause the old disagreement about Politicks.

"I have just returned from Mr. Wm. Bayards—where Hamilton is—I did not see him—he suffers great pain—which he endures like a Hero—Mrs. Hamilton is with him, but she is ignorant of the cause of his Illness, which she supposes to be spasms—no one dare tell her the truth—it is feared she would become frantic.

"Gen'l Hamilton has left his opinion, in writing, against Duelling, which he condemns as much as any man living—he determined not to return the fire of his adversary—and reasoned himself into a belief, that though the custom was in the highest degree *criminal*, yet there were peculiar reasons which rendered it proper for *him*, to expose *himself to Col. Burr in particular*. This instance of the derangement of intellect of a great mind, on a single point, has often been noticed as one of the most common yet unaccountable frailties of human nature.

"Genl Hamilton has of late years expressed his conviction of the truths of the Christian Religion, and has desired to receive the Sacrament—but no one of the Clergy who has yet been consulted will administer it." (Hamilton, *Intimate Life*, 405–06.)

Bill for Alexander Hamilton's Coffin

[New York, July 13, 1804]

The Committee Appointed by the Corporation [1] to Conduct the Funeral of the Late General Hamilton Dr

1804	To Fenwick Lyell [2]	
July 13	To a Mahogany Coffin	£ 10..0..0
		$25 [3]

D, Historical Documents Collection, on deposit at Queens College, City University of New York.

1. On July 13, 1804, the Common Council of the City of New York "Resolved unanimously that the Common Council of the City of New York entertain the most unfeigned sorrow and regret for the death of their fellow citizen Alexander Hamilton, and with a view to pay all the respect due to his past

life and future memory and to afford the most unequivocal testimony of the great loss which in the opinion of the Common Council not only this City, but the State of New York and the United States have sustained by the death of this great and good Man the Common Council, do, unanimously Recommend that the usual business of the day. for tomorrow be dispensed with by all classes of inhabitants.

"And, resolved, unanimously that the Ordinance prohibiting the tolling of Bells, at funerals, be on this occasion suspended, and that it be recommended to those who have the charge of the Church Bells in this City to cause them to be muffled and tolled at suitable intervals during the day of his interment

"And also resolved unanimously that the members of the Common Council will in a body attend and join in the funeral procession of the deceased at the time and place appointed.

"Likewise, resolved unanimously that a Committee of three to make such arrangements on the behalf and at the expence of the Common Council of the City of New York for performing the funeral obsequies of the deceased Alexander Hamilton as the said Committee shall judge necessary and expedient.

"Alderman [Jacob] Morton ⎤ Were appointed a committee to carry
  [Wynant] Van Zandt [Jr.] ⎬ into effect the preceding Resolutions,
    & [Jacob] De la Montagnie ⎦ and the same were ordered to be pub-
                                            lished in the newspapers employed by
                                            the Board."

(*Minutes of the Common Council*, III, 568–69.)

On November 29, 1804, the Common Council "Resolved that a Committee be appointed to wait on Colonel [John] Trumbull and employ him in behalf of this Board and at their expence to paint a full length likeness of the late General Hamilton . . ." (*Minutes of the Common Council*, III, 636). Trumbull's bill in April, 1805, "for a whole length portrait . . . of General Hamilton" was five hundred dollars (AD, Historical Documents Collection, on deposit at Queens College, City University of New York). This full-length portrait is now in the New York City Hall.

2. Lyell was a New York City cabinetmaker.

3. On December 10, 1804, the Common Council ordered that Mayor DeWitt Clinton issue a warrant to pay Lyell (*Minutes of the Common Council*, III, 650).

Coroner's Inquest [1]

[New York, July 13–August 2, 1804]

City & County ⎤
of Newyork ⎦ ss   An Inquisition Indented taken for the
                 People of the State of Newyork

At the third Ward of the City of Newyork in the County of Newyork, the thirteenth day of July in the year of Our Lord One thou-

DS, in the handwriting of John Burger and signed by Burger and fifteen other individuals. Mr. C. P. Greenough Fuller, New York City.

1. On July 26, 1804, Nathaniel Pendleton wrote to William Bard: "The Coronor's Inquest have been sitting here ever since the day after his death.

sand Eight hundred and four, and Continued by adjournment until
the Second day of August in the year Aforesaid, before me John
Burger Coroner for the Said City and County of Newyork, On View
of the body of Alexander Hamilton, then and there to wit on the
Said thirteenth day of July in the year last aforesaid, at the Ward
City and County aforesaid lying dead, Upon the Oath of Alexander
Anderson, George Minuse, John A Hardenbrook, Peter Bonnett,
Elam Williams, John Coffin, John Mildeberger, David A Brower,
David Lydig, Abraham Bloodgood, James Cummings, Amos Curtis,
Isaac Burr Benjamin Strong and John D Miller
Good and Lawful men of the Said City and County of New york,
duly chosen and Who being then and there duly sworn and Charged
to enquire for the People of the State of Newyork, When Where
how and by What means the said, Alexander Hamilton, Came to
his death, do Upon their Oath say that Aaron Burr, late of the
Eighth Ward of the Said City in the Said County Esquire and Vice
President of the United States, not having the fear of God before
his eyes, but being moved and seduced by the Instigation of the
devil, on the eleventh day of July in the year last aforesaid, with
force and Arms, in the County of Bergen and State of New Jersey
in and upon the Said Alexander Hamilton in the peace of God and
of the people, of the Said State of New Jersey, then and there being,
feloniously wilfully and of his Malice aforethought, did make an
Assault, and that the Said Aaron Burr, a Certain Pistol of the Value
of One Dollar Charged and loaded with Gun powder and a leaden
bullet Which he the Said Aaron Burr, then and there had and held
in his right hand, to, at, and against the right-Side of the Belly of the
Said Alexander Hamilton did then and there shoot off and discharge,
by means Whereof he the Said Aaron Burr feloniously Wilfully and

They have examined many witnesses and among others myself. But on my
representations that what I could say would be of a nature necessarily to im-
plicate myself they acquiesced & examined no farther. They have had Matth L
Davis before them who refused to answer certain questions, and they Committed him to Bridewell with one of the Boatman who refused to answer. They
have arrested Colo. [Marinus] Willet, & had a warrant against Irvine who has
fled as I understand. Their object was to ascertain the truth of a report that
at a caucus of these and some others it was agreed Burr should fight one or
the other of four or five characters. You will see by the Evening Post that
Coleman is Endeavoring to prove that it was predetermined, and induced by
motives of revenge" (ALS, Bard College, Annandale-on-Hudson, New York).

of his Malice aforethought, did then and there give unto him the Said Alexander Hamilton, With the leaden bullet aforesaid, so as Aforesaid Shot off and discharged out of the Pistol Aforesaid by the force of the Gun powder aforesaid upon the right Side of the belly of him the said Alexander Hamilton a little above the Hip, one mortal Wound, penetrating the Belly of him the Said Alexander Hamilton of Which said mortal wound he the Said Alexander Hamilton, from the Said Eleventh day of July in the year aforesaid, until the twelfth day of July, in the Same year, as well in the County of Bergen in the State of New Jersey, aforesaid, as also at the Eighth Ward of the City of New york in the County of New-york aforesaid, did languish and languishing did live; on Which twelfth day of July in the Said year the Said Alexander Hamilton at the Said Eighth Ward of the said City in the Said County of New york, of the mortal wound aforesaid died, and the Jurors aforesaid on their Oath Aforesaid do further say that William P Van Ness late of the first Ward of the City of Newyork in the County of Newyork aforesaid Attorney at Law, and Nathaniel Pendleton late of the Same place Counsellor at Law, at the time of Committing the felony and Murder Aforesaid feloniously, wilfully and of their Malice aforethought ware present, abetting aiding assisting Comforting and maintaining the said Aaron Burr to kill and murder the Said Alexander Hamilton in manner aforesaid, And so the Jurors aforesaid upon their Oath aforesaid do say the Said Aaron Burr and the Said William P Van Ness and Nathaniel Pendleton him the Said Alexander Hamilton in Manner and by the Means aforesaid, feloniously Wilfully and of their Malice Aforethought, did kill and Murder against the peace of the People of the State of New York and their Dignity.

In Witness Whereof as Well the aforesaid Corner as the Jurors aforesaid have to this Inquisition put their seals on the Second day of August and in the year One thousand Eight hundred and four and at the place aforesaid.

John Burger coroner

Alexnd Anderson
Geo. Minuse
John A Hardenbrook
Peter Bonnett
Elam Williams

John Coffin
John Mildeberger
David A Brower
David Lydig
Abm. Bloodgood
James Cummings
Amos Curtis
Isaac Burr
Benj Strong
J. D. Miller [2]

2. Among the audited bills for the coroner's inquest is the following bill, dated August 1, 1804, which the coroner submitted to the Corporation of the City of New York:

"1804

May 1		To View on the body of a Man Unknown Daver St Wharf Drowned		3	75
3	"	Do Catherine Darby No 54 Chamber St	Do	3	75
9	"	Do Newborn Infant at the Catholick B Ground		3	75
20	"	Inquest Joseph Nesme City Tavern,	Suicide	5	25
22	"	View, a man unknown George Slip	Drowned	3	75
23	"	Do Sam a B M—Slave to the keeper of Hoboken ferry Do		3	75
28	"	Do Doctor Watson N355 Water Street—	Sudden	3	75
30	"	Do Man Unknown Jones Wharf	Drowned	3	75
31	"	Do Thomas Dunaway, 168 Broad Way	Accidental	3	75
June 3	"	Inquest, Samuel S Lane—Debtors Goal,	Natural	5	25
5	"	Do Alexander Lamb Do	Suicide	5	25
7	"	Do Henry Hannan Old Slip	Do	5	25
8	"	View Mary Coran Lumbard St	Sudden	3	75
10	"	Do John Dyckman labourer at Debtors Goal	Do	3	75
Do	"	Do Hariott Porter Bedlow St	Do	3	75
Do	"	Do Man Unknown at the Batery	Drowned	3	75
27	"	Do John Cavany Kipses Bay ⎱	Do	3	75
	"	for going and returning ⎰ 6 miles		0	37½
29	"	Do John Van Dolson 38 Barclay St	Accidental	3	75
[July] 2	"	Do Margaret Hughs, White Hall	Drowned	3	75
3	"	Do Henry Boshar Burling Slip	Do	3	75
6	"	Inquest Elizabeth Thomas Greenwich St	Suicide	5	25
9	"	View Newborn Infant N 4 Orange St		3	75
Do	"	Inquest Nathaniel Morrison Dr Goal	Natural	5	25
11	"	Do Alexander Hamilton Robertson St	Murdered	5	25
14	"	View, Man Unknown at Catherine Slip	Drowned	3	75
18	"	Do Black Man Unknown Rutgers Do	Do	3	75
19	"	Inquest Angus McDonall Dr Goal	Natural	5	25
26	"	View Jack, B M, Slave to Peter W Green ⟨-⟩ St	Drowned	3	75
27	"	Do Newborn Infant Pine St Wharf		3	75
			$	121	12½"

(AD, Historical Documents Collection, on deposit at Queens College, City University of New York).

H's residence in New York City in 1804 was at 54 Cedar Street. John B. Church lived at 25 Robinson Street, and it was from that address that H's funeral procession to Trinity Church started.

The Funeral

[New York, July 14, 1804]

On Saturday last the remains of ALEXANDER HAMILTON were committed to the grave with every possible testimony of respect and sorrow. That distant readers may form some idea of what passed on this mournful occasion, we shall here present them with a regular and correct account of the whole scene.

The Military, under the command of Lieutenant Col. Morton,[1] were drawn up in front of Mr. Church's[2] house, in Robinson-street, where the body had been deposited. On the appearance of the corpse it was received by the whole line with presented arms, and saluted by the officers, with melancholy music by a large and elegant Band.

The military then preceeded the bier, in open column and inverted order, the left in front, with arms reversed, the band playing a dead march. At 12 o'clock the procession moved in the following order, through Beekman, Pearl, and whitehall-streets, and up Broadway to the Church:

The Artillery.

The 6th Regiment of Militia.

Flank Companies.

Cincinnati Society.

A numerous train of Clergy of all denominations.

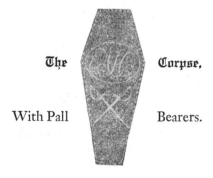

𝕿𝖍𝖊   𝕮𝖔𝖗𝖕𝖘𝖊,

With Pall   Bearers.

New-York Evening Post, July 17, 1804.
1. Jacob Morton.
2. John B. Church.

The General's horse appropriately dressed.

His Children and Relatives.

Physicians.

Gouverneur Morris, the funeral orator, in his carriage.

The Gentlemen of the Bar, all in deep mourning.

The Lieutenant-Governor of the State, in his carriage.

Corporation of the city of New-York.

Resident Agents of Foreign Powers.

Officers of our Army and Navy.

Military and Naval Officers of Foreign Powers.

Militia Officers of the State.

The various officers of the respective Banks.

Chamber of Commerce and Merchants.

Wardens of the Port, and masters of vessels in the harbor.

The President, Professors, and Students of Columbia College,
in mourning gowns.

St. Andrew's Society, mostly in mourning.

Tammany Society.

Mechanic Society.

Marine Society.

Citizens in General.

The Pall was supported by

General Matthew Clarkson

Oliver Wolcott, Esquire,

Richard Harison, Esquire,

Josiah Ogden Hoffman, Esquire,

Richard Varick, Esquire,

William Bayard, Esquire, and

His Hon. Judge Lawrence.

On the top of the coffin was the General's hat and sword; his boots and spurs reversed across the horse. His grey horse, dressed in mourning, was led by two black servants dressed in white, and white turbans trimmed with black.

The streets were lined with people; doors and windows were filled, principally with weeping females, and even the house tops were covered with spectators, who came from all parts to behold the melancholy procession.

When the advanced platoon of the military reached the church, the whole column wheeled backward by sections from the flanks of platoons, forming a lane, bringing their muskets to a reversed order, and resting the cheek on the butt of the piece in the customary attitude of grief. Through the avenue thus formed, the corpse, preceded by the clergy of different denominations, the Society of Cincinnati, and followed by the relations of the deceased, and different public bodies, advanced to the church, the band, with drums muffled, playing all the time a pensive, solemn air.

FUNERAL ORATION.

On the stage erected in the portico of Trinity Church, Mr. Gouverneur Morris,[3] having four of General Hamilton's sons,[4] the eldest

3. On July 13, 1804, Morris wrote in his diary: "Take Mr. Harison [Richard Harison] out to dine with me. Discuss the Points which it may be safe to touch To morrow and those which it will be proper to avoid. To a Man who could fully command all his Powers this Subject is difficult. The first Point of his Biography is that he was a Stranger of illegitimate Birth. Some Mode must be contrived to pass over this handsomely. He was indiscreet, vain and opinionated. These things must be told or the Character will be incomplete—and yet they must be told in such Manner as not to destroy the Interest. He was on Principle opposed to republican and attached to monarchical Government— And then his Opinions were generally known and have been long and loudly proclaimed. His Share in forming our Constitution must be mentioned and his unfavorable Opinion cannot therefore be concealed. The most important Part of his Life was his Administration of the finances. The System he proposed was in one Respect radically wrong—moreover, it has been the Subject of some just and much unjust Criticism. Many are still hostile to it, though on improper Ground. I can neither commit myself to a full and pointed Approbation, nor is it prudent to censure others. All this must, some how or other be reconciled. He was in Principle opposed to Duelling, but he has fallen in a Duel. I cannot thoroughly excuse him without criminating Colo. Burr which would be wrong and might lead to Events which every good Citizen must deprecate. Indeed this Morning when I sent to Colo. [William S.] Smith, who had asked an oration from me last Night, to tell him I would endeavor to say some few words over the Corpse, I told him, in Answer to the Hope he expresst that in doing Justice to the Dead I would not injure the living, that Colo. Burr ought to be considered in the same Light with any other Man who had killed another in a Duel, That I certainly should not excite to any Outrage on him, but, as it seemed evident to me that legal Steps would be taken against him Prudence would I should suppose direct him to keep out of the Way. In Addition to all the Difficulties of this Subject is the Impossibility of writing and committing any thing to Memory in the short time allowed. The Corpse is already putrid and the funeral Procession must take Place to morrow Morning. . . ."

On July 14, 1804, Morris wrote in his diary: ". . . A little before ten go to Mr. Church's House from whence the Corpse is to move. We are detained about sixteen and the youngest about six years of age, with him, rose and delivered to the immense concourse in front an extemporary Oration, which, being pronounced slowly and impressively, was easily committed to memory, and being very soon afterwards placed on paper, is presumed to be correct even to the language. Being shown to several gentlemen who heard it, they all agree that it comes near enough to what was actually delivered to be presented as that oration at length.

FELLOW CITIZENS,

If on this sad, this solemn occasion, I should endeavour to move your commiseration, it would be doing injustice to that sensibility which has been so generally and so justly manifested. Far from attempting to excite your emotions, I must try to repress my own, and yet I fear that instead of the language of a public speaker, you will hear only the lamentations of a bewailing friend. But I will struggle with my bursting heart, to pourtray that Heroic Spirit, which has flown to the mansions of bliss.

Students of Columbia—he was in the ardent pursuit of knowledge in your academic shades, when the first sound of the American war called him to the field. A young and unprotected volunteer, such was his zeal, and so brilliant his service, that we heard his name be-

---

till twelve. While moving in the Procession I meditate, as much as my feelings will permit—on what I am to say. I can find no Way to get over the Difficulty which would attend the Details of his Death. It will be impossible to command either myself or my Audience—their Indignation amounts almost to frenzy already. Over this, then a Veil must be drawn. I must not either dwell on his domestic Life—He has long since foolishly published the Avowal of conjugal Infidelity. Something however must be said to excite public Pity for his family which he has left in indigent Circumstances. I speak for the first Time in the open Air, and find that my Voice is lost before it reaches one tenth of the Audience. Get thro' the Difficulties tolerably well—Am of Necessity short especially as I feel the Impropriety of acting a dumb Shew which is the Case as to all those who see but cannot hear me. I find that what I have said does not answer the general Expectation. This I knew would be the Case—It must ever happen to him whose Duty it is to allay the Sentiment which he is expected to rouse. How easy it would have been to make them for a Moment absolutely mad! This Evening Mr [William] Coleman Editor of the Evening Post calls. He requests me to give him what I have said. He took Notes but found his Language so far inferior that he threw it in the fire. Promise, if he will write what he remembers, I will endeavor to put it into the Terms which were used. He speaks very highly of the Discourse—More so than it deserves" (AD, Gouverneur Morris Papers, Library of Congress).

4. Alexander, James Alexander, John Church, and William Stephen Hamilton.

fore we knew his person. It seemed as if God had called him suddenly into existence, that he might assist to save a world!

The penetrating eye of Washington soon perceived the manly spirit which animated his youthful bosom. By that excellent judge of men he was selected as an Aid, and thus he became early acquainted with, and was a principle actor in the most important scenes of our Revolution.

At the seige of York, he pertinaciously insisted—and he obtained the command of a Forlorn Hope. He stormed the redoubt; but let it be recorded, that not one single man of the enemy perished. His gallant troops emulating the heroism of their chief, checked the uplifted arm, and spared a foe no longer resisting. Here closed his military career.

Shortly after the war, your favour—no, your discernment called him to public office. You sent him to the convention at Philadelphia: he there assisted in forming that constitution which is now the bond of our union, the shield of our defence and the source of our prosperity. In signing that compact he exprest his apprehension that it did not contain sufficient means of strength for its own preservation; and that in consequence we should share the fate of many other republics and pass through Anarchy to Despotism. We hoped better things. We confided in the good sense of the American people: and above all we trusted in the protecting Providence of the Almighty. On this important subject he never concealed his opinion. He disdained concealment. Knowing the purity of his heart, he bore it as it were in his hand, exposing to every passenger its inmost recesses. This generous indiscretion subjected him to censure from misrepresentation. His speculative opinions were treated as deliberate designs; and yet you all know how strenuous, how unremitting were his efforts to establish and to preserve the constitution. If, then, his opinion was wrong, pardon, oh! pardon that single error, in a life devoted to your service.

At the time when our government was organised, we were without funds, though not without resources. To call them into action, and establish order in the finances, Washington sought for splendid talents, for extensive information, and, above all, he sought for sterling, incorruptible integrity—All these he found in Hamilton. The system then adopted has been the subject of much animadversion.

If it be not without a fault, let it be remembered that nothing human is perfect. Recollect the circumstances of the moment—recollect the conflict of opinion—and above all, remember that *the minister of a republic must bend to the will of the people.* The administration which Washington formed, was one of the most efficient, one of the best that any country was ever blest with. And the result was a rapid advance in power and prosperity, of which there is no example in any other age or nation. The part which Hamilton bore is universally known.

His unsuspecting confidence in professions which he believed to be sincere, led him to trust too much to the undeserving. This exposed him to misrepresentation. He felt himself obliged to resign. The care of a rising family, and the narrowness of his fortune, made it a duty to return to his profession for their support. But though he was compelled to abandon public life, never, no, never for a moment did he abandon the public service. He never lost sight of your interests. I declare to you, before that God in whose presence we are now so especially assembled, that in his most private and confidential conversations, the single objects of discussion and consideration were your freedom and happiness.

You well remember the state of things which again called forth Washington from his retreat to lead your armies. You know that he asked for Hamilton to be his Second in command. That venerable sage well knew the dangerous incidents of a military profession, and he felt the hand of time pinching life at its source. It was probable that he would soon be removed from the scene, and that his Second would succeed to the command. He knew, by experience, the importance of that place—and he thought the sword of America might safely be confided to the hand which now lies cold in that coffin. Oh! my fellow citizens, remember this solemn testimonial, that he was not ambitious. Yet, he was charged with ambition: and wounded by the imputation, when he laid down his command, he declared in the proud independence of his soul, that he never would accept of any office, unless in a foreign war he should be called on to expose his life in defence of his country This determination was immoveable. It was his fault that his opinions and his resolutions could not be changed. Knowing his own firm purpose, he was indignant at the charge that he sought for place or power. He was ambitious only of glory, but he was deeply solicitous for you. For himself he feared nothing, but he feared that bad men might by false professions, acquire your confidence and abuse it to your ruin.

Brethren of the Cincinnati—There lies our chief! Let him still be our model. Like him, after a long and faithful public service, let us cheerfully perform the social duties of private life. Oh! he was mild and gentle. In him there was no offence; no guile. His generous hand and heart were open to all.

Gentlemen of the Bar—You have lost your brightest ornament. Cherish and imitate his example. While, like him, with justifiable, with laudable zeal, you pursue the interests of your clients, remember, like him, the eternal principles of justice.

Fellow Citizens—You have long witnessed his professional conduct, and felt his unrivalled eloquence. You know how well he performed the duties of a Citizen—you know that he never courted your favour by adulation, or the sacrifice of his own judgment. You have seen him contending against you, and saving your dearest interests, as it were, in spite of yourselves. And you now feel and enjoy the benefits resulting from the firm energy of his conduct. Bear this testimony to the memory of my departed friend. I CHARGE YOU TO PROTECT HIS FAME—It is all he has left—all that these poor orphan children will inherit from their father. But, my countrymen, that Fame may be a rich treasure to you also. Let it be the test by which to examine those who solicit your favour. Disregarding professions, view their conduct and on a doubtful occasion, ask, *Would Hamilton have done this thing?*

You all know how he perished. On this last scene, I cannot, I must not dwell. It might excite emotions too strong for your better judgment. Suffer not your indignation to lead to any act which might again offend the insulted majesty of the law. On his part, as from his lips, though with my voice—for his voice you will hear no more—let me entreat you to respect yourself.

And now, ye ministers of the everlasting God, perform your holy office and commit these ashes of our departed brother to the bosom of the Grave!

The oration being finished the corpse was carried to the grave, where the usual funeral service was performed by the Reverend Bishop Moore. The troops who had entered the church yard, formed

Photograph by William Prince

an extensive hollow square and terminated the solemnities with three vollies over the grave.

During the procession there was a regular discharge of minute guns from the Battery, by a detachment from the regiment of artillery. The different merchant vessels in the harbor wore their colors half mast, both this and the preceding day.

His Britannic Majesty's ship of war Boston, Capt. Douglass, at anchor within the Hook, appeared in mourning the whole morning, and at ten o'clock she commenced firing minute guns, which were continued forty-eight minutes. His Majesty's packet Lord Charles Spencer, Capt. Cotesworth also was in mourning, and fired an equal number of guns. The French frigates Cybelle and Didon, were also put into full mourning both this and the preceding day, with yards peeked; they also fired minute guns during the procession. It deserves also to be mentioned that the French Surgeons of these frigates went out to Mr. Bayards [5] before his death and offered their services. These affecting marks of attention will be gratefully received by our fellow-citizens, as evidence how highly the deceased was respected and esteemed by the French and English officers.

We have no observations to add. This scene was enough to melt a monument of marble.[6]

5. William Bayard.

6. On August 20, 1804, the New York City Common Council ordered the mayor to issue a warrant to "Selah Strong to pay to Sundry persons on account of the funeral expences of Gen. Hamilton 700 41/100" (*Minutes of the Common Council*, III, 593).

In the Historical Documents Collection on deposit at Queens College, City University of New York, is the bill for nine dollars which was submitted on August 27, 1804, to the Corporation of the City of New York for "tolling three Bells at the funeral of General Hamilton viz in Trinity St. Pauls St George Chappele."

William P. Van Ness to Nathaniel Pendleton

[New York, July 14, 1804]

Dr Sir

I left you for the purpose of procuring & examining my own papers relative to the late Duel unfortunate affair—& was sorry to find on my return that you had left Dr Hosacks. The statement which you hastily read to me, contained things that rendered it desirable for me to recur to my own Notes. As I presume no publication will take place in the morning papers I will have the honor of seeing you again On my return to the City which will be about 9 o clock in the morning.

W. P Van Ness

N. Pendleton Esqr July 14, 1804

ADfS, New York State Historical Association, Cooperstown, New York.

Nathaniel Pendleton to William P. Van Ness

[New York, July 15, 1804]
Sunday evening Nine O Clock

Sir

Having thought it expedient on consideration to make a small addition to the statement which I had the honor of communicating to you on Friday last, I wished to have given you an opportunity of seeing it previous to its publication; and for that purpose I called at your house in town this evening supposing you had been prevented from calling upon me at five oClock this afternoon according to appointment. I judge it proper that the publication should appear in the afternoon's paper of tomorrow. I hope therefore it will be convenient for you to call upon me at an early hour tomorrow morning, that you may have an opportunity of pointing out any inaccuracy if there should be any. It may be proper to apprise you that my friends concur with me in opinion that the publication should not be delayed.

I have the honor to be   Sir   Your most Obedient servt.

Nathl: Pendleton

William P. Van Ness Esqr.

ALS, New York State Historical Association, Cooperstown, New York.

William P. Van Ness to Nathaniel Pendleton

[New York] July 16, 1804

Dr Sir

I went to the City yesterday for the express purpose of conferring with [you] on the subject of the contemplated publication. One of my children was extremely unwell when I left home and a short time after my arrival in town, a Servant was sent to inform me that she was in extreme danger. To this unfortunate situation of my family I beg you to ascribe my apparent inattention to the appointment of yesterday. I regret extremely that your first determination to publish on tuesday has been abandoned, because it will be extremely inconvenient & difficult for me to meet you this day. I shall however be in town by 12 o clock & inform you of my arrival & where I should be happy to see you. The objections that occurred to me upon a slight veiw of your statement were, first that my reasons for not receiving the last communication from Genl Hamilton were not explicitly assigned.[1] I allude to the paper you offered the day after the Message had been delivered,[2] and the answer received.[3]

2d to the introduction of a copy of a paper which you read to me at your house [4]—but was not delivered me, and of course never seen by my principal and as you afterwards furnished me with a written communication [5] of an import somewhat different I think that the only one that should be noticed. One or two other things were presented to my mind at the moment of perusal, but of inferior importance. [It is solely for the purpose of conversing with you on these points, that I should prefer a short suspension of the publication and not to create unnecessary delay. While however the Coroners Jury is sitting,[6] and the public mind is highly excited, I conceive that good rather than evil consequences would result from the proposed delay.] [7] Of this however you will judge & will I trust pursue such measure as are best calculated to allay the irritation which prevails. Pardon me for not copying this letter. The gentleman is waiting for it, and when we meet I will solicit of you permission to transcribe it.

I shall advise you of my arrival, which will be as early as the state of my family's health will permit certainly by One oclock—in the meantime I will prepare my statement & submit it to your inspection.

ADf, New York State Historical Association, Cooperstown, New York.
    1. See "Remarks on the letter of June 27. 1804," June 28, 1804.
    2. See Aaron Burr to H, June 22, 1804; Van Ness to Pendleton, June 26, 27, 1804.
    3. See "Nathaniel Pendleton's Narrative of the Events of June 27–28, 1804"; "Remarks on the letter of June 27. 1804," June 28, 1804.
    4. See "Nathaniel Pendleton's First Account of Alexander Hamilton's Conversation at John Tayler's House," June 25, 1804; "William P. Van Ness's Narrative of Later Events of June 25, 1804."
    5. See "Nathaniel Pendleton's Second Account of Alexander Hamilton's Conversation at John Tayler's House," June 25, 1804; "William P. Van Ness's Narrative of Later Events of June 25, 1804."
    6. See "Coroner's Inquest," July 13–August 2, 1804.
    7. Van Ness crossed out the material within brackets.

Nathaniel Pendleton to William P. Van Ness

New York. July 16, 1804
½ After one.

Dear Sir

It will not be possible for me to give you another opportunity of seeing the Statement, before it is printed. Arrangements were made to have it appear this day,[1] reserving a few lines of addition for your examination until after the hour you mentioned; as to which too we had before conversed. I have added in explicit terms the reason assigned by you for not having received the last paper I offered you from Genl. H—. I could by no means consent to omit the paper I read to you, as you seem to desire; as you must have supposed it was deemed particularly material by having been put into writing.

I trust you will find no reason to complain of any want of accuracy or precision in the publication I have authorised.

I have the honor to be   Sir,   Your Obed Servt.

Nathl: Pendleton

William P Van Ness Esq

ALS, New York State Historical Association, Cooperstown, New York.
   1. Pendleton's narrative was printed in the *New-York Evening Post* on
July 16, 1804. See "Nathaniel Pendleton's Narrative of the Events of June 22,
1804," note 1.

Joint Statement by William P. Van Ness and Nathaniel Pendleton on the Duel between Alexander Hamilton and Aaron Burr [1]

[New York, July 17, 1804]

Col: Burr arrived first on the ground as had been previously agreed.
When Genl Hamilton arrived the parties exchanged salutations and
the Seconds proceeded to make their arrangments. They measured
the distance, ten full paces, and cast lots for the choice of positions
as also to determine by whom the word should be given, both of
which fell to the Second of Genl Hamilton. They then proceeded
to load the pistols in each others presence, after which the parties
took their stations. The Gentleman who was to give the word,
then explained to the parties the rules which were to govern them
in firing which were as follows: The parties being placed at their
stations The Second who gives the word shall ask them whether
they are ready—being answered in the affirmative, he shall say
"present" after which the parties shall present & fire when they
please. If one fires before the other the opposite second shall say
one two, three, fire, and he shall fire or loose his fire. [2] And asked
if they were prepared, being answered in the affirmative he gave the
word *present* as had been agreed on, and both of the parties took
aim, [3] & fired in succession, the Intervening time is not expressed as
the seconds do not precisely agree on that point. The pistols were
discharged within a few seconds of each other and the fire of Col:
Burr took effect; Genl Hamilton almost instantly fell. [4] Col: Burr
then advanced toward Genl H——n with a manner and gesture that
appeared to Genl Hamilton's friend to be expressive of regret, but
without Speaking turned about & withdrew. Being urged from the
field by his friend as has been subsequently stated, with a view to

prevent his being recognised by the Surgeon and Bargemen who were then approaching.[5] No farther communications took place between the principals and the Barge that carried Col: Burr immediately returned to the City. We conceive it proper to add that the conduct of the parties in that interview was perfectly proper as suited the occasion.[6]

ADf, in the handwriting of Van Ness and with revisions in the handwriting of Pendleton, New York State Historical Association, Cooperstown, New York; AD (incomplete), in the handwriting of Pendleton, New-York Historical Society, New York City; [New York] *Morning Chronicle,* July 17, 1804; *New-York Evening Post,* July 19, 1804.

1. In the [New York] *Morning Chronicle,* July 17, 1804, where this document appeared as item No. 13 in Van Ness's account of the duel, it was preceded by the following statement: "The occurrences of that interview [the duel] will appear from the following statement, No. 13, which has been drawn up and mutually agreed on by the seconds of the parties." On the cover of his incomplete statement Pendleton wrote: "facts agreed between N. P. & Wm. V. Ness."

Minor word variations between the document printed above and the newspaper versions of this document have not been noted

2. Up to this point, the Van Ness and Pendleton documents are alike. The rest of Pendleton's incomplete document reads: "The Gentleman who was to give the word asked if they were prepared, being answered in the affirmative he gave the word 'present.' Both the parties presented. The Pistols were both discharged successively, (but the time intervening between the two is not here Stated the seconds not agreeing on that fact. The fire of Colo."

3. On July 18, 1804, an item entitled "A Correction" appeared in the *New-York Evening Post,* which reads: "It is agreed by the gentlemen who attended General Hamilton and Colonel Burr in the late unfortunate affair, that the document No. 13, in the statement which appeared in the Morning Chronicle of yesterday, should be corrected in the following manner:

"In the interview between General Hamilton and Col. Burr, both parties agreeably to the word of command *presented:* this term should therefore be employed as more correct than the expression *"took aim,"* inserted in document No. 13, of the statement published in the Morning Chronicle of yesterday."

The [New York] *Morning Chronicle* published this correction on July 19, 1804.

4. This sentence originally read: ". . . ⟨and⟩ the body of Genl Hamilton who instantly fell. . . ." The word "almost," which was substituted for "who," is in the handwriting of Pendleton.

5. These two sentences, which were revised, originally read: "Col: Burr then advanced toward [the] gentleman with an expression of concern on his countenance and gestures, but was stopped by his Second with a view as has been subsequently stated to prevent his being recognized by the Surgeon and Bargemen who were then approaching." Some of the changes are in Pendleton's handwriting.

6. This sentence was revised by Pendleton. Van Ness originally wrote: "We conceive it proper to add that the conduct of both parties was perfectly correct and honorable."

On July 18, 1804, Burr wrote to Charles Biddle a brief, one-paragraph description of the duel. In this letter he emphasized that the actual firing was delayed by H's insistence on taking his glasses from his pocket and placing them on his nose (copy, New York State Historical Association, Cooperstown, New York). In an undated letter Burr asked Van Ness to explain in detail the duel to Biddle and to stress the fact that H's decision to use his glasses had delayed the duel (AL, New-York Historical Society, New York City). In an undated letter that was apparently sent to Biddle, Van Ness wrote:

"After the necessary pre-arrangements heretofore detailed, had been made—the parties had taken their stations, & received their pistols cocked (Mr. Hamilton's being a remarkably high-finished pair, of a very large bore carrying, I should judge, nearly an ounce ball). After the mode of proceeding had been explained and Mr. Pendleton was about to give the word, 'Stop', said Mr. Hamilton, 'in certain states of the light one requires glasses.' He then levelled his pistol in several directions, as if to try the light; then drew from his pockets & put on, a pair of spectacles, and again levelled his pistol in different directions. and once, as appeared to me, at Mr. Burr who was all this time silent at his station. After the latter experiments of the light, and begging pardon for the delay Genl. H. said, keeping on his spectacles, 'this will do; now you may proceed.'

"The Gentleman whose duty it was to give the word then asked the parties whether they were prepared?—which being replied to in the affirmative, the word *present* was given; on which both parties presented, and Genl. H. fired. After a few seconds of time Coll. B. fired; and instantly Genl. H. fell. Mr. B immediately approached, but Mr. P. at the same time called out very loudly for Doctr. Hossack; and hearing the Doctr. coming through the bushes, I urged the propriety of his (Mr. B's) repairing immediately to the barge: he accordingly retired and I soon followed him. When I arrived at the barge I found Coll B. in the act of stepping from it, and as I approached he said 'I must go & speak to him.' I observed that it would be obviously imprudent, as Genl. H. was then surrounded by the Surgeon & Bargemen by whom he (Mr. B.) ought not to be seen; but that if *he* would remain *I* would go & see the General again, which I did; and on my return ordered the bargemen to proceed immediately to the City.

"On the point of the first firing, although in my opinion of no consequence, I am so unfortunate as to differ from the friend of Genl. H.:—and without doubting the sincerity of his opinion, I can safely declare that I can not conceive the slightest ground to question the fact as above stated; and I was never more confident of any matter subject to the examination of my senses. If any doubt had even existed it would have been removed by the following circumstances: 1st. When Genl. H. fired I observed a jar or slight motion in Mr. B's body, from which I supposed he was struck; but seeing him immediately afterwards standing firm on his station—I concluded the wound could not be serious: Under the impression still, however, that he was wounded, as soon as I had an opportunity I enquired where he was struck?—and after explaining to him the reason of my impression, he informed me that his foot had got upon a stone or piece of wood which gave him pain and had sprained his Ancle. "2 It is agree'd, I believe, by all who were within hearing, but particularly attested by Doctr. Hossack, that several seconds intervened between the two discharges; and it is also agree'd that Genl. H. fell *instantly* on Mr. B's firing, which contradicts the idea that Mr. B. fired first. "3d. Immediately after our getting into the boat I asked Mr. Burr why he had so long delayed his fire? He answered that the smoke of Mr. H's pistol for a moment obscured his sight, and that as Mr. P. did not instantly begin to count, there was nothing to hurry him. It is here to be observed that there was, at the time, a light breeze from the north and that Mr. H. had the northerly position:

besides, the bushes surrounding the place caused the Wind to move in eddies.

"Thus, Sir, have I detailed to you, as minutely as I am able, such circumstances relative to the late unfortunate interview between the Vice President and Genl. Hamilton as have not hitherto been published.

"As to the pretence that Genl. H. did not intend to fire and that Coll. B. knew it, it is more dishonorable to the deceased than the survivor: but nothing appears more destitute of foundation. The above circumstances, as well as every other which fell under my notice or observation throughout the transaction, indicated on the part of Mr. H. a determination to take, if possible, the life of his adversary. If Genl. H. did not intend to fire it is most certainly a fact never intimated to me before the rencounter—of which I had not the least expectation—and which I am convinced from every circumstance, & most conclusively so from that of his having made & committed to me final arrangements respecting his pecuniary Affairs & business generally.

"It is but justice to add that the Vice President so far from manifesting any degree of levity upon the occasion which is the subject of my letter, or from expressing any satisfaction at the result, his whole conduct whilst in my company was expressive of regret & concern." (AL, New-York Historical Society, New York City.)

List of Papers Given to Nathaniel Pendleton

[New York, July 19, 1804]

There were inclosed under this cover and delivered to me after the death of General Hamilton

1. His will [1]
2. Deed of trust to John B Church, Jno Laurence, & Genl Clarkson [2]
3. State of his Property & Debts with remarks [3]
4 Remarks explanatory of his conduct motives & views in his expected interview [4]
5 Note to myself [5]
6. Letter to Mrs. Hamilton [6]
7. Letter to John B Church inclosing an Assignment of some debts. [7]
8. Letter to Mrs. Mitchell inclosing 400 dollars as was mentioned on the outside. Sealed [8]
9. Letter to Geo: Mitchell inclosing a lottery ticket, as mentioned on the outside. Sealed. [9]
10 Memorandum of some fees received after his Engagement which he considers as part of his debts [10]

> The packet was Opened by me in the presence
> of David A Ogden and Washington Morton [11] on the
> day of his death

Nathl Pendleton
made July 19th. 1804

ADS, New-York Historical Society, New York City.

1. See "Last Will and Testament of Alexander Hamilton," July 9, 1804.

2. See "Deed of Trust to John B. Church, John Laurance, and Matthew Clarkson," July 6, 1804.

3. See "Statement of my property and Debts July 1. 1804" and "Alexander Hamilton's Explanation of His Financial Situation," July 1, 1804.

4. See "Statement on Impending Duel with Aaron Burr," June 28–July 10, 1804.

5. See H to Pendleton, July 4, 1804.

6. H wrote two letters to Elizabeth Hamilton before his death. See H to Elizabeth Hamilton, July 4, 10, 1804.

7. See "Assignment of Debts and Grant of Power of Attorney to John B. Church," July 9, 1804. The covering letter from H to Church has not been found.

8. For this "letter not found," see H to Ann Mitchell, June 28–July 10, 1804.

9. For this "letter not found," see H to George Mitchell, June 28–July 10, 1804.

10. See "Debts Owed for Services Not Rendered," July 10, 1804.

11. Morton, who was married to Elizabeth Hamilton's sister Cornelia, and Ogden were New York City lawyers.

Nathaniel Pendleton's Amendments to the Joint Statement Made by William P. Van Ness and Him on the Duel between Alexander Hamilton and Aaron Burr [1]

[New York, July 19, 1804]

The statement containing the facts that led to the interview between General Hamilton and Col. Burr, published in the Evening Post on Monday,[2] studiously avoided mentioning any particulars of what past at the place of meeting. This was dictated by suitable considerations at the time, and with the intention, that whatever it might be deemed proper to lay before the public, should be made the subject of a future communication. The following is therefore now submitted.

In the interviews that have since taken place between the gentle-

New-York Evening Post, July 19, 1804.

1. On July 18, 1804, the following item appeared in the New-York Evening Post: "A difference of opinion having taken place between the friends who accompanied General Hamilton and Colonel Burr, on the late distressing affair, relative to some circumstances which happened at the time and place of the interview, a statement will be laid before the public tomorrow from an authentic source."

2. See "Joint Statement by William P. Van Ness and Nathaniel Pendleton on the Duel between Alexander Hamilton and Aaron Burr," July 17, 1804.

men that were present, they have not been able to agree in two important facts that passed there—for which reason nothing was said on those subjects in the paper lately published as to other particulars in which they were agreed.

Mr. P. expressed a confident opinion that General Hamilton did not fire first—and that he did not fire at all *at Col. Burr.* Mr. V. N. seemed equally confident in the opinion that Gen. H. did fire first— and of course that it must have been *at* his antagonist.

General Hamilton's friend thinks it to be a sacred duty he owes to the memory of that exalted man, to his country, and his friends, to publish to the world such facts and circumstances as have produced a decisive conviction in his own mind, that he cannot have been mistaken in the belief he has formed on these points.

1st. Besides the testimonies of Bishop Moore, and the paper containing an express declaration, under General Hamilton's own hand, enclosed to his friend in a packet, not to be delivered but in the event of his death, and which have already been published, General Hamilton informed Mr. P. at least ten days previous to the affair, that he had doubts whether he would not receive and not return Mr. Burr's first fire. Mr. P. remonstrated against this determination, and urged many considerations against it, as dangerous to himself and not necessary in the particular case, when every ground of accommodation, not humiliating, had been proposed and rejected. He said he would not decide lightly, but take time to deliberate fully. It was incidentally mentioned again at their occasional subsequent conversations, and on the evening preceding the time of the appointed interview, he informed Mr. P. he had made up his mind *not to fire at Col. Burr the first time, but to receive his fire, and fire in the air.* Mr. P. again urged him upon this subject, and repeated his former arguments. His final answer was in terms that made an impression on Mr. P's mind which can never be effaced. "My friend, it is the effect of a RELIGIOUS SCRUPLE, and does not admit of reasoning, it is useless to say more on the subject, as my purpose is definitely fixed."

2d. His last words before he was wounded afford a proof that this purpose had not changed. When he received his pistol, after having taken his position, he was asked if he would have the hair spring set? His answer was, *"Not this time."*

3d. After he was wounded, and laid in the boat, the first words he uttered after recovering the power of speech, were, (addressing himself to a gentleman present, who perfectly well remembers it) *"Pendleton knows I did not mean to fire at Col. Burr the first time."*

4th. This determination had been communicated by Mr. P. to that gentleman that morning, before they left the city.

5th. The pistol that had been used by General Hamilton, lying loose over the other apparatus in the case which was open; after having been some time in the boat, one of the boatmen took hold of it to put it into the case. General Hamilton observing this, said *"Take care of that pistol—it is cocked. It may go off and do mischief."* This is also remembered by the gentleman alluded to.

This shews he was not sensible of having fired at all. If he had fired *previous* to receiving the wound, he would have remembered it, and therefore have known that the pistol could not go off; but if *afterwards* it must have been the effect of an involuntary exertion of the muscles produced by a mortal wound, in which case, he could not have been conscious of having fired.

6. Mr. P. having so strong a conviction that if General Hamilton had fired first, it could not have escaped his attention (all his anxiety being alive for the effect of the first fire, and having no reason to believe the friend of Col. Burr was not sincere in the contrary opinion) he determined to go to the spot where the affair took place, to see if he could not discover some traces of the course of the ball from Gen. Hamilton's pistol.

He took a friend with him the day after General Hamilton died, and after some examination they fortunately found what they were in search of. They ascertained that the ball passed through the limb of a cedar tree, at an elevation of about twelve feet and a half, perpendicularly from the ground, between thirteen and fourteen feet from the mark on which General Hamilton stood, and about four feet wide of the direct line between him and Colonel Burr, on the right side; he having fallen on the left. The part of the limb through which the ball passed was cut off and brought to this city, and is now in Mr. Church's possession.

No inferences are pointed out as resulting from these facts, nor will any comments be made. They are left to the candid judgment and feelings of the public.

William P. Van Ness's Amendments to the Joint Statement Made by Nathaniel Pendleton and Him on the Duel between Alexander Hamilton and Aaron Burr [1]

[New York July 21, 1804]

The second of G H having considered it proper to subjoin an explanatory note to the statement mutually furnished,[2] it becomes proper for the gentleman who attended Col Burr to state also his impressions with respect to those points on which their exists a variance of opinion. In doing this he pointedly disclaims any idea disrespectful to the memory of G H, or an intention to ascribe any conduct to him that is not in his opinion perfectly honorable & correct.

The parties met as has been above related & took their respective stations as directed: the pistols were then handed to them by the seconds. Gen Hamilton elevated his, as if to try the light, & lowering it said I beg pardon for delaying you but the direction of the light renders it necessary, at the same time feeling his pockets with his left hand, & drawing forth his spectacles put them on. The second then asked if they were prepared which was replied to in the affirmative. The word *present* was then given, on which both parties took aim. The pistol of General Hamilton was first discharged, and Col Burr fired immediately after, only five or six seconds of time intervening. On this point the second of Col Burr has full & perfect reccollection. He noticed particularly the discharge of G H's pistol, & looked to his principal to ascertain whether he was hurt, he then clearly saw Col Bs pistol discharged. At this moment of looking at Col B on the discharge of G H's pistol he perceived a slight motion in his person, which induced the idea of his being struck. On this point he conversed with his principal on their return, who ascribed that circumstance to a small stone under his foot, & observed that the smoke of G Hs pistol obscured him for a moment in the interval of their firing.

When G H fell Col B advanced toward him as stated & was checked by his second who urged the importance of his immediately repairing to the barge, conceiving that G H was mortally wounded,

& being desirous to secure his principal from the sight of the sur-geon & bargemen who might be called in evidence. Col B complied with his request.

He shortly followed him to the boat, and Col B again expressed a wish to return, saying with an expression of much concern, I must go & speak to him. I again urged the obvious impropriety stating that the G was surrounded by the Surgeon & Bargemen by whom he must not be seen & insisted on immediate departure.

AD, New York State Historical Association, Cooperstown, New York; [New York] *Morning Chronicle*, July 21, 1804.

1. On July 11, 1804, Aaron Burr wrote to Van Ness: "There is in circula-tion a report which is ascribed to Mr Pendleton & which he must forthwith Contradict. If you cannot call at my house, I will make some arrangement for seeing you in town—but the latter would you know, not be very pleasant" (ALS, New York State Historical Association, Cooperstown, New York).

2. See "Joint Statement by William P. Van Ness and Nathaniel Pendleton on the Duel between Alexander Hamilton and Aaron Burr," July 17, 1804; "Nathaniel Pendleton's Amendments to the Joint Statement Made by William P. Van Ness and Him on the Duel between Alexander Hamilton and Aaron Burr," July 19, 1804.

The People *v* Aaron Burr:
Indictment for fighting a duel &c [1]

[New York, August 14, 1804]

City and County of New York ss: The Jurors of the People of the State of New York in and for the Body of the city and County of New York upon their oath present That Aaron Burr late of the Eighth Ward of the City of New York in the County of New York Esquire on the Eleventh day of July in the year of Our Lord one thousand eight hundred and four at the Ward City and County aforesaid with force and arms did unlawfully wickedly and mali-ciously provoke excite and challenge one Alexander Hamilton late of the Ward City and County aforesaid Esquire (in the peace of God and of the said people then and there being) unlawfully to fight a duel with and against him the said Aaron Burr to the great

D, MS Division, New York Public Library.

1. Indictments were also issued against William P. Van Ness and Nathaniel Pendleton. For contemporary opinions concerning the legality of these indict-ments, see "*William P. Van Ness* adm *The People*," August, 1804 (AD, in Van Ness's handwriting, New-York Historical Society, New York City).

damage of the said Alexander Hamilton to the evil example of all others in like case offending and against the peace of the people of the State of New York and their Dignity. And the Jurors aforesaid upon their Oath aforesaid do further present That the said Aaron Burr afterwards to wit on the said Eleventh day of July in the year of our Lord one thousand eight hundred and four at the said eighth ward of the City of New York in the County of New York aforesaid did request and invite the said Alexander Hamilton to meet him the said Aaron Burr with intent to fight a Duel with him the said Alexander Hamilton he the said Aaron Burr then and still being a Citizen of the State of New York against the form of the Statute [2] in such case made and provided and against the peace of the people of the State of New York and their Dignity.

And the Jurors aforesaid upon their Oath aforesaid do further present that the said Aaron Burr afterwards to wit, on the said Eleventh day of July in the year of Our Lord one thousand eight hundred and four in the County of Bergen and State of New Jersey to wit, at the said eighth Ward of the City of New York in the County of New York aforesaid with arms or deadly Weapons commonly called Pistols lo[a]ded with Gun powder and leaden bullets unlawfully and wilfully fought a duel with the said Alexander Hamilton he the said Aaron Burr then and still being a Citizen of the State of New York against the form of the Statute in such case made and provided and against the peace of the people of the State of New York and their dignity. And the Jurors aforesaid upon their oath aforesaid do further present That the said Aaron Burr afterwards towit on the said Eleventh day of July in the year of our Lord one thousand eight hundred and four in the County of Bergen and State of New-Jersey to wit at the said Eighth Ward of the City of New York in the County of New York aforesaid with arms or deadly weapons commonly called Pistols loaded and charged with gunpowder and leaden balls unlawfully and wilfully fought a duel with the said Alexander Hamilton, and that he the said Aaron Burr, did on the day and year last aforesaid in the County of Bergen and State of New Jersey towit at the ward City and County aforesaid unlawfully wilfully wickedly and designedly fire and discharge a certain Pistol which he then and there held in his right hand loaded

2. "An Act to prevent Duelling" (*New York Laws*, 26th Sess., Ch. LXXI [April 2, 1803]).

and charged with gun powder and a leaden Ball at him the said
Alexander Hamilton he the said Aaron Burr then and still being a
Citizen of the state of New York against the form of the Statute in
such case made and provided and against the peace of the people
of the State of New York and their dignity. And the Jurors aforesaid upon their oath aforesaid do further present That the said Aaron
Burr afterwards, to wit, on the said eleventh day of July in the year
of our Lord one thousand eight hundred and four in the County of
Bergen and State of New Jersey and without the limits of the State
of New York did actually fight a duel with the said Alexander Hamilton, he the said Aaron Burr then and Still being a Citizen of the
State of New York against the form of the Statute in such case made
and provided and against the peace of the people of the State of
New York and their dignity. And the Jurors aforesaid upon their
oath aforesaid do further present That the said Aaron Burr afterwards towit on the said Eleventh day of July in the year of our
Lord one thousand eight hundred and four at the County of Bergen
in the State of New Jersey towit at the said Eighth ward of the City
of New York in the County of New York aforesaid with arms or
deadly weapons commonly called pistols loaded and charged with
gunpowder and leaden balls unlawfully and wilfully fought a duel
with the said Alexander Hamiton and that he the said Aaron Burr
did on the day and year last aforesaid in the County of Bergen and
State of New Jersey to wit at the ward City and County aforesaid
unlawfully wickedly wilfully and designedly fire and discharge a
pistol loaded and charged with gun powder and a leaden ball as
aforesaid to at and against the said Alexander Hamilton, and by
which firing as aforesaid he the said Aaron Burr gave to the said
Alexander Hamilton a mortal wound; of which said mortal wound
he the said Alexander Hamilton afterwards towit on the twelfth day
of July in the year aforesaid at the Ward City and County aforesaid
died against the form of the Statute in such case made and provided
and against the peace of the people of the State of New York and
their dignity.[3]

Riker Dist. Atty [4]

3. On October 14, 1804, Burr wrote to Van Ness: "My friends have left me
to this day ignorant of all those Circumstances which ought to accelerate or
retard my return to N.Y. I may hope that you will devote half an hour to
inform me how you & N. P—— have got on. Whether any difficulty about

bail & What has been demanded—what A. B. may expect on that head—When a Court will sit & Who will preside. Please also to inclose me a Copy of the Inquisition & of the Indictment if any—you have a right to demand these on your own Account" (ALS, New York State Historical Association, Cooperstown, New York).

4. Richard Riker was attorney for the First District of New York.

David Hosack to William Coleman

[New York] August 17th, 1804.

Dear Sir,

To comply with your request is a painful task; but I will repress my feelings while I endeavour to furnish you with an enumeration of such particulars relative to the melancholy end of our beloved friend Hamilton, as dwell most forcibly on my recollection.

When called to him, upon his receiving the fatal wound, I found him half sitting on the ground, supported in the arms of Mr. Pendleton. His countenance of death I shall never forget. He had at that instant just strength to say, "This is a mortal wound, Doctor;" when he sunk away, and became to all appearance lifeless. I immediately stripped up his clothes, and soon, alas! ascertained that the direction of the ball must have been through some vital part.* His pulses were not to be felt; his respiration was entirely suspended; and upon laying my hand on his heart, and perceiving no motion there, I considered him as irrecoverably gone. I however observed to Mr. Pendleton, that the only chance for his reviving was immedi-

---

* For the satisfaction of some of General Hamilton's friends, I examined his body after death, in presence of Dr. Post [1] and two other gentlemen. I discovered that the ball struck the second or third false rib, and fractured it about in the middle; it then passed through the liver and diaphragm, and, as nearly as we could ascertain without a minute examination, lodged in the first or second lumbar vertebra. The vertebra in which it was lodged was considerably splintered, so that the spiculæ were distinctly perceptible to the finger. About a pint of clotted blood was found in the cavity of the belly, which had probably been effused from the divided vessels of the liver.

[William Coleman] *A Collection of the Facts and Documents, Relative to the Death of Major-General Alexander Hamilton; with Comments: Together with the Various Orations, Sermons, and Eulogies, That Have Been Published or Written on His Life and Character* (New-York: Printed by Hopkins and Seymour, For I. Riley and Co. Booksellers, No. 1, City-Hotel, Broadway, 1804), 18–22.

1. Wright Post, a New York City physician, was professor of anatomy at Columbia College.

ately to get him upon the water. We therefore lifted him up, and carried him out of the wood, to the margin of the bank, where the bargemen aided us in conveying him into the boat, which immediately put off. During all this time I could not discover the least symptom of returning life. I now rubbed his face, lips, and temples, with spirits of hartshorne, applied it to his neck and breast, and to the wrists and palms of his hands, and endeavoured to pour some into his mouth. When we had got, as I should judge, about 50 yards from the shore, some imperfect efforts to breathe were for the first time manifest: in a few minutes he sighed, and became sensible to the impression of the hartshorne, or the fresh air of the water: He breathed; his eyes, hardly opened, wandered, without fixing upon any objects; to our great joy he at length spoke: "My vision is indistinct," were his first words. His pulse became more perceptible; his respiration more regular; his sight returned. I then examined the wound to know if there was any dangerous discharge of blood; upon slightly pressing his side it gave him pain; on which I desisted. Soon after recovering his sight, he happened to cast his eye upon the case of pistols, and observing the one that he had had in his hand lying on the outside, he said, "Take care of that pistol; it is undischarged, and still cocked; it may go off and do harm;—Pendleton knows, (attempting to turn his head towards him) that I did not intend to fire at him." "Yes," said Mr. Pendleton, understanding his wish, "I have already made Dr. Hosack acquainted with your determination as to that." He then closed his eyes and remained calm, without any disposition to speak; nor did he say much afterwards, excepting in reply to my questions as to his feelings. He asked me once or twice, how I found his pulse; and he informed me that his lower extremities had lost all feeling; manifesting to me that he entertained no hopes that he should long survive. I changed the posture of his limbs, but to no purpose; they had totally lost their sensibility. Perceiving that we approached the shore, he said, "Let Mrs. Hamilton be immediately sent for—let the event be gradually broken to her; but give her hopes." Looking up we saw his friend Mr. Bayard standing on the wharf in great agitation. He had been told by his servant that Gen. Hamilton, Mr. Pendleton, and myself, had crossed the river in a boat together, and too well he conjectured the fatal errand, and foreboded the dreadful result. Perceiving, as we came nearer, that Mr. Pendleton and myself only sat up in the stern sheets, he clasped his hands together in the most violent apprehension; but when I called to him to have a cot prepared, and he at the same moment saw his poor friend lying in the bottom of the boat, he threw up his eyes and burst into a flood of tears and lamentation. Hamilton alone appeared tranquil and composed. We then conveyed him as tenderly as possible up to the house. The distresses of this amiable family were such that till the first shock was abated, they were scarcely able to summon fortitude enough to yield sufficient assistance to their dying friend.

Upon our reaching the house he became more languid, occasioned probably by the agitation of his removal from the boat. I gave him a little weak wine and water. When he recovered his feelings, he complained of pain in his back; we immediately undressed him, laid him in bed, and darkened the room. I then gave him a large anodyne, which I frequently repeated. During the first day he took upwards of an ounce of laudanum; and tepid anodyne fomentations were also applied to those parts nearest the seat of his pain. Yet were his sufferings, during the whole of the day, almost intolerable.* I had not the shadow of a hope of his recovery, and Dr. Post, whom I requested might be sent for immediately on our reaching Mr. Bayard's house, united with me in this opinion. General Rey,[2] the French Consul, also had the goodness to invite the surgeons of the French frigates in our harbour, as they had had much experience in gunshot wounds, to render their assistance. They immediately came; but to prevent his being disturbed I stated to them his situation, described the nature of his wound and the direction of the ball, with all the symptoms that could enable them to form an opinion as to the event. One of the gentlemen then accompanied me to the bed side. The result was a confirmation of the opinion that had already been expressed by Dr. Post and myself.

During the night, he had some imperfect sleep; but the succeeding morning his symptoms were aggravated, attended however with a diminution of pain. His mind retained all its usual strength and composure. The great source of his anxiety seemed to be in his sym-

---

* As his habit was delicate and had been lately rendered more feeble by ill health, particularly by a disorder of the stomach and bowels, I carefully avoided all those remedies which are usually indicated on such occasions.

2. Antoine-Venance Gabriel Rey was the French commissary of commercial relations in New York City.

pathy with his half distracted wife and children. He spoke to me frequently of them—"My beloved wife and children," were always his expressions. But his fortitude triumphed over his situation, dreadful as it was; once, indeed, at the sight of his children brought to the bed-side together, seven in number, his utterance forsook him; he opened his eyes, gave them one look, and closed them again, till they were taken away. As a proof of his extraordinary composure of mind, let me add, that he alone could calm the frantic grief of their mother. *"Remember, my Eliza, you are a Christian,"* were the expressions with which he frequently, with a firm voice, but in pathetic and impressive manner, addressed her. His words, and the tone in which they were uttered, will never be effaced from my memory. At about two o'clock, as the public well knows, he expired.

> Incorrupta fides—nudaque veritas
> Quando ullum invenient parem?
> Multis ille quidem flebilis occidit.[3]

I am, Sir,   Your friend and humble serv't,   DAVID HOSACK.[4]

Wm. Coleman, Esq.

3. The correct quotation of Horace's ode on the death of Quintilius Varus of Cremona reads:
> "Incorrupta fides, nudaque veritas,
> Quando ullum invenient parem?
> Multis ille bonis flebilis occidit" (Horace, *Odes*, 1.24.7-9).

The translation reads:
> "When will incorruptible Faith and naked Truth
> Find another his equal?
> He has died wept by many."

4. Hosack's bill for services rendered to H in 1804 reads:
"The Estate of General Hamilton

		To D Hosack Dr
1804	To med and adv in January—February—March—May and June	$37.50
	To attendance &c during his last illness	50
		$87.50
		Recd payment

New York Augt. 8th. 1805   D Hosack"
(DS, New-York Historical Society, New York City).

On August 11, 1804, Hosack prepared the following statement: "I David Hosack Physician of the City of New [York] being first deposed upon the Evangelists of Almighty God do declare that Alexander Hamilton late General in the armies of the United States departed this life in the Month of July at the house of William Bayard in the City County and State of New York in the year one thousand Eight hundred and four and that I attended him as his Physician and was with him when he died" (DS, New Jersey Archives, Trenton).

The State of New Jersey *v* Aaron Burr: *Indictment for Murder* [1]

[New Barbadoes,[2] New Jersey, October 23, 1804]

Bergen County Ss: The Jurors for the Body of the County of Bergen in behalf of the State of New Jersey upon their oath present that Aaron Burr late of the Township of Bergen in the County of Bergen esquire not having the fear of God before his eyes but being moved and seduced by the instigation of the Devil on the eleventh day of July in the year of our Lord one thousand eight hundred and four at the Township of Bergen in the County of Bergen aforesaid and within the jurisdiction of this Court, feloniously Wilfully and of his malice aforethought did make an assault upon Alexander Hamilton in the peace of God and of the said State then and there being. And that the said Aaron Burr a certain pistol of the Value of five dollars then and there loaded with gun powder and a leaden ball, which pistol he the said Aaron then and there in his right hand had and held to, against, and upon the said Alexander Hamilton then and there wilfully Maliciously and feloniously and of his malice aforethought did shoot and discharge. And that the said Aaron with the leaden ball aforesaid out of the Pistol aforesaid then and there by force of the gun powder shot discharged and sent forth as aforesaid. The aforesaid Alexander Hamilton in and upon the right side of the belly near the short ribs of him the said Alexander then and there with the leaden ball aforesaid out of the Pistol aforesaid by the said Aaron so as aforesaid shot discharged and sent forth feloniously wilfully and of his malice aforethought did strike penetrate and wound giving the said Alexander with the leaden ball aforesaid so as aforesaid sent forth shot and discharged out of the pistol aforesaid by the said Aaron Burr in and upon the right side of the belly of the said Alexander near the short ribs of the said Alexander one mortal wound did give of the depth of four inches and of the breadth of two inches of which said mortal wounds he the said Alexander from the said eleventh day of July in the year aforesaid untill the twelfth day of the same month of July in the year aforesaid did languish and languishing did live on which said twelfth day of July in the year aforesaid at the Township and in the County aforesaid the said Alexander Hamilton of the said Mortal wounds died. And so the Jurors aforesaid upon their oath aforesaid do say that the said Aaron Burr the said Alexander Hamilton in manner and form aforesaid feloniously wilfully and of his Malice aforethought did kill and murder contrary to the act of the Legislature in such case made and provided against the peace of this State the government and dignity of the same.[3]

Aaron D. Woodruff }   Witnesses
Atty for the State }   John M. Mason

DS, New Jersey Archives, Trenton.

1. In a statement written in November, 1806, Henry Datsun, clerk of the New Jersey Court of Oyer and Terminer, stated that Burr had been indicted "at a Court of Oyer and Terminer & General Goal delivery held at New Barbadoes in and for the County of Bergen on the fourth Tuesday In October In the year of our Lord one thousand and Eight hundred and four . . ." (ADS, New Jersey Archives, Trenton).

2. Present-day Hackensack.

3. On November 13, 1807, the following document was filed in the New Jersey Supreme Court:

"The State } On Indictment for Murder
v } of Alexander Hamilton
Aaron Burr }

"The Indictment having been found at the Court of Oyer and Terminer for the County of Bergen and certified hither by Certiorari and upon Inspection of the said Indictment, it appears that the mortal wound and Death of the said Alexander Hamilton as charged in the said Indictment at the Township of Bergen in the County of Bergen and State of New Jersey and whereas it is suggested and fully appears that the said Alexander did actually die in the City of New York and State of New-York out of the Jurisdiction of this State and a Trial upon the said Indictment would be totally ineffectual, as the said Aaron Burr could not be convicted on the same under the Statute in such Case made and provided—It is ordered by the Court, by the Assent and on motion of the Attorney General, that the said Indictment be quashed." (D, New Jersey Archives, Trenton.)

For the statute, see Section 56 of "An Act for the Punishment of Crimes" (*New Jersey Laws*, October, 1795, Sess., Ch. DC).

ADDITIONAL LETTERS AND DOCUMENTS,

1774–1799

1774

To Alexander McDougall [1]

[New York, 1774–1776]

Dr. sir

It is with the utmost chagrin I am obliged to inform you, that I am not able to return you all your pamph[l]ets; and what is still worse the most valuable of them is missing. I beg you will not impute it to carelessness; for I assure you upon my honor the true state of the case is this—I put your pamphlets in the case with my other books; and some person about the College [2] got into my room through the window, broke open my case, & took out The friendly address,[3] Bankrofts treatise,[4] Two volumes of natural philosophy and a latin author. I have procured another Friendly address to replace the one lost; and have taken all possible pains to recover Bankroft's treatise or to get another in its stead; but my endeavors have hertofore been fruitless. Mr. Abram Livingston [5] thinks he can get one for me, and has promised, if possible, to do it.

I beg Sir you will not take amiss an accident, which has been unavoidable, for be assured, I have had no small uneasiness on account of it. I am Sir

Your most respectful servant A Hamilton

Be pleased to let me know the proper title of Bankrofts pamphlet (which I have forgotten) and I will publish it with the offer of a reward to any person that will restore it.

I have delayed the discovery of the true state of the matter hitherto; because I was still in hopes to have regained the pamphlet; and was unwilling, in the mean time to let you know it was missing.

ALS, W. Wright Hawkes Collection of Revolutionary War Documents on deposit at Union College, Schenectady, New York.

1. McDougall, a native of the Hebrides, was a New York City merchant. In the years immediately preceding the outbreak of the American Revolution he was among the city's most prominent and active opponents of British rule. Ap-

pointed colonel of the First New York Regiment in 1775, he was made a brigadier general in the Continental Army in 1776 and a major general the following
year.

On February 23, 1776, McDougall ". . . recommended Mr. Alexander Hamilton for captain of a company of artillery . . ." (*Journals of the Provincial
Congress, Provincial Convention, Committee of Safety and Council of Safety
of the State of New-York, 1775–1776–1777* [Albany, 1842], I, 321). See H to
McDougall, March 17, 1776 (*PAH*, I, 181–82).

2. H was a student at King's College. See "Matricula of King's College," 1774
(*PAH*, I, 80).

3. Thomas Bradbury Chandler, *A friendly address to all reasonable Americans, on the subject of our political confusions: in which the necessary consequence of violently opposing the King's Troops, and of a general non-
importation are fairly stated* (New York, 1774).

This book is attributed to Myles Cooper, president of King's College, in
Charles Evans, ed., *American Bibliography: A Chronological Dictionary of
All Books, Pamphlets and Periodical Publications Printed in the United States
from the Genesis of Printing in 1639 down to and Including the Year 1820*
(Chicago, 1931), 5, 20. Chandler, however, in his correspondence and in his
memorial to the royal commission on Loyalist claims, maintained that he was
the author. See Clarence Hayden Vance, "Myles Cooper," *Columbia University Quarterly*, XXII (1930), 275–76.

4. Edward Bancroft, *Remarks on the Review of the Controversy between
Great Britain and her Colonies. In Which The Errors of its Author are exposed, and The Claims of the Colonies vindicated, Upon the Evidence of Historical Facts and authentic Records. To which is subjoined, A Proposal for
terminating the present unhappy Dispute with the Colonies; Recovering their
Commerce; Reconciliating their Affection; Securing their Rights; and establishing their Dependence on a just and permanent Basis. Humbly submitted to
the Consideration of the British Legislature* (London: Printed in the year 1769;
New-London, in New-England: Reprinted and sold by T. Green, 1771).

5. Abraham Livingston, the son of Philip Livingston, was a New York merchant and delegate to the Continental Congress from 1774 to his death in 1778.
On March 16, 1776, the Committee of the Convention of New York contracted
with him to supply the troops "employed for the defence" of New York (*Journals of the Provincial Congress of the State of New-York*, I, 365). Congress
ratified the contract on April 16, 1776, and at his request released him from
the contract on May 10, 1776 (*JCC*, IV, 260, 346). On December 1, 1776, the
Secret Committee of Congress appointed Livingston and William Turnbull
agents "to repair to the eastern states, for the purpose of purchasing and collecting cloathing for the use of the army" (*JCC*, VII, 220).

1777

Statement Concerning James Ledlie

Philadelphia, February 11, 1777. "From the general character of Mr. James Ledly and from my own Observations. . . , I have all Reason to Believe him Discreet well Behaved man and a good Soldier. . . ."[1]

Copy, Reel 91, Item 78, II, p. 311, Papers of the Continental Congress, National Archives.

1. Ledlie was master-at-arms of the *Repulse*, a xebec in the Continental Navy.
The statement printed above appears in a report of Ledlie's court-martial in which he was tried for desertion and for taking four muskets and four cartridge boxes. H's statement was written before Ledlie's offence was committed and before the court-martial on November 25, 1777. Ledlie was found guilty and was sentenced "to be hung off the Yard Arm of any Continental Vessell . . ." (DS, Reel 91, Item 78, II, p. 311, Papers of the Continental Congress, National Archives).

To John Laurance [1]

[Morristown, New Jersey, March 1–April 10, 1777]

My dear Jack

Agreeable to your request, I inquired of Gen: Knox,[2] concerning a vacancy of a Captain's birth in his Corps. I find there is such vacancy; and upon being pressed to mention my reason for the inquiry, contrary to your prohibition, I ventured to inform him, that you had signified to me an intention of taking a more active part in our military affairs, than you had heretofore done—and that, I was in hopes you might be prevailed with to accept a company in the Artillery. He was much pleased with the idea, and begged me to urge it upon you, and as an extra-inducement desired me to make you a tender of the remains of my old company,[3] which will be a considerable help to you, in case you should resolve upon embracing the proposal. I shall be very happy if you determine to enter in a Corps so respectable in itself, and at the head of which is a gentleman for whom I have a particular esteem, and who I know is capable of distinguishing merit and willing to reward and encourage it. If you have not a better prospect, I would by all means have you to improve this. You will oblige me with a speedy answer, as General Knox will wait till he hears from you, even if he should have an opportunity of filling his vacancies to his satisfaction.

I am   Dr Sr   Yr. Assured friend & servant   A Hamilton

ALS, New-York Historical Society, New York City.
    1. Laurance, who was born in England and came to New York in 1767, was admitted to the bar in 1772. During the American Revolution he was aide-de-camp to his father-in-law, Brigadier General Alexander McDougall, and the paymaster of the First New York Regiment until April 10, 1777, when he became judge advocate.
    2. Henry Knox was commissioned a colonel in the Continental Regiment of Artillery on November 17, 1775, and became brigadier general and chief of artillery on December 27, 1776.
    3. H had been a captain in command of a company of New York artillery. See H to McDougall, March 17, 1776 (*PAH*, I, 181–82). On March 1, 1777, he became George Washington's aide-de-camp. See "General Orders, Appointing Alexander Hamilton Aide-de-Camp to General Washington," March 1, 1777 (*PAH*, I, 196).

To Captain Francis Grice [1]

Head Quarters Camp at Middle Brook [New Jersey] May 30th. 1777.

Sir

By His Excellency's command, I am to acknowledge the receipt of yours [2] per Mr. Grace.[3]

Colo. Biddle [4] has given Mr. Grace an order to make use of the waggons at Hackets Town,[5] for the purpose of transporting the twelve boats you mention. The General expects it will be done with all possible dispatch, as it is absolutely necessary we should have all the boats we can collect at and about Coryel's ferry,[6] in case we should want to make use of them.

The General expected, that by this time, all the boats were removed from Trenton to Coryel's. He desires it may be done, without loss of time; since by remaining there, they can answer no good end to us, and may be serviceable to the Enemy, should they make a sudden push that way; and it would be difficult to move them up the River in a hurry, should it be necessary, whereas nothing would be more easy than to carry them down, if there was occasion.

You will be careful to keep your boats together, so that they may all be had at a moment's warning, which cannot be the case, if you allow them to be scattered up and down the River.

I am Sir &ca.   A. Hamilton A.D.C.

Varick transcripts, George Washington Papers, Library of Congress.

1. This letter is listed in *PAH*, I, 258, as a "letter not found."
Grice was assistant deputy quartermaster general of the Pennsylvania militia.
2. On May 30, 1777, Grice wrote to George Washington: "We have at Trenton lower Ferry twenty boats built to transport 100 men each, & five artillary scows five other scows will be ready at our return built to carry two field pieces the company & apparatus; the last mentioned boats & scows are large & will be expensive pooling them to Corells, therefore request your Excellency's order for that particular purpose should your Excellency think it necessary to have them up" (ALS, George Washington Papers, Library of Congress).
3. Captain Richard Grace of the Second Maryland Regiment.
4. Colonel Clement Biddle was deputy quartermaster general of the Flying Camp from July 8 to December 1, 1776. On July 1, 1777, he became commissary general of forage.
5. Hackettstown, Warren County, New Jersey.
6. Coryell's Ferry was approximately twenty-five miles north of Trenton on the Delaware River.

To Major General Benjamin Lincoln [1]

Head Quarters Camp at
Middle Brook [New Jersey] June 4th.
1777

As the enemy appear from different Quarters to be in motion it is necessary that the army be in readiness to march, it is therefore ordered that the tents be immediately struck—the baggage and camp equipage loaded—the horses to the Waggons and all the men at their respective incampments paraded and ready to march at a moments warning.

Alexand Hamilton
A D C

ALS, University of California at Berkeley.

1. Lincoln, who before the American Revolution was a Massachusetts farmer and an officer in the Suffolk County militia, was commissioned a major general in the Continental service on February 19, 1776.

When the letter printed above was written, Lincoln was stationed at Bound Brook, New Jersey, on the Raritan River.

See also George Washington to Major General Philip Schuyler, July 24, 1777 (*PAH*, I, 291).

To Colonel Clement Biddle [1]

[Middlebrook, New Jersey, June 17, 1777]

The whole army immediately to strike their tents, pack them up, and get themselves in every respect ready for an instant march. The Quarter Master General [2] to have every thing in his department ready.

A Hamilton A D C

Head Quarters Camp at
Middle Brook June 17th. 1777

Colonel Biddle will communicate the above order, to the Commissary [3] & Pay Master General [4] & Judge advocate.[5]

A Hamilton A D C

ALS, MS Division, New York Public Library.

1. Although George Washington anticipated a British attack on his headquarters at Middlebrook on June 17 (*GW*, VIII, 262–63), no attack occurred. The British troops did not leave their camps at Middlebush and Somerset, New Jersey, until June 19, when they retreated toward New Brunswick.

2. Major General Thomas Mifflin.

3. Joseph Trumbull, commissary general of stores and provisions.

4. Lieutenant Colonel William Palfrey.

5. John Laurance.

To Hugh Knox [1]

Head Quarters Camp
at Middle Brook [New Jersey]
July 1. [-28] 1777.

Dear Sir

I had the pleasure of writing to you about four Months ago from Philadelphia,[2] since which I have neither had leisure nor opportunity to give you a line, on what is transacting in this part of the world, and in which I know you are deeply interested. I am uncertain even now, whether there may be any mode of conveyance for this letter; but I will do my part, and leave the rest to fortune. I shall write, and send what I have written to some friend in Philadelphia, begging his Aid to transmit it to you.

Soon after my last, I found General Washington at Morris Town, and have been with him ever since.[3] The time intervening between that at which I ended my narration, and the present moment, has been provocative of no military event of any great importance, 'till within this fortnight past.

It has been employed wholly in circumscribing the enemy, within the bounds in which their misfortune at Prince Town left them [4] —that is, within the compass of that little strip of land contained between Amboy, and Brunswick; and in preparing the means of strengthening our opposition to their future attempts. There have been a number of trifling skirmishes, which have been of no other

Copy, The Sol Feinstone Collection, Library of the American Philosophical Society, Philadelphia; copy, Catherine S. Crary Collection, Columbia University Libraries.

1. This letter, the first part of H to Hugh Knox, July, 1777 (*PAH*, I, 299–301), had not been found when *PAH*, I, was published.

Knox, a Presbyterian minister who settled on St. Croix in 1772, was also an apothecary and journalist. At times he edited the local paper, *The Royal Danish American Gazette* (*PAH*, I, 34–35). Knox helped H make arrangements to go to the mainland.

2. Letter not found. See Knox to H, April 31, 1777 (*PAH*, I, 244).

3. See "General Orders, Appointing Alexander Hamilton Aide-de-Camp to General Washington," March 1, 1777 (*PAH*, I, 196).

4. This is a reference to the Battle of Princeton, January 3, 1777.

consequence than as they served to harrass, and waste away the enemy, and teach our own men to look them in the face with confidence.

On the 20th of June, the Campaign may be said to have opened by a general movement of the British army, to put in execution a project they had been preparing for all the winter—the possessing themselves of Philadelphia.

But they have been disappointed in their expectation. Our army was situated in a strong position on the heights of Middlebrook, a small distance in the rear of Bound Brook; and could bid defiance to any attempt they might meditate to make an impression of on it.

It was necessary to give us a blow before they could pretend to prosecute their march for the Delaware; for no military principle could justify them to cross a river, with an army equal, if not superior to themselves, hanging upon their rear, and a respectable force on the opposite bank of the river in front. No success could be promised to so hazardous an undertaking, and there was therefore a necessity for them previously to dislodge, and disperse the army. After which they might continue their march in safety. They manoeuvered a while for this purpose, but finding they could not bring us to a battle, that the country people were gathering with great spirit to reinforce us, and that their flanks and rear were continually galled by light parties hovering about them—they were compelled to decamp from their new position, and return to their old, where they could be in greater security. They afterwards evacuated Brunswick, and the intermediate posts, and concentered their forces at Amboy. Concluding that their next step would be to abandon the Jersies altogether, we judged it expedient to move the chief part of our army nearer to them: in order to be more conveniently posted, to take advantage of any favorable moment that might offer itself, and to avail ourselves of the prejudices prevailing by keeping up the idea of a pursuit.

From this movement of ours, they were induced to sally out from Amboy. Their design seems to have been by the rapidity of their march, to surprise and cut off some of our most advanced parties, and if possible to gain the passes of the mountains on our left, and keep us on the plain, which would have obliged us to fight them perhaps on disadvantageous terms. In all this they were again disappointed. Our out parties escaped the snare, and retired without

much loss to the heights of which the whole army repossessed themselves. After looking at us in vain about four and twenty hours, they
returned to Amboy, and we have just received information from one
of our Generals, that they have taken their leave of the Jerseys, and
that he is now in possession of Amboy.[5] In the course of these Operations, they have sustained no inconsiderable diminution of numbers, from the frequent and smart skirmishes our light parties have
had with them: on our side we have lost few men, and should have
nothing to regret, had we not lost three field pieces in the last affair
with them. Thus after vapouring, and parading, plundering, & burn-
ing in the Jerseys, for about nine months, they have been obliged to
quit it with disgrace, and set about some new plan of devastation.
They are now encamped on Statten Island, and seem to be making
preparation for a Water expedition: it is all conjecture where they
will next bend their attention. Some think to Philadelphia by water,
Others up the North River on their last years scheme of cutting
off the communication between the Eastern and Southern States.
Others that they will push further to the Southward, and others that
they will push further to the Northward. For my own part I am lost
in conjecture, and unable to form any conclusion satisfactory to my
own judgment. If they go to Philadelphia, they have to surmount the
Chevaux de Frize, and other impediments in the river, and have the
same army, seconded by a large body of Militia to dispute their
descent. If they try the north River, the passes they have to gain
will be defended by their natural strength, and a respectable body
of troops, who if they do their duty, and the enemy even carry their
point, it must disable them to proceed any farther, and make it easy
for this army to put a finishing stroke to their ruin. I can see no
object to carry them far to the Southward; and I think they will
hardly be mad enough to plunge again into that nest of Hornets,
the Eastern States. What signifies it for them to take Newport, they
must either let go their hold if they do, or divide their forces, and

5. On July 1, 1777, George Washington wrote to Israel Putnam: "The Enemy
totally evacuated Amboy Yesterday Evening and are now encamped opposite
to it on Staten Island. Genl. Scott entered it shortly after, and posting guards
to secure any Stores they might have left, he withdrew his Brigade about four
Miles, It being Night. He will reenter this Morning and bring off whatever he
may find" (Df, George Washington Papers, Library of Congress).
    At this time, Putnam, a resident of Connecticut, was a major general in com-
mand at Princeton. Charles Scott of Virginia became a brigadier general in
the Continental Army on April 1, 1777.

make it easy to destroy them. On the whole, if they understand their true interest, they will remain quiet where they are now, and draw their whole force to a single point, and make a bold effort against our main army. If they could defeat that, there is no saying what may follow: if they do not, all they can do will be in vain, and will only serve to make them the easier prey to the Cautious and enterprising General they have to deal with. Whether they will observe this conduct or not, it is hard to say, for the calculation is against it, for they have generally acted like fools.

July 28th.

On finishing the above, I laid it by to be shortly forwarded to you, but a thousand circumstances have concurred to put it out of my mind, and occasions a delay to this time. I parted with the enemy encamped on Statten Island, they did not remain long in that situation, but in a day or two after embarked on board their Transports, and have since lain at, and about the watering place on Statten Island. Some disagreeable events have taken place to the Northward: Ticonderoga, and severall depending Fortresses have been evacuated, and together with their Stores.[6]

6. On July 2, 1777, British forces under the command of General John Burgoyne attacked Fort Ticonderoga. During the night of July 5, the Americans, led by General Arthur St. Clair, were forced to evacuate the fort.

Receipt to Captain Caleb Gibbs [1]

[Wilmington, Delaware, September 2, 1777]

	paid at Mr James in Cecil Aug 26th
for Lodging &c &c	£ 6
Amt. the within [2]	6.6.6
	£ 12.6.6

Wilmington Sept. 2. 1777
    Received the above of Capt Gibbs   Alex Hamilton [3]

ADS, George Washington Papers, Library of Congress.
    1. Gibbs was an aide-de-camp to George Washington and captain and commander of Washington's Guards.

2. Having embarked from New York on July 23, 1777, with fifteen thousand troops, Sir William Howe landed at the Head of Elk, Maryland, on August 25. Washington did not know Howe's destination, but subsequent intelligence reports indicated that it might be Philadelphia. Washington thereupon moved his army to the vicinity of Trenton and Philadelphia and by mid-August had established a camp near the Neshaminy River in Bucks County, Pennsylvania. On August 23 Washington, having learned that British transports were proceeding up Chesapeake Bay, broke camp and started south. By August 25 his troops had reached Naamans Creek, Delaware, and Washington, who had been informed that the British had landed near Cecil County Court House, established headquarters in Wilmington. On August 26, Washington, the Marquis de Lafayette, Major General Nathanael Greene, a troop of horse, and the headquarters staff went on a scouting expedition that brought them within two miles of the British camp at the Head of Elk. The scouting party was about to return to Wilmington when a storm forced them to spend the night of September 26 at a farmhouse (which, it was subsequently learned, belonged to a Tory). The night passed without incident, and on the following day the scouting party rejoined the army at Wilmington. For accounts of this expedition, see Washington to the President of Congress, August 27, 1777 (LS, George Washington Papers, Library of Congress); Washington to Landon Carter, October 27, 1777 (*GW*, IX, 451–52); *Mémoires, Correspondance et Manuscrits du Général Lafayette, Publiés par Sa Famille* (Paris and London, 1837), I, 21–22; George Washington Greene, *The Life of Nathanael Greene, Major-General in the Army of the Revolution* (New York, 1867), I, 443–44.

3. Attached to this document is the following bill:
"General Washingtons Bill

18 Breakfasts	3 12	
Spirits	7 6	
Rum to Servts.	4	
5 Breakfasts to Do.	15	
	£ 4 18 6	
Oats	1 8	
	6 66	

"Received the above of Col: Hamilton

Christiana   By me
Augt. 26. 1777   Barnaby Sanigan."
The receipt on this bill is in H's handwriting and signed by Sanigan.

Christiana is a town on a creek of the same name, which flows into the Delaware River near Wilmington.

To George Washington

[*New Windsor, New York, November 12, 1777.*[1] *Letter not found.*]

"List of Letters from General Hamilton to General Washington," Columbia University Libraries.

1. Two letters from H to Washington on November 12, 1777, are listed. One of these letters is printed in *PAH*, I, 360–62.

1778

To Charles Pettit [1]

[May 23, 1778–1781]

Col: Hamiltons Compliments to Mr Petit will be obliged to him, if he can give him any hope of soon having the saddle, he was so kind to undertake to procure for him. At present he is a sad dismounted knight.

May 23d.

AL, Yale University Library.
  1. Pettit, a resident of New Jersey, was assistant quartermaster general in the Continental Army from March 2, 1778, to June 20, 1781.

To George Washington

[*Hopewell, New Jersey, June 23, 1778. Letter not found.*]

"List of Letters from General Hamilton to General Washington," Columbia University Libraries.

To Elias Boudinot [1]

[*New Brunswick, New Jersey, July 5, 1778.* The description in the dealer's catalogue reads: ". . . introducing the Marquis de Vienne,[2] whom Hamilton had met through Lafayette. 'Though a young man, he has been a long time in service. . . . I am not well acquainted with his pretensions in our service, but as I dare say they will be reasonable, I shall request you will give him your interest.'" *Letter not found.*]

1. ALS, sold by Parke-Bernet Galleries, Inc., April 9, 1968, Item 87.

Boudinot, a New Jersey lawyer, was appointed commissary general of prisoners by the Continental Congress on June 6, 1777, with the pay and rations of a colonel. In November, 1777, he was elected a delegate to Congress.

2. Louis-Pierre, marquis de Vienne, was a major in the French army. Congress commissioned him a brevet lieutenant colonel in the Continental Army on July 15, 1778. See H to Boudinot, first letter of July 5, 1778, note 17 (*PAH*, I, 514).

To Colonel Charles Stewart [1]

[Fredericksburg, New York, November 18, 1778]

Sir

His Excellency desires to know the number of rations issued daily to the Park of Artillery including officers and all others. I am Sir

Yr Obed ser

A Hamilton
Aide de Camp

Head Qrs.
Novr 18 1778
The Commissary General of Issues

1. ALS, sold by Kenneth W. Rendell, Kingston Galleries, Inc., Somerville, Massachusetts, 1965, facsimile on cover of Catalogue 18, Item 77; ALS, dated November 10, 1776, sold by Patrick Madigan, New York City, 1914, New Series 2, Item C9175.

Stewart, a resident of New Jersey, was commissary general of issues from June 18, 1777, to July, 1782.

George Washington to Henry Laurens [1]

Fredericksburg [*New York*] *November 18, 1778.* Recommends Count Kotkowski,[2] a Polish officer, for "the rank of Captain and the pay of Lieutenant" in the Continental Army.

LS, in the handwriting of H, Reel 168, Item 152, VI, p. 515, Papers of the Continental Congress, National Archives.

1. Laurens, a merchant from Charleston, South Carolina, was a member of the Continental Congress from January, 1777, to November, 1779, and served as president of that body from November 1, 1777, to December 9, 1778.

2. Count Stanislas Kotkowski was a Knight of the Holy Cross and a friend of Count Casimir Pulaski.

1779

To Brigadier General Henry Knox

[*Headquarters, Middlebrook, New Jersey, March 26, 1779.* "This will be delivered to you by Mr. Garranger, who comes to pass through a probation with you.[1] He is to give you such proofs of his knowledge in the theory and practice of artillery as you shall deem satisfactory. He will, on your certificate of the same, be recommended to Congress for an appointment as Preceptor to the artillery, or something of that kind, with the honorary rank of Captain, as you proposed at Philadelphia. If he really is what he pretends to be, I imagine such a man might be made very useful." *Letter not found.*]

The Collector: An Historical Magazine for Autograph and Book Plate Collectors, IX (January, 1896), 51.
    1. In *PAH*, II, 25, this letter is listed as a "letter not found."
    Lewis Garanger was a captain of bombardiers in Major General Philippe Charles Jean Baptiste Tronson du Coudray's French artillery. Garanger was captured by the British and released in November, 1778, after a year in prison. On June 2, 1779, he requested that Congress grant him on account two thousand dollars for his service and "misfortunes" he had suffered, as well as an additional sum to enable him "to go to camp and to stay in it," where he would be "in the park of artillery in which . . . I will continue to execute the orders of the Generals and expect patiently the time where his Excellency General washington will propose to the honorable congress, under what title, and to what functions he will think the most useful to appoint me in the service of the united states" (ALS, Reel 95, Item 78, X, p. 145, Papers of the Continental Congress, National Archives). On June 10, 1779, Congress granted him fifteen hundred dollars on account and ordered "That Mons. Garanger . . . proceed to the grand army, there to exhibit such proofs of his talents and merit as may be deemed necessary to enable the Commander in Chief to certify to Congress the propriety or inexpediency of retaining him in the service of the United States, and in what rank, if he shall entitle himself to a favorable certificate from General Washington" (*JCC*, XIV, 710–11). Washington endorsed this proposal (Washington to the Board of War, July 27, 1779 [*PAH*, II, 114]), and in September, 1779, the Board of War again approved the arrangement (*JCC*, XIV, 711, note 1). Garanger was tested by Major Sebastian Bauman at West Point (H to Bauman, February 14, 1781; two letters of April 13, 1781 [*PAH*, II, 559–60, 590–91]), but he failed to exhibit "proofs of his talents" (Bauman to Knox, April 17, 1781 [ALS, George Washington Papers, Library of Congress]; Knox to Washington, April 18, 1781 [LS, George Washington Papers, Library of Congress]). On April 28, 1781, Knox issued him a certificate of service and

granted him permission to return to France (DS, Henry Knox Papers, Massachusetts Historical Society, Boston). Although Knox wrote to H on June 28, 1779 (printed in this volume), that Garanger had "renounced all claims to rank or command," Garanger maintained in a memorial to Congress, dated October 28, 1783, that that was not the case because "When I joined the army I could not speak English at all: General Knox thought himself proficient enough in French to treat of my affairs in that language but really we could not understand one another . . ." (ADS, Reel 95, Item 78, X, p. 459, Papers of the Continental Congress, National Archives). Garanger was still petitioning Congress in 1783 to employ him in some capacity in the military establishment. On June 18, 1783, he sent Elias Boudinot, President of Congress, two memorials, one "Containing some projects of Military Establishments, and the proposal of some means which would improve and Extend those now existing in the United States . . ." and another "Containing some Demands, which I think myself Intitled to form, and some which are relative to the Execution of my proposals . . ." (ADS, Reel 95, Item 78, X, p. 437, Papers of the Continental Congress, National Archives). One of Garanger's requests was "a Commission of Captain Bombardiers for himself, and one of Lieutenant for his Brother entered in the same time as him in the Continental Service, and both dated from the first of October, 1776" (ADS, "Second Memorial of Captain Garanger, Reel 95, Item 78, X, p. 441, Papers of the Continental Congress, National Archives). See also "Reflections, observations, and Proposals relative to the Military Service of the United States" (ADS, Reel 95, Item 78, X, pp. 445–58, Papers of the Continental Congress, National Archives). On June 19, 1783, this letter was read in Congress (JCC, XXIV, 402).

On October 28, 1783, Garanger, who was then in debtors' prison in Philadelphia, addressed another memorial to Congress, containing a history of his military service in America and copies of correspondence from Generals Knox and Washington concerning his earlier wartime activities. Garanger requested an advance of two hundred pounds Pennsylvania currency on the sum he believed the Government owed him (ADS, Reel 95, Item 78, X, pp. 455–62, Papers of the Continental Congress, National Archives). In November, 1783, he received an unspecified amount from the Government in the form of Treasury certificates ("Petition of Lewis Garanger in behalf of himself and his brother Charles Garanger, relative to the principal and interest of their certificates, subsistence, &c," February 11, 1793 [ADS, RG 46, Records of the United States Senate, Petitions and Memorials, Resolutions of State Legislatures and Related Documents, National Archives]).

In January, 1792, Garanger petitioned Congress on behalf of himself and his brother for additional compensation. His petition was referred to a select committee which made a favorable report on April 26, 1792, and the House passed a bill on January 2, 1793, entitled "An Act to authorize the settlement of the accounts of Lewis Garanger for military services during the late war," but the Senate failed to pass it (Journal of the House, I, 587, 628, 630, 634, 660; "Report on the petition of Lewis Garanger, in behalf of himself, and his brother Charles Garanger, referred on the 24th of January last" [D, RG 233, Records of the House of Representatives, Select Committee Reports, I, National Archives]). Garanger petitioned Congress, again unsuccessfully, in 1793, 1810, and 1813.

To Colonel Israel Shreve [1]

Head Quarters
Middle Brook [New Jersey] May 26. 1779

Sir,

I am commanded by His Excellency to inform you that you are to march on Saturday with your regiment for this camp where you will receive further orders.[2]

I am Sir   Yr. Obed serv   Alex Hamilton
                                                    Aide De Camp

ALS, University of Houston Libraries.
   1. Shreve was a colonel in command of New Jersey's Second Regiment, which was stationed at Elizabethtown, New Jersey.
   2. The "further orders" directed Shreve to proceed to Easton, Pennsylvania, to join General John Sullivan's campaign against the Indians (George Washington to John Sullivan, May 28, 1779 [Df, George Washington Papers, Library of Congress]).
   On May 28, 1779, Shreve asked Washington for permission to march directly to the forks of the Raritan River in central Somerset County, New Jersey, without stopping at Middlebrook (ALS, George Washington Papers, Library of Congress; copy, dated May 27, 1779, University of Houston Libraries). Although no reply from Washington has been found, the journal of Lieutenant Samuel M. Shute of New Jersey's Second Regiment indicates that Shreve's request was granted. On May 29, 1779, Shreve's troops left Elizabethtown and marched fourteen miles to Samptown, and on the following day they marched sixteen miles to the forks of the Raritan ("Journal of Lieutenant Samuel M. Shute," Journals of the Military Expedition of Major General John Sullivan against the Six Nations of Indians in 1779 With Records of Centennial Celebrations [Auburn, New York, 1887], 267–68).

To Jeremiah Wadsworth [1]

[New Windsor, New York, June 27–29, 1779]

Sir

There is some rum just brought to New Windsor the property of speculators, which his Excellency desires you would come down and press for the public use.

I am Sir   your huml Servt

Alex Hamilton
Aide De Camp

Col Wadsworth

Please to call first at Head Quarters. [2]

LS, Connecticut Historical Society, Hartford.
1. Wadsworth was commissary general of purchases and a business partner of John B. Church, who was the husband of Angelica Schuyler, the sister of H's future wife. Wadsworth resigned from the Continental Army in January, 1780.
2. This sentence is in H's handwriting.

From Brigadier General Henry Knox [1]

[New Windsor, New York]
Mr Ellisons Junirs House [2] 28th June 1779.

Dear Sir

Mr Garanger having positively renounced all claims to rank or command in the Corps of artillery, it is my opinion that he can be Employed in the Corps in a manner honorable to himself, and useful to the service. There can be no objection to his receiving a brevet of a Captaincy in the army.

I am Dear Sir affectionately your huml Sert.

Knox

Colonel hamilton

Copy, Reel 95, Item 78, X, p. 460, Papers of the Continental Congress, National Archives.

1. Knox wrote this letter in answer to H to Knox, June 27, 1779 (*PAH*, II, 84).
For background to this letter, see H to Knox, March 26, 1779 (printed in this volume).
2. There were two Ellison houses in New Windsor. Thomas Ellison's house, which was near the Hudson River, was used by George Washington for his headquarters while he was in New Windsor. Knox's headquarters, however, were in the house of John Ellison, the son of Thomas Ellison. The John Ellison house was in the country and some distance from the river.

To Colonel Joseph Ward [1]

[New Windsor, New York, July 8, 1779]

Sir

This will be accompanied by a general order [2] respecting your department which you will be pleased to have executed without delay. The positions are to comprehend all such as are enlisted upon the alternative of three years or during the war who are to be constructed as engaged during the war.

I am with great regard,   Your most obed. ser   Alex Hamilton
                                                    Aide-de-Camp

Head Quarters
July 8, 1779.

ALS, sold by Walter M. Hill, Chicago, November, 1909, Catalogue 28, Lot 42.
1. Ward was commissary general of musters from April 1, 1777, to April, 1780, when he became commissary general of prisoners.
2. For this general order, which is dated July 8, 1779, see *GW*, XV, 380–81.

To Baron von Steuben [1]

[New Windsor, New York] July 9 [1779]

Dr. Baron

The General will adopt the arrangement you propose; [2] that is Nixons & Larneds will form one division Patterson's [3] & North Carolina another. [4]

Yr. Affectionate humble ser.   A Hamilton

The Collector: An Historical Magazine for Autograph and Book Plate Collectors (July-August, 1946), 160.

1. Frederick William Augustus Henry Ferdinand, baron von Steuben, arrived in America from Germany in the autumn of 1777 after serving as one of Frederick the Great's titular aides. He first appeared at Valley Forge on February 23, 1778, and on March 28, 1778, George Washington appointed him volunteer inspector general. On May 5, 1778, he became a major general and inspector general in the Continental Army.

2. For the "arrangement" proposed by Steuben, see "Formation of the Army Commanded by his Excellency General Washington, for the present Campaign" (copy, New-York Historical Society, New York City) and "Formation of Nixon, Patterson, Learned & No. Carolina Brigades" (copy, New-York Historical Society, New York City).

3. John Nixon, Ebenezer Learned, and John Paterson were all from Massachusetts, and each held the rank of brigadier general. Although Learned had resigned in 1778, the brigade which he had commanded was still known by his name.

4. Brigadier General Lachlan McIntosh of Georgia was the commanding officer of the North Carolina brigade.

George Washington to ——————— [1]

[*New Windsor, New York, July 12, 1779.* The newspaper description of this letter reads: ". . . a Revolutionary War letter from Washington, in Alexander Hamilton's hand, sketching out military strategy in a planned attack on British-held Stony Point." [2] *Letter not found.*]

1. LS, in the handwriting of H, sold by Charles Hamilton Autographs, Inc., to Charles Sessler, Inc., Philadelphia (*The New York Times*, April 14, 19, 1968).

2. On the night of July 15–16, 1779, Brigadier General Anthony Wayne captured the British fort at Stony Point, on the west bank of the Hudson River in Orange County, New York. See *PAH*, II, 96, 99, 104, 105.

To Brigadier General Henry Knox [1]

[West Point, July 24, 1779]

Dr Sir

I have communicated your letter [2] to The General. He thinks Col Harrison's [3] regiment not intitled to a ⟨part⟩ of the present supply.

I inclose you by the General's order a letter from General Gates, with sundry papers respe⟨cti⟩ng powder Springfield &c.[4] on which yo⟨ur opi⟩nion is requested. The question is—W⟨hat is t⟩o be done?

Col Nixon sent to Springfield ⟨to be in⟩ charge of the Massachusettes ⟨–⟩ writes that he has obtained a partial supply of arms but no Cartrige boxes.[5] His Excellency requests your attention to this matter that measures may be taken to have a sufficient number ready here to furnish the men as they arrive.

D Genl   Yr. Affect. huml ser   A Hamilton
                                                                ADC

H Qrs. July 24 1779

ALS, Virginia Historical Society, Richmond.
   1. In *PAH*, II, 107, this letter is listed as a "letter not found."
   2. Letter not found.
   3. Charles Harrison, a resident of Virginia, was a colonel in the First Continental Artillery.
   4. On July 18, 1779, Major General Horatio Gates wrote to George Washington that he was waiting for orders from Washington and Knox concerning military supplies in the eastern department. He requested Washington to send Colonel John Lamb of the Second Continental Artillery to inspect the stores at Springfield, which he believed were being poorly managed. Gates also suggested that more powder be manufactured at Andover because of the scarcity of musket and cannon powder throughout his department (LS, George Washington Papers, Library of Congress).
   Gates, a native of Britain who had served with the British army in North America during the French and Indian War, settled in America in 1772. In 1775 he was commissioned a brigadier general in the Continental Army and in 1776 was promoted to major general. He was the commanding officer of the victorious American army at Saratoga. When the letter printed above was written, he was the commanding officer of the eastern department of the Continental forces.
   5. Thomas Nixon to Washington, July 18, 1779 (ALS, George Washington Papers, Library of Congress).

To Abraham Parley [1]

[*West Point, July 24, 1779*. Letter listed in dealer's catalogue. *Letter not found.*]

   1. ALS, sold by Stan V. Henkels, Jr., December 6, 1892, Item 106.
   Parley (Perlee, Perley), a resident of Massachusetts, was a surgeon's mate in the Seventh Continental Infantry Regiment in 1776.

To Major General Nathanael Greene [1]

[*West Point, July 27, 1779*. Document listed in dealer's catalogue. *Document not found.*]

1. ADS, listed by Thomas F. Madigan, New York City, in *Autograph Notes,* I (January-February, 1919), 3, Item 203.

Greene, a Rhode Island Quaker who served in the state militia in 1774 and 1775, was appointed a brigadier general in the Continental Army on June 22, 1775. After the British evacuated Boston in March, 1776, he commanded the army of occupation, and in May, 1776, he was placed in charge of the defenses at New York City. On August 9, 1776, he was promoted to major general, and on March 2, 1778, he was appointed quartermaster general. Although he resigned as quartermaster general in July, 1780, he continued to serve in that capacity until September 30, 1780.

To Major General Nathanael Greene [1]

[West Point, September 10, 1779]

Dr Sir

I really do not think it would be an adviseable measure to detach a brigade, for though I should not apprehend any material danger here, yet I think without some substantial object, it would hardly be prudent to lessen our force. There are *possible* events that might at least embarrass us. But my principal objection arises from my considering a compliance rather as a bad precedent; if you yield to the *impotunity* of one state, you must not only do the same to others in similar circumstances but you encourage that *importunity* and ultimately multiply your embarrassments. I hope the General's letter in answer to the Governor pointing out some errors in his information will appease his apprehensions. The General appears *much averse* to the measure.[2]

I am convinced you can have no other motive than those you profess and I can hardly help chiding you for thinking it possible I could suppose what you hint.

I have the honor to be   Very truly and Affecty   Yr obedient ser

A Hamilton

Sep. 10th.

I have mentioned General Howe's matter [3] to the General, by the way. His answer as I expected *in the negative.*

ALS, The Andre deCoppet Collection, Princeton University Library; copy, Columbia University Libraries.

1. In *PAH*, II, this letter is printed as H to ——.
2. This and the preceding sentence concern a request which Governor Jona-

than Trumbull of Connecticut made to George Washington in a letter dated August 30, 1779. This letter has not been found, but it obviously concerned a request that troops be dispatched to Connecticut on the ground that the arrival at New York of British troops in a convoy under Admiral Marriot Arbuthnot's command posed a threat to the state (Charles J. Hoadly, ed., *The Public Records of the State of Connecticut, From May, 1778, to April, 1780, inclusive, With the Journal of the Council of Safety from May 18, 1778, to April 28, 1780, and an Appendix* [Hartford, 1895], 392; Trumbull to Oliver Wolcott, Sr., August 31, 1779 [ALS, Connecticut Historical Society, Hartford]; Trumbull to Jeremiah Powell, August 31, 1779 [ALS, Massachusetts Archives, Vol. 201, p. 266, Boston]). On September 3, 1779, Washington wrote to Trumbull acknowledging his letter and stating that he did not think that the enemy was about to attack Connecticut, and that on the basis of his information he did not feel justified in ordering additional troops to Connecticut at the present time (*GW*, XVI, 220–21).

3. Robert Howe of North Carolina became a brigadier general in the Continental Army on March 1, 1776, and a major general on October 20, 1777. When the letter printed above was written, Howe was in command of the troops at Verplanck's Point, New York.

On August 23, 1779, Howe asked Greene's aid in securing another brigade (ALS, The Huntington Library, San Marino, California). On September 12, 1779, Howe again wrote to Greene: "I am much obliged to you for those Efforts you have made to obtain me the addition I wish'd for, and *have* to *lament* that the kindness you have shewn me upon this Occasion has not been attended with success" (ALS, William L. Clements Library of the University of Michigan).

To James Duane [1]

[West Point, October 1, 1779]

I am much obliged to you my dear Sir for your two letters of the 16th and 23d.[2] In haste I snatch up my pen by an express going off to the Governor,[3] to give you the news as it is runs. The most important and best ascertained is that Cou[n]t D'Estaing was arrived in the coast of Georgia.[4] The tale stands thus. We are in possession of a Charles Town paper of the 8th. of September, which mentions that the Viscount De Fontanges [5] had arrived at that place sent by the Count to announce his approach.[6] Mr. Mitchel [7] who transmits the paper adds that by the express which brought it Mr. Gerard [8] had received dispatches from the Count informing him of his intention to attack the enemy in Georgia on the 9th—that in consequence of this intelligence Mr. Gerard had pos[t]poned his voyage a few days to be the bearer of the event. This I hope puts a period to the danger of the Southern states, for which I could not help having strong apprehensions, notwithstanding the presumption drawn from the enemys past folly against their persuing any plan favourable to their interests. I acknowlege the force of the argument; but I was afraid they might for once blunder upon the right way. The departure of Cornwallis on the 25th. with the Grenadiers, light infantry and one British regiment, had increased my horrors on this subject.[9] The nature of this corps pointed to a temporary service for some important coup de main. Charles Town presented itself as the only object. They would hardly separate the flower of their troops for any remote and permanent station. They are continuing their embarkation. The accounts we have of the particular corps carry them to between five and six thousand.

I send you A Boston paper of the 23 containing some interesting European advices.[10]

You ask me How I like the new Minister.[11] I answer that with the help of his Secretary [12] he appears qualified to do his Masters business very well. He is a good deal of a Courtier and has had experience in the diplomatic line. He is of course acquainted with Mankind and with the arts of imposing upon them. He is affable in his manners and affects to accommodate himself to our simplicity. He makes a point of being pleased with every thing he sees, because he knows it is the surest method to please. I believe he will not want *dexterity* though I do not take him to be profound. But if I am not much mistaken he has an excellent mentor in his secretary. This appears to be a man of solidity has something in his countenance and behaviour that gains upon you at first sights—rather grave than gay but without being dull or reserved; he courts conversation as if with design to discover the talents and character of those with whom he converses. He is communicative but collected, and seems always ready to satisfy your curiosity—the better to penetrate your thoughts. He seems to be skilled in more sciences than those of politics and the world and capable of adapting himself as well to the philosop[h]er as statesman and man of private life. He was particularly inquisitive about the natural history of this Country. From several traits of his conduct to the minister, he appears to me to have a degree of influence which implies an unlimited deference to his judgment. There was however nothing inconsistent with the greatest respect.

I have ventured to give a picture in which per⟨haps – ima⟩gination has furnis⟨hed – –⟩ colors. Our acq⟨uaintance has been too⟩

short to admit ⟨‒ ‒ ‒⟩ accurate—pe⟨rhaps ‒ ‒ ‒⟩ superficial ⟨‒ ‒ ‒⟩ better judges ⟨‒ ‒ ‒ ‒⟩ will determ⟨ine ‒ ‒ ‒ ‒ ‒ I⟩ have only to beg you will pardon the defects which hurry and a paroxism of unusual dulness have produced—and will be assured that I am not the less Yr. most respectful and affectionate servant

Alex Hamilton

October 1st

The General is happy in the hopes you give him of a speedy visit from General Schuyler [13] and yourself and orders me to present his respects to both. The family join in every sentiment of perfect esteem.

ALS, Lloyd W. Smith Collection, Morristown National Historical Park, Morristown, New Jersey.

1. When *PAH*, II, was published, only an incomplete transcript of this letter had been found. See *PAH*, II, 194–95.

Duane was a delegate from New York to the Continental Congress. When the letter printed above was written, he was at Livingston Manor, New York, which was the home of his father-in-law, Robert Livingston, Jr., the third lord of the manor.

2. *PAH*, II, 180–82, 185–87.

3. George Clinton.

4. On September 8, 1779, the French fleet, which had been operating in the West Indies under the command of Vice Admiral Charles Henri Hector, comte d'Estaing, arrived at the mouth of the Savannah River. In mid-September troops from the French vessels and a force commanded by Major General Benjamin Lincoln began the siege of Savannah. After the failure of an assault on the city by the combined French and American forces on October 9, the French fleet withdrew, and the siege was lifted.

5. François, vicomte de Fontanges, commanded a legion of blacks at the siege of Savannah. In the course of the fighting he was wounded.

6. See the [Charleston] *Gazette of the State of South Carolina*, September 8, 1779.

7. Colonel John Mitchell, deputy quartermaster general.

8. Conrad Alexandre Gérard was French Minister to the United States.

9. Cornwallis did not actually sail for Charleston, South Carolina, until December 26, 1779.

10. See *The* [Boston] *Continental Journal, and Weekly Advertiser*, September 23, 1779, which contains accounts of hearings in the House of Commons on a plan to send peace commissioners to America, an Irish non-importation agreement, an agreement negotiated by Benjamin Franklin with France, and the dispute between Silas Deane and Arthur Lee.

11. Anne Cèsar, chevalier de la Luzerne, had succeeded Gérard as French Minister to the United States and was officially received by Congress on November 17, 1779.

12. François, marquis de Barbé-Marbois.

13. Philip Schuyler, H's future father-in-law, had resigned from the Conti-

nental Army on April 19, 1779, and was a member of the Board of Commissioners for Indian Affairs.

From Marquis de Lafayette [1]

Havre 7th October. 1779.[2]

What is the matter with my dear Hamilton and by what chance do I live in fruitless expectation of some lines from him? Does it begin to be the play in your, or rather in our Country, to take European airs, and forget friends as soon as they have turned their heels— Indeed my good friend I cannot help being somewhat angry against you, which makes into my heart a ridiculous fighting between love and anger, and as the first will never go off, you must behave better with me that anger might be more decently dismissed. Many Ships & Pacquets are arrived in France—letters were spread every where, and not a word from any friend any fellow soldier of mine in all the Army—Not even from my dear and respected General, from the family, from that idle fellow Col Hamilton. Is it not too much.

Copy, Francis Baylies Papers, Library of Congress.

1. Lafayette first came to America in June, 1777, and received a commission from Congress as a major general in the Continental Army on July 31, 1777. On October 21, 1778, Congress granted him a furlough (JCC, XII, 1034–35), and he returned to France in January, 1779. See Lafayette to H, January 8, 1779 (PAH, II, 1).

2. On the same day Lafayette wrote a similar letter to George Washington (Louis Gottschalk, ed., The Letters of Lafayette to Washington, 1777–1799 [New York, 1944], 78–81).

To Samuel Huntington [1]

[Little Egg Harbor, New Jersey, October 19, 1779. On October 27, 1779, Huntington wrote to Louis Le Bèque Du Portail [2] and Hamilton [3] acknowledging the receipt of a "letter . . . from Colo Hamilton of the 19th instant." Letter not found.]

1. Huntington, a resident of Connecticut and a signer of the Declaration of Independence, was a member of the Continental Congress from 1776 to 1784 and President of Congress from September 28, 1779, to July 6, 1781.

2. Du Portail, a native of France, was a brigadier general of engineers and commandant of the Corps of Engineers and Sappers and Miners.
3. Printed in this volume.

Brigadier General Louis Le Bèque Du Portail and Lieutenant Colonel Alexander Hamilton to Samuel Huntington

[*Great Egg Harbor Landing, New Jersey, October 26, 1779.* On October 27, 1779, Huntington wrote to Du Portail and Hamilton:[1] "I am favored with your letter of yesterday." *Letter not found.*]

1. Printed in this volume.

Samuel Huntington to Brigadier General Louis Le Bèque Du Portail and Lieutenant Colonel Alexander Hamilton[1]

Philada Octr 27th 1779

Gentlemen,

I am favour'd with your letter of yesterday[2] also one from Colo Hamilton of the 19th instant.[3]

I have not receiv'd any official or particular intelligence from the Count D'Estaing[4] or the southern Army since you left this City.

The enclos'd papers contain all the information I am able to give you either from the southern, northern or eastern Armies.

I am with esteem & regard your hble Servt   S. H. Prest.

LC, Reel 24, Item 14, p. 214, Papers of the Continental Congress, National Archives.
1. For an explanation of the contents of this letter, see H to Nathanael Greene, October 7, 1779 (*PAH*, II, 199–200).
2. Letter not found.
3. Letter not found.
4. Charles Henri Hector, comte d'Estaing.

To James Duane

[Great Egg Harbor Landing, New Jersey]
Oct. 29. 1779

Dr Sir

Mr Laurance is setting out for Philadelphia to obtain a determination respecting the promotion which he may expect by continuing in his present station. It seems his pay has been lately reduced—and he stands in the predicament of the civil staff in general, without any assurances of having his depreciation made good; though certainly there can be no reason for excluding him from this piece of Justice; as he has been all along exercising a very laborious office upon a fixed and moderate salary, in which he has given the most perfect satisfaction. He will show you a certificate he has lately obtained from the General; though you are I presume so well acquainted with his character, that no testimonials are requisite to convince you of his merit. From a long and intimate knowlege of him, I esteem him highly as a man of sense and integrity. All he will request your assistance in will be to procure him a speedy answer to the applications he may make,[1] that he may determine whether he can continue in the service or must quit. This I am persuaded you will chearfully afford him—and will do every thing that depends on you to have Justice done him.

I importune you often with the causes of Brother officers. I do it upon two principles—a convinction of your friendship to the army and to Dear Sir

Your most obed ser   A Hamilton

ALS, Lloyd W. Smith Collection, Morristown National Historical Park, Morristown, New Jersey.

1. On December 18, 1779, John Laurance wrote to Samuel Huntington, President of the Continental Congress, asking for an increase in pay (ALS, Reel 98, Item 78, IV, p. 299, Papers of the Continental Congress, National Archives). On December 21, 1779, "A letter, of 18, from J. Lawrance, judge advocate general, was read; whereupon,

"*Resolved,* That until the further order of Congress, the subsistence of a judge advocate be the same as the present subsistence of a colonel . . ." (*JCC,* XV, 1397).

To Lieutenant Colonel John Taylor [1]

[*Great Egg Harbor Landing, New Jersey, October 29, 1799.* The description of this letter in the dealer's catalogue reads: ". . . is sending clothing to Taylor by pilot boat. 'I am getting sick & cant say any more.'" *Letter not found.*]

1. ALS, sold by G. A. Baker & Company, Inc., May 4, 1943, Item 25.

When this letter was written, H and Brigadier General Louis Le Bèque Du Portail were at Great Egg Harbor on the New Jersey coast awaiting the arrival of the French fleet under Charles Henri Hector, comte d'Estaing (John Holker to H, October 21, 1779 (*PAH*, II, 205, note 1); H and du Portail to George Washington, November 2, 1779 [*PAH*, II, 219]). Washington had assigned a similar task to Major Henry Lee and in addition had asked him to report on British activities in and around New York Harbor (*GW*, XVI, 279–80). In his instructions to Lee, Washington also wrote: "I would advise you to keep up a communication . . . with Lt. Colo. Taylor at Elizabeth town, forwarding your dispatches to him and send them by Express to me." Taylor was a lieutenant colonel and colonel of the First New Jersey State Regiment. See also Lee to H, October 22, 1779 (*PAH*, II, 208–09); Washington to Taylor (*GW*, XVI, 455–56).

1780

To Brigadier General Henry Knox

[Morristown, New Jersey, January 30, 1780]

Dr. Sir

The General ⟨consents to – –⟩ officers to recover your deserters and to reimburse their reasonable expences. He only makes two conditions, that you will send as few as possible & that they keep and exact and particular account of their expences.

The sentence of The Court Marti⟨al⟩ will probably be determined tomorrow; it is too late for to day's orders.[1]

I am ordered to return you the inclosed and to tell you, that if a couple of 18 or a couple of twelve pounders can be spared it will be well to send them, but that two of each will probably be more than we afford & may not be essential. You are the best judge of the quality of stores necessary and will take yr measure accordingly.[2]

I have the honor to be   Yr. most hum ser   Alex Hamilton
                                                         A D C

Hd. Qrs. Jany 30th. 1780

ALS, Hamilton Papers, Library of Congress.
    1. This is a reference to the court-martial of Major General Benedict Arnold.
    George Washington's general orders, which were not issued until April 6, 1780, read: "At a General Court Martial whereof Major General [Robert] Howe was President, held on the 1st. of June last at Middle Brook and afterwards at Morristown from the 23rd. of December to the 26th. of January, in consequence of a resolution of the Honorable the Congress, for the trial of Major General Arnold on the following Articles contained in the proceedings of the Executive Council of the State of Pennsylvania at the City of Philadelphia the 3rd. of February 1779. Vizt.
    "First. 'That while in the Camp of General Washington at Valley Forge last spring, he gave permission to a Vessel belonging to persons then voluntarily residing in this City, with the enemy, and of disaffected characters to come into a Port of the United States without the knowledge of the authority of the State or of the Commander in Chief tho' then present.
    "2nd. In having shut up the Shops and stores on his arrival in the City, so as even to prevent officers of the army from purchasing, while he privately made considerable purchases for his own benefit as is alleged and believed.
    "3rd. In imposing menial offices upon the sons of Freemen of this State, when called for by the desire of Congress, to perform militia duty, and when remonstrated to hereupon, justifying himself in writing upon the ground of having

power so to do. For that when a citizen assumed the character of a soldier, the former was intirely lost in the latter, and that it was the duty of the militia to obey every order of his Aids (not a breach of the laws and constitution) as his (the General's) without judging of the propriety of them.

"4th. The appropriating the waggons of this State, when called forth upon a special emergency last autumn, to the transportation of private property and that of Persons who voluntarily remained with the enemy last winter, and were deemed disaffected to the Interests and Independence of America.'" (GW, XVIII, 222–23).

The Court acquitted Arnold of the second and third charges, found him guilty of the first and last charges, and sentenced "him to receive a reprimand from His Excellency the Commander in Chief" (GW, XVIII, 225). On February 12, 1780, Congress confirmed the sentence (JCC, XVI, 161–62), and on April 6, 1780, Washington stated in his general orders: "The Commander in Chief would have been much happier in an occasion of bestowing commendations on an officer who has rendered such distinguished services to his Country as Major General Arnold; but in the present case a sense of duty and a regard to candor oblige him to declare, that he considers his conduct in the instance of the permit as peculiarly reprehensible, both in a civil and military view, and in the affair of the waggons as 'Imprudent and improper'" (GW, XVIII, 225).

2. No evidence has been found concerning the destination of the artillery and stores mentioned in this paragraph, but they may have been intended for Fort Pitt. On January 4, 1780, Washington wrote to Colonel Daniel Brodhead, who was commanding officer at Fort Pitt: "I shall write to the Board of War recommending you may be supplied with a few pieces of Artillery and a proportion of Stores to be ready against there may be a call for them" (GW, XVII, 351). See also Washington to the Board of War, February 8, 1780 (GW, XVII, 502); Brodhead to Lieutenant Colonel Archibald Lochry of the Pennsylvania militia, May 10, 1780 (Mary C. Darlington, Fort Pitt and Letters from the Frontier [Pittsburgh, 1892], 235–36).

Major General Arthur St. Clair and Lieutenant Colonels Edward Carrington and Alexander Hamilton to George Washington [1]

[ENCLOSURE]

[Amboy, New Jersey, March 21, 1780]

Plan of exchange for the Troops of Convention, in three Divisions to be formed as equally, as the exchanging by Corps will allow, from the Strength of the Rank & file, each of the two first Divisions to have a Major General and a Brigadier General, and the third The Lieutenant General and a Brigadier General exchanged with them. The Regiments to which the Brigadier Generals belong to be exchanged with them, the other Regiments in a distribution of two

British, then two German to be taken by lott, except certain broken parts of Corps, which it is proposed to exchange in the first Division. The Estimate for these exchanges is formed according to the Tarif annexed to the proposal which gave rise to a meeting of Commissioners.

Amboy March 21st. 1780

Plan proposed for the exchange of the first Division.

Corps	Valuation by Tarif	Total amount	No. of Rank & file to be exchanged
Brigadeir General Hamilton			
Leut. Colo. 21st Regt	200	200	
Brigade Major Kirkman Captain			
21st. Regt.	16	16	
		216	
Royal Artillery			
2 Captains	16	32	
1 Lieutenant	6	6	
6. 2d. Lieutenants	4	24	
8 Sergeants	2	16	
150 Rank & file	1	150	158
		228	

D, Reel 184, Item 167, p. 101, Papers of the Continental Congress, National Archives.

1. This document is enclosure No. 3 to St. Clair, Carrington, and H to Washington, second letter of March 26, 1780 (*PAH*, II, 296–301). For background to this document, see Washington to St. Clair, Carrington, and H, March 7, 8, 1780 (*PAH*, II, 273–74); "Minutes of the Proceedings at Amboy," March 10–14, 1780 (*PAH*, II, 275–85); H to Washington, March 17, 1780 (*PAH*, II, 287–88); "A Proposition," March 18, 1780 (*PAH*, II, 289–91); St. Clair, Carrington, and H to Major General William Phillips and Lieutenant Colonels Cosmo Gordon and Chapel Norton, March 19, 1780 (*PAH*, II, 291–92); St. Clair, Carrington, and H to Washington, first letter of March 26, 1780 (*PAH*, II, 295–96).

From 1775 to 1777 St. Clair rose from a colonel in the Pennsylvania militia to a major general in the Continental Army. In June, 1777, he was in command of the defenses at Fort Ticonderoga and ordered the evacuation of the post in the face of a British attack on the night of July 5. He was court-martialed in September, 1778, but was fully exonerated.

Carrington, a resident of Virginia, was commissioned a lieutenant colonel in the First Continental Artillery on November 30, 1776.

Canada Companies

4 Captains	16	64	
13 Lieutenants	6	78	
15 Serjeants	2	30	
126 Rank & file Drummers	1	126	126
		298	

Lieutenant Nutts Detatchmt.

1 Lieutenant	6	6	
3 Serjeants	2	6	
30 Rank & file & Drummers	1	30	30
		42	

German Detatchmt. of Prince Frederick

10 Rank & file and Drummers	1	10	10

Regiment of Dragoons

1 Captain	16	16	
1 2d. Lieutenant	4	4	
4 Serjeants	2	8	
26 Rank & File & Drummers	1	26	26
		54	

Hesse Hanau Artillery

1 Captain	16	16	
1 Lieutenant	6	6	
9 Serjeants	2	18	
29 Rank & file & Drummers	1	29	29
		69	

62d. British Regiment

1 Major	28	28	
5 Captains	16	80	
6 Lieutenants	6	36	
4 Ensigns	4	16	
1 Surgeon	6	6	
1 Mate	4	4	
17 Sergeants	2	34	
83 Rank & file & Drummers	1	83	83
		287	

21st British Regiment
1 Lieutenant Colonel estimated as
  a Brigadier

1 Major	28	28	
3 Captains	16	48	
7 1st. Lieutenants	6	42	
4 2d. Lieutenants	4	16	
1 Surgeon	6	6	
1 Mate	4	4	
22 Serjeants	2	44	
226 Rank & file and Drummers	1	226	226
		414	

German Battalion of Light
  Infantry

1 Captain	16	16	
2 1st. Lieutenants	6	12	
3 2d Lieutenants	4	12	
1 Surgeon	6	6	
2 Mates	4	8	
12 Serjeants	2	24	
73 Rank & file and Drummers	1	73	73
		151	

German Battalion of
  Grenadeirs

1 Major	28	28	
1 Captain	16	16	
2 1st. Lieutenants	6	12	
4 2d. Lieutenants	4	16	
1 Surgeon	6	6	
2 Mates	4	8	
15 Serjeants	2	30	
150 Rank & file & Drummers	1	150	150
		266	

Major General de Reidesel	372	372
Captain Gerlack	16	16
Captain Poelnitz	16	16
Captain Willoe	16	16

Ensign Freeman   4   4
Chaplain Milias
Private Secretary Langeman
                                           ‾‾‾‾
                                           424

Total Number of Men to be
  exchanged
Drummers   60
Rank & File 843

Plan proposed for the Exchange of the second
Division of the Troops of Convention

Amboy [New Jersey] March 21. 1780

Corps	Valuation by Tarif	Total amount	No. of Rank & file to be exchanged
Major General Phillips	372	372	
Lieutenants Bibby	6	6	
Valancy	6	6	
Campbell	6	6	
2d. Lieutenants Collier	4	4	
Noble	4	4	
Smith	4	4	
Revd. Mr. Brudenell			
		402	
20th. British Regiment			
1 Lieutenant Colonel	72	72	
4 Captains	16	64	
8 Lieutenants	6	48	
5 Ensigns	4	20	
1 Quarter Master	6	6	
1 Surgeon	6	6	
1 Mate	4	4	
25 Serjeants	2	50	
180 Rank & file and Drummers	1	180	180
		450	
24th. British Regiment			
1 Major	28	28	

6 Captains	16	96	
6 Lieutenants	6	54	
6 Ensigns	4	24	
1 Adjutant	6	6	
1 Surgeon	6	6	
1 Mate	4	4	
18 Serjeants	2	36	
169 Rank & file and Drummers	1	169	169
		423	

German Regiment of Rheitz

1 Major	28	28	
2 Captains	16	48	
2 Lieutenants	6	12	
6 2d. Lieutenants	4	24	
3 Ensigns	4	12	
1 Advocate	4	4	
1 Surgeon	6	6	
3 Mates	4		
37 Serjeants	2	74	
224 Rank & file and Drummers	1	224	224

German Regiment of Specht

1 Colonel estimates as a Brigadier

1 Major	28	28	
2 Captains	16	32	
3 1st. Lieutenants	6	18	
5 2d. Lieutenants	4	20	
3 Ensigns	4	12	
1 Advocate	4	4	
1 Surgeon	6	6	
3 Mates	4	12	
32 Serjeants	2	64	
220 Rank & file and Drummers	1	220	220
		416	
Brigadier General Specht	200	200	

Total Number of Men to be
  exchanged
Drummers   48
Rank & file 745

To Marquis de Barbé-Marbois [1]

[*Morristown, New Jersey, May 10, 1780.* The description of this letter reads: "Giving military information." *Letter not found.*]

Victor Hugo Paltsits, ed., *American Book-Prices Current* (New York, 1916), 812.
    1. François, marquis de Barbé-Marbois.

To Brigadier General Henry Knox

[Morristown, New Jersey, June 4, 1780]

Dr Sir

Mr Gilliland,[1] the most helpless mortal in the world, and the most ignorant of every thing he ought to know, represents that he has been two years without pay. He begs this line to you to have justice done him and seems even not to know to whom he ought to apply. In pity give him such information and advice as you can and at least enable him to have some idea of his own affairs & to give me some idea of what may have prevented his being paid like other people.

Very Affectionately   Dr Sir   Yrs   A Hamilton

June 4. 1780

ALS, Hamilton Papers, Library of Congress.
    1. James Gilliland had been a lieutenant in H's artillery company. When this letter was written, he was a captain lieutenant in the Continental Sappers and Miners.

George Washington to Major General William Alexander, Lord Stirling [1]

[*Near Springfield, New Jersey*] *June 8* [*1780*]. States that "a detachment of three batalions under General Hand" [2] will cooperate with the militia "to harass the enemy." Asks him "to have the Militia put into some form and endeavour to ascertain their number" and then to "permit them to act in their own way."

LS, in the handwriting of H, Park Collection, Morristown National Historical Park, Morristown, New Jersey.

1. Although Alexander was a native of North America, in 1755 he instituted legal proceedings to secure the title of Earl of Stirling, to which his father had been heir presumptive before leaving Scotland for America. He lost the suit, but he used the title and was generally known by it. He was commissioned a brigadier general in the Continental Army in 1776 and a major general in 1777.

2. Edward Hand, a native of Ireland, had served with the British forces in America from 1767 to 1774, when he resigned to practice medicine in Lancaster, Pennsylvania. He had been a lieutenant colonel in a Pennsylvania rifle battalion as early as 1775, and when the letter printed above was written he was a brigadier general in the Continental Army.

George Washington to —————

Headquarters, Ramapo, New Jersey, June 30, 1780. Returns "the Proof Sheet of the Proclamation . . . with some corrections." [1] Requests that five hundred copies be "struck off and forwarded . . . with great secrecy and dispatch."

LS, in the handwriting of H, The Sol Feinstone Collection, Library of the American Philosophical Society, Philadelphia.

1. Although the enclosure has not been found, it was undoubtedly one of several proclamations offering pardons to deserters on the condition that they return to their units. See, for example, the proclamations issued by Washington, dated May 31 and August 29, 1790 (Df, George Washington Papers, Library of Congress).

George Washington to Major General Alexander McDougall

Headquarters [*Preakness, New Jersey*] *July 2, 1780.* "I wish to see you here the day after tomorrow morning at furthest to consult you on a matter of the greatest importance to the combined operations."[1]

LS, in the handwriting of H, from the W. Wright Hawkes Collection of Revolutionary War Documents on deposit at Union College, Schenectady, New York.
   1. When this letter was written, McDougall was at West Point.
   Although it cannot be stated with certainty, it appears likely that Washington wished to consult with McDougall concerning cooperation with the French forces. On July 4, 1780, Washington wrote to Colonel Daniel Brodhead: "We are in hourly expectation of a considerable French Land and Sea force which is intended to cooperate with us agt. the common enemy. We are, for this purpose, endeavouring to draw out a competent reinforcement of Men and supplies to enable us in conjunction with our Allies, to strike decisively at the enemy" (Df, George Washington Papers, Library of Congress).

To Brigadier General Henry Knox

[Preakness, New Jersey, July 9, 1780]

Dr Sir

We wish to know the number of heavy cannon we might bring into an operation against New York—already in the possession of The Continental distinguishing the Iron from the Brass.[1] We are writing to The French General.[2]

Yr most Obed   Alex Hamilton

Sunday

also the Mortars their different sizes.[3]

ALS, Hamilton Papers, Library of Congress.
   1. These cannons were to be used for an attack on New York City, which Washington hoped could be undertaken by combined French and Continental forces during the summer or autumn of 1780 (Washington to Nathanael Greene, July 15, 1780 [LS, George Washington Papers, Library of Congress]; Washington to Knox, July 15, 1780 [*PAH*, II, 357]; Washington to Major

General Alexander McDougall, July 2, 1780 [printed in this volume]). The French, however, were unwilling to cooperate on this project (Washington to James Duane, October 4, 1780 [Df, George Washington Papers, Library of Congress]), and the attack never took place.

2. The French fleet arrived at Newport, Rhode Island, on July 11, 1780, and on July 15 Washington drew up a plan for the joint attack on New York City. This plan was in the form of a memorandum to the French commanders at Newport, Lieutenant General Jean Baptiste Donatien de Vimeur, comte de Rochambeau, and Charles Henri d'Arsac, chevalier de Ternay, and it was delivered to them by Lafayette ("Memorandum for Concerting a Plan of Operations" [GW, XIX, 174–76]).

3. Knox endorsed this letter: "A note from, and to, Colo Hamilton, Sunday 9th July 1780." Knox's letter to H has not been found.

From Brigadier General Henry Knox

[*Preakness, New Jersey, July 9, 1780.* Knox's endorsement on Hamilton's letter to him of July 9, 1780,[1] reads: "note . . . to, Colo Hamilton, Sunday 9th July 1780." *Letter not found.*]

1. Printed in this volume.

From Marquis de Fleury [1]

[Newport, Rhode Island, August 29–30, 1780]

I beg you would tell Dr McEnnery [2] that I shall write to him in a few days. I keep for him a gratitude for his friendly services equal to my esteem & friendship.

My respects to all the gentlemen of your Familly.

We have here one deputation of our yellow brothers,[3] we treat them like kings—they are drunk all day long.

Je vous priè de faîre papier cette lettre au M Hazon [4] pour une main sure. Je pouvais le   [5] icy plusieurs personnes seraient bienàise mais s'il repond *ad Rem,* avec clarte, cela devendre au même & eté prie de vous communiquer ma lettre, & de me prendre votre avis.

Seal Hazen's letter and forward it to him.

Col. Alexdr Hamilton
General Washingtons A.D.C.
Head Quarters.

Copy, Francis Baylies Papers, Library of Congress.

1. François Louis Teisseydre, marquis de Fleury, a native of France and a veteran of the French army, served with the Continental Army from 1777 to 1779, when he was a lieutenant colonel of engineers. He returned to France in 1779 and arrived back in the United States with the French army in the summer of 1780.

2. James McHenry, a native of Ireland, came to Philadelphia in 1771 and studied medicine under Dr. Benjamin Rush. He was a medical officer in the Continential Army from 1776 to 1778, when he was appointed secretary to George Washington. In August, 1780, he was transferred to Lafayette's staff.

3. On August 31, 1780, Jean Baptiste Donatien de Vimeur, comte de Rochambeau, wrote to George Washington: "Before yesterday, I received a deputation composed of 19 Indians of Different nations who have been led here by Mr. [James] Deane, and who have been sent me by Mr [Philip] Schuyler from Albany. . . . I showed them yesterday the French Toops mixed with the American. . . . They will go to Day, on board the fleet. . . ." (LS, George Washington Papers, Library of Congress). The purpose of the visit was to demonstrate to the Indians the unity of the French and the Americans and the hostility of both to the English. In a statement to the Indian chiefs, dated August 20, 1780, Rochambeau wrote: "The King of France your father has not forgot his children. . . . he learned with concern that many nations, deceived by the English, who are his enemies, had attacked and Lifted up the hatchet against his good and faithfull allyes the United States of America. he hath desired me to tell you that he is a firm and faithfull friends to all the friends of America, and sworn enemy to all its foes. he hopes that his children whom he loves sincerely, will take part with their father, in this war against the English" (DS, George Washington Papers, Library of Congress). See also Schuyler to Lafayette, August 18, 1780 (ALS, George Washington Papers, Library of Congress); Washington to Rochambeau, September 3, 1780 (*PAH*, II, 420).

4. Colonel Moses Hazen, Second Canadian Regiment.

5. Space left blank in MS.

To Marquis de Barbé-Marbois [1]

[New Bridge, New Jersey, September 13, 1780]

This would be the most dangerous stroke they could give to our cause.[2] It would not only conciliate the greatest part of the people immediately in their power, but would prepare the minds of their neighbours to yield an early submission. This argument aided by the prevailing eloquence of a military force would become almost irresistible. I would not for the world that the tories throughout the Continent were armed with such a weapon to extend the influence of their party. It may be objected that the Commissioners offered every thing, which I suppose in this instance to be granted—and that the popular voice as well as that of Congress rejected their offers.[3] But you my dear Sir, know too much of human nature not to perceive, there is a wide difference between the same thing in prospect and in practice. When it was nothing but an offer to people out of their power, it was an affair of speculation. There was room to insinuate doubts about the sincerity of the offers—to give what interpretations suited out purpose—to influence the opinions and passions of the people as we wished. But if the enemy after having subdued two states, should exemplify their offers, by establishing governments agreeable to the ancient habits of the people it will be urged, as a proof of their moderation and sincerity. The people *feeling* themselves in the same situation which they formerly were will soon be reconciled to it—and emissaries from among them will endeavour to persuade those of the neighbouring states, that they have gained by the change. These, tired of resisting under discouraging circumstances, and seeing those in the conquered states in the same predicament in which they themselves were formerly happy, will insensibly learn to think that they are contending for an unreal good, and incurring certain ills. They will feel no aversion, or not enough, to returning to the dominion of Britain.

Two things ought to be well attended to in this matter, one that This contest was undertaken on a speculation of evils that were expected to result from an usurpation on the rights of this country—not from oppressions actually subsisting and felt by the people. As the people commonly act more from their feelings than from their understandings, there is great danger that present sufferings will overcome the apprehension of speculative ills, and make them regret having drawn upon themselves the former to avoid the latter.

The other—that the people of the Southern states are not actuated by the same principles with those of the Northern—a hereditary hatred of the English nation—a hereditary love of republican government—the enthusiasm of a different and more persecuted religion. The only motive in the first instance with the Southern states was, an attachment to liberty, with a predilection however in favour of Monarchical government, which has since worn off, but has not been succeeded by an *aversion* to it. In the progress of the revolution a desire of independence has infused itself, but this passion will act less powerfully in the minds of the common people than of their leaders, and cannot be relied on for a perservance in opposition under all extremities.

The result of these observations is, that it is of the greatest importance France should give the most vigorous assistance to this
Country and at this juncture, particularly to remove the war from
the Southern states—and that if the war continues, she should do
everything possible to procure for us a considerable loan, or we
must sink under it. 'Tis impossible a country can carry on a war
without finances, and we have no sufficient funds within ourselves.

I beg you my Dear Sir to understand me rightly, I am not one
of those who forgets the gratitude we owe to France for saving us
hitherto from ruin, in an expectation of greater services, as if we
paid her a subsidy to be at our disposal. Do the justice to my sentiments to believe that I have the liveliest sense of our obligations to
your country—and that I speak as one sincerely anxious for her
interests as well as those of America. If I had the honor to be a
Frenchman, and had influence in the councils of France, my advice
would have been from the beginning—"tran[s]fer the weight of
your exertions to the American continent and do the rest afterwards." Your situation and still more your talents give you that
influence; and I use with confidence the liberty you have indulged
me with of offering you my ideas of our affairs.

I am mortified that the neglect of our Commissary of prisoners[4]
puts it out of my power to say any thing more about your brothers.
Notwithstanding the most particular charge to him, I have not heard
from him since I wrote you last on the subject.[5] I desired him
however to write to you from Elizabeth Town. I hope he has not
neglected this also.

With the truest esteem & attachment I have the honor to be   Yr.
Most Obed ser   A Hamilton

New Bridge
Sepr. 13th. 80

ALS (incomplete), William L. Clements Library of the University of Michigan.
    1. The first part of this letter is missing.
    2. This is a reference to British efforts to secure support of citizens in the
southern colonies. Following the British seizure of Charleston, South Carolina,
on June 1, 1780, Sir Henry Clinton and Admiral Marriot Arbuthnot, acting
as commissioners appointed by the king "to restore peace and good government in the several colonies in rebellion in North America," issued a proclamation which stated that all "deluded subjects as have been perverted from

their duty by the factious arts of self-interested and ambitious men, . . . will be received with mercy and forgiveness, if they immediately return to their allegiance, and a due obedience to those laws and that government which they formerly boasted was their birthright and noblest inheritance, and upon a due experience of the sincerity of their professions, a full and free pardon will be granted for the treasonable offences which they have heretofore committed. . ." (Lieutenant Colonel Banastre Tarleton, *A History of the Campaigns of 1780 and 1781 in the Southern Provinces of North America* [London, 1787; reprinted, New York, 1968], 74–75).

3. On August 5, 1780, Congress expressed its determination to retake the states of South Carolina and Georgia (*JCC*, XVII, 698–99).

4. Colonel Joseph Ward, a resident of Massachusetts, was appointed commissary general of prisoners in the Continental Army on April 15, 1780.

5. H to Barbé-Marbois, August 17, 1780 (*PAH*, II, 379–80).

From Lieutenant Colonel Richard Varick [1]

[*Robinson's House*,[2] *Highlands, New York, October 22, 1780.* On October 24, 1780, Varick wrote to Hamilton: [3] "I wrote You on the 22nd." *Letter not found.*]

1. Varick, a native of Hackensack, New Jersey, was admitted to the bar in New York City in 1774. On June 28, 1775, he enlisted as a captain in the New York Regiment and in June, 1776, became a military secretary to General Philip Schuyler, H's future father-in-law. On September 25, 1776, he was appointed deputy muster master general to the Northern Army, and on April 10, 1777, he was promoted to lieutenant colonel and given the title of deputy commissary general of musters. He served in this capacity until Congress abolished the office on January 12, 1780, at which time he returned to civilian life (*JCC*, XVI, 47). In early August, 1780, six weeks before Major General Benedict Arnold's treason was discovered, Arnold, at General Schuyler's suggestion, invited Varick to become his military secretary at West Point, New York.

2. Robinson's House, which was about two miles southeast of West Point, was Benedict Arnold's headquarters when his treason was discovered. It was owned by Beverly Robinson, one of New York's leading Tories.

3. Printed in this volume.

From Lieutenant Colonel Richard Varick

[*Robinson's House, Highlands, New York, October 23, 1780.* On October 24, 1780, Varick wrote to Hamilton: [1] "I wrote You on the . . . 23rd." *Letter not found.*]

1. Printed in this volume.

From Lieutenant Colonel Richard Varick [1]

R. House [Highlands, New York] Oct. 24th. 1780.

My Dear Hamilton

I wrote You on the 22nd & 23rd.[2] I now set myself down to trouble You once More.

ADfS, Harvard College Library.

1. An extract of this letter from a dealer's catalogue is printed in *PAH*, II, 488–89.

This letter concerns Varick's attempt to clear himself before a board of inquiry of suspicion of treason or the misuse of government supplies because of his close association with Major General Benedict Arnold, under whom he served as military secretary. For the full record of the proceedings against Varick, see Albert Bushnell Hart, ed., *The Varick Court of Inquiry to Investigate the Implication of Colonel Varick (Arnold's Private Secretary) in the Arnold Treason* (Boston, 1907).

On September 25, 1780, the day that Arnold's treason was discovered, George Washington placed Varick under arrest, but assured him that no one had voiced suspicions of disloyalty concerning him. Varick immediately submitted all his own papers and those of Arnold to Washington, and on September 28 he requested a court of inquiry stating: "I mean to make the most of this favorable opportunity, in showing to the world a true portrait of my conduct from the earliest period of the war, from stage to stage, till the memorable 25th of Sept. last . . . that I might wipe off from my reputation the odious reproach and suspicions, into which my unhappy connection with the guilty Arnold has traduced it" (Hart, *Varick Court*, 58). Washington granted Varick's request and appointed Major General William Heath of Massachusetts to appoint the court of inquiry (Washington to Heath, October 21, 1780 [*PAH*, II, 485]).

At the inquiry, which took place on November 2, 3, 4, and 5, 1780, Varick conducted his own defense and presented depositions on his behalf which he had gathered from his military associates, including Major David S. Franks, former aide-de-camp to Arnold, Colonel John Lamb, Major General Samuel H. Parsons, and Lieutenant Colonel Robert Hanson Harrison, secretary to Washington. Varick presented evidence that he was neither implicated in Arnold's treason nor was he "an agent in, or conniving with Mr. Arnold's abuse of power in his embezzlement of the public stores and provisions" (Hart, *Varick Court*, 61; for Arnold's misuse of government property, see H to Henry Knox, January 30, 1780, note 1 [printed in this volume]). Before the court of inquiry had convened, Heath had ordered Henry Dorne Tripp, commissary to the Flying Hospital at Colonel Beverly Robinson's house who was charged with running supplies up the Hudson River, to investigate the possibility that Varick had been involved with Arnold in the misappropriation of government property. Tripp gave testimony at the court of inquiry which proved Varick's innocence. See "Deposition of Mr. Henry Dorne Tripp, Commissary to the Flying Hospital," November 5, 1780 (Hart, *Varick Court*, 155–56).

As neither Cols. Meades or Harrison's Depositions [3] may ever reach me & if they do, As they will contain no Information respecting the Papers taken in Andre's Hand [4] I am to beg you, to be so Obliging, as to send me Your Deposition, by the first Conveyance; Of what my Conduct was, or appeared to be to You, from the Morning of the 25th. after You arrived here till that of the 28th Sept when you left us. Whether any Part of my Conduct, or language betrayed any Privity of Arnolds rascally Designs agt. his Country or of his Flight to the Enemy.[5] God only knows that my then unsuspicious Mind would not admit the Idea, till Mrs. Arnolds Declarations in her Phrenzy, "*That he was gone forever*," Alarmed my fears & that I soon after waited on His Excy., fearful to discover but anxious that he should have my Apprehensions & beg'd him to see Mrs. Arnold at her Request.[6] As I was suspected by Hooglandt [7] & others who came Expresses on that Business I could draw no Information from them.

On November 5, 1780, the court unanimously acquitted Varick and declared him "entitled (thro' every part of his conduct) to a degree of merit which does him great honor as an officer, and particularly distinguishes him as a sincere friend to his country" (Hart, *Varick Court*, 63).

The letter printed above also concerns Varick's attempt to be reinstated in the Continental Army as of April 10, 1777, the date of his appointment as lieutenant colonel. When the mustering department was abolished on January 12, 1780, Varick lost his commission in the Army. On August 25, 1780, shortly after he became Arnold's secretary, he sent a memorial to Congress requesting reappointment (ADS, Reel 52, Item 41, X, p. 317, Papers of the Continental Congress, National Archives). The memorial was read before Congress on September 12, but Congress denied Varick's request (*JCC*, XVIII, 824, 871).

On November 12, 1780, after the court adjourned, Varick wrote to Washington stating that he wanted to return to the Army and requesting Washington to present his case to Congress (ALS, George Washington Papers, Library of Congress). Washington did not make such a request to Congress, but in 1781 he appointed Varick as his recording secretary to copy and organize all the papers of the headquarters of the Continental Army.

2. Letters not found.

3. See H to Varick, October 28, 1780 (*PAH*, II, 494). For the depositions of Harrison and Richard Kidder Meade, one of Washington's aides-de-camp, see Hart, *Varick Court*, 113–17.

4. See H to John Laurens, October 11, 1780 (*PAH*, II, 460–70).

5. See H's "Deposition in Favor of Lieutenant Colonel Richard Varick," October 31, 1780 (*PAH*, II, 495–96).

6. See H to Elizabeth Schuyler, September 25, 1780 (*PAH*, II, 441–42).

7. Jeronimus Hoogland, a resident of New York and a captain in the Second Continental Dragoons, was one of three officers who escorted John André to West Point on the night of September 25, 1780 (Winthrop Sargent, *The Life and Career of Major John André, Adjutant-General of the British Army in America* [New York, 1902; reprinted, New York, 1929], 378).

I wish you, in your Depn. to declare whether any & which of the
Papers found on Andre were in my Hand writing. I am told one of
Sheldons Returns is.[8] I can very well account for it. I recd. but one
from the Lines which I always inclosed (if it came in Season) to
Scammell [9] & if I had Time, took a Copy of it. As we had at first no
D. Adjt. Genl. Let me entreat You to forward this, as much as your
hurry in Public Business will admit.

Genl Schuylers Deposition [10] or the Papers from him are not yet
come to Hand, Nor the Deposn. of Heron who carried Arnolds
intercepted Letter in & out again to Parsons—which Genl. Parsons
promised to send under Cover [11] to Genl. Greene. Those from Genl.
Schuyler were requested to be sent to me, under Cover to Genl
Greene also who then commanded here.[12] Genl. Heath had power
to open the Packets & deliver Me my Papers. Should either of the
Packets have followed Genl Greene to Head Quarters, will you be
so good as to Open them or rather advise them opened & forward

8. Colonel Elisha Sheldon had been stationed at South Salem, New York.
Arnold had attempted to use him (without informing him of the reason) as a
middleman for arranging a meeting with André. None of the papers found on
André were in Varick's handwriting. For a return of Sheldon's forces, see
"Estimate of the Forces at Wt. Point and its dependencies," September 19, 1780
(AD, in Arnold's handwriting, John André Papers, New York State Library,
Albany).

9. Colonel Alexander Scammell of New Hampshire was an adjutant general
in the Continental Army on George Washington's staff.

10. For Philip Schuyler's deposition, see "Copy of a letter from the late
Major-General Schuyler addressed to the President of the Court for inquiring
into the conduct of Lieutenant-Colonel Varick," October 15, 1780 (Hart,
Varick Court, 67–69).

11. For William Heron's deposition and Samuel H. Parsons's covering letter,
see "Certificates of the Honorable Brigadier-General Samuel H. Parsons and
of Mr. William Heron," October 26, 1780 (Hart, Varick Court, 99–102). Parsons became a major general on October 23, 1780.

12. Major General Nathanael Greene had resigned as quartermaster general
of the Army on July 26, 1780, after his opponents in Congress had adopted a
new plan for the quartermaster's department on July 15 (JCC, XVII, 615–35).
Congress accepted his resignation on August 3 (JCC, XVII, 680, 690–91), and
Greene returned to Washington's headquarters on the Hudson River at the
beginning of September. When Arnold's treason was discovered later that
month, Washington appointed Greene president of the board of general officers that tried and convicted John André. On October 6, 1780, Washington
ordered Greene to assume command at West Point, replacing Arnold (Washington to Greene, two letters of October 6, 1780 [LS, George Washington Papers, Library of Congress; LS, Massachusetts Historical Society, Boston]). On
October 14 Washington chose Greene to succeed Major General Horatio Gates
as commander of the Southern Army (LS, George Washington Papers, Library
of Congress), and Greene left West Point to assume his new duties.

my Papers to Me without Delay. Genl Greene obligingly promised to send them, in Case they should follow him. I have written to both Genls Schuyler & Parsons last Eveng. & have requested Colo Hughes [13] to send Expresses to both, on my Accot.

I fear Genl Schuylers private Affairs, which, since the Devastation, of Balls Town, West or South West of Saratoga, have prevented his Attention to my *little* Matters.[14] I am convinced of his benevolence & Disposition to Oblige Me. however a few Days will send me what I want.

Matters between Genl. Heath & Myself as a free *Citizen* are accommodated. I have been in some Measure imposed on by *Tripp*.[15] Heath was very polite in our Interview more so than I should have been after receiving such a ⟨–⟩ & we are friendly again & some what ceremonious. Inclosed is copy of My Letter to him since our Meeting, produced by his appart candour to me. I can't help faulting his Conversations with a Hospl. Commsy in these matters when I was on the Spot. In giving him a state of Matters with respect to the trifling Stores I had he acquiesced in the propriety of my Conduct. You may perhaps be surprized why I am so very sedulous for a Retrospective Enquiry into my Conduct. I answer, to support the Facts charged in & insure Success to the inclosed Memorial, sent to Congress by Advice of Genl Schuyler & Mr. Duane,[16] when on their way from Albany to Camp in August last.[17] It was forwarded by the Genl. from Orange Town, or Never sink.

I am anxious how to continue in a more properly ⟨–⟩ service provided I can do it with Honor to Myself. I am therefore solicitous to regain my Rank of Which, I was ungenteely deprived last winter. The Utter ruin of the ⟨–⟩ of our State has destroyed my prest.

13. Hugh Hughes, a resident of New York, was assistant quartermaster general.

14. See Schuyler to H, October 19, 1780 (*PAH*, II, 480–81).

15. See note 1.

Varick thought that Heath was undertaking the investigation with an "air of mean & ungenerous suspicion." Varick, moreover, was not a soldier of the line and disliked being treated as one while his memorial for reinstatement was still before Congress (Varick's "Observations on General Heath's Conduct," October, 1780 [ADS, New-York Historical Society, New York City]; Varick to Heath, October 23, 1780 [ALS, New-York Historical Society, New York City]).

16. James Duane.

17. See note 1.

Prospects in private life. I was heartily weary of the mustering Departmt. where I had the Labor & another the Honor. It often reminded Me of the Inscription mentioned in Virgil's Preface

Hos ego Versiculos feci tulit alter Honores.[18]

This was really & truly the Case between Colo Ward [19] & Myself.

I wish You to detain the Copy of the Memorial till I see You, or if you should leave Colo Deys [20] before I can pay You a Visit, pray leave it with him under Cover to Me.

I have protracted my Scrall so much longer than I tho't my Quill & Supply of Paper would afford when I sat down, that it now appears more like a Lawyers Draft than a Letter. however this is excusable to a *Friend*.

With Every Affect. Sentiment   I remain Your Friend & Hbl. Servt.   Rich. Varick

P.S. I fear the papers will have followed Greene Southward. Be so good as to enquire.   R.V.

Colo Hamilton

[ENCLOSURE]

*Lieutenant Colonel Richard Varick to
Major General William Heath* [21]

Rob. House [Highlands, New York] Oct. 24th. 1780

Sir

I think it my Duty as a Man of Candour & Generosity, to inform You, that for your Information in our Interview of yesterday, I had every reason to convince Me, That Mr. Tripp's Information, so distressing to Me, & in which my warm & pointed letter of the 21st. to

18. When Bathyllus claimed credit for a distich praising Caesar that Vergil had written, Vergil wrote beneath the distich a verse beginning "Hos ego versiculos feci tulit alter honores" with several uncompleted lines appended. Bathyllus could not complete the lines, and Vergil did.

19. On April 10, 1777, Congress appointed Joseph Ward commissary general of musters (*JCC*, VII, 252).

20. Colonel Theunis Dey of the New Jersey militia lived in Paterson, New Jersey. H had stayed at Dey's house on at least one previous occasion (H to Elizabeth Schuyler, July 6, 1780 [*PAH*, II, 353–54]).

21. Copy, in Varick's handwriting, Harvard College Library.

You, was founded; was communicated to me in a very disingenuous Manner & Air & that he mentioned to Me more, than was contained in the written Information, I shewed You: All which I believe to have been done, with an unjustifiable Design.

I confess myself much indebted to You for your then intended & unmerited Friendship, in writing me your letter of the 23rd. (As you supposed me to be an Officer) instead of pursuing those Measures, which Your Duty & Propriety, as Chief in Command here, would have justified. The Obligation is equal, altho your good Intentions could not take Effect.

I am sorry that I ever had the painful reason, for inditing a letter, which must have hurt, your Tender feelings very sensibly. I shall ever consider your intended Friendship in its proper point of View & shall be happy if this Part of my Duty to a Gentleman, came remove the unfavorable Impressions, which my Letter of the 21st. may have made in your Breast to my Prejudice.

I am Sir with respect, Your Obedt. Servt.   R V

Commission as Lieutenant Colonel [1]

[Philadelphia, October 25, 1780]

The United States of America In Congress Assembled

To Alexander Hamilton Esq. Greeting. We, Reposing especial trust and confidence in your Patriotism, Valour, Conduct, and Fidelity, DO by these presents constitute and appoint you, to a Lieutenant Colonel in the Army of the United States, to take rank as such from the first day of March A. D. 1777. You are therefore carefully and diligently to discharge the duty of a Lieutenant Colonel by doing and performing all manner of things thereunto belonging. And to Strictly charge and require all Officers and Soldiers, under your command, to be obedient to your orders, as Lieutenant Colonel. And you are to observe and follow such orders and directions, from time to time, as you Shall receive from this, or a future Congress of the United States, or Committee of Congress for that purpose appointed, a Committee of the States, or Commander in chief for the time being of the Army of the United States, or any other your Superior Officer, according to the rules and discipline of War, in pursuance of the trust reposed in you. This commission to continue in force until revoked by this, or a future Congress, the Committee of Congress beforementioned, or a Committee of the States.

Entered in the War Office and examined by the Board Attest Ben Stoddert Secretary of the Board of War	Witness his Excellency Samuel Huntington Esq President of the Congress of the United States of America, at Philadelphia the 25th. day of October A D 1780, and in the fifth Year of our Independence.

Sam. Huntington President

DS, Hamilton Papers, Library of Congress.
   1. For background to this document, see Robert Hanson Harrison to H, October 27, 1780, note 11 (*PAH*, II, 492).

To Colonel Timothy Pickering [1]

[Totowa, New Jersey, October 25, 1780] [2]

Sir

You will have the boats at Dodd's [3] and those now with the army, properly furnished with oars, transported by horses for the sake of expedition—brought to the Notch,[4] tomorrow evening precisely at five O Clock (i e half an hour before sunset) where they will receive further orders. You will have with each set a confidential person on whom you can absolutely rely for punctuality to a moment. The greatest secrecy is necessary, and it is essential that the boats should not arrive a moment sooner nor later than the time fixed.

You will have fresh teams ready at the same place at the same time under a confidential person also, to relieve those in the Waggons, in order to transport the boats with the more celerity.

I am Sir   Yr. most Obed ser   Alex Hamilton
                                                          Aide De Camp

Hd. Qrs. Octr. 25. 80

If you will be so good as to call at Head Quarters this evening there may be some other points.

The note mentioned by Mr. Garanger [5] was of a personal nature.[6] Your messenger went away this morning before I could write an answer. The boats are to be kept in readiness 'till further order. Good night My Dear Sir

A H

ALS, RG 93, War Department Collection of Revolutionary War Records, Manuscripts #26393, National Archives.

1. Pickering, a resident of Salem, Massachusetts, a lawyer, and a member of the state militia, held several local and state offices before leading a contingent of his state's militia to join the Continental Army during the winter of 1776–1777. On May 7, 1777, he was appointed adjutant general to George Washington, and on November 7, 1777, he was elected to the Board of War, but he continued to serve as adjutant general until January 13, 1778. On August 5, 1780, he was appointed colonel and quartermaster general of the Army.

The preparations described in this letter arose because Washington thought that the British might attack his headquarters near the falls of the Passaic River in the present-day city of Paterson, New Jersey (H to Joshua Mersereau, October 24, 1780 [*PAH*, II, 488]). See also Washington's "Disposition for opposing the Enemy while we were Encamped at the Falls of Passaic," 1780 (AD, George Washington Papers, Library of Congress).

2. Totowa is on the Passaic River and is immediately west of Paterson in Passaic County, New Jersey.

3. Dodd's Tavern was on a branch of the Passaic River four or five miles west of Little Falls, which, in turn, is directly south of Totowa.

4. The "Notch" is a cleft in Weasel Mountain, which lies between present-day Clifton, New Jersey, and Little Falls, New Jersey.

5. Lewis Garanger.

6. In MS, "natural."

From Marquis de Lafayette [1]

[*Light Camp, New Jersey, October 30, 1780.* Letter listed in dealer's catalogue. *Letter not found.*]

1. ALS, sold by C. F. Libbie and Company, Boston, December 12, 1895, Item 312.

Certificate for Major Robert Forsyth [1]

[Philadelphia, November 10, 1780]

I certify that Major Forsyth had served in the Army of the United States as aid de Camp to Major General Stevens [2] during his continuation in the service.

> Alex Hamilton
> aid de Camp
> to the Commander in Chief

Copy, Auditor's Item 70, Revolutionary Section, File for Major Robert Forsyth, Virginia State Library, Richmond.

1. Forsyth had been a captain in Henry Lee's Battalion of Light Dragoons from July 1, 1778, to September 5, 1779, when he resigned to take a commission in the Virginia militia.

2. Edward Stevens was brigadier general of the Virginia militia from 1779 to 1782.

Continental Congress
Nomination as Minister to France [1]

Philadelphia, December 9, 1780. On this date John Sullivan [2] nominated Hamilton "for the office of minister to the Court of Versailles." [3]

JCC, XVIII, 1138.

1. For background to this document, see Marquis de Lafayette to H, December 9, 1780, note 7 (*PAH*, II, 518–21).

2. Sullivan, a resident of New Hampshire, was appointed a brigadier general in the Continental Army on June 22, 1775, and was promoted to major general on August 9, 1776. He resigned his commission on November 30, 1779, and in 1780 he was a delegate to Congress.

3. The other nominees were John Laurens, Alexander McDougall, and Jonathan Trumbull, Jr., of Connecticut (*JCC*, XVIII, 1138). On December 11, 1780, Congress elected Laurens to be Minister to France (*JCC*, XVIII, 1141).

Continental Congress
Nomination as Minister to Russia

Philadelphia, December 15, 1780. On this date John Mathews [1] nominated Hamilton Minister to Russia. [2]

JCC, XVIII, 1155–56.

1. Mathews was a delegate to the Continental Congress from South Carolina.

2. Francis Dana of Massachusetts and Arthur Lee of Virginia were the other nominees (*JCC,* XVIII, 1155–56). On December 19, 1780, Congress named Dana as Minister to the Court of Russia (*JCC,* XVIII, 1166).

Three months later, on March 6, 1781, John Sullivan wrote to George Washington: "I shall this Day nominate him [H] as Secretary of Foreign Affairs . . ." (Burnett, *Letters,* VI, 11). On May 10, 1781, John Armstrong of Pennsylvania wrote to his father, General John Armstrong: "Dr Arthur Lee, [James] Lovell, and Young Hamilton are in nomination for the foreign correspondence" (copy, Peter Force Papers, Library of Congress).

No other evidence has been found that H was nominated for this position.

1781

To Charles Stewart

[New Windsor, New York, January 21, 1781]

The Commissary will issue a ration pr. individual to the Commandants and their crews that is per the inclosed return [1] to fifty five persons till further orders a return of the issues to be made to the Qr. Mr. General [2] that the rations may be paid for in a settlement of accounts with the said persons.

By His Excellency's order

Hd. Qrs. Jany. 21st. 81   Alex Hamilton
To The Commissary of Issues   Aide De Camp

ADS, George Washington Papers, Library of Congress.
1. "Return of Vessels, Employd. in Public Service the Last Season The Crews Belonging to them and their familys," January 2, 1781 (ADS, in the handwriting of John Palmer, George Washington Papers, Library of Congress).
2. Timothy Pickering. See H to Pickering, January 21, 1781 (*PAH*, II, 538).

To Lieutenant Colonel John Laurens [1]

[New Windsor, New York, February 4, 1781]

I had finished my letter [2] when I received a respite of another quarter of an hour which I shall improve in writing you another ⟨let⟩ter.

The Marquis [3] thinks the Generals ⟨lett⟩er [4] will have more weight if the Ministry ⟨see⟩ it, as it were undesignedly by you, than if you formally communicate it to them; and with a view to this he has mentioned the letter to them and advised them to ask for a sight of it. He observes that in this way we shall avoid the suspicion of ⟨the⟩ letters having been *calculated* for their ⟨ins⟩pection and of course they will have less ⟨reser⟩ve in giving faith to its contents.

⟨There⟩ is weight in this observation and ⟨it⟩ is worthy to be considered by you. At all events however, The Ministry ought to see the letter.

I have sincerely told you My Dear Laurens that I was happy the commission has been entrusted to you.[5] ⟨I have⟩ implicit confidence in your talent⟨s and⟩ integrity; but in the frankness of fri⟨endship⟩ allow me to suggest to you one apprehension. It is of the honest warmth of your ⟨temper.⟩ A politician My Dear friend must ⟨be at all⟩ times supple—he must often dissemble ⟨– –⟩ and resentments. I suspect the ⟨French⟩ Ministry will try your temper; but ⟨you⟩ must not suffer them to provoke it. When Congress is spoken of, you must justify and extenuate with the dignity and coolness of a politician, not with the susceptibility of a republican—sometimes even you must acknowlege errors and ascribe ⟨them⟩ to inexperience, and if you he⟨ar animad⟩versions perhaps not over delicate ⟨you must⟩ affect to receive them as the conf⟨ident –⟩ freedoms of allies concerned for ⟨– –⟩. When you wish to show the def⟨iciency⟩ of the French Administration, do it indirectly by exposing the advantages of measures not taken rather than by a direct ⟨criticism⟩ of those taken. When you exp⟨ress⟩ your fears of consequences have the tone of lamentation rather than of menace.

In the nature of things, the French Court must consider us as the obliged party, and I do not see the policy of rejecting this idea, though I would take every proper occasion of showing the advantages of the revolution to France without however seeming to insist upon them. One good way of doing this will be by showing the immense advantages which England would have derived from a continuance of the ⟨u⟩nion.

I believe in fine My friend ⟨the⟩ French Court is jealous and susceptible. You will not give food to this disposition.

These cautions I am sure you will receive as proofs of My friendship & confidence. ⟨Betsy⟩ sends her love and best wishes

Adieu   A H

ALS, Columbia University Libraries.
1. When this letter was written, Laurens was preparing to sail to France. On December 11, 1780, Congress had elected him to be Minister to France "for the special purpose of soliciting the aids requested by Congress . . ." (*JCC*, XVIII, 1141, 1178). For Laurens's commission, letter of credence, and instructions, see *JCC*, XVIII, 1183–88.

2. H to Laurens, February 4, 1781 (*PAH*, II, 549–51).

3. Marquis de Lafayette.

4. George Washington to Laurens, January 15, 1781 (Df, George Washington Papers, Library of Congress).

5. H had also been nominated as Minister to France. See "Continental Congress. Nomination as Minister to France," December 9, 1780 (printed in this volume).

To Colonel Hugh Hughes

Head Quarters [*New Windsor, New York*] *February 9, 1781.*
Requests temporary replacement for his stolen bridle and repairs on his saddle. Also requests a bridle for George Washington's servant's horse.

LC, New-York Historical Society, New York City.

To Colonel Timothy Pickering

[New Windsor, New York, February 9, 1781]

Dr Sir.

The bad condition of my horses and the scarcity of forage in Camp induced me to leave them at Saratoga [1] to recruit against the Campaign. I am shortly to make a journey with the General to Rhode Island for which I shall want horses.[2] I therefore request the favour of you to furnish me with a couple of the best Continental horses that can be found. One for myself—the other for my portmanteau. The last need only be strong. I wish the former if possible to be decent. I shall want them in three or four days. I am Dr Sir

Yr most Obed   A Hamilton

Feby. 9

ALS, RG 93, Revolutionary War Records, Miscellaneous Records, National Archives.

1. H had been in upstate New York in December, 1780, for his marriage to Elizabeth Schuyler at her father's house in Albany. See "Registry of Marriage of Elizabeth Schuyler and Alexander Hamilton," December 14, 1780 (*PAH*, II, 521).

2. H was preparing to accompany George Washington to Newport, Rhode Island, for a conference with the French commander, Jean Baptiste Donatien de Vimeur, comte de Rochambeau. Washington postponed the trip until March 2. See Washington to Rochambeau, February 15, 1781 (LS, George Washington Papers, Library of Congress).

From Colonel Hugh Hughes

Fishkill [New York] February 16, 1781. Has obtained horses requested by Hamilton for the journey to Rhode Island.[1] Asks whether they should be delivered to the west bank of the Hudson River or kept at Fishkill.

LC, New-York Historical Society, New York City.
   1. See H to Timothy Pickering, February 9, 1781 (printed in this volume).

To Colonel Hugh Hughes

[New Windsor, New York] February 27, 1781. "I thank you for the Trouble you have taken about the Horses.[1] Our Journey is postpon'd, but is Still in Contemplation.[2] When we do set out I shall be obliged to depend on the Public for Horses, as mine were so low that I do not intend to bring them from above [3] 'till near the opening of the Campaign. . . ."

LC, New-York Historical Society, New York City.
   1. See Hughes to H, February 16, 1781 (printed in this volume).
   2. See George Washington to President of Congress, February 26, 1781 (*GW*, XXI, 300–02).
   3. See H to Timothy Pickering, February 9, 1781 (printed in this volume).

To Colonel Hugh Hughes

[De Peyster's Point, New York] May 5, 1781. ". . . I shall . . . thank you if you can conveniently do it, to let me have a Boatman to remain with me, while I stay here.[1] I have requested a Soldier from Col Scammell,[2] if I get him the Boatman may return. . . . I

should be glad of a Qur. of a pound of Chalk for a particular purpose."

LC, New-York Historical Society, New York City.
   1. When H wrote this letter, he and his wife were living at De Peyster's
Point, where they had moved in mid-April, 1781, after H had left his position
as aide-de-camp to George Washington. See H to Philip Schuyler, February 18,
1781 (*PAH*, II, 563–68); H to Jeremiah Wadsworth, April 16, 1781 (*PAH*, II,
593). H lived at De Peyster's Point until late May, when he moved to Schuyler's house in Albany. During this period, he returned at least once to Washington's headquarters at New Windsor, New York, to assist Washington. See
Washington to Comte de Rochambeau, April 30, 1781 (*PAH*, II, 636).
   2. Alexander Scammell.

From Colonel Hugh Hughes

Fishkill [*New York*] *May 5, 1781.* Has forwarded Hamilton's
request to Colonel Alexander Scammell and has ordered that "a
Hand" and "½ a pound of Chalk" be sent to Hamilton.[1]

LC, New-York Historical Society, New York City.
   1. See H to Hughes, May 5, 1781 (printed in this volume).

To Stewart and Totten [1]

de Peyster's Point [New York] May 20, 1781.

Gentlemen,

   I have received your favour of the 5th instant,[2] with the one
hundred and sixteen dollars of the emission of this State.[3] *Every kind
of paper money is so out of credit here, that it has been with great
difficulty I have been able to put off any part of the sum you sent
me.* I have no method of employing it but in current expences, and
for the articles I wanted *it will scarcely be received at all.* I have
however been able to part with about sixty dollars which has neated
about one for three. I should return the rest, but as I learn it is in
a worse state in Philadelphia—even than here. I have thought it more
for your interest to retain it, and still endeavour to put it off on the
best terms I can, unless you should desire me to deliver it to any

person here with whom you may be concerned. Whatever it produces, I shall carry to your credit and advise you of. Five for one of this currency has been offered for hard money.

I am with great esteem, Gentlemen,   Your most obedient humble servant,   A. Hamilton

Messrs. Stewart and Totten,
Merchants Philadelphia.

The [New York] *Royal Gazette,* June 13, 1781.
   1. The firm of Stewart and Totten was located in Philadelphia. The proprietors were Robert Totten and James and Alexander Stewart.
   2. See *PAH*, II, 638.
   3. For the "emission of this State," see Charles Pettit to H, April 30, 1791, note 3 (*PAH*, VIII, 318-20).

To Colonel Hugh Hughes

[*Dobbs Ferry,*[1] *New York*] *July 13, 1781.* "I beg your particular Care in forwarding the enclosed. It . . . covers a letter to Mrs. Hamilton [2] and some of my Letters to the General. . . ." [3]

LC, New-York Historical Society, New York City.
   1. H had gone to George Washington's headquarters on July 8, 1781, in an effort to obtain a command for the approaching campaign.
   2. Elizabeth Hamilton was at her father's house in Albany. See H to Elizabeth Hamilton, July 10, 1781 (*PAH*, II, 647-48).
   3. H is presumably referring to copies of letters which he wrote to Washington to obtain a new command and which he forwarded to Philip Schuyler, his father-in-law. See H to Elizabeth Hamilton, July 10, 1781 (*PAH*, II, 647-48).

To Colonel Hugh Hughes

[*Dobbs Ferry, New York*] *July 15, 1781.* Asks Hughes to send "the enclosed" [1] to Albany.

LC, New-York Historical Society, New York City.
   1. See H to Elizabeth Hamilton, July 13, 1781 (*PAH*, II, 652-53).

From Colonel Hugh Hughes

Fishkill [New York] July 18, 1781. States that Hamilton's letters have been forwarded "by careful Hands." [1] Also states that "there are some very inquisitive Gentry on the Route." Requests "a line now & then, on the appearance of a Phenominon &c."

LC, New-York Historical Society, New York City.
  1. See H to Hughes, July 13, 15, 1781 (printed in this volume).

To Colonel Hugh Hughes

[Dobbs Ferry, New York] July 21, 1781. Requests "particular Care in forwarding the Enclosed."

LC, New-York Historical Society, New York City.

To Colonel Hugh Hughes

[Dobbs Ferry, New York] July 25, 1781

My Dear Sir

I beg your Care of the enclosed. I can inform you of Nothing which I believe will be new to you.[1] You have heard of our late reconnoitre? [2] You have seen the Accounts from Green of the Reduction of Augusta.[3] He was obliged by the approach of Rawdon to abandon the Seige of 96, when on the Point of Success—but he was resolved Still to Maintain the Contest in that Quarter.[4] Fayette has had a severe brush with Cornwallis.[5] He lost an hundred and odd Men Killed, wounded and Missing, and two Pieces of Cannon—in all probability the Enemy's loss in Men was not less. Cornwallis had recrossed James River and was supposed to be proceeding to Portsmouth—thence perhaps in whole or in part to N York & South Carolina. All this & more I suppose you know.

  Adieu. your's   A Hamilton

LC, New-York Historical Society, New York City.

1. See Hughes to H, July 18, 1781 (printed in this volume).

2. For George Washington's description of this reconnoitre of what is now the Bronx, see John C. Fitzpatrick, ed., *The Diaries of George Washington, 1748–1799*, II (Boston and New York, 1925), 241–45.

3. On June 6, 1781, the Tories and Indians surrendered Fort Cornwallis in Augusta, Georgia, to the American forces under the command of Lieutenant Colonel Henry Lee.

4. On June 18, 1781, Major General Nathanael Greene began a siege of the fort in the town of Ninety-Six, Greenwood County, South Carolina. A larger British force under Lieutenant Colonel Sir Frances Rawdon came to relieve the fort, but Greene withdrew on June 20, the day before Rawdon arrived. See Greene to the President of Congress, June 20, 1781 (ALS, Reel 175, Item 155, II, p. 175, Papers of the Continental Congress, National Archives).

5. On July 6, 1781, General Cornwallis defeated Lafayette at Green Spring, Virginia, near Jamestown.

To Colonel Hugh Hughes

[Dobbs Ferry, New York, July 28th, 1781]

Dear Sir

I beg your particular Care of the Enclosed. The only News we have here is a Report from Philadelphia, that Rawdon after throwing a small succour into 96, had retired to Charles Town, & that Greene had renewed the Seige of that Place.[1] You heard the British Fleet had put to Sea from the Hook, supposed to be going to escort Cornwallis back.[2]

Adieu my Dear Sir   your most obedt.   A Hamilton

July 28th. 1781

LC, New-York Historical Society, New York City.

1. See H to Hughes, July 25, 1781 (printed in this volume).

Lieutenant Colonel Sir Francis Rawdon took the fort in the town of Ninety-Six on June 21, 1781, and ordered its evacuation. He left a small force at Ninety-Six, but moved the main portion of his troops to Orangeburg, a town forty miles southeast of Charleston, South Carolina.

2. When six or seven ships left Sandy Hook under Admiral Thomas Graves on July 21, George Washington expected them to return to New York with all or part of Cornwallis's forces. Both Washington and H were mistaken, for the vessels were bound for Pensacola, Florida, to pick up and return to New York parolled British soldiers who had been captured by the Spanish under Bernardo de Galvez in May, 1781.

Account of Cloathing Purchased for the Officers of Colo Hamiltons Battalion at the first Sterling price [1]

[August, 1781]

2 pieces linnen	No 150—40 yds	1/7			
2 Do	145—50	1/2¾			
1 piece Bandannoes		1/2	0	14	0
12 Yards Mode		3/6	2	2	0
8 Yards Satten		4/2	1	13	4
7 Yards Callico		2/3	0	15	9
8 pieces of Nankeen		7/3	2	18	0
17½ yards of Russia sheeting		1/4	1	3	4
1 piece of linnen	No. 4—26 yards	1/6	1	19	0
1 Do	2—22	1/5	1	11	2
1 Do	4—22	1/6	1	13	0
Remnent 12 yards	12	1/9½	1	1	6
Do 15	8	2/	1	10	0
2 pieces of Jean	60½ yards	2/3	6	16	1½
6 pair shoe Brushes		1/4		8	0
16 sticks black ball		/7		9	4
4½ yards super fine white Broad cloath			3	8	0
10 yards Buff Cassamer		7/6	3	15	0
8½ Do Do		7/6	3	3	0
6 Yards drab white		5/3	1	11	6
9½ yards white velvet		3/6	1	13	3
3 pair white silk raw hoes		7/	1	1	0
3 pair white spun		7/6	1	2	6
3 Do Coulard		8/6	1	5	6
3 Do Do		12/	1	16	0
2 Do pr White		11/9	1	3	6
1 Dozen White thread		47/	2	7	0
1 Dozen fine Cotton hoes		60/	3	0	0
3 pair brown Cotton Do		4/9		14	3
3 pair leather gloves		3/9		11	3
3 pair Do		2/3		6	9

		£	s	d
12 fine Cambrick handkerchs	3/4½	2		6
5 linnen Ditto	3/		15	0
10 Ditto Do	2/3	1	2	6
2 yards 1/8 super fine scarlet Cloath	20/	2	2	6
6 Dozen white Coat Buttons	1/5		2	6
3 Do Gilt Do	1/6		4	6
1 piece linnen No. 6—25 yards	1/7	1	19	7
1 Ditto Do 5—24	1/5	1	14	0
1 Do Do 6—25	1/6	1	17	6
13 Yards 3/4 white Cordory	4/	2	15	0
7 Bandannoes	4/1	1	8	0
12 Bassalana Hankerchiefs	3/4½	2		6½
7 Bandannoes	4/6	1	11	6
15 yards White shalloon	23/	1	3	0
7½ Yards ½ ell dyed Janet	2/9	1		7½
1 piece fine Linnen N—24 yds	2/	2	8	0
1¼ yard Cassimer	7/9		9	8½
11 Yards Cotton Denim	3/5	1	17	7
19½ yards Cordaroy	2/8	2	11	4
11 3/4 yards Scarlet Cassamer	8/3	4	16	11
3 yards of Mersilus Quilting	5/6		16	6
10 Yards Mode 8 Ells	4/6	1	16	
7½ Do Do	2/6		18	
Capt. Clifts Acct [2]				
7 pr shoes	4/7	0	4	7
6 yards of Taffity	2/8		16	
10 yards of Amezeen	7/3	3	12	16
1 piece of Chints		2	8	0
2 stiks Mohair	/3			6
2 Silk Hankerchiefs	4/	7	9	7
1½ yards scarlet Cloath	19/6	1	9	3
1 Hatt	10/		10	
1 Set of Buckles	12/		12	6
7 yards of Black serge Denim	5/1	1	5	1
10½ yards of Ribband	/8		7	
17 yards black lace	/8	0	11	4
3 Silver Hat bands	2/6		7	6
4 Sticks twist	6/4		6	4

35 Skeins of Silk		7/4	7	4
3 pair of Gilt sleeve buttons		/6	1	6
3 pair Cotton Hoes		4/7	13	7
15 Yards white flannel		1/6	1 2	6
2 pair Gilt shoe buckles		12/	4 4	4
3 pound of thread		2/	6	
1 Do	No. 19	15/	15	
3 pair of brawn thread hoes		2/5	7	3
2 pair of white Do.		4/9	9	6
5 pair brawn Cotten Hoes		4/2	1	10
6 pair of Cotton Do.		2/3	13	6
5 Hats		19/		
5½ yards shalloon		2¾ [3]		

D, RG 53, Vol. 158, War Department Collection of Revolutionary War Records, National Archives.

1. In MS, "Starling prise."

On July 31, 1781, H had been given command of a battalion for the Yorktown campaign. See "General Orders," July 31, 1781 (*PAH*, II, 658).

2. Captain Lemuel Clift of Connecticut, who had been serving in the Fourth Connecticut Regiment, was transferred to the First Connecticut Regiment on January 1, 1781. In August, 1781, this regiment was assigned to H's battalion. See "A List of officers and Mens Names who have Recd. one months pay in Colo Hamiltons Battaln," September 7, 1781 (printed in this volume).

3. This list is endorsed: "Received the within Articles pr Garret Lansing 2nd New York Regt."

A List of officers and Mens Names who have Recd. one months pay in Colo Hamiltons Battaln sept 7th 1781 [1]

[Head of Elk, Maryland, September 7, 1781]

Names	Company	Regiment	Whole Amount	
			Dol	90th
Thads Weed Capt		Colo Swift	50	2nd
Cornelius Russell Lt	Capt Weed	Colo Swift	32	2nd
William Lord Ensn	Selden	Butler	25	4th
Thomas Warson Sergt	Strong	Swift	10	2nd
Joseph Whipple	Morris	Swift	10	2nd

Names	Company	Regiment	Whole Amount		
			Dol	90th	
Luther Page	Ten Eyke	Butler	10		4th
James Bradley	Selden	Butler	10		4th
Isaac Olmsted Corpl	Weed	Swift	7	30	2nd
Charles Porter do	Walker	Webb	7	30	3rd
Harmon Rose Corpl	Reed	Butler	7	30	4th
Isaiah Atkins Do	Munson	Butler	7	30	4th
Rufus Holdridge Drum	Reed	Butler	7	30	4th
Oliver Mun Fife	Humphrey	Butler	7	30	4th
David Bradley	Selden	Butler	6	60	4th
Benjn Brown	Hopkins	Webb	6	60	3rd
Willm. Batison	Wright	Swift	6	60	2nd
Joseph Batison	Converse	Swift	6	60	2nd
Artimus Bloget	Selden	Butler	6	60	4th
David Chester	Riley	Webb	6	60	3rd
Willm Carr	Ten Eyke	Butler	6	60	4th
Jonah Carter	Baldwin	Swift	6	60	2nd
Joseph Cheney	Riley	Webb	6	60	3d
Stephen Batison	Converse	Swift	6	60	2nd
Joseph Cole	Lay	Butler	6	60	4th
Daniel Davis	Hopkins	Webb	6	60	2nd
Joseph Elwood	Monson	Butler	6	60	4th
Daniel Fin	Strong	Swift	6	60	2nd
Samuel Furgo	Williams	Webb	6	60	3d
Thomas Green	Wright	Swift	6	60	2nd
David Headon	Walker	Webb	6	60	3d
Eli Hull	Ten Eyke	Butler	6	60	4th
Jedediah Hibbard	Munson	Butler	6	60	4th
Jabez Lewis	Baldwin	Swift	6	60	4th
Abner Lilly	Starr	Butler	6	60	4th
Seth Montigue	Hopkins	Webb	6	60	3d
Henry McLane	Selden	Butler	6	60	4th
Samuel Price	Billings	Swift	6	60	2d
Azor Patchen	Morris	Swift	6	60	2nd
Jesse Rice	Morris	Swift	6	60	2nd
Newcomb Raymond	Converse	Swift	6	60	2nd

Names	Company	Regiment	Whole Amount		
			Dol	90th	
Willm Short	Buckley	Webb	6	60	3d
Benjn Scofield	Chaimberlin	Swift	6	60	2nd
Asa Solomon	Starr	Butler	6	60	4th
Henry Stish	Lay	Butler	6	60	4th
Willm Sedgwick	Weed	Swift	6	60	2nd
Nathan Tubbs	Ryley	Webb	6	60	3d
Amos Tharpp	Butler	Butler	6	60	4th
Moses Woster	Baldwin	Swift	6	60	2nd
John Wheler	Riley	Webb	6	60	3d
James Wilman	Billings	Swift	6	60	2nd
Daniel Welch	Converse	Swift	6	60	2nd
Hesekiah Wealey	Strong	Swift	6	60	2nd
Lemuel Willis	Monson	Butler	6	60	4th
Ephraim Watkin	Chamberlin	Swift	6	60	2nd
Ebenezer Young	Weed	Swift	6	60	2nd
James L. Dean	Selden	Butler	6	60	4th
Daniel Woodard	Reed	Butler	6	60	4th
			£484	30	Total

D, RG 93, Vol. 158, War Department Collection of Revolutionary War Records, National Archives.

1. The men on this list were from Connecticut.

In his general orders of August 19, 1781, George Washington ordered the formation of two companies from the Connecticut line to join the battalion placed under H's command on July 31, 1781, for the Yorktown campaign (*GW*, XXIII, 19; "General Orders," July 31, 1781 [*PAH*, II, 658]; "Account of Cloathing Purchased for the Officers of Colo Hamiltons Battalion at the first Sterling price," August, 1781 [printed in this volume]).

State of the *Arms Accoutrements & ammunition in Lt. Colo. Hamiltons Battalion of Light Infantry* [1]

September 24th 1781

	Musquetts	Swords	Bayonets	Cartridge Boxes	Gun Slings	Gun Worms	Screw Drivers	Brushes and Prickers	Drums	Fifes	Flints	Cartridges
Good	230	2	232	238	114	10	18	10	2	2	577	8688
Bad	7		5		3			1			10	200
Wanting	1	9	1		121	23	220	228	1	2	127	632
Total	238	11	238	238	238	33	238	238	4	4	724	9220

Ale Hamilton
Lt Col Comt

DS, Harvard College Library.
1. On July 31, 1781, H had obtained command of a battalion for the Yorktown campaign. See "General Orders," July 31, 1781 (*PAH*, II, 658).

To Colonel Hugh Hughes [1]

[*Albany*,[2] *November, 1781.* "Mrs. Hamilton begs me to assure you how much she is indebted to you for your obliging offer. She requests the favour of you to let the waggon, on its way to Albany, call on a certain duchman a tavern Keeper at Rynbeck for some apples and cyder purchased by him for General Schuyler. . . . If you do not leave this side of the river tomorrow, we shall be happy to see you at dinner."[3] *Letter not found.*]

1. ALS, sold by American Art Association, November 22, 1915, Lot 466.

2. After the Battle of Yorktown, in which H had participated (H to Marquis de Lafayette, October 15, 1781 [*PAH*, II, 679–81]; H to Vicomte de Noailles, November-December, 1781 [printed in this volume]), he traveled to Albany, where Elizabeth Hamilton was staying with her father, Philip Schuyler. See H to Elizabeth Hamilton, October 18, 1781 (*PAH*, II, 683).

3. Text taken from the dealer's catalogue.

To Vicomte de Noailles [1]

[November-December, 1781]

Sir,

You have read with astonishment in several American papers, that a man who in various actions of this war has owed his success to his valour, who in the field has been rather the first soldier than the General of his army, has, during the siege of York-Town, entirely lost his reputation of bravery and ability.[2] You inquire of me as of a person too well acquainted with Lord Cornwallis to add a sanction to the injurious pieces written against a defenceless enemy.[3] Your knowledge of our nation induces you to think, that after a victory, in the tranquil moment of reflection, we can judge with calmness, and even protect the person whom the preceeding hour we had attacked with eagerness; though for myself I disclaim the loss of animosity, certain that a constant and eternal hatred is the only method to humble our enemy—like Rome who inflexible in her enmity, even after the destruction of Carthage, could not forgive her former glory. To merit your confidence, I will endeavour to discard every sentiment of passion and prejudice. I must first take a retrospect of his Lordship's conduct. After the arrival of a French fleet in the Chesapeake, had he marched to attack the detachment commanded by Marquis de la Fayette, the same prudence which conducted the American army during eight months in Virginia, had prevented an engagement.[4] The march of the British army had been useless; time had been better employed to erect field-works. After the junction with the French troops from the West Indies, the number of the two armies, and their excellent disposition, amounted to a certainty of success. Some experienced persons condemned the desertion of the two redoubts of Pigeon Quarter,[5] which made it

easy for the combined forces to establish their lines: But that seem-
ingly timid manœuvre was to flatter the enterprising genius of the
assailants, and the probability of success was founded on the example
of Savannah [6] and St. Lucia.[7] The establishment of the parallels
being finished, it were absurd to suppose it possible for the enemy
to make frequent sorties from a place without cover'd way, against
lines flank'd with palissaded redoubts.[8] The attempt which the
British made was a proof, that such a manœuvre exposed them to be
followed to their works. A more heavy fire from the enemy when
the trenches were opened had undoubtedly retarded the work, and
rendered it more difficult, but could not have prevented our
succeeding at last. Without speaking of a cave, and those other
reports so injurious to Lord Cornwallis, which have been circulated
only to flatter those weak minds who take pleasure in lessening the
real merit of an enemy,[9] I chuse rather to find the cause of our
victory in the superior number of good and regular troops,[10] in the
uninterrupted harmony of the two nations, and their equal desire to
be celebrated in the annals of history, for an ardent love of great and
heroic actions. For the private conduct of Lord Cornwallis, I consult
only his army; for, who can better judge of the bravery of a General,
than the soldiers under his immediate command? Who ought rather
to be believed in a matter of such importance to every military
man, than those who, tho' suffering, render homage to truth, and
accuse not their chief of the misfortunes in which they are plunged?
We have seen a General in America unjustly accus'd; but where
shall we find an instance in history that a General has been praised
after a defeat, without deserving it. I have seen that army so
haughty in its success; not an emotion of the soldiers escap'd me; and
I observed every sign of mortification with pleasure. I insinuated
myself into their confidence, but could not hear a word to the prejudice of Lord Cornwallis. The soldiers were the echo of their officers
—and every marquee lamented the fate of their General in England,
more than their own captivity in America. The execution of Byng,[11]
and what is still more painful to a sensible heart, the disgrace of
Burgoyne,[12] fill them with apprehensions for their chief. Our im-
petuous nation, say they, will revenge upon his Lordship the fate of
his army. Cruel in its vengeance, England will not believe that every
project of conquest in America is vain; that a hundred thousand men

could not extend their arms from Quebec to St. Augustine; and that every army which penetrates the country is infallibly lost, whenever a superior fleet will permit the united powers of France and America to assemble their various resources. How proud soever a Frenchman may be to serve in a cause in which the universe is interested, he cannot help feeling that his stay in America is unnesessary to the success of it; that the efforts of France are only to keep a useful population in America, and preserve a good discipline in part of her army. I hope two examples will not persuade England that those are the true reasons which have contributed to his Lordship's defeat.

The attention of an author is not to tire his reader; the indulgence of friendship allows long letters, and I have made it my duty to answer your request. I am satisfied if you can find yourself sufficiently acquainted with the particulars of our glorious campaign. My warmest wish is, that England may direct her armies on the same principles that she has done since the beginning of this contest, and still with the same discipline. It seems that injustice and cruelty enslave the genius of her ministry. May next year furnish the allied nations another opportunity to convince the world, that no people upon the earth are more worthy competetors in war, or will be more faithful friends during a peace.

I have the honor to be, &c.

The [Boston] *Independent Chronicle, and the Universal Advertiser*, December 27, 1781; copy, Papiers de Noailles, Archives Nationales, Paris.

1. Louis-Marie, vicomte de Noailles, a French officer, participated in the siege of Savannah in 1778, played a distinguished role at Yorktown, and represented the French army in negotiating the terms for surrender after the battle. He left Boston for France on December 25, 1781, took part in the early stages of the French Revolution, became an *émigré* in 1792, and arrived in the United States in 1793, where he remained until 1800.

2. Although most Americans and their newspapers condemned Cornwallis for his alleged brutality and cruelty during his campaign in the South before the Battle of Yorktown, little significant evidence has been found that the press thought he had lost "his reputation of bravery and ability" during the siege itself. The principal criticism of Cornwallis's conduct during the battle was that he spent his time in a cave near the York River, "where it was next to an impossibility that the shot or shells of the assailants could reach the person of this renowned warrior" ([Philadelphia] *Freeman's Journal: or, the North-American Intelligencer*, November 14, 1781; see also Franklin and Mary Wickwire, *Cornwallis and the War of Independence* [London, 1970], 377, 382, 383).

3. For examples of criticisms of Cornwallis's conduct before Yorktown, see the [Philadelphia] *Freeman's Journal: or, the North-American Intelligencer*, November 7, 14, 1781; the [Philadelphia] *Pennsylvania Journal, and the Weekly Advertiser*, October 31, November 21, 1781; *The* [Philadelphia] *Pennsylvania*

Gazette, and Weekly Advertiser, October 31, November 14, 1781; *The [Boston] Independent Chronicle, and the Universal Advertiser,* October 18, 1781.

4. This sentence refers to the campaign conducted by Lafayette in Virginia during the months immediately preceding the Battle of Yorktown. After the failure of a plan to capture Benedict Arnold in Maryland in March, 1781, Lafayette was ordered south with his troops to join Nathanael Greene in the Carolinas. He arrived in Richmond on April 29 in time to prevent its destruction by the British. When Cornwallis advanced northward into Virginia, Lafayette first retreated before the British forces and then with reinforcements harassed them. Cornwallis gradually retreated to Portsmouth, and it was Lafayette's task to prevent the escape of the British from the trap that resulted in the Battle of Yorktown. For Lafayette's description of part of this campaign, see Lafayette to H, May 26, 1781 (*PAH,* II, 643–45).

5. To the southwest of Yorktown was a marshy region in the vicinity of Wormeley's Pond and Creek and an open area known as Pigeon Quarter. The British had erected two redoubts in Pigeon Quarter, but abandoned them on the night of September 29–30, 1781.

6. On December 29, 1778, British regulars and Loyalists captured and occupied Savannah.

7. In December, 1778, the British captured St. Lucia, one of the Windward Islands, from the French.

8. This is a reference to the two "parallels" or trenches devised by the Franco-American forces to penetrate and confine the British forces at Yorktown.

9. See notes 2 and 3 above.

10. The combined French and American troops numbered close to 17,000, while the British force consisted of no more than 8,000 men.

11. In 1756 Admiral John Byng, after being defeated by the French in his effort to relieve the British garrison at Minorca, withdrew to Gibraltar. He was arrested, court-martialed, found guilty of neglect of duty, and shot.

12. Following his army's defeat at Saratoga, General John Burgoyne was permitted by the Americans to return to England. On May 26, 1778, he was unable to defend himself successfully from charges in the House of Commons, that he had been responsible for the defeat at Saratoga (*The Parliamentary History of England, From the Earliest Period to the Year 1803* [London, 1814], XIX, 1175–1199).

1782

To Colonel Jeremiah Wadsworth

[*Philadelphia, February 1, 1782.* The description of this letter reads: "Alexander Hamilton, to Col. Wadsworth, begging the loan of one hundred pounds." [1] *Letter not found.*]

"Original Correspondence of Colonel Jeremiah Wadsworth of Hartford, Connecticut, Commissary General of the Continental Army." Items offered for sale by William Todd (Jeremiah Wadsworth Papers, MS Division, New York Public Library).

1. See H's "Cash Book," March 1, 1782–1791 (*PAH*, III, 13).

To Vicomte de Noailles [1]

[Albany, April 4, May 18, May 24, 1782]

A letter which the Marquis [2] wrote me on his way to Boston was [3] like yours detained till a few days ago. As I take it for granted he will be on his return before a letter from me could possibly reach him, [4] I do not write to him by this opportunity; but hope for the pleasure of seeing him in a few weeks. If it should happen otherwise assure him that I shall often write to him. I will not ask you to assure him of my affection, for of that he is convinced.

General Schuyler [5] desires to be particularly remembered to you; and the ladies present their compliments. Mrs. Hamilton has given

ALS, Papiers de Noailles, Archives Nationales, Paris.
1. For background to this letter, see H to Noailles, April-June, 1782 (*PAH*, III, 83–86).
2. The letter from Lafayette has not been found.
3. Noailles, Lafayette, and other French officers sailed from Boston for France on December 25, 1781, on the *Alliance*.
4. Lafayette returned to the United States for a four-month visit in 1784.
5. Philip Schuyler, H's father-in-law.

me a fine boy,[6] whose birth, as you may imagine, was attended with all the omens of future greatness. Adieu My Dr. Viscount. Believe me to be ever affectionately Yrs.   A Hamilton

Albany April 4th. 82

Though the letter of which the preceding is a duplicate contains nothing interesting, I wish it to get to you as a testimony of my desire to maintain a correspondence. Little has happened since worthy of addition. Clinton has relinquished the command to General Robertson, and it is reported here, though not with certainty, that Careleton has lately arrived at New York to take the command from him.[7] It appears by some late steps taken by the British to restrain the predatory incursions of their refugee parties and by some other circumstances, that they intend to embrace a more complaisant system of war.[8] This might once have been dangerous to us but the time is past. I have seen some late resolutions of the British house of commons that show a revolution in opinions there and that the Ministry have lost their Majority.[9] We are indeed told of a total change of Ministers; but we have no authentic account of it. It appears to be the opinion of the leaders of the opposition that exclusive connexions may be formed between England and this Country, but if they succeed to the administration and act upon this ground, they will find themselves as much mistaken as their predecessors. The popular predilection to them as a nation has given place to a more reasonable way of thinking, and all men of sense are convinced that we are bound by policy and gratitude to hold fast to the friendship of France. It would be idle to dissemble

6. Philip Hamilton was born on January 22, 1782.

7. Sir Guy Carleton was appointed commander-in-chief of the British armies in America on February 23, 1782. News that he had succeeded Sir Henry Clinton reached New York on April 27, and Carleton arrived on May 5. In the brief interval between April 27 and May 5 Lieutenant Colonel James Robertson was in command.

8. An entry in Hugh Gaine's journal under the date of May 1, 1782, reads: "Orders this Day for no farther Hostilities at any of our Ports, and the Refugees not to go out any more without orders." The next entry, under the date of May 2, reads: "More accounts of Peace, and 'tis said our Cruizers will be called in very Soon" (Paul Leicester Ford, ed., *The Journals of Hugh Gaine Printer* [New York, 1902], II, 148). See also Elias Dayton to George Washington, May 6, 1782 (ALS, George Washington Papers, Library of Congress).

9. See Lafayette to H, April 12, 1782, note 3 (*PAH*, III, 72).

that as a trading people, on a general pacification we shall trade with them as far as we shall find it our interest to do it; but beyond this all their hopes are visionary.

I am clearly of opinion at the same time that France on commercial principles ought to have an ascendant in the trade of this Country; but there is one circumstance that will operate in favour of England and against her. The British Merchants have been long in the habit of giving credit to the American Merchants and this will be evidently a strong inducement to a connection between them. In countries which have not been long familiar with commerce the merchants are apt to be diffident and to deal more in prompt payment with foreigners; and the losses some of your merchants have sustained from the depreciation of our currency and the precariousness of the times in their first experiments with us will naturaly increase that diffidence; but too much pains cannot be taken to inculcate confidence and to propagate an opinion among your Merchants of the necessity and advantage of giving large credits to ours. This will make us your customers for whatever you can sell us at as a cheap a rate as other people. Indeed I do not know whether it would not be wise and for the interest of both countries that a trading company with you should be formed under the auspices of government, which should assist their capital by an advance of governmental funds, in order to encourage them to give that credit which individuals may be afraid of risking. I have run into this reflection, because I am sincerely desirous that no adventitious circumstances may diminish the fruits of that magnanimous part which your country has taken in favour of our independence. It will add to it that it is of moment this business should at the outset get into the train we wish, that the current may not take a wrong direction at first, which it might be difficult to change.

Albany May 18th.

24th. We have confirmation of a change of Ministry.[10] I am much mistaken If England has not gained by it. I think she has a more able administration and I dare say it will have the full tide of popularity

10. See the *New-York Gazette, and Weekly Mercury*, May 6, 1782, and the [New York] *Royal Gazette*, May 8, 1782.

in its favour. If a continuance of the war should be the object of the present Ministry they will do it with more vigour and to greater advantage than their predecessors. But can this be their object? England in her present situation, has she any other choice than peace? Will men who have uniformly pronounced the war to be ruinous and impossible of success, who have supplanted the former Ministers for persisting in it who have pledged themselves for peace—who have taken the helm when the nation is exhausted and over head and ears in debt; can these men have the temerity to risk the consequences of a further prosecution of the war? I confess I hardly think it; unless fortune should throw in their way some capital successes. Mr. Rivington [11] indeed tells us that this has happened—that Rodney has lately gained a complete victory over DeGrasse and taken five of his ships.[12] I fear there is too much foundation in this story; it will be a disagreeable stroke; but if the ministry are wise they will only make it the occasion of urging peace with a better grace.

It is said propositions are gone from Carelton to Congress.[13] We

11. James Rivington came to America from London in 1760 and owned book-stores in Philadelphia, New York, and Boston before the American Revolution. He published a newspaper in New York City entitled *Rivington's New-York Gazetteer; or the Connecticut New-Jersey, Hudson's River, and Quebec Weekly Advertiser*, with variations in the title from 1773 to 1776 and from 1777 to 1783. After the war he was a bookseller and stationer in New York City until his death in 1797.

12. See Lafayette to H, June 29, 1782, note 2 (*PAH*, III, 96–97). A letter from Sir George Rodney announcing his victory over the French fleet in the West Indies, along with an extract from the Antigua *Gazette* describing the engagement in more detail, appeared in Rivington's *Royal Gazette*, May 15, 1782.

13. On May 7, 1782, two days after he arrived in New York City, Carleton wrote to Washington: "Having been appointed by His Majesty to the Command of the Forces on the Atlantic Ocean and joined with Admiral [Robert] Digby in the Commission of Peace, I find it proper in this Manner to apprize your Excellency of my Arrival at New York.

"The occasion, Sir, seems to render this Communication proper, but the circumstances of the present Time render it also indispensible, as I find it just to transmit herewith to your Excellency certain papers, from the perusal of which your Excellency will perceive what Dispositions prevail in the Government and People of England towards those of America, and what further Efforts are likely to follow. . . ." (ALS, George Washington Papers, Library of Congress.) In this same letter, Carleton requested a passport for Maurice Morgann, Lord Shelburne's private secretary, to deliver copies of the same papers to the Continental Congress. Washington transmitted the request to Congress, but it was refused on May 14 (*JCC*, XXII, 263).

The "propositions" mentioned by H and the "certain papers" to which Carleton refers were two printed enclosures to Carleton's letter to Washington. Both shall listen to none which do not include independence and our allies.

There are many rumours of an intended evacuation of New York.[14] It would be a natural step in the present ministry and therefore less improbable. However I do not give intire credit to the event.

One more Adieu My Dear Viscount.

Affecty yrs   A H

---

enclosures are in the George Washington Papers, Library of Congress. The first of these enclosures is "A Bill to Enable His Majesty to conclude a Peace, or Truce, with the revolted Colonies in *North America*." The second, which is dated March 4, 1782, and entitled "Votes of the House of Commons," contains the unanimous vote approving a resolution which reads in part: "That, after the solemn Declaration of the Opinion of this House in their humble Address presented to His Majesty on *Friday* last, and His Majesty's Assurance of His Gracious Intention, in Pursuance of their Advice, to take such Measures as shall appear to His Majesty to be most conducive to the Restoration of Harmony between *Great Britain* and the Revolted Colonies, so essential to the Prosperity of both, this House will consider as Enemies to His Majesty and this Country, all those who shall endeavour to frustrate His Majesty's Paternal Care for the Ease and Happiness of His People, by advising, or by any Means attempting, the further Prosecution of Offensive War on the Continent of *North America*, for the Purpose of Reducing the Revolted Colonies to Obedience by Force." For more information concerning the parliamentary debates and maneuvers preceding the fall of the North ministry, see *The Parliamentary History of England, From the Earliest Period to the Year 1803* (London, 1814), XXII, 1064–1109); *The Parliamentary Register; or History of the Proceedings and Debates of the House of Commons* (London, 1782), VI, 310–69; and Ian R. Christie, *The End of North's Ministry: 1780–1782* (London, 1958), 340–72.

14. These rumors were, of course, premature. Most Loyalists evacuated the city in 1783, and the British armed forces began their withdrawal on November 25, 1783.

Appointment as Receiver of Continental Taxes [1]

[Philadelphia, April 15, 1782]

To Alexander Hamilton Esquire

Reposing especial Trust and Confidence in your Zeal, Integrity and Abilities I do hereby in Consequence of the Authorities vested in me by an Act of the United States in Congress assembled of the second Day of November last [2] appoint you Alexander Hamilton Esquire to be the Receiver of the continental Taxes for the State of New York.

Given under my Hand and Seal in the Office of Finance this fifteenth Day of April in the Year of our Lord one thousand seven hundred and eighty two

Robt Morris

DS, Hamilton Papers, Library of Congress.

1. For background to this document, see Morris to H, April 15, May 2, July 2, 1782 (*PAH*, III, 72–75, 86–87, 98–99).

2. On November 2, 1781, Congress passed a resolution recommending that the states "lay taxes for raising their quotas of money for the United States . . . and to pass acts directing the collectors to pay the same to the commissioner of the loan office, or such other person as shall be appointed by the superintendant of finance, to receive the same within the State . . ." (*JCC*, XXI, 1091).

To ——————[1]

[Albany, October 12, 1782]

Dr. Sir

I expect early in next month to go to Philadelphia,[2] and I do not believe Mrs. H will continue house keeping after I am gone. I consider myself as answerable for a years rent of your house, unless we can find some person whom it will be agreeable to you to accept as tenant for the residue of the year. If you hear of any such person I will thank you to inform me of it; but if the house should be let to another it must be with this reserve, that Mrs. Sims must continue in possession till the end of my year, and I will make an allowance in the rent for that purpose.

I am with great regard   Yrs.

A Hamilton

October 12.

ALS, Montague Collection, MS Division, New York Public Library.

1. Although it cannot be stated with certainty, it seems likely that this letter was addressed to Philip Van Rensselaer. See H's "Cash Book," March 1, 1782–1791 (*PAH*, III, 8).

Van Rensselaer, a resident of Albany, was commissary of public stores for the northern department during the American Revolution. He was a first cousin of Catherine Van Rensselaer Schuyler, H's mother-in-law.

2. See "Appointment as Delegate to the Continental Congress," July 22, 1782 (*PAH*, III, 117).

To George Clinton

[Philadelphia, December 25, 1782] [1]

Sir

Perhaps before this reaches you, you will have heard that the British have impliedly acknowleged our independence—by giving a commission of the 23d. of September to Mr Oswald to treat with *The thirteen United States of America.*[2]

Many are sanguine in expecting that peace will be the result of the Negotiations, for my part I have hopes, but if it should not be the case I shall not be much disappointed. There are many jarring interests that will not be easily adjusted.

I have the honor to be   With perfect respect   Sir   yr most obed
A Hamilton

Philadelphia

Decemr. 25. 1782

As Mrs Hamilton may be on the route I take the liberty to inclose a letter [3] for her which I request the favour of you to forward or return as circumstances shall dictate.

ALS, The Miriam Lutcher Stark Library, The University of Texas.

1. This letter is misdated "December 27, 1782," in Richard B. Morris, *The Peacemakers: The Great Powers and American Independence* (New York, 1965), 531, note 37.

2. One of the major obstacles in the Anglo-American peace negotiations in Paris during the summer of 1782 was the British refusal to treat with the American peace commissioners as representatives of an independent nation. On September 21, 1782, however, the British cabinet authorized the British peace commissioner, Richard Oswald, "to treat of, consult, and conclude with any *commissioners or persons vested with equal powers, by and on the part of the thirteen United States of America . . .*" (Francis Wharton, ed., *The Revolutionary Diplomatic Correspondence, of the United States* [Washington, 1889], V, 748–50).

3. Letter not found. Elizabeth Hamilton was on her way from Albany to Philadelphia to join H, who was a delegate to the Continental Congress. See H to ——, October 12, 1782 (printed in this volume). See also H to Elizabeth Hamilton, December 18, 1782 (*PAH*, III, 226).

Continental Congress
Report on a Memorial from the
Legislature of Pennsylvania

[*Philadelphia, December, 1782–January, 1783.* "In a late report which had been drawn up by Mr. Hamilton & made to Congress, in answr. to a Memorial from the Legislatre. of Pa. . . . among other things shewing the impossibility Congress had been under of payg. their Credrs. it was observed that the aid afforded by the Ct. of France had been appropriated by that Court at the time to the immediate use of the army.[1] . . . The report was finally recommitted." *Report not found.*]

William T. Hutchinson and William M. E. Rachal, eds., *The Papers of James Madison* (Chicago and London, 1969), VI, 119–20.

1. Although this report "drawn up by Mr. Hamilton" has not been found, the editors of *The Papers of James Madison* provide in detail the context in which Madison made the statement printed above. They also discuss John C. Hamilton's misinterpretation of that statement (*JCHW*, II, 230–35; Hamilton, *History*, II, 361–63, note). See William T. Hutchinson and William M. E. Rachal, eds., *The Papers of James Madison* (Chicago, 1969), VI, 125 26, notes 17 and 18.

1783

To George Washington

[*Philadelphia, February 24, 1783.* The description of this letter reads: "Referring to a plan for carrying the 8th article of the confederation into execution,[1] etc." *Letter not found.*]

Luther S. Livingston, ed., *American Book-Prices Current* (New York, 1906), 717.
   1. See the first and second "Continental Congress. Motion on Evaluation of State Lands for Carrying into Effect Article 8 of the Articles of Confederation," February 6, 1783 (*PAH*, III, 249–51); "Continental Congress. Motion on Abatements for States in Possession of the Enemy," February 17, 1783, note 1 (*PAH*, III, 255–57); H to George Clinton, February 14, 24, 1783 (*PAH*, III, 259–60, 268–74).

Continental Congress
Motion by Alexander Hamilton and Richard Peters [1] Regarding Lewis Morris [2]

[Philadelphia, February 25, 1783]

Resolved
That Lieut. Col Morris Aid de Camp to Major General Greene be allowed the Pay & Emoluments of a Lieut Colonel & that his Accounts be adjusted accordingly.[3]

D, Reel 163, Item 149, II, p. 224, Papers of the Continental Congress, National Archives.
   1. Peters was secretary of the board of war from 1776 to 1781 with a few interruptions and was elected to Congress from Pennsylvania on November 12, 1782.
   2. Lewis Morris, Jr., was brevetted a lieutenant colonel in the Continental Army on September 9, 1778. He was aide-de-camp to Nathanael Greene from November, 1779, to the end of the war.
   3. At the bottom of this document is written: "negatived Motion of Mr. Peters & Mr Hamilton Feby 25. 1783 negatived." Also see *JCC*, XXIV, 148–49.

To George Washington

[*Philadelphia, March 17, 1783. Letter not found.*[1]]

"List of Letters from General Hamilton to General Washington," Columbia University Libraries.
1. Two letters from H to Washington on March 17, 1783, are listed. One letter is printed in *PAH*, III, 290–93.

To Benjamin Lincoln [1]

[*Philadelphia, April 9, 1783.* In a letter dated May, 1783,[2] Lincoln wrote to Hamilton: "I have been honored with your letter of the 9th ultimo." *Letter not found.*]

1. Lincoln was appointed Secretary at War on October 30, 1781 (*JCC*, XXI, 1087).
2. Printed in this volume.

Continental Congress
Motion Regarding Moving Military Lines

[Philadelphia, April 23, 1783]

R[esolved] That the Secy. at War [1] in Conjunction with the Comr of the Southern Army [2] take preparatory Arrangements for removing the Lines of Virginia Maryland & Pennsylvania now with the southern army to such Places within their respective States as they shall think proper, as soon as Circumstances will permit.[3]

D, in the handwriting of Elias Boudinot, Reel 42, Item 26, II, p. 59, Papers of the Continental Congress, National Archives.
1. Benjamin Lincoln.
2. Major General Nathanael Greene.
3. On April 23, 1783, Congress referred H's motion to a committee consisting of H, Thomas FitzSimons of Pennsylvania, and Oliver Ellsworth of Connecticut (*JCC*, XXIV, 273, note 1). On April 24 the committee reported: "*Resolved,*

That the Secretary at War and the Superintendant of finance, take immediate measures for removing the lines of Virginia, Maryland and Pennsylvania, together with the corps of artillery and cavalry now under the command of Major General Greene, to such places within their respective states as they shall think proper." The resolution passed in the affirmative (*JCC*, XXIV, 275–76).

The regiments of these three states had been sent to join the southern department in accordance with a resolution adopted by Congress on February 20, 1781 (*JCC*, XIX, 176–78). On April 15, 1783, Congress had received the provisional peace treaty between the United States and Great Britain (*JCC*, XXIV, 241), and the resolution to have the troops in question return to their respective states was preparatory to their discharge.

To John Chaloner [1]

[Philadelphia, May 1, 1783]

Col Hamilton's compliments to Mr. Chaloner, incloses him a note which he promised Col Wadsworth to leave with Mr Chaloner. The date is blank which Mr Chaloner will be so good as to fill up from the time Col Wadsworth left this city.

Philadelphia
May 1st 83

AL, Mr. James H. Welch, Canton, Ohio.

1. Chaloner, a Philadelphia merchant, was assistant commissary of purchases for the Continental Army during the American Revolution. After the war, in association with Charles White, his business was conducted under the firm name of Chaloner and White.

Chaloner, while contracting for the Philadelphia office of the commissary department, had come to the attention of Jeremiah Wadsworth, commissary general of purchases and business partner of John B. Church. Church, upon his arrival from England in the United States during the American Revolution, had assumed the name of John Carter. From the numerous contracts he made for supplying the American army and particularly from the contract which he and Wadsworth secured for supplying the French forces in America, Church acquired a fortune. While in the United States, he married Angelica Schuyler, older sister of Elizabeth Hamilton. When the Churches returned to England in the summer of 1783 (H to John Jay, July 25, 1783 [*PAH*, III, 416–17]), Church left the management of his interests in America to H.

All the business affairs of Wadsworth and Carter in Philadelphia were conducted through Chaloner, and when in 1784 the business partners were in Europe, Chaloner received the largest share of the thousands of pounds of merchandise they shipped from Europe to America. The partnership of Wadsworth and Carter was dissolved at the end of July, 1785, but, principally because Chaloner had mismanaged their affairs, several years were required for Chaloner to settle his accounts with the partners.

From John Allan [1]

[Philadelphia, May 28, 1783]

Sir

The memorandum which I had the Honour of delivering you a day or two ago was in General the State of matters in the Indian Eastern Department,[2] from which I presumed the Hono[r]able Committee Appointed by Congress woud Examine into the Matter, And from the Importance of the Subject woud Speedly determine.

I woud not by any means urge matters out of the proper Rule or Channel nor wou'd I be so Impertinent as to press on Gentlemen, whoes Abilities and Liberal sentiments must be well Known by the Conspicuous Characters they now bare in the united States, but probably a thoro Knowledge of those parts may be wanting by attention to Greater Concerns.

The Business of the Eastern Indians, has been View'd in a Serious Light by those who has had an Oppertunity to Know the perticular Situation and State of that Country. The Intercourse and Conection which Subsists between the different Tribes which Inhabits the Micmac (nova scotia) Country, 200 Leagues up the River St Lawrence, These being Interpersed among British Subjects, who have been verry Attentive during the Warr in Endeavouring to Gain their Interests, and will no doubt (as is the Common Custom) urge during peace every Intreaguing mode to draw their attention from the United States.

We have been so Successfull during this warr in that Quarter, that there has no great cause of Alarm to Government, that by a

LS, with a postscript in Allan's handwriting, Reel 163, Item 149, II, p. 565, Papers of the Continental Congress, National Archives.

1. Allan was appointed superintendent of Indian affairs for the eastern department on January 15, 1777 (JCC, VII, 38–39).

2. Allan's memorial to Congress, dated May 24, 1783 (DS, Reel 163, Item 149, II, p. 561, Papers of the Continental Congress, National Archives), was enclosed in Benjamin Lincoln to Elias Boudinot, President of Congress, May 22, 1783 (LS, Reel 163, Item 149, II, p. 557, Papers of the Continental Congress, National Archives). On May 23, 1783, the memorial was referred to a committee consisting of H, James Madison, Oliver Ellsworth, James Wilson, and Samuel Holten (JCC, XXIV, 362, note 3).

Continual Residence & Close attention, Under the Smiles of Providence the Enemy have been prevented in their Design respecting the Indians as well as taking possession of the Country.

Commercial Views, as well as holding them for future Advantages—will Cause the Britains to be Attentive on the Indian Affairs, and there is not wanting among Ourselves persons of such sordid principles who will ever Encourage & Countenance such things where their Interests is Concernd.

Gifts and Promises to Indians are not Sufficient to Keep them. It must be a Constant Attendance given to work upon them, according to their Passions and Dispositions for the Time being.

The Indians thro that country have now constant Meetings. They Try to hear every thing that Passes & by their Acquaintance in Settlements will hear things different ways, they want to Know, what Notice is taken of them, and will direct their Councils Accordingly.

Their External conduct during my Residence, demonstrates, their Wisdom & Subtilty, and that altho they may Appear Satisfyd, Sometimes it is nothing but a Cloak to cover some evil design, they are allways particular to Know in what manner things are Communicated to them—and if it shoud Appear not properly Authenticated they will Treat it with Contempt, which on the Other hand woud be Religiously attended to.

I shall not Trouble you Sir, with more of these Observations. A future time may give me More oppertunity for a better Information Shou'd it be the pleasure of the Honoble. Congress to Continue me in the business.[3] I must Earnestly Request, that I may proceed upon my duty with some thing that may Give Satisfaction & Assurance to the Indians, that I may be Enabled to communicate What the Intention & design of Government is towards them Whereby a Solid and Permanent System may be Established—the sooner it is done will make it more Easy and Eligible.

3. On June 3, 1783, Congress reappointed Allan superintendent of Indian affairs for the eastern department and ordered "That so much of the memorial of Colonel John Allan, superintendant of Indian affairs for the eastern department, as relates to compensation for services, and his request to be enabled to discharge the debts due to the Indians, by virtue of his necessary stipulations in behalf of the United States, be referred to the Superintendant of finance to take order" (JCC, XXIV, 379–80).

I forgot mentioning in the Memorial, the Promise made to the Indians, to Procure them a Priest, this I woud pray might be attended to, as A verry Assential Matter in Securing their Interest.

I have the Honour to be with very Great respect Sir Your most Obdt Hble servt   J Allan.

Phelidelphia May 28th. 1783

NB. I waited upon Genl Lincoln, after I had the pleasure of seeing you yesterday. He mentioned that he had nothing more than the Declaration of Peace to Communicate [4]—but nothing Concerning the present business.

The Honble. Colo Hamilton

[ENCLOSURE]

A Memorandum for Indian Eastern Department [5]

The Indians to have an Exclusive Right of the Beaver Hunt, on the Rivers, which they now live on. To wit—all Eastward of machias, with the Lakes that Extend from Passamaquady River to Penobscot Including the last.

Some methode to prevent Unfair dealing with the Indians, and Embezzleing their property.

A Sum of 250 £ M of massts. for Expresses and other Employment, with presents to Indians who, have been most attentive to business.

A Roman Priest

Instructions for futer management of Indians, and what is Intended with them.

At the present Settlement of Peace. a Speech from the Honble. Congress—allso very necessary a Speech from the Ambassador of His Christian Majesty.

There will be wanting at the Conference a Present. Of Ammunition. Tobacco—Wine, with provisions during the time of Conference.

4. The provisional peace treaty between Great Britain and the United States was read before Congress on April 15, 1783 (*JCC*, XXIV, 243–52).

5. AD, Reel 163, Item 149, II, p. 567, Papers of the Continental Congress, National Archives.

A Small Fortification on the River St Croix or Passamaquody Near the hunting, with a Trifle of Artillery. This will Command respect & Please the Indians.

Some men to be keep'd in the business, not Exceeding Ten with Boats &c

J Allan Agt
for said Department

NB. A Quantity of Ordinance Stores is now at Machias—some of which will Do for the fortification.

Philidelphia May 28th 1783

From Benjamin Lincoln [1]

War-Office May   1783.

Gentlemen,[2]

I have been honored with your letter of the 9th. ultimo in which you request that I would communicate to you my thoughts on a military Peace establishment for the United-States.[3]

As the detail of the System, which I am about to recommend, will more properly rest with the executive Officers of the Engineer and Inspector General's departments—I will confine my information to the following general Heads.

1. The situation and number of Posts to be established on the Frontiers of the United States.

LS, Reel 45, Item 38, p. 317, Papers of the Continental Congress, National Archives.

1. For background to this letter, see H to George Washington, April 9, 1783 (*PAH*, III, 322–23); Washington to H, April 16, May 2, 1783 (*PAH*, III, 331–32, 346–47); "Continental Congress. Report on a Military Peace Establishment," June 18, 1783 (*PAH*, III, 378–83).

2. This letter was addressed to H in his capacity as chairman of the committee for a military peace establishment. For the appointment and membership of this committee, see "Continental Congress. Report on a Military Peace Establishment," June 18, 1783, note 1 (*PAH*, III, 378–79).

3. Letter not found. H made a similar request to Washington on April 9, 1783 (*PAH*, III, 322–23).

2. The number of harbours which it will be necessary to fortify for Continental purposes—and the places which, from their situation and other circumstances, I apprehend will be the most eligible.

3. The number of Magazines to be established for the reception of the continental-stores, and the places at which I would recommend they should be fixed.

4. The number of Academies to be erected for the instruction of military Pupils in the several branches of science required to form an Engineer, Artillerist, or Officer of Infantry and Horse—and the most eligible situations for these establishments.

5. The necessity of a similar organisation for the Militia throughout the United States—and the expediency that Congress should recommend the establishing of State and County Magazines for supplying the Militia with arms, accoutrements, and ammunition, in proportion to the number of the male Inhabitants of each State.

6. The number of regular troops which I suppose will be required for a Peace establishment—and the necessity of an alternation in the articles of war [4] for their government in the time of Peace.

The necessity of establishing a line of Posts upon our frontiers, to serve as a barrier against sudden inroads, and for the protection of our inland trade, as well as to maintain possession of as much of the territory, which has been ceded to us as possible, is the first object which claims our attention.

A more accurate knowledge of the country, than I possess may be requisite to form the best judgment of the number and situation of these Posts. I would however suggest the propriety of erecting one on the east banks of St. Marys river, the western boundary of the United States—One at the conflux of the Mississippi and Ohio—One at the conflux of the Ohio and the Wabash—One near the south end of Lake Mechigan—One at Detroit—One at Niagara—One at Oswego—One in the 45th. degree of north latitude on connecticut river, or somewhere between that river and lake Champlain—One at the source of Kennebeck-river, and One on the

4. For the articles of war, which were adopted by Congress on September 20, 1776 (JCC, V, 788–807), see H to Jonathan Dayton, August 6, 1798, note 11 (PAH, XXII, 50–56).

river St. Croix, which is the eastern boundary of the United-States.

The number of Posts, which I have mentioned, should, I think, be established either by Congress—or, if their right to this arrangement, should (as I hear it has been doubted by some of them) [5] be questioned, an adoption of the Plan should be recommended by Congress to the several States, within whose bounds the places pointed out are.

As it will, in some degree, be essential to the security of our trade, and to protect the flag of the United States from insult, that a small Marine should be kept up—fortified harbours will be required to cover the Marine and to establish Dock-Yards and Stores.

Boston and New York assemble the most advantages in situation, security and the facility of obtaining Sea-Men—and Beaufort [6] being the only harbour South of the Chesapeak which will admit Ships of 60 guns, it is to be prefered, and it may be easily fortified. I beg leave to observe that these three Places appear to me the most eligible.

In my report to Congress on the 3rd day of March [7] last, I stated the necessity of public Magazines, and recommended that five should be established. One at Springfield in Massachusetts—one at

5. Although H's committee for a military peace establishment reported to Congress on June 18, 1783 (note 2 above), Congress did not consider the report until October 23, 1783, when it was resubmitted to that body by a new committee of which H was not a member (*JCC*, XXIV, 492–94; XXV, 722–44). In the interval between the submission and consideration of this report, Lincoln's fears were in part confirmed by the delegates of some of the states to Congress. On August 13, 1783, Ezra L'Hommedieu, a member of Congress from New York, wrote to Governor George Clinton of New York: "A Peace Establishment, which has been reported and on which General Washington is to be consulted (who will be here in a few Days) is a Business of much Consequence and ought soon to be perfected; but I fear delays will be made and some of the eastern States, if I am not much mistaken will oppose the keeping of any Troops on the Frontiers especially those of New York" (Burnett, *Letters*, VII, 266). L'Hommedieu again wrote to Clinton on September 3: "I was observing that I found many of the States disposed to have the frontier Posts garrisoned by the States in whose Territory they were, and not by the Continent . . ." (Burnett, *Letters*, VII, 285). For New York State's opposition to the use of Continental troops on its frontiers, see James Duane and L'Hommedieu to H and William Floyd, September 1, 1783 (*PAH*, III, 435–37). Rhode Island also opposed the creation of a military peace establishment by Congress (James McHenry to Washington, July 31, 1783 [Burnett, *Letters*, VII, 245]).

6. Beaufort, North Carolina.

7. This report is enclosed in Lincoln to Elias Boudinot, March 3, 1783 (LS, Reel 45, Item 38, p. 283, Papers of the Continental Congress, National Archives).

West-Point—one at Carlisle in Pennsylvania—one at New London in Virginia—and one at Camden in south Carolina.

I am still of opinion that this number is requisite—and I would only now propose to place the one intended to be built at New London somewhere high up on James-river in Virginia.

I would recommend that all the Arms and military stores belonging to the United States should be deposited, in equal proportions, at the several Magazines excepting the heavy Ordnance and their stores—which will be disposed of, as may be judged proper, at the several fortified posts where heavy Artillery may be required.

There should, I think, be lodged at each Magazine, as soon as possible, two thousand barrels of powder together with arms, field artillery, and equipments complete for fifteen thousand men, which will be more readily effected if Manufactories and Foundaries are established.

In my report to Congress I have recommended the establishing of Military Academies. I then supposed that an establishment of this Nature, at each of the Magazines, where the Pupils might be taught the Mathematics, and instructed in the several duties of the engineering and artillery departments would be as far as we could go. But, if two such Institutions, on the plan recommended by Baron Steuben,[8] which you inform me has been laid before your Committee, can be established, I think they will answer very beneficial purposes.

I would recommend West Point—and the post at which the Magazine in Virginia may be fixed, as the best situations for the two Academies.

If the Academies are not erected I hope we shall not lose sight of the Manufactories and Foundaries.

I have also reported to Congress my opinion on the importance of

8. Baron von Steuben sent two documents to the Continental Congress concerning military academies. The first is entitled "Projet pour L'establissement des academies et manufactures militaires . . ." (copy, Reel 45, Item 38, pp. 448–65, Papers of the Continental Congress, National Archives), enclosed in Steuben to Richard Peters, n.d. (ALS, Reel 45, Item 38, p. 467, Papers of the Continental Congress, National Archives). The second report is entitled "Etats des Depenses annuels en General pour les Establissements militaires des Etats unis . . ." (copy, Reel 45, Item 38, pp. 475–77, Papers of the Continental Congress, National Archives), enclosed in Steuben to Peters, April 23, 1783 (ALS, Reel 45, Item 38, p. 475, Papers of the Continental Congress, National Archives).

having the militia Laws through the United States framed and conducted on similar principles. I am persuaded it will be necessary for
Congress to recommend that one system be adopted by all the States
for the regulation of their Militia, which may be done with great
propriety, the States having confederated to maintain a well
organised Militia.

As I have none of the Militia-laws before me I dare not attempt
the draught of a law, from recollection, which I should be willing
to recommend.

It will be necessary that Congress should also recommend to the
several States the establishing of State and County Magazines for
the purpose of supplying the Militia in cases of emergency. The
State magazines should contain a sufficiency of ammunition, and the
necessary equipments, of arms &ca for an eighth part of the male
Inhabitants capable of bearing arms—and a train of field Artillery
and ammunition, for the like number of men, should be lodged at
the State Magazines. The County Magazines should be furnished
with lesser supplies, to facilitate the delivery of arms and ammunition to the Militia—when wanted on pressing occasions—and as it
would be proper that part of the ammunition should be fixed—it
will be essentially requisite that the arms are all of the same calibre.

If all the Posts I have mentioned are to be garrisoned by the
United-States, and the number of magazines and academies are
established—It will be necessary to retain four regiments of five
hundred men each.

Whether we consider the line of Posts as a barrier to the United
States—or as places of cover to the trade—I conceive it will be
much best that the Guards should be continental. As such, they
will be under one head—and a communication will be maintained
through the whole which will encrease their strength and safety—
nor will there be any inducements to that partiality which local connexions often produce. It will also tend to support the Union, and
strengthen our Confederacy.

It will be necessary that Congress should make some alterations
in the articles of War. The troops will be so detached that it will be
difficult, perhaps impossible, at times to convene a General Court
Martial.

A recommendation should go to the several States to enact laws for the trial and punishment of Deserters—and for all capital offences. The Soldier should be delivered over to the civil authority of the State in which he is stationed, or doing duty.

I have the honor to be, with perfect respect, Gentlemen, Your most obedient, and most humble Servant   B. Lincoln

The honorable
A. Hamilton
Chairman of the Committee of arrangement on a Peace-establishment

Continental Congress
Motion to Extend the Time Allowed for Appeals from Maritime Courts [1]

[*Philadelphia, June 6, 1783*. Under this date the Register of Reports of Committees sent to Congress reads: "On Mr Hamilton's Motion for extending the time allowed for appeals from maritime courts.—filed." [2] *Motion not found.*]

D, Reel 198, Item 191, p. 40, Papers of the Continental Congress, National Archives.
   1. H's motion concerned the Confederation Court of Appeals in Cases of Captures, also known as the Court of Appeals or the Court of Prize Appeals, which was established by Congress on January 15, 1780, "for the trial of all appeals from the courts of admiralty in these United States, in cases of capture . . ." (*JCC*, XVI, 61–64). On May 24, 1780, Congress passed a resolution concerning the Court of Appeals, which reads: "*Resolved*, That appeals from the courts of admiralty in the respective states, be, as heretofore, demanded within five days after definitive sentence; and in future such appeals be lodged with the register of the Court of Appeals in cases of capture within forty days thereafter, provided the party appealing shall give security to prosecute such appeal to effect" (*JCC*, XVII, 459).
   2. This motion was filed on June 11, 1783 (D, Reel 198, Item 191, p. 40, Papers of the Continental Congress, National Archives). On May 17, 1784, Congress resolved that various reports which it listed should "be referred to the consideration of the next Congress" (D, Reel 198, Item 191, p. 59, Papers of the Continental Congress, National Archives). Among the items listed was: "No 24 Motion Mr Hamilton for extending the time for entering appeals from Judgments of maritime Courts—report thereon" (D, Reel 198, Item 191, p. 61, Papers of the Continental Congress, National Archives). No evidence has been found that any succeeding session of Congress acted on this report.

From George Washington

[*Newburgh, New York, June 7, 1783. Letter not found.*]

"List of Letters from G—— Washington to General Hamilton," Columbia University Libraries.

Continental Congress
Draft of a Proclamation by President of Congress [1]

[Philadelphia, June 24, 1783]

Whereas a body of armed soldiers in the service of the United States quartered in the barracks of this city having mutinously renounced their obedience to their officers did on Saturday the twenty first instant proceed under the command of their sergeants in a hostile and threatening manner to the place in which Congress were assembled and did surround the same with guards, and Whereas Congress in consequence thereof did immediately resolve

insert the resolution [2]

and whereas Congress did at the same time appoint a Committee to confer with the said Supreme Executive council on the practicability of carrying the said resolution into due effect,

And Whereas the said Committee have reported to me that they have not received satisfactory assurance of prompt & vigorous exertions for the purposes above-mentioned— [3]

ADf, Elias Boudinot Papers, Library of Congress.
    1. Elias Boudinot, a resident of Elizabeth, New Jersey, was President of the Continental Congress from November 4, 1782, to November 3, 1783.
    For background to this document, see "Continental Congress. Report on Conference with the Supreme Executive Council of Pennsylvania on the Mutiny," June 20, 1783 (*PAH*, III, 399–401); "Continental Congress. Resolutions on Measures to be Taken in Consequence of the Pennsylvania Mutiny," June 21, 1783 (*PAH*, III, 401–02); "Continental Congress. Report of a Committee Appointed to Confer with the Supreme Executive Council of Pennsylvania on the Mutiny," June 24, 1783 (*PAH*, III, 403–07).
    2. For the text of the resolution, see the first resolution in "Continental Con-

gress. Resolutions on Measures to be Taken in Consequence of the Pennsylvania Mutiny," June 21, 1783 (*PAH*, III, 401–02).

3. H's draft stops at this point. The remainder of the final version of the proclamation reads: "And also whereas the said Committee have reported to me, that they have not received satisfactory Assurances for expecting adequate and prompt exertions of this State for supporting the Dignity of the fœderal Government: And also whereas the said Soldiers still continue in a state of open Mutiny and Revolt, so that the Dignity and Authority of the United States would be constantly exposed to a repetition of Insult, while Congress shall continue to sit in this City. I do therefore, by and with the Advice of the said Committee, and according to the Powers and Authorities in me vested for this Purpose, hereby summon the honourable the Delegates composing the Congress of the United States, and every of them, to meet in Congress on Thursday the Twenty Sixth Day of June instant, at Princeton, in the state of New-Jersey, in order that further and more effectual Measures may be taken for suppressing the present Revolt, and maintaining the Dignity and Authority of the United States, of which all Officers of the United States, civil and military, and all others whom it may concern, are desired to take Notice and govern themselves accordingly" (*By His Excellency Elias Boudinot, Esquire, President of the United States in Congress Assembled. A Proclamation. Whereas a Body of Armed Soldiers* . . . [Philadelphia: Printed by David C. Claypoole, 1783]).

To Elias Boudinot [1]

[Philadelphia, June 24, 1783]

The Committee appointed to confer with the Supreme Executive Council of this state, respecting the practicability of taking effectual measures for supporting the public authority, violated by the mutinous behaviour of a body of armed soldiers, who surrounded the place where Congress and the Executive Council of this state were assembled on saturday last in a hostile and menacing manner—not having received satisfactory assurances of prompt and vigorous exertions for the purpose above mentioned—advise His Excellency the President conformable to the intentions of Congress in that case to summon the members to meet on thursday next at Trenton or Princeton in the state of New Jersey.

Alex Hamilton Chairman

Philadelphia
June 24th 1783

To His Excellency
The President of Congress

ALS, Elias Boudinot Papers, Library of Congress.

1. For background to this letter, see "Continental Congress. Draft of a Proclamation by President of Congress," June 24, 1783 (printed in this volume).

Receipt to Abel James [1]

Philadelphia, July 26, 1783. Receipt for papers relating to lands in the Otsego Patent which had formerly belonged to George Croghan [2] and which were mortgaged to William Franklin.[3]

ADS, anonymous donor.

1. James was a Philadelphia merchant and land speculator.

This document concerns a complicated and protracted dispute over several large tracts of land located in the vicinity of Lake Otsego and Cherry Valley, New York.

For the text of this document and an explanation of its contents, see the discussion of the Otsego Patent of George Croghan in Goebel, *Law Practice*, forthcoming volumes.

2. Croghan, who had died on August 31, 1782, had been a land speculator and an Indian agent and trader. For information on Croghan's landholdings, see Richard Peters to H, February 18, 1795 (*PAH*, XVIII, 277).

3. Franklin, the son of Benjamin Franklin, was the last royal governor of New Jersey. During the American Revolution he was imprisoned as a Loyalist in Connecticut. In 1778 he was exchanged and went first to New York City and then to England.

Account with the State of New York [1]

[Albany, July 30, 1783–March 26, 1784]

The State of New York,

To Alex. Hamilton, Dr.

1783

July 30   To my allowance as a delegate of Congress [2]
          from the 25 of November 1782 to this day   £ 496
          at 5 dollars per day—248 days both days
          included. Days of travelling in going and
          coming, 14 days at ditto   28
                                                              ————
                                                               524

                    Credit
          By an order from Col. Udney Hay on Mr.
             Comfort Sands [3]   2 0 0.

Also from Col. Hay part of an order for
200 in favour of Mr. Floyed and myself [4]

                           60

Drafts on His Excellency the Governor
for   200   460
                                  64

Receipt

26th March 1784. Received the above Ballance of Sixty four pounds from his Excellency Gov. Clinton.

                                     Alex Hamilton

ADS, from a typescript furnished by the New York State Library, Albany; LC, "Audited Accounts," Vol. A, 38, New York State Library, Albany.
1. H sent this bill to Governor George Clinton of New York on August 20, 1783. See H to Philip Van Rensselaer, August 20, 1783 (*PAH*, III, 433–34).
2. See H's "Commission as Delegate to the Continental Congress," October 25, 1782 (*PAH*, III, 188–89).
3. Udny Hay, who had been a lieutenant colonel in the Continental Army and deputy quartermaster general, was state agent for New York. His duties included serving as paymaster general of the state. Sands, a New York City merchant, had been auditor general of New York from 1776 to 1782. In 1783 he was the contractor for supplying Army officers in the district of West Point. For information concerning this transaction, see H to Clinton, January 12, 1783 (*PAH*, III, 240–41).
4. William Floyd, a signer of the Declaration of Independence from New York, was a member of the Continental Congress from 1774 to 1777 and from 1778 to 1783. For this account, see H to Clinton, December 29, 1782, note 1 (*PAH*, III, 231). See also the account for Floyd in "Audited Accounts," Vol. A, 37, New York State Library, Albany.

To George Clinton

[*New York, August 3, 1783. Letter not found.*]

"General Hamilton to Governor George Clinton," Columbia University Libraries.

To John Chaloner [1]

[Albany, August 22, 1783]

Dr Sir

Mrs. Hamilton has requested her sister [2] who left this a few days
since on her way to Philadelphia to purchase a few articles there
for her, and if she found it necessary to apply to you for the money.
I will be obliged to you to advance it on my account and I will in a
short time repay it.

We have accounts here that induce us to believe Carleton has
received final orders for the evacuation of New York.[3] I am Dr Sir
 Yr. Obed serv   A Hamilton

Albany Aug. 22d. 1783
Mr. Chaloner

ALS, Historical Society of Pennsylvania, Philadelphia.
 1. H, who had resigned as a member of the Continental Congress, arrived in
Albany on August 11, 1783. See H to George Clinton, June 11, July 27, 1783
(*PAH*, III, 377, 418–19); H to Robert R. Livingston, August 13, 1803 (*PAH*,
III, 431–32).
 2. Margarita Schuyler, who had married Stephen Van Rensselaer on June 6,
1783, was Elizabeth Hamilton's sister.
 3. On August 17, 1783, Sir Guy Carleton, who had succeeded Sir Henry
Clinton as commander in chief of the British forces in North America in May,
1782, wrote to Elias Boudinot, President of Congress: "The June Packet, lately
arrived, has brought me final Orders for the evacuation of this place; be pleased
Sir to inform Congress of this proof of the perseverance of the Court of Great
Britain in the pacific system expressed by the provisional articles, and that I
shall lose no time, as far as depends upon me, in fulfilling His Majesty's commands" (LS, Reel 66, Item 52, p. 217, Papers of the Continental Congress, Library of Congress). Boudinot presented the letter to Congress on August 21,
1783 (*JCC*, XXIV, 517).
 The British forces completed the evacuation of New York on December 4,
1783.

From John Jay [1]

[Bath, England, November 28, 1783. Letter not found.]

"List of Letters from Mr. Jay . . ." to H, Columbia University Libraries.
 1. Jay had gone to Europe in January, 1780, as Minister Plenipotentiary to

Spain. In June, 1782, he went to Paris to serve as one of the commissioners to negotiate peace with Great Britain. The definitive peace treaty was signed in Paris on September 3, 1783, and in mid-October Jay went to England on the advice of doctors that the waters of Bath would improve his health.

To Abel James

New York, December 4, 1783. Reports on the progress of James's case involving lands in the Otsego Patent.[1]

Copy, in the handwriting of Abel James, anonymous donor.
1. For the text of this letter and an explanation of its contents, see the discussion of the Otsego Patent of George Croghan in Goebel, *Law Practice*, forthcoming volumes.

To John Chaloner [1]

[New York, December 11, 1783]

Dr. Sir

As it now draws towards the time for declaring a dividend of the bank,[2] and I am authorized by Mr. Carter[3] to receive his share I shall wish to be informed in what manner the bank will choose to have an acknowlegement of the receipt of the money from me, when time of payment comes—whether an order from me in favour of yourself—or a bill drawn payable to myself, or a receipt from me will be preferred. I make this inquiry because, the Bank may have some mode of their own for transacting the business in similar cases.[4] I will therefore take it as a favour if you will inquire and let me know by a line. It is my wish that you would in the first instance receive the amount and pay it to my order. Let me know also if you please whether there are any persons disposed to *sell* bank stock and whether it yet begins to sell at an advanced price and the rate.[5]

Mrs. Schuyler[6] when I left Albany[7] gave me a memorandum

about some shoes she expected you would send her. I wish you would forward them to me here and I will send them on.

Compliments to Mrs. Chaloner.

I am with esteem   Sir   Yr. most Obed ser   Alex Hamilton

City of New York
December 11th. 1783

ALS, Historical Society of Pennsylvania, Philadelphia.
   1. This letter is listed as a "letter not found" in *PAH*, III, 480.
   2. The Bank of North America in Philadelphia, which Congress had chartered on December 3, 1781 (*JCC*, XXI, 1187–89). See also Chaloner to H, November 26, 1783, note 1 (*PAH*, III, 477).
   3. See H to Chaloner, May 1, 1783 (printed in this volume).
   4. See Chaloner to H, December 18, 1783 (*PAH*, III, 481).
   5. See Chaloner to H, November 26, 1783 (*PAH*, III, 477–78).
   6. Catherine Van Rensselaer Schuyler, H's mother-in-law.
   7. The Hamiltons had moved from Albany to New York City in November, 1783. See H to Elizabeth Hamilton, 1783–1789, note 1 (*PAH*, III, 482).

1784

To James Madison [1]

[*New York, April 18, 1784.* "I take the liberty to introduce him to you, as to one who will be disposed, so far as your situation will permit and the circumstances of the State may render practicable, to patronise any just or equitable claims which he may have upon the State. What those claims are he will himself explain to you, I have assured him that he will find in you a friend to justice and an able advocate for whatever ought and is possible to be done for him. . . ." *Letter not found.*]

Frederick B. McGuire Catalogue of "President Madison's Correspondence" (Philadelphia, February 26, 1917), Item 52.

1. This letter of introduction was written on behalf of Joseph François Perrault, a French fur trader and merchant, who in 1784 petitioned Virginia for reimbursement for the supplies he had furnished that state's troops in the Illinois country in 1778–1779.

The extract printed above, the text of which is taken from the dealer's catalogue, is also printed and fully annotated in Robert A. Rutland and William M. E. Rachal, eds., *The Papers of James Madison* (Chicago, 1973), VIII, 19.

This extract poses two distinct problems. In the first place, the year in which it was written does not appear on the extract, and it has been tentatively assigned 1784 in the *Madison Papers* on the grounds that the Virginia House of Delegates and Governor William Harrison in Council considered and ultimately rejected a petition by Perrault in May and June, 1784. On the other hand, no evidence has been found that Perrault passed through New York and proceeded to Virginia in 1784 or in any other year. No mention of such a trip appears in his autobiography or in any other available source (P. Bender, *Old and New Canada 1753-1844. Historic Scenes and Social Pictures, or the Life of Joseph-François Perrault* [Montreal, 1882]; Louise Kellogg, ed., *Publications of the State Historical Society of Wisconsin. Collections,* Vol. XXIV, *Frontier Retreat on the Upper Ohio 1779-1781* [Madison, 1917], 86–87).

In the second place, because no manuscript of this document has been found, it is possible that this letter was not written by H. In H's extant correspondence no other reference to Perrault can be found. In addition, among H's contemporaries there were other Alexander Hamiltons. For example, in 1790 an Alexander I. Hamilton lived in New York City, and there were three Alexander Hamiltons in Maryland (*Heads of Families at the First Census of the United States Taken in the Year 1790 New York* [Washington: Government Printing Office, 1908], 122; *Heads of Families at the First Census of the United States Taken in the Year 1790 Maryland* [Washington: Government Printing Office, 1907], 50, 94).

To Thomas Pearsall [1]

[*New York*] *May 20* [*1784*]. Apologizes for "a too sudden opinion . . . relating to confiscated property." Sends new opinion.[2]

ALS, Columbia University Libraries.
   1. Pearsall was a partner in the firm of merchants in New York City known
as Thomas Pearsall and Son.
   2. For the text of H's opinion and a discussion of Pearsall's case, see Goebel,
Law Practice, I, 251–53.

To James Bowne [1]

[*New York*] *June 17, 1784.* "Let me know if you please Whether
Philip Palmer and Joseph Palmer [2] are both alive or not, and
whether Mr. Leonard Lawrence [3] is Executor or Administrator to
his father, if the former whether there are any other Executors
named in his will and now alive. . . ." [4]

ALS, Mr. Samuel A. Mehlman, New York City.
   1. In *PAH*, III, 565–66, this letter is listed as a "letter not found."
   Bowne, a resident of Flushing, New York, was a member of the firm of
Bowne and Company of New York City, stationers and printers, founded by
Daniel Bowne in 1775.
   For H's account with Bowne, see his "Cash Book," March 1, 1782–1791
(*PAH*, III, 24).
   This letter concerns the suit of *Leonard Lawrence executor of Stephen Law-
rence deceased* v *Philip Palmer*, which was brought in the January, 1785, term
of the New York Supreme Court to recover on a bond of one hundred pounds
(Narrative and Oyer [two copies, Hamilton Papers, Library of Congress];
Bond, August 16, 1774 (DS, Hamilton Papers, Library of Congress). Upon the
defendant's default, judgment was entered for the plaintiff on October 19, 1786
(MS Minutes of the New York Supreme Court, 1786 [Hall of Records, New
York City]).
   2. Philip and Joseph Palmer lived at Throgs (Frogs) Neck in what was at
that time the town and county of Westchester, New York.
   3. Lawrence, a resident of Flushing, New York, had been a Loyalist during
the American Revolution.
   4. At the bottom of this letter is written: "Philop Palmer is living
                                    Jos: do: is Dead
                                    Leonard Lawrence is Executor."

To Aaron Burr [1]

[*New York*] *July 17, 1784.* ". . . the Defendant in the above cause intends to bring into Court at the ensuing term Twenty five pounds and Eight shillings, being the amount of what he acknowleges to be due to the Plaintiff. . . ." [2]

ALS, Sleepy Hollow Restorations, Inc., Tarrytown, New York.
    1. H addressed this letter to "Aaron Burr Esqr. Attorney for the Plaintiff."
    2. On the document there is no indication of the names of the plaintiff or defendant in "the above cause."

Receipt to John Thomas [1]

New York October 14. 1784

Received of John Thomas by the hands of John Laurence [2] Twenty seven pounds for damages in the above suit [3] and Twenty six pounds for Costs.

Alex Hamilton

ADS, New-York Historical Society, New York City.
    1. Thomas had served or was serving as sheriff of Westchester County, New York.
    2. After resigning as judge advocate of the Continental Army in 1782, Laurance resumed the practice of law in New York City.
    3. *Peter and Elizabeth King* v *John Thomas* was a case which concerned the conversion of goods. The case was tried at the circuit of the New York Supreme Court held for Westchester County in September, 1784 (Narrative [copy, Hamilton Papers, Library of Congress]; Issue Roll, Parchment 76-D-10 [Hall of Records, New York City]; Nisi Prius Roll, Parchment 174-C-3 [Hall of Records, New York City]).

To George Clinton [1]

[November 26, 1784–July 17, 1787] [2]

Dr Sir

It is the wish of several of the Regents of the University that a Meeting should be appointed on some business of importance; and I am requested to write to you on the subject. It will be only necessary for you to write to Mr. Harpur who is secretary of the University desiring him to publish an advertisement according to mode prescribed in the act.

I am Dr Sir with great respect & regard   your Obed ser

A Hamilton

ALS, Mrs. Robert Crimmins, Darien, Connecticut.

1. H wrote this letter in his capacity as a member of the Board of Regents of the University of the State of New York, a position to which he was appointed on November 26, 1784 ("An Act to amend an Act, entitled, An Act for granting certain Privileges to the College heretofore called King's College, for altering the name and Charter thereof, and erecting an University within this State" [*New York Laws*, 8th Sess., Ch. XV (November 26, 1784)]). H served as a regent until his death in 1804.

The MS of the letter printed above has no addressee, but it was presumably addressed to Governor George Clinton. The statute creating the University of the State of New York, which was passed on May 1, 1784 ("An Act for Granting certain Privileges to the College heretofore called King's College, for altering the Name and Charter thereof, and erecting an University within this State" [*New York Laws*, 7th Sess., Ch. XL]) provided for a governing board to be called the Board of Regents. It also named the members of the board beginning with the "Governor, Lieutenant-Governor, the President of the Senate for the Time being. . . ." The act of November 26, 1784, which is cited in the preceding paragraph, named additional members to the board, including H, and also stated: "That to constitute a legal Meeting of the Regents, the Time and Place for holding the same, shall be previously fixed by the Chancellor, or in his absence the Vice-Chancellor, or in the Absence of both, the Regent next nominated in the said Act, by writing under his Hand, and Notice thereof signed by the Secretary of the University, shall previously be advertised in one of the public News-Papers, for at least two Weeks, to give all Regents within a convenient Distance, an Opportunity of attending' (*New York Laws*, 8th Sess., Ch. XV).

Clinton was governor of the State of New York and chancellor of the University of the State of New York from May 5, 1784, to January 20, 1796. Pierre Van Cortlandt was lieutenant governor and vice chancellor from May 5, 1784, to July 17, 1787.

2. This letter is undated; the dates which have been assigned to it indicate the period during which Robert Harpur, to whom H refers in the letter printed above, was secretary of the University of the State of New York.

1785

To Richard Varick [1]

[*New York, January 13, 1785.* Letter listed in dealer's catalogue *Letter not found.*]

1. ALS, sold by Patrick Madigan, New York City, 1914, New Series 2.

From Abel James [1]

Philadelphia, January 21, 1785. Apologizes for not answering Hamilton's letter of December 4, 1783, and states that he has been ill. Sends part of information requested by Hamilton.[2]

ALS, anonymous donor.
1. For the text of this letter and an explanation of its contents, see the discussion of the Otsego Patent of George Croghan in Goebel, *Law Practice,* forthcoming volumes.
2. James enclosed in this letter an extract from two of Croghan's mortgages (copy, in James's handwriting, anonymous donor).

Petition of John Lamb [1]

[New York, February 1–9, 1785]

To The Honorable The Representatives of the United States in Congress assembled.

The Memorial and Petition of John Lamb of the State of Connecticut humbly sheweth

That Your Memorialist believing it to be the interest of the United States to form some treaty of amity and Commerce with the States of Barbary; and inferring from the general sense of persons with whom Your Memorialist has conversed, that it is the desire of

Congress to set on foot negotiations for that purpose, Your Memorialist is induced to offer his services for conducting those negotiations.

Your Memorialist can offer no other inducements to this trust than his zeal for the service of the United States and his knowlege of the Country, to which he desires to be sent, acquired by an intercourse of five years; and asks no rewards for his services, all he requires being to have the sanction of the United States and the necessary powers to treat.

Your Memorialst to this end prays that the Honorable the Congress if they think him worthy of such Confidence would be pleased to vest him with such character & power correspondent thereto as they may judge necessary & expedient. And Your Petitioner as in duty bound shall pray &c

Df, in the handwriting of H, Hamilton Papers, Library of Congress.

1. John Lamb should not be confused with John Lamb of New York City, who had been one of the leaders of the Sons of Liberty in that city and had had a distinguished military career during the American Revolution. When the document printed above was written, John Lamb of New York was collector of customs in New York City for the State of New York.

John Lamb, the author of this petition, was a resident of Norwich, Connecticut, a ship's captain, and a merchant. On January 10, 1785, Samuel Huntington wrote from Norwich to John Jay, Secretary for Foreign Affairs: "Capt. John Lamb of this Place will have the honor of delivering this Letter. He hath formed the Design of going to the Coast of Barbary where he is well acquainted, having made several Voyages to those Parts before the late War, and resided considerable Time in that Country. He is desirous to obtain some aid from Congress as a Protection, and willing to do any national Service for us in his Power. Capt. Lamb is a Gentleman of Fidelity and mercantile Knowledge, especially in the Marine Department, of an enterprising Genius and intrepid Spirit" (Burnett, *Letters*, VIII, 73). Lamb's petition was read before Congress on February 9, 1785, and on February 15 Congress appointed him United States representative to the Barbary States (*JCC*, XXVIII, 54 note, 67 note; Burnett, *Letters*, VIII, 72). Lamb was instructed to report in Europe to Thomas Jefferson and John Adams, both of whom had unwittingly named Thomas Barclay for the same position. A compromise was arranged by which Barclay was assigned the mission to Morocco and Lamb the mission to Algiers (Burnett, *Letters*, VIII, 250). Both missions were unsuccessful. Lamb arrived in Algiers on March 25, 1786, with instructions to try to ransom twenty-one Americans who had been captured by the Algerines in June, 1785. He was unable to negotiate a treaty of peace, and in September, 1786, he was ordered to return to the United States (Ray W. Irwin, *The Diplomatic Relations of the United States with the Barbary Powers, 1776–1816* [Chapel Hill, 1931], 37–40). Lamb arrived in New York in April, 1788 (*JCC*, XXXIV, 129).

To John Chaloner [1]

[*New York, February 2, 1785.* "I have received your letter with the state of the case enclosed. If you can make no arrangement for securing Mr. Carter without the assistance of the law, I am upon the whole of opinion it will be advisable to rely on the first bill of exchange, instituting another suit against Turnbull Marmie & Co.[2] Though it may be a question whether they are not discharged by the acceptance of the second bill, yet there is law enough to the contrary to justify an experiment to make them answerable. And it will be prudent to hold fast all the security to which you have any pretensions. I suppose there has [been] no receipt or other thing past considering the second bills as absolute payment for so much of the first. No doubt . . . you have employed able counsel in the matter on the first who know the genius of your courts. You will do well to follow their advice rather than my opinion. I shall be happy at all times to give you the best I can in whatever relates either to our friend or yourself." [3] *Letter not found.*]

1. ALS, sold by The Rendells, Inc., Catalogue 119, Item 103.
For background to this letter, see H to Chaloner, May 1, 1783, note 1; December 11, 1783 (both printed in this volume).
2. Turnbull, Marmie, and Company was a mercantile firm in Philadelphia. See John Trumbull to H, September 4, 1784 (*PAH*, III, 578).
3. Text taken from the dealer's catalogue.

Conveyance from James Barclay and Others [1]

[*New York, September 17, 1785*]. James Barclay and others convey "All that certain messuage or dwelling house and the store house thereunto adjoining, as also the lott of ground whereon the said dwelling house and store house do stand and which is thereunto belonging situate lying and being in the South Ward of the City of New York Fronting to a certain street called Wall Street. . . ." [2]

Certified copy, recorded under the date of May 27, 1786, Conveyances in the Office of the Register, City of New York, Liber 43, 379–80, Hall of Records, New York City.

1. Barclay was an auctioneer at 14 Hanover Square, New York City.

2. This document concerns H's purchase of the house at 58 Wall Street, New York City, which he had been renting for at least a year. See H's "Cash Book," March 1, 1782–1791 (*PAH*, III, 18); H to Elizabeth Hamilton, March 17, 1785 (*PAH*, III, 599), May 28, 1789 (*PAH*, V, 342–43). When H was appointed Secretary of the Treasury and moved to Philadelphia in 1790, he rented the house to William Maxwell, a tobacconist and a director of the Bank of New York (William Duncan, *The New-York Directory, and Register, for the Year 1791* [New York, 1791], 85). On April 27, 1793, H sold the house to Gulian Verplanck, president of the Bank of New York ("Conveyance by Lease and Release to Gulian Verplanck," April 27, 1793 [*PAH*, XIV, 352–53]).

To ——————— Townsend [1]

[*New York, December 27, 1785.*] Instructs Townsend on how to proceed with the execution of a conveyance.[2]

AL, Hamilton Papers, Library of Congress.

1. This letter concerns the settlement of the estate of Noah Townsend, a resident of Oyster Bay, Long Island, New York. The "Mr. Townsend" to whom it is addressed was either William Townsend or Micajah Townsend, two of Noah Townsend's four executors. See Noah Townsend's will, February 12, 1760 (copy, Hamilton Papers, Library of Congress). See also H's "Cash Book," March 1, 1782–1791 (*PAH*, III, 38).

2. This letter is endorsed: "Directions to execute a Deed or other Insmt. in the state of Pennsylvania."

To Egbert Benson [1]

[*1785–1787.*] Recounts the facts in the case of *Mary Franklin, Executor of Henry Franklin v Teunis Slingerlands.*[2]

LS, from a photostat in the New York State Library, Albany.

1. Benson, a New York lawyer, was a member of the first New York State Assembly in 1777, a delegate to the Continental Congress from 1781 to 1784, and attorney general of New York from 1777 to 1787. He was a member of the House of Representatives from 1789 to 1793.

2. For information on this case, see Goebel, *Law Practice*, I, 230–31. See also H's "Cash Book," March 1, 1782–1791 (*PAH*, III, 33).

1786

To Samuel H. Parsons [1]

[New York] January 11, 1786. "Some time since I transmitted you a Commission issuing out of the Court of Appeals in cases of Capture the object of which was to examine you on the subject of a certain Agreement stated in your letter [2] and affidavit that no prejudice should arise from not lodging the appeal in time in the cause of the Brig Hope. . . . Not having yet had the pleasure of hearing from you on the subject I am induced to trouble you with this letter to ascertain whether the Commission has reached you & whether the proposed arrangement is agreeable to you. . . ."

ALS, RG 267, Records of the Supreme Court of the United States, Records of the Court of Appeals in Cases of Capture, Revolutionary War Prize Case Files, 1776–1786, Box 12, No. 103, Brig Hope, National Archives.

1. Parsons, a lawyer and a veteran of the American Revolution, lived in Middletown, Connecticut. On September 22, 1785, Congress appointed him a commissioner to extinguish Indian claims to the Territory Northwest of the River Ohio.

This letter concerns *Richard Blake Jr. Appt.* v *Brig Hope John Hurlbutt Appee*, a Revolutionary War prize case, in which H acted as counsel for the appellants and which was heard before the Confederation Court of Appeals in 1787. For material concerning this case, see RG 267, Records of the Supreme Court of the United States, Records of the Court of Appeals in Cases of Capture, Revolutionary War Prize Case Files, 1776–1786, Box 12, No. 103, Brig Hope, National Archives. See also Goebel, *Law Practice*, II, 892.

2. Letter not found.

Receipt to Andrew Craig and William Cooper [1]

New York, January 23, 1786. Receipt for a deed to a tract of land in George Croghan's Otsego Patent.[2]

ADS, anonymous donor.

1. Cooper, who later founded Cooperstown, New York, was the father of James Fenimore Cooper, the novelist. Cooper and Craig were residents of Burlington, New Jersey, and both were land speculators.

2. For the text of this document and an explanation of its contents, see the discussion of the Otsego Patent of George Croghan in Goebel, *Law Practice*, forthcoming volumes.

Conveyance. Isaac Moses, Nicholas Low, Daniel Ludlow, and Alexander Hamilton to Alexander Macomb [1]

New York, February 15, 1786. ". . . Isaac Moses of the City of New York Merchant of the first part Nicholas Low and Daniel Ludlow Merchant and Alexander Hamilton Counsellor at law all of the same place assignees of the real and personal estate of the said Isaac Moses . . . for and in consideration of the sum of Four thousand four hundred and fifty pounds New York currency to them in hand paid by . . . Alexander Macomb . . . have granted . . . unto the said Alexander Macomb . . . All those three certain messuages or tenements and lots of ground situate, lying and being in the Dockward of the City of New York bounded northwesterly by great dock street southwesterly by a lot of ground of William Constable southeasterly by little Dock street and northeasterly by a lot of ground late of Thomas Doughty and a lot now or late of John Oothout. . . ."

Certified copy, recorded under the date of February 9, 1790, Conveyances in the Office of the Register, City of New York, Liber 46, 31–33, Hall of Records, New York City.

1. Moses, a New York City auctioneer, was a partner with Moses Myers, an Amsterdam merchant, in the mercantile firm of Isaac Moses and Company in New York City. Moses became a bankrupt in early 1785, and the dissolution of the firm was announced in a supplement to *The New-York Journal, or the Weekly Register*, June 23, 1785. See "Transfer of Property: Isaac Moses and Company to Low, Ludlow, and H," November 25, 1785 (copy, Division of Corporations and State Records, New York Department of State, Albany). See also Jeremiah Wadsworth to H, April 3, 1785; H to Wadsworth, April 7, 1785 (*PAH*, III, 600, 601–02). Wadsworth and John B. Church held some of the notes of Isaac Moses and Company.

For additional information concerning Moses's business affairs and H's role in them, see Goebel, *Law Practice*, forthcoming volumes.

Macomb, a native of Ireland, had engaged in trade with the Indians in the North American West during the American Revolution and was a partner with his brother William and William Edgar in the Detroit firm of Macomb, Edgar, and Macomb, which supplied the British Indian department. After the war, he

settled in New York City, where he became a wealthy businessman and speculator.

To Andrew Craig and William Cooper

New York, March 2, 1786. Advises Cooper and Craig how to secure their interest in their portions of George Croghan's Otsego
Patent.[1]

ALS, anonymous donor.
1. For the text of this letter and an explanation of the contents, see the discussion of the Otsego Patent of George Croghan in Goebel, *Law Practice*,
forthcoming volumes.

To Isaac Gouverneur, Junior [1]

[New York, March, 1786]

Sir

Mr Bremar [2] last evening delivered me your Letter inclosing a
Copy of your Correspondence with Mr Lewis.[3]

In a personal Altercation between two Gentlemen where their
passions have evidently become pritty warmly engaged, and for both
whom I always had Esteem, I should not be willing to give my Opinion on the conduct of one of them, especially when the appeal was
not made to me by both. On this head I shall only take the Liberty
to say, that I would not advise *publication* which has always a disagreeable appearance, and seldom turns out to the Advantage of
either party.

In another respect I feel myself painfully Situated. Having received
favourable impressions of your Character, I am sorry to observe any
thing to have come from you which I am oblige[d] to consider as
exceptionable. Your Second Letter to Mr Lewis contains a *general*
and of Course an unjustifiable Reflection on the profession to which
I belong and of a Nature to put it out of my power to attempt to
render you any service in the line of that profession. I readily believe
you did not attend to the full force of the Expression, when you tell

Mr Lewis *"Attorney like"* to make the most of his bill of Costs: but it contains in it an insinuation which cannot be pleasing to any man in the Profession and which must oblige anyone that has proper dilicacy to decline the business of one who professedly entertains such an Idea of the Conduct of his profession.

I make allowances for your feelings when you wrote that Letter, and am therefore reluctantly drawn into these Observations.[4]

I remain with Esteem Sir your Obedient sevt. A Hamilton

Copy, Hamilton Papers, Library of Congress.

1. James A. Hamilton gives the addressee of this letter as "Mr. Gouverneur" (*Reminiscences*, 6). Allan McLane Hamilton states that the addressee was Isaac Gouverneur, a New York City merchant (Hamilton, *Intimate Life*, 169), and in the Lodge edition of Hamilton's works the addressee is Nicholas Gouverneur, who was also a New York City merchant (*HCLW*, IX, 500). The *New York Herald*, which printed this letter on May 21, 1856, dates the letter "New York, 1796," while James A. Hamilton and Lodge date it "1792." Allan McLane Hamilton suggests that it was written during the protracted series of cases involving Louis Le Guen on the one hand and Isaac Gouverneur and Peter Kemble on the other.

This letter was actually written in reply to Isaac Gouverneur, Jr., to H, February 24, 1786, which is calendared in *PAH*, III, 650. The full text of the calendared letter reads: "As I wish to have you my principal attorney for what I may have occasion to do in the law way—before I publish to the World the enclosed correspondence between Col. Lewis and myself, shoud be glad to submit it to your opinion as a Gentleman and a Man of honour: whether this treatment from that person ought to be consider'd otherways than extremely indecent and improper.

"I was this morning obliged to find Bail for Mr. Bremar, and have now to request you also take measures to set the Suit aside, for reasons that have already been assigned both to Col. Lewis & Mr. Curson.

"I woud waite on you in person, but am confined to my Room by ill health; that I have for some time been troubled with." (ALS, Hamilton Papers, Library of Congress.)

Gouverneur was the son of Samuel Gouverneur and was called junior to distinguish him from his uncle, Isaac Gouverneur.

Samuel Curson and Gouverneur were New York merchants and business partners. In July, 1785, H had served as their attorney in the New York Supreme Court in *George Cherry* v *Samuel Curson and Isaac Gouverneur* (defendant's plea, July 21, 1785 [copy, Hamilton Papers, Library of Congress]). See also *PAH*, III, 63; "Bill of Costs, Curson & Gouverneur adsm Cherry," December 29, 1785 (AD, Hamilton Papers, Library of Congress).

By 1788 Gouverneur's partnership with Curson had expired or dissolved, and Gouverneur became a partner with his older brother, Nicholas, and his brother-in-law, Peter Kemble, in the New York mercantile firm of Gouverneur and Kemble. For H's role as attorney to Gouverneur and Kemble, see Goebel, *Law Practice*, II, 48–164.

In addition, H helped Isaac Gouverneur obtain a divorce from his wife, Elizabeth, on the ground of adultery. For H's role in this matter in the New York legislature in 1787, see *PAH*, IV, 70–71. H also represented Gouverneur in the proceedings concerning the settlement of the divorce in the Court of

Chancery. See *Isaac Gouverneur [Junior]* v *Elizabeth Gouverneur* (MS Minutes of the New York Court of Chancery, 1785–1789, under dates of January 18, 30, October 10, 1788 [Hall of Records, New York City]; Bill of Chancery, filed March 31, 1787, and decree, dated October 18, 1788, and enrolled May, 1789 [Historical Records Collection, on deposit at Queens College, City University of New York]).

2. "Mr. Bremar" may have been John Bremar of Rensselaerwyck, Albany County, New York.

3. Morgan Lewis was a New York City attorney.
On the MS "Mr Lewis" has been inked out at this point and twice in the following paragraph.

4. The endorsement on this letter, much of which has been inked out, reads: "I am much gratified to learn the addressee of this letter. It is my opinion that no publication ought to be made of any of the correspondence referring to private differences and should this be given to the public, it ought to be done without the name of the person to whom it was addressed.   A H
"Perhaps it would do best to publish this letter as it gives the opinion of the author on the question."

To Aaron Burr [1]

[New York, April 4, 1786]

ALS, Greenfield Village and Henry Ford Museum, Dearborn, Michigan.
1. This letter has not been released for publication.

To Elihu Marshall and James Bingham [1]

[*New York, April 19, 1786*. Sends a notice for trial in the New York Supreme Court in the case of *Robert McWilliams* [2] v *Elihu Marshall and James Bingham.* [3] Document not found.]

1. ADS, sold by American Art Association-Anderson Galleries, New York City, February 1, 1921.
Marshall was a mariner in New York City; Bingham was a gauger in New York City.

2. McWilliams was a New York City grocer.

3. H's law agenda for 1785 states that a narrative of the case was filed and that bail was demanded for Marshall and Bingham (AD, Agenda No. 2 for October Vacation [1785], Hamilton Papers, Library of Congress).
H had been McWilliams's attorney in other cases. See H's "Cash Book," March 1, 1782–1791 (*PAH*, III, 61, 66, 67).
This case was an action to recover a debt of £250. The defendants did not appear and did not enter a plea. The court ordered that an inquiry to assess the amount of the damages be made (MS Minutes of the New York Supreme

Court, 1786, under the dates of January 28, May 6, 1786 [Hall of Records, New York City]; Pleadings, 1754–1837, M-168 [Hall of Records, New York City]). On April 28, 1786, the sheriff returned the writ of inquiry with an inquisition by which the jury assessed the plaintiff's damages at £210.13.11 and costs (DS, in H's handwriting, Hall of Records, New York City). On May 25, 1786, the court ordered judgment for the plaintiff for the damages and £21.15.1 for costs and charges (Judgment Roll, Parchment 112-A-7 [Hall of Records, New York City]).

Receipt to Robert Morris

New York, April 19, 1786. Acknowledges receipt of "Nine pounds twelve shill⟨ings⟩" as a retainer for a case concerning "Patents . . . adjacent to the Jersey line in the County of Orange. . . ."

ADS, Yale University Library.

From Murray, Sansom, and Company [1]

[New York, April, 1786]

Murray, Sansom & Co. present their Compliments to Mr. Hamilton and inform him that there is a Vessel that will sail on Sunday next for London, they would be obliged to him if he would have the Commission made out to go by that conveyance. At foot are the names they wish to have nominated as Commissioners.

[Mark Lane London] [2]

No 1 [Henry] Adams—Attorney at Law
　　3 Robert Barclay
　　4 Joseph Woods
　　5 Effingham Lawrence　　　[of the City of London
　　2 Thomas Powell　　　　　　Merchants]
　　6 John Freeman [3]

L, Hamilton Papers, Library of Congress.
　1. This letter concerns the case of *Robert Murray, John Murray, and Philip Sansom* v *James Arden* in the New York Supreme Court. In 1779 Arden, a New York merchant, requested that the New York firm of Murray, Sansom, and Company purchase goods for him in London and ship them to New York. The goods were sent on the ship *Martha*, which was first taken by an Ameri-

can privateer and retaken by a British vessel which carried it to Halifax. There the goods were condemned on the ground that the ship was cleared for Halifax, not New York. Murray, Sansom, and Company employed H as counsel and sued Arden for the cost of the seized goods. Arden contended that Murray, Sansom, and Company were at fault for not having the *Martha* cleared for New York ("State of the Case between Murray Sansom & Co & James Arden" [D, Hamilton Papers, Library of Congress]; Narrative, New York Supreme Court, October term, 1784 [D, Hamilton Papers, Library of Congress]). See also Issue Roll, 1785 (Parchment 130-L-6, Hall of Records, New York City); Affidavit of John Murray, April 26, 1786 (BM-2564-M, Chancery Papers, Hall of Records, New York City). In 1786 H, on behalf of his clients, obtained permission from the Court of Chancery for the issuance of a commission to London to examine witnesses whose testimony was material to the plaintiff's case (MS Minutes of the New York Court of Chancery, 1785–1789, under date of April 26, 1786 [Hall of Records, New York City]).

The letter printed above indicates the men in London whom Murray, Sansom, and Company wished to have named commissioners.

In July, 1787, a jury in the New York Supreme Court sitting on circuit in New York City found a verdict for the plaintiffs of £1,383.2.3 damages and costs (Nisi Prius Roll and Postea, July, 1787 [Parchment 2-H-1, Hall of Records, New York City]).

2. The material within brackets is in H's handwriting.
3. The name is crossed out on the MS.

To John Delafield [1]

[New York, May 22, 1786]

Mr. Hamilton requests Mr. Delafield to send him a list of the bills negotiated for Lady Anne Polnitz [2] on or account of the house.[3]

May 22d

AL, Hamilton Papers, Library of Congress.
1. Delafield, who came to New York from England in 1783, was a broker in securities.
2. Anne Stuart, baronne von Poellnitz, the wife of Frederick Charles Hans Bruno, baron von Poellnitz, had purchased twenty-two and one-half acres of land in Manhattan, situated on present-day Broadway between Eighth and Tenth streets. The land was part of the former estate of Andrew Elliot, receiver general of the Province of New York under the Crown. Poellnitz, who was in England in May, 1786, used the land as an experimental farm that became widely popularized. In 1790 he sold the farm to Robert Richard Randall, founder of Sailors' Snug Harbor and one of H's clients (H to William Beekman, June 15, 1801, note 4 [*PAH*, XXV 389]). See "Alexander Hamilton. Certificate to cancel a mortgage from Frederick Charles Hans Bruno Poellnitz, N. Y.," June 5, 1790 (DS, MS 225, New York State Library, Albany).

H was involved in the purchase and sale of this land because he managed

Poellnitz's business and personal affairs in America. See H's "Cash Book," March 1, 1782–1791 (*PAH*, III, 28–29).

3. Following this letter is a list, which is not in H's handwriting and which **reads:**

"Read & Bogardus	£400	**2 of 200**
S Franklin & Co	300	1 of 300
J & H Waddington	400	1 of 400
Haydock & Warr	250	1 of 250
J & H Shotwell	150	1 of 150
Robt. Bowne	301.10	81.10
		60
		60
		60
		40
E. K. Royston	110	1 of £110
J Delafield	200	2 of 100."

In the Hamilton Papers, Library of Congress, there are three documents concerning the bills of exchange which H mentions in his letter. The first is entitled "Account of Bills of Exchange sold for Mr. White Matlack drawn by Lady Anne Poelnitz," which is a list similar to the one printed above. The second document, entitled "Bills sold for W. Matlack," contains the same list as the first document as well as a statement by Matlack concerning payment of the bills, dated May 24, 1786. The third document is dated April 11, 1785, and is a bill of exchange for £200 drawn by Lady Poellnitz on Jacob Read and Robert Bogardus, New York City merchants.

Receipt to Robert Cambridge Livingston [1]

[*New York, June 8, 1786.* On June 17, 1796, Walter Livingston wrote to Hamilton: "In examining my fathers papers yesterday I found a receipt of yours in the following words Viz. Received New York June 8. 1786 of Robert C. Livingston Esquire Twenty five Dollars as a retainer for the Manor of Livingston. Alex Hamilton." *Receipt not found.*]

1. Robert Cambridge Livingston, a merchant, was the fourth son of Robert Livingston, Jr., the third lord of Livingston Manor.

For background to this document, see Walter Livingston to H, June 17, 1796 (*PAH*, XX, 228–29).

Stephen Van Rensselaer to the Tenants of Rensselaerwyck [1]

[July-August, 1786]

Sir

The situation in which you occupy the lands in your possession in the manor of Rensselaærwyck must of course make you anxious to be put upon a more certain and explicit footing. On my part it is my wish not merely to do justice but to act liberally towards those with whom I have any concerns of property. In this disposition I have concluded to give you a lease in fee for the farm in your possession on such terms and conditions as will be reasonable in respect to you and consistent with a due regard to myself and my family. You will therefore call upon me at my house on   [2] in order that what is necessary may be done.

I am Sir   Your hum ser   A Hamilton

ADfS, in H's handwriting and signed by H, Mr. Ben Weisinger, Brooklyn, New York.

1. Van Rensselaer was the eighth patroon of the Manor of Rensselaerwyck. On June 9, 1783, he married Margarita Schuyler, one of Elizabeth Hamilton's younger sisters.

In 1769, when Van Rensselaer was five years old, his father, Stephen Van Rensselaer, died, leaving the management of the estate to Abraham Ten Broeck, the husband of the younger Van Rensselaer's aunt, Elizabeth Van Rensselaer. In 1786, after Van Rensselaer reached his majority, he assumed his role as patroon and in an effort to increase the cultivation of the manor lands granted perpetual leases at moderate rentals to his tenants.

See Philip Schuyler to H, July 11, 1786 (*PAH*, III, 678), in which Stephen Van Rensselaer is incorrectly identified as John Van Rensselaer and the word "lands" was read for the word "leases."

2. Space left blank in MS.

To the Corporation of Albany [1]

[*New York*] *October 28, 1786.* Gives legal advice concerning settlers on Corporation land.

ALS, Pierpont Morgan Library, New York City.
1. For the full text of this document and for an explanation of its contents, see Goebel, *Law Practice,* forthcoming volumes. See also H's "Cash Book," March 1, 1782–1791 (*PAH,* III, 21).

Moses Myers to Nicholas Low, Daniel Ludlow, and Alexander Hamilton [1]

Philadelphia, November 23, 1786. Describes his efforts in Baltimore and Philadelphia to collect money to cover his firm's debts.

ALS, Hamilton Papers, Library of Congress.
1. For background to this letter, see "Conveyance. Isaac Moses, Nicholas Low, Daniel Ludlow, and Alexander Hamilton to Alexander Macomb," February 15, 1786, note 1 (printed in this volume).

1787

Certificate of Clerkship for Dirck Ten Broeck [1]

New York January 26th 1787

I hereby certify that Mr. Dirck Ten Broeck entered a Clerkship with me on the Tenth day of January in the year One thousand seven hundred and Eighty four and served as a Clerk in my office until the fifteenth day of October last past and that he is of good moral character.   Alexander Hamilton

ADS, Pleadings, 1754–1837, T-540, Hall of Records, New York City.

1. Ten Broeck was the son of Abraham Ten Broeck, who had been a member of the colonial Assembly, the New York Provincial Congress from 1775 to 1777, and a brigadier general of the Albany County militia during the American Revolution. H was related to the Ten Broecks by marriage. In 1763 Abraham Ten Broeck had married Elizabeth Van Rensselaer, the aunt of Stephen Van Rensselaer, eighth patroon of Rensselaerwyck and the husband of Elizabeth Hamilton's sister, Margarita.

When Dirck Ten Broeck left H's law office in October, 1786, he went to Albany and completed his clerkship with John Lansing, Jr. (Lansing's Certificate, January 20, 1787 [ADS, Pleadings, 1754–1837, T-540, Hall of Records, New York City]). Ten Broeck was admitted to practice law on August 1, 1787 ("Roll of Attorneys" [D, Hall of Records, New York City]).

On June 1, 1789, H certified that he had appointed Dirck Ten Broeck as his agent in Albany for such matters as serving notices on opposing attorneys and filing rules with the clerk of the court (D, Pleadings, 1754–1837, H-231, Hall of Records, New York City).

To  [1]

[*Philadelphia, June 2, 1787*. The dealer's catalogue description of this letter reads: ". . . autograph postscript in which . . . [Hamilton] suggests that if his correspondent breaks his journey at Elizabethtown he should go to the house either of Mr. Bondinot [2] or Governor Livingstone." [3] *Letter not found.*]

1. ALS, sold at Sotheby's of London, Ltd., June 11–12, 1973, Lot 602.
2. Elias Boudinot.
3. William Livingston, a lawyer and a native of New York State, was head of the liberal faction in state politics from 1758 1770, when he was defeated by the conservative De Lancey faction. In 1772 he retired temporarily from public life and moved to a farm in New Jersey. He was a delegate from New Jersey to the First and Second Continental Congresses and served as governor from 1776 until his death in 1790.

To Aaron Burr

[*New York, June-October, 1787.*] [1] "As I wished the cause of Bayard vs Breese [2] and others to be regularly at issue & as the Chancellor could not readily be come at to procure from him an order to serve subpoenas on the Clerk in Court, I sent you a request some time since [3] to file rejoinders. . . . I have not, however, received any notice of its having been done. I will thank you particularly to have it done in the course of the day. . . ."

ALS, American Antiquarian Society, Worcester, Massachusetts.

1. In Worthington C. Ford, "Some Papers of Aaron Burr," *Proceedings of the American Antiquarian Society*, new series, XXIX (1919), 99–100, this letter is dated "1797."

2. This letter concerns a case in Chancery, *Catherine Bayard v John Cruger, Augustus Van Horne, William Malcom, Samuel Breese, and Aaron Burr*, in which H was Catherine Bayard's attorney. See Catherine Bayard to H, April 24, 1787 (*PAH*, IV, 154); H to Breese, Malcom, and Burr, April, 1787 (*PAH*, IV, 155). Breese, Malcom, and Burr were the executors of the estate of Samuel Bayard, Catherine Bayard's deceased husband. Cruger and Van Horne were the executors of the estate of Elizabeth Carpenter, Catherine Bayard's mother. Catherine Bayard charged the executors with defrauding her by refusing to convey to her a house which her husband had purchased from the estate of his mother-in-law, Elizabeth Carpenter, and she also maintained that she was entitled to a larger sum from her mother's estate than the executors had given her (Bill, *Catherine Bayard v John Cruger, Augustus Van Horne, William Malcom, Samuel Breese, and Aaron Burr*, May 11, 1786 [New York Chancery Decrees before 1800, B-108 F, Historical Documents Collection, on deposit at Queens College, City University of New York]). On December 18, 1787, Chancellor Robert R. Livingston decreed: "That the Executors of Elizabeth Carpenter do pay the Complainant the Ballance confessed to be in their Hands after deducting the Costs of Suit and the said sum of Three hundred and Fifty pounds due on the purchase of the said House And that the said John Cruger and Augustus Van Horne . . . Do convey to the said Executors of the said Samuel Bayard . . . The House and Lot which the said Samuel Bayard . . . did agree to purchase of the said Executors of the said Elizabeth Carpenter for the said Sum of Three hundred and fifty Pounds Currency . . ." (MS Minutes of the New York Court of Chancery, Hall of Records, New York City).

3. Letter not found.

Receipt to Philip Van Cortlandt [1]

[*New York, July 5, 1787.* "Received of Phil. Van Cortlandt, Treasurer to the Society of the Cincinnati for the State of New York, Five thousand Dollars in Certificates Issued by John Pierce,[2] commonly called New York finals, being part of the Funds belonging to Said Society, and for which we are to be accountable." [3] *Receipt not found.*]

Dossier File, Van Cortlandt-Van Wyck Papers, MS Division, New York Public Library.
1. Van Cortlandt, who during the American Revolution was a colonel in the Second New York Regiment and a member of George Washington's staff for a brief period, was brevetted a brigadier general in 1783. In 1788 he was a delegate to the New York Ratifying Convention.
H was a member of the New York State Society of the Cincinnati and had been appointed by the state society as chairman of a committee of correspondence. See "Circular Letter to the State Societies of the Cincinnati," November 1, 1786 (*PAH*, III, 693–96). He had attended the general meeting of the Society of the Cincinnati in Philadelphia in May, 1787. See "Credentials as Delegate to the General Society of the Cincinnati," May 18, 1787 (*PAH*, IV, 158).
2. Pierce was commissioner of Army accounts.
3. This document, which is Item No. 1 on a handwritten list of calendars of documents, is described: "Society of the Cincinnati. Rev. Officers & Legal Items. Document Signed by Alexr Hamilton, M[arinus] Willett, John Lamb Rich C Platt and D[avid] Brooks. Written by one of the signers."

From Marquis de Lafayette [1]

Paris october the 26 [1787]

My dear friend
    As I am writing By a Gentleman Who goes through England and Carries my letter Himself, I shall Content Myself with inclosing the Copy of Some favourable Arrangemens of Commerce [2]—and Reminding You of Your loving, grateful, and devoted am My dear Hamilton
    Yours for Ever   Lafayette

My Best Respects to Mrs Hamilton.

ALS, The Sol Feinstone Collection, Library of the American Philosophical Society, Philadelphia.

1. For background to this letter, see Lafayette to H, October 15, 1787 (*PAH*, IV, 282–83).

2. This enclosure has not been found. It may have been a preliminary draft of the French "Arrêt du Conseil d'Etat du Roi, Pour l'encouragement du Commerce de France avec les Etats-Unis d'Amérique" of December 29, 1787, which granted the United States several trading privileges, including the right to store United States goods in French ports for six months subject to a minimum duty. See "View of the Commercial Regulations of France and Great Britain in Reference to the United States," 1792–1793, note 58 (*PAH*, XIII, 419).

To Peter Van Schaack [1]

[*New York, October, 1787.* Letter listed in dealer's catalogue. *Letter not found.*]

1. ALS, sold by Robert K. Black, Upper Montclair, New Jersey, 1949, Catalogue 13, Item 182.

Van Schaack was banished to England in 1778 because of his Loyalist sympathies. The New York legislature restored his citizenship in 1784, and he returned to New York in 1785.

Bill and Receipt from Francis Childs [1]

[New York, November 12, 1787]

Alexander Hamilton Esqr.

to Francis Childs Dr.

1787

Nov. 12. to advertising the Farm for Sale on Frog's Neck [2]—9 weeks   £1.1⟨–⟩

Received payment
Frans Childs

ADS, MS Division, New York Public Library.

1. Childs was the editor and publisher of *The* [New York] *Daily Advertiser,* a newspaper that he had established on March 1, 1785.

2. Throgs (Frogs) Neck is a peninsula at the eastern end of the East River in what was then Westchester County and is now the Bronx, New York City.

1788

Subscription to the Ohio Company for Education and Worship in the Territory Northwest of the River Ohio

[*New York*] *March, 1788.* Subscribes ten pounds to the Ohio Company for "the Education of Youth, and the Promotion of Public Worship, among the first Settlers." [1]

DS, Princeton University Library.

1. The other subscribers were Richard C. Platt, William Edgar, Alexander Macomb, William Constable, and William Duer, all New York City merchants.

H owned five and one-half shares in the Ohio Company. See Benjamin Tallmadge to H, June 20, 1795, note 2 (*PAH*, XVIII, 383–84); Rufus Putnam to H, November 19, 1796 (*PAH*, XX, 401–02); H to William R. Putnam, July, 1800 (*PAH*, XXV, 48–49), December 6, 1802, October, 1803 (printed in this volume); William R. Putnam to H, January 17, 1803 (printed in this volume); H to Oliver Wolcott, Jr., October 3, 1802 (printed in this volume).

To Nicholas Low [1]

[New York, May 6, 1788]

I send you the questions answered.

Yrs.   A Hamilton

ALS, Mr. Cyril Clemens, Kirkwood, Missouri.

1. Low, a prominent New York merchant, for whom H had on various occasions served as attorney, was seeking election as a delegate to the New York State convention to ratify the Constitution of the United States. See H to Gouverneur Morris, May 19, 1788 (*PAH*, IV, 650–52).

Certificate by Ezra L'Hommedieu, Egbert Benson, and Alexander Hamilton of a Statement by Abraham Yates, Junior, Respecting His Vote on the Constitution of the United States [1]

[New York, August 8, 1788]

We do certify that Mr Yates has delivered to us a Paper subscribed by him (of which the preceeding is a Copy) [2] as declaritive of his

Principles on which he will vote in Congress in the affirmative on the final Question on the Ordinance for putting the new Constitution for the United States into Operation.

Ezra L Hommedieu
Egbt. Benson
Alexander Hamilton

DS, in the handwriting of Ezra L'Hommedieu, Abraham Yates Papers, MS Division, New York Public Library; copy, in the handwriting of Abraham Yates, Jr., Abraham Yates Papers, MS Division, New York Public Library.
1. L'Hommedieu, Benson, Yates, and H were New York delegates to the Continental Congress. See H's "Appointment as Delegate to the Continental Congress," February 2, 1788 (*PAH*, IV, 492–93).
L'Hommedieu, a lawyer from Suffolk County, served in the New York Assembly from 1777 to 1783, in the Continental Congress from 1779 to 1783, and the New York Senate from 1784 to 1792. Benson, a New York lawyer, was attorney general of New York from May 8, 1777, to May 14, 1788. Yates a resident of Albany, was a delegate to the Provincial Congress from 1775 to 1777 and a member of the New York Senate from 1778 to 1790.
2. The document printed above was written at the bottom of the draft of a statement by Yates in which he expressed his opposition to the Constitution but stated that he would vote to approve it if his vote were needed. (ADfS, Abraham Yates Papers, MS Division, New York Public Library; copy, Abraham Yates Papers, MS Division, New York Public Library). On September 12, 1788, when Congress voted to assemble and "commence Proceedings under the Said Constitution," Yates did not vote (*JCC*, XXIV, 516–19).

From Philip Schuyler

Albany, September 2, 1788. Sends information for his defense against a bill filed in Chancery by Charles John Evans and Agatha Evans.[1]

ADfS, Schuyler Papers, MS Division, New York Public Library.
1. For information concerning this document, see Benjamin Walker to H, September 3, 1803 (printed in this volume).

John H. Livingston, Thomas Jones, Alexander Hamilton, and Brockholst Livingston [1] to Richard Morris [2]

New York, September 8, 1788. Petition by the administrators of Philip Livingston's estate to Morris, Chief Justice of the State of

New York, to examine and to settle a claim made by Livingston's estate against the estate of Philip Skene,[3] a Tory whose lands had been confiscated by New York State.

DS, Columbia University Libraries.

1. This document is listed as a "document not found" in *PAH*, V, 215.

The two Livingstons, H, and Jones wrote this petition in their capacities as administrators of the estate of Philip Livingston, a signer of the Declaration of Independence, a New York City merchant, and a member of the Continental Congress, who died in 1788.

John Henry Livingston, who had practiced law in Poughkeepsie, New York, from 1762 to 1764, received the degree of Doctor of Theology from the University of Utrecht in May, 1770. He became minister of the Dutch Reformed congregation in New York City after the American Revolution and in 1784 was elected professor of theology for the General Synod of the Dutch Reformed Church. In 1775 he married Sarah, the daughter of Philip Livingston.

Henry Brockholst Livingston was an aide-de-camp to General Philip Schuyler during the American Revolution. In 1779 he went to Spain as the private secretary of John Jay, the new Minister to the Court at Madrid. In 1783 he was admitted to the bar and began to practice law in New York City, using the name Brockholst Livingston. He was the son of William Livingston, one of Philip Livingston's younger brothers.

Jones was a New York City physician who had married Margaret Livingston, the daughter of Philip Livingston.

When Philip Livingston died his estate was insufficient to meet his debts, and the executors whom he named in his will renounced the administration of the estate. An act passed by the New York legislature on February 25, 1785, entitled "An Act for vesting the Estate of Philip Livingston, late of the City of New-York, Esquire, deceased, in Trustees for the Payment of his Debts, and other Purposes therein mentioned" named Philip Philip Livingston, Philip Livingston's son and heir, Isaac Roosevelt, and Robert C. Livingston trustees to administer Livingston's property, pay all debts, and discharge the pecuniary legacies. Roosevelt, a New York City merchant, was president of the Bank of New York from 1786 to 1791. He was the husband of Cornelia Hoffman Roosevelt, whose father, Martin Hoffman of Red Hook, New York, married as his second wife Alida Livingston Hansen, widow of Henry Hansen and younger sister of Philip Livingston. Robert C. Livingston, a New York City merchant, was a son of Robert Livingston, Jr., third lord of the manor, and a nephew of Philip Livingston. The act of 1785 provided that in the case of Philip Philip Livingston's death, which occurred in 1787, Roosevelt and Robert C. Livingston could grant "to such Person or Persons as may be nominated and appointed with the assents of" the surviving heirs power "to Administer the Goods and Chattels, Rights and Credits aforesaid" and the "Completion of the Trusts aforesaid," and shall "stand in the Place of said Philip Philip Livingston, Isaac Roosevelt, and Robert C. Livingston" (*New York Laws*, 8th Sess., Ch. XXI). The trustees then appointed Jones, John H. Livingston, H, and Brockholst Livingston to administer the estate.

For the text of this petition and additional information concerning this action, see Goebel, *Law Practice*, I, 253–58.

2. Morris, who was admitted to the bar in New York City in 1752, was appointed judge of the Vice Admiralty Court having jurisdiction over New York, New Jersey, and Connecticut in 1762. In 1778 he was named to the state Senate from the Southern District, and in 1779 he was appointed Chief Justice of the state Supreme Court.

3. Philip Skene, founder of Skenesborough (now Whitehall), Vermont, was lieutenant-governor of Crown Point and Ticonderoga and surveyor of His Majesty's woods near Lake Champlain before the American Revolution. In 1777 he volunteered for service with General Burgoyne's expedition from Canada, and later in the same year he surrendered with the British army at Saratoga.

From Theodore Sedgwick [1]

[Boston, November 12, 1788. Letter not found.]

"Letters from T. S. [Theodore Sedgwick] to Genl. A. Hamilton," William Livingston Papers, Book 3, Massachusetts Historical Society, Boston.
  1. Sedgwick, a lawyer in Berkshire County, Massachusetts, was a member of the state legislature in 1780, 1782, 1783, 1787, and 1788, a delegate to the Continental Congress from 1785 to 1788, and speaker of the Massachusetts House of Representatives in 1788.

From Philip Schuyler [1]

Albany, November 21, 1788. Encloses the "papers" which he had "promised to prepare" concerning his financial transactions with and for John Bradstreet.

ADf, Schuyler Papers, MS Division, New York Public Library.
  1. For information concerning this letter, see Benjamin Walker to H, September 3, 1803 (printed in this volume). See also Schuyler to H, September 2, 1788 (printed in this volume).

Conveyance. Isaac Roosevelt and Robert C. Livingston to Thomas Jones, John H. Livingston, Alexander Hamilton, and Brockholst Livingston [1]

New York, December 4, 1788. ". . . By an act of the Legislature of the State of New York Entitled 'An act for vesting the Estate of Philip Livingston late of the City of New York Esquire deceased in Trustees for the payment of his Debts and other purposes therein mentioned' " [2] the heirs of Philip Livingston convey his entire estate to the trustees "for one whole year bearing date the day before the date of these presents and by force of the Statute made for transferring of uses into possessions. . . ."

Certified copy, recorded under the date of March 24, 1792, Conveyance in the Office of the Register, City of New York, Liber 27, 140–43, Hall of Records, New York City.
1. For background to this document, see John H. Livingston, Thomas Jones, H, and Brockholst Livingston to Richard Morris, September 8, 1788, note 1 (printed in this volume).
2. *New York Laws*, 8th Sess., Ch. XXI (February 25, 1785).

Receipt to Baron von Steuben

[New York, December 12, 1788]

I certify that William Constable [1] hath delivered me for the Baron De Steuben by way of loan One Hundred pounds December 12th 1788.[2]   Alex Hamilton

ADS, anonymous donor.
1. Constable, a native of Ireland, was a prominent New York City merchant. In 1784 he became a partner with John Rucker of New York in the firm of Constable, Rucker, and Company. Rucker died in 1788, and Constable continued the firm under the name of William Constable and Company. In 1784 Robert and Gouverneur Morris invested £10,666 in Constable, Rucker, and Company, an association that continued until 1791. Constable was a director of the Bank of New York from 1787 to 1792.
2. At the bottom of this document Benjamin Walker wrote: "Colo. Walker promises to pay the Amt in May next. January 12th. 1789."
The endorsement in H's handwriting reads: "oct 6 89 paid by A Hamilton & charged." See H's "Cash Book," March 1, 1782–1791 (*PAH*, III, 51, 52); "Receipt from Benjamin Walker," April 5, 1790 (*PAH*, VI, 353).
A native of London, Benjamin Walker had emigrated to America before the American Revolution and settled in New York City. During the war he was aide-de-camp to Baron von Steuben. In 1786 he was appointed commissioner to settle the accounts of the hospital, marine, and clothing departments.

1789

Certificate of Clerkship for Joseph Strong

[New York, January 20, 1789]

I certify that Joseph Strong has served a clerkship of three years in my office in the business of an Attorney and that he is of good moral character.[1]

Alexander Hamilton

New York January 20th 1789

ADS, Pleadings, 1754–1837, S-486, Hall of Records, New York City.
1. Following his clerkship, Strong practiced law first in Cooperstown, New York, and then in Albany. See Strong to H, August 11, 1796 (*PAH*, III, 303–04).

Certificate of Good Character for Peter Ogilvie [1]

[New York, February 13, 1789. The dealer's catalogue description of this document reads: "certifying the character of Peter Ogilvie." *Document not found.]*

1. ADS, sold at Swann Auction Galleries, October 1, 1942, Lot 28.
Ogilvie was a New York attorney, a member of the New York Assembly from Orange County in 1778 and 1779, and judge of the Court of Probates of New York State from 1787 to 1799.

To Isaac Ledyard [1]

[Jamaica, New York, February 18, 1789]

Dr. Sir:

I understand you are to have a meeting at this place to morrow on the subject of the ensuing elections and accordingly inclose you to be laid before the meeting an address to the Inhabitants of your Township in regard to the appointment of a Governor. It is much to be wished the meeting may agree with their fellow citizens in New York and come to a resolution on the subject—For in Politics as in war the first blow is half the battle. The sooner we declare the better.

I am on my way to Huntington as a Messen⟨ger⟩ from the committee of New York to the Supervisors of the two Count⟨ies⟩ [2] who are to assemble there.

Yrs. with great regard   A Hamilton

Jamaica Feby 18 89

Copy, Columbia University Libraries.
    1. Ledyard, who was a veteran of the American Revolution and lived in Newtown, Long Island, has been credited as the author of "Mentor's Reply," published in 1784 as an attack on H's "Phocion" essays. See "Second Letter from Phocion," April, 1784, note 1 (*PAH*, III, 530–58).
    For an explanation of the contents of this letter, see "Appointment as Member of Committee of Correspondence," February 11, 1789 (*PAH*, V, 253–54); H to the Supervisors of the City of Albany, February 18, 1789 (*PAH*, V, 255–61); the Electors of Queens County to H, February 19, 1789 (*PAH*, V, 261–62).
    2. Queens and Suffolk counties.

Conveyance to George Anthon [1]

New York, April 25, 1789. Conveys to Anthon in return for eight hundred pounds "All that certain messuage or dwelling house and lot of Ground situate lying and being in the dock Ward of the City of New York on the Easterly side of a Certain Street there called and known by the name of Broad Street. . . ." [2]

DS, Hamilton Papers, Library of Congress; certified copy, recorded under the date of August 29, 1789, Conveyances in the Office of the Register, City of New York, Liber 45, 501, Hall of Records, New York City.
    1. Anthon was a New York City physician.
    2. The lot that H sold to Anthon adjoined the rear of H's property at 58 Wall Street, which he purchased in 1785. See "Conveyance from James Barclay and Others," September 17, 1785 (printed in this volume).

From George Washington

[New York, June 4, 1789. Letter not found.]

"List of Letters from G—— Washington to General Hamilton," Columbia University Libraries.

From Samuel Jones [1]

[New York, August 5, 1789]

The Duties to be collected are imposed only upon Goods imported into the United States after the first of August.[2] Consequently no Goods imported on or before that Day are charged with those Duties. And I am of Opinion that all such Goods may be carried to and landed at any other Port of the United States Duty free. The Act regulating the Collection of the Duties requires the Master or Person having the Charge or Command of any Ship or Vessel (Ships and Vessels of War excepted) coming into any Port of the United States to make Report, and deliver Manifests of the Loading to the Collector and take an Oath therein prescribed And provides that no Goods shall be unladen without a Permit.[3] These Regulations are necessary to prevent Frauds; And in my Opinion apply as well to Vessels coming from one Port of the United States to another as to Vessels coming from a foreign Port and must be complied with by the master of all Vessels coming into this Port. I think all Goods imported into any of the United States on or before or since the first of august may be carried to any other port in the United States duty free. It may be doubtful what is an Importation, particularly whether a Vessel's going to a Port is an Importation of her Cargoe without entering or landing it But I should suppose that a Clearance from any Port of the United States under the present Regulations would be sufficient Evidence that the Goods cleared out had been imported into such Port.[4]

Samuel Jones
New York 5 August 1789

ADS, Museum of the City of New York; ADfS, Museum of the City of New York.

1. Jones, a prominent lawyer of Queens County, New York, was a member of the New York Assembly from 1786 to 1790. A member of the New York Ratifying Convention in 1788, he was one of the few prominent Loyalists among the Antifederalists and one of the first Antifederalists at the Convention to support the Constitution. Occasionally H asked Jones for his interpretation of Federal legislation. See H to Jones, September, 1789 (printed in this volume); Jones to H, October 4, 1789 (printed in this volume); H to Richard Harison, November 9, 1789 (*PAH*, V, 504–06); Harison and Jones to H, November 18, 1789 (*PAH*, V, 521–22).

2. For the duties laid on imports after August 1, 1789, see Sections 1 and 2 of "An Act for laying a Duty on Goods, Wares and Merchandises imported into the United States" (1 *Stat.* 24–27 [July 4, 1789]).

3. See Sections 11 and 12 of "An Act to regulate the Collection of the Duties imposed by law on the tonnage of ships or vessels, and on goods, wares and merchandises imported into the United States" (1 *Stat.* 29–49 [July 31, 1789]).

4. Jones wrote the draft of this document on the back of a draft of a bond which the Collection Law required to be posted against the payment of import duties. See Sections 19, 20, and 21 of "An Act to regulate the Collection of Duties imposed by law on the tonnage of ships or vessels, and on goods, wares and merchandises imported into the United States" (1 *Stat.* 29–49).

The draft of the bond reads: "Know all Men by these Presents that WE of the City of Newyork are held and fairly bound unto the United States of America in Dollars to be paid to the Said United States For Payt. whereof WE do bind ourselves our Heirs and Executors and Administrators jointly and severally firmly by these Presents—Sealed with our Seals—Dated this day of in the Year .

"The Condition of this Obligation is such that if the above bounden or either of them or either of their Heirs Executors or Administrators shall and do on or before the day of next well and truly pay or cause to be paid unto John Lamb Collector for the District of the City of New York or to the Collector of the said District for the Time being Dollars being the Amount of Duties on certain Goods Wares and Merchandise imported in the then the above Obligation to be paid otherwise to be and remain in full Force and Virtue." (Df, Museum of the City of New York.)

Lamb was nominated collector of customs for New York on August 3, 1789, and the Senate approved the nomination on the same day (*Executive Journal*, I, 10, 12). Before his appointment Lamb had held the same position under the state government.

Appointment as Secretary of the Treasury [1]

[New York, September 11, 1789]

Know Ye, that reposing special Trust and Confidence in the Patriotism, Integrity, and Abilities of Alexander Hamilton of the City of New York in the State of New York, Esquire, I have nominated, and by and with the Advice and Consent of the Senate, do appoint him Secretary of the Treasury of the said United States, and do authorize and empower him to execute and fulfil the Duties of that Office according to Law; and to have and to hold the said Office, with all the Powers, Privileges, and Emoluments to the same of Right appertaining, during the Pleasure of the President of the United States for the Time being. In Testimony whereof I have caused these Letters to be made patent, and the Seal of the United States to be hereunto affixed. Given under my Hand at the City of New York the eleventh Day of September in the Year of our Lord one thousand seven hundred and Eighty-nine.

Go: Washington

LS, Hamilton Papers, Library of Congress.
   1. See "Alexander Hamilton's Nomination by George Washington for the Office of Secretary of the Treasury of the United States," September 11, 1789 (PAH, V, 365–66).

To Sharp Delany [1]

Treasury Office
New York September 13th. 1789.

Sir

   Mr. Duer my assistant goes to Philadelphia to transact some business with the bank there in which your co-operation will probably be wanted.[2] He will give you the necessary explanations; and I doubt not will have your acquiescence in whatever may be requisite to complete his arrangments. The other principal Officers of the Department not being on the spot some informality may be unavoidable. But the necessity will justify it; and as soon as the Comptroller [3] and Treasurer [4] arrive, things will be put in their proper train.

   I am, Sir   Your obedient servant   Alexander Hamilton
                                              Secretary of the Treasury

Sharpe Delaney Esq.

LS, The Sol Feinstone Collection, Library of the American Philosophical Society, Philadelphia.
   1. Delany was collector of customs at Philadelphia.

In *PAH*, V, 369, this letter is listed as a "letter not found."

2. William Duer, a financier and merchant who came to America from England and the British West Indies in 1773, was a member of the Continental Congress from 1777 to 1779 and was also on the Board of War. He held some of the largest contracts from Congress for supplying the Army during the American Revolution. In 1784 he helped to found the Bank of New York, and in 1786 he was appointed secretary of the Board of the Treasury. In 1786 he represented New York City in the New York Assembly. In September, 1789, he became Assistant to the Secretary of the Treasury.

For Duer's "transactions" in Philadelphia, see H to Thomas Willing, September 13, 1789; Willing to H, October 1, 1789 (*PAH*, V, 370-71, 416-19).

3. Nicholas Eveleigh of South Carolina, who had served in the American Revolution as deputy adjutant general for South Carolina and Georgia during the American Revolution, was a member of the South Carolina House of Representatives in 1781 and the Continental Congress in 1781 and 1782. On September 11, 1789, he was appointed comptroller.

4. Samuel Meredith of Pennsylvania, a brigadier general of the Pennsylvania militia during the American Revolution, was a member of the Continental Congress from 1786 to 1788 and surveyor of the port of Philadelphia from August, 1789, to September 11, 1789, when he resigned to become Treasurer of the United States.

See H to Meredith, September 13, 1789 (*PAH*, V, 369).

To John B. Church

[*New York, September 28, 1789.* On November 4, 1789, John Rutledge, Jr., wrote to William Short [1]: "Church read me a letter from Hamilton dated the 28th of Septr—he says 'Mr Jay [2] is appointed chief Justice, Mr Osgood [3] Post Master—Wilson [4] one of the 5 circuit Judges & Mr Jefferson [5] will have offered him the foreign department.' " *Letter not found.*]

1. ALS, William Short Papers, Library of Congress.

Rutledge, a lawyer from Charleston, South Carolina, was governor of South Carolina from 1779 to 1782 and a delegate to the Continental Congress in 1782 and 1783. In 1784 he was elected as a judge of the Chancery Court of the state, and from 1784 to 1790 he was a member of the South Carolina House of Representatives.

While Jefferson was in France, Short, a resident of Virginia, served as his private secretary and secretary of the legation from 1785 to 1789, when Jefferson returned to America and Short became chargé d'affaires at Paris.

2. After the Definitive Treaty of Peace was signed at Paris in September, 1783, John Jay returned to the United States and in 1784 became Secretary for Foreign Affairs. On September 24, 1789, George Washington nominated him as Chief Justice of the United States. Jay served as Secretary of State *ad interim* under the new constitution until March 22, 1790, when Jefferson assumed the office.

3. Samuel Osgood of Massachusetts, a veteran of the American Revolution

and a member of the Continental Congress from 1781 to 1784, was appointed one of three commissioners of the Treasury on January 25, 1785. On September 26, 1789, he was appointed Postmaster General.

4. James Wilson, a native of Scotland and a lawyer in Philadelphia, was a member of the Continental Congress from 1775 to 1777 and from 1785 to 1787. On September 29, 1789, the Senate approved his nomination as associate justice of the Supreme Court of the United States.

5. Jefferson was appointed Secretary of State on September 25, 1789.

To Samuel Jones [1]

[New York, September, 1789]

I   Are the duties recoverable on goods imported between the first of August and the time the custom house was organised in a state recoverable?

II May vessels arriving in any port leave that port without paying or securing the duties prior to the expiration of 48 hours and go *where they please* or not?

III May they only go prior to the same period to another state?

IV May they after that period go to another state? If in any case must it appear that they were *originally bound* to that other state or not.

V   Can a vessel go from one district to another in the same state before or after the 48 hours without paying or securing the duties in the first district?

AD, Museum of the City of New York.

1. H's questions concern the interpretation of the provisions of "An Act to regulate the Collection of Duties imposed by law on the tonnage of ships or vessels, and on goods, wares and merchandises imported into the United States" (1 *Stat.* 29–49 [July 31, 1789]) and "An Act for Registering and Clearing Vessels, Regulating the Coasting Trade, and for other purposes" (1 *Stat.* 55–65 [September 1, 1789]).

From Samuel Jones [1]

[New York, October 4, 1789]

Answer,

I am of Opinion that the Duties upon Goods imported into any District after the first Day of August and before a Custom House was established and organized in such District are recoverable by Action of Debt in the Name or by Information on Behalf of the United States against the Importers.

The Acts for Collection of the Duties and regulating the coasting Trade suppose and some of their Provisions clearly imply that the Duties are to be paid at the Port of Entry in the District where the Goods first Arrive. I think the Duties become due upon the Importation of Goods And that the Master of every Vessel coming into any Port of the United States is bound to make a Report and Entry within 48 Hours after his arrival And that the Vessel has not a Right either before or after the Expiration of that Time to leave the Port and go to any foreign Port or to another State or to another District in the same State without paying or securing the Duties unless the Port at which such Vessel arrives is not the Port to which She was bound and She is compelled to come into such Port by Distress of Weather or other sufficient Cause.

Samuel Jones
New York
4 October 1789

ADS, Museum of the City of New York.
  1. The first part of this document has not been printed because it contains the same questions which H had asked in H to Jones, September, 1789 (printed in this volume).

From Jedediah Huntington [1]

Custom House N London [Connecticut]
7 Octor. 1789

Sir

I have this day the Honour of receiving your Letter of the 1st.[2] inst. Upon my entering into Office I found the Light house at this Port furnished with Oil for three or four days only and no Provision made for further Supply. I immediately purchased a little for temporary use and have since laid in a Stock for the Winter. The Light House is built of Stone & the walls are good but the Roof was very leaky and that & the inner work in a ruinous Condition. I therefore thought it prudent to have a thorough Repair of the Roof which will be completed as soon as I can procure some more Sheet Lead. The Lamps requires abt. Eight hundred Gallons of Oil in a year which costs abt. three hundred Dollars & 50 dols the hire of a Man to tend the Lamps & contingent Expences arise to abt. 100 dollars yearly. The Superintendance of the whole was under the State Naval Officer. I am willing to take the Charge of it for the present. Sir

I remain most respectfully   your obedt. Servant   J H

The Genl. Assembly of this state last May ordered some Buoys to be fixed in the Harbour[3] but nothing has been done in Consequence of their Act although the Merchants are very anxious that it should be complied with.

ADfS, New London Customs House Records, Federal Records Center, Boston.
    1. Huntington, a veteran of the American Revolution, was collector of customs at New London, Connecticut.
    2. "Treasury Department Circular to the Collectors of the Customs," October 1, 1789 (*PAH*, V, 415–16).
    3. The resolution of the Connecticut General Assembly reads: "*Resolved by this Assembly* that the Naval Officer for the Port of New London be and he is thereby authorized and directed to fix Buoys on the Rocks or Ledges called Black Ledge and Race Rock and on the South East Point of the Reef called Goshen Reef on the Sound off against the Port of New London, and cause the same to be kept in proper Condition and Repair from Time to Time, the expence to be paid out of the Monies appropriated for support of the Light House near the Port of New London" (Leonard Woods Labaree, comp., *The Public Records of the State of Connecticut from May 1789 through October 1792* [Hartford, 1948], 54–55).

To Jeremiah Wadsworth [1]

[New York, October 9–15, 1789]

Col Hamilton requests Col Wadsworth as often as convenient to make inquiry and take minutes of the circumstances relating to the navigation of different nations—the construction and quality of their ships with respect to bulk duration and expedition—the expence of materials construction & equipment—the number of men with which they are navigated—the wages to the seamen, subsistence &c., so as to form a general idea of the comparitive advantages for navigation between this and other countries.

AH

ALS, Connecticut Historical Society, Hartford.
   1. Although this letter is undated, H wrote similar letters to Stephen Higginson on October 9, 1789, and to William Bingham and to John Fitzgerald on October 10, 1789 (*PAH*, V, 432, 432–33, 433, 466–71). See also "Treasury Department Circular to the Collectors of the Customs," October 15, 1789 (*PAH*, V, 446–47).

To Jedediah Huntington [1]

[*New York, October 11, 1789.* Letter listed in dealer's catalogue. *Letter not found.*]

   1. LS, sold by John Heise, Syracuse, New York, 1923, Catalogue 2531, Item 62.

To Sharp Delany [1]

Treasury Department
October 17th 1789

Sir

   As some of the Circular Letters to the Collectors of the Different Ports containing an Instruction to receive Notes of the Bank of New York, as well as of that of North America [2]—may have been sent to you among others, either through hurry, or from its having been blended with other matters which were equally applicable to you—You will be pleased to understand that so much of any such instruction as relates to the Notes of New York is inapplicable to you, being inconsistent with the arrangements taken with the Bank of North America.[3]

   I am   Sir   Your Obedient Servant   A Hamilton
                                                Secy of the Treasury

Sharp Delany Esquire
Collector of the Customs
For Philadelphia

LS, Mr. Pierce Gaines, Fairfield, Connecticut.
   1. This letter is referred to in Delany to H, October 16–31, 1789, note 3

(*PAH*, V, 448), where it is erroneously stated that Delany was mistaken concerning its date.

2. "Treasury Department Circular to the Collectors of the Customs," September 22, October 14, 1789 (*PAH*, V, 394–95, 444–46).

3. This is a reference to the articles of agreement between William Duer, Assistant to the Secretary of the Treasury, and the Bank of North America for a loan of fifty thousand dollars. See H to Thomas Willing, September 13, 1789 (*PAH*, V, 370–71); Willing to H, October 1, 1789 (*PAH*, V, 416–19); H to Delany, September 13, 1789 (printed in this volume).

From Jedediah Huntington

New London [*Connecticut*] *October 29, 1789*. "Having just returned from the Genl Assembly of this state where a public Engagement called me & the post going out I have only to acknowledge the Honour of your several Communications. . . ." [1]

ALS, New London Customs House Records, Federal Records Center, Boston.

1. On October 7, 1789, in a letter printed in this volume, Huntington acknowledged receipt of H's "Treasury Department Circular to the Collectors of the Customs," October 1, 1789 (*PAH*, V, 415–16). H's subsequent circulars to the collectors of customs are dated October 2, 3, 6, 10, 12, 14, 15, 20 (*PAH*, V, 419–21, 422, 427, 434–35, 440–441, 444–46, 446–47, 454–56).

From Oliver Wolcott, Junior [1]

[*New York, October, 1789.*] Sends [2] "Estimate of Debts contracted by the State of Connecticut during the late War and remaining unpaid September 1, 1789."

Copy, Connecticut Historical Society, Hartford.

1. Wolcott was the son of Oliver Wolcott, Connecticut jurist and governor. Wolcott, who served during the American Revolution in the quartermaster department, was admitted to the bar in 1781, and in 1788 was appointed comptroller of public accounts in Connecticut. He was appointed auditor of the Treasury Department on September 12, 1789.

This document is similar to, and formed the basis for, H's statement on Connecticut in Schedule E ("Abstract of the Public Debt of the States . . .") in his "Report Relative to a Provision for the Support of Public Credit," January 9, 1790 (*PAH*, VI, 120–21).

2. The covering letter has not been found, but Wolcott endorsed this docu-

ment: "Estimate of the Debt of Connecticut sent to the Honble. Alnr Hamilton Oct. 1789."

To Otho H. Williams

Treasury Department Nov. 7th. 1789.

Sir,

Your letters of the 26th and 29th. of October have duly come to hand.

The difficulties you state as arising from some provisions (and the want of others) in the laws of Impost and Tonnage [1] are doubtless well founded, and indicate the propriety of some future correction of the System. With regard to the method of keeping accounts, by the establishment of the Treasury Department, the Forms are first to be prepared and reported by the Comptroller, and afterwards decided upon by the Secretary of the Treasury.[2] The absence of the Comptroller,[3] who is not yet arrived has of course retarded the business; but the Auditor [4] and the Chief Clerk [5] of the Comptroller are now engaged in it. I have submitted to them your plan, and the reasons for it, which appear to me to deserve attention. The forms as decided upon by me, will ere long be transmitted.

You will have found by my Circular of the 20th. ultimo,[6] that my opinion of the Construction of the Tonnage Act agrees with that which governed you in the case of the *Polly*.[7] I am not sure that the law will not in this respect require relaxation; but this must be matter of future regulation by the Legislature.

The oath prescribed by the sixth Section of the Act for register-ing &c. must of course be your guide in respect to the Brig Sarah.[8] Unless that oath be taken, she cannot be registered; and unless registered she can only be considered as a foreign Vessel, and must enter and clear as such. The oath requires some alteration, but this also must be the subject of legislative regulation.

The hurry of Business has prevented my sooner thanking you for having found means to take up the Treasurer's drafts; though not in Cash for that purpose.[9] Your attention to the advancement of the public service on this occasion merits acknowledgement: Though it was not my intention that such a necessity should have existed, and I shall take care that it be avoided in future.

I am, Sir   Your Obedient Servant   Alexander Hamilton
                                                       Secy of the Treasury

Otho H. Williams Esqr.
Collector of the Customs for the Port of Baltimore

LS, The Sol Feinstone Collection, Library of the American Philosophical Society, Philadelphia.
1. "An Act to regulate the Collection of the Duties imposed by law on the tonnage of ships or vessels, and on goods, wares and merchandises imported into the United States" (1 *Stat.* 29–49 [July 31, 1789]) and "An Act imposing Duties on Tonnage" (1 *Stat.* 27–28 [July 20, 1789]).
2. See Section 3 of "An Act to establish the Treasury Department" (1 *Stat.* 65–67 [September 2, 1789]).
3. Nicholas Eveleigh.
4. Oliver Wolcott, Jr.
5. Henry Kuhl.
6. "Treasury Department Circular to the Collectors of the Customs," October 20, 1789 (*PAH*, V, 54–56).
7. In Williams to H, October 29, 1789, which is calendared in *PAH*, V, 477, Williams wrote: "The Ship Polly, a British Vessel . . . was cleared at Philadelphia on the Ninth Instant 'for amsterdam, *to touch at Baltimore*' and arrived here the 15th. . . . As I know of no Authority which the Officers of one District have to privilege Vessels to touch at another in the United States I thought it my duty to demand The tonnage agreeably to the third section of the Act imposing a duty on tonnage. This demand has incurred some displeasure against this office as being more rigid than another, for the Master was fortified with opinions of Gentlemen . . . that I would have no right to receive the tonnage here if he produced a Certificate of its having been paid in Philadelphia. . . ."
For the text of Section 3 of "An Act imposing Duties on Tonnage" (1 *Stat.* 27–28 [July 20, 1789]), see Sharp Delany to H, February 8, 1790, note 5 (*PAH*, VI, 250).
8. "An Act for Registering and Clearing Vessels, Regulating the Coasting Trade, and for other purposes" (1 *Stat.* 55–65 [September 1, 1789]).
In Williams to H, October 29, 1789, which is calendared in *PAH*, V, 477, Williams wrote: ". . . a Citizen of the United States went down the Mississippi to New Orleans where he purchased the Brig Sarah . . . which he was informed was built in Virginia about five or six Years ago. . . . this Vessel . . . Sailed for the United States and arrived here the 21st. Instant without Register Clearances or any other papers. The Master & owner both say the Officer of the Spanish Port would not grant them any thing but a permit to pass the Bellize or out port. . . .
"The Law for Registering &c Sec 6 requires that one of the Owners shall swear or affirm where the Vessel was built. . . . The Owner of the Sarah is a consciencious man, and cannot swear Where she was built. . . . I request to know if he can be permitted to Enter, and *Clear* without a Register . . . ?"
9. See Williams to H, October 23, 1789 (*PAH*, V, 459–60).

From Charles Lee [1]

Alexandria [Virginia] 21st. November 1789.

Sir

Upon the River Powtomack there are five Collectorships, two in Maryland and three in Virginia.[2] I will forbear to give my opinion till more mature consideration, what alterations ought to be made, but, at present I can venture to say that they are not all necessary, either for mercantile convenience, or for the better collection of the revenue. The distance from Georgetown to Alexandria is seven miles and from Alexandria to Dumfries twenty five miles. The trade of the Powtomack being dispersed and not brought to a point does not appear to a stranger to be so considerable as it really is, and especially the exports are immensely great. From the highest tide water which is about twelve miles from this Town to the mouth of the river 160 miles from thence to the Capes is   [3] miles from the highest tide water to Fort Cumberland (which is expected to be made navigable for boats and the work is already considerably advanced and in a probable way of success) is   [4] miles. The extensive country through which this river passes is remarkably fertile and well inhabited with industrious and healthy people. The trade of the Powtomack is considerable now—at this moment there are 40 sea vessels at this Town and what is very pleasing it is daily increasing. I observe by the Judiciary establishments that the State of Virginia is made a district whereby this river is a boundary, and its inhabitants are remote from the places of holding the Courts and from the Officers of such Courts.[5] This

Copy, RG 56, Letters to and from the Collector at Alexandria, National Archives.

1. Lee was appointed collector of customs for the port of Alexandria in August, 1789.
Lee wrote this letter in reply to "Treasury Department Circular to the Collectors of the Customs," October 2, 1789 (*PAH*, V, 419–21).
2. The two collectorships on the Potomac in Maryland were Nanjemoy and Georgetown. The three in Virginia were Yeocomico, Dumfries, and Alexandria.
3. Space left blank in MS.
4. Space left blank in MS.
5. Section 2 of "An Act to establish the Judicial Courts of the United States" reads in part: "That the United States shall be, and they hereby are divided

will be found very inconvenient to the Revenue Officers in cases of seizure as well as to the Merchants. To send 100 miles or perhaps 150 miles in all cases for the process of the Court and to the officers of the court will be very expensive and tedious for though the district Judge may hold a Court for some purposes whenever he shall please [6] yet the inconveniences in the first instance will not be removed. While Virginia remains a district some parts of it will be subject to great expenses and inconveniences and as I conceive it to be too large for a speedy and energetic execution of the continental laws, it ought to be otherwise modified from what it is now. As to the Powtomack Country an agreeable form at once offers itself for a district and the other part of Virginia will be as large as a district should be. Let the western shore of Maryland and the northern neck of Virginia make a district: the law of the revenue might then be executed with certainty dispatch and convenience and unless this should be done I fear many offences will probably pass un-prosecuted and unpunished on account of the trouble and expense which will arise to prosecutors and witnesses. Some time ago I had occasion to seize a cask of wine of mean quality it happened to be and not of the value of fifty dollars. The owner was content that the same should be forfeited, and therefore by his consent it may per-haps be sold as condemned goods. To have prosecuted for this under the present system, would have cost more than the wine would sell for. This also may serve to show that though a district court be appointed for the Country on the Potowmack which is almost the unanimous wish of its inhabitants there should be some tribunal more convenient than a district court to try seizures under

---

into thirteen districts, to be limited and called as follows . . . one to consist of the State of Virginia, except that part called the District of Kentucky, and to be called Virginia District" (1 *Stat.* 73 [September 24, 1789]). Section 5 of the same act reads in part: ". . . And the sessions of the said circuit court shall be held . . . in the district of Virginia, alternately at Charlottesville and Wil-liamsburgh . . ." (1 *Stat.* 75).

6. Section 3 of "An Act to establish the Judicial Courts of the United States" reads in part: "That there be a court called a District Court, in each of the afore mentioned districts, to consist of one judge. . . . That the stated District Court shall be held . . . in the district of Virginia, alternately at Richmond and Williamsburgh . . . and that the special courts shall be held at the same place in each district as the stated courts, or in districts that have two, at either of them, in the discretion of the judge, or at such other place in the district, as the nature of the business and his discretion shall direct" (1 *Stat.* 73–74).

the value of a certain sum for instance 200 dollars. The district I
am suggesting is larger than the State of Maryland, and the eastern
shore of Maryland might be united (as indeed it is by nature) to
Delaware State—such a modification in this as well as other
instances would tend to confirm and consolidate the powers of the
present government of the United States. Under the state laws the
bonded duties were recoverable in a summary way in our courts,
viz: on ten days notice and motion.[7] By the act of congress it seems
they are to be sued for in the ordinary and tardy forms of law
which is a mode of recovery that will be unseasonable some time
hence I apprehend.[8] I have been at a loss in what manner the Bonds
were to be made payable and I now enclose a copy of the form
used in my Office which appeared to me to be the most proper. I
have not allowed any discount on the bonded duties and shall act
according to your letter on this subject.[9] Under the State regulations there were two sloops employed concerning the revenue
which were armed with a few small cannon and swivels and manned
with a few Marines, they drew a small depth of water being intended to penetrate as high as possible up all our tide waters and

7. Section 15 of "An Act to amend and reduce the several Acts of Assembly
for ascertaining certain taxes and duties, and for establishing a permanent
revenue, into one Act" reads in part: "*And be it further enacted*, That it shall
and may be lawful to and for the said Collectors and Clerks to recover the
said duties so bonded by motion made in the General Court, or the County
Court wherein the principal or either of his securities respectively reside, and
such Court shall give judgment for the sum due on such bonds, with costs and
interest of five per centum on the same, until paid. Provided always ten days
previous notice in writing shall be given by such Collector or Clerk, to the
person or persons so to be moved against" (*Virginia Laws*, October, 1782, Sess.,
Ch. CIII).

8. Section 19 of "An Act to regulate the Collection of Duties imposed by
law on the tonnage of ships or vessels, and on goods, wares and merchandises
imported into the United States" reads in part: "That all duties on goods,
wares and merchandise, imported, shall be paid by the importer, before a permit shall be granted for landing the same, unless the amount of such duties
shall exceed fifty dollars, in which case it shall be at the option of the party
making entry, to secure the same by bond . . ." (1 *Stat.* 42 [July 31, 1789]).
Section 21 of the same act reads: "That where any bond for the payment of
the duties shall not be satisfied on the day it become due, the collector shall
prosecute for the recovery of the money due thereon, by action or suit at law,
in the proper court, having cognizance therein; and in all cases of insolvency,
or where any estate in the hands of executors or administrators shall be insufficient to pay all the debts due from the deceased, the debt due to the United
States on any such bonds shall be first satisfied" (1 *Stat.* 42).

9. See "Treasury Department Circular to the Collectors of the Customs,"
October 6, 1789 (*PAH*, V, 427).

were under the direction of the executive who occasionally sent them whenever it might be required and generally employed them in the Bay and at the mouths of the great rivers. I think the expense of these vessels, was about six thousand dollars annually and I am of opinion that such an establishment would be of use in preventing frauds that I fear will otherwise be attempted some time hence upon the revenue when the Bonds shall be coming due. The masters of these vessels were in duty bound to examine such vessels as they met with and to know whether the laws had been complied with by inspecting the papers on board each vessel: three vessels would be sufficient for Maryland and Virginia, whether the vessels belonging to Virginia have been sold or not I am not sure but I believe they have been sold. At this port there was in use under that state laws a small row boat for the purpose of boarding vessels which I think is necessary in order that upon an emergency the public officers may not be dependent on the courtesy of others, this boat cost one hundred dollars and one person was hired to take care of her and was paid by the public Officer. As the public revenue hath not yet needed a boat the business having been conducted without much difficulty or embarrassment I have not applied for it, and shall wait your orders as to purchasing any boat of this kind. The 16th section of the act to regulate the collection of the duties [10] &c which obliges all vessels to stop at the mouth of our river viz: at St Mary's or Yeocomico excited a general uneasiness and complaint among the merchants and others on the Patowmack. The regulations was conceived to have a most injurious effect in diverting foreign commerce to Baltimore or Norfolk, where it might freely go without any similar interruption. The regulation was thought useless and unnecessary with respect to protecting the public revenue from fraud

10. Lee is mistaken; he is referring to Section 4 of "An Act to regulate the Collection of the Duties imposed by law on the tonnage of ships and vessels, and on goods, wares and merchandises imported into the United States," which reads in part: "That the master or commander of every ship or vessel . . . if bound to any district on the Potomac, shall, before he pass by the rivers St. Mary's and Yeocomico, and immediately after his arrival, deposit with the surveyor at St. Mary's, or the collector at Yeocomico, as may be most convenient, a true manifest of the cargo on board such ship or vessel, including a declaration of the port at which the same is to be entered; . . . and the said surveyor and collector respectively, shall, after registering the manifests, transmit the same duly certified to have been so deposited to the officer with whom the entries are to be made, without which certificate no such entry shall be received" (1 *Stat.* 36).

or evasion of the laws. It was thought oppressive and detrimental to the merchants, as it would create delay and expense to their vessels in their voyages as it would expose their ships in time of bad weather to danger, as in case of a mistake in the master it would be very troublesome, embarrassing and tedious to rectify the same in consequence of the great distance from their residence to the mouth of the river; for no entry can be made but exactly according to the certified manifest. It was moreover thought partial as a similar regulation was not made as to other parts of America to which with equal reason it might have been applied for example the river Delaware, and to many it appeared unaccountable as the Virginia representatives well knew that a regulation somewhat like it had been made by one assembly and repealed by the next after a trial and conviction of its impropriety impolicy and injustice.[11] These sentiments produced a memorial from the people of the Patomack [12] to the Congress who suspended this obnoxious regulation till May next [13] but they still hope it will be repealed at the next session as

11. Section XVII of "An Act to amend the several acts of Assembly concerning NAVAL OFFICERS, and the collection of the DUTIES" reads in part: "BE it enacted, That no goods, wares, or merchandises, of greater value than ten pounds, shall be waterborne in any one vessel at one time from any port or place, to another port or place within the said district of South Potowmack and river Pocomoke, unless it shall be certified under the hand and seal of the Naval Officer of the district, or of a Searcher, or some justice of the peace within the same, that he has sufficient reason to believe that the duties have been paid or secured to be paid thereon . . ." (*Virginia Laws*, October, 1786, Sess., Ch. XL). This provision was repealed by Section LXII of "An Act to amend the several Acts of Assembly concerning Naval Officers, and the Collection of the Duties," which reads: "THE act intituled 'An act to amend the several acts of Assembly concerning naval officers and the collection of the duties,' except the twenty-fourth, twenty-fifth, twenty-sixth, twenty-seventh, twenty-eighth, twenty-ninth, and thirty-second clauses thereof concerning importation of goods by land, and all other acts coming within the purview of this act, except the act, intituled, 'An act to impose certain duties,' shall be, and they are hereby repealed" (*Virginia Laws*, October, 1787, Sess., Ch. IV [January 7, 1788]).

12. On August 22, 1789, a "memorial of the merchants and other inhabitants" of the Virginia towns of Alexandria and Dumfries was presented to the House of Representatives "praying that so much of the act of Congress to regulate the collection of duties, as restricts ships or vessels bound up the river Potomac to stop at Saint Mary's or Yeocomico, and there obtain a certified manifest of their cargoes before entry made, be repealed, or that the like regulation may be made general throughout the United States." A similar memorial was submitted to the House by Maryland merchants from Georgetown, Bladensburgh, and Piscataway on August 24 (*Journal of the House*, I, 89, 90, 91, 92, 110).

13. Section 1 of "An Act to suspend part of an Act, intituled 'An Act to regulate the collection of the Duties imposed by Law on the Tonnage of Ships or Vessels, and on Goods, Wares and Merchandises, imported into the United

in their opinion it will produce the most ruinous consequences to their commerce. For my own part I have no difficulty in declaring that this regulation appears to me to be useless as to the public revenue oppressive as it respects the merchants and in itself unjust and offensive for its partiality. The allowances of drawbacks under any terms is objectionable as it will tend to introduce confusion in the Custom House books than which nothing ought to be more plain and correct.[14] I will only observe at present that the term of twelve months is unreasonably long for the exportation of duried goods. Under the State laws only three months was allowed.[15] It is thought by some uncertain what fees are due in some cases to the surveyor and in this respect a collector is placed in a most disagreable situation. On the one hand he is liable to public censure or perhaps to individual loss or punishment if he demands and receives for the surveyor any fees not lawfully due and on the other hand he is liable to a suit from the Surveyor if he omits to receive all that is due. I own if the surveyors fees were ever so explicitly ascertained, I should feel it the most irksome part of my duty to be his cashier

---

States,' and for other purposes" reads: "That so much of the act, intituled 'An act to regulate the collection of the duties imposed by law, on the tonnage of ships or vessels, and on goods, wares, and merchandises, imported into the United States,' as obliges ships or vessels bound up the river Potomac, to come to and deposit manifests of their cargoes, with the officers at St. Mary's and Yeocomico, before they proceed to their port of delivery, shall be and is hereby suspended until the first day of May next" (1 *Stat.* 69 [September 16, 1789]).

14. Section 3 of "An Act for laying a Duty on Goods, Wares and Merchandises imported into the United States" reads: "That all the duties paid, or secured to be paid upon any of the goods, wares and merchandises as aforesaid, except on distilled spirits, other than brandy and geneva, shall be returned or discharged upon such of the said goods, wares, or merchandises, as shall within twelve months after payment made, or security given, be exported to any country without the limits of the United States, as settled by the late treaty of peace; except one per centum on the amount of the said duties, in consideration of the expense which shall have accrued by the entry and safe-keeping thereof" (1 *Stat.* 26–27 [July 4, 1789]).

15. Section LX of "An Act to amend the several Acts of Assembly concerning Naval Officers, and the Collection of the Duties" reads in part: "DRAWBACKS shall be under the limitations and restrictions herein after mentioned: No drawbacks shall be allowed for any merchandise liable to duty, exported out of this state, unless exported within ninety days after importation thereof by the original importer, and by water, and unless exported in the original cask or package in which they were imported unbroken, and in vessels belonging to a citizen or citizens of the United States, or in the vessel in which they were originally imported . . ." (*Virginia Laws*, October, 1787, Sess., Ch. IV [January 7, 1788]).

and clerk and therefore wish that the law could be so altered as to make the Surveyor his own receiver subject in cases of difference with the masters of vessels to the direction of the Collector. I have no difficulty with respect to the fees due to a collector, they being plainly expressed: [16] But the Surveyor [17] of my district conceives and others think with him, that every Licensed Vessel [18] coming from one district into another should pay a fee of two thirds of a dollar to the Surveyor [19] and also all fees under the coasting law: [20]

16. Section 29 of "An Act to regulate the Collection of the Duties imposed by law on the tonnage of ships or vessels, and on goods, wares and merchandises imported into the United States" (1 *Stat.* 44–45) provided that all fees due to the surveyor were to be paid to the collector by the master or owner of the ship and that the collector was to pay the surveyor weekly.

17. Samuel Hanson.

18. For the regulations concerning the licensing of vessels engaged in trade along the coast of the United States, see "An Act for Registering and Clearing Vessels, Regulating the Coasting Trade, and for other purposes" (1 *Stat.* 55–65 [September 1, 1789]).

19. Section 29 of "An Act to regulate the Collection of the Duties imposed by law on the tonnage of ships or vessels, and on goods, wares, and merchandises" (1 *Stat.* 44–45) provided that the surveyor was entitled to two-thirds of a dollar "on all vessels not having on board goods, wares and merchandise, subject to duty. . . ."

20. Section 31 of "An Act for Registering and Clearing Vessels, Regulating the Coasting Trade, and for other purposes" reads: "That the fees and allowances for the several duties to be performed in virtue of this act, and the distribution of the same, shall be as follows, to wit:

"For the first register or certificate of record granted for every ship or vessel, there shall be paid to the collector granting the same, the sum of two dollars.

"For every subsequent one, one dollar and fifty cents.

"For every certificate of enrolment, fifty cents.

"For every license to trade between the different districts of the United States, or to carry on the bank or whale fishery for one year, fifty cents.

"For every entry of inward cargo directed to be made in conformity with this act, and for receiving of, and qualifying to every manifest of vessels licensed to trade as aforesaid, sixty cents.

"For a permit to land goods of foreign growth or manufacture, twenty cents.

"For every permit to proceed to the place of destination, twenty-five cents.

"And for taking every bond required by this act, twenty cents.

"The whole amount of which fees shall be accounted for by the collector, and where there is a collector, naval officer and surveyor, shall be equally divided between the said officers, and where there is no naval officer, between the collector and surveyor, and where there is more than one surveyor in any district, each of them shall receive his proportionable part of such fees as shall arise in the port for which he is appointed. *Provided always,* That in all cases where the tonnage of any ship or vessel shall be ascertained by any person specially appointed for that purpose, as is herein before directed, that such person shall be allowed and paid by the collector a reasonable compensation for the same, out of the fees aforesaid, before any distribution thereof as aforesaid." (1 *Stat.* 64.)

my opinion is that a Licensed Vessel ought not to pay any fees excepting directed by the coasting law. The fee of two thirds of a dollar claimed by the Surveyor is under the collection law which I think does not apply to licensed Vessels. I am uneasy that the Surveyor here may possibly be losing any thing to which the law entitles him and there being no counsel for the United States to whom I could apply to with propriety on this subject I have taken the liberty to make this representation hoping that your instruction will settle the doubt. I have been induced to do this also because in a public point of view, it is important that it be universally understood what are the fees of the public Offices that there may be a uniformity. I must beg pardon for this long letter which I fear will be more tiresome than useful and am Sir most respectfully your obedt. servant,   Charles Lee.

To Thomas Smith [1]

Treasury Department
Novr. 21st. 1789

Sir

In Consequence of your Application,[2] I have this day issued a warrant in your Favor on the Treasurer of the United States [3] for 22.250 Dollars in Indents of Interest,[4] which he is directed to forward without Delay.

I am, Sir, Your Obedt. & humble Servt.

A Hamilton
Secy of the Treasury

For Thomas Smith Esqr.
Commr. of the Loan-Office for the State of Pensilvania.

LS, Breckinridge Long Papers, Library of Congress.
   1. For background to this letter, see "Treasury Department Circular to the Continental Loan Officers," October 12, 1789 (PAH, V, 440–41).
   2. Letter not found.
   3. An item in the Blotters of the Office of the Register of the Treasury under the date of November 21, 1789, reads: "Dr. to Samuel Meridith Treasurer of the United States h/a of Interest Indents
   "For the . . . following Warrants drawn by the Secretary of the Treasury

and countersigned by the Comptroller, on said Treasurer in favor of the following Loan Officers for which said Loan officers are accountable and subject to a charge hereafter of such Fractional parts of a Dollar as they may add to said Indents.

"Thomas Smith Commissioner of the Loan Office for the State of Pennsylva h/a of Interest Indents for Warrt. No. 1 in his favor for 22250." (RG 39, Records of the Bureau of Accounts [Treasury], Blotters of the Office of the Register of the Treasury, 1782–1810, National Archives.)

4. For "indents of interest," see Nathaniel Appleton to H, February 5, 1791, note 1 (*PAH*, VIII, 8–9).

To Peyton Short [1]

[*Treasury Department, December 1, 1789.* In his "Memd. Book begun the 6th March 1792," Short stated: "Wrote a Letter [2] in Ansr. to one recd. from the Secy of the Treasy. of the U. S. acquainting him with my resignation & desiring him to acquaint the President therewith, provided he has not recd. my letter to him, to the same effect. The above Letter from the Secy. of the Treasy. dated 'Treasury Departmt. Decr. 1st. 1789.' " [3] *Letter not found.*]

1. Short, the brother of William Short, was collector of customs for Louisville, Virginia. After resigning as collector, Short served in the state Senate from 1792 to 1796.
2. Letter not found.
3. ADS, Short Family Papers, MS Box No. 1, Library of Congress.

From Charles Lee

Alexandria [Virginia] December 24, 1789. ". . . Having sent a copy of your queries [1] to some of the principal merchants in this state, I have the answer of one of them Mr. Alexander Donald of Richmond,[2] this Gentleman formerly and since the American Independence has been extensively engaged in the Commerce of this State, and I take the liberty to enclose his letter as one containing a description of our Trade. . . ."

Copy, RG 56, Letters to and from the Collector at Alexandria, National Archives.

1. See "Treasury Department Circular to the Collectors of the Customs," October 15, 1789 (*PAH*, V, 446–47).

2. Donald, a merchant in Richmond, Virginia, was a close friend of Thomas Jefferson, an agent in Virginia for Robert Morris, and a partner in the London firm of Donald and Burton.

From Charles Lee

Alexandria [Virginia] 30th December 1789

Sir!

I have received your letter of instruction upon the subject of calculating the duties, accompanied with the opinions of counsel concerning the fees under the coasting law.[1] As to the former the practice of my office has corresponded with your directions since the receipt of the form of making quarterly returns.[2] As to the latter the opinion of the learned Counsel agree with my own and according thereto the fees have been demanded except as to the fee for a license to a vessel under twenty tons. The trouble and expense of licensing such a Vessel is the same as of one above that size—and the 31st. section is general in its language not making any discrimination according to the burden of vessels.[3] Besides by an amendatory law made afterwards, the privilege of being exempt from entering and clearing is extended to licensed vessels under fifty tons, having on board only American produce and manufactures[4] by which it would seem that a vessel of forty tons and one of fifty tons were to be in the same predicament if licensed and loaded with American produce or manufactures only. I shall however acquiesce cheerfully in the opinions of those Gentlemen and conform the conduct of my office in this instance to their construction of the law.

I have the honor to be Sir!   Your Obedient Servant

Charles Lee, Collector
at Alexandria

Copy, RG 56, Letters to and from the Collector at Alexandria, National Archives.

1. "Treasury Department Circular to the Collectors of the Customs," November 30, 1789 (*PAH*, V, 575–78).

2. See "Treasury Department Circular to the Collectors of the Customs," October 10, 1789 (*PAH*, V, 434–35).

3. For Section 31 of "An Act for Registering and Clearing Vessels, Regulating the Coasting Trade, and for other purposes" (1 *Stat.* 55–64 [September 1, 1789]), see Lee to H, November 21, 1789, note 20 (printed in this volume).

4. Section 2 of "An Act to explain and amend an Act, intituled 'An Act for registering and clearing Vessels, regulating the Coasting Trade, and for other

purposes'" reads: "That so much of the twenty-second section of the said re-cited act, as exempts vessels of less than twenty, and not less than five tons burthen, employed between any of the districts of the United States, in any bay or river, and having a license from the collector of the district to which such vessel belongs, from entering and clearing for the term of one year, be extended to vessels not exceeding fifty tons: *provided,* such vessels shall not have on board goods, wares or merchandise, other than such as are actually the growth or produce of the United States" (1 *Stat.* 94–95 [September 29, 1789]).

From Charles Lee [1]

Alexandria [Virginia] 31st. December 1789.

Sir!

The people here concerned in trade have been long accustomed to a due execution of Impost laws and have been in the habit of punctuality in payment of their duties so that I hope there will seldom be occasion to apply to legal remedies. Your instruction as expressed in your letter to me of the 18th. Instant shall be duly obeyed.[2] A Vessel which was Registered in Rhode Island in the year 1787 and appears to be the property of two Citizens of that State and one of Virginia claims the benefit of the Act passed the 16th. September 1789,[3] so as to pay only American Tonnage and to have a deduction of ten per cent on the Duties on the Goods, but as the vessel is not the property of Citizens of Rhode Island only, I am at a loss what ought to be done.[4] It has been treated as an American Vessel as to the Tonnage, which I apprehend is an error. There have several instances occurred at this Office which have exposed me to some uneasy sensations as my conduct has appeared rigid, and the Merchants have not been well pleased. I have demanded from an American Vessel lately Registered at New York, and transporting American produce from that District to this without a License, the same Tonnage as a foreign Vessel in such a case is liable to pay, that is to say 50 Cents per Ton. under the 23rd Section of the Coast-ing Law.[5] The New Yorkers particularly think it hard on them, because they come from the Metropolis where the Laws should be best understood, and they were not told at the Custom House there, that a License was necessary, or useful on such a Voyage.

I am, most respectfully Sir! Your most Obedt. Humble Servant.

Charles Lee, Collector
at Alexandria

Copy, RG 56, Letters to and from the Collector at Alexandria, National Archives.

1. In *PAH*, VI, 40, this letter is listed as a "letter not found."

2. "Treasury Department Circular to the Collectors of the Customs," December 18, 1789 (*PAH*, VI, 18–19).

3. Section 2 of "An Act to suspend part of an Act, intituled 'An Act to regulate the collection of the Duties imposed by Law on the Tonnage of Ships or Vessels, and on Goods, Wares, and Merchandises, imported into the United States,' and for other purposes" reads: "That all the privileges and advantages to which ships and vessels owned by citizens of the Untied States, are by law entitled, shall be, until the fifteenth day of January next, extended to ships and vessels wholly owned by citizens of the States of North Carolina, and Rhode Island and Providence Plantations. *Provided,* That the master of every such ship or vessel last mentioned, shall produce a register for the same, conformable to the laws of the state in which it shall have been obtained, showing that the said ship or vessel is, and before the first day of September instant, was owned as aforesaid, and make oath or affirmation, before the collector of the port in which the benefit of this act is claimed, that the ship or vessel for which such register is produced, is the same therein mentioned, and that he believes it is still wholly owned by the person or persons named in said register, and that he or they are citizens of one of the states aforesaid" (1 *Stat.* 69 [September 16, 1789]).

4. For H's answer to Lee's question, see H to Lee, February 12, 1790 (*PAH*, VI, 263).

5. Section 23 of "An Act for Registering and Clearing Vessels, Regulating the Coasting Trade, and for other purposes" reads in part: ". . . and if any vessel of the burthen of twenty tons or upwards, not having a certificate of registry or enrolment, and a license, shall be found trading between different districts, or be employed in the bank or whale fisheries, every such ship or vessel shall be subject to the same tonnage, and fees, as foreign ships or vessels" (1 *Stat.* 61 [September 1, 1789]).

For H's decision concerning unlicensed vessels trading between districts, see "Treasury Department Circular to the Collectors of the Customs," December 23, 1789 (*PAH*, VI, 30–31).

Tax Assessment [1]

New York, 1789. Hamilton's house at 58 Wall Street was assessed at £1,200 and his personal property at £750.[2]

Tax Assessment Record for New York City (Manhattan), Municipal Reference Library, New York City.

1. For background to this document, see "Conveyance from James Barclay and Others," September 17, 1785 (printed in this volume).

2. New York currency.

1790

From Pierpont Edwards [1]

[*New Haven, Connecticut, January 4, 1790.* On January 30, 1790,
Hamilton wrote to Edwards [2] and referred to "your letter of the 4th.
instant." *Letter not found.*]

1. Edwards was United States attorney for the District of Connecticut.
2. Printed in this volume.

To John Holker [1]

[New York, January 8, 1790]

Dr Sir

You will naturally imagine, that as well on public, as personal
accounts, I must be anxious that Mr. Duer should be extricated from
the embarrassments, with which he is perplexed, from the unsettled
state of his affairs.[2] The nature of Our connection will apologise to
you for my interference in a matter, which is purely of private concern between you and him—so far as to express a wish that you
could find means of coming to an amicable settlement. He assures
me that he will do every thing that impartial persons could say he
ought to do to this end. And I feel intire confidence in the sincerity
of a declaration of this sort *made to me.*

I think Sir, on reflection, you will perceive that it must be your
interest to prefer an amicable settlement *with security* for payment
of any ballance which may appear in your favour to a *litigious* one,
without that advantage.

And allow me to add that it would give me real pleasure, could
you see it your interest to embrace the former part of the alternative.

I remain with esteem   Dr Sir   Your Obed sr   A Hamilton

ALS, John Holker Papers, Library of Congress.

1. This letter concerns Holker's efforts to collect the funds owed him from the bankrupt Daniel Parker and Company, with which William Duer was associated. See H to Holker, January 29, 1789 (*PAH*, V, 250); John Ross to H, November 29, 1791 (*PAH*, IX, 544–46); John Murray to H, July 12, 1794 (*PAH*, XVI, 595–96).

2. Duer's financial difficulties arose from his extensive speculations in land and securities. H's "public" and "personal" concern arose from the fact that Duer was Assistant to the Secretary of the Treasury and that he and H were friends.

From Charles Lee

Alexandria [Virginia] 8th. January 1790.

Sir!

I have received your Circular letter of the 23rd December Ultimo.[1] and have the satisfaction to find your opinion on the several points therein stated corresponds with what has already been done in my Office as occasion has required except with regard to Vessels going in Ballast for an outward cargo or to finish her load of an outward Cargo, from one District into another and in such cases I suppose no Tonnage was payable at the last port. This opinion was founded on the Tonnage Act, whereby it was enacted that every foreign Vessel transporting American produce or manufactures coastwise, shall on each entry pay fifty cents, which in my mind implied that such a vessel should not pay fifty cents unless thus employed.[2] I suppose if she were in Ballast or going from one District to another to complete her outward cargo that nothing was demandable at the last port; for if in every case such a vessel was liable to pay 50 cents it was unnecessary for the Legislature to have made provision for a particular case. Herewith I send the weekly and monthly returns in course and by next post will transmit the quarterly returns, which is as soon as I have found it practicable to put the business into the Forms prescribed.

I have the honor to be   Sir! Your most obedt. Servant

Charles Lee, Collector
at Alexandria.

Copy, RG 56, Letters to and from the Collector at Alexandria, National Archives.

1. *PAH*, VI, 30–31.

2. For the text of Section 3 of "An Act imposing Duties on Tonnage" (1 *Stat.* 27–28 [July 20, 1789]), see Sharp Delany to H, February 8, 1790, note 5 (*PAH*, VI, 250).

From William Ellery [1]

Newport R Island Jany. 10 1790

Sir

My last letter to the late Commrs of the Treasury was dated June 9th 1789.[2] to which I received no answer, nor have I received any information from them since the 25th. of May last, and that was in a letter from their Secry.

Not receiving any letter from them after the meeting of Congress under the New-Government; not from you since you was placed at the head of the Treasury, and Congress not having passed any act respecting the Loan-Officers I thought it was my duty to proceed in issuing Indents [3] up to the end of 1787, and I continued to issue them accordingly until the close of the last year.

In December last I was accidentally informed that the Loan-Officer for the State of Massachusetts [4] had received directions from you to cease issuing indents at the end of the last year,[5] and conceiving that there was the same reason for my discontinuing to issue, as for his I stopped at the time before mentioned.

I wrote to him on the subject, and found that my information was good.

The late Board of Treasury in their circular letter of the 14 March 1788 informed me that it would not be necessary to state or transmit my accounts to the Treasury more than once in six months instead of once every quarter.

My accounts for the six months which terminated the last day of last Septemr. are ready for transmissn, and wait only for your direction; and I shall prepare those for the last quarter immediately.

I should be greatly obliged to you if you would issue a warrant for the payment of at least a part of what is due to me. The ballance due to me the first of Jany. current will be about 1500 dolls.

I have suffered exceedingly from the want of punctuality in the payment of my salary &c; [6] but I blame not the late Comms of the Treasury. They knowing my situation and circumstances exerted themselves in my behalf. There was little or no money in the Treasury, and I could receive nothing in the mode prescribed by them for the payment of the Loan-Officers. They were to be paid out of the monies received by them from the States where they officiated. This State has not paid a farthing since I have held the Loan-Office, and of course I have received nothing in this channel. Hence I have suffered, hence the deficiency peculiar to me. Hoping by your attention to be speedily relieved from it, and with sentiments of great respect

I have the honour to be   Sir,   Your most obedt. Servant

William Ellery

The Secry of the Treasury

LC, Newport Historical Society, Newport, Rhode Island.

1. Ellery, a signer of the Declaration of Independence, was a delegate from Rhode Island to the Continental Congress from 1776 to 1781 and from 1783 to 1785. He was Continental loan officer for Rhode Island from April 16, 1786, to January 1, 1790. Although he had ceased being loan officer, the letter printed above concerns his activities when he held that position.

2. On June 9, 1789, Ellery wrote to Arthur Lee, Walter Livingston, and Samuel Osgood, members of the Board of Treasury: "I have received a letter from the Secry of your Honble Board [William Duer] dated May 25-1789, enclosing a Warrant upon me in favor of Michael Hillegas Esqr. Treasr. of the United States for 12.239—63 Dollars in Certificates for Loaning Service &c with his receipt thereon for that sum, which sum corresponds with my entry" (LC, Newport Historical Society, Newport, Rhode Island).

For an explanation of "Certificates," see Nathaniel Appleton to H, February 5, 1791, note 1 (*PAH*, VIII, 8–9).

3. For an explanation of indents and their use under the Articles of Confederation, see Nathaniel Appleton to H, February 5, 1791, note 1 (*PAH*, VIII, 8–9).

4. Nathaniel Appleton.

5. "Treasury Department Circular to the Continental Loan Officers," October 12, 1789 (*PAH*, V, 440).

6. See the Treasury Department circular cited in note 5 for the Government's policy on paying the Continental loan officers.

From John Holker

Philadelphia ye 13th January
1790

Dear sir

I have Received the favor of your Letter without date,[1] Respecting the settlement of my private Concerns with Mr: Duer: you may rest assured that I shall always feel happy to do any thing which may afford you pleasure or satisfaction & that on this occasion in particular I shall most chearfully conform to your wishes & recommendation. It is very probable I shall be able to go to New york next week, when I shall be more explicit on the Subject: at Same time you'll permit me to add, that was it not for your interference I should not have altered my Course, having deemed myself ill used By Mr Duer, particularly during my late stay in New york.

    I Remain with every sentiment of Respectfull esteem, Dear sir, your most obedient & very humble Servant   Holker

Pray deliver the inclosed to Mr Duer.

A: Hamilton Esqr.

ALS, Sleepy Hollow Restorations, Inc., Tarrytown, New York.
  1. H to Holker, January 8, 1790 (printed in this volume).

To the President, Directors, and Company of the Pennsylvania Society for the Encouragement of Manufactures and the Useful Arts [1]

Treasury Department, January 25, 1790. Requests information concerning manufacturing in Pennsylvania.

Copy, Papers of Tench Coxe in the Coxe Family Papers at the Historical Society of Pennsylvania, Philadelphia.

1. The society to which this letter was addressed was founded in August, 1787. It was an actual manufacturing company as well as a society, and it produced textiles until its building was destroyed by fire in March, 1790.

This letter, which was one of many which H wrote in an effort to obtain material for his "Report on the Subject of Manufactures," December 5, 1791, is identical to H to Benjamin Lincoln, January 25, 1790 (*PAH*, VI, 207–08).

For a list of letters H received concerning manufacturing in the United States, see "Report on the Subject of Manufactures," December 5, 1791, note 26 (*PAH*, X, 10).

From Charles Lee [1]

Alexandria [Virginia] 29th January 1790

Sir!

The amount of my fees under the collection law [2] from the 1st. of August 1789 to the 1st. of Jany 1790 $294.40

Amount of my fees, under the coasting law [3] within the same period   46.40

Amount of my Commissions, on the sums paid,[4] within the same period   23.42

    364.22

Having stated above the gross amount of the emoluments of my office suffer me to add an account of the charges which have been incurred on account of the office, within the same period of time.

Amount of Stationary including Books   79.43
An Iron Chest   52.50
An Office at the rent of 60 Dollars per ann. for 5 months   25.00
A clerk, at the rate of 270 Dollars per annum for 5 months   112.50
Net proceeds to the 1st. of January 1790   94.79
    364.22

Though the Iron Chest and Office Books seem to me to be proper articles of debit against the United States, I have not charged them least they should be disallowed and I thought it better to wait for your approbation. According to the present system of Duties I expect the annual amount in this District will be 40.000 dollars. Total amount of Surveyor's [5] fees from the 1st. of August 1789 to the 1st. of January 1790. $182.56 and, as he is at no expense of office the collector being his Clerk, it may be considered as the net produce.

I have the honor to be Sir!   Your most Obedt. H'ble Servant

Charles Lee, Collector at Alexandria

Copy, RG 56, Letters to and from the Collector at Alexandria, National Archives.

1. This letter was written in reply to "Treasury Department Circular to the Collectors of the Customs," January 20, 1790 (*PAH*, VI, 204).

2. See Section 29 of "An Act to regulate the Collection of the Duties imposed by law on the tonnage of ships or vessels, and on goods, wares and merchandise imported into the United States" (1 *Stat.* 44–45 [July 31, 1789]).

3. These fees were stipulated by Section 31 of "An Act for Registering and Clearing Vessels, Regulating the Coasting Trade, and for other purposes" (1 *Stat.* 64 [September 1, 1789]). For the text of this section, see Lee to H, November 21, 1789, note 20 (printed in this volume).

4. Section 29 of "An Act to regulate the Collection of the Duties imposed by law on the tonnage of ships or vessels, and on goods, wares and merchandise imported into the United States" (1 *Stat.* 45) allowed collectors "one per centum on the amount of all monies by them respectively received and paid into the treasury of the United States."

5. Samuel Hanson.

To Pierpont Edwards

Treasury Department 30th Jany 1790.

Sir

My time has been for some Weeks past so much occupied with preparing business for the consideration of the legislature, as to preclude an earlier attention to your letter of the 4th. instant.[1]

I have considered the question you have stated on the subject of the Bonds which have been put into your hands by the Collectors [2] in your district; and have, as well as yourself, considerable doubts, whether the Jurisdiction of the foederal district Courts extends to them.

You will however, after maturely considering what will be the most probable mode of recovering the money due on these Bonds in a summary manner proceed against the parties, either in the District Court, or in one of the State Courts, as you shall judge most adviseable. The defendant in the former case might, perhaps, not avail himself in season of pleading to the Jurisdiction of the

Court; but as this must depend in a great measure on the character of the party or his Council, or on the doubts which have started abroad on this subject, it is probable, that much dependance cannot be placed on this Circumstance.

I am Sir Your most obedt. & hble Servant.   A Hamilton

Pierpoint Edwards Esqr.
Judge of Connecticut District [3]

LS, James Biddle Collection of the Biddle Family Papers, Andalusia, Pennsylvania.
  1. Letter not found.
  2. Sections 19 and 21 of "An Act to regulate the Collection of the Duties imposed by law on the tonnage of ships or vessels, and on goods, wares and merchandises imported into the United States" (1 *Stat.* 28–49 [July 31, 1789]) stipulate the circumstances under which importers could deposit bonds instead of making immediate payment of duties. Section 28 of the same act made provision for posting bonds with sureties as means of guaranteeing the faithful performance of their duties by the collectors.
  3. H was mistaken. Edwards was United States attorney for Connecticut.

To Benjamin Lincoln [1]

Treasury Department, January 30, 1790. Writes concerning the payment of pensions to invalids.

LS, Massachusetts Historical Society, Boston.
  1. Lincoln was collector of customs at Boston.
  This letter is listed as a "letter not found" in *PAH*, VI, 233. It is the same as H to Jedediah Huntington, January 30, 1790 (*PAH*, VI, 232–33), and H to Jeremiah Olney, February 4, 1790 (*PAH*, VI, 246), and it is similar to H to John Haywood, February 2, 1790 (*PAH*, VI, 240–41).

To George Washington [1]

[New York, January 31, 1790]

Sir

I have made the inquiry of General Schuyler [2] which you directed. He says that he thinks Kirkland's [3] fidelity may be relied on; but does not entertain a very favourable opinion of his judgment or veracity. He says also that there is a Mr James Deane[4] at Onieda who is a man of more discernment discretion and integrity, and who may probably be got here in twelve days.

I shall make the inquiry you direct in your letter of this day & will wait on you with the result.

I have the honor to be   Sir   Your Affect & Obedt Ser

A Hamilton

New York Jany 31. 1799[5]
The President of the U States[6]

ALS, RG 59, Miscellaneous Letters, January 1, 1799–December 27, 1800, National Archives.

1. When this letter was written, Washington was reviewing the relations of the United States with Indians along the country's entire frontier. He undertook this review as a result of the report of the commissioners sent to negotiate with the Creek Indians. For this report, which is dated November 20, 1789, see *ASP, Indian Affairs*, I, 68–80. For Washington's reaction to the report and his concern over relations with the Indians, see John C. Fitzpatrick, ed., *The Diaries of George Washington, 1748–1799* (Boston, 1925), IV, 54, 57, 58, 60–61, 69, 74, 81.

2. Philip Schuyler.

3. Samuel Kirkland was a missionary to the Oneida Indians and lived among them during most of his adult life. He was generally credited with keeping the Oneidas neutral during the American Revolution. In 1793 he founded the Hamilton Oneida Academy, which in 1812 became Hamilton College.

4. Deane, like Kirkland, had been a missionary to the Oneidas. One of the first settlers of what is now Utica, during the American Revolution and the years immediately following it he had served as agent and interpreter for the commissioners of indian affairs for the northern department.

5. This is a mistake and should read "1790."

6. Washington endorsed this letter: "From Colonel Hamilton 31st. Jan. 1790."

Draft of An Act Making Further Provision for the Payment of the Debts of the United States[1]

[New York, January–July 12, 1790]

An Act making further provision for the Payment of the Debts of the United States

Whereas by an Act intitled "An Act for laying a duty on goods

ADf, RG 46, Records of the United States Senate, Committee Reports and Papers, National Archives.

1. This draft was the basis for "An Act making further provision for the payment of the debts of the United States" (1 *Stat.* 180–82 [August 10, 1790]).

After H had submitted his "Report Relative to a Provision for the Support

wares and merchandizes imported into the United States" [2] divers
duties were laid on goods wares and merchandize so imported for
the discharge of the debts of the United States and the encouragement and protection of Manufactures: And whereas the support of
government and the discharge of the said Debts render it necessary
to increase the said duties

Be it enacted by the Senate and House of Representatives of the
United States of America in Congress Assembled, that from and
after the last day of December next the duties specified and laid in
and by the Act aforesaid shall cease and determine, and that upon
all goods wares and merchandize (not herein particularly excepted)
which after the said day shall be brought into the United States
from any foreign port or place there shall be levied, collected and
paid the several ⟨and⟩ respective duties following that ⟨is to⟩ say—
Madeira Wine of the quality of

London particular	per Gallon	35 Cents
other Madeira Wine	per Gallon	30 Cents
Sherry Wine	per Gallon	25 Cents
other Wines	per Gallon	20 Cents

of Public Credit," January 9, 1790 (*PAH*, VI, 51–168), to the House of Representatives on January 14, the Committee of the Whole House on April 27, 1790,
reported a series of resolutions revising the duties on wines and distilled spirits
and appointed a committee to bring in a bill "pursuant to the said resolutions."
On May 5 the committee presented a bill for laying new duties on imported
and domestic distilled spirits "as well as to discourage the excessive use of those
spirits, and promote agriculture, as to provide for the support of the public
credit, and for the common defence and general welfare." On June 21 the
House defeated the bill and appointed a second committee "to devise a plan
for payment of the interest on the debt of the United States." On July 2, after
the committee had reported, the House passed a series of resolutions and appointed a third committee, which presented a bill on July 13 "making further
provisions for the payment of the debts of the United States." The House
passed the bill on July 19, and on August 6 the House agreed to the Senate
amendments to the bill (*Annals of Congress*, I, 1600–01, 1604–05, 1699–1700,
1711, 1715, 1716, 1733, 1741, 1761).

The similarities between this draft and the act as passed are numerous and
striking, and they far outweigh the differences between the two documents.

Some, but far from all, of the provisions in both the draft and the act as
passed can also be found in H's "Report Relative to a Provision for the Support of Public Credit," January 9, 1790. See especially *PAH*, VI, 102–04.

There are two documents attached to H's draft. The first, entitled "The
Committee report the following amendments," contains an amendment to the
preamble of H's draft as well as changes in the wording of other sections. The
second document is entitled "Estimate of Interest & Ways & Means."

2. 1 *Stat.* 24–27 (July 4, 1789).

Distilled Spirits—

If more than ten per Cent below proof according to Dycas's Hydrometer	℔ Gallon	12 Cents
If under five and not more than ten per Cent below proof according to the same Hydrometer	per Gallon	12½ Cents
If of proof and not more than five per Cent below proof according to the same Hydrometer	per Gallon	13 Cents
If above proof but not exceeding twenty per Cent according to the same Hydrometer	per Gallon	15 Cents
If of more than twenty and not more than forty per Cent above proof according to the same Hydrometer	per Gallon	20 Cents
If of more than forty per Cent above proof according to the same Hydrometer	per Gallon	25 Cents
Molasses	per Gallon	3 Cents
Beer ale and porter in casks	per Gallon	5 Cents
Beer ale porter and cyder in bottles	per dozen	20 Cents
~~Loaf and lump Sugar~~	~~per lb~~	~~5 Cents~~
~~Brown Sugar~~	~~per lb~~	~~1½ Cents~~
~~Other Sugar~~	~~per lb~~	~~2 Cents~~
~~Coffee~~	~~per lb~~	~~4 Cents~~
~~Cocoa~~	~~per lb~~	~~1 Cent~~
~~Candles of Tallow~~	~~per lb~~	~~2 Cents~~
~~Candles of Wax or Spermaceti~~	~~per lb~~	~~6 Cents~~
~~Cheese~~	~~℔ lb~~	~~4 Cents~~

Teas from China and India in Ships or Vessels of the United States

Bohea	per lb	10 Cents
Souchong and other black teas	per lb	18 Cents
Hyson	per lb	32 Cents
other Green Teas	pr. lb	20 Cents

Teas from Europe in Ships or Vessels of the United States

Bohea	pr. lb	12 Cents
Suchong and other black Teas	pr. lb	20 Cents
Hyson	pr. lb	40 Cents
other Green Teas	℔ lb	24 Cents

Teas from any other place or in any other Ships or Vessels

Bohea	pr. lb	15 Cents
Souchong and other black teas	pr. lb	27 Cents
Hyson	pr. lb	50 Cents
other Green Teas	pr. lb	30 Cents

Coffee	per lb	4 Cents
Cocoa	per lb	1 Cent
Loaf sugar	per lb	5 Cents
Brown sugar	per lb	1½ Cents
Other Sugar	per lb	2½ Cents
Candles of Tallow	per lb	2 Cents
candles of Wax or Spermaceti	per lb	6 Cents
Cheese	per lb	4 Cents
Soap	per lb	2 Cents
Pepper	per lb	6 Cents
Pimento	per lb	4 Cents
Manufactured Tobacco	per lb	6 Cents
Snuff	per lb	10 Cents
Indigo	per lb	25 Cents
Nails and spikes	per lb	1 Cent
Cotton	per lb	3 Cents
Bar and other lead	per lb	1 Cent
Steel unwrought	per 112 lbs	75 Cents
Hemp	per 112 lbs	60 Cents
Cables	per 112 lbs	150 Cents
Tarred Cordage	per 112 lbs	150 Cents
untarred Cordage and yarn	per 112 lbs	180 Cents
Twine and pack thread	per 112 lbs	400 Cents
Salt	per bushel	12 Cents
Malt	per bushel	10 Cents
Coal	per bushel	3 Cents

Boots	per pair	50 Cents
Shoes slippers and Goloshoes made of leather	per pair	7 Cents
Shoes and Slippers made of silk or stuff	per pair	10 Cents
Wool and Cotton Cards	per dozen	50 Cents
Playing Cards	per pack	10 Cents

coaches Chariots Phaetons Chaises chairs solos or other Carriages or parts of Carriages } 15 per Centum ad valorum

All goods wares and merchandizes (except Teas) from China or India in Ships or vessels not of the United States
All china ware
Looking Glasses window and other Glass and all manufactures of Glass (black quart bottles excepted) } 12½ per Centum ad valorum

Marble Slate and other stones bricks tiles Tables mortars and other utensils of Marble or Slate and generally all Stone and earthen ware
Blanck books
Writing paper and wrapping paper paper hangings paste boards Parchment and Vellum
Pictures and Prints
Painters colours including lamp black, except those commonly used in dying
Gold Silver and plated ware
Gold and silver lace
Jewellery and paste work } 10 per Centum ad valorum

Clocks and watches ⎤
Shoe and knee buckles ⎥
Grocery (except the articles before ⎥
   enumerated) namely cinnamon ⎥
   Cloves Mace Nutmegs Ginger ⎥
   Anniseed currants dates figs ⎥
   plumbs Prunes Raisins Sugar ⎬ 10 per Centum
   candy Oranges lemons limes and ⎥ ad valorum
   generally all fruits and comfits ⎥
   Olives Capers and pickles of every ⎥
   sort ⎥
Oil ⎥
Gun powder ⎥
Mustard in flour ⎦

Cabinet Wares ⎤
buttons ⎥
Saddles ⎥
Gloves of leather ⎥
Hats of beaver felt wool or a mix- ⎥
   ture of any of them ⎥
Millenary ready made ⎥
Castings of iron and slit and rolled ⎥
   iron ⎥
Leather Tanned or tawed and all ⎥
   manufactures of which leather ⎬ 4½ per Centum ad
   is the article of Chief Value ex- ⎥ valorum
   cept such as are herein otherwise ⎥
   rated ⎥
canes walking Sticks and Whips ⎥
Cloathing ready made ⎥
Brushes ⎥
Anchors ⎥
All wares of Tin Pewter or Copper ⎥
   ~~or of a mixture of~~ all or any of ⎥
   them ⎦

Medicinal Drugs except those commonly used in dying carpets and carpeting All Velvets velverets Sattins and other wrought silks cambricks muslins muslinets lawns laces Gauzes Chintzes and colored Callicoes and Nankeens	5½ per Centum ad valorum

All other goods wares and merchandize except bullion tin in pigs tin plates, Old Pewter, brass Teutenague, iron and brass wire, copper in plates Salt petre, plaister of paris, dying woods and dying drugs raw hides and skins, furrs of every kind the sea stores of Ships or vessels the cloaths books household furniture and the tools or implements of the trade or profession of persons who come to reside in the United States, philosophical apparatus specially imported for any seminary of learning, all goods intended to be re-exported to a foreign port or place in the same Ship or vessel in which they shall be imported and generally all articles of the growth product of manufacture of the United States, five per Centum ad valorem.

And be it further enacted that after the last day of December next ~~which will be in the year 1791~~ there shall be paid on Hemp imported as aforesaid at the rate of sixty Cents for 1½ pounds and on Cotton imported in like manner at the rate of three cents per lb.

And be it further enacted that an addition of ten per Centum shall be made to the several rates of duties above specified and imposed in respect to all goods wares and merchandize which after the said last day of December next shall be imported in ships or vessels not of the United States except in the cases in which an additional duty is hereinbefore specially laid on any goods wares or merchandizes which shall be imported in such Ships or Vessels.

And be it further enacted that all duties which shall be paid or secured to be paid by virtue of this Act shall be returned or discharged in respect to all such goods wares or merchandize whereupon they shall have been so paid or secured to be paid as within twelve Calendar Months after payment made or security given shall be exported to any foreign port or place; except one per Centum on the amount of the said duties which shall be retained as an indemnification for whatever expence may have accrued concerning the same.

And be it further enacted that there shall be allowed and paid on dried and pickled fish of the Fisheries of the United States and on other provisions salted within the said states; which after the said last Day of December next shall be exported therefrom to any foreign port or place, in lieu of a drawback of the duty on the salt which shall have been expended thereupon, according to the following rates viz

Dried fish per Quintal	Nine Cents
Pickled Fish and other salted provisions per barrel	Nine Cents

And be it further enacted that where duties by this act are imposed or drawbacks allowed on any specific quantity of goods the same shall be deemed to apply in proportion to any quantity less than such specific quantity.

And be it further enacted that all duties which by virtue of the Act entitled "An act for laying a duty on goods wares and merchandize imported into the United States" accrued between the time specified in the said act for the commencement of the said duties and the respective times when the Collectors entered upon the duties of their respective offices in the several districts be and they are hereby remitted and discharged and that in any case in which they may have been paid to the United States, restitution thereof shall be made.

And be it further enacted and declared that the several duties imposed by this act shall continue to be collected and paid until the debts and purposes for which they are pledged and appropriated shall be fully discharged and satisfied. ~~Provided that nothing herein contained shall be construed to prevent the Legislature of the United States from substituting other duties or taxes of equal value to any or all of the said Duties and imposts.~~

From Otho H. Williams [1]

[*Baltimore, February 15, 1790.* The description of this letter in the dealer's catalogue reads: "Interesting letter about the legality of a matter relating to the Collection of duties at the port of Baltimore." *Letter not found.*]

1. ALS, sold by Paul C. Richards, Autographs, Catalogue No. 4, Item No. 348.

From Tench Coxe [1]

[Philadelphia, February, 1790]

to british Goods and habits in trade than any other Circumstance. Mr. De Marbois [2] & Mr. De Cheamont [3] & the Count de Moustier [4] & Mr. de la forest [5] in Newyork have so far enterd into those Ideas

Copy (incomplete), Papers of Tench Coxe in the Coxe Family Papers at the Historical Society of Pennsylvania, Philadelphia.

1. The first part of this letter is missing.

Coxe, a resident of Philadelphia, had been a Loyalist and then a Patriot during the American Revolution. During the seventeen-eighties he was a leading Philadelphia merchant. He was a delegate to the Annapolis Convention in 1786 and a member of the Continental Congress in 1787 and 1788. He became Assistant to the Secretary of the Treasury on May 10, 1790, and commissioner of the revenue on May 8, 1792.

When this letter was written, Coxe was probably the best-known exponent in the United States of plans for promoting domestic manufactures (Davis, *Essays,* I, 349–56), and the letter printed above undoubtedly was designed to provide H with information for what was to become the "Report on the Subject of Manufactures," December 5, 1791 (*PAH*, X, 1–340; Coxe's version of the Report printed in this volume). This letter may also be at least in part a reply to H to the President, Directors, and Company of the Pennsylvania Society for the Encouragement of Manufactures and the Useful Arts, January 25, 1790 (printed in this volume), for although Coxe was not an official of that society, he was one of its founders and most prominent members.

2. François, marquis de Barbé-Marbois.

3. Jacques Donatien Le Ray de Chaumont was a contractor for the French government.

4. Eléanor François Elie, comte de Moustier, the French Minister Plenipotentiary to the United States.

5. Antoine René Charles Mathurin de la Forest, who served in the French legation in the United States during the American Revolution, was made

that in several conversations with them they have conceded to me that it was therefore *the Interest of france* to promote the growth of manufactures in America & nothing is more evident in my View of things.

Our success in Manufactures thus far has exceedingly increased our Reputation as an energetic and sensible people. When the Idea was first seriously adgitated in 1787 [6] it was matter of Ridicule among the foreigners here and among a considerable number of our own people. But when they see a Manufacturing interest grow up in our Country in a ratio of advance unequalled by any thing but the rise of new lands and that the means of further improvement & final success have become matter of absolute demonstration here and that orders for certain Species of Goods are yearly decreas'd abroad, they consider the versatility, industry & capacity of our people in a very favorable point of light. I do assure you, Sir, I have known an English Mercht. of considerable eminence on a Visit here, to be so extravagantly affected by the beginning of things (for it is only a beginning) that he express'd before me a determination to discontinue all importations on his own Account.

There is one circumstance which renders manufactures of extraordinary value to Pennsylvania. Nature has thrown into the heart of our State a fine canal, the Susquehannah, navigable every where but towards the Sea. Of consequence we are oblig'd at present to cart our produce from 60 to 120 Miles after it reaches the places of deposit on that River—to an Atlantic Philada. New port, Wilmington or Baltimore. The Medium land Carriage is at this time

---

French vice consul at Savannah in 1783. He assumed the duties of consul general in 1785, but was not officially appointed to the post until March 2, 1792.

6. See Tench Coxe, "An Enquiry into the Principles on which a Commercial System for the United States of America should be founded; to which are added some Political Observations connected with the Subject, Read before the Society for Political Enquiries, convened at the house of his Excellency Benjamin Franklin, Esq., in Philadelphia, May 11, 1787" (*The American Museum, or Repository of Ancient and Modern Fugitive Pieces, Prose and Poetical*, I [Philadelphia: Printed by Mathew Carey, 1787], 496–514) and "An address to an assembly of the friends of American manufactures, convened for the purpose of establishing a society for the encouragement of manufactures and the useful arts, read in the university of Pennsylvania, on Thursday the 9th of August, 1787—by Tench Coxe, esq. and published at their request" (*The American Museum*, II [Philadelphia: Printed by Mathew Carey, 1787], 248–54).

5/ or 2/3d. of a dollar pr. 112 or £5 ₩ ton. If our manufacturers can be collected on the Banks of that River to meet their provisions & conserve them there, & to meet their Raw materials & work them up there, this expence of transportation will be entirely saved so far as the fabrics are used on the Susquehannah & so far as the difference of value between the Raw material and the manufacture the expence will be sav'd on goods brought to the above Atlantic Markets. Iron is 3d. ₩ lb Nails on a medium 9d., Hemp 6d. Sail Cloth ₩ lb is worth 2/3 and so of other Articles. This applies more or less in other parts of the United States.

It may be of use next, Sir, to notice the difficulties under wch. manufactures labor, or with which they are threatened.

The duty on hemp, wh. is not produced in sufficient quantity for our present demand and which demand will be very much increas'd by the time the duty will be in operation [7] is menacing circumstance to the makers of those indispensable Articles, Cardage & Sail Cloth. If the new invention of the hemp & flax spinning Mill does not prove a deception this duty will be a very unfortunate thing. The duty on Cotton is liable to the same Remarks. We know it can be purchas'd at Bombay & Surat for 4d. or 4/90 of a dollar ₩ lb & that it can be imported to very great advantage in aid of the Cotton Mills wch. also are secured. Every raw material of this kind applicable to labor-saving Machines, shou'd be free of duty. England who exempts them all from duty must else out do us.

The fall of Exchange below par by reducing foreign goods almost deprives our Manufactures of the protection of duty on non enumerated goods.[8] But as the introduction of money is the Consequence the Evil carries a Comfort with it, for

The want of capitalists in Manufactures is yet a very great diffi-

7. Section 2 of "An Act for laying a Duty on Goods, Wares and Merchandises imported into the United States" reads: "That from and after the first day of December, which shall be in the year one thousand seven hundred and ninety, there shall be laid a duty on every one hundred and twelve pounds, weight of hemp as aforesaid, of sixty cents; and on cotton per pound, three cents" (1 *Stat.* 26 [July 4, 1789]).

8. Section 1 of "An Act for laying a Duty on Goods, Wares and Merchandises imported into the United States" contains a list of goods and their specified duties and then states: "On all other goods, wares and merchandise, five per centum on the value thereof at the time and place of importation . . ." (1 *Stat.* 26).

culty. The great labor-saving machines, extensive breweries and other very profitable branches require large funds. Time and particularly a stable value to the public Securities will give us these.

The Credits given by the European manufacturer prove a considerable impediment to the sale of ours. They particularly interfere with wholesome dealing for the man here who wou'd buy in wholesale, finds it more convenient to pay a large advance for a Credit than to buy with Cash of our Manufacturers. This affects the business even in this money'd town, but it is easy to suppose it must be more injurious in Baltimore, Richmond &ca.

The prejudices in favor of foreign Goods I have already noticed, & in the Case of British Goods they are very great. They are however very handsome & often very good.

Our not being yet in full possession of Workmen, machines & Secrets in the Useful Arts are existing but decreasing disadvantages.

The want of a patent office is an inconvenience that will be quickly removed.[9]

Apologizing for haste and incorrection I conclude myself—most respectfully dear Sir

Yr. obedient humble Servant

9. On April 10, 1790, Congress passed "An Act to promote the progress of useful arts" (1 *Stat.* 109–12), which provided for the establishment of a Federal patent office.

From William Ellery [1]

Newport [Rhode Island] March 8th 1790

Sir,

I have received your letter [2] and now transmit by the Post my receipts from the 1st. of Apl. to the last of Sepr. 1789 and from Oct. the 1st to the last day of Dece. 1789. I have authorized Benjamin Huntington Esqr.[3] by a power of Attorney to receive on my account the sum of One thousand dollars which you advise me you shall be ready to advance on account of my Salary on the settlement of my account at the Treasury to the end of the last year. I hope that such provision will be made as will authorize the payment of the ballance in a short time. Please to inform me what you would have done with the Indents and blank Loan-Office Certificates remaining in my hands.

I am   Sir, your obedt. hble servant   William Ellery

The Secretary of the Treasury

LC, Newport Historical Society, Newport, Rhode Island.
   1. For background to this letter, see Ellery to H, January 10, 1790 (printed in this volume).
   2. Letter not found.
   3. Huntington, a Norwich, Connecticut, lawyer, was a member of the Continental Congress from 1780 to 1784, in 1787 and 1788, and a member of the House of Representatives from 1789 to 1791.

Contract with Melancton Smith

[New York, March 15, 1790]

Agreement between Alexander Hamilton Secretary of the Treasury on behalf of the United States of America, and Melancton Smith of the City of New York Merchant.[1]

First. That the said Melancton Smith shall supply the posts of Westpoint on Hudsons River and of Springfield on Connecticut River, with all Rations which may be required for the use of the said posts, from the 1st. day of January to the last day of December 1790 including both days.

Secondly. That the Ration shall consist of the following Articles, to wit:

One pound of Bread or Flour.
One pound of Beef, or three quarters of a pound of Pork.
One Gill of Common Rum.
One quart of Salt.
Two quarts of Vinegar
Two pounds of Soap   } per 100 Rations.
One pound of Candles

Thirdly. That the said Secretary on behalf of the United States shall pay to the said Melancton Smith the sum of Eight Cents and four tenths of a Cent for each ration issued as aforesaid and that such payment shall be made Monthly, upon the Accounts being passed at the proper Offices of the Treasury Department.

In Witness whereof the said Secretary of the Treasury on behalf of the said United States of America hath herewith subscribed his hand and affixed the Seal of the Treasury; and the said Melancton Smith has werewith subscribed and set his hand and seal the fifteenth day of March in the Year of our Lord One thousand seven hundred and Ninety, and of the Independence of the said United States the fourteenth.

Alexander Hamilton
Secy of the Treasury

Melancton Smith

Sealed and delivered in
the presence of

DS, The Sol Feinstone Collection, Library of the American Philosophical Society, Philadelphia.

1. Smith was a large landholder in Dutchess County, New York, and a merchant and lawyer in New York City. During the American Revolution he was one of three commisioners appointed by Congress to search out and punish Tories. Throughout his adult life he was a close political associate of Governor George Clinton and played a leading Antifederalist role in the New York Ratifying Convention until he finally decided to vote for ratification.

The fact that Smith was selected as contractor to supply the posts at West Point and Springfield, Massachusetts, places him in that small body of Antifederalists (another was John Lamb, collector of customs at New York) who received patronage from the Federalist administration.

For background to this document, see H to Nathaniel Gorham, December 8, 1789 (*PAH*, VI, 8); "Request for Bids," November 4, 1789 (*PAH*, V, 496).

To Benjamin Huntington [1]

Treasury Department 19th march 1790

Sir

Be pleased to inform me whether a draft on the Cashier of the Bank of Boston for the sum of One thousand dollars, on account of Salary due to William Ellery, will be as agreeable as Cash. The former mode of payment will be most convenient to the present state of the Treasury.

I am, Sir, Your obedt. Servt.   A Hamilton

The Honorable Benjamin Huntington Esquire

LS, The Thomas Bright Collection, Jervis Library, Rome, New York.
1. For background to this letter, see William Ellery to H, January 10, March 8, 1790 (both printed in this volume).

From Benjamin Huntington [1]

N York March 19th 1790

Sir

In answer to your Letter of this Day I have to say I act as an Atty to Wm Ellery Esqr for the Sole Purposes of Receiving and Remitting his Money to him & have no interest of my own in the Business nor am I able to say whether the Mode of Payment you propose will be agreeable to him or not.

In his Directions to me on this Subject he says "When you have Received the Money, send me three Hundred Dollars by the first Packet & keep the Rest untill I give further Directions about it." By this it Seems that he has present Use for three hundred Dollars & will not Expect the Remainder untill the Question you ask may be put to him & his answer Received. If it is agreeable to you to order the three Hundred Dollars I am Content the Remainder should be in the Treasury untill Mr Ellerys Answer Can be obtained and on my own Account Prefer this Measure to being at the Risque in holding the Money in my Possession.[2]

ADf, The Thomas Bright Collection, Jervis Library, Rome, New York.
1. For background to this letter, see William Ellery to H, January 10, March 8, 1790; H to Huntington, March 19, 1790 (all printed in this volume).
2. For the payment to Ellery, see "Report on the Receipts and Expenditures of Public Monies to the End of the Year 1791," November 10, 1792 (*PAH*, XIII, 47). See also Oliver Wolcott, Jr., to H, July 31, 1790 (*PAH*, VI, 513–14).

To Robert Morris [1]

[New York, March 19, 1790]

Dr Sir

I find that I cannot answer as soon as I expected. The absence of a Gentleman, who has taken a ride out of town, will probably postpone my decision till afternoon. The moment I am ready, you shall hear from me.

Yrs. sincerely   A Hamilton

March 19th. 1790

ALS (facsimile), sold by Charles Hamilton Autographs, Inc., April 23, 1970, Item 94.

1. When this letter was written, Morris was a member of the United States Senate from Pennsylvania.

Although it cannot be stated with certainty, it seems likely that this letter concerns H's efforts to sell to Morris stock in the Bank of North America owned by John B. Church. Church was Elizabeth Hamilton's brother-in-law, and H acted as his agent or representative while (as was now the case) he was in his native England. For the negotiations concerning this sale, see Morris to H, November 13, 1789, April 4, 1790 (*PAH*, V, 513–14; VI, 348–49); H to Thomas Willing, February 20–23, March 22, 30, 1790 (*PAH*, VI, 273–74, 308, 322); Willing to H, February 24 1790 (*PAH*, VI, 278–79); H to Brockholst Livingston, March 30, 1790 (*PAH*, VI, 329–30); Livingston to H, April 4, 1790 (*PAH*, VI, 347–48). See also Church's account in H's "Cash Book," March 1, 1782–1791 (*PAH*, III, 55), and the introductory note to Morris to H, June 7, 1795 (*PAH*, XIII, 359–66).

Conversation with George Beckwith [1]

[New York, March 22–April, 1790] [2]

7.[3] [Beckwith] I am directed by Lord Dorchester to thank You for those expressions of civility, which You were pleased to use with

Copy, PRO: C.O., 42/67, ff 237–44; copy, MG 11, Q Series, Vol. Q-44, part 1, Public Archives of Canada, Ottawa.

1. Beckwith served in the British army during the American Revolution and in 1782 became aide-de-camp to Sir Guy Carleton. After Carleton—elevated to the peerage as Lord Dorchester—was appointed governor of Quebec, a position

respect to him, when I had the pleasure of seeing You in autumn,[4] and for the confidence You reposed in His Lordship, in the com-

---

he held from 1786 to 1791, he again called on the services of Beckwith. As Great Britain had no legation in the United States, Beckwith was designated the unofficial Minister of the British Government. Like that of an accredited minister, Beckwith's job was to forward to officials in London information collected in the United States which might affect British-American relations. His communiqués were sent to Dorchester who forwarded them to William Wyndham Grenville (created Baron Grenville in November, 1790), Pitt's Secretary of State for Home Affairs from June, 1789, to June, 1791, and after the latter date Secretary of State for Foreign Affairs. In 1787 Beckwith spent six months observing events in the United States, and in 1788 he returned to study the effects which the adoption of the Constitution might have on relations between the United States and Great Britain. He returned to England late in 1788 and was still there when Grenville, in August, 1789, received news of the passage of tariff and tonnage acts by the recently assembled United States Congress. Beckwith was sent back to the United States with instructions to inform American officials that his government was disturbed by the restrictions which these acts proposed to put on English commerce, and that persistence in a policy of discrimination would lead to retaliation by the British. Beckwith arrived in New York City, temporary capital of the United States Government, in October, 1789.

The document printed above was enclosed in Dorchester to Grenville, May 27, 1790 (ALS, PRO: C.O., 42–67, f 235).

The topics discussed in this document were in large part a product of the American Revolution and the treaty of peace between the United States and Great Britain (Miller, *Treaties,* II, 96–106). These topics are:

1. The refusal of the British to evacuate the Northwest posts (Article 2 [Miller, *Treaties,* II, 97–98]).
2. The inability of southern planters to regain the slaves who had been carried off by the British in violation of the treaty (Article 7 [Miller, *Treaties,* II, 99–100]).
3. The refusal of the British to permit Americans to enter the trade with the British West Indies.
4. The failure of Great Britain to send an envoy with the rank of minister to the United States.
5. The obstacles placed by the states (especially in the South) to the collection of debts owed by Americans to the British (Article 4 [Miller, *Treaties,* II, 98]).
6. The inability of the two countries to reach a settlement on the boundary of northeastern United States (Article 2 [Miller, *Treaties,* II, 97–98]).

2. This inclusive date has been assigned to the document printed above for two reasons. The first date has been chosen because H states in his conversation: "Mr. Jefferson arrived last night." Jefferson arrived in New York City on March 21, 1790 (Jefferson to Thomas Mann Randolph, March 28, 1790 [Boyd, *Papers of Thomas Jefferson,* XVI, 277–78]). Secondly, Beckwith stated that he planned to remain in New York "Until about the middle of April," and on the continuation of the conversation he stated: ". . . the time is drawing near when I intend returning to Quebec."

3. "7" was Beckwith's code number for H.

4. See "Conversation with George Beckwith," October, 1789 (*PAH,* V, 482–90).

munications made by me upon that occasion; they have been transmitted home, and although the delays incident to the season of the year have not hitherto enabled His Lordship to hear from Great Britain in reply he has judged it necessary to defer no longer the expressing his approbation of the principle, You then laid down *"that it is expendient that a solid friendship should be established between the two countries."* I am desired to explain this to You, and to remain a short time here, in case any information from home, subsequent to my leaving Quebec, may enable His Lordship to throw further light on this subject.

[Hamilton] I am happy to find Lord Dorchester's sentiments are in favor of that general principle, which I hold to be so evidently compatible with the welfare both of Great Britain and of this country. [5] My communications with You, You will of course always consider to be informal, but on this particular point I think I speak the sentiments of the majority of those, who are to conduct the affairs of this country; as to my own part my ideas naturally extend to objects, which I hold to be favorable for the general interests of the States, in which view I contemplate a connexion with You, and further than they may have that tendency, I certainly should not go, but with us different gentlemen may view this matter in different lights; the President of the United States I am inclined to think considers this subject in a favorable one.[6] Mr. Jefferson, the

5. At this point in the document Beckwith left a space of several lines and in the margin wrote: "expressions of personal civility omitted."

6. Despite H's assertion, George Washington had been very guarded in his statements concerning relations between the United States and Great Britain. Perhaps his views on the matter are best expressed in the first two letters of three which he wrote to Gouverneur Morris on October 13, 1789. In the first letter, he wrote that it was "important to both Countries, that the Treaty of Peace between Great Britain and the United States, should be observed and performed with perfect and mutual good Faith; and that of a Treaty of Commerce should be concluded by them on Principles of reciprocal Advantage to both." He then asked Morris to ascertain on an informal basis "the Sentiments and Intentions of the Court of London on these interesting Subjects" (*GW*, XXX, 439–40). The second letter, which covers some of the same points discussed in the conversation printed above, reads: "My letter to you, herewith enclosed, will give you the credence necessary to enable you to do the business, which it commits to your management, and which I am persuaded you will readily undertake.

"Your inquiries will commence by observing that, as the present constitution of government, and of the courts established in pursuance of it, removes the objections heretofore made to putting the United States in possession of their frontier posts, it is natural to expect from the assurances of his Majesty and

Secretary of State, who lately returned from Paris [7] on his private affairs, the condition of France not requiring his presence, and who did not know of his appointment until his arrival in America,[8] is of opinion that the struggle for freedom in that country will be successful, and when completed, that it will be productive of great commercial benefits to the States, from the influence of the Marquis de la Fayette, who is greatly attached to this country, as well as

---

the national good faith that no unnecessary delays will take place. Proceed then to press a speedy performance of the treaty respecting the object.

"Remind them of the article by which it was agreed, that negroes belonging to our citizens should not be carried away, and of the reasonableness of making compensation for them. Learn with precision, if possible, what they mean to do on this head.

"The commerce between the two countries you well understand. You are apprized of the sentiments and feelings of the United States on the present state of it; and you doubtless have heard that in the late session of Congress a very respectable number of both houses were inclined to a discrimination of duties unfavorable to Britain, and that it would have taken place but for conciliatory considerations, and the probability that the late change in our government and circumstances would lead to more satisfactory arrangements.

"Request to be informed therefore, whether they contemplate a treaty of commerce with the United States, and on what principles or terms in general. In treating this subject, let it be strongly impressed on your mind, that the privilege of carrying our productions in our vessels to their Islands, and of bringing in return the productions of those Islands to our own ports and markets, is regarded here as of the highest importance; and you will be careful not to countenance any idea of our dispensing with it in a treaty. Ascertain if possible, their views on this point; for it would not be expedient to commence negotiations without previously having good reasons to expect a satisfactory termination of them.

"It may also be well for you to take a proper occasion of remarking, that their omitting to send a minister here, when the United States sent one to London, did not make an agreeable impression on this country; and request to know what would be their future conduct on similar occasions.

"It is in my own opinion very important, that we avoid errors in our system of policy respecting Great Britain; and this can only be done by forming a right judgment of their disposition and views. Hence you will perceive how interesting it is that you obtain the information in question, and that the business be so managed as that it may receive every advantage which abilities, address and delicacy can promise and afford." (*GW*, XXX, 440–42.)

As far as H's conversations with Beckwith are concerned, there is no evidence that Washington knew anything about them until July 8, 1790, when H reported to the President on a conversation (subsequent to the one printed above) that he had had with Beckwith (*PAH*, VI, 484–86). See also H to Washington, July 15, 1790 (*PAH*, VI, 493–96).

7. Jefferson had arrived in Norfolk, Virginia, on November 23, 1789 (Jefferson to John Jay, November 23, 1789 [Boyd, *Papers of Thomas Jefferson*, XV, 553]).

8. See Jefferson to Washington, December 15, 1789 (Boyd, *Papers of Thomas Jefferson*, XVI, 34–35).

from that general bias, which those, who guide that party, have always shewn towards us.[9] From these considerations I am the more strongly disposed to view the present time as particularly favorable for the consideration of a commercial Treaty. As to Spain no doubt the navigation of the Mississippi does attract the attention of discerning men with us, and it is looked forward to as the probable source of coldness, possibly of differences with that court at a future period, but it does not appear to me, that it could come under immediate consideration. With regard to your Court having a Minister here I am clear, that would be a measure, which would give general satisfaction, the particular rank might depend on the pretensions of the gentleman in question for that station; high appointments in our situation woud not be thought eligible; I am not versed in diplomatic distinctions, but am led to think that a Minister Plenipotentiary is of a scale adequate for the purposes of both countries, concluding that a parity of rank would be proper for each.

I am authorized further to say, that it is for Your consideration whether in the present stage of this business You may judge it expedient to make any further communications to Lord Dorchester.

I cannot at this moment determine, whether it may be proper to communicate further with Lord Dorchester on this subject, or to carry it forward through a regular official channel. Mr. Jefferson arrived last night, and these matters are in his department. Pray how long do You intend to remain here?

[Beckwith] Until about the middle of April.

[Hamilton] It is probable that before that time I shall have it in my power to give You some information on this point.

We observe a paragraph from a London paper, that mentions Lord Hawkesbury and Mr. Grenville being engaged in the framing the outline of a commercial Treaty with us,[10] pray in what official station is His Lordship?

9. It cannot be determined with certainty where H obtained the information in this sentence. On the other hand, most, but not all, the views which H attributed to Jefferson can be found in Jefferson to Jay, September 19, 1789 (Boyd, *Papers of Thomas Jefferson*, XV, 454–60). When Jefferson wrote to Jay he was about to leave Paris and return to the United States, and Jay was serving as acting secretary of the State Department. In the last paragraph of his letter Jefferson wrote: "Expecting within a few days to leave Paris, and that this is my last letter on public subjects, I have indulged myself in giving you a general view of things. . . ."

10. In the [Philadelphia] *Gazette of the United States*, March 20, 1790, the following "Extract of a letter from London, 1st January, 1790" appeared: "Lord

[Beckwith] His Lordship has presided at a Committee of the Privy Council for commercial affairs.[11]

In continuation

[Hamilton] Nothing has happened since I had the pleasure of seeing You, to render it requisite for me to change my opinions on the different subjects touched upon in that conversation. A Treaty of Commerce with Great Britain is generally wished, and the full consideration of the subject is desirable. The reciprocal appointment of Ministers is also very agreeable, the particular grade is a secondary consideration, and may be readily accomodated to the mutual convenience of both countries.

NB. Mr. —— added something with respect to the States having sent a Minister to Our Court, which we never acknowledged, and hinted, as if it was expected, that it was for Us to make the first offer; I replied that the condition of the States at that time had been such, as to have rendered it impracticable for a Minister from *us* to have remained at New York, and if otherwise, from the nature of their then government he could have been of no service.[12]

In continuation

[Beckwith] I have requested to see You as the time is drawing near when I intend returning to Quebec; I conceive it to be neces-

---

Hawkesbury and Mr. Grenville are now actually employed in preparing the plan of a commercial treaty with your States, which I doubt not will *shortly* be fully matured and put into a train of negociation."

Charles Jenkinson, first Earl of Liverpool and first Baron Hawkesbury, was Undersecretary of State in 1761, a member of the House of Commons from 1761 to 1786, created Baron Hawkesbury in 1786, a member of the Privy Council from 1773 to 1808, and appointed President of the Privy Council for Trade and Plantations in 1786.

11. In December, 1790, Grenville referred "An Act for laying a Duty on Goods, Wares, and Merchandises imported into the United States" (1 *Stat.* 24–27 [July 4, 1789]) and "An Act imposing Duties on Tonnage" (1 *Stat.* 27–28 [July 20, 1789]) to the Privy Council for Trade and Plantations, of which Hawkesbury was chairman and Grenville a member. The council, however, did not report until January 28, 1791, when it stated that as of 1790 the United States trade regulations did not discriminate against England. See *A Report of the Lords of the Committee of the Privy Council, appointed for all Matters relating to Trade and Foreign Plantations, on The Commerce and Navigation between His Majesty's Dominions, and the Territories belonging to the United States of America. 28th January 1791* (London, 1791). This report was reprinted in *Collection of Interesting and Important Reports and Papers on the Navigation and Trade of Great Britain* (London, 1807).

12. John Adams was United States Minister to Great Britain from 1785 to 1788. During this period Great Britain did not send to the United States an envoy with a rank equal to that of Adams.

sary and not improper for me to remark that I take it for granted, the different communications, You have been pleased to make to me, flow from that source, which under Your present government, is alone competent to make them.

[Hamilton] I am not authorized to say to You in so many words, that such is the language of the President of the United States, to a gentleman, who has no public character such a declaration cannot be made, but my honor and character stand implicated in the fulfilment of these assurances. The gentlemen at the head of the different departments may not have precisely the same way of thinking on all public concerns. I therefore speak with the greatest caution on all points in which they have a direct share, but where it respects the President to whom this must have reference, I can speak with more precision. I can say this, that his mind is perfectly free from any bias whatever on this subject and that he is ready to go into the discussion of every thing unsettled between the two countries.

[Beckwith] If I comprehended You the last time I had the honor of seeing You You suggested some difficulty in the appointment of a minister to us.

[Hamilton] Yes I did so, we have had a Minister at Your Court You did not send one in return, we should find a difficulty in taking the lead again in such a nomination.

[Beckwith] I am sorry to observe the disputes upon Your North east frontier relative to the boundary,[13] and the publications in Your newspapers on the subject.

[Hamilton] Yes, that matter ought to be settled as soon as possible, as some accident may possibly happen.

[Beckwith] It is to be hoped, that Your government most inter-

13. The northeastern boundary dispute between the United States and Great Britain grew out of the peace treaty of 1783 which stipulated in Article 2 that the boundary should be the St. Croix River (Miller, *Treaties*, II, 97–98). Although the map used by the peace commissioners contained such a river, a dispute arose as to which of three rivers, the Magaguadavic, the Cobscook, or the Schoodic, was actually the St. Croix. On February 9, 1790, Washington requested the opinion of the Senate on the dispute, and on March 9, 1790, a Senate committee suggested that a consultation be held with the British government (*ASP, Foreign Relations*, I, 20–100). For the nature of the dispute, see John Bassett Moore, ed., *International Adjudications; Ancient and Modern, History and Documents, Together with Mediatorial Reports, Advisory Opinions, and the Decisions of Domestic Commissions, on International Claims* (New York, 1929), I, 1–10.

ested in this matter (Massachusetts bay) will not become intemperate.

[Hamilton] I think it right to remark to You in this place, that a degree of moderation and good sense, has been conspicuous in the conduct of the Eastern Governments since the peace, which has not been equally so to the southward of Pensylvania, at the different periods, in which I have been a member of Congress under the late Constitution,[14] I have had frequent occasions to observe this, and at first I acknowledge with some surprize, cool, plain good sense, determines their decisions without either animosity or partiality; it is not so much so, I am sorry to say to the southward, and I have been frequently led to consider the cause; I am inclined to think that the sentiments of one or two gentlemen in the southern States, whose characters give them influence, has led to this, they have been esteemed men of superior capacity, And certain causes have induced them to keep alive distinctions neither wise nor proper; but these persons are not at present in office, and possibly the private circumstances of too many of our southern planters, and their dread of the operation of the federal Courts, may also have an influence.[15]

[Beckwith] As Enthusiasm cannot suppose that with respect to *us*, there exists the smallest necessity to compel the consideration of commercial subjects with the States, and however embarrassed You may still continue in many respects, as candor must admit, that Your

14. H was a member of the Continental Congress from 1782 to 1783 and in 1788.

15. It would be difficult, if not impossible, to "prove" H's assertions in this paragraph. At the same time, there is much to what he says, for many southerners felt very strongly about the slaves who had been carried away by the British and the provision in the treaty concerning the collection of debts owed by Americans to the British (notes 1 and 6). If, indeed, the South was more anti-British than the "Eastern Governments," this attitude can hardly be explained, as H does, by the activities of "one or two gentlemen in the southern States." A far more plausible explanation is the fury of the war in the South and the relative peace that prevailed throughout much of the Revolution in New England.

The final statement in this sentence concerning the "federal Courts" is a direct reference to Article 4 of the treaty, which in its entirety reads: "It is agreed that Creditors on either side, shall meet with no lawful Impediment to the Recovery of the full value in Sterling Money of all bonâ fide Debts heretofore contracted" (Miller, *Treaties*, II, 98). The southern states had established "lawful impediments," and the Confederation government, with neither an executive branch nor a national court system, could not enforce this provision of the treaty.

situation is better, than it was two years ago, I should hope if there shall be any discussions on this subject they will be entered upon with temper and candor.

[Hamilton] It is the duty of every man in Office to do so; we have still much to do, but the foundation is laid, and our difficulties are chiefly owing to ourselves; it will require time, but in the course of things we must become a very considerable people. I have ever thought it undesirable, that we should be *courted* by one power in Europe only; I do not mean this in the common acceptation of the word, but that our connexions should be more extended.

From William Ellery [1]

Newport [*Rhode Island*] *March 30, 1790.* States that there is an error in his "Account Current of money received and paid" and that the "charge for my quarter's salary commencing Oct. 1st. and ending Dece. 31 1789 instead of 150 Dollars is carried out 300 Dolls."

LC, Newport Historical Society, Newport, Rhode Island.
   1. For background to this letter, see Ellery to H, January 10, March 8, 1790; H to Benjamin Huntington, March 19, 1790; Huntington to H, March 19, 1790 (all printed in this volume).

To Benjamin Lincoln

Treasury Department, April 13, 1790. Writes concerning the payment of pensions to invalids.[1]

LS, Massachusetts Historical Society, Boston.
   1. See H to Lincoln, January 30, 1790 (printed in this volume).

To Thomas Smith [1]

[*Treasury Department, April 17, 1790.* The description in the dealer's catalogue of this letter reads: "At his request, Hamilton has issued a warrant in his favor on Samuel Meredith for $20,000.[2] 'I wish you had indicated to me what sum would be requisite to execute the object of exchanging the certificates of your State.' " *Letter not found.*]

1. LS, sold by Kenneth W. Rendell, Inc., Catalogue No. 70, Lot 56.
For background to this letter, see "Treasury Department Circular to the Continental Loan Officers," October 12, 1789 (*PAH*, V, 440–41).
2. An entry for May 13, 1790, in the Blotters of the Office of the Register of the Treasury reads: "Thomas Smith Receiver of Continental Taxes and Loan Officer for Pennsylvania his Account of Interest Indents Dr. to Samuel Meredith Treasurer of the United States his Account of ditto For a Warrant No. 7 drawn the 17th Ultimo, on said Treasurer in favor of said Loan Officer for Twenty thousand Dollars in Indents of Interest for which he is to be charged and held Accountable subject hereafter to a charge of such Fractional parts of a dollar as he may add to the indents   20,000" (RG 39 Records of the Bureau of Accounts [Treasury], Blotters of the Office of the Register of the Treasury, 1782–1810, National Archives).
For "indents of interest," see Nathaniel Appleton to H, February 5, 1791, note 1 (*PAH*, VIII, 8–9).
See also Oliver Wolcott, Jr., to H, July 31, 1790 (*PAH*, VI, 513–14).

To Abraham Van Vechten [1]

[*New York, April 20, 1790.* Letter listed in dealer's catalogue. *Letter not found.*]

1. ALS, sold by Stan V. Henkels, Jr., April 24, 1894, Item 72.
Van Vechten was an Albany lawyer and Federalist politician.

Certificate of Clerkship for Henry W. Livingston [1]

[New York, April 29, 1790]

I Certify that Henry W. Livingston served as a Clerk in my Office from the third day of October, in the Year One Thousand Seven Hundred and Eighty Seven, until the Eleventh day of September in the year One Thousand Seven Hundred and Eighty Nine, and that he is of good moral Character.

New York April 29. 1790
A Hamilton
Attorney at Law

ALS, Pleadings, 1754–1837, L-126, Hall of Records, New York City.

1. Livingston, the son of Walter and Cornelia (Schuyler) Livingston, subsequently practiced law in New York City, was a member of the state Assembly from Columbia County in 1802 and 1810, and was a member of the House of Representatives from 1803 to 1807.

On the reverse of the document printed above a certificate by Brockholst Livingston states that Henry W. Livingston served as his law clerk from September 11, 1789, to October 9, 1790.

To Otho H. Williams [1]

[*New York, April 29, 1790.* The description of this letter reads: "asking statement of facts relative to vessels exempted from duties." *Letter not found.*]

1. LS, sold by Harvard Trust Company, 1962.
For background to this letter, see Robert Purviance to H, April 22, 1790 (*PAH*, VI, 372).

From Jedediah Huntington

[*New London, Connecticut*] *April 30, 1790.* "I am favd. with your Letter of the 21st. respecting Light Houses &c and am much obliged to the president for the Appointment therein announced to me. I do not know of any Beacons Buoys or piers in this state that come within the Description of the Act of Congress [1] but will make Enquiry. The Legislature of this state in May last ordered the buoys fixed at certain places in the Harbour of N. London of which I once made Mention to you [2] but the order has never been executed. I shall endeavour to prevail with the Legislature to include those places in their Act of Cession in hopes that Buoys may be fixed. . . ." [3]

ADf, New London Customs House Records, Federal Records Center, Boston,
1. Section 1 of "An Act for the establishment and support of Lighthouses, Beacons, Buoys, and Public Piers" reads: "That all expenses which shall accrue from and after the fifteenth day of August, one thousand seven hundred and eighty-nine, in the necessary support, maintenance and repairs of all lighthouses, beacons, buoys and public piers erected, placed, or sunk before the passing of this act, at the entrance of, or within any bay, inlet, harbor, or port of the United States, for rendering the navigation thereof easy and safe, shall be defrayed out of the treasury of the United States . . ." (1 *Stat.* 53–54 [August 7, 1789]). Section 3 of the same act required the Secretary of the Treasury

"to provide by contracts, which shall be approved by the President of the United States, . . . for rebuilding when necessary, and keeping in good repair, the lighthouses, beacons, buoys and public piers in the several States, and for furnishing the same with all necessary supplies . . ." (1 *Stat.* 54).

2. Huntington to H, October 7, 1789 (printed in this volume).

3. For "An Act for ceding, and vesting in the United States the Buoys, and Light House at the Port of New London," which was passed by the Connecticut General Assembly in May, 1789, see Leonard Woods Labaree, comp., *The Public Records of the State of Connecticut from May 1789 through October 1792* (Hartford, 1948), 122.

To Jeremiah Lansing [1]

[*Philadelphia, May 17, 1790.* Letter listed in dealer's catalogue. *Letter not found.*]

1. LS, sold by John Heise, Syracuse, New York, 1926, Catalogue 1644, Item 39. Lansing was surveyor for the port of Albany, New York.

From Jedediah Huntington

[New London, Connecticut, May 27, 1790]

Sir,

The Brig Maria James Stephenson Master Luke Fortune Consignee Arrived here in Feby last from Grenada—where she was put in Seizure for a Breach of the Laws of Trade. She sails under a british Register. It is said she has since been condemned at Grenada. The Captain repents his assisting in bringing her away and demands her Register of me that he may carry her back. Luke Fortune the Consignee who came in her who is a Citizen of the U States who I believe has some property in her—refused to allow the Captain to have any thing to do with the Register or Vessel. I promised Capt Stephenson to lay the Case before you for Your Opinion for which I shall be obliged to You &

I am Sir &c

May 27 1790
Secy of Treasury

ADf, New London Customs House Records, Federal Records Center, Boston.

From Otho H. Williams [1]

[*Baltimore, May 30, 1790.* The description of this letter reads: "stating facts relative to . . . vessels exempted from duties." *Letter not found.*]

1. ALS, sold by Harvard Trust Company, 1962.
This letter was written in reply to H to Williams, April 29, 1790 (printed in this volume).

From William Ellery [1]

Newport [*Rhode Island*] *June 1, 1790.* "I have received your letter of the 17th. of the last month,[2] and . . . now transmit to you . . . four bundles of Indents . . . and another package of blank Loan-Office Certife. . . . I have no bills of credit, known by name of the New Emissions.[3] I find by the News papers that an appropriation is made by law for discharging the demands which exist against the United States, and that . . . a payment of the salaries to the late Loan-Officers of the several States to the 31st. day of Dece. 1789 is authorized. . . .[4] The ballance due to me to that period is 544 89/100 Dolls. . . ."

LC, Newport Historical Society, Newport, Rhode Island.
1. For background to this letter, see Ellery to H, January 10, March 8, 30, 1790; H to Benjamin Huntington, March 19, 1790; Huntington to H, March 19, 1790 (all printed in this volume).
2. "Treasury Department Circular to the Continental Loan Officers," May 17, 1790 (*PAH*, VI, 418–19).
3. For an explanation of the contents of this sentence, see Nathaniel Appleton to H, February 5, 1791, note 1 (*PAH*, VIII, 8–9).
4. See Section 5 of "An Act making appropriations for the support of government for the year one thousand seven hundred and ninety" (1 *Stat.* 104–06 [March 26, 1790]).

From Alexander Martin [1]

North Carolina. June 1st. 1790.

Sir

I do myself the Honour to inclose you herewith a bill of exchange payable to me as Governor of the State of North Carolina from Mr Daniel Carthy [2] agent for Royal Flint Esquire [3] in New york drawn upon that Gentleman for sixteen Hundred Spanish Milled Dollars being his first Bill dated 23d. of April 1790. The second and third of same Tenor & date in my possessetion and not yet forwarded but will be the first opportunity—being for fifty six thousand weight of public Tobacco contracted with Mr. Flint by my predecessor Governor Johnston [4] in behalf of the State and late delivered to his said agent. By a Resolution of the General Assembly I beg leave to inform you Sir that the said Monies are to be appropriated to the sole purpose of discharging this State's Quota of the Interest due on the foreign Debt of the United States.[5] Be pleased to place the above when paid to the Credit of this State as aforesaid, and favour me with your advice thereupon.

I have the Honour to be with very great respect Sir your most Obedient Humble Servant   Alex. Martin

The Honourable Alexander Hamilton Esquire
Secretary of the Treasury of the United States

LC, Governor's Letter Book, 1789–1791, North Carolina Department of Archives and History, Raleigh, North Carolina.

1. Martin, a member of the colonial Assembly of North Carolina and an officer in the Continental Army, was a member of the state Senate from 1779 to 1782 and from 1785 to 1788, and was governor of North Carolina from 1782 to 1784 and from 1789 to 1792.

2. Carthy was a merchant of New Bern, North Carolina, who was affiliated with several New York City merchants and speculators.

3. Originally a resident of Connecticut, Flint became a prominent New York merchant and speculator in both land and securities. During the American Revolution he was paymaster for Connecticut, and he subsequently served as a commissioner for settling the accounts of the eastern states with the Federal Government. In the seventeen-eighties he had been closely associated in several ventures with William Duer and Jeremiah Wadsworth.

4. Samuel Johnston, a native of Scotland, had been a member of the colonial Assembly of North Carolina, the first four provincial Congresses, the state Senate in 1779, 1783, and 1784, and the Continental Congress from 1780 to 1782. He was elected governor of North Carolina in 1787 and twice re-elected, but he resigned in 1789 to become a United States Senator.

5. See "An Act for Emitting One Hundred Thousand Pounds Paper currency, for the Purposes Therein Expressed" (Walter Clark, ed., *The State Records of North Carolina* [Goldsboro, North Carolina, 1905], XXIV, 722–25). This act, which was passed on December 29, 1785, opens with the following statement: "Whereas the pressing circumstances of our domestic and foreign debts, evince the necessity of emitting a further sum of one hundred thousand pounds in paper currency, to be applied to discharge a part of the foreign debts due from the United States, and a part of the current expences of the federal government." In addition this act provided: "And be it further Enacted . . . , That a further sum, not exceeding thirty-six thousand pounds, shall be paid to such persons as shall be elected by ballot . . . for the express purpose of purchasing tobacco . . . ; which said tobacco shall be purchased by the . . . commissioners, and shall be by them shipped to such ports in Europe, or the West Indies, or elsewhere . . . to such persons from whom bills of exchange or monies may be procured for the payment of the proportionable part of this State, of the debt due from the United States. . . ." For amendments to this act, see Clark, *Records of North Carolina*, XXIV, 812–13, 892–93.

For a reference to Flint's role as purchaser of North Carolina tobacco, see *Journal of the House of Commons. State of North Carolina. At a General Assembly, begun and held at Fayetteville, on the Second Day of November, in the Year of Our Lord One Thousand Seven Hundred and Eight-nine, and in the Fourteenth Year of the Independence of the United States of America: Being the First Session of this Assembly* (Edenton: Printed by Hodge & Wills, Printers to the State, n.d.), 69.

From Bennett Wheeler [1]

[*Providence, June 5, 1790.* On June 14, 1790, Hamilton wrote to Wheeler: [2] "I have received . . . your letter of the 5th Instant." *Letter not found.*]

1. Wheeler, a native of Nova Scotia, was the publisher of the [Providence] *American Journal and General Advertiser* from 1779 to 1781 and *The* [Providence] *United States Chronicle* from 1784 to 1802. The second of these two papers supported ratification of the Federal Constitution and Federalist party policies.

2. Printed in this volume.

To William Ellery

[*New York, June 7, 1790.* On June 22, 1790, Ellery wrote to Hamilton: [1] "Your letter of the 7th. instant . . . did not come into my hands until the 19th." *Letter not found.*]

1. Printed in this volume.

To Jedediah Huntington [1]

Treasury Department
June 7th 1790

Sir

The case of the Brig Maria has been stated substantially in Conformity with your letter by Captain Stephenson.

The following are my Ideas on the subject   The Cap⟨t.⟩ Stephenson on entering the Vessel deposited his Register with you as usual, and if he clears out & applies to you for the Register again in order to depart, it is in the ordinary Course of business that you deliver it to him, with your clearences &ca. unless Mr Luke Fortune or some other person claiming interest in the Vessel, should forbid it. If such prohibition should take place, it will be prudent for you to obtain a sufficient indemnification from Mr Fortune to save you harmless, from any consequences of detaining the Register. If the Captain however should require the Register and should offer sufficient security to indemnify you, I do not discover any hazard in your persuing the ordinary course of business on the delivery of it and the usual clearance to him. Should both offer you indemnification, it does not immediately appear to me how you can suffer by delivering the Register to the Captain taking sufficient security from him to save you harmless. This indeed would rather seem to me the safest course.[2]

Your duty does not require you to decide upon the respective rights of Mr Fortune & Captain Stephenson, to direct this Vessel—

and you will of Course avoid any thing that may bear that Construction.

These are my Ideas of what prudence requires, to which I may add that the Case as stated does not appear to involve any question in regard to the Revenue, wherefore & because my opinion could not save you harmless, were you to infringe the legal rights of the parties, I recommend your taking the advice of Council and if equally convenient, perhaps the Attorney of the United States for your District [3] would be the most proper adviser. It will always place you in a blameless situation in the view of the President if you govern yourself by the opinion of a Gentleman to whom government has given its approbation.

I am Sir   very respectfully   Your Obedient Servant

Alexander Hamilton

Jedediah Huntington Esqr
Collector
New London

LF, Mr. Leland F. Leland, St. Paul, Minnesota.
    1. This letter is calendared in *PAH*, VI, 458. It is printed in full in this volume for it is in response to Huntington to H, May 27, 1790, which is also printed in this volume.
    2. This sentence is in H's handwriting.
    3. Pierpont Edwards.

To Bennett Wheeler

Treasury Department, June 14, 1790. "I have received . . . your letter of the 5th Instant. . . .[1] The resolution of your Association, relative to smuggling will be very useful, and is highly laudable. . . .[2] I return my thanks for the Pamphlet you enclosed, & reciprocate very sincerely your Congratulations on the Accession of your State to the General Government." [3]

LS, Rhode Island Historical Society, Providence.
    1. Letter not found.
    2. Wheeler was a charter member and the first secretary of the Providence Association of Mechanics and Manufacturers, which had been founded in 1789.

On June 4, 1790, the association adopted the following resolution: "This Association believing it to be the duty of every citizen, in a republican government, to observe and support the laws thereof, by which alone freemen ought to be governed, and highly approving of the commercial regulations of the Legislature of the Union, by which commerce is put on a just and equal footing throughout the United States, and by which, if duly observed, the manufactures of our country will be greatly encouraged and promoted; and anxious to give a permanent proof of their attachment to the general government, DO RESOLVE, that we will collectively and individually do all in our power to support the said laws, particularly by discountenancing and discouraging smuggling, which we consider injurious to the fair trader, and prejudicial to the morals of those concerned in it: and as we deem it to be disreputable and dishonest to defraud the public revenue as it is to defraud an individual, and consider it to be the duty of every good citizen to give information of any person they shall know to be guilty of smuggling, WE DO FURTHER RESOLVE, that if any person shall hereafter be guilty thereof, to the knowledge of any of us, we will give information thereof to the proper officers of government; and that one half of the reward any of us shall be entitled to, in consequence of such information, shall be the property of the Association, and be paid into the treasury accordingly" (*Mechanics' Festival, An Account of the Seventy-first Anniversary of the Providence Association of Mechanics and Manufacturers . . . Together with a Sketch of the Early History of the Association . . . and Brief Notices of Deceased Officers.* Prepared by Edwin M. Stone [Providence, 1860], 36–37).

3. Rhode Island ratified the Constitution on May 29, 1790.

To William Ellery

[*New York, June 19, 1790.* In June, 1790, Ellery wrote to Hamilton:[1] "I had the honour of receiving your letter of the 19th. the currt." *Letter not found.*]

1. Printed in this volume.

From William Ellery[1]

Newport [*Rhode Island*] *June 22, 1790.* "Your letter of the 7th. instant . . .[2] did not come into my hands until the 19th. . . . I hope and trust that the computation of the Auditor[3] will conform with my account. . . . I have authorized Benjamin Huntington, Esqr. to receive of you on my account Four hundred and Sixty Dollars and twenty six Cents, the sum which by your letter you are ready to pay."

LC, Newport Historical Society, Newport, Rhode Island.
    1. For an explanation of the contents of this letter, see Ellery to H, January 10, March 8, 30, June 1, 1790; H to Benjamin Huntington, March 19, 1790; Huntington to H, March 19, 1790 (all printed in this volume).
    2. Letter not found.
    3. Oliver Wolcott, Jr. See Wolcott to H, July 31, 1790 (*PAH*, VI, 513–14).

To Robert Morris [1]

[New York, June 25, 1790]

Mr. Hamilton wishes to converse with Mr. Morris on the subject of the 44 Shares of bank Stock but being unwell he will be obliged to Mr. Morris to call on him at his house sometime before he goes to Senate.

Friday

AL, Montague Collection, MS Division, New York Public Library.
    1. For background to this letter, see H to Morris, March 19, 1790 (printed in this volume).

From Charles Lee [1]

Alexandria [Virginia] 20th. June 1790.

Sir!

Within the last ten days a process was served on Captain William Simpson of the Brig Ranger on account of the Penalty for a false entry of his Cargo 70 pairs of Cotton Stockings having been omitted. By the laws of Virginia special bail is not required in cases of prosecutions for penalties except in certain instances where the same is demanded by the Acts of Assembly.[2] The Laws of the Congress do not expressly require bail to be given in prosecutions for penalties and thus Captain Simpson has not been ruled to bail. This is a serious defect in the Laws of Congress concerning the revenue.[3]

The difficulty of getting process in time and of obtaining evidence at the Trial in such a District as Virginia, added to the former defect will prevent the Laws being duly enforced.

I have the honor to be, Sir!   Your most Obedt. Servant

Charles Lee, Collector
at Alexandria.

Copy, RG 56, Letters to and from the Collector at Alexandria, National Archives.

1. In *PAH*, VI, 475, 498–99, this letter is listed as a "letter not found."

2. See Section XXVIII of "An Act to amend the Several Acts of Assembly concerning Naval Officers, and the Collection of the Duties" (*Virginia Laws*, 1786 Sess., Ch. XL); Section XXVIII of "An Act to amend the several Acts of Assembly concerning Naval Officers, and the Collection of the Duties" (*Virginia Laws*, October, 1787, Sess., Ch. IV [January 7, 1788]).

3. For the legislation concerning the problem raised by Lee in this paragraph, see "An Act to regulate the Collection of the Duties imposed by law on the tonnage of ships or vessels, and on goods, wares and merchandises imported into the United States" (1 *Stat.* 30–49 [July 31, 1789]) and "An Act to provide for mitigating or remitting the forfeitures and penalties accruing under the revenue laws, in certain cases therein mentioned" (1 *Stat.* 122–23 [May 26, 1790]).

From William Ellery [1]

[Newport, Rhode Island, June, 1790]

Sir

I had the honour of receiving your letter of the 19th. the currt.[2] with the Acts of the United States, and the copies of circular letters which accompanied it. I have not had time as yet to peruse them. I mean to read them with attention, and to act conformably to them. I wish that the forms of the papers to be used in the Custom Houses had been drawn, and transmitted by you to the several Offices; it would have prevented error, and produced and preserved uniformity. The Colle. for the District of Providence [3] brought with him from N. york copies of most of the Forms, and has been so kind as to furnish me with copies. This and your explanations of the coasting act will releive me from that embarrassment, in which a difference in the forms I had collected and the complication of the Act to regulate the Collection of the Duties &c and the Act for registering Vessels and regulating the Coasting trade had involved me.[4]

A case new to me has occurred on which I request your opinion. Last Saturday arrived here from a whaling voyage the Brigantine Fame late from St. Helena Aaron Sheffield master with a cargo of nine hundred, & forty seven barrels of whale Oil, and twelve thousand pounds of Whalebone and produced his papers consisting only of an American Register, and a French Pass copies of which are inclosed. He requested that a Register might be granted to him and was ready to make oath that he was sole owner of the said Brigantine. As the American Register is of a date anterior to the french pass and by the latter she is declared to be du *Batiment Francois* &c I am at a loss to determin whether to deem her French property or the property of the said Sheffield. Captn. Sheffield not having been in France since he entered upon his said whaling voyage if she was French property when he sailed, the property has not since been transferred to him. Captn. Sheffield has been absent several years & has made several whaling Voyages; but his wife & family have resided during his absence on a farm which he owns on this island, and he considers himself, I think properly, as a citizen of the United States. Francis Roche [5] who is mentioned in the American Register as part owner of the said Vessel is I am informed an Inhabitant of Nantucket in the State of Massachusetts.

To encourage the Whale Fishery the French give a bounty on whale Oil, and to obtain that bounty some of the former inhabs. of the United States have made Dunkirk, I believe it is, the place of their residence, and employed their vessels which were built in the United States in the Whale fishery, and when engaged in this business they take along with them their American Registers and French passes to be used occasionally.[6] I should take this to be the case of the vessel about which I am writing, if Capt. Sheffield was not so ready to sware that he was the only owner of her. If She is to be deemed French property She is not I presume entitled to a register and the whale Oil must pay the duty of six per Cent. ad valorem. As this is I believe a new case and as it is expected that a number of vessels under similar circumstances, excepting that they may possibly come in Ballast, are coming to the United States to procure New Registers, under an Apprehension that France may be engaged in War, and their Registers are too old to be good for any thing. I should be happy to have your opinion on the case I have stated as soon as may be convenient; because it would give me great uneasiness to have Capt. Sheffield detained one moment by my doubts.

I am &c

LC, Newport Historical Society, Newport, Rhode Island.
    1. Ellery wrote this letter in his capacity as collector of customs at Newport, Rhode Island, a position to which he had been appointed on June 14, 1790

(*Executive Journal*, I, 51). The delay in his appointment arose from the fact that Rhode Island did not ratify the Constitution until May 29, 1790. See Jeremiah Olney to H, June 7, 1790, note 2 (*PAH*, VI, 458–59). In his previous correspondence with H (Ellery to H, January 10, March 8, 30, June 1, 22, 1790 [all printed in this volume]), Ellery was attempting to obtain the money which he thought was owed to him for his services as Continental loan officer for Rhode Island.

2. Letter not found.

3. On June 14, 1790, or the same day on which Ellery was appointed collector at Newport, Olney was appointed collector of customs at Providence (*Executive Journal*, I, 51). See also H to Olney, June 17, 1790 (*PAH*, VI, 467).

4. For the Treasury Department circulars in which H discusses the measures mentioned in this sentence, see "Treasury Department Circular to the Collectors of the Customs," November 30, December 23, 1789; February 17, April 16, 1790 (*PAH*, V, 575–78; VI, 30–31, 269–70, 367).

5. Francis Rotch.

6. For on explanation of the contents of this sentence, see George Cabot to H, December 18, 1791, notes 2 and 3 (*PAH*, X, 390–91).

From William Ellery

Newport [*Rhode Island*] *July 6, 1790.* "Last Tuesday . . . Capt. Sheffield presented a protest . . . and requested that he might be permitted to unlade part of his cargo in order that he might take out his masts . . . and a permission was granted to him for that purpose. I shall take the *foreign* tonnage of him, and permit him to proceed to L Orient the place of his destination; but shall not give him a Register unless it should appear by your answer to my letter that his vessel is to be considered as American property. . . .[1] The whole expence of the Light-house which is in the Port of Newport for one year, is nearly Four hundred and forty five Dollars. . . ."[2]

LC, Newport Historical Society, Newport, Rhode Island.

1. See Ellery to H, June, 1790 (printed in this volume).

2. Ellery sent this information in response to a request contained in H's "Treasury Department Circular to the Collectors of the Customs," October 1, 1789 (*PAH*, V, 415–16). See also schedule A of "Reports on Additional Sums Necessary for the Support of the Government," August 5, 1790 (*PAH*, VI, 528).

From William Ellery

Newport [*Rhode Island*] *July 12, 1790.* ". . . I have read over the circular letter which contains the opinion of two eminent lawyers . . .[1] which respects the exemption of Vessels under twenty tons from paying fees for their licences. . . . if Licensed Vessels under Twenty tons may trade between the difft. districts of the United States, or carry on the bank or whale fisheries . . . it would seem to me that a fee for their licences is demandable. . . . I cannot conceive that it was the intention of the Legislature of the United States that its servants should do something for nothing. I could have wished that the fees for every Service had been precisely ascertained. . . ."

LC, Newport Historical Society, Newport, Rhode Island.

1. See Richard Harison and Samuel Jones to H, November 18, 1789 (*PAH,* V, 521–22), a copy of which was enclosed in "Treasury Department Circular to the Collectors of the Customs," November 30, 1789 (*PAH,* V, 575–78).

Draft of a Secret Article Concerning the Treaty of Peace with the Creeks [1]

[New York, July 20–August 4, 1790]

The President of the United States states the following Question for the consideration and advice of the Senate.

If it should be found essential to a Treaty for the firm establishment of peace with the Creek Nation of Indians that an article to the following effect should be inserted therein Will such an article be proper [2] viz

And whereas the Trade of the said Creek Nation is now carried on wholly or principally through the territories of Spain and obstructions thereto may happen by war or prohibitions of the Spanish government.

It is therefore agreed between the said parties that in the event of any such obstructions happening it shall be lawful for such persons as the   [3] shall designate to introduce into and transport through the territories of the UStates to the Country of the said Creek Nation any quantity of goods wares and merchandise not exceeding in value in any one year sixty thousand Dollars and that free from any duties or impositions whatsoever but subject to such regulations for guarding against abuse as the United States shall judge necessary, which privilege shall continue as long as such obstruction shall continue.[4]

ADf, Massachusetts Historical Society, Boston.

1. This document is a draft of a secret article which George Washington submitted to the Senate on August 4, 1790, during negotiations in New York City for a treaty of peace and friendship between the United States and the Creek Indians. See "Conversation with George Beckwith," August 7–12, 1790, note 5 (*PAH*, VI, 546–49). In his message to the Senate accompanying this article Washington stated: "In preparing the articles of this treaty, the present arrangements of the trade with the Creeks have caused much embarrassment. It seems to be well ascertained, that the said trade is almost exclusively in the hands of a company of British merchants, who, by agreement, make their importations of goods from England, into the Spanish ports.

"As the trade of the Indians is a main mean of their political management, it is therefore obvious, that the United States cannot possess any security for the performance of treaties with the Creeks, while their trade is liable to be interrupted or withheld, at the caprice of two foreign Powers.

"Hence it becomes an object of real importance, to form new channels for the commerce of the Creeks through the United States. But this operation will require time, as the present arrangements cannot be suddenly broken, without the greatest violation of faith and morals.

"It therefore appears to be important, to form a secret article of a treaty, similar to the one which accompanies this message." (*ASP, Indian Affairs*, I, 80; *Annals of Congress*, I, 1063.) On the same day the Senate "*Resolved*, That the Senate do advise and consent to the execution of the secret article referred to in the message, and that the blank in said article be filled with the words 'President of the United States'" (*Annals of Congress*, I, 1064). On August 7, 1790, Washington submitted the treaty to Congress, and on August 12 the Senate ratified the treaty (*Annals of Congress*, I, 1068, 1074).

2. H originally wrote the word "admissable." The word "proper" is not in H's handwriting.

3. H wrote and then crossed out "Alexander McGillivray." McGillivray was chief of the Creek Indians. On July 20, 1790, he and twenty-nine other leaders of the Creek nation arrived in New York City to negotiate the treaty with the United States Government. In the final form of the secret article, the blank was filled with the words "President of the United States." See note 1.

4. H wrote and crossed out at this point: "unless the United States shall make substantial and effectual arrangement for carrying on the said trade and furnishing the said Creek Nation with the usual supplies by or through their own Agents or Citizens."

To Alexander Martin [1]

Treasury Department, July 29, 1790. "I had the honour of receiving the three . . . draughts from Governor Johnston, and yourself for 18,136 39/90 Dollars, 8507 46/90 Dollars & 1680 Dollars which were remitted to this office. They . . . will be duly passed to the Credit of the State of North Carolina."

Copy, Governor's Letter Book, 1789–1791, North Carolina Department of Archives and History, Raleigh, North Carolina.

1. This letter was written in reply to Martin to H, June 1, 1790 (printed in this volume).

From William Ellery

Newport [Rhode Island] August 2, 1790. States that the land on which the Newport lighthouse is located does not belong to the state of Rhode Island.[1] Discusses means of eliminating smuggling in his district. Asks whether Section 40 of the Collection Law applies to both vessels owned by citizens of the United States and those owned by foreigners.[2]

LC, Newport Historical Society, Newport, Rhode Island.

1. See "Treasury Department Circular to the Collectors of the Customs," October 1, 1789 (*PAH*, V, 415–16).

2. For Section 40 of "An Act to regulate the Collection of the Duties imposed by law on the tonnage of ships or vessels, and on goods, wares and merchandises imported into the United States", see 1 *Stat.* 48–49 (July 31, 1789). See also "Report on Defects in the Existing Laws of Revenue," April 22, 1790 (*PAH*, VI, 373–97), and H to William Webb, May 5, 1790 (*PAH*, VI, 404). Ellery endorsed this letter: "Answered." H's answer has not been found.

From William Ellery

Newport [Rhode Island] August 9, 1790. Asks whether drawbacks are allowable on pickled fish which has been imported, repacked, and then exported to the West Indies.[1]

LC, Newport Historical Society, Newport, Rhode Island.

1. For H's reply to this question, see "Report on Defects in the Existing Laws of Revenue," April 22, 1790 (*PAH*, VI, 373–97).

Report on the Petition of Moses Hazen [1]

[*New York, August 9, 1790.* An entry in the *Journal of the House* for this date reads: "The Speaker laid before the House a

letter and report of the Secretary of the Treasury on the petition of
Moses Hazen, which were read and ordered to lie on the table."
Letter and report not found.]

Journal of the House, I, 296.

1. Hazen had been a lieutenant in the British army on half pay when he was
appointed colonel of the Second Canadian Regiment on January 22, 1776. He
was brevetted brigadier general on June 29, 1781, and retired on January 1,
1783. For correspondence concerning Hazen's request for a settlement of his
charges against the United States as an officer in the Continental Army, see
Tobias Lear to H, December 18, 1789; Oliver Wolcott, Jr., to H, March 13,
1790 (*PAH*, VI, 17, 302).

Hazen had originally petitioned Congress on March 29, 1790, "praying a settlement of certain claims against the United States" as an officer "in the late
Army." The next day, the House ordered that Hazen's petition be referred to
the Secretary of the Treasury for his examination and report to the House
(*Journal of the House*, I, 184, 185). The House did not take action on H's report before it adjourned on August 12, 1790. Hazen petitioned Congress again
in 1791, 1795, and 1802, without success (*Journal of the House*, I, 452; II, 284;
IV, 324), before he died on February 3, 1803. On January 23, 1805, Congress
passed "An Act for the relief of Charlotte Hazen, widow and relict of the late
Brigadier-General Moses Hazen," which granted her a pension of two hundred
dollars a year for life beginning on February 4, 1803 (6 *Stat.* 56).

To Jedediah Huntington [1]

Treasury Department
Augst. 14th 1790

Sir

By this mail will be transmitted to the honorable Richard Law
Esquire Judge of the district court for Connecticut, the decision
on the report upon the petition of Richard Savage; to which & to
my letter [2] accompanying the same be pleased to refer.

I am, Sir, with respect Your obedt. Servt.   A Hamilton

Jedidiah Huntington Esqr.
Collector
New London

LS, anonymous donor.
1. For a somewhat similar letter on the same subject as that printed above,
see H to ——, 1789–1795 (*PAH*, VI, 41).
2. Report and letter not found.

From Thomas Jefferson

[*August 15–21, 1790*. Letter listed in Jefferson's "Summary Journal of Letters." [1] *Letter not found.*]

AD, Thomas Jefferson Papers, Library of Congress.
1. See Boyd, *Papers of Thomas Jefferson*, XVII, 409.

From William Ellery

Newport [*Rhode Island*] *August 23, 1790.* "The arrival of the President of the U. S.[1] the last Tuesday morning prevented my sending the returns last week. I send them this. . . . The Person appointed to collect Light Money[2] by the Govr. of this State[3] continues to do it, and the trade complains of being obliged to pay tonnage to the United States and Light money to the State.[4] I wish for your directions respecting the Light-House. . . ."

LC, Newport Historical Society, Newport, Rhode Island.
1. For a description of George Washington's visit to Newport, see the *Newport* [Rhode Island] *Mercury*, August 23, 1790.
2. Robert Crooke.
3. Arthur Fenner was governor of Rhode Island from 1790 to 1805.
4. The question concerning the payment to the state for the maintenance of the lighthouse at Newport arose because Rhode Island had not ratified the Constitution until May 29, 1790, and the lighthouse was still under the state's jurisdiction. For the resolution of this problem, see Ellery to H, September 14, 1790, notes 1 and 2 (printed in this volume).

To George Washington

[New York, August 23, 1790]

The Secretary of the Treasury presents his respects to the President of the United States and sends him the Draft of a power concerning the intended Loans.[1] If any thing more particular should occur to the President it may be the subject of a distinct instruction.

Monday

LC, George Washington Papers, Library of Congress.
1. For information concerning this document, see Tobias Lear to H, August 26, 1790 (*PAH*, VI, 566); Washington to H, two letters of August 28, 1790 (*PAH*, VI, 578–81).

Account with Tench Coxe

[New York, August 24, 1790]

Recd. August 24th. 1790. from the hon. Alexr. Hamilton Esqr two hundred dollars, which I promise to repay on demand.[1]

Tench Coxe

ADS, Papers of Tench Coxe in the Coxe Family Papers at the Historical Society of Pennsylvania, Philadelphia.
1. At the bottom of this document Coxe wrote: "(repaid in Philada. ℔ Acct. in sundries & Cash)."

To William Ellery [1]

[*New York, August 27, 1790.* Letter listed in dealer's catalogue. *Letter not found.*]

1. LS, sold by Robert Black, Upper Montclair, New Jersey, 1962, Catalogue 87, Item 49.

To Samuel R. Gerry [1]

[*Treasury Department, September 3, 1790.* The description of this letter in the dealer's catalogue reads: "Interesting letter to the newly appointed Collector of Customs at Marblehead (Massachusetts) enclosing a communication for the former incumbent of that office,

Mr. Burrell Devereux,[2] which will enable Gerry 'to receive every thing in his hands relative to the duties of your office.' " *Letter not found.*]

1. LS, sold by Thomas F. Madigan, New York City, 1929, Catalogue 54, Lot 54–102.

2. Gerry replaced Richard Harris, who had been appointed on August 3, 1789, and had died in office. Devereux was never appointed to the position and apparently performed the duties of the office on a temporary basis until Gerry's appointment on August 3, 1790. See *Executive Journal*, I, 12, 53–54.

No letter from H to Devereux has been found.

To Nicholas Gilman [1]

[New York, September 10, 1790]
Private

Dr Sir

I take the liberty to request you will name to me to be submitted to the consideration of the President such persons your way as appear to you best qualified, (and who would be willing to serve) as officers on Board a Revenue boat to be employed on your Eastern Coast.[2]

Prudence activity Vigilance and strict integrity are the *desiderata*.

Yours with great esteem & regard   A Hamilton

New York Sepr. 10. 1790
The Honble Mr Gilman

ALS, from the Rokeby Collection, Barrytown, Dutchess County, New York, courtesy of Mr. Richard Aldrich and others.

1. Gilman, a veteran of the American Revolution, was a Federalist member of the House of Representatives from New Hampshire.

2. For additional information concerning the subject of this letter, see "Report on Defects in the Existing Laws of Revenue," April 22, 1790 (*PAH*, VI, 380–81); H to George Washington, September 10, 29, October 28, 1790 (*PAH*, VII, 31–32, 77–79, 104–05); Joseph Whipple to H, October 9, 1790 (*PAH*, VII, 130–31); H to Gilman, November 19, 1790 (*PAH*, VII, 158).

To Benjamin Lincoln [1]

[New York, September 10, 1790]
Private

My Dear Sir

I have now under consideration the subject of boats for protection of the Revenue. Though they might be built collectively in certain places with most œconomy; as the saving would not be material, and umbrage might be given, I conclude it will be best to make a partition of them among the states. Accordingly, if the President approves my proposition, *One* will be built at Boston *another* at Portsmouth.

The President has received but little information about proper character as officers of the one to be built with you. Capt John Foster Williams [2] is the only person before him who it seems is recommended by Governor Hancock.[3] You will oblige me by your opinion of that Gentleman and by naming any others who may appear to you preferable. And I will request you to turn your attention at the same time to the *inferior* officers whose number & emoluments you will find in the last Collection Bill.[4] Your communications will of course be considered by me as *confidential*. No one can be more sensible than yourself how much the utility of the boats will depend on the characters to whom they are committed— or a better judge of the qualities they ought to possess.

It enters into my views to purchase the Duck of your manufacture for the whole number of boats say ten—by way of encouragement to it.[5] Is it really of the good quality we are told? Can it be had nearly of the same price with the European Duck & what is that price? The dimensions of the boats will be from forty to fifty feet keel. When the President's instructions arrive, you will hear further from me.[6]

I remain Dr Sir   Yr Affect & Obed ser   A Hamilton

New York Sepr. 10. 1790

What can such a boat be completed with you for?

General Lincoln

ALS, Mr. and Mrs. Charles E. Kern, II, Washington, D. C.

1. In *PAH, VII,* 30, this letter is listed as a "letter not found."

2. See H to George Washington, September 29, 1790; Washington to H, October 6, 1790 (*PAH,* VII, 77–79, 97–98).

3. John Hancock, a Boston merchant and signer of the Declaration of Independence, was governor of Massachusetts from 1780 to 1785 and again from 1786 until his death in 1793.

4. For Section 62 of "An Act to provide more effectually for the collection of the duties imposed by law on goods, wares and merchandise imported into the United States, and on the tonnage of ships or vessels" (1 *Stat.* 175 [August 4, 1790]), see H to Washington, September 10, 1790, note 1 (*PAH,* VII, 31).

5. For a description of the Boston Duck or Sail Manufactory, see the enclosure to Nathaniel Gorham to H, October 13, 1791 (*PAH,* IX, 372–73).

6. See "Treasury Department Circular to the Collectors of the Customs," October 1, 1790 (*PAH,* VII, 87).

From William Ellery

Newport [*Rhode Island*] *September 14, 1790.* ". . . The Genl. Assembly of this State at their Session in Bristol, the last week repealed the Acts of the State relative to the Light House,[1] and it is now expected that I should see that the light is kept. . . . I have engaged William Martin . . . to take care of it . . . until I shall have received directions from you. Nothing was done by the Genl. Assembly respecting a Cession of the Light House &c. . . ."[2]

LC, Newport Historical Society, Newport, Rhode Island.

1. The Rhode Island General Assembly passed the following resolution: "*Whereas* the Provision made by Congress, for defraying the Expence of Light-Houses within the United States, is extended to this State:

"*It is therefore Voted and Resolved,* That the Act of this State, made and passed in the Year 1786 entitled 'An Act for regulating the Light-House,' &c. and all other Acts relating to the same, be and they are hereby repealed." (*At the General Assembly of the Governor and Company of the State of Rhode-Island and Providence-Plantations, begun and held by Adjournment at Bristol, within and for the State aforesaid, on the First Monday in September, in the Year of our Lord One Thousand Seven Hundred and Ninety, and in the Fifteenth Year of Independence* [n.p.: Printed by J. Carter], 13.)

For "the Provision made by Congress," see "An Act for the establishment and support of Lighthouses, Beacons, Buoys, and Public Piers" (1 *Stat.* 53–54 [August 7, 1789]).

2. Rhode Island did not cede the lighthouse at Newport until May, 1793. See "An Act granting to the United States of America the public Light-House within this State" (*At the General Assembly of the Governor and Company of the State of Rhode-Island and Providence-Plantations, begun and holden at*

Newport, within and for the State aforesaid, on the First Wednesday in May, in the Year of our Lord One Thousand Seven Hundred and Ninety-three, and in the Seventeenth Year of Independence [Providence: Printed by Bennett Wheeler], 21). See also Ellery to H, March 7, May 9, July 4, November 11, 1791 (*PAH*, VIII, 163–64, 332–32, 528–30; IX, 493–94).

Ellery endorsed this letter: "This letter was answered Sept. 27th 1790." Letter not found. H evidently wrote two letters to Ellery on this date. See H to Ellery, September 27, October 7, 1790 (*PAH*, VII, 74, 99–100).

Treasury Department Circular to the Commissioners of Loans [1]

	Treasury Department
Circular.	September 16 1790

Sir

I have already transmitted [2] a Copy of an act of Congress passed on the fourth day of August 1790, making provision for the debt of the United States, & I now transmit such forms as have been devised for the government of your conduct as Commissioner of Loans in the State of ——.

On the opening of your Office, two books will be provided by you for the purpose of receiving subscriptions, agreably to the form marked (A)—one of these books will be used for receiving subscriptions in Certificates of the domestic debt of the United States [3]—and the other for subscriptions in Certificates of the debt of the State.

The account marked (B) is the form of a statement designed to accompany the Certificates of public debt which may be presented by the Creditors—this account you will endeavor to have made out

Df, in the handwriting of Oliver Wolcott, Jr., with insertions in H's handwriting, Connecticut Historical Society, Hartford.

1. In *PAH*, VII, 57, this document is listed as not having been found. The material within brackets in this document is in H's handwriting.

2. "Treasury Department Circular to the Commissioners of Loans," August 31, 1790 (*PAH*, VI, 588–90).

3. Section 3 of "An Act making provision for the (payment of the) Debt of the United States" (1 *Stat.* 138–44 [August 4, 1790]) described the variety of paper which could be subscribed to the new Federal loan. See Nathaniel Appleton to H, February 5, 1791, note 1 (*PAH*, VIII, 7–9).

by the subscribers to the Loan in cases where you can rely upon their accuracy.

After the statement (B) is examined by you and found right, it will be recorded in the *book of Loans*, marked (C) which is intended to serve as a Waste Book from which entries are to be made in your Journal.

For the amount ascertained to be due by the statement (B) three Certificates will be issued for the different species of stock created by the act of Congress agreably to the forms marked D E F.

When the three species of Certificates of *Funded Debt* before mentioned are issued; duplicate receipts are to be taken therefor, agreably to the form marked (G) one of which will be cut out from the receipt book as a voucher for the account marked (B).

The amount of the loans will be entered in a book agreably to form (H) a copy of which will be the form of a return to be made by you to the Treasury once in each month.

The return to the Treasury agreably to the form (H) will be accompanied by the accounts (B) and the original certificates previously cancelled by you; and will also be supported by a set of the duplicate receipts marked (G).

To prevent forged or counterfeit Certificates from being received on loan, it has been judged necessary that the *Loan Office Certificates* and those issued by *State Commissioners*, should be received *only at the Treasury* and by the *Commissioners of Loans in those States in which such Certificates were issued: the Certificates issued by the Register of the Treasury*—by the *Commissioners of army accounts* and by the *Commissioners appointed to settle the accounts of the five great departments—Indents of Interest* and *bills of old emissions*, are to be recd. indiscriminately *at the Treasury* and by the *Commissioners in all the States* under the limitations and cautions hereafter provided.

All Certificates issued by the *Register of the Treasury* and *all other Certificates* of which you have *no Checks or Registers*, or of the *authenticity of which you entertain doubts*, are previously to a settlement in your office, to be transmitted to the Treasury for examination—to accomplish which with safety & as much dispatch as the nature of the business will admit, the form (J) has been prepared.

In this account you will enter the date number and description of each certificate, with the apparent specie value in the first money column, leaving the other columns blank—on one copy of this account you will pass a receipt to the claimant, in case he requests it—specifying the number and amount of the Certificates presented —and that they are to be transmitted to the Treasury for examination and two Copies of the said Acct. with the Certificates previously cancelled will be by you transmitted to be examined—when the examination is made at the Treasury, the true amount of each Certificate will be inserted, in the second money column of the accounts, one of which with such remarks thereon as will enable you to compleat the business will be transmitted from the Treasury.

As the transmission of Certificates, will be attended with much trouble and delay, which ought to be avoided by every expedient which can be reconciled with a due attention to the public interest—[Notice will be given] to the public creditors, that the necessary arrangements with respect to the Loan would be facilitated [and expedited] in case the applications of holders of *Treasury Certificates* and *those issued by the Commissioners of army accounts, and by the Commissioners for settling the accounts of the five great departments were made in the first instance at the Treasury.* [It will be well for you to repeat this intimation personally to such as may apply to you with any of those Certificates, accompanied with a proper explanation.]

[But] where the Creditors [do not think fit] to apply at the Treasury this Certife. must be received by you, under the limitations before mentioned, taking care to exercise the discretion with which you are invested, for transmitting certain species of Certificates to the Treasury, in such manner that on the one hand, the public be not charged with counterfeit evidences of debt, [and] on the other the public Creditors be [not] exposed to improper delays and inconvenience.

For the renewal of Certificates to such of the public creditors as may not choose to subscribe to the proposed loan, the following forms are to be pursued.

The Certificates which may be presented by non subscribers are to be accompanied with an account agreably to the form marked (K)—which account is nearly of the same form as the account marked (B.) and is also to be made out by the Creditors in all cases where it can be conveniently done—however, instead of consolidating the arrearages of Interest to the first day of January 1791, into a new capital, as is to be done in respect to the *Funded Debt,* you will issue a Certificate agreably to the form marked (L) which Certificate is to bear interest from such a period, that interest being computed at the rate of six ⅌ Centum ⅌ Annum on the amount thereof, to the first day of January 1791 will give the sum of Interest arising from imputations on the Certificates presented agreeable to the statement (K).

For the Certificates issued to non subscribers agreably to the form (L) duplicate receipts are to be taken according to the form (M) one of which will be cut out from the receipt book and filed as a voucher for the account marked (K).

The account (K) is to be recorded in a book agreably to the form (N), which book will be nearly of the same form as the Book of Loans marked (C) and this book (N) is also to serve as a Waste Book, from which the entries relative to *Unfunded Stock,* are to be made in the Journal.

The aggregate amount of the several species of Certificates recd. from non subscribers will be entered in a book agreably to the form (O)—a copy of which will be the form of a return which you will make to the Treasury once in each Month.

The return last mentioned will be accompanied with the accounts marked (K) and the original Certificates previously cancelled by you, and also with one sett of the duplicate receipts marked (M).

The forms and accounts before described are indispensibly necessary to enable the Officers of the Treasury, to close the accounts relative to the several species of Certificates now open in the public books—and for the purpose of ascertaining the amount of Stock which may be credited in the books of your Office, and though a compliance with them will be attended with considerable trouble, you will have the satisfaction of reflecting, that they will become unnecessary, when the Loans are compleated.

When the records are made in the books marked (C & O) you will be prepared to make the necessary entries in your Journals. The cases which will occur with respect to accounts of *principal Stock* are the following viz

1st. When Stock is subscribed in your Office or is to be credited to a non subscriber on his receiving a new Certificate.

2d. When Stock is to be transfered *on* your books.

3d. When Stock is to be transfered *from* your books.

4th. When Stock is transfered *to* your books, by Warrant from the Secretary of the Treasury.

In the *first* instance the proper *Accot. of Stock* will be debited to the *Stock holder* or *Non subscriber,* as the case may happen.

In the *second instance,* the *Assignor,* will be debited to the *Assignee,* for the sum transfered.

In the *third* instance, the *Stock holders* or *Non subscribers* account will be debited to the account of *Stock* for the sum proposed to be transfered.

In all instances where applications are made for transfering Stock from your books, to those of the Treasury or of some other Commissioner the Certificate thereof is to be taken up by you & cancelled, and another issued agreably to the form (P) which Certificate is to be filled up in such manner, as [to] specify the species of Stock and the time from which Interest is payable.

In the *fourth* instance before mentioned, the *account of Stock* will be debited to the *Stockholder or Non Subscriber,* for the sum contained in the Warrant from the Secretary of the Treasury, directing the transfer to be made.

The proper entries to be made in most of the Cases before mentioned are exemplified [4] in the first & fourth pages of the form of the Journal marked (Q).

It will be expedient for you to keep distinct Ledgers for the different kinds of Stock both for the purpose of preventing errors in transfers, and to enable you more expeditiously to balance your books, when the quarterly dividends of Interest are to be made, by employing several Clerks on that business—the forms of the Ledgers in which the accounts of *Stock* are to be kept are marked (R).

For the payment of Interest on the *Funded Debt,* the following regulations are to be observed.

For the term of [fourteen] days before interest becomes due in each quarter, your Office will be closed and no transfers permitted,

4. In MS, "exemplied."

of which regulation, notice ought to be given to the public Creditors.

During this time you ought carefully to balance your books; in case no errors have happened, the credits to individuals, will correspond with the amount debited to the several accounts of *Stock*.

When this is done an account of all the Stock credited to individuals will be entered in the *Book of Dividends* agreably to the form (W). On the sums of Stock credited to each individual the interest will be computed; which Intt. will be for the term of *one quarter;* on the stock subscribed before the expiration of the quarter ending March 31st. 1791—for *the term of two quarters*, on the Stock subscribed between Apl. 1st. & June 30th. 1791 & for *the term of three quarters* on the Stock subscribed between July 1st. & Sept. 30th. 1791—After the Loans are compleated, all the dividends will be made for one quarters interest only, except that it may sometimes happen, that Stock transfered by Warrant from the Secretary of the Treasury may not be credited in your books during the same quarter in which the account for said Stock was closed in the books from which the same was transfered.

When the computations of Interest are made in the Dividend Book, they may be proved to be right by computations on the gross sums of Stock, bearing interest from one period. After the Book of Dividends is thus compleated an Inden thereto ought to be made.

Duplicate Receipts for the interest settled in the Dividend Book are in the next place to be filled up in books to be prepared agreably to the form (X); these receipts are to be numbered progressively, and their numbers inserted in the Column for that purpose in the dividend Book against each Stock holders name. A copy of the Dividend Book being then made out to be transmitted to the Treasury, you will be prepared to open your office for the payment of Interest; which you will be able to do with dispatch, by means of the Inden to the Dividend Book, which will shew you the sum to be paid and the number of the Receipts which are to be signed.

After a payment of Interest, you will cut out of the Book one of the Receipts which you will take therefor, which being regularly filed, will serve in the first instance to govern the charge which is to be made, and afterwards as a Voucher for the account to be transmitted to the Treasury.

At the end of each quarter after the payments of Interest commence, you will render an accot. Current to the Treasury agreably to the form (Y) accompanied with a statement of the Interest paid; which statement will be of the same form as the Dividend Book, and will agree therewith so far as payments have been made, this statement will be supported by one sett of the duplicate Rects. for Interest marked (X).

At the end of the third quarter after the Dividend Book has been settled, an account of all the Interest unclaimed, is to be made out agreably to the form (Z) and transmitted to the Treasury. This account will consist of all the sums appearing due on the Dividend Book for the quarter to which it refers, and will agree with the receipts for Interest remaining unsigned. When this account is rendered the Dividend Book ought to be closed & the unsigned receipts cancelled.

As your Books will contain compleat evidence of all the claims of the Stockholders, both as respects *Principal & Interest,* it will not be necessary that any endorsements should be made on the Certificates of *Funded Debt* which may be issued. In cases of transfers of *Funded Debt* the new Certificate will bear Interest only from the first day of the quarter in which the transfer is made—and any demands for Interest settled in the Dividend Book, will be made only by the person in whose favour the Dividend was made, or his special Assignee.

For the payment of Interest to *Non Subscribers,* a book is to be prepared agreably to the form (No. 1). The documents on which these payments are to be made, will be the Certificate of *Unfunded Debt* issued by you agreably to the form (L).

In each part of the account (No 1) the description of these Certificates is to be entered, and the arrearages of Interest to the 1st. day of January 1791, are to be inserted in the Columns for that purpose. On the *principal sum* contained in each Certificate Interest is to be calculated at the rate of *four ℔ Centum ℔ Annum,* and on the *arrearages of Interest,* at the rate of *three ℔ Centum ℔ Annum* which Interest [will be] payable quarterly during the year 1791.

When the Interest is thus calculated and the payment made, the Creditors or their Attorneys will affix their signatures in the column for that purpose, which signatures will be considered as duplicate Receipts for the sums opposite to their names.

At the end of each quarter, you will cut out from the Interest

Book (No 1) one sett of the accounts, which you will transmit to the Treasury, as a Voucher for the amount, which will be charged in your Account Current.

In this part of the business, it will be necessary that endorsements should be made on the Certifics. for all the Interest which may be paid, and in cases of transfers the same endorsements must be made on the Certificates issued as appeared on those which were given up in consequence of the transfers.

To prevent a multiplicity of entries it will perhaps be expedient that the Interest, paid to non Subscribers should be carried into the Journal, only once in each quarter, on this point however, you can exercise your discretion.

The accounts relative to the payment of Interest being very simple may be kept by you either with those respecting *Principal Stock* or in separate Books as you judge most convenient, and will be opened under the tittles of *United States, Cash,* and *Interest Account,* agreably to the form of a Ledger (No. 2)

The *United States* will be credited by *Cash* for all monies recd. from the Treasury, and will be debited to *Interest Account,* for the gross amt. of all Dividends of Interest which may be settled in favour of the Stock holders, and also for the amount of the Interest paid to *Non Subscribers.* This account therefore, by calculating the demands which will be made by Non Subscribers, and adding the same to the balance of the account, as it will stand on your books, will enable you to judge what monies ought to be [drawn] from the Treasury for the use of your office.

The *Interest Account,* will be credited for the gross amount of all Interest settled in the Dividend Book, and for the Interest paid to Non Subscribers—and will be debited to *Cash* for all payments of Interest made—the balance of this account will shew the amount of Interest unclaimed at your Office.

At the end of the third quarter after a dividend is made, and on the return to the Treasury of unclaimed Interest agreably to the Form (Z) the *Interest Accots.* is to be debited to the *United States* for the amount thereof, as said Interest will no longer be demanded at your Office.

The entries to the account of *Cash,* will consist of credits for money received and debits for money paid, and a transcript thereof will form the Account Current which you are to render to the Treasury.

The Salary to which you are intittled will be paid quarterly, on your drafts or assignments upon the Treasury, and will not therefore be blended with your accounts.

The papers marked (No. 3, 4 & 5) contain forms to be used in transfering Stock, either by personal appearance or by power of attorney; also forms of powers of attorney for transfering Stock & for receiving dividends of Interest, which forms ought to be published for the information of the public Creditors.

As nothing definitive can be done, with respect to the Loan offered for the State debts untill the first day of October 1791, it will not be necessary at present that you should proceed farther in this business than to open a subscription book agreable to the form before described—to keep a correct Register of the Certificates deposited in your Office agreably to the form (No. 6.)—to give descriptive receipts therefor to the subscribers and to report quarterly the amount of the subscriptions to the Secretary of the Treasury.

If the business of your Office shall permit it may be useful for you, to investigate by the best means in your power whether the Certificates deposited in your office possess the properties required by the Act of Congress to render them receivable on the Loan, and to make such remarks as will facilitate the settlement, when the amot. of the Subscriptions is ascertained.

In issuing the several species of Certificates which have been before described your special attention is requested to the following check which has been devised to detect the alteration of the sums for which the Certificates may be issued

In the [blank] margin of the Certificate paper, you will find five Tables, in which the numerical characters are inserted in an uniform order.

In the first Table at the left hand side, each Unit is designed to represent Ten Thousand Dollars—in the second table—One thousand Dollars—in the third table—One hundred Dollars—in the fourth table—Ten Dollars—& in the fifth table each character represents one or more Units.

The rule for reading the figures, is to consider the highest character in each table as significant of a certain sum according to the power of the table.

The highest sum which can be expressed by means of all the Tables is 99.999 Dollars—the figure 9 being the highest in each table.

Supposing the figure (9) in the table expressing ten thousand dollars to be cut out, the table would then express 89.999.—supposing the figure (9) in the table of one thousand dollars, to be cut out & the figure (9) in the table of ten thousand Dollars restored, the table would then express the sum of 98.999.

By attending to this rule it is evident that the different tables may be by an indenture made to express any sum up to 99.999 Dollars—and as each figure has a definite place—and as the highest number in each table is significant of a certain sum in case you are careful in making the indenture it will be impossible that any Certificate should be altered to a larger amount than the sum for which it was issued without being detected by means of this Check.

As a guide to you in making the indenture, it will be well after a Certificate is filled up, to mark the numbers which express the amount thereof, after which the indenture may be made in any way, provided the significant numbers are the highest remaining in the Table.

A form of the tables, and an example of an indenture to be made so as to express the sum of 85.417 Dolls is herewith transmitted [as explanatory of the process. It is marked (No. 7).]

Conveyance: Alexander Hamilton to Jane Moncrieff

New York, September 20, 1790. Recites an indenture dated November 1, 1788, purportedly made by Jane Moncrieff, a widow, selling a lot on William Street to Hamilton for £1752.15.4. States that Mrs. Moncrieff inserted Hamilton's name without his consent and that he refused to accept the indenture.

Certified copy, recorded under the date of February 12, 1791, Conveyances in the Office of the Register, City of New York, Liber 46, 389–90, Hall of Records, New York City.

From William Ellery

Newport [Rhode Island] September 20, 1790. Wishes to suggest some changes in the provisions of the Coasting Act.[1] Proposes that Section 11 be changed so that when a ship or vessel is sold or transferred "a production of such bill of sale to the Collector by the owner be made a condition of his receiving a new Certificate of Registry." States: "By the 12th Sec: when the master of a *registered* Vessel is changed a memorandum of such change is to be endorsed on the Certificate of Registry &c. I have observed such memorandums on some *Enrollments*. Are they necessary?" Proposes that "every licenced vessel be her tonnage, her lading, her destination what it may, or wheresoever she may be employed, be obliged to enter and clear."

LC, Newport Historical Society, Rhode Island.
1. "An Act for Registering and Clearing Vessels, Regulating the Coasting Trade, and for other purposes" (1 *Stat.* 55–65 [September 1, 1789]). See also "Report on Defects in the Existing Laws of Revenue," April 22, 1790 (*PAH*, VI, 373–97). On July 22, 1790, a "bill for registering Ships or Vessels, for regulating those employed in the Coasting Trade and Fisheries, and for other purposes" was presented to the House of Representatives. On July 26, however, the House "*Ordered*, That the farther consideration of the bill . . . be postponed until the next session of Congress" (*Journal of the House*, I, 275–76, 282). A new coasting bill was not passed until February 18, 1793 ("An Act for enrolling and licensing ships or vessels to be employed in the coasting trade and fisheries, and regulating the same" [1 *Stat.* 305–18]).

From Brockholst Livingston and Edward Greswold [1]

New York September 23rd. 1790

Sir,

Please to pay to Mr. James Rivington or order Thirty One Pounds Twelve Shillings for the Sett of Pickerings Statutes [2] purchased of him by the Trustees of the New York Society Library [3] and which you have agreed to take of them for the Office of the Treasury of the United States.[4]

    We are Sir,   Your very obedt. Servants,   Brockholst Livingston
                                               Edw Greswold

To the honorable Alexr. Hamilton Esqr

LS, RG 217, Miscellaneous Treasury Accounts, 1790–1894, Account No. 1196, National Archives.

   1. Greswold was a New York City attorney.

   2. Danby Pickering, ed., *The Statutes of the United Kingdom of Great Britain and Ireland: The Statutes at Large, from Magna Charta to 46 George III*, Vols. 1–46 (London: Printed by G. E. Eyre and W. Spottiswoode, 1761–1806).

   3. The New York Society Library, founded in 1754 and granted a charter by the Province of New York in 1772, was re-established by an act of the state legislature on February 18, 1789 ("An Act to remove doubts respecting the Charter granted to the members of the New-York Society Library" [*New York Laws*, 12th Sess., Ch. XXV]), and housed in the New York City Hall building where it served as a congressional library for the Federal Government.

Both Livingston and Greswold were appointed trustees of the library by the 1789 act.

It is, of course, still in existence.

   4. At the bottom of this letter Tench Coxe, Assistant to the Secretary of the Treasury, wrote the following note to John Myer, a clerk in the Treasury Department: "Pay the above out of the contingent monies in yr. hands.
                                             Tench Coxe
                                           Septr. 29th. 1790."

From Charles Lee [1]

Alexandria [Virginia] 25th. September 1790

Sir!

    The Officers of the Customs are sometimes put to inconvenience in boarding vessels as they arrive. Hitherto they have been obliged to use such as the Merchants would lend. I think it would be proper that a small boat should be provided for the use of this District the cost of which may be computed at from seventy to one hundred Dollars, and with your directions such an one shall be procured as will suit the public purposes.

   I am respectfully Sir!   Your most Obedt. Hble Servt.

                                      Charles Lee, Collector
                                      at Alexandria

Copy, RG 56, Letters to and from the Collector at Alexandria, National Archives.

1. In *PAH*, VII, 73, this letter is listed as a "letter not found." For H's reply to this letter, see H to Lee, October 10, 1790 (*PAH*, VII, 106).

To Pierpont Edwards

[*New York, September 26, 1790.* Hamilton's frank appears on an envelope which is addressed to Edwards and postmarked "New York Sept. 26." *Letter not found.*]

DS, The Filson Club, Louisville, Kentucky.

From William Ellery

Custom House
Newport [Rhode Island] Sept. 27th 1790

Sir,

This letter will be accompanied by a weekly return of cash.

In my last [1] I ventured to offer some hints respecting the Coastg. Act, permit me in this to make some additional remarks, and to propose some other questions.

By the 22nd. Sect: of that Act whenever the property of an enrolled vessel is changed the Owner or Owners thereof are required to make known such change to the Colle. of the District where he or they may reside and a new Certif: of enrollment is to be granted. Is the former Certife. of Enrollment to be recited in the bill of sale as in the case of Registered Vessels?

In the proviso of this Sect: Before any new License shall be given for a succeding year to the master of a vessel less than twenty tons, he shall on oath or affirmation declare that no illicit trade has been carried on &c. The master may be a new one, and entirely unacquainted with the transactions of the preceding year, and neither of the former masters may be to found.

The masters of such vessels as well as of Registered vessels may be changed during the year. Should not notice of such change be given to the Collector, and a memorandum thereof be endorsed on their Licences &c.

By the 26th. Sec: of the same Act the masters of vessels under the circumstances therein mentioned [2] are required to deliver duplicate manifests to the Collect. &c but no penalty is enjoined for neglect or refusal.

There are several other instances in this Act in which certain duties are commanded to be performed, and no penalty annexed to disobedience. Laws without penalties are dead Letters.[3]

I am, Sir,   Yr. most obedt. servant   W Ellery Colle

Alexander Hamilton Esq
Secry of the Treasy.
of the U. S.

LC, Newport Historical Society, Newport, Rhode Island.
    1. Ellery to H, September 20, 1790 (printed in this volume).
    2. Section 26 of "An Act for Registering and Clearing Vessels, Regulating the Coasting Trade, and for other purposes" reads in part: ". . . That the master of every ship or vessel of the burthen of twenty tons or upwards, licensed to trade as aforesaid, having on board goods, wares or merchandise of the growth or manufacture of the United States only, and being bound from a district in one state to a district in any other than an adjoining state, shall deliver to the collector, or where the collector and surveyor reside at different places within the same district, to the collector or surveyor as the one or the other may reside at or nearest to the port where such ship or vessel may be, duplicate manifests of the whole cargo on board . . ." (1 Stat. 62 [September 1, 1789]).
    3. Ellery endorsed this letter: "Answered." H's reply has not been found, but see H to Ellery, September 27, 1790 (printed in this volume).

To William Ellery [1]

Treasury Department, September 27, 1790. "I learn by your letter of the 14th Instant [2] that you have continued William Martin as keeper of the Light House. . . . He will be notified to the President for a regular appointment. . . .[3] The collection of Light Money by the State being a contribution of your Trade to an object the expence of which the United States defray, ought to be discontinued. . . .[4] A cession from the Legislature of their right & Title to the Light House would . . . be desireable. . . .[5] A Bill of Sale reciting the Register of the Vessel sold must be exhibited prior to granting a new Certificate of Registry, and it is proper that the name of the new Master of an Enrolled Vessel at the time of the change should be endorsed on the Certificate of Enrollment and on the licence.[6] Sensible of the danger to the Revenue from the latitude given to licensed Vessels I have inserted some additional Checks in the plan of a new Bill for the regulation of Coasters submitted to the House of Representatives at their late Session. . . ." [7]

LS, The Sol Feinstone Collection, Library of the American Philosophical Society, Philadelphia.
1. This letter is listed as a "letter not found" in *PAH*, VII, 74.
2. Printed in this volume.
3. See H to George Washington, October 5, December 7, 1790 (*PAH*, VII, 94–95, 202); Tobias Lear to H, December 14, 1790 (*PAH*, VII, 342).
4. See H to Ellery, October 7, 1790 (*PAH*, VII, 99–100).
5. See Ellery to H, September 14, 1790, note 2 (printed in this volume).
6. See Ellery to H, September 20, 27, 1790 (printed in this volume).
7. See Ellery to H, September 20, 1790, note 1 (printed in this volume).

To Tench Coxe

[New York, October 1–20, 1790]

Dr Sir

If I understand the statements rightly the money paid by the Collector of Baltimore [1] namely 30000 Dollars is still an advance; but as nothing more is now asked, and as it is presumeable the expences of the expedition [2] and supplies to the end of the year will exceed the sum advanced all is well.

I have only conjecture as to what will be the situation of the troops after the termination of the expedition; but I presume it will be for the Winter pretty much as before the movements commenced. When the Secretary at War [3] returns, I will request him to transmit more particular information.

I recollect nothing in particular about which I wish to see Mr. Williams; [4] but if there be any thing about which he may have expressed a desire to see me I shall be glad to see him at any time before he goes.

To avoid the noise of our confused house I am now at the Baron De Steubens.[5] I shall be all the afternoon at home.

Yrs. very truly   A Hamilton

In the letter to the President I will thank you to let the ⟨– – – –⟩

October ⟨–⟩ 1790

ALS, Papers of Tench Coxe in the Coxe Family Papers at the Historical Society of Pennsylvania, Philadelphia.

1. Otho H. Williams, collector of customs at Baltimore.

2. H is referring to a campaign by the United States Army and the Kentucky militia under the command of Brigadier General Josiah Harmar in September and October, 1790, against several Indian tribes in the West. See "Conversation with George Beckwith and William Macomb," January 31, 1791 (*PAH*, VII, 608–13). See also *ASP, Indian Affairs*, I, 96, 97–98, 101, 104–06.

3. On September 15, 1790, Secretary of War Henry Knox left New York for Boston to attend to his own business affairs (Knox to George Washington, September 15, 1790 [ALS, George Washington Papers, Library of Congress]). Knox did not return to New York until after October 20 (Henry Jackson to Knox, October 24, 1790 [ALS, Massachusetts Historical Society, Boston]).

4. Elie Williams, brother of Otho H. Williams, was the partner of Robert Elliot in the Maryland firm of Elliot and Williams, which had contracted to supply the western posts. See Elie Williams to H, October 10, 1789 (*PAH*, V, 435–47); H to Williams, October 17, 1789 (*PAH*, V, 450–51).

5. Baron von Steuben lived in New York City at 89 Broadway.

The Hamilton family was preparing to move to Philadelphia. See "Notice of Removal from New York City," Ocober 7, 1790 (*PAH*, VII, 100). H rented a house in Philadelphia which was owned by Benjamin Rush (Rush to Tench Coxe, September 13, 23, 1790 [ALS, Papers of Tench Coxe in the Coxe Family Papers at the Pennsylvania Historical Society, Philadelphia]). See also H to Thomas FitzSimons, September 1, 15, 1790 (*PAH*, V, 34–35).

To Joseph Nourse [1]

[*New York, October 2, 1790.* An entry dated December 31, 1792, in Nourse's blotters concerning a special indent issued to Gerard Bancker [2] refers to "general Instructions recd from the Secy of the Treasury ⅌ his letter dated Oct 2 1790." *Letter not found.*]

RG 39, Records of the Bureau of Accounts (Treasury), Blotters of the Register of the Treasury, 1782–1810, National Archives.

1. Nourse was register of the Treasury Department.

2. Bancker, a merchant, was treasurer of the State of New York from 1782 to 1798.

From William Ellery [1]

Newport [Rhode Island] October 5, 1790. ". . . I wish to know whether it would be convenient to you to pay the balance due to me of Eighty four Dolls as late Commr. of the Loan Office in this State."

LC, Newport Historical Society, Newport, Rhode Island.
    1. For background to this letter, see Ellery to H, January 10, March 8, 30, June 1, 22, 1790; H to Benjamin Huntington, March 19, 1790; Huntington to H, March 19, 1790 (all printed in this volume).

To William Ellery

[New York, October 6, 1790. On October 18, 1790, Ellery wrote to Hamilton [1] and acknowledged receipt of Hamilton's letter of October 6. Letter not found.]

    1. Printed in this volume.

From William Ellery [1]

[Newport, Rhode Island, October 11–18, 1790.] "I received your particular letter of the 27th of your circular letter of the 30th. of Sept. last. . . . I will make a provisional Contract with William Martin for his allowance for keeping the Light. . . . The Collection of Light money by the State has been discontinued. . . . I expect the Legislature will make a ⟨mo⟩tion of their right and title to the Light House &c to the United States. . . . Jerathmael Bowen who claims the fee of the Land on which the Light House and Dwelling House stand lives at Swansey in the State of Massachusetts. I will take the earliest and best measures in my power to find out his ideas on this matter. . . . the forms which, in your Circular letter, you requested to be furnished with will accompany this letter. . . ."

LC, Newport Historical Society, Newport, Rhode Island.
    1. For background to this letter, see Ellery to H, July 6, August 2, 23, September 14, 1790; H to Ellery, September 27, 1790 (all printed in this volume). See also "Treasury Department Circular to the Collectors of the Customs," September 30, 1790 (*PAH*, VII, 83–84).

From Charles Lee

Alexandria [Virginia] 16th. October 1790

Sir!

I have received your letter of 24th. September last covering a letter to me from the Collector of Providence,[1] and your answer to him respecting the Sloop Nancy, Christopher Thornton master.[2]

The Merchants to whom she was consigned at Alexandria have informed my deputy Mr Gray [3] that she returned without any Cargo on board when she left our Town, and whatever she had on board on her arrival at Rhode Island must have been put on board after her departure from Alexandria. Thus my books contain no part of her export cargo. Captain Thornton was told at my Office of the necessity of obtaining a certified manifest and permit for the Cargo which he meant to carry to Rhode Island and his observation was, that he could do well enough without any such documents. He never applied for such documents and of course sailed without them.

I suppose he may have [been] led into this error from what had just before happened to him when he left Providence, where he believed the Laws were better understood than at Alexandria.

The various forms, used by me officially which you have directed to be transmitted,[4] shall be sent.

I am most respectfully Sir!   Your most Obt. Hble Servant

Charles Lee, Collector
at Alexandria.

Copy, RG 56, Letters to and from the Collector at Alexandria, National Archives.
    1. Jeremiah Olney. See Olney to H, September 8, 1790, note 3 (*PAH*, VII, 27–28).
    2. H to Olney, September 24, 1790 (*PAH*, VII, 68–69).
    3. Vincent Gray was deputy collector of customs at Alexandria.
    4. See "Treasury Department Circular to the Collectors of the Customs," September 30, 1790 (*PAH*, VII, 83–84).

From William Ellery

Newport [Rhode Island] October 18, 1790. Encloses a provisional contract made with William Martin "in conformity to your letter of the 27th of Sept." Requests opinion whether, under the provisions of "The Act to provide more effecty. for the Collection of the Duties on goods &c," duties are to be repaid on "Goods &c of the growth or manufacture of the United States or of this State . . . exported to a foreign Country before this State had become a member of the Union, and . . . since that event . . . brought back and the duties paid in this Office on their importation." [1] Acknowledges receipt of Hamilton's letter of October 6. [2] States: "I . . . have written to Jabez Bowen Esqe. [3] informing him that I was ready to deliver to him or his order the Books, Documents, Checks and papers in my hands relative to the late Continental Loan Office in our State." [4]

LC, Newport Historical Society, Newport, Rhode Island.

1. The provisions of "An Act to provide more effectually for the collection of the duties imposed by law on goods, wares and merchandise imported into the United States, and on the tonnage of ships or vessels" to which Ellery is referring reads: "Sec. 23 . . . And whereas by the letter of the act, intituled 'An act for laying a duty on goods, wares and merchandises imported into the United States,' articles of the growth or manufacture of the United States, exported to foreign countries, and brought back to the United States, are subject to duty on their importation into the said states; and whereas it was not the intention of Congress that they should be so subject to duty:

"Sec. 24. *Be it therefore further enacted,* That in every case in which a duty may have been heretofore paid on goods, wares or merchandises of the growth or manufacture of the United States, exported to a foreign country, and brought back to the said states, the amount thereof shall be repaid to the person or persons by whom the same shall have been paid, or to his, her or their representatives; and that in every case in which such duty may have accrued, but may not have been paid, the same be remitted, and that no such duty shall hereafter be demanded: *Provided,* That the regulations herein after prescribed for ascertaining the identity of such goods, wares or merchandise, be observed and complied with, and that as well in respect to those heretofore imported, as far as may be practicable, as to those hereafter to be imported.

"And also to ascertain the identity of articles of the growth, product or manufacture of the United States, which having been exported to any foreign port or place, shall be brought back to the said states. . . ." (1 *Stat.* 162 [August 4, 1790].)

2. Letter not found.

3. On August 7, 1790, George Washington nominated Bowen to succeed Ellery as commissioner of loans for Rhode Island and Providence Plantations,

and the Senate approved the appointment the same day (*Executive Journal*, I, 57, 58).

    4. Ellery endorsed this letter: "Answered." H's answer has not been found.

From William Ellery

    Newport [*Rhode Island*] *October 25, 1790.* "I received your letter of the 7th., . . . with the Act of the United States therein enclosed.[1] . . . Your idea is perfectly right that the Light money mentioned by me was for the purpose of supporting the Light-House establishments in this State, and distinct from the imposition you refer to to which Congress have declared their consent. . . .[2] I have delivered to the order of Jabez Bowen Esqe. all the books, checks, documents & papers,[3] with the marking instruments in my hands, excepting the Registers. These I conceive I may retain as a species of evidence in my behalf, until the bond I gave for my faithful conduct as Commr. of the Loan Office be delivered up or cancelled. . . . If you should think my holding them unnecessary . . . they will be delivered to him immediately. . . . Two hundred barrels of pickled fish, and forty three casks of dried fish of the fishery of the United [States] were shipped on board the Brigantine Happy Return Benjamin Sayre Master for Cape Francois, and there landed as appears by a Certificate of two merchants of that port. The weight of the dried fish is specified in the manifest of the outward cargo of said Brigantine which was cleared out from this Port last July; but the pickled and dried fish were laden on board said Brig without notice and without inspection. Is the owner entitled to the allowance allowed by law in lieu of a drawback on the duties imposed on the importation of salt.[4] Please to favour me with an answer to this Question."[5]

LC, Newport Historical Society, Newport, Rhode Island.
    1. *PAH*, VII, 99–100.
    2. See H to Ellery, September 27, 1790 (printed in this volume).
    3. See Ellery to H, October 18, 1790 (printed in this volume).
    4. For the regulations governing the payment of drawbacks, see Sections 57, 58, 59, 60, and 61 of "An Act to provide more effectually for the collection of the duties imposed by law on goods, wares and merchandise imported into the United States, and on the tonnage of ships and vessels" (1 *Stat.* 173–75 [August 4, 1790]); Section 4 of "An Act making further provision for the pay-

ment of the debts of the United States" (1 *Stat.* 181–82 [August 10, 1790]).
  5. Ellery endorsed this letter: "Answered the Owner not allowed the draw-back." H's reply has not been found.

To John Langdon [1]

(Private)
Philadelphia, October 26, 1790

Dear Sir:—

I received a day or two before my departure from New York [2] your letter [3] recommending Mr. Keith Spence,[4] as a proper person for the loan officer of your State and intimating that your brother [5] would not probably incline to accept that appointment.

On receiving information of the resolution of Mr. Gilman [6] to decline the office, I took occasion to remind the President, by a line, of your brother; adding that the information I had received concerning him induced me to consider him as an eligible character.[7]

Yesterday came to hand a letter from the President to your Brother inclosed in one to me announcing his nomination to the office.[8] I have concluded to send it forward, not withstanding your intimation to me; in the hope, that upon the whole he will determine not to refuse.

The convenience of the States is concerned that the business to be executed by the loan officer should not be longer delayed; and if the office does not at this moment exhibit a lucrative aspect, it ought to be considered that it is of the nature to be likely to be permanent; and that it must necessarily stand or be put on a footing to command the services of the best men; & that its importance and emolument will in all probability be progressive.

With regard to Mr. Spence as well from other information as from what you say of him, I am satisfied that he is a man of merit and competent to the trust; but I am informed, that he has lately experienced all the embarrassment of Insolvency. Unless this matter can be explained so as to shew that these embarrassments are effectually done away, I cannot help thinking, that the situation will appear to the president a weighty objection to the person.

As he is to have the actual disposition of considerable sums of money, it is a **strong reason** for looking for a man unembarrassed in his circumstances. Should one in a different situation be appointed from a confidence in his personal character the prudence of it might be questioned in the first instance & if an accident of any kind should happen it would not fail to be severely censured. I have the honor to be with great esteem & regard

    Sir   Your most Obed. Servt.   Alex. Hamilton

Letters by Washington, Adams, Jefferson and Others Written During and After the Revolution to John Langdon, New Hampshire (Philadelphia: Press of Henry B. Ashmead, 1880), 77–78.

1. Langdon, a New Hampshire merchant, was speaker of the state legislature from 1777 to 1781, a member of the Continental Congress in 1775, 1776, and 1783, a state senator in 1784, and president of New Hampshire in 1785 and 1788. In 1789 he became a United States senator.

2. See "Notice of Removal from New York City," October 7, 1790 (*PAH*, VII, 100). See also H to Tench Coxe, October 1–20, 1790, note 5 (printed in this volume).

3. Letter not found.

4. Spence was a Portsmouth, New Hampshire, merchant.

5. Woodbury Langdon, the brother of John Langdon, was a New Hampshire merchant and politician. In June, 1790, after he had served five years on the state superior court, he was impeached for neglect of duty by the lower house of the state legislature. The trial was not held until January, 1791, and Langdon was allowed to resign.

6. Nathaniel Gilman.

7. See H to George Washington, October 6, 1790 (*PAH*, VII, 96–97).

8. See Washington to H, October 15, 1790 (*PAH*, VII, 115).

To William Ellery

[*Philadelphia, October 29, 1790.* On November 16, 1790, Ellery wrote to Hamilton: [1] "I have received your letter of the 29th of Octe." *Letter not found.*]

1. Printed in this volume.

From William Ellery

Newport [*Rhode Island*] *November 1, 1790.* Submits questions concerning the interpretation of "the second clause in the 17th.

page" and "the 27th. page" of the Collection Law.[1] States that the
state legislature has postponed passage of a motion ceding its right
and title to the Newport lighthouse to the United States.[2]

LC, Newport Historical Society, Newport, Rhode Island.
    1. See Sections 16 and 38 of "An Act to provide more effectually for the
collection of the duties imposed by law on goods, wares and merchandise imported into the United States, and on the tonnage of ships and vessels" (1 *Stat.*
145–78 [August 4, 1790]).
    2. See Ellery to H, September 14, October 11–18, 1790 (printed in this
volume).
    Ellery endorsed the letter calendared above: "answered Nov. 14." H's letter
has not been found.

From William Ellery

[*Newport, Rhode Island*] *November 8, 1790.* ". . . In my letter
of the 12th. of July [1] I expressed a wish that the fees for every service had been precisely ascertained. I hope that this will take place
in the new Coasting Act. . . ." [2]

LC, Newport Historical Society, Newport, Rhode Island.
    1. Printed in this volume.
    2. See Ellery to H, September 20, 1790, note 1 (printed in this volume).

To Thomas Mifflin [1]

Philadelphia, November 13, 1790. Introduces R. J. Vanden Broeck
who was "a Clerk for a considerable period in the office of the Auditor of the State of New York and afterwards in that of the Secretary at War. . . ."

ALS, Schuyler Papers, MS Division, New York Public Library.
    1. Mifflin, a former Quaker and Philadelphia merchant, was a veteran of the
American Revolution, during which he had achieved the rank of major general.
He was a member of the Continental Congress from 1782 to 1784 and served
as president of that body from December 13, 1783, to June 3, 1784. He was
president of the Supreme Executive Council of Pennsylvania from 1788 to 1790,
when he was elected governor of the state.

To William Ellery

[*Philadelphia, November 14, 1790.* Ellery endorsed his letter to Hamilton of November 1, 1790: [1] "answered Nov. 14." [2] *Letter not found.*]

1. Printed in this volume.
2. See William Ellery, Jr., to H, November 30, 1790.

From William Ellery

[*Newport, Rhode Island*] *November 16, 1790.* "I have received your letter of the 29th of Octe.[1] with the inclosed Acts. . . ."

LC, Newport Historical Society, Newport, Rhode Island.
1. Letter not found.

From Walter Livingston

New York Novr. 20. 90

Sir

Mr. Sands [1] informs me that you promised him to procure the Opinion of the Attorney General of the Union [2]; Whether the powers of the Comptroller [3] extended to the Settlement of the Demand exhibited by Sands Livingston & Co. against the united States and by them, with the consent of the Parties submitted to Referrees. Our Claim is of such magnitude, that few persons can submit, without very great inconvenience to the (perhaps unavoidable delays on the part of government,) to be ranked among those chosen for your Claimants have not the smalest pretensions, If the Attorney General is in Philadelphia we are persuaded no unnecessary delay will take place. If not we must perforce wait for justice.[4]

I am Sir   your H St.

The Honble Alexr Hamilton Esqr.
Philadelphia

LC, New-York Historical Society, New York City.

1. At the time this letter was written Comfort Sands was a director of the Bank of New York, which he had helped to found in 1784.

2. Edmund Randolph.

3. Nicholas Eveleigh.

4. For information concerning the claims of Sands, Livingston, and others against the United States Government, see "Report on the Petition of Comfort Sands and Others," February 24, 1791 (*PAH*, VIII, 138–41).

To Israel Ludlow [1]

Treasury Department, November 20, 1790. Commissions and instructs Ludlow to make "the Surveys which still remain to be made towards a complete demarkation of the boundaries of the several Tracts of land which have been contracted for with the persons respectively denominated The Ohio Company, The Scioto Company, and the Miami Company."

Extract, RG 217, Miscellaneous Treasury Accounts, 1790–1894, Account No. 2472, National Archives.

1. This letter, which had not been found when *PAH*, VII, was published, is printed in full in Arthur St. Clair to H, May 25, 1791, note 2 (*PAH*, VIII, 362).

Ludlow was a New Jersey surveyor and land speculator. He also acted as an agent for William Duer on the frontier. See Arthur St. Clair to H, July 21, 1791 (*PAH*, VIII, 563).

See also "Report on Appropriations of Money for Certain Purposes," January 6, 1791 (*PAH*, VII, 416–18); Ludlow to H, May 5, 1792 (*PAH*, XI, 361–64).

From Hugh Hughes [1]

Yonkers [New York] Novbr. 21st. 1790

Sir,

Happening very lately to see an Act of Congress, which was passed the last Session, making certain Appropriations of Monies

ADfS, Papers of Hugh Hughes, Library of Congress.

1. Hughes was assistant quartermaster general from May 11, 1776, to December 6, 1781.

This letter concerns the payment of debts incurred by the quartermaster's department after August 5, 1780, when Timothy Pickering became quartermaster general. By 1780, because of an empty treasury, army contractors and suppliers were given in lieu of money certificates which amounted to promises arising from Duties on Goods, Wares and Merchandize imported, as well as on the Tonnage of Ships &c. which Act has the following Clause—"The Sum of forty thousand Dollars towards discharging certain Debts contracted by Colonel Timothy Pickering late Quarter Master General, and which Sum was included in the Amount of a Warrant drawn in his Favour by the late Superintendant of the Finances of the United States, and which Warrant was not discharged." [2] It immediately occurred to me that this must mean the 40,000 Dollars which Colonel Pickering first gave me a Draught on Mr. Tillotson [3] for, and next, on ye late Board of Treasury; but as neither Mr. Tillotson, who was the Receiver of Taxes in this State, nor the Board of Treasury, was in Cash, not either of the Draughts was paid and the last was deposited with Messrs. Osgood and Liv-

---

to pay. The question of redeeming these certificates was further complicated by various changes in the relationship of individual states to first the Confederation and then the Federal Government.

As the letter printed above indicates, the matter was still not settled after H had been Secretary of the Treasury for more than a year, and the complexities attending the various attempts to collect such payments often rested on circumstances for which any kind of specific proof appeared to be lacking. Then, too, there was the question of just how responsible the officials in the quartermaster's department were for pledges they had made. For example, on August 5, 1790, H wrote: "The then Quarter Master General alleges, and the allegation is supported by some evidence, that he and his assistants relying on being enabled to make due payment, have rendered themselves in a number of cases personally answerable for its being done. . . .

"It has happened, that several persons have brought in the Certificates they received from the Quarter Master General and his deputies, to the Commissioner for settling the accounts of that department, to be cancelled and have received other certificates in lieu of them which now constitute a part of the general debt. To what extent this has been done is not ascertained, nor can be so without going over an immense mass of cancelled papers." (PAH, VI, 522.)

Finally, Hughes's demand represents a special problem, for as H reported on November 30, 1792: "The books and vouchers of Mr. Hughes having been destroyed by fire, no aid to his recollection can be supposed to have been drawn from that source" (PAH, XIII, 260).

2. This quotation is from "An Act making certain Appropriations therein mentioned" (1 Stat. 185–86 [August 12, 1790]).

For the transaction mentioned in this quotation, see "Report on a Particular Statement of the Warrants Issued by the Late Superintendent of Finance, and by the Board of Treasury," September 25, 1789 (PAH, V, 400–03). See also "Report on the Estimate of the Expenditure for the Civil List and the War Department to the End of the Present Year," September 19, 1789 (PAH, V, 379–92); "Report on Additional Sums Necessary for the Support of Government," August 5, 1790 (PAH, VI, 520–42).

Robert Morris resigned as Superintendent of Finance on November 1, 1784.

3. Thomas Tillotson. For his accounts with Pickering, see references in note 2.

ingston, who composed the Board at the Time of Presenting it, which as near as my Memory serves, was, in the Spring of '84,[4] when, I received for Answer, "That whenever Congress were invested with sufficient Funds, it should be discharged." From which, to the Time that the Legislature of this State made a Specie Grant of 1,80000 Dollars to Congress, which, if I mistake not, was in '85,[5] as I resided in another State and often severely indisposed, and heard no further of it. But on hearing of that Grant, which, as I was informed by several Persons of Veracity, was the more readily made, from an Apprehension that 40,000 Dollars of it would go to satisfying the just Claims of their Constituents. In Fact, this was confided to me by several Members of the Legislature, themselves. I applied for that Sum, I was told that it had been issued for the current Service, & dischargg some Part of the Interests of the Dutch Loan, and was told that there were no Hopes of it untill a more efficient Government took Place. From all which it will evidently appear that I never lost Sight of it, tho' sometime prevented by Sickness & Locality from attending.

What the whole Intention or Design of those who have made this last Application to Congress for the sd. 40,000 Dollars is, I can not say, as I have never been consulted on it, but beg to be believed, when I assure you, Sir, that the original Intention of giving me the aforesd. Draughts, was to enable me to fulfil my Engagements and which were made at the ⟨–⟩ Request of the QMG to the Inhabitants of this State in particular as having afforded him more ⟨supplies⟩ than any other ⟨whatsoever⟩, and that not only in an official Capacity, but in a private one, as there was a Time, when neither the QMG, nor my Self, could obtain what the Service required without becoming responsible in a private Capacity,[6] and, which he, I ⟨am⟩

4. Samuel Osgood and Walter Livingston did not become commissioners of the Board of Treasury until January 25, 1785 (JCC, XXVIII, 18).

5. Hughes may have been mistaken in the figure in this sentence and may have intended to write "100,800." In any event, "An Act directing the Treasurer of this State, to pay into the Treasury of the United States, 147,734 9–90 Dollars" authorized the "Treasurer of this State . . . to pay into the Treasury of the United States . . . , in Specie, amounting to One Hundred and Ten Thousand and Eight Hundred Dollars, and fifty-one ninetieths of a Dollar . . ." (New York Laws, 8th Sess., Ch. LIII [April 4, 1785]).

6. For example, see Pickering to Hughes, January 22, 1782 (ALS, Massachusetts Historical Society, Boston); Hughes to Sickles, January, 1782 (ALS, Massachusetts Historical Society, Boston).

very confident, must well remember. Then it was, Sir, that I became answerable, in my private Character, for Services and Supplies for the Publicke, and received repeated ⟨written⟩ Assurances, that I should be furnished with Monies to pay for whatever I procured on that Condition but which I have not paid, tho' often called on, and threatened with Suits. Nay, the QMG. authorized me to promise Payment, *in Specie,* at three Months Credit, for all Services and Supplies from the Beginning of the Year 1782, as well to that Branch of his Department, under my Direction, as to the Country at large, and this I did, in the most perfect Confidence & solemn Manner, but without being enabled to fulfil my Promises to this Day, tho' it was in Consequence of those very Assurances in my private Capacity that I not only procured large Supplies, but retained a good Number of the most useful Persons in the Service—however my Zeal then might have had the ascendancy of Prudence.

This being an incontestable State of Facts, Sir, I appeal to your well known Love of public, as well as private, Justice, whether the 40,000 Dollars first mentioned ought to be diverted from the Original Design of granting them, and whether the Persons to whom they are due, are not as fairly & justly entitled to Interest on their respective Sums, as any other public Creditor whatever without Deduction of any Kind? specially when the liberal Services and Supplies, as well as the Length of Time that they have lain out of their Property, are considered, and that many others withheld, when they so cheerfully and nobly contributed to the Salvation of their Country? If this original Design be done, ⟨and⟩ is but carried into Execution, I care not who does it; as I wish not to receive any public Money but what is fairly and honestly due to me, and that, I know your Candor will allow me the same Right to as others, as you are very sensible, that I have not ⟨–⟩ it less faithfully.

Impressed with these Ideas of the Services and Supplies rendered the Public by the worthy Inhabitants of this State, at my special Insistance and being that the Money in Question were not paid, I could do no less, in Justice to them as well as myself, than address you on the Subject, Sir,—

Whatever, in this, relates to Colonel Pickering, the late QMGeneral, I am very confident, from repeated Experience, he will confirm.

Whenever you may think it proper to favor me with a Line I will thank you, as I reside in the Country, to order it under Cover to General Lamb.[7]

Should personal Attendance be requisite, I will do myself the Honor, Sir—

If I have trespassed on your Time, I know you have Goodness to forgive the Prolixity of Age especially in one whom you have so often favor'd with your Confidence & Friendship.

I have the Honor to be, with every Sentiment of Esteem and Regard Sir, your most obdt. Humble Servant   H H

7. John Lamb, collector of customs at New York.

From William Ellery

Newport [*Rhode Island*] *November 22, 1790.* "William Bright-man Master of the Schooner Fly a British built vessel of the burthen of Twenty two tons & ¾ as measured by the Surveyor of this Port [1] arrived here last tuesday and reported his vessel and Cargo consisting of about fifty Quintals of dried Codfish and ten Tons of Train Oil. Upon inquiry we found that he had no Register or any other ship-ping paper and that said vessel was purchased so lately as the first of last Oct, and not entitled to the Privileges of a vessel of the United States; and under the circumstances in which the fish were caught and the Oil extracted and imported, it became a question whether both vessel and cargo were not subject to seizure and for-feiture by the first clause in the 40th. page of the new Collecting Law; [2] and if not so subject whether her cargo was not subject to the foreign duty. . . . Capt. Brightman has consented . . . to wait until I shall receive your Sentiments on this subject. . . ." [3]

LC, Newport Historical Society, Newport, Rhode Island.
  1. Daniel Lyman.
  2. This is a reference to Section 70 of "An Act to provide more effectually for the collection of duties imposed by law on goods, wares, and merchandise imported into the United States, and on the tonnage of ships and vessels" (1 *Stat.* 177 [August 4, 1790]).
  3. See Ellery to H, January 17, 1791 (printed in this volume).
  Ellery endorsed this letter: "Answered Dece. 6th." H's reply has not been found.

From William Ellery, Junior [1]

Newport [*Rhode Island*] *November 30, 1790.* "I have received your Letter of the 14th. inst: [2] shall transmit by the first convenient opportunity the Registers of the Business done by the Late Loan Offices. . . ." [3]

LC, Newport Historical Society, Newport, Rhode Island.
1. Ellery, the son of William Ellery, was deputy collector of customs at Newport.
2. Letter not found.
3. See William Ellery to H, October 18, 25, 1790 (printed in this volume).

To Tench Coxe

[Philadelphia, November, 1790–1794]

Dr. Sir

Inclosed is a letter, which came under cover to General Knox, and which he sent to me as probably intended for me—on opening it, it appears to be your's & I send it accordingly.

Yrs   A H

ALS, Papers of Tench Coxe in the Coxe Family Papers at the Historical Society of Pennsylvania, Philadelphia.

To Tench Coxe

[Philadelphia, November, 1790–1794]

Dr Sir

If you are not otherwise engaged I will call on you at 12 to day & ask you to accompany me to complete my visits to members of Congress. I am afraid I shall never finish without a guide.

Yrs   A Hamilton

Sunday

ALS, Papers of Tench Coxe in the Coxe Family Papers at the Historical Society of Pennsylvania, Philadelphia.

To Samuel Bosworth [1]

Treasury Department
Dec. 2⟨d⟩ 1790.

Sir

I have received you⟨r l⟩etter [2] relative to the hydrometer [3] which will be sent to you as soon as finished. Should it be in your power to borrow one for the short time before it reaches you it will be convenient.

The Bond [4] sent on by you is right in all respects except that it should be to *"The United States of America"* and not to me as Secretary of the Treasury. You and your Surety will be pleased to execute another with that alteration and to transmit it to me.

I am, Sir,   Your obedient servant   A Hamilton

Samuel Bosworth Esq.
Surveyor, Bristol
R. Island.

LS, Rhode Island Historical Society, Providence.
    1. See Jeremiah Olney to H, June 23, 1790 (*PAH*, VI, 470).
    2. Letter not found.
    3. See "Treasury Department Circular to the Collectors of the Customs," December 18, 1790 (*PAH*, VII, 368–72).
    4. See Section 52 of "An Act to provide more effectually for the collection of the duties imposed by law on goods, wares and merchandise imported into the United States, and on the tonnage of ships or vessels" (1 *Stat.* 171 [August 4, 1790]).

To William Ellery

[*Philadelphia, December 6, 1790.* Ellery endorsed his letter to Hamilton of November 22, 1790: [1] "Answered Dece. 6th." *Letter not found.*]

    1. Printed in this volume.

To Edmund Randolph [1]

[*Philadelphia, December 10, 1790.* On July 9, 1791, Randolph wrote to Hamilton: [2] "In answering your communication of the 10th. of december last." *Letter not found.*]

1. Randolph, a native of Virginia, was an aide-de-camp to George Washington in 1775, a member of the Continental Congress from 1779 to 1783, governor of Virginia from 1786 to 1789, and attorney general of the United States from 1789 to 1794.
2. *PAH,* VIII, 541.

To Sharp Delany [1]

Treasury Department
December 12th. 1790.

Sir

I find it necessary to be more fully informed as to some particulars attending the case stated to me by Messrs. Warder & Co.[2] on the 6th. Instant.[3]

It is said in your Notes and additions to their statement that the Teas were surveyed by the Wardens with *the consent* of the Collector. I wish to know, if the appointment was made by you according to the directions of the 16th. Section of the then collection Law [4] and if the Surveyors were sworn by you. I also request a copy of the return, or if more convenient to you of the original.

The statement of the Importers declares the importation to have been made in December 1789, and altho' the Bond remained unpaid the case was never made known at the Treasury till the 6th. Instant.

The credit must then have expired about six months. I request you will inform me if there were any circumstances attending this case which prevented as full and accurate a statement and as equitable an adjustment in May or June as can be made at this time.

I am, Sir, Your Obedt. Servt.   A Hamilton

Sharp Delany Esqr.
collr Philadelphia.

LS, Mr. Ben Weisinger, New York City.

1. This letter was written in response to an undated letter which Delany wrote to H and which in *PAH*, VII, 398, has been dated "December, 1790." The letter printed above makes it clear that a more appropriate date for Delany's letter would be "November, 1790." A second undated letter from Delany in *PAH*, VII, 398–99, which has been dated "December, 1790," is Delany's reply to the letter printed above and should be dated "December 13–31, 1790."

2. John and Jeremiah Warder were Philadelphia merchants.

3. Statement not found.

4. Section 16 of "An Act to regulate the Collection of the Duties imposed by law on the tonnage of ships or vessels, and on goods, wares and merchandises imported into the United States" reads: "That if any goods, wares or merchandise, on which duties are payable, shall receive damage during the voyage, or shall not be accompanied with the original invoice of their cost, it shall be lawful for the collector to appoint one merchant, and the owner or consignee another, who being sworn or affirmed by the collector well and truly to appraise such goods, shall value them accordingly, and the duties upon such goods shall be estimated according to such valuation; and if any package, or any goods stowed in bulk, which shall have been entered as is herein before directed, shall not be duly delivered, or if any of the packages so entered shall not agree with the manifest, or if the manifest shall not agree with the delivery, in every such case the person having command shall forfeit and pay the sum of two hundred dollars, unless it shall appear that such disagreement was occasioned by unavoidable necessity or accident, and not with intention to defraud the revenue" (1 *Stat.* 41 [July 31, 1789]).

To Nathaniel Appleton [1]

Treasury Department
Dec. 13. 1790.

Sir

I am of opinion it will be most proper that a person having a general power to transfer stock should not transfer to himself. He may as well transfer to a third person, who can afterwards transfer to him, which will avoid all question.

When you issue new certificates on a transfer of stock, it will be well that on the back of the cancelled certificate (or file of cancelled certificates, if there be several) you take a receipt or receipts for that or those you give in lieu thereof.

As notaries public are not to be found in the interior part of the States, I shall have no objection to your acting upon powers of Attorney authenticated by a Judge of the superior or inferior courts of Massachusetts, with the seal of the Court; or without seal if the hand writing of the Judge be known, or can be satisfactorily proved, to you.

I am, Sir, Your obedt. servant   A Hamilton

Nathaniel Appleton Esq.
Commissioner of Loans
Boston.

LS, The Sol Feinstone Collection, Library of the American Philosophical Society, Philadelphia.
1. This letter was written in reply to Appleton to H, November 20, 1790 (*PAH*, VII, 160–61).

To William Ellery

[*Philadelphia, December 13, 1790*. On January 17, 1791, Ellery wrote to Hamilton: [1] "On my return from the Eastward . . . I found that four letters had been received from you. . . . The third dated Dece. 13. 1790 respects the Departure of the Ship Warren from the District of Providence without a coasting licence or register." [2] *Letter not found.*]

1. Printed in this volume.
2. See Jeremiah Olney to H, November 29, December 24, 1790 (*PAH*, VII, 168–69, 210); H to Olney, December 13, 1790 (*PAH*, VII, 381).

To Nathaniel Phillips [1]

[*Philadelphia, December 13, 1790*. On June 6, 1791, William Ellery wrote to Hamilton: [2] "I received a letter from the Surveyor of the Port of Warren some time ago inclosing a letter from you of the 13th. of Decr. 1790." *Letter not found.*]

1. Phillips was surveyor of the ports of Warren and Barrington, Rhode Island.
2. Printed in this volume.

From Willem Six [1]

[Amsterdam, December 17, 1790]

Permettez, Monsieur, quoique je n'aye pas l'avantage d'être connu de vous, que j'ajoute quelques lignes a la Lettre des deux Maisons,[2] de la derniere desquelles je Suis un des Associés.

L'Auteur du Federaliste est connu en Europe peutêtre plus, qu'il ne pense peutetre luy même. Elevé dans la carriere politique, que les evenemens des dernieres années m'ont fait échanger contre des occupations differentes, j'aÿ crû de mon devoir, non de lire, mais d'etudier cet ouvrage; et bientot l'agrement et l'Interet se sont reünis au devoir: Il ne conviendrait pas a votre delicatesse, Monsieur, d'entendre, ni a la mienne peutêtre de vous dire ce que j'en pense. Permettes moy seulement de vous assurer, que depuis ce temps j'ay ambitionné en silence la satisfaction d'entrer en Correspondance avec vous. L'occasion s'en est offerte, et je m'empresse de la saisir.

J'aime l'Amerique, Monsieur, comme l'on aime le spectacle d'un Etat jeune & fier de toute sa force & de toute sa beauté. J'y aÿ placé une partie de ma fortune, persuadé, que je rendrais service a ceux qui viendront aprés moÿ. Je suis egalement convaincu, qu'a la Paix les relations entre nos deux Patries deviendront très interessantes; qu'il ÿ aura plus d'*intercourse* entre les hommes eclairés des deux Paÿs, et que vraisemblablement et l'Ancien et le Nouveau Monde n'y pourront que gagner.

Pour peu que vous m'encouragies, Monsieur, je desirerais vous entretenir de plusieurs objets, qui regardent la prosperité *generale*. L'etude de l'Economie politique et des ouvrages immortels des Ecossais, et Surtout d'Adam Smith dans cette partie, a toujours eté mon occupation favorite. Ils peuvent adoucir assez les loisirs de l'homme retiré des affaires publiques, et qui, comme de raison, doit s'interdire de toucher a cette Arche Sacrée.

J'ay l'honneur d'etre avec des Sentimens d'une consideration particuliere Monsieur! Votre tres humble & très obeissant Serviteur!
Six

Amsterdam ce 17 de Decr. 1790.

Si vous me faites l'honneur, Monsieur, de me repondre, ajoutez y la bonté de le faire en Anglais. Je le lis, comme le Francais, ne l'ecrivant que difficilement.

ALS, Hamilton Papers, Library of Congress.
  1. Six, a merchant in Amsterdam, was a member of the firm of Couderc, Brants, and Changuion.
  2. Letter not found.

From Walter Livingston

New York Decr. 18. 1790

Sir

On the 20 of last month [1] I applied to you respecting the Claims of Sands Livingston & Co. against the united States. Tho hurried with the most important business, permit me to call your attention to our demand, by requesting you to inform me, if application has been made to the Attorney General, for his opinion respecting the authority of the Comptroller either to allow or reject the Claims established by the Award.

LC, New-York Historical Society, New York City.
  1. This letter is printed in this volume.

From William Ellery, Junior

Newport [Rhode Island] December 21, 1790. "I have received your Letter of the 6th instant,[1] and have acted accordingly. . . ."

LC, Newport Historical Society, Newport, Rhode Island.
  1. Letter not found.

From Charles Lee

Alexandria [Virginia] 22 December 1790

Sir!

Application has been made to me by Mr. William Lowry of this Town for the refund of the foreign Tonnage paid upon the Entry of the Brig Rachel on the 24th day of April last who alledges that this case is within the relief of the Act of the last Session of Congress entitled an act Imposing Duties on the Tonnage of Ships or Vessels.[1] Before the late change of Government the Brig Rachel had an American Register under the State of Massachussetts, and in December 1789 she sailed from hence with her old Register by permission of Mr Lowry, who was informed of the propriety of taking out for her a Congressional Register in order that she might be entitled to the privileges of an American Vessel when she should return. Though it was in his knowledge that this was necessary it was omitted and when the vessel returned, she was treated as foreign Vessels are directed to be treated—lately a Congressional Register has been obtained for her, bearing date the 6th. of August last.

Considering the late Act of Congress before mentioned and your letter of the 20th. of August[2] as expressive of your construction of it, I have a doubt whether the refund should be made in this case, and am to request your direction in this particular. I ought to have before stated to you that the Brig Rachael sailed from hence to London in December 1789 and returned from thence to this Port in April 1790, and was not trading Coastwise or in the Fisheries.

I am with respect, Sir!   Your most Obedt. Hble Servant

Charles Lee, Collector
at Alexandria.

Copy, RG 56, Letters to and from the Collector at Alexandria, National Archives.
  1. 1 *Stat.* 135–36 (July 20, 1790).
  2. "Treasury Department Circular to the Collectors of the Customs," August 20, 1790 (*PAH*, VI, 561–62).

From William Duer [1]

[New York, December 24th. 1790]

My dear Friend,

I learn with inexpressible Concern, that your Health still Continues in an Equivocal State: all your Friends here Entertain on this Subject the most serious Anxiety, and I am constantly required to Impress on you the necessity of some Relaxation from the laborious Duties of your Office. In the Executing this Task, I obey the Impulse of my own Heart, let me therefore Entreat in public Considerations (for private ones have I am sensible little Camparative Influence with you) to mind what the Baron w[r]ites to you on this Subject.[2]

I have read with Attention your Plan of the Bank; and the Report on the Duties.[3] I love you too well to say what Even I think of them, less you may suspect me disposed to treat you as Public Men generally are by those who profess themselves their Friend. The Effects which have been produced by them are the best Proof of the Soundness of your Principles. The Sources of Public Confidence, are at length open'd. Wise and Solid Characters begin to Consider the Public, as the most Eligible Creditors: and if they are not checked in their first Speculations by a Fall in the Stocks, will I am certain bring forth such Resources as will Establish Public Credit on the most Solid Basis. Some objections have been stated by a few who pretend to be vested in Banking Principles, that it is not proper to Combine Specie, with Stocks at the same Rate. whilst they are below Par. But this if it is Examined has not the weight which the Objectors make; and it is in your Power to remove it altogether.

For my own Part I cannot see why the Bank Stock in your Plan should not rise at least to the same Rate with that of Ireland. The comparative Resources of this Country are greater; and the Dividend of the Bank is not more than 6 ⅌ Ct. whilst the Capital is one hundred, and Forty five. In a few days I will Enlarge on these Desultory Ideas—in the mean while, Pursue with firmness the Principles you have adopted; they will Establish your Reputation in the Happiness and Prosperity of the Country, to whom you have devoted your Services.

God bless you!   Wm. Duer

Alexander Hamilton Esqr.
New york. Decb 24th. 1790.

ALS, Sleepy Hollow Restorations, Inc., Tarrytown, New York.
    1. Duer, who had known H since at least 1777 (H to Duer, May 6, 1777 [*PAH*, I, 246–47]), was a native of England and first visited New York in 1768, where, with the help of Philip Schuyler, he purchased timberlands in the vicinity of Saratoga, New York. He settled permanently in New York in 1773, was a delegate to the provincial Congress in 1775, a delegate to the New York

Constitutional Convention in 1776, a delegate to the Continental Congress from 1777 to 1779, Secretary to the Board of Treasury from 1786 to 1789, and Assistant to the Secretary of the Treasury under H from the autumn of 1789 to March or April, 1790.

Both in and out of office he participated in a variety of business enterprises and speculative ventures. For example, during and immediately after the American Revolution he in association with Daniel Parker held large and lucrative contracts for supplying the Army; he speculated in lands in several states; he was instrumental in establishing the Bank of New York in 1784 and was perhaps the leading figure in the Society for Establishing Useful Manufactures and the Scioto project; and finally, he was heavily involved in speculating in securities issued by the new Federal Government. It was this last activity that paved the way for his ruin during the speculative boom in securities in the first three months of 1792. By mid-March of that year he was unable to meet his obligations to his creditors. At the same time, the Federal Government announced a suit against him for two unbalanced charges in his books as Secretary of the Board of Treasury. On March 23 he was imprisoned for debt, and he remained in debtors' prison in New York City until his death in May, 1799.

2. Baron von Steuben to H, December 16, 1790 (*PAH*, VII, 344–45).

3. "First Report on the Further Provision Necessary for Establishing Public Credit," December 13, 1790 (*PAH*, VII, 210–36); "Second Report on the Further Provision Necessary for Establishing Public Credit (Report on a National Bank)," December 13, 1790 (*PAH*, VII, 236–342).

To William Ellery

[*Philadelphia, December 28, 1790.* On January 17, 1791, Ellery wrote to Hamilton: [1] "On my return from the Eastward . . . I found that four letters had been received from you. . . . The letter of the 28th. of Dece. requires no answer." *Letter not found.*]

1. Printed in this volume.

1791

From Samuel R. Gerry [1]

[*Marblehead, Massachusetts, January 1, 1791.* On February 1, 1791, Tench Coxe wrote to Gerry: "Your letter to the Secretary of the Treasury, of the 1st. ultimo, has been received." [2] *Letter not found.*]

1. Gerry was collector of customs at Marblehead, Massachusetts.
2. LS, Beverly Historical Society, Beverly, Massachusetts.

To Walter Livingston

[*Philadelphia, January 5, 1791.* On January 15, 1791, Livingston wrote to Hamilton [1] and referred to the "receipt of your favor of the 5." *Letter not found.*]

1. This letter is printed in this volume.

From Thomas Jefferson

[*Philadelphia, January 11, 1791.* Letter listed in Jefferson's "Summary Journal of letters." [1] *Letter not found.*]

1. AD, Thomas Jefferson Papers, Library of Congress.

Treasury Department Circular to the Commissioners of Loans [1]

(Circular)

Treasury Department
January 11. 1791.

Sir

It has been stated to me that bills of the old emissions,[2] expressed to have been issued in pursuance of an Act of Congress of 2d. July

1777, have been presented to the loan officers. As no such resolution of Congress appears on their Journals all bills of that description must be rejected by you as counterfeits.

I am, Sir, Your obedt. servant   A Hamilton

LS, to Nathaniel Appleton, from a private collection.
1. This letter is listed as a "letter not found" in *PAH*, VII, 425.
2. For "bills of the old emissions," see Nathaniel Appleton to H, February 5, 1791, note 1 (*PAH*, VIII, 7–9).

From Walter Livingston [1]

N York Jany. 15. 91

Sir

On the receipt of your favor of the 5.[2] covering the Opinion of the Attorney General on the Claims of the Contractors of the moving Army & the Post of West Point—The Parties concerned determined on an application to Congress praying them to empower the Proper Officers of the Treasury to determine on the Award presented to Congress by the referees.

Mr. Joshua Sands now waits on you with our Memorial, which you are requested to examine and to give him your Advice. He will wait in Philadelphia till the Sentiments of Congress are known.

LC, New-York Historical Society, New York City.
1. For an explanation of the contents of this letter, see "Report on the Petition of Comfort Sands and Others," February 24, 1791 (*PAH*, VIII, 138–41). See also Livingston to H, November 20, December 18, 1790 (printed in this volume).
2. Letter not found.

From William Ellery

Custom House [Newport, Rhode Island]
Jany. 17th 1791

Sir,

On my return from the Eastward, where by extreme bad roads, and severe weather, I had been detained I found that four letters had been received from you. On the receipt of the first dated Nove. 14 [1] in answer to mine of the 25th of Octe., the Registers of my late business as Continental Loan Offe. were immediately transmitted and delivered to Mr. Bowen.[2] On receipt of the second, dated Dece. 6.,[3] application was made to the Attorney [4] and the Judge of the District Court,[5] and Capt. Brightman's attention directed to the mitigating act.[6] The Judge has transmitted the Proceedings to you.[7] The third dated Dece. 13. 1790 [8] respects the Departure of the Ship Warren from the District of Providence without a coasting licence or a register.[9] If there were wrong conduct in this Office it was not owing to any aversion in my Deputy [10] to proceed in the execution of his duty; or to a want of application to the Attorney of the District, or advising with the Naval Officer and Surveyor.[11] They all approved of his letter to Col. Olney, and it was then and now is the opinion of the District Attorney that as the Penalty for the Ship's Departure, from Providence without the necessary papers was incurred in that District the prosecution ought to have been commenced by the Collector thereof. In conformity to that opinion, and not to a disposition to decline to do any thing with the Ship in my absence the reference was made to him.

The master of the ship made a verbal report on the 26th of Nove, within 24 hours after his arrival in this port. He declared among

LC, Newport Historical Society, Newport, Rhode Island.

1. Letter not found.
2. Jabez Bowen. See Ellery to H, October 18, 25, 1790; William Ellery, Jr., to H, November 30, 1790 (all printed in this volume).
3. Letter not found.
4. William Channing was United States attorney for the District of Rhode Island and Providence Plantations.
5. Henry Marchant was United States judge for the District of Rhode Island and Providence Plantations.
6. Section 1 of "An Act to provide for mitigating or remitting the forfeitures and penalties accruing under the revenue laws, in certain cases therein mentioned" provided: "That whenever any person . . . is . . . liable to a fine, penalty or forfeiture, or interested in any vessel, goods, wares or merchandise, or other thing which may be subject to seizure and forfeiture, by force of the laws of the United States . . . for collecting duties . . . ," he could petition the judge of the district to review the facts of the case and to submit his findings to the Secretary of the Treasury who had the "power to mitigate or remit such fine, penalty or forfeiture" (1 Stat. 122–23 [May 26, 1790]).
7. See Marchant to H, December 20, 1790 (PAH, VII, 373).
8. Letter not found.
9. See Jeremiah Olney to H, November 20, December 24, 1790 (PAH, VII, 168–69, 210); H to Olney, December 13, 1790 (PAH, VII, 381).
10. William Ellery, Jr.
11. Robert Crooke and Daniel Lyman.

other things that the ship was ordered from Providence by his owners, the wind and tide being favorable, to avoid her taking the ground, and being stopped by ice; and that he expected his papers would be immediately sent down by his Owners. She did not make a regular entry, nor was she charged with foreign tonnage. On the 30th. the Master produced to the Depy. Collector of this District a Register, a license, a certified manifest and a permit to proceed to this Port, granted and issued by the Colle. of the District of Providence. This gave a new complexion to the case, and the misconduct of the Capt. seemed to be cured. She entered here as a Coaster and on the 24th. of Dece. was cleared out for Calcutta in India, and sailed the next day, previously to the receipt of your letter now before me. If your letter had arrived before her Departure the Capt. would have been prosecuted agreeably to your direction.

Without questioning the propriety of the Colle. of the District of Providence granting a Register, a license certified manifest, and a Permit to the Ship Warren to proceed to this Port, which was actually in this Port when those papers were issued, this act, and his not prosecuting the master for departing from his district without the necessary official papers, which it is conceived it was his province to do, led to the conduct in this office which has incurred your disapprobation. You may rely upon it, Sir, that the Officers of the Customs in this Port, are attentive, and faithful, and decisive in executing their duty when understood, and that when they err it is from a want of information and knowledge only, and mistakes of this sort it is hoped will be viewed with candour: And altho' it is with reluctance yet I must say that if I had not been well assured from experience in the Loan Office as well as in this office of the capacity, diligence, fidelity and resolution of my son I should not have employed him as my Deputy. I have applied to the Attorney of this District with respect to proceding against the Ship Warren for not having a regular entry, and for the foreign tonnage. It is his opinion that the Master only is liable to prosecution in both cases, and as he departed before the receipt of your letter, and it is uncertain whether he has any attachable property, and if he should have, no determination could be had until his return home he advised not to commence a prosecution until I should have received your directions.

Copies of the manifest, permit, and of Col. Olney's letter of the

29th of Nove. last are herewith transmitted. My Depy. did not insert the words *to stop at Newport,* after the words *East Indies* in the head of the manifest agreeably to Col. Olney's request; because the latter words were not therein, and because he conceived there would be an impropriety in his making addition or alteration in it, especially as thereby the head would become a proper one for a General Clearance, and thus not consistent with his Permit.

A Statement of the case of William Almy[12] marked A., of the Case of Hezekiah Usher & George Usher[13] marked B., a copy of the Entry of House-hold furniture &c by John Sly. A Weekly return of Cash. Two drafts upon me by Saml. Meredith Trease. of the United States, No. 848 for 800 Dollars and 861 for 400 Dollars are herewith transmitted.

I am with great esteem   Sir   Yr. most obedt. Servt.

W Ellery Colle

P. S. The letter of the 28th. of Dece.[14] requires no answer. I have recd. a letter from the Assist. Secry.[15] acknowledgg. the receipt of a letter of the 21 Dece.,[16] and a pay draft of the Treasy. No. 809. for 200 Dolls.[17]

W E   C.

Alexr Hamilton Esqe.
Secry. of the Treasy.

12. Almy was a Providence merchant. See also Ellery to H, April 25, 1791 (*PAH*, VIII, 310).
13. See Marchant to H, February 14, 1791 (*PAH*, VIII, 30); Ellery to H, February 15, May 9, August 29, October 4, 1791 (*PAH*, VIII, 37–38, 333; XI, 118, 283).
14. Letter not found.
15. Tench Coxe.
16. William Ellery, Jr., to H, December 21, 1790 (printed in this volume).
17. Ellery endorsed this letter: "Answd. May 30th." H's letter has not been found.

To Benjamin Lincoln

[*Philadelphia, January 22, 1791.* On February 23, 1791, Lincoln wrote to Hamilton[1] and referred to "your letter of the 22nd ultimo." *Letter not found.*]

1. *PAH*, VIII, 61–62.

From William Ellery

[*Newport, Rhode Island, January 25, 1791.* ". . . By the last Post I received the substitute hydrometer with the apparatus which you transmitted, with your letter of the 18th of the last month,[1] and a description of Dycas's Hydrometer, with directions for the use of it, and directions also for the use of the Substitute. . . ."

LC, Newport Historical Society, Newport, Rhode Island.
1. "Treasury Department Circular to the Collectors of the Customs," December 18, 1790 (*PAH*, VII, 368–72).

From William Ellery

Newport [*Rhode Island*] *January 31, 1791.* ". . . The greatest part of the business of the Customs Houses is done by the Collectors, and yet the nett income of the Naval Officer [1] and of the Surveyor [2] of this port is far superior to mine. . . . Seventy three or Seventy four dollars for six months and one third of a months service it will be allowed is a very trifling consideration. Let me therefore intreat you, Sir, to lay this matter before the Honble Congress, and to use your influence that I may receive an allowance and a compensation adequate to the attention, responsibility, and respectability of my office." [3]

LC, Newport Historical Society, Newport, Rhode Island.
1. Robert Crooke.
2. Daniel Lyman.
3. See "Treasury Department Circular to the Collectors of the Customs," January 20, 1790, April 14, 1791 (*PAH*, VI, 204; VIII, 287–88); H to Jeremiah Olney, April 11, 1791, note 1 (*PAH*, VIII, 273–74).

From William Ellery

Newport [*Rhode Island*] *January 31, 1791.* ". . . Imported, dutiable goods are exported to draw back the duty, and for want of a market are returned, may they be entered and landed on the duties being paid upon them or secured to be paid? The law respecting Drawbacks [1] doth not appear to me to have had such cases in contemplation. I wish for your opinion on this subject.[2] Nathan Saunders Master of the Sloop Polly belonging and bound to Pawcatuck in this District, lately arrived off Stonington, from Cadiz. An inspector from the District of New London went on board her and demanded a manifest of the master which he refused. . . . the said Master had taken out of said Sloop his Chest and Bedding a Kegg of Wine, a box of Lemons, and part of a hamper of raisins without a Permit, and against the remonstrance of the Inspector. I have desired the Surveyor [3] to search for & seize those goods, and the Attorney of this District [4] to prosecute the Master for violating the 27th Section of the Collection Law. . . ." [5]

LC, Newport Historical Society, Newport, Rhode Island.
    1. See Sections 57, 58, 59, 60, and 61 of "An Act to provide more effectually for the collection of the duties imposed by law on goods, wares and merchandise imported into the United States, and on the tonnage of ships or vessels" (1 *Stat.* 173–75 [August 4, 1790]).
    2. For H's reply, see H to Ellery, April 11, 1791 (*PAH*, VIII, 271–72).
    3. Daniel Lyman.
    4. William Channing.
    5. Section 27 of the Collection Law reads in part: "That no goods, wares or merchandise brought in any ship or vessel from any foreign port or place, shall be unladen or delivered from such ship or vessel, within the United States, but in open day . . . nor at any time without a permit from the collector for such unlading or delivery . . ." (1 *Stat.* 163).

To William Ellery

[*Philadelphia, January 31, 1791.* On February 15, 1791, Ellery wrote to Hamilton: [1] "I received your letter of the 31st. of last month." *Letter not found.*]

    1. *PAH*, VIII, 37–38.

To Tench Coxe [1]

[Philadelphia, February 1, 1791]

Dear Sir

I send you a Check on the Bank of New York, for three thousand Dollars, to be delivered Mr. Francis [2] another for Mr. Tilghman [3] on the Cashier of the Bank [4] here for *3275 Ds* * & 94 Cts. which I compute to be the amount of the bills. I will be obliged to you to complete this negotiation for me & take a receipt for the money.

On reflection, I am not quite at my ease about the request made of the Bank, as the accommodation is perhaps irregular. But I cannot in time make a different arrangement & therefore must go on. It would however relieve me if the thing could be put in the shape of a purchase of my draft on the Bank of New York; in which I should not scruple a discount of half per Cent. Be so good as to speak to Mr. Francis for me & endeavour to arrange the matter so as to put me *more in order.*

Yrs. sincerely   A Hamilton

I shall stay at home to day to *go over* the Report on Manufactures [5] and make such additions &c. as occur.

Feby. 1.

* Note I have 6 or 700 Drs in Bank here beside the 3000.

ALS, Papers of Tench Coxe in the Coxe Family Papers at the Historical Society of Pennsylvania, Philadelphia.

1. For an explanation of the contents of this letter, see William Seton to H, February 3, 1791 (*PAH,* VIII, 4–5).
2. Tench Francis was cashier of the Bank of North America.
3. Presumably William Tilghman, Coxe's cousin, who was a native of Maryland, a lawyer, and a Loyalist or neutral during the American Revolution. He was a member of the Maryland Assembly from 1788 to 1790, and in 1791 he became a member of the Maryland Senate.
4. Tench Francis.
5. For Coxe's part in the preparation of the Report on Manufactures, see the introductory note to "Report on the Subject of Manufactures," Decem-

ber 5, 1791 (*PAH*, X, 1–15); Coxe's draft of the Report (printed in this volume).

To John Cochran [1]

[*Treasury Department, February 8, 1791.* The description of this letter in the dealer's catalogue reads: "Concerning 'the Payment of Pensions to Invalids for the space of one year. . . . The allowance for your trouble will be two per cent on what you pay.' " [2] *Letter not found.*]

The Collector: A Magazine for Autograph and Historical Collectors, LXXXI, (1968), 806, Item B242.
    1. Cochran was commissioner of loans for New York from 1790 to 1795.
    2. This quotation also appears in H to Jedediah Huntington, January 30, 1790 (*PAH*, VI, 232–33). See also H to Nathaniel Appleton, February 8, 1791 (*PAH*, VIII, 13–14).

To John Neufville [1]

[*Philadelphia, February 8, 1791.* On May 5, 1796, Neufville wrote to John Davis: [2] "The Secretary of the Treasury advised me by letter of 8th. February 1791, that the Secretary of War [3] would write to me concerning the evidences upon, and under which those payments were to be made, but . . . nothing of that sort had come to my hands." *Letter not found.*]

    1. Neufville, who wrote this letter in his capacity as commissioner of loans for South Carolina, is discussing the payment of invalid pensions.
    For information concerning invalid pensions, see H to Nathaniel Appleton, February 8, 1791, note 1 (*PAH*, VIII, 13–14).
    2. Copy, Miscellaneous Treasury Accounts, 1790–1894, Account No. 7997, National Archives.
    Davis was comptroller of the Treasury.
    3. Henry Knox.

To Tench Coxe

[Philadelphia, February-May, 1791]

Dr. Sir

I send you some letters to be copied also the draft of instructions to Commanders of Revenue Cutters to be considered &c.[1]

The preparation of the other letters concerning Cutters ought to be a primary object. As Registers cannot pursuant to the Registering Act[2] be furnished to them will it not be proper they should have some Treasury paper as equivalent to it? If it will a Survey ought to be directed to be transmitted to the Treasury.

I remain at home this forenoon. Send me the note of monies in hands of Collectors when ready & whatever papers require signing.

I wish also to have your draft and my alterations of the manufacturing Report[3] as I am about to review the whole and give it its final form. I want to see the papers in their original state as there are some minute things which have been altered perhaps not for the better—& on a revision may be reinstated.

Yrs. sincerely   A Hamilton

Tuesday Morning

ALS, Papers of Tench Coxe in the Coxe Family Papers at the Historical Society of Pennsylvania, Philadelphia.
  1. See "Treasury Department Circular to the Captains of the Revenue Cutters," June 1, 4, 1791 (*PAH*, VIII, 406–07, 426–33).
  2. "An Act for Registering and Clearing Vessels, Regulating the Coasting Trade, and for other purposes" (1 *Stat.* 55–65 [September 1, 1789]).
  3. See H to Coxe, February 1, 1790 (printed in this volume); "Report on the Subject of Manufactures," December 5, 1791 (*PAH*, X, 1–340); Coxe's draft of the Report (printed in this volume).

From Tench Coxe [1]

[Philadelphia, March 19, 1791]

Dear Sir

Mr. Jefferson has sent for the Bills of 99000 Guilders, which on application to Mr. Meredith,[2] are said to have been countermanded.

I had transmitted to Mr. Jeffn. the three letters of advice[3] to be sealed by a wafer to the Bills. Will you be good enough to give me your instructions as Mr. Jefferson's opty will be tomorrow.[4]

yr. most obedt. Servant
                                             Tench Coxe
                                             March 19th. 1791

ALS, Papers of Tench Coxe in the Coxe Family Papers at the Pennsylvania Historical Society, Philadelphia.

1. For background to this letter and an explanation of its contents, see H to Wilhem and Jan Willink, Nicholaas and Jacob Van Staphorst, and Nicholas Hubbard, March 18, 1791 (*PAH*, VIII, 204–05); George Washington to H, March 19, 1791 (*PAH*, VIII, 205–06).

2. Samuel Meredith was treasurer of the United States.

3. Letters not found. A letter of advice is a note advising a commercial or financial correspondent that a certain arrangement, of which the correspondent is a part, has been made.

4. At the bottom of this letter H wrote: "Let the bills be sent to Mr. Jefferson. Yrs. A Hamilton."

Conversation with George Beckwith [1]

[*Philadelphia, March–April, 1791.* ". . . the Vice-president,[2] Secretaries of the Treasury & War[3] & myself met on the 11th. . . . I mentioned to the gentlemen the idea of suggesting thro' Colo. Beckwith, our knowlege of the conduct of the British officers in furnishing the Indians with arms & ammunition, & our dissatisfaction. Colo. Hamilton said that Beckwith had been with him on the subject, and had assured him they had given the Indians nothing more than the annual present, & at the annual period. it was thought proper however that he should be made sensible that this had attracted the notice of government. . . ."

Thomas Jefferson to George Washington, April 17, 1791 (ALS, RG 59, Miscellaneous Letters, January 1-July 31, 1791, National Archives).

1. For background to this document and an explanation of its contents, see Washington to Jefferson, April 4, 1791 (*GW*, XXXI, 267–68). See also "Conversation with George Beckwith and William Macomb," January 31, 1791 (*PAH*, VII, 608–13).

2. John Adams.

3. Henry Knox.

To John Rutherfurd [1]

[Philadelphia, March, 1791-January, 1795]

General Hamilton will have the pleasure of Dining with Mr. Rutherford agreeable to his polite Invitation.

Tuesday 15th.

AL, anonymous donor.
1. Rutherfurd was a New York City lawyer until 1787, when he moved to New Jersey, where he was a member of the General Assembly in 1788 and 1789. He was a Federalist member of the United States Senate from March 4, 1791, to December 5, 1798.

From Jeremiah Wadsworth [1]

[*Hartford, April 24, 1791.* In a letter to Wadsworth in April, 1791,[2] Hamilton referred to "your letter of the 24th of April 1791." *Letter not found.*]

1. After the American Revolution, Wadsworth continued his mercantile pursuits in Hartford, Connecticut. He was elected to Congress in 1787 and 1788, and he was also a member of the state Ratifying Convention in 1788. He was a founder of the Bank of North America in Philadelphia, a director of the Bank of the United States, president of the Bank of New York, and a promoter of the Hartford Woolen Manufactory, established in 1788.
2. Printed in this volume.

From Théophile Cazenove [1]

Mr. A. Hamilton   Philade. du 26 avril 1791

Je vous prie de me faire savoir si les éclaircissemens que vous désirés [2] rélativemt. aux piastres seront fournis par la réponse aux questions detaillées sur la Notte que j'ai l'honnr. de vous envoyer.

Mes amis d'hollande m'ont authorisés á leur assurer quelque intérét dans les entreprises utiles qui se formeroient ici: je considere comme tel le plan de la Compe. de manufactures[3] que Mr. Duer m'a communiqué de votre part!

Vous avés, Monsieur, acquis de si justes droits a la Confiance des Capitalistes hollandois, qu'il leurs suffira de savoir que vous avés formé un projet, ou que vous vous intéressés a sa réussite, pour désirer & chercher d'y contribuer de leur côté.

LC, Gemeentearchief Amsterdam, Holland Land Company. In 1964 the Holland Land Company documents were transferred from the Nederlandsch Economisch-Historisch Archief, Amsterdam.

1. Cazenove, a native of Holland, conducted a brokerage and commercial business in Amsterdam from 1763 to 1788. In 1789 he was appointed by four Dutch banking houses—Peter Stadnitski and Son, Nicholaas and Jacob Van Staphorst, P. and C. Van Eeghen, and Isaac Ten Cate and Hendrick Vollenhoven—to handle their speculations in American securities. Cazenove arrived in the United States in 1790. In 1792 he persuaded his employers to invest in western lands in the United States. For that purpose the Dutch bankers were joined by Wilhem and Jan Willink and Rutger Jan Schimmelpenninck. Although the banking firms did not formally organize as the Holland Land Company until February 13, 1796, Cazenove from 1792 to 1794 purchased five million acres of land in western New York and northern and western Pennsylvania for his Dutch principals. He also purchased considerable amounts of Federal and state debts, bought substantial shares in the Bank of the United States, and invested in a number of canal promotions.

2. The inquiries mentioned in this paragraph concern information about coinage which H wished to obtain in connection with the establishment and operation of the United States Mint. In a letter, which has not been found, H had written to Cazenove, as he had to several others on this subject. See H to William Seton, December 3, 1790 (*PAH*, VII, 190–92); Seton to H, January 10, 1791 (*PAH*, VII, 422–23); H to Thomas Jefferson, April 14, 1791 (*PAH*, VIII, 284–86); H to Pierre Charles L'Enfant, May 24, 1791 (*PAH*, VIII, 354–55); John B. Church to H, August 2, 1791 (*PAH*, IX, 4–5); William Short to H, September 23, 1791 (*PAH*, IX, 226–29). See also "Report on the Establishment of a Mint," January 28, 1791 (*PAH*, VII, 462–607).

3. For H's efforts to secure the financial support of Cazenove and his Dutch associates for the Society for Establishing Useful Manufactures, see H to William Duer, April 20, 1791 (*PAH*, VIII, 300–01). For Cazenove's expressions of interest in the S.U.M., see, for example, Cazenove to "Mrs. M. M.," April 13, 27, 1791 (LC, Gemeentearchief Amsterdam, Holland Land Company).

To Théophile Cazenove [1]

[Philadelphia, April 26, 1791]

Sir

The minute of questions you have been so obliging as to prepare (and which is return'd) comprises all the points about which I was desirous of information, and adds others; eclaircissements concerning which cannot fail to be useful. I will thank you to have the inquiry pursued, and any expense, which may attend the making of assays &ca will with pleasure be reimbursed.

I learn with Satisfaction the light in which you view the plan for a manufacturing society communicated to you by Mr Duer, in consequence of my suggestions,[2] and feel myself indebted for the dispositions toward me, on the part of the Dutch Capitalists, which you so politely assure me of. These dispositions are not merely flattering— I regard them as a real resource towards the Success of my public views. And shall cherish a sincere wish to preserve them.

The readiness with which, You, Sir, enter into the Plan proposed by me is a new proof of that liberal and elightened judgment which has led you, on every occasion that has occured since your arrival in this Country, to discern the perfect harmony that subsists between the interests you represent and measures tending to give solidity to the affairs of the United States.

It is also an additional title to that real esteem with which I have the honor to be   Sir   Your obdt & hbl. servt.   A Hamilton

LC, Gemeentearchief Amsterdam, Holland Land Company. In 1964 the Holland Land Company documents were transferred from the Nederlandsch Economisch-Historisch Archief, Amsterdam.
1. This letter was written in reply to Cazenove to H, April 26, 1791 (printed in this volume).
2. In MS, "suggestered."

To Jeremiah Wadsworth [1]

[Philadelphia, April, 1791]

My Dear Friend

You will think me a sad delinquent and You will have reason. I plead guilty & crave the mercy of the Court.

The two Credits of July 31. 1786 stand in my book as different

sums— $\left. \begin{array}{l} 3500 \\ \\ 3000 \end{array} \right\}$ Dollars. This renders it less probable that they should

be one payment as you appear by your letter of the 24 of April 1791 [2] to think possible. I have not on examination found any additional light. If none can be found by you it must stand as *two* payments; though I wish you to examine: because when I came to render an Account to Mr. Church July 87. I found myself considerably more in arrear to him than from what I had supposed to be the course of my remittances I had imagined.

We have nothing new here. The News Paper fire has abated. The beginning of next Month I begin a certain undertaking.[3]

Yrs. affecy & truly   A Hamilton

J Wadsworth Esq.

ALS, Connecticut Historical Society, Hartford.
    1. For background to this letter, see H to Wadsworth, April 12, 1791 (*PAH*, VIII, 279–80); "Account with John B. Church," May 1, 1791 (*PAH*, VIII, 320). See also H's account with Church in H's "Cash Book," March 1, 1782–1791 (*PAH*, III, 55–56).
    2. Letter not found.
    3. On May 9, 1791, H wrote to Tench Coxe (printed in this volume) that he was "about to leave the City for a Fortnight." He did not, however, state where or why he was going, and the purpose of this trip has not been ascertained. In addition, on May 20, 1791, John H. Livingston wrote to H from New York concerning a visit in Philadelphia where he had consulted H on a legal matter and then said: "When I had the pleasure of seeing you I recollect you told me of your intention to take a tour into the Country. I hope you have found it a beneficial and seasonable recreation—if you can extend your Journey and gratify your friends at New York with a visit, I can assure you it will give them great pleasure to see you" (calendared in *PAH*, VIII, 349).

From George Cabot

[*Beverly, Massachusetts, May 2, 1791.* On May 30, 1791, Cabot wrote to Tench Coxe: [1] "I have the satisfaction of acknowledging the receipt of your obliging letter of the 14th in reply to mine of the 2d instant addressed to the Secretary of the Treasury." [2] *Letter not found.*]

    1. ALS, Papers of Tench Coxe in the Coxe Family Papers at the Historical Society of Pennsylvania, Philadelphia.
    Cabot was a Salem, Massachusetts, merchant and Federalist. He was a delegate to the state Constitutional Convention in 1780; he was elected to, but did not attend, the Annapolis Convention; and he was a member of his state's Ratifying Convention in 1788. In June, 1791, he was chosen United States Senator from Massachusetts.

2. Coxe had replied to Cabot's letter in his capacity as Assistant to the Secretary of the Treasury. During a brief absence from Philadelphia, H left Coxe in charge of the Treasury Department (H to Coxe, May 9, 1791 [printed in this volume]).

To Tench Coxe

Treasury Department
May 9th 1791

Sir

Being about to leave the City for a Fortnight [1]—I have requested the Bank of North America to advance to your order such sums as you may find necessary for the current service of the Government during my absence to the extent of Twenty thousand dollars. This provision is designed to enable you to answer such demands as may arise in relation to the civil list (including the contingencies of the several executive departments and of the two houses of Congress) [2] to the Act making provision for the Debt of the United States,[3] & to the several acts of the last session concerning the duties on distilled spirits and compensations for the officers of the Judicial Courts of the United States and for jurors and Witnesses.[4] Your disbursements will of course be confined to objects, for which there have been appropriations by law, and you will in each case obtain some voucher of a nature to operate as a discharge of the warrants which must hereafter issue to cover the sums paid.

I remain with great consideration and esteem   Sir   Your obedient servant   Alex Hamilton
Secy of the Treasury

PS If the 400.000 Guilders for drawing which directions have been given [5] shall have been sold or *nearly* sold in my absence you will direct the drawing for two hundred thousand more (say 200.000).

To Tench Coxe Esqr
Assistant Secretary

ALS, Papers of Tench Coxe in the Coxe Family Papers at the Historical Society of Pennsylvania, Philadelphia.

1. See H to Jeremiah Wadsworth, April, 1791, note 3 (printed in this volume).

2. "An Act making appropriations for the support of Government during the year one thousand seven hundred and ninety-one, and for other purposes" (1 *Stat.* 190 [February 11, 1791]).

3. "An Act making provision for the (payment of the) Debt of the United States" (1 *Stat.* 138–44 [August 4, 1790]).

4. "An Act repealing, after the last day of June next, the duties heretofore laid upon Distilled Spirits imported from abroad, and laying others in their stead; and also upon Spirits distilled within the United States, and for appropriating the same" (1 *Stat.* 199–214 [March 3, 1791]); "An Act providing compensations for the officers of the Judicial Courts of the United States, and for Jurors and Witnesses, and for other purposes" (1 *Stat.* 216–17 [March 3, 1791]).

5. See H to William Seton, May 9, 1791 (*PAH*, VIII, 334–35).

From John Neufville [1]

[*Philadelphia, May 15, 1791.* On May 5, 1796, Neufville wrote to John Davis: [2] "The Secretary of the Treasury advised me under date of 15. May 1791. that on enquiry at the war office it was found that the Secretary of that Department had not been able to transmit the requisite certified roll of the Invalids for want of Information from South Carolina." *Letter not found.*]

1. For background to this letter, see Neufville to H, February 8, 1791 (printed in this volume).

2. Copy, Miscellaneous Treasury Accounts, 1790–1894, Account No. 7997, National Archives.

From David Wolfe [1]

New York 16th June 1791.

Sir

Mr. Walcot [2] informs Mr. Anspach by letter that Colo. Pickering late QMG was Consulted by you with respect to the Debts of his department & that Colo. Pickering expressly stated "that in all cases where printed Certificates [3] had been issued he consider'd the Claim for payment in specie as extinguished." And in Consequence of the aforesaid Consultation &c. payment of a number of Certificates have been refused at the Treasury office.

This I conceive to be unjust for the following reasons—

1st because they are included in the Estimates in the Treasury Office under the term *specie Certificates* signed by Col. Pickering

2d because Colo Pickering has paid in specie at Divers times, principal & Interest of those certificates to the Amount of Several thousand dollars as may appear by his Accounts render'd at the Treasury Office

More reasons might be added if necessary, But those are sufficient to prove that Colo. Pickering has not heretofore considered the Claim of printed certificates for payment in specie as extinguished.

Your examining into these matters and directing the payment of the Certificates held by Mr. Graham [4] will abate the Censure now reflected on the Treasury Department.

I am sir   Your Obt servant   David Wolfe

Colo. A. Hamilton

Copy, in Wolfe's handwriting, The Sol Feinstone Collection, Library of the American Philosophical Society, Philadelphia.

1. In *PAH*, VIII, 485, this letter is listed as a "letter not found."

Wolfe had been assistant deputy quartermaster general at Claverack, New York, during the American Revolution.

For background to this letter, see H to Timothy Pickering, November 19, 1789 (*PAH*, V, 528–29); Pickering to H, November 19, 25, 1789, August 28, 1790 (*PAH*, V, 527–28, 558; VI, 576–77); H to Peter Anspach, December 5, 1789, December 2, 20, 1790 (*PAH*, VI, 6–7; VII, 174, 372); Anspach to H, December 30, 1789, January 20, July 2, December 7, 1790, January 24, 1791 (*PAH*, VI, 38, 192, 478; VII, 198–200, 450–51); "Report on Additional Sums Necessary for the Support of the Government," August 5, 1790 (*PAH*, VI, 520–42); H to Wolfe, July 12, 1791 (*PAH*, VIII, 547). For correspondence subsequent to the letter printed above, see Wolfe to H, September 8, 1792 (printed in this volume); John Campbell to Pickering, August 29, 1792, and enclosures, Wolfe to Pickering, January 31, 1792, Pickering to Wolfe, March 18, 1792 (all ALS, Massachusetts Historical Society, Boston); Oliver Wolcott, Jr., to Pickering, January 25, 1793 (LS, Massachusetts Historical Society, Boston). See also Hugh Hughes to H, November 21, 1790 (printed in this volume).

2. Oliver Wolcott, Jr.

3. Certificates were issued in lieu of specie by the quartermaster general's department during the American Revolution. They were originally handwritten notes; but subsequently printed forms were used. Continental Army officers issued these certificates to individuals from whom supplies were impressed for the Army.

4. William Graham, Wolfe's attorney. For payments which Wolfe received after the letter printed above was written, see "Report on the Receipts and Expenditures of Public Monies to the End of the year 1791," November 10, 1792 (*PAH*, XIII, 96).

To Henry Marchant

[*Philadelphia, June 30, 1791.* On September 14, 1791, Marchant wrote to Hamilton [1] and referred to "Your very polite Letter of the 30th of June." *Letter not found.*]

1. Printed in this volume.

From John Jay

[*New York, July 8, 1791. Letter not found.*]

"List of Letters from Mr. Jay . . ." to H, Columbia University Libraries.

To Tench Coxe

[Philadelphia, July 13, 1791–1792] [1]

Dr. Sir

You will find in the Closet blank warrants signed by me as follow

Upon the Treasurer	45
Upon Collectors	22
of Transfer	226 [2]

Yrs. sincerely   A Hamilton

July 13

ALS, Papers of Tench Coxe in the Coxe Family Papers at the Historical Society of Pennsylvania, Philadelphia.

1. The date has been taken from Coxe's endorsement, which reads: "A. Hamilton. July 13 1791. or 2."

2. A note in Coxe's handwriting at the foot of the letter reads: "(13 Cancelled as within)."

Conveyance to Isaac Moses

New York, July 21, 1791. ". . . that for and consideration of the sum of One thousand and eight hundred pounds current lawful money of New York to the said Alexander Hamilton and Elizabeth his wife in hand paid by the said Isaac Moses at or before the unsealing and delivery of these presents the receipt whereof is hereby acknowledged they have granted bargained sold aliened released and conveyed . . . unto the said Isaac Moses . . . All that certain lot of ground situate in the Dock Ward of the City of New York fronting Northerly to the Street commonly called Dock Street. . . ." [1]

Certified copy, recorded under the date of July 28, 1791, Conveyances in the Office of the Register, City of New York, Liber 46, 528–29, Hall of Records, New York City.
1. See Moses to H, April 24, 1791 (*PAH*, VIII, 306).

From Elizabeth Hamilton

[*Albany, August 6, 1791.* On August 12, 1791, Hamilton wrote to his wife [1] and referred to "your letter of the 6th instant." *Letter not found.*]

1. This letter is printed in this volume.

To Elizabeth Hamilton

[Philadelphia, August 12, 1791]

You cannot imagine My beloved Betsey how much I am afflicted at learning by your letter of the 6th instant,[1] that you had not received one from me. It is wholly inconceivable. I wrote you from New York before my departure from that place which was the Sunday after you left it,[2] and sent the letter to the Post Office by

Charles. I write by this opportunity to him to Endeavour to trace it.

On my arrival here I also wrote to you and twice Since.[3] For let me be ever so busy, I could not forbear to allow myself the only Converse which your distance from me permits. I could not endure that you should be pained by my silence.

Be of good Chear my Darling; but if you Cannot make yourself happy come to me, for the only thing that can reconcile me to your absence is that your health might benefit by it, but this cannot be the case if you are anxious and uneasy.

Heaven bless my Charmer & my dear infants   Yr. Ever Affect.

A Hamilton

Aug 12
Mrs. Hamilton

Copy, Columbia University Libraries.
    1. Letter not found.
    2. Letter not found.
    3. See H to Elizabeth Hamilton, August 2, 9, 10, 1791 (*PAH*, IX, 6, 24, 25–26).

Account with John B. Church [1]

[*Philadelphia, August 13, 1791.* The description of this document reads: "Credit Side of John Barker Church's Account. . . ." *Document not found.*]

Edward Lazare, ed., *American Book-Prices Current, Index 1960–1965* (New York, 1968), 1917.
    1. See "Account with John B. Church," May 1, 1791 (*PAH*, VIII, 320). See also H's "Cash Book," March 1, 1782–1791 (*PAH*, III, 55–56).

From William Duer [1]

[New York, August 16, 1791]

My dear Friend.

Mr. King delivered me your Letter [2] on the Subject of the Sudden
Rise of Scrip,[3] which I observe has occasioned in your mind a great
Alarm. Those who impute to my Artifices the Rise of this Species of
Stock in the Market, beyond its true Point of Value do me infinite
Injustice. The Fact is that as far as my Opinion public or Private
could have an Effect I have mentioned to the Dealers, in Stocks, par-
ticularly Scrip that were Straining it beyond its true Point of Value.
For the latter I never gave but in one Instance more than 175—al-
though in my Judgment they are fa[i]rly worth £200. And if we
do not Support them at that Price *at least*, you may be Assured (and
I speak it from Facts arising within my own Knowledge) that the
Major Interest in the Bank will be Foreign Property: how far this is
desireable, I leave to your Judgment.

The Instance in which I gave more than 175 for the Sprips is as
follows—and Mr. Robert Morris (then in this City) can Witness to
the Truth of it. When the Arts of Designing men (combined with
the heated Imagination of new Adventurers) had carried the Price
of scrip to Nearly 300, and they were then practising on the Fears
of the Unskilfull to Induce them to sacrifice them as an Article
worth nothing; I united with one or two Gentlemen of Patriotic
Principles—and agreed to take about 400, at 240, provided the Sellers
would deposit them with us Immediately, and Wait for their Pay till
the first day of December. This they did, and the Consequences were
allowed by all the City to be Extremely beneficial. Instead of an Instant Depression of the Stock, which would have Involved hundred
in Utter Ruin, a Pause of Reflection Succeeded, the true Value of
the Article became an Object of Discussion, and of Course a gradual
Reduction in Price; the only thing, which by averaging the Loss,
can rescue some of the Unvary Adventurers from Utter Ruin.

This is the plain History of my Conduct in this Matter, and of its
Motives. I shall Conclude with one Observation; as it Relates to myself, I wish to have avoided it, but Exposed as I find myself to Un-

just Clamours in your City, I am Constrained to say what otherwise I would have left to others.

During the whole Time I have been Engaged in Operations of the Public Debt, I can with Truth Aver that I have Scrupulously adhered to the most rigid Principles of Candor, and fair Dealing. Instead of Entering into Combinations to Entrap the Unwary I have Endeavored to make any Knowledge I possest on this Subject, a Common Stock. By my advice & Example, Numbers in this City have by Embark'g in the Funds, supported the Public Credit, and advanced their own Fortunes. If the Price of Stock in the New-York market has had a powerful Influence in other Parts, I can with Truth say that its Effects (if beneficial) are in no small Degree imputable to me. Feeling therefore in this Instance (as I have in the whole Course of my Life) that the Public Good has been a primary Object of my Pursuit, I despise the malicious aspersions of those who Aim to destroy my character in your, and the Public Esteem. The Citizens amongst whom I live have I am persuaded too good an opinion of my heart and head to think me so Weak, and Wicked to pursue that Line, of Conduct, which your Letter Intimates. I feel a Consciousness, that it cannot have made an Impression (even for a moment) on your Mind; and if it has you will I trust do me the Justice not only to Efface Every Trace of such an opinion, in your Breast—but in that of Every other Person within the Circle of your Friends, whose Esteem is Worthy of Preservation.

I have the honor to be with Sentiments of Esteem & Sincere Affection   Yours   Wm. Duer

Alexr. Hamilton Esqr.
New york. Augt. 16th. 1791.

ALS, Sleepy Hollow Restorations, Inc., Tarrytown, New York.
    1. In *PAH*, IX, 71, this letter is listed as a "letter not found."
    For background to the letter printed above, see Fisher Ames to H, August 15, 1791 (*PAH*, IX, 55–59); Rufus King to H, August 15, 1791 (*PAH*, IX, 59–61); "Meeting of the Commissioners of the Sinking Fund," August 15, 1791 (*PAH*, IX, 67–68); H to William Seton, August 15, 16, 1791 (*PAH*, X, 68–69, 71–73); Seton to H, August 15, 1791 (*PAH*, IX, 69–70); H to the President and Directors of the Bank of New York, August 16, 1791 (*PAH*, IX, 71); H to Duer, August 17, 1791 (*PAH*, IX, 74–75); H to King, August 17, 1791 (*PAH*, IX, 75–76).
    2. Letter not found.

3. "Scrip" was the name given to the certificates or receipts for the initial payment of $25 to those buying stock in the Bank of the United States. Such receipts were first issued on July 15, 1791, and in the following weeks intensive speculation in scrip led to a tremendous rise in the price of both scrip and securities issued by the Federal Government. Joseph Stancliffe Davis reports that the price of scrip had risen to $50 by the end of July and to $280 by August 11 (Davis, *Essays*, I, 202–03). According to Bray Hamomnd, these certificates "in August . . . rose to a market price of $300 or more" (Hammond, *Banks and Politics in America from the Revolution to the Civil War* [Princeton, 1957], 123).

To Elizabeth Hamilton

[Philadelphia, August 17, 1791]

My Loved Eliza:

I wrote you two or three times last week.[1] But since my last I have received another letter from you [2] which does not remove my anxiety. The state of our dear sick angel [3] continues too precarious. My heart trembles whenever I open a letter from you—The experiment of the Pink root alarms me but I continue to place my hope in Heaven.

You press to return to me. I will not continue to dissuade you. Do as you think best. If you resolve to come I should like best your coming by land & I wish you could prevail on Doctor Stringer [4] to accompany you. It would be a matter of course & pleasure to make him a handsome compensation. If you want money, you may either get it from your father or draw on Mr. Seton [5] at New York for it.

But let me know beforehand your determination that I may meet you at New York with an arrangment for bringing you, or rather write to Mr. Seton who I will request to have things ready—All you will have to do will be to inform him that you leave Albany on a certain day. All here are perfectly well & join in love to you.

Adieu, my Angel

A. H.

Aug 17
Mrs. Hamilton

Copy, Columbia University Libraries.
1. See H to Elizabeth Hamilton, August 9, 10, 1791 (*PAH*, IX, 24, 25–26), August 12, 1791 (printed in this volume).
2. Letter not found.

3. James Hamilton, H's third son and fourth child, who was three years old.

4. Samuel Stringer, a native of Maryland, received his medical education in Philadelphia and was director general of hospitals in the northern department during the American Revolution. After the war he settled in Albany and continued to practice medicine. He was the Hamilton family's doctor in Albany.

5. William Seton, cashier of the Bank of New York.

From Philip Schuyler

Albany September 1st 1791.

Dr Sir

Mr. Henry Glen [1] has Exhibited certain accounts of expences accrued by him as an Agent for Indian Affairs appointed by the board of Commissioners in the Northern department, to the Auditor of the Treasury [2] he informs, objections arise to the liquidation on a Supposition that they were not presented within the time limited by the late Congress.[3] The inclosed Copy of a Certificate given by Mr. Barber [4] the Commissioner in the part of the United States to settle accounts with the citizens of this State will Evince that application was made to him at an early day.[5]

Mr Dow [6] one of the Commissioners whose accounts are also with the Auditor was appointed by the board to receive what monies were granted for the Indian service, to pay it out, and to account, requested me to apply to Mr. Barber when here to know when he would attend to the Settlement of his account. Mr. Barbers reply to me was Substantially the same as that given by him to Mr: Glen.

I have advanced to an amount exceeding Fifteen hundred Pounds, and delivered my accounts to Mr. Dow, who if he had been in Cash would have discharged it, it is inclosed in his account and if Mr. Dow, or Mr. Glen had not even attempted an adjustment of their accounts I conceive it ought not to injure the individual Claimants as they applied for payment to the Officers who contracted the debts and who received their accounts, and who was to discharge them when enabled by the public. Anxious for an adjustment of both these accounts permit me to intreat your interference as far as may be proper & Consistent with your Situation.

The bearer Mr. Van Ingen [7] is Empower'd by Mr. Glen to Solicit the Settlement of his Accounts.

I am Dear Sir   Affectionately Yours &c

Honble. Alexander Hamilton Esqr.

Copy, Schuyler Papers, MS Division, New York Public Library.

1. Glen, a Schenectady, New York, merchant, had been a member of the Provincial Congress, a deputy quartermaster during the American Revolution, and a member of the New York Assembly in 1786 and 1787.

2. Oliver Wolcott, Jr.

3. On March 17, 1785, Congress adopted the following resolution: "*Resolved, That all persons having unliquidated claims against the United States, be, and they are hereby required, within twelve Months from the date hereof, to deliver a particular abstract of such claims to some Commissioner in the State in which they respectively reside, who is authorised to settle accounts against the United States; And any person or persons, neglecting to deliver their claims as aforesaid, shall be precluded from any adjustment of the same, except at the board of treasury . . ." (JCC, XXVIII, 169).

4. William Barber's full title was commissioner of accounts for the State of New York. He had been appointed in accordance with a congressional resolution of February 20, 1782, which stated that such "a commissioner for each State . . . be appointed," and that among other things he was "fully empowered and directed to liquidate and settle, in specie value, all certificates given for supplies by public officers to individuals, and other claims against the United States by individuals for supplies furnished the army, the transportation thereof, and contingent expences thereon, within the said State . . ." (JCC, XXII, 84–85).

5. On March 17, 1786, Glen submitted a petition to Congress "stating that as Agent for the Comrs. of Indian Affairs in the northern department he performed services and Advanced considerable sums of money his accounts for which are not finally adjusted or settled and praying that William Barber Comr. for the State of New York may be permitted to settle his Accts. and issue a certificate for the balance as from several circumstances his certificates are of more immediate value than those issued by the board of treasury" (JCC, XXX, 116). For Barber's statement on Glen's claim, see H to Glen, June 26, 1792, note 3 (PAH, XI, 570). The petition was submitted to the Board of Treasury, but no report from the board has been found. Glen petitioned Congress again on February 3, 1795, and February 16, 1796, with no results (Journal of the House, II, 313, 444; III, 260).

6. Volkert P. Douw. This claim was presumably related to "a certain quantity of Provisions furnished for the Oneida Indians under the directions of Philip Schuyler, and Volker P. Dow Commissioners of Indian Treaties for the Northern District in the year 1780 . . ." (JCC, XXX, 208).

7. William Van Ingen, a resident of Schenectady, New York, was Glen's son-in-law.

To George Gale [1]

Treasury Department, September 3, 1791. Sends commission of "Philip Thomas Esq. Inspector of the Revenue for Survey No. 2 in the District of Maryland." [2]

LS, Tusculum College, Greeneville, Tennessee.
    1. In *PAH,* IX, 164, this letter is listed as a "letter not found." Gale was supervisor of the revenue for the District of Maryland.
    2. See "To the Senate and the House of Representatives," October 31, 1791 (*PAH,* IX, 426–31).

From Robert Troup [1]

[New York] 12 Sep. 1791

My dear friend

I have reced. your favor [2] respecting the special authority necessary to be given to those who represent the original holders of Bank Shares in the choice of Directors and have done as you requested. The speculations in those shares have been prodigious & much money has been made & lost by them. The fluctuations in their value have excited alarm in the minds of the well wishers to public credit as tending to exhibit an unsound state of our finances. The truth is that the fluctuations are principally owing to the arts & contrivances of mere jobbers & amongst these our friend Brockholst stands in the foremost ranks.[3] A few days ago a cursed scheme of depression was planned & executed under his immediate patronage as is universally said & believed.[4] It frightened the Directors of our Bank [5] & seriously injured many persons amongst whom are some of Brockholst's particular friends. The current has since taken a contrary direction but it is conjectured it will not carry the shares to as high a value as they have generally been at since the bubble first broke. By the by our friend Brockholst some how or other has an unfortunate story eternally pursuing him—And as he rises in fortune he appears to sink in reputation. His last maneuvre has occasioned a separation between him & several who were his warmest supporters. Duer on the contrary is mounting fast above him. The basis of his conduct as a speculator is frankness & I have not heard him even suspected here of any dishonorable combination or of any stratagem to deceive—so that he really Stands amongst us upon better ground in point of character than ever. There is between him & me an amnesty of all past bickerings & I mean to do every thing in my power to promote his election. I have already formed some arrangments upon this subject & am preparing the way generally for him. The event is certainly doubtful but I hope & am determined to hope for the best. Pray write an answer to the enclosed letter by the first post. I wish you to be careful of what you say with respect to the speculations in paper—the value of Stock &c. You have been quoted upon some occasions for the purposes of mere jobbing. God bless you

Yours   Robt Troup.

A Hamilton Esqre

ALS, Sleepy Hollow Restorations, Inc., Tarrytown, New York.
1. Troup, who had been a close friend of H since their undergraduate days at King's College, was a New York lawyer and land speculator.
2. Letter not found.
3. The stockholders of the Bank of the United States elected the directors of the bank on October 21, 1791 ([Philadelphia] *Gazette of the United States,* October 26, 1791). For H's plans and proposals on how the election should be conducted, see LeRoy and Bayard to H, September 1, 11, 1791 (*PAH,* IX, 157–58, 201–02); Oliver Wolcott, Jr., to H, September, 1791 (*PAH,* IX, 255–60); Edmund Randolph to H, October 18, 1791 (*PAH,* IX, 406–11).
4. Brockholst Livingston, a New York lawyer, and certain associates (including Edward and John R. Livingston) were speculating as "bears" in the New York securities market in the summer and fall of 1791 (Davis, *Essays,* I, 283). Following a sharp rise in the prices of funded securities in July and August, 1791, there was a precipitous drop in the market. In October the security prices began to recover and reached new highs in January, 1792 (*ASP, Finance,* I, 231; Davis, *Essays,* I, 210; H to William Seton, September 7, 1791 [*PAH,* IX, 185]). In the same period the scrip of the Bank of the United States followed a somewhat similar pattern, but the fluctuations were much more pronounced (William Duer to H, August 16, 1791, note 3 [printed in this volume]; Davis, *Essays,* I, 211).
5. Bank of New York.

From William Constable

[New York] 14th Septr 1791

I have a Ship here lately arrived from Londo. particularly circumstanced, she is Eastern built as can be made appear & was seized some years ago at Tobago & condemned for Contraband, & has since been employed in the French Colony trade. She was sold at Londo. & purchased in the name of Captn. Jones the mr. an american, for his accot. Messrs. Hoffman & Sons [1] & our house,[2] & brot. out a Cargo of Goods on frt. We have been obliged to allow the importers the 10 ⅌ ct. foreign Duty which she was liable to from not having an American Register.[3] May I presume to ask your opinion whether a petition to Congress would probably obtain us a Register (the fact being fully ascertained that she is American built) & whether we might hope for a remission of the extra 10 pr. Cent. Mr. Langdon [4] will be able I believe to identify the Ship. With sentiments of perfect respect I am

Yours &ca.

LC, William and James Constable Letter Book, 1791–1793, MS Division, New York Public Library.

1. Nicholas Hoffman and Son was a mercantile firm at 12 Little Dock Street in New York City.

2. William Constable and Company, merchants, was located at 89 Great Dock Street in New York City.

3. Section 5 of "An Act for laying a Duty on Goods, Wares, and Merchandises imported into the United States" reads: "That a discount of ten per cent. on all the duties imposed by this act, shall be allowed on such goods, wares and merchandises, as shall be imported in vessels built in the United States, and which shall be wholly the property of a citizen or citizens thereof, or in vessels built in foreign countries, and on the sixteenth day of May last, wholly the property of a citizen or citizens of the United States, and so continuing until the time of importation" (1 *Stat.* 27 [July 4, 1789]).

4. Presumably John Langdon, United States Senator from New Hampshire.

From Henry Marchant

Newport Rhode Island
Sepr. 14th. 1791.

Sir,

I have the Honor to transmit You the Petition of Peleg Saunders upon the mitigating Act; and the Proceedings thereon.[1] I feel myself much obliged by Your very polite Letter of the 30th of June;[2] The interesting Concern You are pleased to take in the Situation of Officers of Government residing at a distance; and the flattering Hopes We have reason to entertain of a Speedy Relief in the mode of Payment of their Salaries. With all possible Esteem I am,

Sir,   Your most obedient and very humble Servt.

Henry Marchant.

Alexander Hamilton Esq.
Secretary of the Treasury of the United States
Philadelphia.

ALS, Independence National Historical Park, Philadelphia.
  1. See Marchant to H, September 14, 1791 (*PAH*, IX, 205–06).
  2. Letter not found.

From John Armstrong [1]

[Fort Washington,
Territory Northwest of the River Ohio,
September 17, 1791]

Dear Sir:

Permit me Sir to intrude so fancy to call your attention for a moment on a subject that to me is very interesting. In a report I made to Gel. Knox the 21st of February last a copy of which I am told was sent to your Office, I stated some facts relative to the Conduct of the late contractors,[2] and having since learnt that they have by

some means procured certificates contradicting this report, I therefore concieve it necessary to inform you that when called on I can
Support the facts therein stated by the Testimony of Captain Beatty,
Captain Strong Lt Sedam Lt Kingsbury [3] & in short almost every
Officer in the Rgt. Major Ferguson [4] to whom I showed a copy of
that Report in reply to that part wherein I speak of the due bills,
Says he always compeled the contractors to pay the Articles on Soap
in Lieu thereof. I wrote General Knox more fully on the Subject
on the 15th. July, but perhaps that letter may have miscarried. Major
Hamtramck [5] who was commanding Officer at Post Vincennes informs me that Messrs Elliot & Williams directed their agent to call
on him to certify that the troops had been well furnished, which certificate he refused giving as the troops had often been on half allow-
ence. Their agent was also requested to take his deposition before a
Magistrate on this Subject, but he had too just a sense of their rights
to do so.

It will appear by the Merchants books at Fort Washington that
during the last Summer they sold to the Individual Soldiers more
than Six thousand weight of Bacon beef &c. It is therefore evident if
the Soldiers had drawn their rations they could have had no use for
that quantity, this proves also that there was plenty of provisions to
be had & I believe it was offerd the contractors at a time when the
troops were in a sterving condition as mentioned in my report. I
have in my possession an account renderd by the contracters wherein
I stend charged 22/6 pr. hundrid for flour & 7/6 pr Gallon for whisky
as mentiond in my report. It is a fact Sir that every imposition has
been played off against the Soldiery, & that they have been the continual Subject of Speculation.

Copy, Indiana Historical Society Library, Indianapolis.
    1. Armstrong, who fought in the line of the Twelfth and Third Pennsylvania
Regiments during the American Revolution, was brevetted a captain on September 30, 1783. He received a commission in the United States Infantry Regiment on August 12, 1784, and in 1786 was transferred to the western frontier.
In 1790 he was promoted to captain in the First United States Infantry Regiment and in the same year explored the Spanish territory in the West and the
Missouri and Wabash rivers. Armstrong served in the expeditions against the
Indians led by Brigadier General Josiah Harmar in 1790 and by Major General Arthur St. Clair in 1791. In 1793 he resigned from the Army, and in 1796
he became treasurer of the Territory Northwest of the River Ohio and founded
one of the first settlements in what is now Indiana.
    2. Armstrong is referring to Robert Elliot and Elie Williams, of the Balti-

more firm of Elliot and Williams. See H to Otho H. Williams, December 7, 1791 (*PAH*, X, 348).

3. Erkurius Beatty, David Strong, Cornelius Sedam, and Jacob Kingsbury were all members of the First Infantry Regiment.

4. William Ferguson of Pennsylvania was a major commandant in the artillery battalion of the United States Army. He was killed on November 4, 1791, during St. Clair's expedition against the western Indians.

5. John F. Hamtramck of New York was a major in the First Infantry Regiment.

From Walter Livingston

New York Octobr. 5 91

Sir

In the month of June last Mr. Seton Cashier of the Bank of New York gave me the perusal of a letter of yours to him purporting that monies for shares in the United States Bank, to a certain amount might be paid to him.[1] Mr. Seton asked me if I chose to avail myself of the priviledge. I replyed in the affirmative and gave him a check for 2500 Dollrs. being the first payment for my Subscription for 100 Shares. Mr. Setons certificate for my Subscription was given to Mr. Constable[2] who applied on the morning of the 4th. of July to the Commissioners appointed to receive Subscriptions to the Bank of the United States[3] for the above 100 Shares (not all in my own name) and was refused. The money was lodged in the Bank at Philadelphia where I believe it still remains. The above information was not communicated to me until the 2d. Instant on my return from the Country or I should have written to you on the Subject sooner.

Will you be so kind as to inform me what steps I must pursue to obtain my Shares in the Bank, to which I am legally entitled.

To the Honbl: Alexr. Hamilton Eqr. Philadel:

LC, New-York Historical Society, New York City.

1. See William Seton to H, June 24, 1791 (*PAH*, VIII, 503); H to Seton, June 25, 1791 (*PAH*, VIII, 504).

2. William Constable.

3. See H to Tobias Lear, March 23, 1791 (*PAH*, VIII, 210).

To Catharine Greene [1]

Philadelphia Nov. 2 91

You are right My Dear friend in conjecturing that your letter from Charles Town did not reach me. I am still to learn whether you received mine in answer to one you wrote me from Georgia.[2]

I hope in ten days to be able so far to extricate my self as to report on your Memorial.[3] Indeed I will do it & if possible sooner.

God forbid I should think it possible that my departed friend could violate honor or truth. I admit every thing he says and only doubt on the score of public precedent, in a case in which every requisite precaution was omitted.

But whatever may be my ultimate opinion on the merits of the question referred, I cannot but endeavour to do you service. And surely the family of General Greene will not be permitted to be the Victims of his want of caution in an instance of great zeal for the public service. I write in the most intense confidence.[4]

ALS, sold by Charles Hamilton Autographs, Inc., Auction No. 101, December 9, 1976.

1. Catharine Greene was the widow of Major General Nathanael Greene, who died in 1786.
2. Letter not found.
3. See "Report on the Petition of Catharine Greene," December 26, 1791 (*PAH*, X, 406–68).
4. Text taken from the dealer's catalogue.

To John Rutherfurd

[November 4, 1791–October 8, 1792] [1]

My Dear Sir

I called at your Lodgings to converse with you on a certain subject and wish much to see you. If you will be at home at two today, I shall then find you.

Yrs.   A Hamilton

Saturday

ALS, Columbia University Libraries.

1. This letter has been dated on the basis of a list written on the back of the letter which contains the names of twenty-four senators who were members of the Second Congress, which lasted from March 4, 1791, to March 3, 1793. On the list is the name of Stephen Bradley of Vermont, who took his seat on November 4, 1791, and Richard Henry Lee, who resigned on October 8, 1792.

To Ann Pemberton

[Philadelphia, December 2, 1791]

Mr. Hamilton presents his respects to Mrs. Pemberton—having no copy of the agreement respecting the hire of the house & lot in use of the Treasury Department [1] he will be much obliged to her for one. If not convenient to furnish a copy & she will please to send the original it will be copied & returned.

Decr. 2. 1791

AL, Papers of Tench Coxe in the Coxe Family Papers at the Historical Society of Pennsylvania, Philadelphia.

1. During the period when H was Secretary of the Treasury and the Treasury Department was in Philadelphia (October, 1790, through January, 1795) theTreasury Department's main office was at 100 Chestnut Street. During the same years Mrs. Ann Pemberton, a widow, owned an adjoining house at 102 Chestnut Street.

The Treasury Department also rented two houses on Chestnut Street from a Mrs. McIntire for six hundred dollars per year. See Tench Coxe's account with the United States, March 13, 1791 (ADS, Tench Coxe Papers in the Coxe Family Papers at the Historical Society of Pennsylvania, Philadelphia); Coxe's "Memm of Mrs. McIntires rent," August 1, 1791 (AD, Tench Coxe Papers in the Coxe Family Papers at the Historical Society of Pennsylvania, Philadelphia).

Report on the Subject of Manufactures

[Philadelphia, December 5, 1791]

Introductory Note

When *The Papers of Alexander Hamilton*, X, was published in 1966 the Tench Coxe Papers in the Coxe Family Papers, which then, as now, were located in the Historical Society of Pennsylvania, were not open to scholars. Through the courtesy of Mr. Daniel M. Coxe, however, the editors received a copy of a draft by Coxe of a paper on manufacturing. This was printed under the title "Tench Coxe's Draft of the Report on the Subject of Manufactures," 1790.[1]

Since 1966 an examination of the Tench Coxe Papers has revealed additional contributions by Coxe to Hamilton's "Report on the Subject of Manufactures." [2] In the first place, Coxe wrote a first draft, dated September, 1790, which consists of three manuscript pages.[3] This document is printed below under the title of "Tench Coxe's First Draft." In the second place, Coxe's draft printed in *The Papers of Alexander Hamilton* in 1966 [4] has proved to be incomplete. A more complete and accurate version of this document is printed below as "Tench Coxe's Second Draft." Some doubts remain concerning the order in which Coxe's draft was written, for various pages of the manuscript are not numbered and were originally scattered throughout the Tench Coxe Papers. When questions concerning the order have arisen, the editors have used as a guide "Alexander Hamilton's First Draft of the Report on the Subject of Manufactures," 1790,[5] on the assumption that Hamilton reproduced Coxe's material in the same order in which Coxe had presented it.[6]

As Jacob E. Cooke has pointed out in detail, Hamilton relied far more heavily than had originally been suspected on Coxe's work in drawing up his own first draft.[7] At the same time, Coxe's influence can be seen to diminish progressively and drastically in each of Hamilton's subsequent drafts and his final report.[8] In any event, this is a subject not worth pursuing, for readers can easily reach their own conclusions by comparing the various documents in question.

No attempt has been made to annotate the two Coxe documents printed below, for the points which they raise have been explained in either the originally published "Tench Coxe's Draft of the Report on the Subject of Manufactures," 1790,[9] or "Alexander Hamilton's First Draft of the Report on the Subject of Manufactures," 1790.[10]

1. *PAH*, X, 15–23.
2. For discussions of these materials, see Keiji Tajima, "Tench Coxe's 'Drafts' of the 'Report on the Subject of Manufactures,'" *The Aoyama Journal of Economics*, XXVII (March, 1976), 101–13; Jacob E. Cooke, "Tench Coxe, Alexander Hamilton, and the Encouragement of American Manufactures," *William and Mary Quarterly*, 3rd ser., XXXII (July, 1975), 369–92.
3. This draft is printed in Tajima, "Tench Coxe's 'Drafts' . . . ," 110–11.
4. *PAH*, X, 15–23.
5. *PAH*, X, 23–49.
6. In the articles cited in note 2 above, Tajima and Cooke appear to differ widely on the question of the order in which Coxe presented his ideas. In addition, Tajima's version is briefer than that outlined by Cooke.
7. See note 2.
8. *PAH*, X, 49–340.
9. *PAH*, X, 15–23.
10. *PAH*, X, 23–49.

TENCH COXE'S FIRST DRAFT [11]

Treasy. Dept. September   1790

The Secretary of the Treasury in obedience to the order of the house of Representatives of the fifteenth day of January last has applied his attention at as early a period as his other duties would permit, to the subject of manufactures, and particularly to the means of promoting such as will tend to render the United states independent on other nations for military and other essential Supplies.

The expediency of encouraging manufactures in the United States, tho recently deemed very questionable appears now to be universally admitted.

The advantages of the landholder in furnishing raw materials, food, fuel & other supplies to the manufacturers, the aid which the fisheries derive from manufactures by the consumption of articles derived from them, their assistance to commerce by promoting the importation of raw articles and the exportation of manufactured commodities, their favorable effects on population by inducing the emigration of foreign workmen, their encreasing and rendering more certain the means of national defence, and other essential supplies, the promotion of individual industry and œconomy which naturally result from them, and lastly the reduction of the prices of imported supplies, which has already taken place on the appearance of competition in the American Market are considerations which entitle this important object to a share of Legislative attention.

Among the methods devised by Other nations to encourage manufactures protecting duties have been very generally adopted. It cannot be unobserved by those who are engaged in these pursuits nor by those capitalists and workmen who may intend to transfer their property and business to the United States that the duties already imposed by the legislature for the purposes of Revenue afford great & certain advantages to the American Manufacturer. Whether any additions to these duties be necessary to encourage particular

11. ADf, Papers of Tench Coxe in the Coxe Family Papers at the Historical Society of Pennsylvania, Philadelphia.

branches is a question respectfully suggested to the wisdom of the house.

Prohibitions of rival articles, or duties equivalent, frequently present themselves in the laws of foreign Nations. Tho this measure may seem of doubtful propriety for the United States, in most instances, it does not appear advisable to decide against it so far as regards military supply. From the present flourishing condition of some manufactories of warlike stores, such as gunpowder, leaden & iron ball, iron cannon, & cartridge paper, it may not be deemed hazardous, in a season of profound peace, to encrease the duty so as to effect an exclusion of them.

Besides military stores there are certain Articles manufactured from materials with which the United states abound which do not appear unfit subjects of excluding duties. Among Articles here contemplated are Malt liquors, Spirits made from grain of every sort & from several kinds of fruit, the oils of sea & land animals & of flax seed, Starch, Snuff, chewing & smoking Tobaccoes, spirits of turpentine, and other things manufactured from such productions of our lands & fisheries as are constantly exported in large quantities. The wisdom of the house however will render them duly aware of the Danger of extending too far the application of duties equivalent to prohibitions should they be induced to impose them on some articles necessary for defence and on certain manufactures highly & extensively beneficial to the landed interest.

TENCH COXE'S SECOND DRAFT [12]

Treasury Department
the   1790

The Secretary of the Treasury, in obedience to the order of the house of Representatives of the fifteenth day of January last, has

12. ADf, Papers of Tench Coxe in the Coxe Family Papers at the Historical Society of Pennsylvania, Philadelphia.

Material within broken brackets in this document has been taken from H's first draft of the Report (*PAH*, X, 23–49).

applied his attention, at as early a period as his other duties would permit, to the subject of manufactures, and particularly to the means of promoting such as will tend to render the United States independent on foreign Nations for military and other essential supplies.

The expediency of encouraging manufactures in the United States, tho recently deemed very questionable, appears at this time to be generally admitted. The advantages of the Landholder in furnishing raw materials, subsistence, fuel and other supplies to the workmen—the support which the fisheries derive from them by their consumption of articles drawn from the ocean—the assistance given to external commerce by promoting the importation of raw articles and furnishing manufactured commodities for exportation—their favorable effects on population by inducing the emigration of foreign artists and laborers—the introduction of money by offering a new & promising field to capitalists of other nations—the promotion of individual industry & œconomy which naturally result from manufactures and particularly when engrafted upon an extensive agriculture—their encreasing and rendering more certain the means of defence and other articles of prime necessity and lastly the Reduction of the prices of convenient & essential supplies for public & private use, which has already taken place on the appearance of competition from the American manufacturer are among the considerations, which have produced more favorable opinions concerning this Object.[13]

In addition to these advantages manifestly resulting to the U.S. from the small share of attention which manufactures have hitherto obtained several circumstances present themselves, strongly encouraging the sedulous & steady promotion of them.

It is a position in commerce of indisputable "truth" that the greatest resort will ever be to those marts wherein the supplies while equally valuable are most various. Each difference of kind holds out their proper inducements to those who need or desire it. Thus the trade of the grain states is animated by the conversion of a part of the various species of that commodity into meal and bread,

13. In the margin at this point Coxe wrote: See [page] 100." Below these words he wrote in the margin and then crossed out: "Further inducement a brief statement of our capacity in the essential points." Beside this note he wrote "X X" and "* *." Coxe was referring to an insertion he wished to make consisting of the following ten paragraphs.

and the portions of Hemp, flax, iron, leather, wool & cotton which are manufactured into sail cloth & cordage, anchors, implements of husbandry, & fabrics for apparel occasion more foreign orders to the mercantile citizens than the raw materials would have drawn. Consumers abroad, who would never resort to a market of un-manufactured commodities, being unable to work them up, will be inivited to the same port when it shall present them with the fabrics for which they have occasion. The operation of these facts is equally certain and beneficial, whether an original export or remit-trances for prior importations be the End in View.

Should the United States decline or omit to encourage manu-factures their local situation will subject them to some peculiar dis-advantages. Their commodities, which are generally very bulky, will sustain in the freight & other charges of exportation to their distant foreign consumers a proportionate deduction &, as the equality & moderation of individual property & the great portion of unim-proved lands occasion an unusual demand for coarse manufactures a corresponding weight of expence will be imposed on all their supplies. In Seasons of profound peace these circumstances occasion an immense annual deduction from the gross value of their produc-tions, but in the time of a war that shall involve their principal carriers the charges of expor[ta]tion on some of the most bulky raw ma-terials, perhaps the most profitable, must become a grievous burden to the farmer, if the introduction of factories should not be pre-viously effected.

It is unnecessary to suggest to the house the sound policy of pursuing such measures as will retain at home the a[c]tive capital, which will certainly flow with due œconomy, out of the affairs of industrious & sensible people. That Manufacturing in a considerable degree, is necessary to this purpose appears highly probable since we know not of any great manufacturing nation, however incon-siderable its agriculture may be, that does not abound with money, nor is there any instance of a country, which does not manufacture that can retain its Specie, however blest its soil or abundant its sources of the precious metals. The reason is obvious. The importa-tions of manufactured supplies, incessantly drains the merely agri-cultural people of their wealth. Hence it is that the West India Islands, the soils of which are the most fertile, and the Nation that supplies Europe with Coin, exchange to a loss with every country in the world. In further illustration of this point it may be observed that undisputed Statements in a principal manufacturing Country of Europe render it more than probable that their exports including their various fabrics never exceeded one third of the gross value of their Manufactures. Had they entirely neglected this domestic branch of trade, and had they as freely consumed foreign articles similar to those they make for themselves, it is evident that national & individual poverty must have been the consequences. That the U. S. have heretofore felt the inconvenience of that situation in a very great degree is a matter of notoriety. To prevent the increase, and gradually to diminish the evil was the Object of the house, it is humbly presumed, in the resolution which calls for this report.

Altho agricultural employments are generally speaking the most proper for the great body of the inhabitants of these States, yet when the variety of human talent is duly remembred, and it is considered that minds of the strongest & most active powers for their proper objects, may fall below mediocrity, or labor without effect, if confined to incongenial pursuits, it will appear unwise so to arrange our political œconomy as to impel to agriculture the whole body of the people. It is interesting to the prosperity and advancement of the U. S. that those who have been peculiarly qualified by nature for the useful arts, should find the encouragement necessary to call forth their various talents. All employments, that are comprehended in the general plan of a well formed community, were doubtless intended to be pursued, & that nation, whose citizens have attained to facility and eminence in the greatest variety, will be found at once the most independent and the most respectable.

If a doubt should remain of the expediency of encouraging manufactures in the United States an appeal to the substantial Evidence of facts may be safely made. The house may be respectfully reminded that those parts of the Union in which Manufactures have most strikingly encreased have recovered in the greatest degree from the injuries of the late war, and that those States, which have given the most liberal encouragement to this branch of trade, are now among the most flourishing. Nor is this less manifest in the states that possess extensive bodies of vacant Land, than in those that are most numerously populated.

It may be useful in a survey of this subject to advert to the capacity of the U. S. in the business of Manufactures, especially as it was the opinion of a former period, not very remote, that they were incapable of any thing considerable in this branch of trade. To a body, as accurately informed as the honorable house, it is unnecessary to adduce proofs that a very considerable number of manufacturers in a great variety of branches have already established themselves in the United States, not a small part of whom carry on branches depending entirely on manual labor. It may be reasonably argued that what has succeeded in so many instances, notwithstanding the disadvantages supposed to exist, may succeed in many more. The cheapness of provisions which is likely to encrease, the trivial taxes & internal duties (compared with those of other countries) which a workman pays, the exemption from tythes & from corporation restraints, the growing cheapness of raw materials, together with the heavy charges of importing rival Articles have produced this success, and promise the same advantage to all prudent & œconomical attempts to establish even handicraft manufactures of articles in general Use. But when it is remembered that the great objection to American manufactures (the price of labor) is in the most valuable branches obviated by the agency of fire, or by that of water, or by that of labor saving machines moved by fire, water, or hand a doubt of success cannot be entertained.

But the rate of labor it is believed will not be found on consideration so weighty an objection as it is by some supposed to be. Many branches are conducted wholly or in a great degree in the U. S. & all other countries by the thrifty industry of private families in hours that would otherwise be unemployed. The wages in others, do not exceed, in some parts of the Union, the rates which successful manufacturers in Europe pay in the same branches. Women are known to perform the work, in the making of some kinds of fabrics, which in other parts of the World is executed by men. This useful habit may be extended, & the labor of Children. It is moreover a reasonable expectation, that European workmen will be induced, by the supposed high rates of labor, whenever they really exist, to transplant themselves from that consideration to the United States.

After these preliminary observations which have been rendered as brief as the nature of the subject would admit the immediate object of the resolution of the honorable house remains to be considered.

Capitals, it is urged, are wanting in the U. S. for manufacturing establishments. This seems to be no more than an unduly confined assertion of an obvious & comfortable truth—that the opening affairs of this rising country afford profitable objects for more capital than it has yet acquired. It is true as well with regard to foreign commerce as manufactures else why do the American Merchants import so largely upon credit. That it is also true with regard to agriculture our millions of uncultivated acres fully prove. The past success of many branches of manufacture shew that our own industry & funds, if wisely directed, may be advantageously applied to them. But when the European manufacturer & capitalist shall be accurately informed of the situation of this country—of the cheapness of provisions & raw materials, of the duties on the importation of his European fabrics & the exemption of our own—of the cheapness of mill seats & buildings—when he shall advert to the expences of freight & insurance with which his commodities are loaded and the facility of establishing the great labor-saving works by water & fire, he must be convinced that no profit can accrue in Europe adequate to what must follow a well conducted establishment with a suitable capital in the many parts of the United States.

Among the means devised by the European nations to encourage manufactures protecting duties have been very generally adopted. It cannot be unobserved by those, who are engaged in these pursuits nor will it escape the notice of those capitalists, and workmen who may intend to transfer their property and business to the United States, that the duties already imposed by the legislature, tho principally for the purposes of Revenue, afford very considerable and certain advantages to the American manufacturer. Tho it may be very doubtful whether general addition to these duties be necessary further to encourage the manufactures of the United States, yet it is humbly conceived a few articles may be very properly aided by a moderate encrease. Among those in View is Sail Cloth which is important to defence, to domestic & foreign commerce, the fisheries, &c, as it relates to the raw materials, to agriculture likewise.

Prohibitions of rival articles, or duties equivalent, frequently present themselves in the laws of foreign nation. Tho this measure, in most instances, may be of doubtful propriety in the United States, it appears to merit consideration in regard to particular Articles.

From the present flourishing condition of some manufactories of military supplies, such as Gunpowder, leaden & iron balls, iron cannon & cartridge paper it may not be deemed hazardous, in a season of profound peace, to encrease the duty so as to prevent the Importation of them. Besides warlike stores there are certain Articles manufactured from materials with which the United States abound, that do not appear unfit Subjects of excluding duties. Among the objects here contemplated are Malt liquors, spirits made from grain of every sort & from fruit (excepting that made of the grape), the oils of sea and land animals, flaxseed, the spirits of turpentine, snuff, chewing & smoking tobacco, starch and other things manufactured from such productions of the Earth & of the fisheries as are constantly exported in large quantities which are encreasing on our hands, and for which a sufficient vent is consequently difficult to procure. The wisdom of the house however will render them duly aware of the injuries that may be occasioned by an indiscriminate & too extended an application of duties equivalent to prohibitions should they be induced to impose them in favor of certain manufactures necessary for defence, or highly and universally beneficial to the landed interest.

Pecuniary Bounties upon home made articles have been tried in several European countries with great success. The linen branch in Ireland is a well known instance. But under the present circumstances of this country the Secretary cannot discover sufficient inducements to these expensive encouragements to justify a strenuous recommendation of them to the consideration of the legislature. This aid to manufactures however is less necessary at the present moment in the United States than in any European country, because their fabrics being generally wanted for hom⟨e consumption, are free from the heavy expences of importation, which rival foreign⟩ goods sustain to the amount, of fifteen, and twenty five ℞ Cent on their Value according to their bulk. But if it should on consideration be deemed inexpedient to grant bounties in money to encourage manufacture⟨s⟩ it may nevertheless appear advisable ⟨to⟩ reward certain great and useful promoters of them by other means. The United States having a very large quantity of unappropriated lands the Secretary humbly submits to the house the propriety of setting apart the quantity of five hundred thousand acres, of a good quality and advantageously situated, for the purpose of rewarding the first introducers or establishers of new and useful manufactories, arts machines, & secrets not before possessed, known or carried on in the United States. The objects here contemplated, and the mode of applying this landed fund will be more clearly explained by the plan contained in the paper (A) which accompanies this report. A measure of this nature would evince to the manufacturers of Europe the disposition of the legislature to encourage and reward them, and would afford to persons ⟨who⟩ transfer their capitals and establishments to ⟨the United States a certain⟩ tho ⟨not⟩ an immediate compensation ⟨even in unsuccessful⟩ instances.

In addition to these rewards for the Importation of manufacturing Machinery and secrets of great value, acts may be passed, if sufficiently warranted by the extraordinary utility of the object and the difficulty of attaining ⟨it,⟩ granting to the introducers such exclusive privileges for a term of years as would have been secured by patent had they been the inventors. Public Advantage, if derived from each in an equal degree, will justify this favor to the one as well as to the other, and the successful practice of the principal manufacturing nations of Europe establishes the prudence of the measure.

As a substitute for pecuniary bounties on particular articles beneficial to the landed interest to merit that expansive and inconvenient encouragement, the revenue may be calculated to assist them by diminishing the use of rival tho in some instances different commodities. Thus the Duties on ardent spirits may be rendered a virtual bounty on beer ale or porter & the impost on foreign spirituous liquors an encouragment to those made at home. By careful attention to regulations of this Nature it is believed very effectual aid may be given to our manufactures without any hazard of public inconvenience or injurious frauds. An examination of the Articles imported for consumption in the United States, and of the capacity of our manufacturers to make succedanea for them out of our own produce, and imported raw Materials will suggest many objects to which it is supposed this Idea may be advantageously applied.

A drawback of the amount of the duty on the raw Material on the ex⟨portation of manufactured⟩ Articles is a measure recommended ⟨by policy, and rendered in some degree necessary⟩ by the practice of nations, who will hold a competition with us in foreign

Markets. The duty on Molasses, if the idea here suggested should meet the approbation of the legislature, might be allowed on the exportation of American rum—that on Muscovado sugars on the exportation of refined—that on Cocoa on the exportation of Chocolate—and in such other instances as shall admit of due security against deception & fraud, the danger of which is the only Objection that occurs to this mode of encouragement.

The Admission of the tools and implements of their trade and the household furniture of manufacturers, free from import duty is a regulation, which the legislature have already been pleased to make in their favor, in common with other emigrants. The continuance of this exemption appears to be perfectly safe and politic.

The promotion of friendly intercourse & fair trade with the indian Tribes will have a favorable effect upon some valuable branches of Manufacture, the raw materials ⟨for which are derived from the western Country. Towards these ends the wisdom⟩ of the Legislature and of the ⟨Chief Magistrate⟩ have been already successfully directed, but some objects of great consequence to the Indian trade & consequently to the Manufacturer dependent on it remain to be obtained. The pursuit of them however rests upon considerations of so much more Importance than any which arise on the present topic, that it is sufficient merely to present them to the attention of the house as connected with the subject of this report.

Facility of communication, and cheapness of transportation are matters of primary importance in the business of every country; but under the existing circumstances of the United States they call for the earliest & most efficient exertions of government. The good condition of the post roads especially where they happen to connect places of landing on the rivers & bays, and those which run into the western country will conduce exceedingly to the cheapness of transporting and the facility of obtaining raw materials, fuel & provisions. But the most useful assistance perhaps, which it is in the power of the legislature to give to manufactures and which at the same time will equally benefit the landed & commercial interests, is the improvement of inland navigation. Three of the easiest and most importan⟨t⟩ operations of this kind are the improvement of communication between New York, Connecticut, Rhode Island & Boston by cutting a passage thro the peninsula of cape Cod, the Union of

Delaware and Chessapeak bays by a canal from the waters of the former to those of the latter, and the junction the Chessapeak bay & Albermarle sound by uniting the Elizabeth & the   .[14] The accomplishment of these and other objects of the same nature seems likely to afford greater & more various aids to our growing manufactures than any other measure that has occured to the Secretary in the investigation, which he has been directed to make.

A fur⟨ther measure⟩ of pro⟨moting⟩ the cheap transportation of raw materials & provisions presents itself in the abolition of the duty of Tonnage imposed on coasting vessels. This appears to be a burden on the produce of lands, as substantially as if it were imposed on working waggons, and seems hardly consistent with sound policy.

The principal production of the fisheries may not improperly be considered as articles of the nature of manufactures, & the remainder are of great Utility as raw materials or cheap & wholesome food. Whalebone cutters, the makers of whips, umbrellas, stays, millenary, fishing tackel & philosophical apparatus consume whalebone, Ivory turners use the Seahorses teeth, druggists, chemists instrument makers, hatters, tanners watchmakers, sadlers, & shoemakers work up the skins & furs of various Sea animals, Shipbuilders, riggers, soap & candle makers, and leather dressers consume the oils or spermaceti, and the workmen & manufacturers are enabled to observe a more beneficial œconomy by the use of the oils in lighting their shops & houses & of the fish in their sustenance. Aiding the fisheries therefore appears to be a very safe & efficient method of promoting manufactures: but as[15] the means of encouraging that important branch of trade have been refered by the house to the Secretary of State it is unnecessary and improper to enlarge upon it here.

The establishment of impartial and judicious inspections by which frauds upon consumers at home & exporters to foreign countries might be prevented and proper standards might be ascertained,

14. This space and subsequent spaces left blank in MS.
15. In the margin opposite the first sentence of this paragraph Coxe wrote: "oil of every kind whale bone." Coxe wrote the second sentence and the portion of the third sentence up to this point on a separate sheet of paper. He did not, however, indicate where he wished to insert the material on whalebone. In placing it after the first sentence the editors have followed H's first draft of the Report.

would have a favorable effect upon the quality & character of our manufactures. The reputation of flour in some ports, and of potash in others have been established by that method. The same good name may be derived to those articles by similar means in all the ports of the U. S. from whence they are usually shipt; and inspection may be advantageously extended to other commodities. The manufactory of Gunpowder, it is conceived, is now in a train to be perfected by placing it under this wholesome regulation, & it is not to be doubted that reflexion & time will suggest other objects.[16]

The regulation of inland bills of exchange, so as to ensure due caution in drawing them and strict punctuality in paying them, must have a favorable effect on the purchases of raw Materials & sales of manufactured Articles in a country so extensive as the United States.

⟨The⟩ ability to place funds with celerity & ease in every part of the Country for the purchase of raw materials and provisions is a matter of great importance to the manufacturer. To aff⟨ord⟩ the accomodation of a general paper circulation of the nature of Bank Notes payable with absolute certainty in specie on demand is therefore very desirable. This benefit will immediately result from a national bank, & from such arrangements of Government with that ⟨Institution⟩ as soon as it shall be erected as may give ⟨uni⟩versal circulation to their cash notes.

The want of sufficient capital being deemed one of the principal difficulties in a national view, with which the manufactures of the United states have at this time to contend a steady pursuit of such measures as will give full and unfluctuating value to the public funds appears of the utmost importance to the increase and prosperity of American Manufactures. Having enlarged upon the beneficial circulation that ever grows out of a well funded national debt in the report upon public credit, which he had the honor to make in January last, the Secretary conceives it sufficient at this time to repeat his thorough convictions of what is therein stated on that point.

16. Coxe wrote this paragraph on a separate sheet of paper which he endorsed: "part of Rept. on Manufs." He did not, however, indicate where in his draft he wished to have the paragraph placed. In putting it at this point in Coxe's draft, the editors have followed H's lead, who inserted it at the same point in his first draft of the Report.

The ⟨Importation of⟩ raw materials and ingredients, and of colors, drugs & other articles necessary to com⟨plete⟩ manufactures, free of duty, is an encouragement ⟨of⟩ obvious propriety, generally consider⟨ed⟩ but when it is remembered that the principal nations of Europe afford this aid to their manufactories, and that we are to meet them as competitors in our own & in foreign markets it appears to be almost indispensible. Proceeding, it is presumed, on these principles the legislature have been pleased to exempt from impost a number of articles of the nature above described thereby giving the sanction to the principle here contemplated. An extension of this exemption further than has yet taken place particularly to include cotton & hemp, the Secretary humbly conceives to be necessary to success in the business of manufactures.

The peculiar value to the U. S. of improved implements and machinery for manufacturing, and the inducements to export those we have already obtained or may hereafter procure, which the interest of our competitors obviously creat⟨es, seem to⟩ render a penalty for such exportations an eligible me⟨asure.⟩ It is manifestly proper to guard carefully against extending this f⟨urther⟩ than is absolutely necessary to preve⟨nt⟩ a deprivation of any particular ⟨im⟩plement or machine, lest in the formation of the law, the export trade of well Known articles, applicable in manufactures may be unfavorably affected.[17]

Besides the measures for the encouragement of manufactures, which it appears eligible that the legislature should pursue there are some of considerable importance which fall more immediately within the sphere of the other branches of government, and on which for obvious reasons arising out of the nature of those measures, the Secretary refrains from enlarging.

Under the existing circumstances of this Country the foregoing Ideas, are respectfully submitted as the constituent parts of a general plan for the encouragement of national manufactures. The requisite aid to those particular branches, which are necessary for defence, or which may be deemed essential to the Government & citizens of the United States are yet to be considered.

17. In the margin opposite the end of this paragraph Coxe wrote and crossed out: "right to cut Logwood of Mahogany import cocoa, melasses, ⟨-⟩ & Spanish cotton."

The manufactory of Gunpowder has been rapidly advanced, & principally by individual exertion within the few last years. Tho it may be considered as established yet its importance & utility renders its extension thro the Union very desirable. Sulphur, which is a very considerable ingredient in its composition, has been made liable to the non-enumerated duty of five ℔ Cent. No quantity of that article has yet been produced from internal sources. The addition of Sulphur to the class of free goods appears therefore to merit consideration. It may be further observed that another principal use of this commodity is in finishing the bottoms of Ships, a manufactory that cannot be deemed secondary to that of gun powder, they being at once powerful instruments of defence, and the necessary vehicles of all the productions and all the supplies of the United States.

The annual importation of a certain quantity of Salt petre, rough or refined, has been made an indispensible Obligation on one of the most successful East India companies of Europe. This, it is understood, has been required with a view to assisting the manufactures of gun Powder. The trade to China being now well established, a moderate regulation of this nature, duly proportioned to the Tonnage of each vessel, might perhaps be conveniently enacted. The United States not having factories established in other parts of the East Indies the requisition could not be reasonably extended to Vessels from any other than the port of Canton.

Leaden Ball & Shot employ but few hands & require little skill to make them & therefore may be expected to succeed. To aid the exertions of the owners of lead mines the foreign commodity has been charged with a duty of one cent per pound, which may be safely extended, it is believed, to shot, ball and all the manufactures of this Article. These are liable at present to the lowest rate of duty, tho the foreign raw material is subjected to one of the highest, which operates to encourage the importation of the foreign manufactures.[18]

The brass foundries, that are already introduced into the U. S., tho at present confined to common wares, may be considered as

18. At the beginning of the next paragraph Coxe placed an asterisk to indicate an insertion he wished to make. This insertion is written on a separate sheet of paper. The editors have followed H's lead in his first draft of the Report and placed Coxe's insertion after the next two paragraphs.

furnishing the future means of manufacturing ordinance of that metal. In the new impost law iron Castings and copper wares are rated at seven and one half per cent & those of brass are included in the non enumerated class which pay the lowest duty. If this raw material be continued among the free articles, and copper (the ingredient in brass) in pigs & bars should be added to that class, there appears to be perfect safety in placing manufactured brass in the list of wares subject to the duty of seven and one half ℔ Cent. This metal being also used in the manufactory of some kinds of small arms & instruments in the Arts & Sciences, and other useful articles the influence of the duty, which cannot be deemed high, will be extensive.

Musquets and all the class of small fire arms, swords and other military weapons of that nature, and the connected articles of Surgical instruments and cutlery might be rated it is conceived without injury at seven and one half ℔ Cent; Iron & Steel of which they are made, being among the most abundant productions of the United States.

The several Species of wood & timber ordinarily used in cabinet work & Ship building are free of duty in foreign Countries, when imported in their national Vessels. Cabinet Wares being in general use, and frequently exported, and the manufactory of ships being the most perfect in the United States it appears both safe & politic to give the workers in wood support, wch. other nations have universally extended to them. A further inducement to this regulation arises from its favorable tendency in regard to our Magazine of ship timber. The encreasing scarcity and the growing importance of that Article in European countries admonish the United States to commence & systematically to pursue measures for the preservation of their stock.

In the enumeration of the several kinds of paper wch. are subjected to a duty of 7½ ℔ Cent, sheathing and cartridge paper are omitted, being the most simple manufactures of that nature, and necessary to military supply, as well as the national shipping the addition of these to the specification appears to be recommended by the considerations that apply to the other articles.

The duty on nails, and spikes, however various in size & value is laid upon their weight. The Effect of this is to reduce the impost on the smaller Kinds below ℔ Cent, while the larger pay a considerable ad valorem duty. Of the persons employed in this branch a great proportion are boys, whose early habits of industry are of importance to the community to the present relief of their families, & to their own future comfort. The raw material is a native production of almost every state—the necessary fuel is abundant in all. An addition therefore of ℔ Cent upon the Value of nails only does not appear unworthy of consideration.

Glue starch, hair powder, and wafers are left in the mass of non enumerated articles at five ℔ Cent. No manufactures are more simple. The first, like paper, is an entire œconomy of materials, which if not manufactured, must be left to perish. The three last are made with the utmost ease from the most abundant productions of the Earth. They all appear suitable additions to the class of Articles rated at 12½ ℔ Cent. In Europe they are generally objects of excluding duties, or expressly prohibited.

The progress, which has been made within a few years in the manufactory of Sail Cloth and other coarse linen articles, their importance in equipment of fleets and in the appointment of armies, the universal capacity of the states to produce the raw materials, both flax and hemp, and the precious effects of the linen branch upon individual industry & domestic œconomy recommend all the fabrics of that Kind in a peculiar degree to the protection of the legislature. To these considerations may be added the example of a more encouraging duty upon the principal manufactures of cotton, which are rated, & with sound policy it is conceived, at seven & a half ℔ Cent. There appears to be no hazard of injury from placing a little above non-enumerated goods, two descriptions of merchandize, the *cotton* & the *linen,* capable of being manufactured by the great labor saving machines.

It is not possible to do complete justice to the subject of this report without bringing into the view of the house those great Instruments of manufacture in the European Nations, labor-saving Machines. The United States, by the bountiful distribution of mill seats over the face of their Territories & by their skill in Mechanism, are peculiarly qualified for their profitable modes of manufacture. A fitness, no less peculiar arises from the State & nature of their population. By the qualities of their soil & the activity of their

Merchants they can command the raw materials to which these machines best apply, on the most advantageous Terms. The requisite Machinery is already obtained: but the enterprize has hitherto appeared too novel for individuals. The capital required is not inconsiderable and the risque of injury in the attempt consequently greater than a private person has yet ventured to encounter. Tis seldon adviseable for a government to interest itself in these undertakings & however promising the calculations, because they too often suffer in the execution of projects that would have been profitable to individuals. It is also true that a loan of capital to individuals, even upon indubitable security is a measure that should be very rarely adopted, and that such aid should never be extended to objects of confined Utility. Yet there may be cases of such obvious safety & from which such extensive national benefits will certainly result, as to justify a deviation from those rules, by which a wise government will circumscribe itself in all ordinary instances. Whether that now contemplated may be deemed of a nature, that will warrant the advancement of an adequate capital, is humbly submitted with the other suggestions in this report by

Alexander Hamilton
Secy of the Treasy.

To the President and Directors of the Bank of the United States

[*Treasury Department, December 21, 1791.* The description of this letter in the dealer's catalogue reads: "On banking matters and suggesting that they give 'such information as you can prudently impart to enable them [the Collectors of Impost and tonnage throughout the United States] to detect counterfeits which may be offered them.'" *Letter not found.*]

The Collector: A Magazine for Autograph and Historical Collectors, LXVII, No. 1–2 (January-February, 1954), 7, Item e 45.

To Ann Pemberton

[Philadelphia, December, 1791]

Coll Hamilton with his Respects to Mrs. Pemberton returns the Agreement for the House the same having been copied at the Treasury.[1]

Wednesday afternoon

Copy, Papers of Tench Coxe in the Coxe Family Papers at the Historical Society of Pennsylvania, Philadelphia.
1. See H to Ann Pemberton, December 2, 1791 (printed in this volume).

To Tench Coxe

[Philadelphia, 1791–1794]

Dr. Sir

I am engaged at home to day. If any thing requires my attention at the Office will you send it to me.

Mr. Horsefield[1] takes a family dinner with me at three OClock. Can you be of the party.

Yrs.   A Hamilton

Tuesday
T Coxe Esq

ALS, Papers of Tench Coxe in the Coxe Family Papers at the Historical Society of Pennsylvania, Philadelphia.
1. Joseph Horsfield of Northampton County was a delegate to the Pennsylvania Ratifying Convention and was appointed postmaster at Bethlehem, Pennsylvania, on June 12, 1792.

To William Webb [1]

[*1791–1792*. The description of this letter in the dealer's catalogue reads: "In regard to 'expenses incurred in consequences of the action against Jonathan Williams.'"[2] *Letter not found.*]

1. LS, sold at Goodspeed's Book Shop, Boston, Catalogue 174, Item 4819B. Webb was collector of customs at Bath, District of Maine.

2. The "expenses" mentioned in the description printed above were the costs to the Federal Government in the case of *The United States* v *Jonathan Williams*. This case was first heard in the September, 1790, term of the United States District Court for Maine. The United States through William Webb sued Williams, who was a resident of Bowdoin in the District of Maine and the master of the schooner *Hannah* on a return voyage from St. Eustatius. Williams was charged with having unloaded from the *Hannah* at Bath on June 6, 1790, "five hogsheads of foreign Rum, five hogsheads of brown Sugar, & eight bags of Coffee" without having obtained a permit from the collector required by "An Act to regulate the Collection of the Duties imposed by law on the tonnage of ships or vessels, and on goods, wares and merchandises imported into the United States" (1 *Stat.* 29-49 [July 31, 1789]). At the June, 1791, term of the same court a jury ruled in favor of the United States, and the court ordered the collector to "recover against the said Jonathan Williams, the sum of four hundred dollars debt or damage" (RG 21, Records of the United States District Court for Maine, Final Record Book, Vol. 1, National Archives).

1792

To John Kean [1]

[*Philadelphia, February 28, 1792*. Letter listed in dealer's catalogue. *Letter not found.*]

1. LS, sold by George H. Richmond, New York City, 1906, "Autograph Letters, Manuscripts. . . ," Item 183.
Kean was cashier of the Bank of the United States.

From William Banks [1]

[*Philadelphia*] *March 1, 1792*. Recommends various ways by which the collectors of customs could improve their record keeping and reports on exports.

Copy, Papers of Tench Coxe in the Coxe Family Papers at the Historical Society of Pennsylvania, Philadelphia.
1. Banks was a clerk in the register's office of the Treasury Department. On at least one other occasion Banks made similar recommendations concerning management or administrative matters in the Treasury Department. See Joseph Nourse to H, August 17, 1792 (*PAH*, XII, 222).

From John Langdon

[*Philadelphia, March 5, 1792*. On June 18, 1792, Hamilton wrote to Langdon [1] and referred to "your letter to me of the 5th of March." *Letter not found.*]

1. Printed in this volume.

To Tench Coxe

[Philadelphia, March 12, 1792]

Dr Sir

I shall not attend the Office to day. Send me whatever may require my attention & save me as much as possible from interruption.

Yrs. sincerely   A Hamilton

Tuesday
March 12
T Coxe Esq

ALS, Papers of Tench Coxe in the Coxe Family Papers at the Historical Society of Pennsylvania, Philadelphia.

To the President and Directors of the Bank of the United States [1]

Treasury Department, March 19, 1792.

Gentlemen:

It has been represented to me that a sum of money, unusually large, has and will become due to the United States, from the importers into the district of Philadelphia, in the course of the current month. On this occasion I think it proper to remind you that the collector of that district,[2] in consequence of standing circular instructions to the custom-houses,[3] will receive from the merchants, upon equal terms with cash, the post-notes of the Bank of the United States, if not issued for a longer term of payment than thirty days after date. You will judge how far it may be convenient to you to make operations payable in such notes, which might not be convenient if payable immediately in specie or in cash notes.

It has occurred that such an operation may have special reference to those who have the payments to make, and it is particularly desirable, at the present crisis, that every reasonable accomodation should be afforded.

I am, gentlemen, &c.,   A. Hamilton, Secretary

The President and Directors of the Bank of the United States.

ASP, Finance, IV, 267–68.
    1. In *PAH*, XI, 152, this letter is listed as a "letter not found."
    Thomas Willing was president of the Bank of the United States.
    2. Sharp Delany.
    3. See "Treasury Department Circular to the Collectors of the Customs,"
September 22, 1789; January 2, 1792 (*PAH*, V, 394–95; X, 501–03).

From William Duer [1]

New york. March 21st 1792

My dear Friend

Your Letter of the 14th [2] has been a Balm to my Soul, in the Midst of my affliction. The Advice you give, I had laid down as the previous Rule of my Conduct—and with Rigidity adhere it. Whatever may happen, you shall never blush to Call me your Friend. Of this no more!

This Letter will be presented to you by my Friend Mr. Vandenbenden,[3] the Principal Support of the Flourishing Colony of Gallipolis [4]—⟨-⟩ my dear Friend, at the Expense of my Fortune, unaided, and unprotected by the Government. Let me my dear Sir, Entreat all your Influence to call the attention of Government to this Valuable Settlement, which has introduced Arts, and the Cultivation of objects which will prove a Source of wealth to the western world; whilst it serves as a Medium to preserve under proper Encouragement, the Friendship of the Savage Tribes.[5]

They are at present altogether Destitute of Protection; whilst Marietta [6] an older Settlement—as well as that of Symmes,[7] has Experienced Constantly the fostering Care of Government, as far as our military Force will admit of. I have assured this Gentleman, you had the Interest of that Settlement much at heart, and that as far as depended on you, you would use your Influence to Extend Protection to them.

God bless you & Yours!   W Duer.

ALS, Sleepy Hollow Restorations, Inc., Tarrytown, New York.

1. In *PAH*, XI, this letter is listed as a "letter not found."

The letter printed above was written two days before Duer was imprisoned for debt.

The Panic of 1792, of which Duer was both a major cause and a principal victim, was the product of many complex developments. In part the fervid speculation in the Government funded debt which drove the New York securities market to new highs in January, 1792, was merely an intensification of the speculative binge in the last months of 1791 (*ASP, Finance*, I, 231; *PAH* XIV, 121–27; Davis, *Essays*, I, 210). A further impetus to speculation arose out of the efforts of various businessmen and speculators to create three new banks in New York City in one week in January, 1792 (H to William Seton, January 18, 1792 (*PAH*, X, 525–26); Seton to H, January 22, February 6, 1792 [*PAH*, X, 528–30; XI, 17–19]). Also, many of the principal speculators in securities were involved and overextended in several other enterprises. For example, Duer at the time had a contract to supply the United States Army, was mixed up in the new banking ventures, and had plunged heavily in numerous other land speculations. Further, almost all the New York directors of the Society for Establishing Useful Manufactures, including Duer, were leading speculators in securities who as a result of the panic went into bankruptcy or avoided it by a variety of subterfuges. Among the leading speculators in the Federal funded debt in addition to Duer were Alexander Macomb, Richard C. Platt, John Pintard, Isaac Whippo, Brockholst Livingston, and John R. and Edward Livingston. These men and many others were at times bound to each other by their cooperation in other business undertakings and by debts and endorsements of notes. Other times, they found their interests in conflict, as when the three Livingstons were "bears" and Duer and his associates, including Walter Livingston, were "bulls."

Duer had the unhappy distinction of being more responsible than any other individual for precipitating the Panic of 1792. On or shortly after March 9, he was "obliged to stop payment of a Certain Description of Notes" (Duer to Jeremiah Wadsworth, March 12, 1792, quoted in Davis, *Essays*, I, 289), and by March 15 securities on the New York exchange had declined to such an extent that he was unable to meet his numerous and enormous obligations.

Duer's final collapse, however, occurred not because of his personal debts, but rather because of his obligations to the Federal Government. On March 12, 1792, Oliver Wolcott, Jr., comptroller of the Treasury, wrote to Richard Harison, United States attorney for the District of New York, that there were two unbalanced charges against Duer dating back to his service as Secretary to the Board of Treasury. Wolcott instructed Harison that if Duer could not balance his accounts or provide evidence that he could and would do so, he should be sued (copy, Connecticut Historical Society, Hartford). When Duer failed to meet the requirements set by Wolcott, he was arrested on March 23, 1792, and sent to prison.

The progress, if any, of the Government's suit against Duer has remained a mystery, but see *ASP, Claims*, I, 259–62; U. S., Congress, House, Committee of Claims, *Rep. No. 133*, 29th Cong., 1st sess., January 27, 1846; H to Duer, March 14, 1792, note 2 (*PAH*, XI, 132). For an example of an individual's suit against Duer, see Jonathan Williams to H, June 8, 1796 (*PAH*, XX, 217–18).

For an outstanding account of the Panic of 1792 and Duer's role in it, see Davis, *Essays*, I, 278–315. See also Duer to H, March 12, 1792 (*PAH*, XI, 126–27); H to Duer, March 14, 1792 (*PAH*, XI, 131–32); Robert Troup to H, March 19, 1792 (*PAH*, XI, 155–58).

2. Printed in *PAH*, XI, 131–32.

3. Louis Vanden Benden was one of the largest landholders in the French settlement of Gallipolis on the Ohio River (Carter, *Territorial Papers*, II, 425, 428).

4. This sentence and the remainder of this letter concern the Scioto Company, which was an offshoot or product of the negotiations that secured a land grant for the Ohio Company. The Ohio Company had been organized in Boston in 1786 by Benjamin Tupper and Rufus Putnam. As a result of the efforts of the Reverend Manasseh Cutler, Congress on July 23, 1787 (*JCC*, XXXII, 311–13; XXXIII, 399–401), approved an arrangement under which on July 27, 1787, the Board of Treasury, of which Duer was Secretary, sold to the Ohio Company almost one million eight hundred thousand acres in the Ohio country for one million dollars. In addition, provision was made for an option on approximately five million acres. This option was then assigned to the Scioto Company, a group of speculators headed by Duer. The trustees of the company were Duer, Royal Flint, and Andrew Craigie. The company sent Joel Barlow to France to sell land, but he was generally unsuccessful, and the only settlement in the lands owned by the Scioto Company was Gallipolis, which was settled by Frenchmen in 1790. The Scioto Company went down in the Panic of 1792, for its directors were unable to meet their obligations and defaulted on their contract with the Government. See Davis, *Essays*, I, 124–50, 213–53. See also H to Duer, April 4–7, 1790 (*PAH*, VI, 346–47); William Short to H, April 4, 1790, note 6 (*PAH*, VI, 349–52); H to Arthur St. Clair, May 19, 1790 (*PAH*, VI, 421–22); H to George Washington, August 28, 1790 (*PAH*, VI, 577–78); Benjamin Walker to H, December 28, 1790 (*PAH*, VII, 388–89); William Playfair to H, March 30, 1791, September-December, 1791 (*PAH*, VIII, 227–33; IX, 253–55).

5. As might be expected, this was a not altogether accurate description. In the winter of 1791–1792, the French settlers had had to depend "on outside sources for their supplies" (Theodore T. Belote, "The Scioto Speculation and the French Settlement at Gallipolis," *University Studies Published by the University of Cincinnati*, III, No. 3 [September-October, 1909], 55).

6. Marietta was the principal settlement in the lands owned by the Ohio Company.

7. For the Symmes purchase in the Ohio country, see H to William Rawle, January 6, 1793, note 2 (*PAH*, XIII, 472).

From William Duer [1]

[New York] March 22d. 1792.

My dear Friend

I know not how to Express to you the Consolation I have derived in reading your Letter: [2] to preserve your Affection, and to deserve it—is my Principal, and Ardent wish—this I am sure will be the Case, if I strictly *follow the Line you mark out*.

The Object of this Letter which I send by Express—is to know precisely what Idea you Assess to the Term *fair Creditor*—which you use in your Letter. The Practice of Usary has so Infected all

Classes in this City where this Doctrine is maintained by Persons whose Names, you would be astonished to Learn—"That their Claims ought to Come in for an Equal Dividend with all others." At present neither my judgment, or Feelings accord with this Opinion; and I have rigidly opposed it in the Spite of all Measures, (and (shall I tell you my Friend) Even at the Risque of Life). If on the best Estimate I can at present form of my affairs the admission of this description of a Man to a Dividend, would pare down to almost nothing, the bonâ fide claims of Creditors of other Descriptions, or the honorable Claims of Friends. Shall I consent to this new System of Morality? The Bulk of the present Claims was contracted by an Agent,[3] on most Extravagant, Usary; with whose appropriations I am at present Unacquainted. Give me your mature, and candid opinion—it shall be (if you chuse), preserved by me in inviolable Confidence—and whatever may happen, I will submit to present Calumny, & Clamors rather than obtain precious Tranquility, at the Expence of solid, and permanent Esteem, of yourself, and the few Valuable Friends I have still left. May heaven preserve your life— and make you and yours as happy, as I am at present miserable.

W Duer.

ALS, Sleepy Hollow Restorations, Inc., Tarrytown, New York.
   1. In *PAH*, XI, 168, this letter is listed as a "letter not found."
   For an explanation of the contents of this letter, see Duer to H, March 21, 1792 (printed in this volume).
   2. Printed in *PAH*, XI, 131–32.
   3. Duer had numerous "agents," and it is impossible to know which one he is referring to in this instance. In commenting on Duer's assertion that his troubles could be ascribed to an agent, Joseph Stancliffe Davis has written: "It is altogether unlikely that Duer had kept closely in touch with the extent to which his obligations were accumulating, but this effort to saddle the blame on his agent must be regarded as a lame excuse" (Davis, *Essays*, 1, 289, note 2).

From Robert Troup [1]

[New York, March 24, 1792]

My dear friend

Things here are in a calamitous state. My heart is nearly broken with the distresses of our friend Duer. Read the enclosed & judge what my feelings must be from your own. Great pains have been taken to excite the public rage agt. him & his friends. Among others I have been marked out as an object of resentment—for being one of his Lawyers. It is true I am so—but I have done nothing but what a sincere friend & an honest man ought to do. But no consideration will influence me to desert him in the present hour of his deep distress. I shall however take care to engage in nothing that will be unbecoming the respect every mans owes himself.

B. L——n [2] & some others are triumphing over this unfortunate Mans distress and they are preying upon the vitals of public credit by every artifice & combination that can be devised to depress stocks. I am obliged to abandon these men as devoid of every sentiment which humanity inspires—and at a future time you will shudder at the tale of perfidy which I shall unfold to you.

Indeed my dear friend I am frantic with the pangs I feel for the public welfare and for the honor & happiness of our friend. I hope for a favorable change but at present shadows clouds & darkness rest upon the prospect of it. No Man's affairs could be more complex & deranged—& few men's more extensive. I have no connexion with him but what is dictated by friendship & benevolence. God prosper you—& let me entreat you to send me the consolation of your friendship.

In haste & in distraction   I am, My dear friend,   Yours

Rob Troup

A Hamilton Esqr
Saturday afternoon 24 March 1792

ALS, Sleepy Hollow Restorations, Inc., Tarrytown, New York.
    1. For background to this letter, see Duer to H, March 21, 22, 1792 (both printed in this volume).
    2. Brockholst Livingston.

To Philip Livingston

[*Philadelphia, March 25, 1792.* On Tuesday, March 27, 1792, Livingston wrote to H: [1] "Your letter of Sunday was brought to me yesterday morning. . . ." *Letter not found.*]

    1. Printed in this volume.

From Nicholas Low [1]

New york 25 March 1792

Dear sir

The Moment I received Information of poor Duer's Stopping payment [2] I apply'd to walker [3] to know the particular State of the Funds of the manufacturing Society—since this A Mercer & John Nielson [4] from Brunswick having called upon me to consult we have had an informal Meeting of such of the Directors as were in Town & find the State of the Funds to be as follows—50 thousand Dollars paid to John Dewhurst [5] in Bills drawn by Alexander Macomb [6] and remitted by Dewhurst for the purpose of importing a Quantity of Cotton Cloths from England. I am not without my Fears (all I say to you is in Confidence and I shall therefore speak with the greater Freedom) that this Money will be misapply'd. I doubt the Integrity of the man & he was constituted the agent upon this Occasion in Defiance of what little Influence I had in the Committe & Interest against him. 5 Thousand Dollars have been paid to walker about

ALS, Sleepy Hollow Restorations, Inc., Tarrytown, New York.

1. In *PAH*, XI, 185, this letter is listed as a "letter not found." For background to the letter printed above, see Archibald Mercer to H, April 6, 1792 (*PAH*, XI, 246–49). See also H to William Duer, March 23, 1792 (*PAH*, XI, 170–72); Philip Livingston to H, March 24, 1792 (*PAH*, XI, 174–75); Philip Schuyler to H, March 25, 1792 (*PAH* XI 186–90).

Low, a New York City merchant, wrote this letter in his capacity as a director of the Society for Establishing Useful Manufactures.

2. See Duer to H, March 21, 1792, note 1 (printed in this volume).

3. Benjamin Walker, a director from New York of the Society for Establishing Useful Manufactures, was a close associate of Duer in the Scioto Company. For Walker's relationship with Dewhurst, see Low to H, April 10, 1792 (*PAH*, XI, 259–60).

4. Archibald Mercer and Neilson were members from New Jersey of the Board of Directors of the Society for Establishing Useful Manufactures.

5. For the fifty thousand dollars entrusted to Dewhurst, a director from New York of the Society for Establishing Useful Manufactures and a close business associate of William Duer, see Low to H, April 10, 1792 (*PAH*, XI, 259–60). Like so many of the New York directors of the Society for Establishing Useful Manufactures, Dewhurst went bankrupt. He was, however, able to escape his creditors by moving to Philadelphia.

6. Alexander Macomb, a director from New York of the Society for Establishing Useful Manufactures and a close business associate of Duer, was imprisoned for debt on April 18, 1792. For his relationship with Dewhurst, see Low to H, April 10, 1792 (*PAH*, XI, 259–60).

three thousand of them expended the Residue subject to the warrants to be drawn upon him by Duer for the purposes of the Society—10 Thousand Dollars paid to Duer—who has given the most solemn assurances and which he repeated to me yesterday that he will at the next meeting of the Directors lay before them an account with proper vouchers of his Expenditures to Amount of about 5 thousand Dollars—and pay them the Balance in money.[7] The Residue of the Stock of the Society is loaned to Alexander Macomb for one year at 7 ℔ Cent upon his Bond with deferred Debt at 14/ in the pound to be transferred at the opening of the Office—as a collateral Security—we agreed that as it would be impossible in the present State of things to command the Attendance of the New york Directors at Brunswick—the Jersey Directors should meet there on the first Tuesday in April next adjourn to powles Hook come here arrange all that is to be done & go over to the Hook to complete the Business of the Meeting.[8] during my visit to Duer yesterday in Jail, I suggested to him in very delicate Terms & applying to his own Feelings of the propriety of signing his appointment as Governor & Seat as a Director of the Society this he refuses in most positive Terms to do [9]—telling me he had that morning been applyd by A Mercer on the same Subject. His Reasons for refusing are that he has the Institution much at Heart & sees clearly that local views will govern upon his Resignation—to you I say that in the present State of his affairs & person—his Continuance as either Governor or Director is in my Opinion not only extremely ridiculous—but dishonorable to him & disgracefull to the Society. If you see the propriety of his resigning you will advise him to the measure and I trust he will take your advice. If he refuses is it in the power of the Directors to supercede his appointment or suspend his Functions as Governor and ought to call a meeting of the Stockholders to chuse another Director. He has signed about one fourth can we appoint another person to sign the Residue of the

7. The money paid to Duer was never accounted for and was never recovered.

8. See Mercer to H, April 6, 1792 (*PAH*, XI, 246–49).

9. Among the directors of the Society for Establishing Useful Manufactures who were not re-elected at a meeting of general stockholders on October 1, 1792, were Duer, Dewhurst, Macomb, and Royal Flint. All were from New York, and all had been ruined by the Panic of 1792 (H to Nehemiah Hubbard, May 3, 1792, note 2 [*PAH*, XI, 356]).

Scrip. The Stockholders are extremely impatient to have them, give me or if you please to A Mercer, such Communications as you wish for the Information of the Directors—we all look up to you for your advise.

you will I am sure do every Thing in your power that can be warranted by the principles of Prudence & Discretion to contribute to the Support of publick & private Credit in this alarming State of it. it seems to me that the Bank of the united States with its Branch in this City might agree with the Bank of North America and of New york that upon this trying Occasion & for a limited period say for 6. 9 or 12 Months—their whole Specie Capital shall be as a Common Stock to be applyd to the aid & Support of each other— that by this mean Discounts might be extended very considerably without fear of a Run upon either—the Specie now in all the Vaults the aggregate Sum will remain none can be wanted to send to any other parts of the Union, nor for Remittances to Europe while Bills are so low and whatever Projects may have been formed by some Individuals among ourselves heretofore for draining the vaults no Man who shall be detected in them hereafter will be permitted to *live* in this City.

Besides Duer—John Bush & Royal Flint are gone to Jail—John pintard & George Knox absconded—Walter Livingston stopped payment.[10] Brockholst told me last Evening that Duer has executed a Bond in Judgment to walter for £160,000 which yesterday was entered upon the Dockets here & will be in other States where Duer

---

10. On March 25, 1792, Seth Johnson wrote to Andrew Craigie: ". . . Pintard has gone off, without clearing up his character, & from all appearances he has been a perfect swindler—he has induced many to sell Stock, or lend money for D[uer]s notes & his endorsements assuring them that he was secure in having property in his hands.—he has put up Stock Transferable at certain periods for cash down—received the cash. & never returned the Stock—& I believe has gone off with a very considerable amount of a mans property whose agent he had been. . . . Bush who has been a great borrower & endorser for Duer is in prison—Knox another borrower & endorser has absconded—I am afraid that . . . Flint by . . . [his] endorsements . . . [is] very much involved. W. Livingston refused to take up a note with his endorsement yesterday, tho' it is said he is secure in all he has done, besides his own property—people cry shame upon him, & will show him no mercy" (Davis, *Essays*, I, 296–97). On April 1, 1792, Johnson again wrote to Craigie: "Flint is I believe a ruined man—he means first to provide for the payment of all his own debts, & to give the residue of his property up on a/c of his endorsements, the extent of which may be 1 or 200000 dollars" (Davis, *Essays*, I, 298).

has real Estate—that Duer had written to walter yesterday forbidding the payment of all Notes given by him to walter—upon which Monies were obtained at usurious Interest, he inform'd me further that walter is desirous of submitting to one of two alternatives—either that he be left in the Management of his own affairs under the Direction of three to be appointed by his Creditors or to surrender all his Estate real & person and take a Discharge. I observed to him upon this that in either Event the usurious Lenders would all be precluded from payment, and that the general Opinion is (and indeed I know walter has declared) that he is amply secured against all his Negociations for Duer—a singular Circumstance that walters Friends—Brockholst—John & Edwd. are most industrious in propagating the Report of his Failure, and that all the Stock Dealers either Doubt the Truth or are not affected by the Event of it. It was brot. forward in the Stock Room yesterday by John & seems to be a matter of perfect Indifference to all whom I converse with. I suspect that most of his Indorsements for Duer are upon usurious Notes.[11] When poor Duer stopped payment no arguments were necessary to convince the Town that he was really Bankrupt. It is hard upon the other Gentm. that with all the Eloquence of his honorable Friends, to aid him he cannot lead us to enterain the same Opinion of him. I Am in Hopes that we have seen nearly the End of Bankrupcies in Consequence of the Shock created by Duers Stoppage. Whippo [12] whom I once thought gone is I now believe secure, he pays up handsomely. my Negociations of late have been pretty much limited & I have no payments due to me which I consider at Hazard unless it be macombs paper—& this I consider as secure & that he will pay punctually.

It will be adviseable that you send for a Mr. Griffiths [13]—a young

11. For the part played in the Panic of 1792 by the various Livingstons mentioned in this paragraph, see Philip Schuyler to H, March 25, 1792 (*PAH*, XI, 186–90); H to Philip Livingston, April 2, 1792 (*PAH*, XI, 218–19).

12. Isaac Whippo, a former New York oysterman, became very much involved in the securities market and was a close associate, if not a partner, of Alexander Macomb. At the time of the Panic of 1792, Duer was heavily in debt to Whippo, Macomb, Walter Livingston, Pintard, Knox and Bush. On April 15, 1792, Seth Johnson wrote to Andrew Craigie: "Whippo has gone off —a reward is offered for him, & a number of persons gone in pursuit of him—it is supposed he has taken a great property with him" (Davis, *Essays*, I, 302).

13. James Griffiths was employed as a clerk by the Society for Establishing Useful Manufactures.

Man employ'd by Governor Duer & whom you will hear of at Mrs. Roberts's in Chesnut Street [14] and direct him to attend the Meeting of the Directors of the Manufacturing Society and to bring with him all the Books & papers &ca. This is a most unfortunate Time for Mr. Carachie's propositions [15] I fear he will not get forward with his Subscriptions—and If he gets Subscribers one half of them may be dead or Bankrupt before the Expiration of the Ten years.

Inclosed is Bill of Loading for the Two Cases of Glass ware sent by Mrs. Church [16] to Mrs. Hamilton. she will please to send me the Invoice on their Arrival. in the Interim I have made a Deposit with the Collector [17] for Duties upon their supposed value £20. Sterling.

I am Dear sir   yours very sincerely &ca &ca.   Nich Low

14. Martha Roberts.
15. Giuseppe Ceracchi. For his "propositions," see H to Richard Harison, March 7, 1792 (*PAH*, XI, 111–12).
16. Angelica Schuyler Church was Elizabeth Hamilton's sister and John B. Church's wife. When the letter printed above was written, she and her husband were living in London.
17. John Lamb, collector of customs at New York.

From Philip Livingston [1]

New York 27th. March 1792.

My dear Sir

Your Letter of Sunday,[2] was brought to me yesterday morning about eight OClock with its inclosures, I immediately delivered

ALS, Sleepy Hollow Restorations, Inc., Tarrytown, New York.
1. This letter concerns H's efforts to have the Federal Government check the Panic of 1792.
For the Panic of 1792 and the events leading up to it, see William Duer to H, December 24, 1790, August 16, 1791, March 21, 22, May 30, 1792; Robert Troup to H, September 12, 1791, March 24, 1792; Nicholas Low to H, March 25, 1792 (all printed in this volume); Duer to H, March 12, 1792 (*PAH*, XI, 126–27); H to Duer, March 14, 23, 1792 (*PAH*, XI, 131–32, 170–72); Troup to H, March 19, 1792 (*PAH*, XI, 155–58).
For H's efforts to check the decline in the price of Government securities through the use of the sinking fund, see H to William Seton, March 19, 1792 (*PAH*, XI, 154–55); H to John Adams, March 20, 1792 (*PAH*, XI, 158–59); H to Thomas Jefferson, March 20, 1792 (*PAH*, XI, 159); Adams to John Jay, March 21, 1792 (*PAH*, XI, 159 61); Seton to H, March 21, 1792 (*PAH*,

them, the one addressed to Mr. Seton,[3] the other for Generl. Schuyler.[4] I called upon Mr. G. Verplank, the President of the State Bank, he appears, perfectly to coincide, in opinion, of the propriety of giving aid to the Dealers, as far as is consistent with prudence.[5] Schuyler thought there woud be no impropriety, in mentioning to the Dealers the loan which has been negotiated at Amsterdam on behalf of the U.S[6]—& the good disposition wh: prevailed, between the two Banks, with you, to afford assistance, to the Dealers, within the bounds of discretion. The circumstance of this Loan I found was no secret, among them who pry into, & some how or other find out every thing. Bronson[7] lately from Philadelphia told me the Trustees were equally divided in opinion about the propriety of purchasing more of the Debt, & that Mr. Jay was sent for.[8] Another Dealer connected with his freinds in Philadelphia, told me that he had heard Burrall[9] was to bring on here for this Department, only

---

XI, 163–64); H to Jay, March 23, 1792 (*PAH*, XI, 172–73); Philip Livingston to H, March 24, 1792 (*PAH*, XI, 174–75); H to Seton, March 24, 1792 (*PAH*, XI, 190–92); "Meeting of the Commissioners of the Sinking Fund," March 26, 1792 (*PAH*, XI, 193–94); H to Seton, March 26, 1792 (*PAH*, XI, 194); Seton to H, March 26, 1792 (*PAH*, XI, 194–95); H to Gulian Verplanck, March 26, 1792 (*PAH*, XI, 195–96); Jay to the Commissioners of the Sinking Fund, March 31, 1792 (*PAH*, XI, 214–16); H to Livingston, April 2, 1792 (*PAH*, XI, 218–19); "Meeting of the Commissioners of the Sinking Fund," April 4, 1792 (*PAH*, XI, 224–25); H to Seton, April 4, 1792 (*PAH*, XI, 225–26); Seton to H, April 9, 1792 (*PAH*, XI, 257–58); Seton to H, April 11, 1792 (*PAH*, XI, 263–64); H to the President and Directors of the Bank of New York, April 12, 1792 (*PAH*, XI, 266–67); "Meeting of the Commissioners of the Sinking Fund," April 12, 1792 (*PAH*, XI, 272); H to Seton, April 12, 1792 (*PAH*, XI, 272–73); Seton to H, April 16, 1792 (*PAH*, XI, 288–89).

For H's views on the Panic of 1792, see H to William Short, April 16, 1792 (*PAH*, XI, 289–91).

2. H's letter to Livingston, dated March 25, 1792, has not been found.

3. H to Seton, March 26, 1792 (*PAH*, XI, 194).

4. Letter not found.

5. See H to Verplanck, March 26, 1792 (*PAH*, XI, 195–96).

6. For a description of this loan, see Short to H, December 23, 28, 1791 (*PAH*, X, 403–04, 472–80).

7. Isaac Bronson was a New York City merchant and moneylender.

8. See Adams to Jay, March 21, 1792; H to Jay, March 23, 1792; "Meeting of the Commissioners of the Sinking Fund," March 26, 1792 (*PAH*, XI, 159–61, 172–73, 193–94).

9. Jonathan Burrall was cashier of the New York branch of the Bank of the United States. Although the bank's branch in New York did not open until April 2, 1792, the cashier had been elected by the bank's board on January 12, 1792 (James O. Wettereau, "The Branches of the First Bank of the United States," *Journal of Economic History*, Supplement [December, 1942], 75).

100,000 Dollars.—& asked if it was true, I answered of course, I knew of no particular Sum, & that he had better information, than I was possessed of, & cut the matter short, either thro' Clerks or Low [10] I know not, but the Dealers do get at, a great deal of Information.

Our Sales of Stock, begin here at Noon, formerly they were in the Eveng. Upon communicating publickly to the Dealers, as I met them, the Loan in Holland, & *my* opinion of the probability of aid from the Bank's, joined probably to what they knew, & personally offering to give 22/, for six per Cents, on any Person's taking my Bills on London well indorsed in payment—six per Cents which had before the Sales, sold at par, rose to 20/.8d—& half shares in the National Bank, wh: were sold in the Morning at 46, pr. Ct. advance, rose to upwards, of 50—so that if they remain here, there will be no necessity of Mr. Seton's coming forward into the Market,—but if he retains the power to do it, & the Harpies know it—there will be no occasion I hope for his assistance. In the Evening last night at the Coffee House, little or none of funded debt was sold, that I could hear of—but half Shares, could not be had at 57. Cash. I heard it frequently offered, & refused. The difference then, between the Morning & Evening in the price of half Shares, was from 46, pr. Ct. advance to 57, Cash—and all this has been effected by the arrival of your dispatches, to Seton Schuyler & myself. I think the fit of despondency is now over, but I hope Seton will remain armed with powers, to defeat any Schemes of the Harpies.

The Dealers last Night had a meeting & appointed a Committee, to confer with the Directors of the two Banks. The Propositions which they are to hold out I hear in general is to offer, funded debt, at your price as pledges for their discounts—& they are to sign an Agreement to bind themselves not to draw any Specie from the Banks, on account of the discounts which they shall obtain and in giving checks to each other, if any one, shall part with the Check— except to those, who engage by the agreement, not to draw out Specie, he shall be deemed, infamous—& held up—& that no one of the signers of the agreement will deal with him. This may last some-time, but the Banks cannot with any degree of certainty depend long upon it. If it shall answer, for a time, & not violently raise Stocks, beyond its real value, it will have the desired effect.

10. Nicholas Low.

I inclose you a Slip, cut out of Child's Paper [11] of Yesterday. I saw Duer in the Gaol on Sunday. The Baron,[12] Walker,[13] & several other Gentlemen were there, Lady Kitty,[14] Madam Duval [15] &

11. This is a reference to *The* [New York] *Daily Advertiser,* which was published by Francis Childs and John Swaine. On March 26, 1792, the following notice was printed in *The Daily Advertiser:*

"To the Holders of Engagements under the signature of the Subscriber.

"*New-York Prison.*

"March 24, 1792,

"It is with regret that the subscriber finds himself disappointed in bringing forward to his creditors, on this day, such specific propositions for the ultimate redemption of his debts, as he had once reason to expect.

"At a meeting of a number of gentlemen (all of whom stiled themselves his friends, and amongst whom some were really so) it was thought adviseable to postpone the publication of the plan he had in view, till it was supported by them in such a manner as they conceived most likely to ensure success.

"But (the causes of such change it is not necessary to detail) the malice of open enemies and the insidious insinuations of pretended friends, have chilled the first glow of benevolence; and left to the subscriber the guardianship of his own fame, and that of the interest of all his creditors. A sacred trust! which the subscriber pledges himself to discharge with fidelity and honor.

"In this view it is proposed by him as follows:

"1st. That he will within nine months, computed from the present date (or sooner, if possible) make a settlement of all his concerns, point out the sources and amount of his losses, and constitute an adequate fund for the ultimate redemption of the principal and legal interest of all his debts.

"2d. That this fund shall be so formed as not to place it within his own reach, to divert it from the objects of its destination.

"3d. That he will make prompt arrangements for the reimbursement in the first instance, of all advances made by distressed widows, or orphans, mechanics and tradesmen, to whom any considerable delay would operate as ruin.

"4th. That, till the above objects are effected, the walls of a prison shall secure that confidence which he feels, might have been justly placed in his honor.

"5thly. That, trusting to time and a conscience void of intended injury for justification, he at present leaves to his enemies the cruel triumph of sporting over his afflictions, and to a generous people who may still be mindful of his public and private services, the protection of a virtuous wife and innocent family. Wm. Duer."

The same issue of the same paper carried notices by Walter Livingston and Isaac Whippo to their respective creditors.

12. Baron Von Steuben.

13. Benjamin Walker.

14. Catharine Alexander, known as "Lady Kitty," was the daughter of William Alexander, known as "Lord Stirling" or the "Earl of Stirling." She was Duer's wife.

15. Mme. Bacler de Leval, a native of France, migrated to the United States in 1790. She hoped to acquire land for a colony of French refugees, and she agreed to buy property in Maine at $1.25 an acre from Duer, Henry Jackson, and Henry Knox. Before completing the purchase, she went to Maine to inspect the lands in question. Although she bought a hundred-acre farm in Maine, largely because of Duer's failure she never obtained the larger tract in

other Ladies. I pitty poor Kitty from my soul, she bears it like an Heroine. Duer was, perfectly composed, & in better spirits, than I have seen him for some time. I took an opportunity to enquire about the Money of the Jersey Manufactoring society [16]—he say's all is right. Low promised to write you on monday last about it in detail wh: I suppose he has done.[17] I am with the greatest regard

Yours sincerely   Ph: Livingston

---

which she was interested (Frances S. Childs, *French Refugee Life in the United States, 1790–1800. An American Chapter of the French Revolution* [Baltimore, 1940], 67–68). See also Bacler de Leval to H, April 12, 1792 (*PAH,* XI, 265–66).
16. See Low to H, March 25, 1792 (printed in this volume).
17. Low to H, March 25, 1792 (printed in this volume).

To John Kean [1]

[Philadelphia, March 28, 1792]

Dear Sir

I request that you will not draw out from the Bank of N America any further *sum* without a previous communication to me.[2]

Yrs.   A Hamilton

March 28th. 92
Cashier of Bank of U States

ALS, Harvard University Library.
1. In *PAH,* XI, 198, this letter is listed as a "letter not found."
2. This letter concerns relations between the Bank of the United States and the state banks. Stuart Bruchey, in a definitive article on this subject, has written: "Thus in the period prior to the opening of the Bank of the United States and its first four branches Hamilton authorized the collection of duties in the notes of the Bank of North America, the Bank of New York, the Bank of Massachusetts, and the Bank of Providence.
"With the Bank of the United States and those branches functioning in the major commercial cities in the spring of 1792 it became possible for the Treasury to implement Section 10 of the act incorporating the Bank, which stipulated that 'the bills or notes of the said corporation, originally made payable, or which shall become payable on demand, in gold and silver coin, shall be receivable in all payments to the United States.' But Hamilton's initial response to the opening of the parent bank was merely to place its notes on an equal footing with those of the Bank of North America, the other major institution in Philadelphia, directing on January 2, 1792, that the former 'be received and

exchanged in like manner.' At a conference later that month with the president and directors of the parent bank, however, Hamilton suggested that it would 'probably be found mutually convenient' to both government and the Bank 'to carry on through you the negotiations concerning the public Revenues.' Accordingly, on February 21, he issued another circular to the collectors of the customs in which he explained that 'in pursuance of arrangements with the Bank of the United States, I have to desire, that after the expiration of a month from the time of the receipt of this letter, you will discontinue the execution of my former instructions concerning the receipt, and exchange for specie, of the Cash Notes and Post Notes of the Banks of North-America and New York.'

"That same month Hamilton wrote the cashier of the Bank of New York: 'You will understand that all the money you may receive for bills or otherwise, on account of the U States, subsequent to the 31st of January last shall be received from you in bills of the Bank of the United States And that no order shall issue to derange this engagement.' And on March 10 the *Gazette of the United States* announced it was informed that the secretary of the Treasury had directed all the collectors of revenue 'to receive no other notes but those of the Bank of the United States.' However, it will be observed that Hamilton's directive of February 21 was to take effect a month later, and it is perhaps for this reason that he appears to have delayed sending it out. For on March 30, in a letter to the president of the Bank of New York, he indicates that the circular will be dispatched on that date, while the acknowledgement of the receipt of the circular by the collector at Providence indicates that it was not mailed before May 10. Hamilton's apparently repeated postponements of the effective date of the new regime must certainly have eased the necessary readjustment on the part of the state banks. And as we shall see, the notes of one state bank—those of the Bank of New York—continued to be receivable for duties in New York City, although probably not elsewhere, until April, 1793, apparent evidence to the contrary notwithstanding." (Bruchey, "Alexander Hamilton and the State Banks, 1789 to 1795," *The William and Mary Quarterly*, 3d. ser., XXVII [July, 1970], 361–63.)

See "Treasury Department Circular to the Collectors of the Customs, January 2, February 21, 1792 (*PAH*, X, 501–02; XI, 42–43); H to William Seton, February 10, 1792 (*PAH*, XI, 27–28); H to Gulian Verplanck, March 30, 1792 (*PAH*, XI, 211–12); Jeremiah Olney to H, June 5, 1792 (*PAH*, XI, 489).

To the President and Directors of the Bank of Maryland

Treasury Department, March 29, 1792.

Gentlemen:

It has been intimated to me that considerable sums of duties have become due, or are to fall due, in Baltimore, in the course of the present month. It is, at all times, my wish to give to the merchants as much facility as the public business will admit of. I have therefore determined to inform you that, if you should incline to make discounts for the importers, to enable them to pay the duties which have become due or which shall fall due on or before the 15th of April, I will leave a sum of money equal thereto in your hands, for sixty days after the dates of the notes.

If you should intend to give the trade this accomodation, the collector of Baltimore, on application to him, will furnish you with names of the obligors and the sums they are, respectively, to pay on or before the said 15th April.[1]

I am, gentlemen, &c. A. H., Secretary

The President and Directors of the Bank of Maryland.

ASP, *Finance*, IV, 268.
 1. See H to Otho H. Williams, March 29, 1792 (*PAH*, XI, 206–07).

To Tench Coxe

[Philadelphia, March–April 15, 1792]

Dr. Sir

Be so good as to inquire of General Irvine[1] the character of Mr. O Hara[2] as a man of business and Integrity and qualifications as for a Quarter Master. If any one else occurs to you I will thank you to mention him. I have thought much of the affair & of characters supposed to be attainable; I am at a loss to satisfy myself.

Yrs. A Hamilton

Send Bowman.[3]
I wish also for Mr. Meyer.[4]
What was the state of Stock last night?

ALS, Papers of Tench Coxe in the Coxe Family Papers at the Historical Society of Pennsylvania, Philadelphia.
 1. William Irvine, a native of Ireland, fought throughout the American Revolution and attained the rank of brigadier general. In 1785 he was in charge of the distribution of lands in western Pennsylvania to veterans of the Revolution, and from 1786 to 1788 he was a delegate from Pennsylvania to the Continental Congress.
 2. James O'Hara, a native of Ireland, had served during the American Revolution in the quartermaster's department. After the war he settled in Pittsburgh,

and in 1790 he was contractor for the Army during the campaign of Brigadier General Josiah Harmar against the western Indians. On April 19, 1792, he was appointed quartermaster general of the newly reorganized United States Army. See "An Act for making further and more effectual Provision for the Protection of the Frontiers of the United States" (1 *Stat.* 241–43 [March 5, 1792]).

3. Joseph Bowman was employed as a messenger in the office of the auditor of the Treasury Department.

4. John Meyer was a clerk in the Treasury Department.

To the President and Directors and Company of the Bank of Maryland

Treasury Department, April 10, 1792.

Gentlemen:

I am induced, by circumstances which have come within my knowledge, to inform you that the operation suggested in my letter of the 29th ultimo [1] continues to be desirable, in relation to those who have payments to make at the custom-house in the course of the current month. You will consider it as it concerns the convenience of the Bank of Maryland.

I am, gentlemen, &c.   A. H., Secretary.

The President, Directors and Company of the Bank of Maryland.

ASP, Finance, IV, 268.
1. Printed in this volume.

Tobias Lear to Samuel Hanson [1]

[Philadelphia April 21st: 1792] [2]

Sir

I am directed by the President [of the U. S.] to acknowlege the receipt of your letter of the 10th of March [3] and to give you the following answer.

The law appears to contemplate the surveyor where there is one at a Port, as the person who is ordinarily to perform the service of measuring Vessels,[4] and it may be inferred that the exercise of the power given to the Collector to appoint persons for the purpose is intended to be auxiliary and occasional only.

Under this view of the matter and as the power of appointment is expressly vested in the Collector, there does not appear to be propriety in a special interposition to produce the arrangement you desire, contrary to his judgment of what the public service requires.

[With esteem & consideration   I have the honor to be Sir   Yr Most Obed ser   Tobias Lear. S. P. U. S.

Samuel Hanson of Samls Esqr]

DfS, in the handwriting of H and Tobias Lear, RG 59 Miscellaneous Letters of the Department of State, 1790–1799, National Archives.
1. Lear was George Washington's secretary; Hanson was surveyor of the port of Alexandria, Virginia.
For information concerning the contents of this letter, see H to Charles Lee, January 18, 1792, note 3 (*PAH*, X, 522–23).
2. The material within brackets in this letter is in Lear's handwriting.
3. ALS, RG 59, Miscellaneous Letters of the Department of State, 1790–1799, National Archives.
4. See Section 44 of "An Act to provide more effectually for the collection of the duties imposed by law on goods, wares and merchandise imported into the United States, and on the tonnage of ships or vessels" (1 *Stat.* 169 [August 4, 1790]).

To George Washington

[*Philadelphia, May 5, 1792.* The calendar description of this letter reads: "Enclosing Application of Thomas Mendenhall [1] for position of Assay Master of the Mint." *Letter not found.*]

RG 104, Preliminary Inventory of the Records of the Bureau of the Mint, National Archives.
1. From September 9 to December 18, 1790, Mendenhall had been superintendent of a paper mill in Chester County, Pennsylvania, that produced paper used for Treasury Department certificates (D, RG 217, Miscellaneous Treasury Accounts, 1790–1894, Account No. 1100, National Archives). See also "Report on the Receipts and Expenditures of Public Monies to the End of the Year 1791," November 10, 1792 (*PAH*, XIII, 108).

Treasury Department Circular [1]

[*Philadelphia, May 9, 1792.* The description of this circular reads: "Concerning the President's (George Washington's) appointment of Tench Coxe to the office of Commissioner of Revenue." [2] *Circular not found.*]

1. LS, sold by B. Altman & Co., New York City (*The New York Times,* December 7, 1969).
2. On May 8, 1792, Washington nominated Coxe to be commissioner of the revenue, and the Senate confirmed the appointment on the same day (*Executive Journal,* I, 124).

To Sylvanus Bourne [1]

Philadelphia May 10. 1792

Sir

You will have heared of the issue of a certain appointment, which was desired by you.

An alteration which has been made in the Treasury Department [2] will lead to the appointment of an additional number of Clerks. If nothing better offers itself to you & an appointment of this Nature can be a temporary accommodation, it is at your service.* I beg you to be always assured of the friendly dispositions of

D Sir   Y Obed ser   A Hamilton

* A corresponding Clerk. The present emolument can only be 500 Ds. A speedy answer is requested.

ALS, Mr. Edward Powis Jones, New York City.
1. Bourne, a resident of Boston, had been United States consul at Santo Domingo from June, 1790, to September, 1791.
For information concerning the contents of this letter, see Bourne to H, May 10, 24, 1792 (*PAH,* XI, 382–83, 419–20).
In *PAH* XI, 383, this letter is listed as a "letter not found."
2. See "An Act making alterations in the Treasury and War Departments" (1 *Stat.* 279–81 [May 8, 1792]).

Receipt to Rufus Putnam [1]

Philadelphia May 21. 1792

Received by the hands of General R. Putnam a deed executed by Rufus Putnam M Cutler,[2] Robert Oliver [3] & G Greene [4] purporting to be a conveyance to me of five shares of the land of the Ohio Company of Associates & bearing date the 14th of May 1792.[5]

Alexander Hamilton

ADS, Dawes Memorial Library, Marietta College, Marietta, Ohio.

1. Putnam was a veteran of the American Revolution and one of the founders of the Ohio Company. See H to Oliver Wolcott, Jr., October 3, 1802, note 3 (printed in this volume).

2. Manasseh Cutler, a Congregational clergyman and botanist from Massachusetts, was in Philadelphia at this time attending a three-day meeting of the board of directors of the Ohio Company. See H to Thomas Jefferson, May 12, 1792 (PAH, XI, 396–97). One of the founders of the Ohio Company, he helped draw up its original articles of agreement. Through skillful lobbying in Congress, he was probably more responsible than any other individual for securing the land grant to the Ohio Company in July, 1787. In December, 1787, he set out for the Ohio country to aid in the establishment of the first settlements by the company. He returned to Massachusetts in 1789.

3. Oliver, a veteran of the American Revolution from Massachusetts, was a director of the Ohio Company.

4. Griffin Greene, a veteran of the American Revolution, a Rhode Island merchant, and a director of the Ohio Company, moved to Marietta, Territory Northwest of the River Ohio, in 1788.

5. For an excerpt from this conveyance, which has not been found, see the enclosure and note 7 to H to Wolcott, October 3, 1802 (printed in this volume).

From William Duer [1]

New york May 30th. 1792.

My dear Friend.

Amidst the Embarassments in which I am involved there is one which perplexes me not a little: not only on my own account, but as to its Consequences respecting others.

The matter I allude to you, is an Agreement, made with the Ohio Company—by Mr. Cragie, Flint, and myself in behalf of the Scioto Proprietors, for the Purchase of a Tract of Land, to accommodate the present Settlers at Gallipolis—the Particulars of which Mr. Cragie will acquaint you with. I had Every Reason to suppose that these Lands would not have been included, in the Tract designated by the Act of Congress for the Ohio Company—and if Genl: Putnam and mr. Cutler, had acted with Candor, I presume they would not have been. The Fact however is, that all the Town of Gallipolis, and 16 Lands more Immediately adjoining it are Included—in Consequence of which the Settlers, are left to the *Tender Mercies* of the Directors who will Covet their Lands, and Improvements. This Apprehension is so strong in their Minds, that it threatens to break up the most Valuable Colony, in all the Western Country—and not only that but to involve Mr. Cragie Flint, & myself in a Contest of a very Disagreeable Nature with the Ohio-Association. I find by the Act relative to the Ohio Purchase, that the Tract, actually defined, does not Include, the whole of the Land, which the Directors Engaged to Convey to us, for the Scioto-Association. If therefore the Supplementary Grant of Lands can be so shaped, as not to include the Residue of the Land which they agreed to give us Title for, we shall stand on a Footing to settle with them on Grounds favorable to the Settlers, as well as ourselves. May I request your friendly Aid, in preventing any further Steps being taken, which will defeat so just an End. This can only be done by a Representation to the President—if you thing any thing which I under my present Circumstances can say, will have any Effect to defeat the Artful Designs of the Ohio Directors, let me know—and I will write such a Letter, as you may judge adviseable.

I received from Baron Steuben, a Letter you wrote to me at Newark: [2] & a Communication of your Letter to him.[3] I will answer this Letter, in a few days, and am in the Mean while,

Your very Affectionate & Obliged Friend.   W Duer

A: Hamilton Esqr.
New york May 30th. 1792

PS At the Time we agreed with Putnam & Cutler, for the Lands alluded to, it was never Understood that we were personally responsible (but clearly, and Explicitly the Reverse)—nor do I think they can make us so. However it has been insinuated to me, that some of the other Directors, mean to Attempt it.

ALS, Sleepy Hollow Restorations, Inc., Tarrytown, New York.

1. In *PAH*, XI, 456, this letter is listed as a "letter not found."

For an explanation of the contents of this letter, see Duer to H, March 21, 1792 (printed in this volume); Theodore T. Belote, "The Scioto Speculation and the French Settlement at Gallipolis," *University Studies Published by the University of Cincinnati*, III, No. 3 (September-October, 1909); Davis, *Essays*, I, 213–53.

2. Letter not found. H had left Philadelphia on May 13, 1792, to attend a meeting in Newark, New Jersey, of the Society for Establishing Useful Manufactures and returned to Philadelphia on May 20. See H to George Washington, May 13, 21, 1792 (*PAH*, XI, 398, 415–16).

3. Letter not found.

From Thomas Jefferson

[*Philadelphia, June 5, 1792.* In "Memorandum re papers and documents received from President Washington, 1790–1795" the following item appears under the date of June 5, 1792: "This day the ratification of the Loan by the Bank of the U.S. of 523500 dollrs. by instalments as therein specified passed the Great Seal in the usual form, and was with a note from the Secy. of State, transmitted to the Secy. of the Treasury." [1] *Letter not found.*]

D, Papers of the Continental Congress, Reel 198, Item 187, p. 135, National Archives.

1. See "Agreement with the President, Directors, and Company of the Bank of the United States," May 25, 1792, note 3 (*PAH*, XI, 421–24).

To Robert Troup [1]

[*Philadelphia, June 7, 1792.* "An application is made to me by a Mr. Sarragon of South Carolina for some copies of vouchers of a claim against James Neilson which he says were sent to me in September 1789; but of which I have no present recollection. If they were sent they are with you." [2] *Letter not found.*]

The Collector: A Magazine for Autograph and Historical Collectors, LXV, No. 8 (August-September, 1952), 169, Item R 1461.

1. Troup, a New York lawyer, and H had been undergraduates together at King's College before the American Revolution. When H became Secretary of the Treasury on September 11, 1789, he turned over to Troup pending litigation in which he was involved as attorney.

2. Text taken from the dealer's catalogue.

To John Hancock [1]

[*Philadelphia June 10, 1792.* "The period of the session did not permit the subject being brought before Congress, with advantage, previous to their rising. Your excellency however may rely that it shall receive the attention which is due to so benevolent a purpose and to the auspices under which it presents itself." [2] *Letter not found.*]

1. ALS, sold by Dodd, Mead and Company, New York City, November, 1901, Catalogue 61, Item 170.
When this letter was written, Hancock was governor of Massachusetts, a position to which he was elected nine times and which he held at his death in 1793.
2. Extract taken from dealer's catalogue.

To John Langdon [1]

Philadelphia, June 18th, 1792

Dear Sir:

In turning over my private letters a day or two since, I found that from Mr. Church,[2] which relates to your demand upon him. The ground on which he places his refusal to pay is that *he was not an owner at the time.* As your letter to me of the 5th of March [3] contains no explanation on this point, nothing tending to shew that the above supposition is an error, Mr. Church's answer to it must of course be the same as to the former.

I am therefore to request that you will state such particulars of the transaction to me as will serve to shew either that Mr. Church was an owner at the time the expense in question was incurred, or that he was under some collateral or incidental engagement, which made him responsible to you.[4] If you remove the doubt on this point, either by a letter to me, or to Mr. Church I presume you will remove all obstacle to the admission of your claim. With respectful & very cordial regard, I have the honor to remain Sir

Your Obed. Serv.   A Hamilton

The Honorable J. Langdon, Esq.

Letters by Washington, Adams, Jefferson and Others Written During and After the Revolution to John Langdon, New Hampshire (Philadelphia: Press of Henry B. Ashmead, 1880), 79–80.
1. In *PAH*, XI, 523, this letter is listed as a "letter not found."
2. John B. Church. Letter not found.
3. Letter not found.
4. For Langdon's reply, see Langdon to H, June 28, 1792 (*PAH*, XI, 592–93).

To Robert Purviance [1]

[*Treasury Department, June 19, 1792.* The dealer's description of this letter reads: "Concerning a fraudulent practice." [2] *Letter not found.*]

1. LS, sold by B Altman & Co., New York City, (*The New York Times*, October 9, 1977).
2. See Purviance to H, June 14, 1792 (*PAH*, XI, 518).

To Edward Wigglesworth [1]

[*Philadelphia, June 28, 1792.* Letter listed in dealer's catalogue. *Letter not found.*]

1. LS, sold by Bruce Gimelson, Fort Washington, Pennsylvania, 1938, Catalogue 306, Item 1792.
Wigglesworth was collector of customs at Newburyport, Massachusetts.

To Henry Marchant

Treasury Department
June 29th 1792

Sir

The Bank of the United States have agreed to undertake the payment of the salaries of the public Officers, and the details of an arrangement for that purpose will be adjusted prior to the expiration of the *next* quarter.[1]

On the point of the quantum of compensation to the District

Judge of Rhode Island,[2] I could not with propriety say any thing, as it is a matter entirely foreign to my department. As an individual, I must always wish liberal allowances to the Judiciary, as of great importance to their independence, and consequently to the well administering of Justice.

With respectful consideration, I have the honor to be, Sir, Your Obed Servant Alexander Hamilton

Henry Marchant Esq.
Judge of the District Court,
Rhode Island.

LS, Rhode Island Historical Society, Providence.
1. See Marchant to H, September 14, 1791 (printed in this volume).
2. For Marchant's compensation as United States judge for the District of Rhode Island, see "Report on the Receipts and Expenditures of Public Monies to the End of the Year 1791," November 10, 1792 (*PAH*, XIII, 54); "Report on the Balance of All Unapplied Revenues at the End of the Year 1792 and on All Unapplied Monies Which May Have Been Obtained by the Several Loans Authorized by Law," February 4, 1793 (*PAH*, XIII, 565).

To Robert Troup [1]

[*Philadelphia, June 30, 1792.* "I think, I sometime since, requested you to settle my account with Judge Hobart.[2] In turning over my papers, I find the enclosed—which I send you, in order that you may have the goodness if anything remains due, to discharge it." [3] *Letter not found.*]

1. ALS, sold by Kenneth W. Rendell, Inc., Catalogue No. 70, Lot 55.
2. John Sloss Hobart, a member from Suffolk County, New York, of the Provincial Congress from 1775 to 1777, was a justice of the New York Supreme Court from 1777 to 1798.
3. Text taken from the dealer's catalogue.

To James Lingan [1]

[*Treasury Department, July 3, 1792.* The description of this letter in the dealer's catalogue reads: "Acknowledges receipt of a draft in the amount of $1500.00." *Letter not found.*]

1. LS, sold by Kenneth W. Rendell, Inc., Catalogue No. 92, Lot 47. Lingan was collector of customs at Georgetown, District of Columbia.

From Benjamin Tallmadge [1]

Col. Hamilton   Litchfield [Connecticut] July 20th 1792

Sir,

The Design of this Letter is to communicate to you the Information which I have collected respecting a Gang of *Counterfeiters*, the Effects of whose Villainy have long been known, but whose Connexions & more particular Operations have never been thoroughly developed.

We have in Custody, at this place, a Man by the name of *Jackson*, who has long been known to be a notorious *horse-thief*, as well as a Purchaser & Seller of public Securities. This Man within a few days, partly from a Compunction for his former Demerits, but principally to avoid punishment, has discovered a wish to disclose the Scene of Villainy. He declares that the Seat or Head Quarters where this business is principally effected is in a *Den* or Cavern of a rock in the State of N. York, near the North river (the particular location of which can at any time be more minutely pointed out) to which place *Adonijah Crane* the principal penman, *Francis Crane* Brother to Adonijah commonly called *Wright—Ephraim Willard* & a very important Character from the Southward, who is said to be a very rich man & a Gentleman but has never had any name among them with many others of smaller Note, frequently resort. He describes the Cavern to be a large room perfectly enclosed & tight, with only one Entrance, which is by a Trap door from the Top. This Door is supported by large hinges, & covered with Turf, Green Ivys &c, & has been in the same Situation ever since the peace, & has never yet been discovered. In this place are kept the Implements for extracting the Ink & counterfieting public Securities; also a plate with which they strike off bank bills &c. I have shewn to him a Bank bill of the U. States which he says they make in the greatest perfection. They have collected a considerable Quantity of thin paper exactly similar to that used by the Bank, on which they are impressing the Bank Stamp of the U. States, as well as that of the State of N. York, & he declares to me that he knows of immense Sums having been sent out & put off lately in different parts of the Continent. He says (what would be very natural to suppose) that they have Agents in different parts of the Continent who are continually purchasing up final Settlement Notes & other public Securities of small nominal amot. which they make into larger Sums, & *these* together with their other Counterfeit paper, are sent abroad & sold to the people. He further informs that the last time he was at this *Pandæmoneum,* they were preparing a Machine to counterfeit Gold Coin. He mentions that he saw at that place, John Sturla, the Man who counterfieted the Checks upon the Banks at N. York, who with some others were waiting for a Vessel to be got ready, on board which they were to sail to the West Indies or some foreign port. The Gang are considerably numerous, tho' seldom all there at a time, but are armed with Guns & pistols & very desperate.

From this general Statement of the business, together with a variety of other Information, a number of Gentlemen in this Quarter have determined to make an Attempt to detect & break up this Gang. Particular reasons require that it should be done without loss of time. I propose accompanying them by all means, unless the State of Mrs. Tallmadge's health (which at present is very critical) totally prevents. At any rate my whole aid & Assistance shall be afforded to further the Expedition. If any thing important should be effected, you may expect to hear further from me on the Subject. At present I tho't it my Duty to lay this information before you, that you may pursue such measures as your prudence may dictate.

I need not request you to consider this as a Confidential Communication for the present. Perhaps it may be proper to lay this Information before the President & Directors of the Bank of the United States.

I have the Honor to be, with the most perfect Regard, Sir, your most Obedt Servt.   Benj Tallmadge

ALS, Connecticut Historical Society, Hartford.
1. Tallmadge, a veteran of the American Revolution and a merchant in Litchfield, Connecticut, was treasurer of the Ohio Company. In 1792 he was appointed postmaster at Litchfield.
For an explanation of the contents of this letter, see H to Jeremiah Wadsworth, November 8, 1789 (*PAH,* V, 503–04); Wadsworth to H, December 17, 1789 (*PAH,* VI, 15–16); H to Joseph Howell, Jr., March 3, 1790 (*PAH,* VI,

285); H to Richard Harison, March 15, 1791 (*PAH*, VIII, 184–85); Harison to H, April 8, 1791 (*PAH*, VIII, 251–53).

To the President and Directors of the Bank of Maryland

Treasury Department, July 25, 1792.

Gentlemen:

I think it proper to inform you that I have directed the collector of Baltimore to divide his deposits, hereafter, between the Bank of Maryland and the Office of Discount and Deposit of the United States Bank, until the 1st of October, ensuing;[1] and thenceforth to deposit the public moneys wholly with the said office or branch bank.[2]

I am, gentlemen, &c.

A. H., Secretary

The President and Directors of the Bank of Maryland.

ASP, Finance, VI, 268.
  1. H to Otho H. Williams, July 25, 1792 (*PAH*, XII, 108).
  2. See H to John Kean, March 28, 1792, note 2 (printed in this volume).

To George Washington [1]

Philadelphia Aug 11. 1792

Sir

I have already written to you to go by the Post.[2] This is barely to inform you, that I have made the communication you desired to Mr. Kean, who promises every possible exertion—and that Mr. Langdon has been here about a fortnight.[3]

With perfect respect & attachment I have the honor to be Sir Your obedient servant

A Hamilton

P.S I have made progress in certain answers;[4] but shall scarcely be ready to send them before Monday's Post.

The President of The UStates.

ALS, M. E. Saltykev-Shchedrin State Public Library, Leningrad, U.S.S.R.
   1. In *PAH*, XII, 195, this letter is listed as a "letter not found."
   2. H to Washington, August 10, 1792 (*PAH*, XII, 185–87).
   3. See Washington to H, August 1, 1792 (*PAH*, XII, 147–48).
   4. See Washington to H, July 29, 1792 (*PAH*, XII, 129–34). For H's "answers," see H to Washington, August 18, 1792 (*PAH*, XII, 228–58).

From William Constable [1]

[London, August 19, 1792]

Conversation between My Ld Hawkesbury & Mr. B—— a Mercht.
August 19th 1792 [2]

Mr. B.   I wait upon your Ldship with the Copy of a letter from the American Secretary of State respecting the Flag of that Nation, stating that all Vessells *actually owned* by Citizens of the States, whether registered or not, are to be Considered as equally entitled to the Protection of their Neutrality.

Ld H   Mr. Jefferson is a Party Man & We know it.

Mr B.   Considerable apprehensions are entertained in the City of a War with America, permit me My Lord to ask if these fears have any foundation.

Ld H   Not the smallest be assured of it, as long as Washington is at the head of the Executive & the Fœderal Party prevail there will be no War with this Country as Peace is the Interest & Wish of both Govmnts.

In the Course of Conversation his Lordship mentioned that a Person of Consequence wou'd shortly go out to America. Be so good as to burn this after reading, especially as a Gentns. Name is mentioned for whose Patriotism I have a sincere respect and of whom I am convinced Ld. Hwkby entertains a very erroneous Opinion. As his Ldship is a very influential Member of the Council I thought it worthwhile to lett you know his ideas of the Parties in our Country & their Sentiments. It is unnecessary for me to sign this.

AL, Hamilton Papers, Library of Congress.
   1. In 1792 Constable was in England attempting to sell 1,800,000 acres of land

in northern New York, which Alexander Macomb, a business associate, had purchased in 1791.

2. Although Constable reported this conversation to H in 1792, it most likely took place between September 30, 1789, when Thomas Jefferson became Secretary of State, and January 28, 1791. During this period, Baron Hawkesbury, as chairman of the Board of Trade, conducted an extensive study of Anglo-American trade which included interviews with many London merchants. Hawkesbury issued his report on American trade on January 28, 1791 (copy, Add. MS 38350, 234–47, British Museum). This report was published. See "A Report of the Lords of the Committee of Privy Council, Appointed for all Matters relating to Trade and Foreign Plantations, on the Commerce and Navigation between his Majesty's Dominions, and the Territories belonging to the United States of America," 28th January, 1791. Reprinted by Order of The Society of Ship-owners of Great Britain. 1806. In *Collection of Interesting and Important Reports and Papers on the Navigation and Trade of Great Britain, Ireland, and the British Colonies in the West Indies and America*. Printed by Order of The Society of Ship-owners of Great Britain (n.p., 1807), 45–154. Additional evidence to support this dating is the mention of "a Person of Consequence." This is presumably George Hammond, British Minister to the United States, who arrived in the United States on November 1, 1791.

Above the dash after the letter "B" someone later wrote in pencil the name "Baring." This is a reference to Sir Francis Baring, a London merchant and founder of the firm of Baring Brothers & Company, which had numerous business connections with the United States. There is no other evidence that Constable was actually referring to Baring.

Honorary Degree from Rhode Island College

Providence, September 4, 1792. "VOTED, That the Degree of Doctor of Laws be conferred on . . . the Hon. Alexander Hamilton, Secretary of the Treasury of the United States." [1]

MS minutes, Brown University—Corporation Minutes, 1764– , Brown University Archives, John Hay Library, Providence.

1. For an account of the commencement of Rhode Island College on September 5, 1792, at which this degree was conferred on H, who was not present, see the *Providence Gazette and Country Journal*, September 8, 1792.

To Tobias Lear [1]

Philadelphia Sepr. 6, 1792

My Dear Sir

I have the pleasure of your letter of the 27 of August,[2] and thank you very much for the trouble you have taken.

We could assure a compensation of 600 Dollars among twelve, and we would consent to an increase of the School to the number requisite to make up the 1000 in the same proportion of compensation—if we did not ourselves prefer to make the addition. This is all that can be now promised. If a competent character is willing to undertake on these terms, the sooner he is here the better.

I am happy to learn the flourishing state of the Country where you are. I believe too, though not in a perfectly equal degree, every part of the country enjoys a large portion of prosperity. But every part of the Country is not happy. The patriots, by way of eminence, will not let them be so. Their creed seems to be that the political like the Celestial heaven is to be obtained "in fear and trembling." [3]

Mrs. Hamilton has lately given me another boy,[4] who and the Mother are unusually well. She adds to her Complements to you her affect remembrances to Mrs. Lear in which let me join. Truly & with the most cordial esteem & regard I remain

Dr Sir   Your Obed ser   A Hamilton

Tobias Lear Esqr.

ALS, New Hampshire Historical Society, Concord.
    1. In *PAH*, XII, 327, this letter is listed as a "letter not found."
    2. *PAH*, XII, 279–80.
    3. Paul's letter to the Philippians, chapter 2, verse 12, reads: "Wherefore, my beloved, as ye have always obeyed, not as in my presence only, but now much more in my absence, work out your own salvation with fear and trembling."
    4. John Church Hamilton, H's fourth son and fifth child, was born on August 22, 1792.

To James Lingan [1]

Treasury Department
September 6. 1792.

Sir

It has been stated to me by Messrs Oliver and Thomson [2] that the Ship Eliza, N Stone Master, entered at Alexandria in November last, and proceeded up the River in *Ballast* to load at George Town, where the said Master had been obliged to pay Tonnage a second time.

If the case is accurately stated, and the Master had paid Tonnage at Alexandria, as may be inferred from the entry said to have been made there, your charge was erroneously made, and the Tonnage Duty paid to you must in that case be refunded.

I am, Sir,   Your Obed. Servant.   Alexander Hamilton

James M Lingan Esqr.
George Town.

LS, Mr. Cyril Clemens, Kirkwood, Missouri.
   1. In *PAH*, XII, 327, this letter is listed as a "letter not found."
   2. For information concerning the contents of this letter, see "Report on the Petition of Robert Oliver and Hugh Thompson," February 2, 1795 (*PAH*, XVIII, 246–47).

From David Wolfe [1]

New York September 8th 1792.

Sir

On the 12th. July 1791 [2] you were pleased to inform me, that "my Observations were duly communicated to the Comptroller and would receive a proper consideration."

it is now unnecessary to bestow much time on them, for I believe Colo Pickering himself will allow the truth of them. Nay stranger yet, he has to a creditor, *denied giving the Officers of the* Treasury the information as stated in Mr. Walcots letters respecting printed certificates bearing interest.

he is in Philadelphia and may be consulted again, he is now older & perhaps Wiser. he may now inform you (and at the same time speak the truth) that all Debts contracted since the 1st Jany 1782 were specially stipulated to be paid in specie, and that receiving a Certificate sign'd by himself Did not ban or in any wise impair any persons claim and further that those certificates were estimated by *his express order*, for the purpose of having them included in the General Estimate deliverd Mr. Morris on the 29th. september 1784.

   I have the Honour to be   Your Obt Servant   David Wolfe

The Secretary of the Treasury

Copy, Massachusetts Historical Society, Boston.
1. For background to this letter, see Wolfe to H, June 16, 1791 (printed in this volume).
2. *PAH*, VIII, 547.

To Tobias Lear

Treasury Department, September 11, 1792. Encloses a letter "left at the office by Mr. Fraunces [1] the Steward . . . of the President of the United States."

LS, from an anonymous donor.
1. Samuel Fraunces, formerly the proprietor of Fraunces Tavern in New York City.

To John Campbell [1]

[*Philadelphia, September 18, 1792.* Letter listed in dealer's catalogue. *Letter not found.*]

1. LS, sold by John Heise, Syracuse, New York, 1914, Catalogue 101, Item 98.
Campbell was a weaver in Philadelphia who was associated with the Society for Establishing Useful Manufactures. See "Contract with James and Shoemaker," November 5, 1792 (*PAH*, XIII, 17); "Agreement with John Campbell and Receipt from John Campbell," November 9, 1792 (*PAH*, XIII, 31–32).

To Nicholas Low [1]

[*Philadelphia, September 18, 1792.* The description of this letter in the dealer's catalogue reads: "Complains humorously 'of the badness of my memory' and promises that "I shall (Deo volente) meet you & other friends at New Ark on the first Monday of October.[2] I am glad to learn that King [3] will be there. . . .' " *Letter not found.*]

1. ALS, sold by Carnegie Book Shop, New York City, 1971, Catalogue 315, Item 226.
2. October 1, 1792, was a Monday. On that date H was in Newark, New Jersey (H to William Short, October 1–15, 1792 [*PAH*, XII, 513–14]). On the same date the directors of the Society for Establishing Useful Manufactures

met in Newark. Low was a director of the society. The minutes of the meeting do not record that H attended ("Minutes of the S.U.M.," 71, 72). This, however, was not unusual, for although he was, of course, one of the leading founders and advisers of the society, he was not one of its directors in 1792 ("Minutes of the S.U.M.," 1, 72).

3. This may be a reference to Joseph King, who was the society's agent in Liverpool. No evidence has been found that he ever visited the United States.

To ——————— [1]

[*Philadelphia, September 22, 1792.* Letter listed in dealer's catalogue. *Letter not found.*]

1. DS, sold by Charles Hamilton Autographs, Inc., October 22, 1970, Item 136B.

From Winthrop Sargent [1]

[*October 24, 1792.* On December 31, 1792, Hamilton wrote to Sargent: [2] "I duly received your letter of the 24th of October." *Letter not found.*]

1. Sargent, who had surveyed the Ohio country in 1786, was elected secretary of the Ohio Company in 1787 and was active in the planting of the Ohio settlements. In 1787 Congress appointed him secretary of the Territory Northwest of the River Ohio.
2. Printed in this volume.

To Thomas Willing [1]

[*Treasury Department, October 24, 1792.* The dealer's catalogue description of this letter reads: "To the President of the Bank of the U.S. extending for an additional thirty days credit on bill sold by the Bank on American Commissioners in Amsterdam 'to such purchasers of bills as have deposited public securities.'" *Letter not found.*]

1. LS, sold by Carnegie Book Shop, New York City, 1948, Catalogue 138, Item 105.

This letter is listed as a "letter not found" (but without a description of its contents) in *PAH*, XII, 619.

For an explanation of the contents of this letter, see "Report on the Balance of All Unapplied Revenues at the End of the Year 1792 and on All Unapplied Monies Which May Have Been Applied by the Several Loans Authorized by Law," February 4, 1793 (*PAH*, XIII, 532–79).

To John Chaloner [1]

[Philadelphia, October 26, 1792]

Mr. Hamiltons Compliments to Mr. Chaloner requests to know who is the other joint Morgagee with Mr. Church of Mr. Holker's land; and whether he is informed of proceedings having been begun for effecting a sale of the land upon the Mortgage.

Friday Morning
Octr. 26

AL, Mr. James H. Welch, Canton, Ohio.
1. For information concerning the contents of this letter, see H to Chaloner, June 11, 1793 (*PAH*, XIV, 533).

From James Lovell [1]

Boston Octr. 1792

Sir

Agreably to the directions of your circular letter of August 31st.[2] covering an order of the Senate passed on the 7th. of may last, I now transmit the demanded account. I cannot, however, refrain from expressing an Hope that *my* statements may not prove injurious to such Officers as have had *usual & necessary* Assistance of Clerks, without being driven to devote their own Nights as well as days to their Offices. Adversity has formed but few such callous Drudges as myself in a similar Line of Life.

I am sir   with Consideration   your obedient   James Lovell
Naval off

To the Secretary of the Treasury of the United States

Copy, in the handwriting of James Lovell, Thomas Jefferson Papers, Library of Congress.
1. This letter was enclosed in Lovell to Thomas Jefferson, January 8, 1803 (ALS, Thomas Jefferson Papers, Library of Congress).

Lovell was the naval officer for the District of Boston and Charlestown, Massachusetts.

2. "Treasury Department Circular to the Collectors of the Customs," August 31, 1792 (*PAH*, XII, 303–04).

From Henry Knox [1]

War department,
3d. November 1792

Sir

I have considered maturely of the magazines of provisions, the meat part whereof to be salted, which the service may require to be kept in advance for the garrisons and divisions of the troops north west of the Ohio. I have the honor to transmit you the result, which has been approved by the President of the United States, and the general subject of which has been transmitted to Major General Wayne.[2]

To wit.

Fort Jefferson. ⎤ The garrisons may be ⎤   *Rations*
—— St. Clair. ⎬ from 120 each, to 150, but ye. ⎬ 450 for 90 days. 40,500
—— Hamilton ⎦ latter number is taken ⎦

Additional quantities.

| | | Fort Jefferson | 50,000 | |
| | | —— St. Clair | 50,000 | 100,000 |

Posts.	Probable garrisons	No of days Subse.			
Fort Knox	120	130		21,600.	
Fort Steuben	60	90		5,400.	
Galliopolis	40	90		3,600.	
Blockhouse dry Ridge	12	90		1,080.	
Marietta	70	90		6,300.	
Fort Franklin	120	180	21,600		
Additional			10,000	31,600	
Big Beaver	40	90		3,600	
General Wayne's encampment				50,000	122.680
				Total	262.680

The garrisons generally ought to be furnished with three months rations in advance. This has been a fixed principle, and is a proper precaution to be taken against the evils of a blockade or siege.

But it seems necessary to place a further quantity in the advance posts at Forts Jefferson and St. Clair. This quantity will probably be required to serve to replenish any desultory parties which may be ordered out during the winter, or early in the spring, or to serve for contingencies which cannot now be specified.

Fort Knox being very distant, and supplies precarious, it is thought proper the garrison should have six months provisions in the Magazine—and it being difficult to communicate with Fort Franklin in winter—and moreover, it being a place to which the friendly Indians must resort, it ought to have for its own garrison six months provisions, and Ten thousand rations for the extra purposes of the Indians.

As Fort Washington will be the main post at the lower parts of the Ohio, and from which detachments and succours will be made to the advanced posts, and also the point from which desultory expeditions will be furnished, it ought to be supplied with One hundred thousand rations in advance.

The position which General Wayne will occupy north of the Ohio, being liable at times to have its communication interrupted, it ought to have the Fifty thousand rations mentioned.

I have the honor to be   Sir   Your obedient servant   H Knox

The hon. the secretary of the Treasury

Copy, Historical Society of Pennsylvania, Philadelphia.
    1. After the defeat of Major General Arthur St. Clair's expedition against the western Indians on November 4, 1791, the newly reorganized United States Army was placed under the command of Major General Anthony Wayne, and preparations were made for a new campaign against the Indians in the Northwest. On August 1, 1792, George Washington requested Knox to report on the supplies necessary for the Army on the western frontier (GW, XXXII, 104), and it was in this context that Knox wrote the letter printed above.
    For background to this letter, see Washington to H, August 1, 1792 (PAH, XII, 146–47); H to Washington, August 10, 1792 (PAH, XII, 185–86).
    On November 9, 1792, Knox sent a copy of his letter to H printed above to Wayne (Richard C. Knopf, ed., Anthony Wayne, A Name in Arms: Soldier, Diplomat, Defender of Expansion Westward of a Nation: The Wayne-Knox-Pickering-McHenry Correspondence [Pittsburgh, 1960], 131).
    2. Knox to Wayne, November 2, 1792 (Knopf, Wayne, 125–28).

To the President and Directors of the
Bank of the United States [1]

[*Treasury Department, November 5, 1792.* "I have to request that you will advance to Messrs. William Young and George Dannaker the sum of two thousand dollars, on account of their contract with the public,[2] for supplying the troops with clothing for the ensuing year. For this advance the contractors are to be charged in a temporary account, until arrangements shall be made to have the payment covered by a warrant." [3] *Letter not found.*]

1. ALS, sold by Kenneth W. Rendell, Inc., Catalogue 80, Item 92.
In *PAH*, XIII, 17, this letter is listed as a "letter not found."
2. See "Contract with George Dannacker and William Young," October 22, 1792 (*PAH*, XII, 608). See also H to the President and Directors of the Bank of the United States, November 28, 1792 (*PAH*, XIII, 241–42).
In the dealer's catalogue Dannacker's name is spelled "Dannakee."
3. Text taken from the dealer's catalogue.

To Theodosius Fowler [1]

[*Philadelphia, November 9, 1792.* On November 13, 1792, Fowler wrote to Hamilton [2] and referred to "the receipt of your favour of the 9th. instant." *Letter not found.*]

1. Fowler, a New York City speculator in securities and land, had also been a contractor for supplying the troops in the western territories.
2. Printed in this volume.

From Theodosius Fowler [1]

New York 13th. November 1792

Alexander Hamilton Esqr.
Dear sir

Immediately on the receipt of your favour of the 9th. instant,[2] I waited on Mr. Duer and informed him it was necessary to forward to Philadelphia without delay all the papers in his possession that any ways concerned the late Expedition under Genl. St. Clair that real facts might be Established.

He in answer assured he would write to you on the subject and forward every Paper in his possession relative to the business and also write to some of the Members of Congress on that head.

I am &c   Theods Fowler

LC, Stevens Family Papers, New Jersey Historical Society, Newark.
1. For an explanation of the contents of this letter, see H to William Duer, April 7, 1791, note 2 (*PAH*, VIII, 247–48). See also Joseph Nourse to H, May 1, 1792 (*PAH*, XI 350–52); H to Richard Harison, August 30, 1792 (*PAH*, XII, 288–89); H to Henry Knox, November 14, 1792 (*PAH*, XIII, 117–18); David Ross to H, November 23, 1792, note 5 (*PAH*, XIII, 218–28), April 25, 1793, notes 1 and 2 (*PAH*, XIV, 343–46); "Statement on Remarks by John F. Mercer," April, 1793 (*PAH*, XIV, 361).
2. Letter not found.

From Henry Knox

[*Philadelphia, November 14, 1792.* On November 14, 1792, Hamilton wrote to Knox [1] and referred to "your letter of this day." *Letter not found.*]

1. *PAH*, XIII, 117–18.

To the President and Directors of the Bank of the United States

Treasury Department, December 8, 1792.

Gentlemen:

I understand there is at present an unusual press for money, proceeding from certain mercantile speculations.

As an accomodation in regard to notes in which the Government is interested may, in this state of things, be of peculiar convenience to the persons concerned, I shall have no objection if the bank will renew such notes for thirty days in all cases where it can be done with perfect safety to the public.

I have the honor, &c.   A. H.

The President and Directors of the Bank of the United States.

ASP, Finance, IV, 268.

To James O'Hara [1]

Treasury Departmt. Dec. 18. 92

Sir

It is indispensable that your Account as Quarter Master General should be render'd to the Treasury, up to the end of the present year as soon as possible—and thenceforth regularly after the expiration of every Quarter.

It is expected that this Arrangement will be strictly observ'd, it being essentially requisite that any future advances must of necessity be regulated by the issue.

I am Sir, with consideration   Your Obt. Servant   Alex Hamilton

LC, The Indiana Historical Society Library, Indianapolis.
  1. In *PAH*, XIII, 339, this letter is listed as a "letter not found."
  For O'Hara's answer to this letter, see O'Hara to H, January 10, 1793 (*PAH*, XIII, 474–75).

To Samuel Hodgdon [1]

[*Treasury Department, December 20, 1792.* "A warrant has been issued this day on the Treasurer in your favor as attorney for James O'Hara [2] Quarter Master General of the Army of the United States . . . to be applied . . . to . . . discharging sundry bills. . . ." [3] *Letter not found.*]

  1. LS, sold by Kenneth W. Rendell, Kingston Galleries, Inc., Somerville, Massachusetts, 1969, Catalogue 37, Item 70.

Hodgdon was commissary of military stores and was stationed at Philadelphia.

2. This is presumably a reference to Warrant 2314 listed in *PAH*, XIII, 570. But also see Warrants 2151, 2186, 2190, 2250 (*PAH*, XIII, 564, 565, 566, 568).

3. Text taken from dealer's catalogue.

To Winthrop Sargent

Treasury Department
December 31. 1792

Sir

I duly received your letter of the 24th of October.[1] An extreme press of business has prevented me, hitherto, from making a Report on your petition; but you may rely upon the promise which I now make you, that one will be very shortly made.[2]

I am, Sir, with consideration, Your Obedt Servant

A Hamilton

Winthrop Sargent Esq.
Cincinnati,
North West of the Ohio

LS, Ontario County Historical Society, Canandaigua, New York.

1. Letter not found.

2. See Sargent to H, October 28, 1793, January 2, 1794 (*PAH*, XV, 379–80, 605–07); "Report on the Petition of Winthrop Sargent," January 31, 1794 (*PAH*, XV, 680–81).

On January 27, 1796, Sargent submitted another petition to Congress, which was referred to the Committee of Claims, but no other action was taken (*Journal of the House*, II, 428).

1793

To Thomas Willing [1]

[Philadelphia, January 8, 1793. Letter listed in dealer's catalogue. Letter not found.]

1. LS, sold by Carnegie Book Shop, New York City, 1938, Catalogue 66, Item 664.

To the President and Directors of the Bank of the United States [1]

[Philadelphia, January 10, 1793. Letter listed in dealer's catalogue. Letter not found.]

1. LS, sold by George H. Richmond, New York City, 1906, "Autograph Letters, Manuscripts . . . ," Item 185.

From Theodosius Fowler [1]

New York Feby 2. 1793

respected Sir

I have observed lately in the public prints another Report of a Committee of Congress on the failure of the Expedition under the Comd of Genl St Clair.

I take the liberty of writing to you in Confidence and beg you to favor me with the particular situation of the Contract that Mr William Duer acted under, whether he has fulfilled on his part and if he has produced Vouchers and other documents sufficient to cover the advances made him by the Public. Do pray write me on this Subject and let me know how the Matter stands for I am distressd beyond description about this afair—tho I am an inocent person in the whole of this Transaction, which no doubt you are perfectly senciable of. My dr Sir permit me to say I must look up to you as my friend and protector in this Business for if I am made an inocent Victim of it [it] will be a most cruel fate to me and my family for ever.

I hope my particular situation in this Business will be a sufficient apology for my taking the liberty of writing to you on this Subject.

Believe me to be with perfect respect & Esteem your most obt & very Humble Sert.   T. Fowler

LC, Stevens Family Papers, New Jersey Historical Society, Newark.
    1. For an explanation of the contents of this letter, see Fowler to H, November 13, 1792 (printed in this volume). See also Fowler to Oliver Wolcott, Jr., December 4, 13, 1794 (LC, Stevens Family Papers, New Jersey Historical Society, Newark).

From Tench Coxe [1]

[*Philadelphia, February 4, 1793.* In an undated letter written sometime in 1797 to Oliver Wolcott, Jr., Coxe reviewed his correspondence with Hamilton concerning the execution of the revenue laws in Pennsylvania. In the course of the letter Coxe wrote: "My letter of the 4th. Feby. 1793 contains a sad exhibition of the disorders in the Service in Pennsa. The letter of Feb. 4. shews the knowledge of the state of things possessed by the Secy. of the Treasury." *Letter not found.*]

    1. ADf, Papers of Tench Coxe in the Coxe Family Papers at the Historical Society of Pennsylvania, Philadelphia.

To William Hull [1]

[*Philadelphia, February 28, 1793.* ". . . The issue is contrary to expectation and is matter of regret. The best, however, must be made of circumstances. The object of your mission being at an end, I am to request that . . . you will return to this place." [2] *Letter not found.*]

The Collector: A Magazine for Autograph and Historical Collectors, LXIV, No. 3 (June, 1951), 128, Item W990.

1. Hull, a native of Derby, Connecticut, a veteran of the American Revolution, and a lawyer in Newton, Massachusetts, was appointed in January, 1793, agent to arrange with Governor John Graves Simcoe for the purchase of supplies for a proposed meeting with the western Indians in the spring. For background to this letter, see "Draft of Instructions for William Hull," January 14, 1793 (*PAH,* XIII, 479–80); Hull to H, February 6, 1793 (*PAH,* XIV, 9–13). See also "Conversation with George Hammond," December 15-28, 1792 (*PAH,* XIII, 326–28); H to Hammond, December 29, 1792 (*PAH,* XIII, 382–84). For the proposed council with the western Indians, see "Conversation with George Hammond." November 22, 1792, note 4 (*PAH,* XIII, 213–15).
2. Text taken from extract in dealer's catalogue.

To the President and Directors of the Office of Discount and Deposit, Baltimore

Treasury Department, March 2, 1793.

Gentlemen:

I find that my letter of the 23d ultimo,[1] (which was written in haste,) proposing an arrangement for the accomodation of merchants who are indebted to the custom-house, does not correctly express the idea which was contemplated.

I therefore request that the following mode may be pursued: The directors are to judge of the safety of the notes which may be presented for discount for the respective sums due to the custom-house, and to take the risk of non-payment upon themselves. When the notes are accepted, the proceeds are subject to checks in favor of the *collector* [2] *only,* which checks the bank receives for the collector as cash.

If the arrangement should be found necessary, it will be proper that this explanation be communicated to the collector.

I have the honor, &c.   A. H.

The President and Directors of the Office of Discount and Deposit, Baltimore.

ASP, Finance, IV, 269.
1. "Treasury Department Circular to the Presidents and Directors of the Offices of Discount and Deposit of the Bank of the United States," February 23–March 5, 1793 (*PAH,* XIV, 137–38).
2. Otho H. Williams.

To John Rutherfurd

[Philadelphia, March 4, 1793–January 31, 1795]

Dr. Sir

I called at your Quarters a while ago to ask you to take with two or three friends a family Dinner with me to day.

A word in answer by the bearer will oblige.

Yrs   A Hamilton

Will you tell Mr. Frelinghuyssen [1] that if he will be of the party I shall esteem it a favour.

ALS, anonymous donor.
1. Frederick Frelinghuysen, a lawyer and a member of the Continental Congress in 1778 and 1782, was a United States Senator from New Jersey.

From Charles Cotesworth Pinckney [1]

[*Charleston, South Carolina, March 30, 1793.* Letter listed in dealer's catalogue. *Letter not found.*]

1. ALS, sold by C. F. Libbie and Company, Boston, December 12, 1875, Item 537.
Pinckney, a leading South Carolina Federalist and lawyer, had been a member of the South Carolina Provincial Assembly, a brigade commander and aide to George Washington during the American Revolution, a member of the state legislature in 1778, 1779, and 1782, and a delegate to the Federal Convention in 1787. Although he held no office when this letter was written, in 1791 Washington had offered and he had declined both the command of the Army and a seat on the Supreme Court.

To John Kean

Treasury Department
April 4 1793

Sir

If you have any Treasurer's Drafts on the Bank of Providence I request they may not be disposed of till you hear further from me and shall be glad to know their amount.[1] With consideration & esteem

I am Sir   Your obedient servant   A Hamilton

John Kean Esquire
Cashier of the Bank of the U States

ALS, New-York Historical Society, New York City.
   1. See H to John Brown, April 5, 1793 (*PAH*, XIV, 283–84).

From Tench Coxe

[Philadelphia, April 13, 1793]

Dear Sir

Notes for discount are to be *presented* to the Bank of the U. S. on Mondays.[1] There will be wanted 2500 Drs. to make up the Sum, which was noted for *this* week—and any part of the remaining sum of 3000 drs. proposed to be paid in April, which may be convenient. The third sum of 3500 Drs. will not be necessary, but in the course of August. That is the proportion, which was noted as to be paid by the first of September.

I have recd. an answer from the gentleman to whom the prior offer of 4000 As. was made.[2] He decides to take that quantity, which being out of Ball & Smith's contract leaves 1000 Drs. to be yet laid out. This of course will also diminish the August payments, and bring the further sum of 1000 Drs. (in lieu of a part of those payments) into the provisions to be made in April current.[3]

yr. mo. respectful serv.   Tench Coxe

April 13th. 1793
A. Hamilton Esqr. Atty. for J. B. Church Esqr.

ALS, Papers of Tench Coxe in the Coxe Family Papers at the Historical Society of Pennsylvania, Philadelphia.
   1. For an explanation of this sentence and the remainder of this paragraph, see "Treasury Department Circular to the Presidents and Directors of the Offices of Discount and Deposit of the Bank of the United States," February 23–March 5, 1793 (*PAH*, XIV, 137–38).

2. For the "prior offer," see Coxe to H, April 10, 1793 (*PAH*, XIV, 304–05). The "gentleman" was William Vans Murray, who on March 31, 1793, wrote to Coxe: "On the most mature consideration I am of opinion clearly that I ought to embrace your friendly offer & if you can yet let me in, hereby agree to pay the money for four thousand acres at the rate of a quarter of a dollar pr. acre . . . on the first of September next" (ALS, Papers of Tench Coxe in the Coxe Family Papers at the Historical Society of Pennsylvania, Philadelphia). In a document entitled "Memn. of Mr. W. V. Murray's Money Sept. 2d. 1793," Coxe wrote: "pd. me for accot of an undivided 4000 As. of Lands bot of Ball & Smith" (ADS, Papers of Tench Coxe in the Coxe Family Papers at the Historical Society of Pennsylvania, Philadelphia).

Murray was a lawyer from Cambridge, Maryland. When he made the agreement with Coxe, he was a Federalist member of the House of Representatives.

3. This paragraph contains the first reference in this volume to a partnership between Coxe and John B. Church, in which H served as the latter's representative and attorney in fact. The agreement between Church and Coxe provided that Church would advance ten thousand dollars to Coxe to purchase lands in Pennsylvania for the partnership and that Coxe would repay half of this amount of money with interest to Church.

The correspondence concerning the partnership and H's role in it extends from 1793 to 1797, and many of the most significant letters on this subject were and are located in the Tench Coxe Papers. These papers were not made available to scholars until recently, and they therefore could not be used in the preparation of *The Papers of Alexander Hamilton*, XIV–XVII (February, 1793–December, 1794). The first letter from this collection to be printed in *The Papers of Alexander Hamilton* is Coxe to H, February 13, 1795 (*PAH*, XVIII, 269). This and four other letters from Coxe to H (three written in 1795 and one in 1796) along with several related documents were released to the editors of *The Papers of Alexander Hamilton* in the early nineteen-seventies, but no search of the collection for other letters and documents was permitted at that time. As a result, the letter printed above and several others that follow it appear in this volume rather than in their proper chronological order in earlier volumes.

For a history of the Church-Coxe partnership and H's role in it, see the introductory note to Coxe to H, February 13, 1795 (*PAH*, XVIII, 262–69). For the correspondence concerning this partnership, see

Coxe to H, April 10, 1793	*PAH*, XIV, 304–05
H to Coxe, April 15, 1793	Printed in this volume
H to Coxe, April 19, 1793	Printed in this volume
H to Coxe, May 17, 1793	Printed in this volume
H to Coxe, June 3, 1793	Printed in this volume
Coxe to H, June 5–8, 1793	Printed in this volume
H to Coxe, June 14, 1793	Printed in this volume
Coxe to H, November 16, 1793	Printed in this volume
Coxe to H, November 21, 1793	Printed in this volume
Coxe to H, January 1, 1794	Printed in this volume
H to Coxe, January 12, 1794	Printed in this volume
Coxe to H, January 25, 1794	*PAH*, XV, 661, and reprinted in this volume
Coxe to H, September 25, 1794	Printed in this volume
Coxe to H, February 13, 1795	*PAH*, XVIII, 269
Coxe to H, February 17–18, 1795	*PAH*, XVIII, 272–74
Coxe to H, February 22, 1795	*PAH*, XVIII, 281–82
H to Joseph Anthony, March 11, 1795	*PAH*, XVIII, 290–92
Coxe to H, May 10, 1795	*PAH*, XVIII, 337–40

From Henry Marchant

Newport [Rhode Island] Apl. 13. 1793

Sir,

I was last Evening honored with yours of the 30th ult.[1] whereby I am informed of the Arrangement which has been concerted for the Accommodation of the public Officers &c; inclosing also a blank Power of Atty and Form of Drafts. I enclose with my Power of Attorney my signature on several pieces of Paper as requested. As I have for some time past found myself happily relieved from Expence or trouble by a regular Remittance of my Salary by the kindness of the Cashier[2] thro' the post office—It will still be most agreeable to me that the Cashier of the Bank remit as heretofore the Monies drawn on my Account (for which He *now* has my Power) either in Bank Post Notes payable to me or Order, or Drafts on the Collector of the Revenue in Newport[3] when such Drafts shall be at the disposal of the Bank. I have drawn my Power to the President &c of the Bank to receive, all such Sums of Money as shall become due to me after the last day of March last. As I presume my last Quarters Salary due the last Day of March last may be on the Way, remitted by the Cashier of the Bank by my former arrangment with Him, I presume upon Your Indulgence that the Cashier will have the Knowledge of this Letter, and that any further Communication by me to him, will not be necessary to induce him to remit my Salary as usual upon the Power he has by the first Post after the ten days are elapsed necessary after my Compensation falls due for settling the accounts at the Treasury and placing the money to my Credit at the Bank. If any thing further should be necessary I hope the Cashier of the Bank will give me notice by Post. I feel myself much obliged by the arrangement the Secretary has kindly effected for the public officers—And with sincere Esteem and best Respects,

 I am Sir your much obliged and humble Servt.   H M

The Honbl Alexander Hamilton Esqr.

ADfS, Rhode Island Historical Society, Providence.
 1. "Treasury Department Circular," March 30, 1793 (*PAH*, XIV, 264-65).
 2. John Kean, cashier of the Bank of the United States.
 3. William Ellery.

To Tench Coxe [1]

[Philadelphia, April 15, 1793]

Dr Sir

 I send you 800 Dollars in Bank bills & my note for 1500 to be presented to the Bank. You may either send it yourself or I will as you think best.[2] Yrs.   A H

April 15

ALS, Papers of Tench Coxe in the Coxe Family Papers at the Historical Society of Pennsylvania, Philadelphia.
 1. For an explanation of the contents of this letter, see the introductory note to Coxe to H, February 13, 1795 (*PAH*, XVIII, 262-69). See also the references cited in Coxe to H, April 13, 1793, note 3 (printed in this volume).
 2. At the foot of this letter Coxe wrote: "for a/c of Mr. J. B. Churchs purchase, & loan." Coxe's endorsement reads: "A. Hamilton April 15. 1793 Note of 1500 endorsed by me & retd. to Mr. Hamilton to procure discount.
 "19th. Cash in lieu pd. me 1500 Drs. ℔ A
 "(Letter B) entd. 800 Drs."
 For "A" see H to Coxe, April 19, 1793 (printed in this volume).

To Joseph Whipple

Treasury Department April 15. 1793.

Sir

Your letter of the 5th of February was duly received.[1]

It is my wish that the journals of the Revenue Cutters be regularly transmitted to me.

I am, with consideration,   Sir,   Your Obed Servant   A Hamilton

Joseph Whipple Esq.
Collr Portsmouth, N H.

LS, Stone Autograph Collection, Library of Congress.

1. When *PAH*, XIV, was published, Whipple's letter to H, February 5, 1793, was not printed on the ground that it was a routine Treasury Department letter. In that letter Whipple enclosed his weekly return of money received and wrote: "Cap. Yeaton has forwarded to me agreeably to My directions Monthly Journals of Occurrences on board the Scammel. If it is your desire that these Journals Should be transmitted to the Treasury be pleased to inform me—& whether to you, or to the Comptrollers office."

Hopley Yeaton was captain of the New Hampshire revenue cutter *Scammell*. In "Treasury Department Circular to the Captains of the Revenue Cutters," June 4, 1791 (*PAH*, VIII, 426–33), H had ordered the captains of the revenue cutters to keep a journal and "that a copy of this journal to the end of each month be regularly forwarded to the Treasury."

To Samuel Hodgdon [1]

[Philadelphia, April 17, 1793]

Mr. Hamilton presents his Compliments to Mr. Hodgsdon. He has signed a warrant in favour of the Qr. M. Generals Departt. for 40000 Dollars [2]—to be forwarded to him in Post Notes of the Bank of the UStates. If Mr. Hodgsdon has not received the warrant he will do well to call for it as time presses.

April 17. 1793

AL, The Sol Feinstone Collection, Library of the American Philosophical Society, Philadelphia.

1. Hodgdon, who was quartermaster general of the United States Army from March, 1791, to April, 1792, was Army storekeeper at Philadelphia.

2. This warrant is dated April 16, 1793, and is numbered 2698 (*PAH*, XVII, 519). The money was for supplies for the troops under Major General Anthony Wayne, who was preparing for an expedition against the western Indians. See also Henry Knox to H, November 3, 1792, note 1 (printed in this volume); Knox to Wayne, April 20, 1793 (Richard C. Knopf, ed., *Anthony Wayne, A Name in Arms: Soldier, Diplomat, Defender of Expansion Westward of a Nation: The Wayne-Knox-Pickering-McHenry Correspondence* [Pittsburgh, 1960], 223).

To Tench Coxe [1]

[Philadelphia] Apl. 19. 1793

with 1500 drs. in lieue of the Note for 1500 Drs. in Mr. H.s last letter—I having retd. that Note to him to procure Discot.[2]

(see Letter B) [3]

AD, Papers of Tench Coxe in the Coxe Family Papers at the Historical Society of Pennsylvania, Philadelphia.

1. For an explanation of the contents of this letter, see the introductory note to Coxe to H, February 13, 1795 (*PAH*, XVIII, 262–69). See also the references cited in Coxe to H, April 13, 1793, note 3 (printed in this volume).

2. This document consists of an envelope addressed to Coxe in H's handwriting. Coxe wrote below H's writing: "A. Hamilton Apl. 19. 1793—a cover only, with Check 1500 Ds. A (Entd. 1500 Drs.)." Coxe's document was written on the reverse side of the envelope.

3. For "letter B," see H to Coxe, April 15, 1793 (printed in this volume).

Treasury Department Circular to the Collectors of the Customs

Treasury Department, April 23, 1793

Sir:

You will find enclosed the copy of a proclamation lately issued by the President of the United States, respecting the war at present existing between certain Powers of Europe therein named.[1]

The preservation of the peace of the country is so very important to its interests, and that must depend so materially upon the conformity of the conduct of our citizens to the spirit which is manifested by the proclamation, that it is deemed particularly interesting to receive the earliest and most exact advice of every appearance in any quarter which may seem to contravene the intention of the Government in this respect.

I therefore request that you will keep an observant eye upon whatever passes in your district having reference to the object of the proclamation; and if any thing comes under your notice inconsistent with it, that you will immediately communicate it to the Attorney of the United States for the judicial district comprehending your district, and to me.

The building of vessels calculated and fitted for war is a circumstance which will merit particular attention, as much danger may be apprehended from that quarter.

I am, sir, &c. Alexander Hamilton.

The Collectors of the Customs

ASP, Foreign Relations, III, 339.
1. For George Washington's proclamation of neutrality, dated April 22, 1793, see John Jay to H, April 11, 1793, note 1 (*PAH*, XIV, 307–10). See also H to Washington, May 4, 1793, note 1 (*PAH*, XIV, 412–14).

To Thomas Jefferson [1]

[Philadelphia, May 9–14, 1793]

A   Perhaps the Secretary of State, revising the expression of this member of the sentence, will find terms to express his idea still more clearly and may avoid the use of a word of doubtful propriety "Contraventions"
B   "but be attentive"
C   "mere" to be omitted
D   Considering that this Letter will probably become a matter of publicity to the world is it necessary to be so strong? Would not the following suffice as a substitute?

"but our unwillingness to believe that the French Nation could be wanting in respect or friendship to us upon any occasion suspends our assent to and conclusions upon these statements 'till further evidence." It will be observed that the words "conclusions upon" are proposed to be added to indicate that some further measure is contemplated, conformably to the declaration to Mr. Hamm⟨ond – – –⟩ measures will be taken ⟨– –⟩ may be in lieu of General Knox's amendment.

E   Suppose the words "bay of" were omitted

F   "Expectation" is proposed to be substituted to "*desire*"

G   For the sentence between (   ) It is proposed to substitute this—

"They consider the rigorous exercise of that virtue as the surest mode of preserving perfect harmony between the UStates and the Powers at War"

A Hamilton
Edm Randolph

DS, in the handwriting of H, Thomas Jefferson Papers, Library of Congress.
    1. For background to this document, see the introductory note to H to George Washington, May 15, 1793 (*PAH*, XIV, 451–54).
    This document contains revisions and suggestions made by H and Randolph to the draft of a letter which Jefferson sent on May 15, 1793, to Jean Baptiste de Ternant, the French Minister to the United States. Jefferson's draft has not been found. The letter that was sent to Ternant reads: "Having received several Memorials from the British minister [George Hammond] on subjects arising out of the present war, I take the liberty of enclosing them to you, and shall add an explanation of the determinations of the government thereon. These will serve to indicate the principles on which it is meant to proceed; and which are to be applied with impartiality to the proceedings of both parties. They will form, therefore, as far as they go, a rule of action for them as for us.
    "In one of these memorials, it is stated that arms and military accoutrements are now buying up by a French agent in this Country with an intent to export them to France. We have answered that our citizens have been always free to make, vend and export arms: that it is the constant occupation and livelihood of some of them. To suppress their callings, the only means, perhaps, of their subsistence, because a war exists in foreign and distant countries, in which we have no concern, would scarcely be expected. It would be hard in principle and impossible in practice. The law of nations, therefore, respecting the rights of those at peace, has not required from them such an internal derangement in their occupations. It is satisfied with the external penalty pronounced in the President's proclamation, that of confiscation of such portion of these arms as shall fall into the hands of any of the belligerent powers, on their way to the ports of their enemies. To this penalty our citizens are warned that they will be abandoned; and that the purchase of arms here, may work no inequality between the parties at war, the liberty to make them will be enjoyed equally by both.
    "Another of these memorials complains that [Michel Ange Bernard Mangourit] the Consul of France at Charleston, has condemned as legal prize, a British vessel captured by a French frigate, observing that this judicial act is

not warranted by the usage of nations nor by the stipulations existing between the United States and France. It is true, that it is not so warranted, nor yet by any law of the Land: that, therefore, it is a mere nullity, can be respected in no court, make no part in the title of the vessel, nor give to the purchaser any other security than what he would have had without it, that consequently it ought to give no concern to any person interested in the fate of the vessel. While we have considered this to be the proper answer, as between us and Great Britain, between us and France, it is an act, to which we cannot but be attentive. An assumption of jurisdiction by an officer of a foreign power, in cases which have not been permitted by the nation within whose limits it has been exercised, could not be deemed an act of indifference. We have not full evidence that the case has happened, but on such an hypothesis, while we should be disposed to view it, in this instance, as an error in judgment in the particular officer, we should rely, Sir, that you would interpose efficaciously, to prevent a repetition of the error by him, or any other of the Consuls of your nation.

"Our information is not perfect on the subject matter of another of these memorials, which states that a vessel has been fitted out at Charleston, manned there, and partly too, with Citizens of the United States, received a Commision there to cruize against nations at peace with us, and has taken and sent a British vessel into this port. Without taking all these facts for granted, we have not hesitated to express our highest disapprobation of the conduct of any of our Citizens who may personally engage in committing hostilities at sea against any of the nations, parties to the present war, and to declare that if the case has happened, or that should it happen, we will exert all the measures with which the Laws and Constitution have armed us, to discover such offenders and bring them to condign punishment. and that the like conduct shall be observed, should the like enterprises be attempted against your nation, I am authorized to give you the most unreserved assurances. Our friendship for all the parties at war; our desire to pursue ourselves the path of peace, as the only one leading surely to prosperity, and our wish to preserve the morals of our Citizens from being vitiated by courses of lawless plunder and murder, are a security that our proceedings, in this respect, will be with good faith, fervor, and vigilance. The arming of men and vessels within our territory, and without consent or consultation on our part, to wage war on nations with which we are at peace, are acts, which we will not gratuitously impute to the public authority of France. They are stated indeed with positiveness in one of the Memorials. but our unwillingness to believe that the French nation could be wanting in respect or friendship to us on any occasion, suspends our assent to, and conclusions upon these statements till further evidence. There is still a further point in this memorial, to which no answer has been yet given.

"The capture of the British Ship Grange, by the French frigate l'Embuscade, within the Delaware, has been the subject of a former letter to you. On full and mature consideration, the Government deems the capture to have been unquestionably within it's jurisdiction, and that according to the rules of neutrality and the protection it owes to all persons while within it's limits, it is bound to see that the crew be liberated and the vessel and cargo restored to their former owners. The Attorney General of the United States, has made a statement of the grounds of this determination, a copy of which I have the honor to enclose you. I am, in consequence, charged by the President of the United States to express to you his expectation, and at the same time his confidence that you will be pleased to take immediate and effectual measures for having the ship Grange and her cargo restored to the British owners, and the persons taken on board her, set at liberty.

"I am persuaded, Sir, you will be sensible on mature consideration, that in forming these determinations, the Government of the United States, has listened to nothing but the dictates of immutable Justice: they consider the rigorous exercise of that virtue as the surest means of preserving perfect harmony between the United States and the powers at war." (LS, letterpress copy, Thomas Jefferson Papers, Library of Congress.)

To Tench Coxe [1]

[Philadelphia, May 17, 1793]

Dr. Sir

Above is a Check for five hundred Dollars. Tomorrow I will make an arrangement for 1000 more. I did not receive your Note [2] till this moment Quarter past two.[3]

Yrs.   A H

ALS, Papers of Tench Coxe in the Coxe Family Papers at the Historical Society of Pennsylvania, Philadelphia.
    1. For an explanation of the contents of this letter, see the introductory note to Coxe to H, February 13, 1795 (*PAH*, XVIII, 262–69). See also the references cited in Coxe to H, April 13, 1793, note 3 (printed in this volume).
    2. Letter not found.
    3. Coxe's endorsement reads: "A H supposed to be 17. May 1793
                                            entd. 500 Drs."
    Coxe made a second note on the back of this letter which reads: "with 500 Drs. pd. into Bk 17. May for J. B. Church."
    On May 20, 1793, Coxe wrote a memorandum which reads: "Mr. Hamilton pd. Drs. 1000 this 20th May 1793 in a Check on Bk U S. wch. I pd. into sd. Bank by E. Forman directly" (AD, Papers of Tench Coxe in the Coxe Family Papers at the Pennsylvania Historical Society, Philadelphia). Ezekiel Forman was a clerk in the office of the commissioner of the revenue.

To Jonathan Jackson [1]

[*Philadelphia, May 18, 1793*. "For a Journey from Newburyport to Wiscasset & back performed this month at the request of The honorable A Hamilton Secretary of the Treasury signified by his letter of May 18th. 1793 to J Jackson." [2] *Letter not found.*]

    1. For background to this letter, see H to George Thacher, May 18, 1793 (*PAH*, XIV, 477).
    Jackson, a resident of Newburyport, Massachusetts, had been United States marshal for the District of Massachusetts from 1789 to 1791.

2. DS, RG 217, Miscellaneous Treasury Accounts, 1790–1894, Account No 4479, National Archives.

To John Cochran [1]

[*Philadelphia, May 25, 1793.* Letter listed in dealer's catalogue. *Letter not found.*]

1. ALS, sold by S. G. Hubbard Company, Cincinnati, Ohio, March 15, 1864, Item 239.
Cochran was commissioner of loans for New York.

To Tench Coxe [1]

[Philadelphia, June 3, 1793]

D Sir

I send you a check for 700 Dollars another for 200. To day I am to pay off the note for 1500 which you endorsed for me & I do not know exactly how I stand in Bank. I believe however there will be enough left to pay both checks—tomorrow the proceeds of the enclosed which I request you to endorse & send in for discount will give you the remainder & leave a sum at my disposal for another purpose.[2]

Yrs.

A Hamilton

ALS, Papers of Tench Coxe in the Coxe Family Papers at the Historical Society of Pennsylvania, Philadelphia.
1. For an explanation of the contents of this letter, see the introductory note to Coxe to H, February 13, 1795 (*PAH*, XVIII, 262–69). See also the references cited in Coxe to H, April 13, 1793, note 3 (printed in this volume).
2. At the bottom of this letter Coxe wrote: "recd. from Gitts June 3d. 1793 with two checks of that date sent into Bk of U. S. for a/c of J. B. Church Also Mr. Hs note for 8000 Drs. for discot. endorsed by me."
Michael Gitts was a messenger in the office of commissioner of the revenue.
Coxe endorsed the envelope: "Entd. 900 Drs."

From Tench Coxe [1]

[Philadelphia] June 5th. [–8] 1793

Dr. sir

The following is a Note of all the payments made by you to me in part for the lands purchased by me of Messrs. Pattersons & Stroud, W. Steedman & Ball & Smith for the joint account of John B. Church esqr. & myself being forty three thousand Acres—That is to say

1793

```
Apl.  9 -  500   x x x ⎤  as ℔ my letter of the 10th & the postscript
      11 -  500     x x ⎦        Note thereto of the 11th. April last.[2]
      15 -  800 √ x x x
      19. 1500 √ x x x
May   1... 500 √ x x x
      17 -  500     x x
      20 - 1000     x x
June  3 -  900 √   x x
          ────
          6200
     5th 300   retained out of Note of 800 Drs ⎤
               the rest being repaid            ⎦
          ────
          6500 Dollars
```

This sum of six thousand five hundred dollars, includes all the payments, which have been made to me on the account of Mr. Church, or the purchases of Lands Some of them appear in my former Correspondence with you.

My Check is inclosed for the Sum of 495 47/100 Drs. the overplus of your Note discounted, which makes every thing square so far as the installments are due, and untill August.

I have the honor to be　your most obedt. Servant　　　T. C

Hon. Alexr. Hamilton, Esqr.

June 8. 1793

The Check was deld. in person on the 5th instant.

T. Coxe

ADfS, Papers of Tench Coxe in the Coxe Family Papers at the Historical Society of Pennsylvania, Philadelphia.
  1. For an explanation of the contents of this letter, see the introductory note to Coxe to H, February 13, 1795 (*PAH*, XVIII, 262–69). See also the references cited in Coxe to H, April 13, 1793, note 3 (printed in this volume).
  2. See Coxe to H, April 10, 1793 (*PAH*, XIV, 304–05).

To Tench Coxe

[Philadelphia, June 14, 1793]

Dr. Sir

Inclosed is my Note for 600 Dollars.[1] I will thank to you the needful as to discount.

  Yrs.

A Hamilton

T Coxe Esq

ALS, Papers of Tench Coxe in the Coxe Family Papers at the Pennsylvania Historical Society, Philadelphia.
  1. At the bottom of this letter Coxe wrote: "recd. June 14, 1793 with a Note in blank made of the same date, for 600 Drs.
  "20th. It was Discod. the sum of 300 Drs. lent by me retained & the remdr. returned in my Ch on Bk of U. S."

From Robert Troup

[*New York, June 15, 1793.* On June 20, 1793, Hamilton wrote to Troup:[1] "Your letters of the 15 & 18 of June have been received." *Letter of June 15 not found.*]

  1. Printed in this volume.

From Robert Troup

[*New York, June 18, 1793.* On June 20, 1793, Hamilton wrote to Troup:[1] "Your letters of the 15 & 18 of June have been received." *Letter of June 18 not found.*]

  1. Printed in this volume.

To Robert Troup

[Philadelphia, June 20, 1793]

Dr Robert

Your letters of the 15 & 18 of June have been received.[1]

The ideas you express in the former appear to me just. But I hope to God you have been able to find the means of instituting prosecutions before this, against the Offenders. The ferment you mention to have been excited is an additional reason for it. Tis indispensable in such cases to take a decided and imposing tone.[2]

If there are *unwilling or timid* persons, whom you have reason to believe are acquainted with facts, why not bring them by *process* before the Magistrate to give their testimony? Have you seen the letter from the consul to the Governor? [3] Mention is there made of the person who was to command. Does not Alderman Randall [4] know persons? Let me intreat you—probe the affair with zeal and decision.

Fitsimmons [5] & myself have adjusted what relates to Mr Church. He informs me that instructions will go from the Fishers [6] to Bogert [7] to stop the proceedings. See Bogert if you please for greater caution & know if he has received instructions.

There is an account between Cock [8] & me for Chancery fees. Do me the favour to adjust the matter with him according to the best materials in your power & pay him what appears to be due, for which draw upon me, if you are not otherwise in Cash on my account.

Yr. Affectionate   A Hamilton

June 20 1793

ALS, Mr. Charles Mather, II, Mather & Co., Philadelphia.
    1. Letters not found.
    2. For an explanation of the contents of this paragraph and the following one, see "Cabinet Meeting. Opinion Respecting the Measures to Be Taken Relative to a Sloop Fitted Out as a Privateer," June 12, 1793 (*PAH*, XIV, 534-36); H to Richard Harison, June 13-15, 1793 (*PAH*, XIV, 539-40); Harison to H, June 21, 1793 (*PAH*, XV, 11-12).
    3. Alexandre Blanc de Lanautte, comte d'Hauterive, was the French consul

at New York. For his letter to Governor George Clinton and related papers, see *ASP, Foreign Relations,* I, 152–53.

4. Thomas Randall, an alderman from the South Ward of New York City and a port warden in the city, was superintendent of the lighthouse at Sandy Hook, New Jersey.

5. Thomas FitzSimons was a Federalist member of the House of Representatives from Pennsylvania.

For an explanation of this sentence and the remainder of the paragraph, see H to John Chaloner, June 11, 1793 (*PAH,* XIV, 533).

6. Samuel and Miers Fisher were members of a Philadelphia firm of merchants.

7. Cornelius I. Bogert was a New York City lawyer.

8. William Cock was a New York City lawyer.

To John B. Church [1]

[Philadelphia, July 6, 1793]

to Angelica [2] & yourself.

Adieu My Dear Sir   A Hamilton

P. S. The deed for the land is in your name—and in case you decline you will have to reconvey or to convey *to the son.*

July 6th.

I send you a duplicate of the bill.

J B Church Esqr.

ALS (fragment), Columbia University Libraries.
 1. For an explanation of the contents of the postscript to this letter, see the introductory note to Robert Morris to H, June 7, 1795, notes 3 and 4 (*PAH,* XVIII, 359–60).
 2. Angelica Schuyler Church, H's sister-in-law.

To Benjamin Brown [1]

[*Philadelphia, July 8, 1793.* Letter listed in dealer's catalogue. *Letter not found.*]

1. ALS, sold by Stan V. Henkels, Jr., May 8, 1895, Item 26.

This letter was presumably written either to Benjamin Brown, a soldier in H's battalion during the American Revolution ("A List of officers and Mens Names who have Recd. one months pay in Colo Hamiltons Battln sept 7th 1781") or to Benjamin Brown, a seaman on board the frigate *Trumbull* during the war ("Report on the Petition of Benjamin Brown," November 21, 1792 [*PAH*, XIII, 187–88]).

To John Cochran

Treasury Department, August 13, 1793. "I have directed the Treasurer of the United States, to furnish you with a draught on the Office of Discount & Deposit at New-York, for Seven Thousand Nine Hundred and Eighty five Dollars; for the purpose of enabling you . . . to discharge a half years pension which will become due to the Invalids of the United States on the 5th of the ensuing month." [1]

LS, Cornell University Library.

1. For the payment to Cochran (Warrant No. 3045, August 14, 1793), see *PAH*, XVII, 526.

To John A. Chevallié [1]

[*Treasury Department, August 14, 1793.* ". . . Every thing with regard to Mr. Beaumarchais' accounts is as far advanced as circumstances now permit. . . ." [2] *Letter not found.*]

1. LS, sold by Charles Hamilton Autographs, Inc., April 23, 1970, Item 96.

For information concerning the contents of this letter, see Pierre August Caron de Beaumarchais to H, October 29, 1796 (*PAH*, XX, 355–61).

Chevallié was a partner with Anthony Rainetaux in the New York mercantile firm of Chevallié and Rainetaux.

2. Text taken from dealer's catalogue.

From Tench Coxe [1]

[*Philadelphia, August 27, 1793.* In an undated letter written sometime in 1797 to Oliver Wolcott, Jr., Coxe reviewed his correspondence with Hamilton concerning the execution of the revenue laws in Pennsylvania. In the course of the letter Coxe wrote: "The Amendments proposed in my letters of the 11th. Decr. 1792 [2] & 27th. of August 1793." *Letter of August 27, 1793, not found.*]

1. ADf, Papers of Tench Coxe in the Coxe Family Papers at the Historical Society of Pennsylvania, Philadelphia.
2. *PAH*, XIII, 305–14.

To Jeremiah Wadsworth [1]

Philadelphia Sepr. 3. 1793

My Dear Wadsworth

Shortly after I came into Office I remember your having told me that Glauback (whom you represented as a worthless and ungrateful fellow) was indebted to General Greenes estate, I think for money lent him, and that it was your intention to endeavour to effect a purchase of his public claim; allowing him some part of it for his immediate necessities and letting the residue be an indemnification to General Greenes estate, or in other words go to the benefit of Mrs. Greene observing withal that he would probably part with it to some one else for a song or something to that effect; and I think I understood from you when you left the City that you had left the business in charge with Flint.

The purchase of the claim was afterwards made though at second hand, & it appears in *fact* that Mrs. Greene has had the benefit of it.

Fraunces lately a Clerk in my department prompted partly by resentment & partly I believe by some political enemies—gives out that I assisted in this affair as a *speculation* & to prove it shews the Draft of a Power for assigning the claim with some corrections which are said to be in my hand writing.

Whether this be so or not, I really do not now recollect, but I think it very possible, that having understood the matter in the light I have stated from you and viewing the transaction even with a favourable eye from my regard to Mrs. Greene, that upon the draft of such a power having been shewn to me probably to know whether it would be deemed competent, I may have been induced to make some corrections.

I will therefore thank you to state with precision the course of the transaction as it stands in your recollection particularly what passed between you & myself in the first instance. If not inconvenient to you I should ever be glad that you would attest to it.

Yrs. Affecty   A Hamilton

Jeremiah Wadsworth Esq

ALS, The Sol Feinstone Collection, Library of the American Philosophical Society, Philadelphia.
1. An incomplete version of this letter is printed in *PAH*, XV, 321.
For background to this letter, see Andrew G. Fraunces to H, May 16, 1793, note 9 (*PAH*, XIV, 462); William Willcocks to H, August 25, September 1, 1793 (*PAH*, XV, 277, 317); H to Catharine Greene, September 3, 1793 (*PAH*, XV, 318–20).

From Abraham Yates, Junior

Albany Sept. 26. 1793
in Common Council

Sir

Your Letter of this days date [1] has been recd—& laid before the Com. Council who have given me in charge to acquaint you that the same will be taken into consideration by them Tomorrow.

I am Sir   with due respect   your most obedt. servt

Abm. Yates Junr. Mayor

ADfS, The Sol Feinstone Collection, Library of the American Philosophical Society, Philadelphia.
1. *PAH*, XV, 343–48.

From George Washington

[*Mount Vernon, October 23, 1793. Letter not found.*]

"List of Letters from G—— Washington to General Hamilton," Columbia University Libraries.

From Tench Coxe [1]

Philada. Novemr. 16. 1793

Sir

Mr. William Steedman of Northumberland County from whom I made the purchase of eight thousand Acs. mentioned in my letter to you of the 10th of April last,[2] has informed me verbally that he has completed the Surveys of about five sixth parts of the whole quantity out of which the part purchased for John B. Church Esqr and myself is to be drawn by lot: he added that he was going on to complete the remainder. As this was some weeks ago I have not the least doubt that the whole quantity out of which our purchase of 8000 acres is to be taken, are surveyed.

My brother John D. Coxe who lately returned from Northampton County informed me, that he saw (at a Tavern near to the lands bought of Pattersons & Stroud) Mr. Joseph Burr [3] whom I employed to inspect the 23000 As. which I bought of those Gentlemen agreeably to my said letter of 10th. April for Mr. Church & myself. Mr. Burr told my brother that all the surveys were completed, & wished to know where I was that he might make his report.

I have written to the sellers under the two contracts above mentioned to attend in Philada. for the division of the parts of the lands bought of them respectively.

Of the Execution of Ball & Smith's Contract, which after deducting the reserved 4000 Acres remains for Mr. Church & myself to the Amount of twelve thousand Acres, I have no advice: but have written urgently to them.[4]

I am sir with great respect   yr. most obedient Servant   T. C.

Alexr. Hamilton, Esqr
Atty. of John Barker Church, Esqr.

ADfS, Papers of Tench Coxe in the Coxe Family Papers at the Historical Society of Pennsylvania, Philadelphia.

1. For an explanation of the contents of this letter, see the introductory note to Coxe to H, February 13, 1795 (*PAH*, XVIII, 262–69). See also the references cited in Coxe to H, April 13, 1793, note 3 (printed in this volume).

2. For this letter, see *PAH*, XIV, 304–05.

3. Burr had been recommended to Coxe by Isaac Jones on June 20, 1793 (ALS, Papers of Tench Coxe in the Coxe Family Papers at the Historical Society of Pennsylvania, Philadelphia). On August 10, 1793, Burr wrote to John Phillips that "the Surveying of Mr. Coxe's Lands had not yet Commenc'd." In the same letter, which was sent from Lower Smithfield, [Pennsylvania,] Burr stated that at present he was "obliged to attend the surveying Of Lands for Gentlemen in Philadelphia" (ALS, Papers of Tench Coxe in the Coxe Family Papers at the Historical Society of Pennsylvania, Philadelphia). In a document entitled "Part of Materials of accot. rendd. June 18. 1797 to J. B. Church," Coxe made the following entry on the debit side under the date of June 25, 1795: "To ½ charge of Inspecting lands of Patterson by Jos. Burr 43 96/100 Drs (16.6.1½)" (AD, Papers of Tench Coxe in the Coxe Family Papers at the Historical Society of Pennsylvania, Philadelphia).

4. Coxe to Blackall William Ball and Francis Joseph Smith, November 7, 1793 (copy, Papers of Tench Coxe in the Coxe Family Papers at the Historical Society of Pennsylvania, Philadelphia). On November 16, 1793, Ball replied to this letter and stated: ". . . there are between twenty three and twenty four thousand acres already surveyed, & that the remainder will be compleated in this & the next month" (ALS, Papers of Tench Coxe in the Coxe Family Papers at the Historical Society of Pennsylvania, Philadelphia).

To William Ellery [1]

[*Philadelphia, November 20, 1793*. Letter listed in dealer's catalogue. *Letter not found.*]

1. ALS, sold by Dodd & Livingston, New York City, April, 1912, Catalogue 7.

From Tench Coxe [1]

[Philadelphia, November 21, 1793]

Mr T. Coxe has the Honor to request of Mr Hamilton as early an Arrangement as may be convenient for the payment to Mr C. of the remaining sum (3500 Drs) for account of John B. Church Esqr. & Mr C.s. joint purchase of Steedman, Patterson & Co. & Ball & Co.[2]

Novr. 21. 1793

Copy, Papers of Tench Coxe in the Coxe Family Papers at the Historical Society of Pennsylvania, Philadelphia.

1. For an explanation of the contents of this letter, see the introductory note

to Coxe to H, February 13, 1795 (*PAH*, XVIII, 262–69). See also the references cited in Coxe to H, April 13, 1793, note 3 (printed in this volume).

2. Coxe endorsed this copy: "Tench Coxe's demands of Money due Sept. 1 1793 of A. Hamilton Esqr. Atty of J. B. Church Esqr. Novr. 21st. 1793—on accot. purchases of Lands."

From Walter Livingston

New York Nov 30 93

Dr. Sir

Mrs. Livingston [1] has requested me to send to your care the enclosed letter for her Son,[2] and will thank you for forwarding it to him agreeably to your polite offer.

Alexr Hamilton Philadelphia

LC, New-York Historical Society, New York City.

1. Cornelia Schuyler Livingston was the daughter of Peter Schuyler, Jr., of Albany and his wife, Gertrude Schuyler. Cornelia married Walter Livingston in 1767.

2. Henry W. Livingston, Walter Livingston's oldest son, had been a clerk in H's law office. See "Certificate of Clerkship for Henry W. Livingston," April 29, 1790 (printed in this volume).

To Hodijah Baylies [1]

[*Treasury Department, December 5, 1793.* "I have to request that you will retain in your hands a sufficient sum of the monies arising from the duties on imports . . . for the purpose of discharging the allowances to fishing vessels which will become due in your district . . . and which are to be paid agreeably to the instructions heretofore given for that purpose.[2] If the funds accruing in your office should fall short of the amount required you will pay the deficiency by draft, according to the enclosed form, on Benjamin Lincoln . . . Collector of Boston; in which case it will be necessary that you transmit your signature to be said collector, and furnish him with weekly statements accurately describing therein the drafts issued. Copies of these statements are also to be regularly forwarded to this office."[3] *Letter not found.*]

1. LS, sold by Kenneth W. Rendell, Inc., Catalogue No. 54, Item 26.
Baylies was collector of customs at Dighton, Massachusetts.
For background to this letter, see H to Benjamin Lincoln, December 5, 1793
(*PAH*, XV, 443–44).
2. See "Treasury Department Circular to the Collectors of the Customs,"
October 25, 1792 (*PAH*, XII, 620–21).
3. Text taken from the dealer's catalogue.

From Tench Coxe [1]

[*Philadelphia, December 13, 1793.* In an undated letter written
sometime in 1797 to Oliver Wolcott, Jr., Coxe reviewed his correspondence with Hamilton concerning the execution of the revenue
laws in Pennsylvania. In the course of this letter Coxe wrote: "In my
letter of the 13 Decr. 1793, I suggest numerous amendments of the
Revenue laws for consideration, plainly or expressly to the end of a
complete execution of the Revenue laws in Pennsa." *Letter not
found.*]

1. ADf, Papers of Tench Coxe in the Coxe Family Papers at the Historical
Society of Pennsylvania, Philadelphia.

From Tench Coxe [1]

[*Philadelphia, December 17, 1793.* In an undated letter written
sometime in 1797 to Oliver Wolcott, Jr., Coxe reviewed his correspondence with Hamilton concerning the execution of the revenue
laws in Pennsylvania. In the course of this letter Coxe wrote: "On
the 17th. Decr. 1793, the letter from this office with those it enclosed,
represented the condition of the service in Pannsa. to be very uncomfortable as to embarrass ⟨–⟩, accounts, and revenue." *Letter not
found.*]

1. ADf, Papers of Tench Coxe in the Coxe Family Papers at the Historical
Society of Pennsylvania, Philadelphia.

From Tench Coxe [1]

[Philadelphia, December 18, 1793]

Sir

Agreeably to you[r] desire I have the honor to report to you in writing the substance of the conversations between Mr. Andrew G. Fraunces and myself, upon the occasion of his applying, through me, to the proper officers of this Department for the payment of certain warrants issued by the late Commissioners of the Treasury.

About the End of July or the beginning of August last I was met in one of the streets of Philadelphia, by Mr. Fraunces, formerly a Clerk in your office, who, after a few words of common salutation, observed that he had been very hardly treated by the officers of the Treasury in regard to the non-payment of some of the warrants of the old board, for which, he observed, an appropriation of money had been made by the present general Government. On asking him to state freely any part of his complaint that might apply to me, he said he did not consider the matter as at all relative to me. I observed to him that I was certain he must be of that opinion as he knew from his own experience in the Department, the particular officers who could have any cognizance of claims against the United States or any agency in causing them to be discharged. He replied, that he knew the regular course of Business, that he was not inclined to present his

ADf, Papers of Tench Coxe in the Coxe Family Papers at the Historical Society of Pennsylvania, Philadelphia.

1. This letter concerns a bitter dispute between Andrew G. Fraunces and H. For an account of this dispute and the roles played in it by the various people mentioned in this letter (except for John Dennis), see the introductory note to Fraunces to H, May 16, 1793 (*PAH*, XIV, 460–71). See also Fraunces to H, June 10, July 1, August 2, 1793 (*PAH*, XIV, 528–30; XV, 45, 164–65, 177); H to Fraunces, May 18, July 2, August 2, two letters of August 3, October 1, 1793 (*PAH*, XIV, 476; XV, 52–53, 165, 171, 171–72, 354–55); George Washington to H, August 3, December 11, 1793 (*PAH*, XV, 175–76, 455–56); H to Washington, August 9, 1793 (*PAH*, XV, 213–22); H to John M. Taylor, August 6, 1793 (*PAH*, XV, 196–97); Oliver Wolcott, Jr., to H, August 7, 1793 (*PAH*, XV, 197–203); William Willcocks to H, August 25, September 5, 1793 (*PAH*, XV, 277, 323–24); Robert Affleck to H, September 7, 1793 (*PAH*, XV, 326–27); H to Frederick A. C. Muhlenberg, December 16, 1793 (*PAH*, XV, 460–67); H to Jeremiah Wadsworth, September 3, 1793 (printed in this volume).

demand formally to the accounting officers as he understood it would probably be suspended under the late law,[2] that he wished for payment in the manner which, as he observed, had been pursued in many other cases of the same kind by you, with whom he expressed himself much dissatisfied. He complained of the difference, which he said was made between him & others who had held the same kind of public paper, he observed that he did not think you would finally venture to refuse payment to him and he added that he laid the matter before the President. On his proceeding to exhibit to me some of his papers, and on his mentioning his intention to publish them all I advised him not to be hasty & I requested him to call at my office the next morning (it being then near sunset) observing to him that I would do any thing in my power in the mean time to procure him either payment or satisfactory reasons for a refusal.

I mentioned to him a similar application through me, by Mr. Dennis,[3] of Brunswick, while I was Assistant Secretary of the Treasury, which had been suspended in like manner by you, tho I could not say, from my change of station, whether that Warrant had been since paid. I also mentioned to him that I understood that the want of a settlement of some of the latest pecuniary transactions of the old Government was the cause of the Suspension in Mr. Dennis's case—& that this state of things might yet exist. I dissuaded him from a publication, as a measure that could not relieve his necessities, noting it would tend to encrease public discord, and I represented to him that it would be manifestly & highly improper at a time when he had an Application pending before the President. In a subsequent Conversation upon the occasion of his calling at my Office, I asked him what he meant by the Observation that you would not finally refuse to pay the Warrant, and whether he had any intention to convey the Idea of your purchasing public securities. He said that he had not meant that, but that you would not venture to make such great differences in your treatment of him and others, as would be the case in this and another instance, adding that he had documents in a regard to a matter very important to you. He observed, with

2. "An Act relative to the claims against the United States, not barred by any act of limitation, and which have not already been adjusted" (1 *Stat.* 301–02 [February 12, 1793]).
3. John Dennis was a resident of New Brunswick, New Jersey, and a veteran of the American Revolution.

emotion, that he was in the greatest Need of the money, that altho some part of his family was dangerously ill, yet he could not return to New York for want of Cash, that his Bank credit was at stake there, that he must be forced to sell his claim at a loss, and that he could sell it or get money on it, which he feared he should be obliged to do tho it distressed him much as the person who would buy it or lend the money was an Enemy of yours in relation to the Subject of public Enquiry into your official Conduct, but that he did not incline to say whether he was in private or public life, tho he was not an inconsiderable man.

He observed that you had cooperated in the purchase of a claim of the Baron Glaubeck upon the U. S. for Mrs. (General) Green, that he had effected the purchase of the assignee of the Baron (a Mr. Bezen [4] I think) under Mr. Duer's [5] direction and yours, that in proof of your knowledge of the transaction you had corrected the power of Attorney, which was to be used in the case, and that the rough draught of that power, written by himself, with alterations in your handwriting, was in his possession, that the purchase was made at a great discount, that an appropriation to pay the full sum was made soon after by Congress, that the seller Mr. Bezen was so much offended with him, as to make a representation to you against him (Mr. Fraunces) on the subject, that Mr Duer had communicated the circumstance of this representation to him & told him that Mr Bezen was then in your Office on the business, that you had sent for him (Mr. Fraunces) that he must go in to you & Mr. Bezen, that he must not mind any warmth or reprehension that you or Mr. Bezen should express towards him on the subject, but that he must make apologies as for himself only & must not say a word of his & your part in the business, that he must endeavour to satisfy Mr Bezen, that it was probable you would even threaten to turn him out of your office—and that he must make submissions to appear to satisfy you, that he accordingly went in, that he received many expressions of Anger and reprehension from you before Mr Bezen, that he bore it all, and made the best apologies he could, that Mr Bezen went away much dissatisfied with him, that he had since spoken to him sharply about the matter & would sue you, if he was acquainted with all the Cir-

4. Thomas Bazen (not Bezen).
5. William Duer.

cumstances which had taken place. He observed that he did not believe you or Mr. Duer had any interest or benefit from the purchase, that he was satisfied it was effected to serve Mrs. Greene, but that you had done all you could to serve her, & he said there was a difference in your conduct to him which hurt his feelings. Mr. Fraunces went away with an Assurance from me that I would immediately attend to the Business. It appearing no less proper to converse on the subject with the accounting officers of the Department than with yourself, I therefore applied immediately to the Comptroller [6] & Auditor,[7] as well as to you. I found these two officers of Opinion, that the claim could only be treated by them according to the directions of the act of the 12th of Febry 1793, and I was instructed by you to inform Mr. Fraunces that the Warrants would not be discharged at that time for the reasons you had previously given to him, drawn from the situation of the latters pecuniary transactions under the authority of the late Board. When Mr. Fraunces called upon me for your answer, I communicated to him the above information. Some conversation ensued which was principally a reiteration of several of the matters already stated in this letter. Mr. Fraunces appearing dissatisfied I finally observed to him that I could not interpose further, that he knew that some of the pecuniary transactions in pursuance of the directions or authorities of the late Board were not settled, he having been one of the Clerks of that Board, that from a desire to promote harmony in the public affairs and a disposition to do any thing in reason which might relieve him I had made Applications not strictly in the line of my duty, and had faithfully represented the substance of his complaints and arguments to all the officers, who according to the constitution of the Department could afford him that relief and particularly to yourself.

It is proper that I should remind you that Mr. Fraunces on my mentioning the extent of my representations in this last conversation, observed to me that he had not particularly wished the various matters & circumstances he had mentioned to be communicated to any other person, tho I had been at liberty to do it if I chose or thought fit. On this I observed, that I had of course viewed every thing he had said as intended by him to be of the nature of Argu-

6. Oliver Wolcott, Jr.
7. Richard Harrison.

ments & considerations, for the officers of the Treasury. I had stated
to each such parts of the conversation as appeared to have a relation
to the office or conduct of each and to you nearly the whole. This,
I continued, was proper and my duty, whether I was considered as
acting in a public capacity only, or as acting at the same time as a
person disposed to render him any lawful & reasonable service in my
power.

Mr. Fraunces went away complaining of the embarrassments of his
situation, and regretting the sacrifice he must make & the steps he
should be obliged to take.

I have the Honor to be, with great respect, Sir, your most
obedient Servant   T. C.

The Secretary of the Treasury

From George Clymer [1]

[December 19, 1793. "Mr John Witman Collector of the revenue
for the County of Bucks informs me that his inspector Mr Collins [2]
being about to resign he intends to offer himself to suppy the vacancy. . . . I cannot refuse at Mr Witman's instance to note what
appear to me his grounds of pretension. . . . He is considered as
respectable in his Character and circumstances, and is doubtless the
best collector in the district. . . . Mr Witman is extremely popular
among the Germans whose language he speaks and who form such
a vast proportion of the inhabitants of the Survey."

LC, Papers of Tench Coxe in the Coxe Family Papers, Historical Society of
Pennsylvania, Philadelphia.
    1. Clymer was supervisor of the revenue for the District of Pennsylvania.
    2. James Collins was inspector of the revenue for Survey No. 2 in the Dis-
trict of Pennsylvania.

From Tench Coxe [1]

[Philadelphia, December 20, 1793. In an undated letter written
sometime in 1797 to Oliver Wolcott, Jr., Coxe reviewed his cor-

respondence with Hamilton concerning the execution of the revenue laws in Pennsylvania. In the course of this letter Coxe wrote: "The Letter of the 20th. December 1793, gives similar information, urges particular attention to the bad state of things in Pennsa. and presses an early movement on the part of the Secy." *Letter not found.*]

1. ADf, Papers of Tench Coxe in the Coxe Family Papers at the Historical Society of Pennsylvania, Philadelphia.

To Daniel Brent [1]

[*Philadelphia, December 26, 1793.* On July 16, 1798, Brent wrote to Hamilton [2] and referred to "a letter which I had the Honor of receiving from you, dated the 26th of December 1793." *Letter not found.*]

1. Brent was a clerk in the office of the Secretary of the Treasury until January 5, 1794. See Brent to H, December 27, 1793; January 27, 1794 (*PAH*, XV, 592, 663).
2. *PAH*, XXII, 22.

To Jabez Bowen

[*Treasury Department, 1793.* The description of this letter reads: "Discharging the interest on certain stocks." [1] *Letter not found.*]

Luther S. Livingston, ed., *American Book-Prices Current* (New York, 1906), 717.
1. See "Report on an Account of the Receipts and Expenditures of the United States for the Year 1793," December 26, 1793 (*PAH*, XVII, 530).

1794

From Tench Coxe [1]

Mr. Coxe has the honor to inform Mr. Hamilton that an offer was made to him last Night of one dollar ℔ Acre for two parcels one on Snow Valley run a water of Mahantango—& the other in Nescopeack—in all about 8500 As. belong to Church & Coxe—of the land purchased for Mr. Church & himself (Mr. C.) last Spring. *The payment will be prompt.* Mr. Coxe intends to accept the offer for his part, and wishes to be informed by *three OClock*, if it will be agreeable to Mr. Hamilton that the part belonging to Mr. Church should also be sold.

Mr. Coxe finds that he has not a copy of the Corn Law of G Britain,[2] but he thinks Mr. Vaughan[3] or Mr. Bond[4] could lend it to Mr. Hamilton.

Jany 1. 1794

AL, Papers of Tench Coxe in the Coxe Family Papers at the Historical Society of Pennsylvania, Philadelphia.

1. For an explanation of the contents of the first paragraph of this letter, see the introductory note to Coxe to H, February 13, 1795 (*PAH*, XVIII, 262–69). See also the references cited in Coxe to H, April 13, 1793, note 3 (printed in this volume).

2. H may have wanted a copy of the "Corn Law" for his "View of the Commercial Regulations of France and Great Britain in Reference to the United States," which is dated 1792–1793 in *PAH*, XIII, 395, but which may have been written in 1794.

There were, of course, numerous "Corn Laws," but this is presumably a reference to "An Act for regulating the Importation and Exportation of Corn, and the Payment of the Duty on Foreign Corn Imported, and of the Bounty of *British* Corn exported" (31 Geo. III, C. 30 [1791]). See also "An Act for indemnifying all Persons who have been concerned in advising and carrying into Execution an Order of Council respecting the Exportation of Wheat and Wheat Flour, for preventing Suits in consequence of the same, and for making further Provisions relative thereto; and also for authorizing his Majesty to prohibit the Exportation of Corn, Meal, Flour, Bread, Biscuit, and Potatoes; and to permit the Importation of Corn, Meal, or Flour, on Low Duties" (33 Geo. III, C. 3 [1793]).

3. This may be a reference to John Vaughan, a Philadelphia wine merchant and importer.
4. Phineas Bond was the British consul at Philadelphia.

To Tench Coxe

[Philadelphia, January 12, 1794]

Dr Sir

My whole supply of Cash having been exhausted in the advance on account of Mr. Church—if you can spare it for some days I will thank you for 300 dollars of the proceeds of the Note by way of loan till I can make some further arrangements.[1]

Yrs
A Hamilton

Jany. 12

Are not some of the British West Indies open to our vessels at this time? Which of them [2]

Tench Coxe Esqr

ALS, Papers of Tench Coxe in the Coxe Family Papers at the Historical Society of Pennsylvania, Philadelphia.
1. For an explanation of the contents of this paragraph, see the introductory note to Coxe to H, February 13, 1795 (*PAH*, XVIII, 262–69). See also the references cited in Coxe to H, April 13, 1793, note 3 (printed in this volume).
Coxe endorsed this letter: "Jany. 12th. 1794 should be 11th.—A. Hamilton—lent Mr. Hamilton 300 Drs. Jany. 11th. I recd. of him a note for 1850 Drs. wch (deducting the above 300 Drs. from the proceeds of the last Note of 600 Drs) is about the balance."
2. See the introductory note to "View of the Commercial Regulations of France and Great Britain in Reference to the United States," 1792–1793 (*PAH*, XIII, 395–401); H to Coxe, January 1, 1794 (*PAH*, XV, 603–04); H to Coxe, January 1, 1794, note 2 (printed in this volume).

To William Ellery [1]

[*Philadelphia, January 23, 1794.* "The Collector of New York informed me . . . that the papers concerning the Brigantine Enterprize requested by you had been forwarded by the district attorney of New York, I doubt not these documents are now in your possession." [2] *Letter not found.*]

1. LS, sold by Kenneth W. Rendell, Kingston Galleries, Inc., Somerville, Massachusetts, 1969, Catalogue 42, Item 67.

For information on the contents of this letter, see Ellery to H, August 26, December 2, 30, 1793 (*PAH*, XV, 277–78, 434–35, 597). Ellery answered this letter on February 10, 1794 (*PAH*, XV, 22–23).

In *PAH*, XV, 658, this letter is listed as a "letter not found," but without a summary of its contents.

2. Text taken from dealer's catalogue.

From Tench Coxe [1]

[Philadelphia, January 25, 1794]

Mr. Coxe has the honor to inclose to Mr. Hamilton a general account of the payments, in Notes & money, of the sum of ten thousand dollars, except a balance of 206 40/100 Drs. for which Mr. Coxe will thank Mr. H. if he can send it to day.[2] Mr. Coxe will at the same time deliver Mr. Hamiltons Note for 300 Drs. of the 11th Jany. last [3] and sign a minute upon the within paper declaring the whole to have been paid. If Mr. Meyer [4] could make a calculation ascertaining the day between Apl. 9 & Jany.   th [5] on which the interest should run upon the whole sum an Obligation in form will be given in exchange for all the other papers.

Jany. 25th. 1794

[E N C L O S U R E] [6]

Account of Cash paid & arising from Notes of hand to come to the credit of John Barker Church Esquire (thro the hands of Alexander Hamltion Esqr.) one half to be credited to account for three parcels of Lands purchased by Tench Coxe for the joint & equal account of sd. Church & said Coxe—AD. 1793

1793	By a Payment of
Apl. 9	500 Dollars one half to be a loan to sd. Coxe on lawful interest payable in three years & one half to be invested in a moiety of said Lands.

11	500 Do	½ do and ½ do
15	800 Do	½ do and ½ do
19	1500 Do	½ do and ½ do
May 1	500 Do	½ do and ½ do
17	500 Do	½ do and ½ do
20	1000 Do	½ do and ½ do
June 3	900 Do	½ do and ½ do

6200 Drs. agreeably to Note of Payments furnished before

Decr 23	600 Do	½ do and ½ do

1794
Jany 8	850 Do	½ do and ½ do
10	293 60/100 Drs*	½ do and ½ do
14	1850 Do	½ do and ½ do

9793 60/100

25th Ball.   260 40/100   remainder to be divided like the foregoing, when rec. into a loan, as to one half & into the investments made in the lands for the other half.

Drs. 10,000 Dollars,   which having been invested in the Lands, one half is the property of Mr. Church, & one half mine, and I am to give my Bond for 5000 Dollars. This completes the arrangement of the Transaction.

* This payment was made in a *Note* for 600 Dollars, discounted & leaving Drs. 593 60/100 of wch. the Rect. was acknowledged, & out of which 300 Drs. were afterwards returned. Wherefore only 293 60/100 Drss are credited in this paper.

Mr. Hamilton pd. the above 206 40/100 Drs this 25th. Jany 1794—and I gave him up the note for 300 Drs. refered in the last Note *, on the transaction of the 10th. & 11th. of Jany. last, which concludes all my demands upon him for the 10000 Drs. invested for our joint Account in Lands & for his own Due to me.

Note Feb. 22d. 1795. I pd. 17000 Acs. C & C's lands for Jackson Steedman & Co with Ruston in June 1793—who advd. 200 Drs. to Ball & Smith in Apl. or May 1792.

AL, Montague Collection, MS Division, New York Public Library.

1. This letter is printed in *PAH*, XV, 661, and is reprinted here because the enclosure has recently been found in the Papers of Tench Coxe in the Coxe Family Papers at the Historical Society of Pennsylvania, Philadelphia.

For an explanation of the contents of this letter, see the introductory note to Coxe to H, February 13, 1795 (*PAH*, XVIII, 262–69). See also the references cited in Coxe to H, April 13, 1793, note 3 (printed in this volume).

2. At the bottom of this letter H wrote: "paid the above mentioned balance this day   AH."
3. See H to Coxe, January 12, 1794 (printed in this volume).
4. John Meyer was a clerk in the Treasury Department.
5. Space left blank in MS.
6. AD, Papers of Tench Coxe in the Coxe Family Papers at the Historical Society of Pennsylvania, Philadelphia.

From Tench Coxe [1]

[*Philadelphia, February 18, 1974*. In an undated letter written sometime in 1797 to Oliver Wolcott, Jr., Coxe reviewed his correspondence with Hamilton concerning the execution of the revenue laws in Pennsylvania. In the course of the letter Coxe wrote: "My letter of the 18th. of Feb. 1794 adds thirteen objects of Amendment to those suggested in Decr. 1792 [2] & Augt. 1793.[3] the 2d 7th. & 13th of which were particularly necessary for Pennsa." *Letter not found.*]

1. ADf, Papers of Tench Coxe in the Coxe Family Papers at the Historical Society of Pennsylvania, Philadelphia.
2. Coxe to H, December 11, 1792 (*PAH*, XIII, 305–14).
3. This letter, which has not been found, is dated August 27, 1793.

To George Washington

[*Philadelphia, April 9, 1794. Letter not found.*]

"List of Letters from General Hamilton to General Washington," Columbia University Libraries.

To Stephen Moylan [1]

[*Philadelphia, April 19, 1794*. The dealer's catalogue description reads: "Requests further particulars regarding the clerks discharged from his office. '. . . whether the services performed were in 1793 or 1794. . . .' " [2] *Letter not found.*]

1. AL, Carnegie Book Shop, New York City, Catalogue 335, Item 204. Moylan was commissioner of loans for Pennsylvania.
2. See Moylan to H, April 14, 19, 1794 (*PAH*, XVI, 257, 298–99).

From Tench Coxe [1]

[*Philadelphia, April 21, 1794.* In an undated letter written some-time in 1797 to Oliver Wolcott, Jr., Coxe reviewed his correspon-dence with Hamilton concerning the execution of the revenue laws in Pennsylvania. In the course of the letter Coxe wrote: "My letter of the 21st. of April 1794 contains explicit notices of the difficulties that attended the service in Pennsa." *Letter not found.*]

1. ADf, Papers of Tench Coxe in the Coxe Family Papers at the Historical Society of Pennsylvania, Philadelphia.

From Tench Coxe [1]

[*Philadelphia, April 26, 1794.* In an undated letter written some-time in 1797 to Oliver Wolcott, Jr., Coxe reviewed his correspon-dence with Hamilton concerning the execution of the revenue laws in Pennsylvania. In the course of the letter Coxe wrote: "My letter of the 26th. of April 1794 contains a full recapitulation and disquisi-tion of certain documents, and proofs concerning the interruptions of the service, which had been brought to the treasury in the several months immediately preceeding its date." *Letter not found.*]

1. ADf, Papers of Tench Coxe in the Coxe Family Papers at the Historical Society of Pennsylvania, Philadelphia.

To George Washington

[*Philadelphia, April 27, 1794. Letter not found.*]

"List of Letters from General Hamilton to General Washington," Columbia University Libraries.

To George Washington

[*Philadelphia, May 21, 1794. Letter not found.*]

"List of Letters from General Hamilton to General Washington," Columbia University Libraries.

To John Clark, Junior [1]

Philadelphia June 17 1794

Dear Sir

It was quite impossible for me to have reported upon your Petition at the last session without giving just dissatisfaction to many others nor whatever may have been my Report, could it have been of any use to you from the extreme pressure of business in the House.[2] You may rely (my health being preserved) on a report at the beginning of the next session.

With esteem & regard I am Dr Sir Your obed ser A Hamilton

John Clark Esq

ALS, RG 46, Records of the United States Senate; Petitions and Memorials, Resolutions of State Legislatures, and Related Documents, Claims (15A-G1), National Archives.

1. During the American Revolution, Clark, a resident of York, Pennsylvania, was successively a lieutenant in the First Continental Infantry, a major in the Second Battalion of the Pennsylvania Flying Camp, and aide-de-camp to Major General Nathanael Greene. From February, 1778, to November, 1779, he was auditor of accounts for the Army under Washington's command.

2. On February 4, 1794, "A petition of John Clark, of the State of Pennsylvania, was presented to the House and read, praying the liquidation and settlement of a claim for services, as Auditor of Accounts to the Army of the United States, during the late war.

"*Ordered,* That the said petition be referred to the Secretary of the Treasury, with instruction to examine the same, and report his opinion, thereupon to the House." (*Journal of the House,* II, 54.)

On January 5, 1795, H returned the petition to the House, where it was referred on January 7 to the Committee of Claims. On March 2, 1795, the Committee of Claims "made a report; which was read, and ordered to lie on the table" (*Journal of the House,* II, 286, 353).

Documents, including accounts and letters from prominent Americans supporting Clark's claim, may be found in RG 46, Records of the United States Senate; Petitions and Memorials, Resolutions of State Legislatures, and Related Documents, Claims (15A-G1), National Archives. In this material is the copy of a petition which Clark sent to Congress on December 23, 1818, when he was sixty-eight. In this petition he based his claim on a wound which he had received in the war and on funds still owed to him as auditor. "An Act for the relief of John Clark," which became law on February 20, 1819, authorized that Clark be issued a "land warrant for the quantity of eight hundred and fifty acres of land" (6 *Stat.* 224).

To Tench Coxe

[Philadelphia, June 19, 1794]

There was a Mr. *Newton* who appeared as President or Secretary of the Democratic Society at Norfolk. Who is he? Had he any connection with the Gentleman of that name lately an Inspector? [1] I will thank you to make inquiry & let me know.

AL, Papers of Tench Coxe in the Coxe Family Papers at the Historical Society of Pennsylvania, Philadelphia.

1. Thomas Newton, Jr., was inspector of the revenue for Survey No. 4 in Virginia from March 8, 1792, until his resignation in November, 1792 (*Executive Journal*, I, 102, 111, 125, 136). His father, a merchant, was president of the Norfolk, Virginia, Republican (or Democratic) Society. See Eugene P. Link, *Democratic-Republican Societies, 1790–1800* (New York, 1942: Reprinted, 1965), 75, 99. For Thomas Newton, Jr.'s, part in forming the Norfolk society, see Link, *Democratic-Republican Societies,* 10.

To John Nicholson [1]

[*Philadelphia, August 25, 1794.* The description of this letter in the dealer's catalogue reads: "Regarding damage done to his house by heavy rains and the need to repair the trouble." *Letter not found.*]

The Collector: A Magazine for Autograph and Historical Collectors, LVI, No. 2 (December, 1942), 28, Item 4866.

1. Nicholson, a native of Wales and a resident of Philadelphia, was the most important fiscal officer in Pennsylvania from 1782 to 1794. In 1782 the legislature appointed him comptroller general of the state. While holding this office he was also appointed receiver general of taxes in 1785 and escheator general in 1787. Although he was impeached in 1794, the state Senate acquitted him on April 11, 1794, and on the same day he resigned as comptroller.

From George Washington

[*Philadelphia, September 5, 1794. Letter not found.*]

"List of Letters from G—— Washington to General Hamilton," Columbia University Libraries.

To Nicholas Low [1]

[*Philadelphia, September 6, 1794.* Introduces Ernst Frederich von Walterstorff. *Letter not found.*]

1. LS, sold by Thomas F. Madigan, New York City, 1935, Item 161.
This letter is exactly the same as H to John Langdon, September 6, 1794 (*PAH*, XVII, 200).

To Samuel Hodgdon

[*Philadelphia, September 11, 1794.* The description of this letter in the dealer's catalogue reads: "Request for arms and accoutrements, tents and other supplies to be held in readiness for the Jersey Militia 'upon the returns of the Commanding Officers of Corps. . . .'" [1] *Letter not found.*]

The Collector: A Magazine for Autograph and Historical Collectors, LX, No. 3 (March, 1947), 59, Item A380.
1. See H to Hodgdon, September 11, 1794 (*PAH*, XVII, 215–16).

To Thomas Willing [1]

[*Philadelphia, September 11, 1794.* Letter listed in dealer's catalogue. *Letter not found.*]

1. LS, listed by Patrick F. and Thomas F. Madigan, New York City, in *The Autograph*, I (November, 1911).

From Tench Coxe [1]

Philadelphia Septr. 25th. 1794.

Sir

As you mentioned your intention of reinvesting the proceeds of the late Sale in lands, I have thought the following Ideas might be worthy of Consideration.

Mr. Church will have, as soon as the papers are completed, in my hands engagements equal in ready money to near 19000 Drs. if the Sale when adjusted includes all his share of the lands under Patterson's & Stroud of which I have no doubt—say—   19000 Drs.

principal when due & interest now due of my Debt—say   5300

                                                    24300 Drs.

For these I will give him, patented—

1st   my third of the valuable purchase of Wm Steed-
      man & Co. intermixed with Mr. Church's *third*   } about 4150 As.
      which you will remember their letters in 1793,
      valued at 17/6

2dly adjoining to that purchase   6800 As

3d—within 2 or 3 miles of the above body   13350

                                              Acres   24300

This property is about 75 80 & 90 miles in a direct line N. W. from Philadelphia. Its longitude west of Philadelphia is not 40 miles & of the city of New York about 100 Miles. It is 50 miles nearer to Philadelphia than Asylum (Tallon, Noailles & Co) [2] & in the route to it from New York & Philada. & 1   miles N. E. & By East of the nearest parts of the 4th. Survey of Pennsa. The Settlers around & beyond it are chiefly Jerseymen, new Englandmen, Germans & Quakers & other people from the old Counties of Pennsa. Priestly Co's [3] purchases are fifty to seventy miles Westward of it, and it is all between the susquahannah & Delaware that is on the East Side of Susquehannah. In order to complete the Land business of Mr. Church I will give 6000 Acres of adjacent land in lieu of so much which Ball & Smith are to furnish to us, with an election of your taking for him within two years instead of those 6000 Acres whatever I may obtain under Mr. Church's share in that contract within that time.

If this arrangement shall appear eligible, Mr. Church would have on this side Susqa. & near to one another about 35000 Acres of land for his original 10,000 Dollars & for my use of a moiety of it for about a year—say 300 Drs. or 35000 Acres for 10300 Drs. The patents might be completed at once & the transaction closed. I will add that I shall be ready to afford my future assistance in Philada. in the sales &ca. of these lands, and in selecting proper agents in the Country, which however I should readily do for his present property without any inducement from the proposed arrangement.

I have the honor to be with gt. respt. Sir Yr. mo. obt. Sr.
T. C.

A Hamilton Esqr.
Atty of J. B. Church, Esq

ADfS, Papers of Tench Coxe in the Coxe Family Papers at the Historical Society of Pennsylvania, Philadelphia.

1. For an explanation of the contents of this letter, see the introductory note to Coxe to H, February 13, 1795 (*PAH*, XVIII, 262–69). See also the references cited in Coxe to H, April 13, 1793, note 3 (printed in this volume).

2. In 1793 Louis Marie, vicomte de Noailles, and Antoine–Omer Talon, chevalier and marquis de Boileau, both of whom were French refugees in Philadelphia, founded the Asylum Company. This company, which was backed by Robert Morris and his associate, John Nicholson, established a settlement for French refugees on a bend in the Susquehanna River between the towns of Towanda and Wyalusing. It eventually had some fifty houses, a chapel, and some small businesses. The undertaking ended in 1802, when Napoleon permitted the refugees to return to France.

3. In 1794 Joseph Priestley, the well-known scientist, educator, and writer on religious subjects, arrived in Philadelphia. See Angelica Church to H, April 1–7, 1794, note 2 (*PAH*, XVI, 225). He attempted to establish a utopian community on land which his son, Joseph, and his brother-in-law, Thomas Cooper, had recommended in Pennsylvania. Morris and Nicholson were associated with the company that was formed to sell the land and provided it with 300,000 acres in Northumberland County. The project failed to attract settlers and was eventually abandoned.

From William Bradford [1]

[*Philadelphia, September 27, 1794.* The description of this letter in the dealer's catalogue reads: "Concerning expenses of 'The Com-

missioners appointed by the President of the United States.' [2] Bradford . . . had apparently advanced the money needed to buy horses,
etc., and he inquires if the sums advanced were to be repaid him by
the Quartermaster or charged in his account against the U.S." [3] *Letter not found.*]

The Collector: *A Magazine for Autograph and Historical Collectors,* LXIX,
No. 11 (November, 1956), 108, Item j 849.
  1. Bradford was United States attorney general.
  2. For the appointment of Jasper Yeates, James Ross, and Bradford as Federal commissioners to confer with the representatives of the insurgents in western Pennsylvania, see H and Henry Knox to George Washington, August 5,
1794, note 3 (*PAH,* XVII, 21–24).
  3. The dealer's catalogue states that on the back of this letter H wrote:
"The Quarter Master will pay for the Horses taken them to the use of that
Department, Sept. 29, 1794."

To Abraham Parley [1]

[*Carlisle, Pennsylvania, October 8, 1794.* Letter listed in dealer's
catalogue. *Letter not found.*]

  1. ALS, sold by Arthur Pforzheimer, New York City, 1937, Rare Books and
First Editions, Item 60.

To Jasper Yeates [1]

[*Carlisle, Pennsylvania, October 11, 1794.* The description of this
letter in the dealer's catalogue reads: "Regarding a young Lieutenant
James Renshaw of the corps of dragoons, who was being recommended as a proper person for some service needed by Judge Yeates."
Letter not found.]

The Collector: *A Magazine for Autograph and Historical Collectors,* LVIII,
No. 3 (April-May, 1945), 84.
  1. Yeates was associate justice of the Pennsylvania Supreme Court from 1791
until his death in 1817. At the time this letter was written Yeates was one of
the Federal commissioners appointed by George Washington to confer with
the representatives of the insurgents in western Pennsylvania. See H and Henry
Knox to Washington, August 5, 1794, note 3 (*PAH,* XVII, 21–24).

Alexander Hamilton, Richard Peters, and William Rawle to David Lenox [1]

Camp Rostraver [Pennsylvania] November 11, 1794

Dear Sir

Altho' we have uniformly during the present Operation received perfect Satisfaction from your Firmness & Exertion in the Duties of your Office, yet we have, with sincere Sympathy, observed the Torture of your Mind, agitated between a Sense of public Duty & your private Affections, owing to the unpleasant Accounts you have received repeatedly of Mrs. Lenox's Illness. We cannot withold longer our Advice, that you forthwith return Home; & we trust that, tho' it may be difficult fully to supply your Place, yet we have a Confidence that such Arrangements will be made, as to prevent the public Service suffering by your Absence.

We are with sincere Esteem, your obedt Servts

Alexander Hamilton
Richard Peters
W Rawle

Major David Lennox

LS, University of Delaware Library.
    1. For an explanation of the contents of this letter, see Lenox to H, September 8, 1794; H to George Washington, November 11, 1794 (*PAH*, XVII, 203–09, 366–67).
    Peters was United States judge for the District of Pennsylvania. Rawle was United States attorney for the District of Pennsylvania. Lenox was United States marshal for the District of Pennsylvania.

To Robert Purviance [1]

[*Philadelphia, November 27, 1794*. Letter listed in dealer's catalogue. *Letter not found.*]

    1. LS, sold by Anderson Galleries, New York City, April 16, 1914, Item 285.

Subscription for Promoting the Cultivation of the Vine [1]

[*Philadelphia, 1794.*] Hamilton purchased one share of the one hundred and thirty-nine shares which were sold to sixty-seven persons in 1794 for "promoting the cultivation of the vine."

Copy, Thomas Jefferson Papers, Library of Congress.
1. This document contains a list of names and is entitled "Extract of the Book. Names of the Gentlemen has subscribed in 1794." It was enclosed in a letter which Peter Legaux, a Frenchman who had emigrated to the United States before the French Revolution and who kept meteorological records for the American Philosophical Society, wrote to Thomas Jefferson on March 25, 1801 (ALS, Thomas Jefferson Papers, Library of Congress). In this letter he described his organization and asked Jefferson to subscribe to it. In addition, Legaux enclosed a document dated March 16, 1801, from the commissioners appointed by Pennsylvania law "for receiving subscriptions for promoting the Cultivation of the vine." This document authorized Legaux "to sollicit subscriptions for the above purpose and to receive one Dollar in part payment of Each share subscribed, at the time of enacting such subscription—the remainder, making in the whole Twenty Dollars for Each share, to be paid in such maner and proportion as the Managers of the Compagny, when the same shall be incorporated shall determine" (copy, Thomas Jefferson Papers, Library of Congress).
For the Pennsylvania law which appointed the commissioners, see "An Act to enable the Governor of this commonwealth to incorporate a company, for the purpose of promoting the cultivation of vines, and for other purposes therein mentioned" (*Pennsylvania Laws,* 1792–1793 Sess., Ch. CXLIV [March 22, 1793]). For amendments to the act, see *Pennsylvania Laws,* 1793–1794 Sess., Ch. CLXXV (January 13, 1794); 1800–1801 Sess., Ch. CCLV (March 7, 1800), Ch. CCV (January 31, 1801).

Views on the French Revolution

[1794]

Facts, numerous and unequivocal, demonstrate that the present AERA is among the most extraordinary, which have occurred in the history of human affairs. Opinions, for a long time, have been gradually gaining ground, which threaten the foundations of Religion, Morality and Society. An attack was first made upon the Christian Revelation; for which natural Religion was offered as the substitute. The Gospel was to be discarded as a gross imposture; but the being and attributes of a GOD, the obligations of piety, even the doctrine of a future state of rewards and punishments were to be retained and cherished.

In proportion as success has appeared to attend the plan, a bolder project has been unfolded. The very existence of a Deity has been questionned, and in some instances denied. The duty of piety has been ridiculed, the perishable nature of man asserted and his hopes bounded to the short span of his earthly state. DEATH has been proclaimed an ETERNAL SLEEP [1]—"the dogma of the *immortality* of the soul a *cheat* invented to torment the living for the benefit of the dead." [2] Irreligion, no longer confined to the closets of conceiled sophists, nor to the haunts of wealthy riot, has more or less displayed its hideous front among all classes.

Wise and good men took a lead in delineating the odious character of Despotism; in exhibiting the advantages of a moderate and well-balanced government, in inviting nations to contend for the enjoyment of rational liberty. Fanatics in political science have since exaggerated and perverted their doctrines. Theories of Government unsuited to the nature of man, miscalculating the force of his passions, disregarding the lessons of experimental wisdom, have been projected and recommended. These have every where attracted sectaries and every where the fabric of Government has been in different degrees undermined.

A league has at length been cemented between the apostles and disciples of irreligion and of anarchy. Religion and Government have both been stigmatised as abuses; as unwarrantable restraints upon the freedom of man; as causes of the corruption of his nature, intrinsically good; as sources of an artificial and false morality, which tyrannically robs him of the enjoyments for which his passions fit him; and as cloggs upon his progress to the perfection for which he was destined.

As a corollary from these premisses, it is a favourite tenet of the sect that religious opinion of any sort is unnecessary to Society; that the maxims of a genuine morality and the authority of the Magistracy and the laws are a sufficient and ought to be the only security for civil rights and private happiness.

As another corollary, it is occasionally maintained by the same sect, that but a small portion of power is requisite to Government; that even this portion is only temporarily necessary, in consequence of the bad habits which have been produced by the errors of ancient systems; and that as human nature shall refine and ameliorate by the operation of a more enlightened plan, government itself will become useless, and Society will subsist and flourish free from its shackles.

If all the votaries of this new philosophy do not go the whole length of its frantic creed; they all go far enough to endanger the full extent of the mischiefs which are inherent in so wild and fatal a scheme; every modification of which aims a mortal blow at the vitals of human happiness.

The practical developement of this pernicious system has been seen in France. It has served as an engine to subvert all her antient institutions civil and religious, with all the checks that served to mitigate the rigour of authority; it has hurried her headlong through a rapid succession of dreadful revolutions, which have laid waste property, made havoc among the arts, overthrow cities, desolated provinces, unpeopled regions, crimsonned her soil with blood and deluged it in crime poverty and wretchedness; and all this as yet for no better purpose than to erect on the ruins of former things a despotism unlimited and uncontrouled; leaving to a deluded, an abused, a plundered, a scourged and an oppressed people not even the shadow of liberty, to console them for a long train of substantial misfortunes, of bitter sufferings.

This horrid system seemed awhile to threaten the subversion of civilized Society and the introduction of general disorder among mankind. And though the frightful evils, which have been its first and only fruits, have given a check to its progress, it is to be feared that the poison has spread too widely and penetrated too deeply, to be as yet eradicated. Its activity has indeed been suspended, but the elements remain concocting for new eruptions as occasion shall permit. It is greatly to be apprehended, that mankind is not near the end of the misfortunes, which it is calculated to produce, and that it still portends a long train of convulsion, Revolution, carnage, devastation, and misery.

Symptoms of the too great prevalence of this system in the United States are alarmingly visible. It was by its influence, that efforts were made to embark this country in a common cause with France in the early period of the present war; to induce our government to sanction and promote her odious principles and views with the blood and treasure of our citizens. It is by its influence, that every succeeding revolution has been approved or excused—all the horrors that have been committed justified or extenuated—that even the last usurpation, which contradicts all the ostensible principles of the Revolution, has been regarded with complacency; and the despotic constitution engendered by it slyly held up as a model not unworthy of our Imitation.

In the progress of this system, impiety and infidelity have advanced with gigantic strides. Prodigious crimes heretofore unknown among us are seen. The chief and idol of

AD (incomplete), Hamilton Papers, Library of Congress.

1. Between the months of April and December, 1793, the French Revolution's Reign of Terror was extended to include attacks on Christianity. One of the manifestations of this movement to dechristianize France occurred on 19 Vendémiaire An II (October 10, 1793) in the capital city of Nevers in the department of La Nièvre, where the National Convention's *représentant en mission,* Joseph Fouché, issued a decree on the subject of cemeteries. In this decree, Fouché ordered that new revolutionary cemeteries be set aside as *sépulture commune* (Article IV of the decree) and that no statues other than one representing *le Sommeil* (Article IV) be erected. Article VI, which H is quoting, reads in part: "On lira sur la porte de ce champ . . . cette inscription: 'La mort est un sommeil éternel.'" Fouché's decree was read and approved during the 25 Vendemiaire An II (October 16, 1793) session of the Conseil-général of the Commune de Paris, and although it does not appear to have become law, it was widely circulated among the provinces and had considerable influence on the escalation of anti-Christian feeling in France. For the complete text of the decree, see *Réimpression de L'Ancien Moniteur. Seule Histoire Authentique et Inaltérée de la Révolution Française Depuis la Réunion des Etats-Generaux Jusqu'au Consulat (Mai 1789-Novembre 1799)* (Paris, 1847), XVIII, 137. For more information on Fouché and dechristianization, see A. Aulard, *Le Culte de la Raison et Le Culte de l'Etre Supreme* (1793-1794), *Essai Historique* (Paris, 1892); Louis Madelin, *Fouché 1759-1820* (Paris, 1903).

2. H is apparently citing a letter to the National Convention which was read on the 15 Brumaire An II (November 5, 1793) session and written by Joseph-François Laignelot and Joseph-Marie Lequinio de Kerblay, the Convention's *représentants en mission* to Rochefort in the department of the Charente Inférieure. This letter reads in part: ". . . il n'y aura plus dans cette ville . . . qu'un seul dépôt des restes inanimés de l'homme, que la superstition faisait revivre sans cesse pour tourmenter les vivants." For the complete text of this letter, see *Réimpression de L'Ancien Moniteur,* XVIII, 348. See also Lequinio's address of 20 Brumaire An II (November 10, 1793), delivered at Rochefort, in which he charges that Catholic priests, whom he refers to as "imposteurs," hold the French people "dans l'asservissement et la misère en maîtrisant son imagination, et en le frustrant des jouissances d'ici bas, sous la fausse promesse d'un bonheur éternel dans l'avenir!" (*Du Bonheur: Par Lequinio, Représentant du Peuple, Envoyé dans le Département de la Charente inférieure, prononcé dans le Temple de la Vérité, ci-devant l'Église catholique de Rochefort, le deuxième décade de Brumaire, l'an second de la République française, une et indivisible* [Angoulème, 1793], 3, [Bibliothèque Nationale #41/3484]).

1795

To Noah Webster, Junior [1]

[New York, September 30, 1795–1798]

Mr. Hamilton presents his Compliments to Mr. Webster requests the favour of him to strike off & send him in the course of the day thirty Copies of the Inclosed Letter, with his account of the Cost.

Sep 30th

AL, inserted in a grangerized edition of George Shea, *Illustrated Life of Alexander Hamilton* (New York, 1877), Columbia University Libraries.

1. Webster, the famous lexicographer, was a native of Connecticut and a graduate of Yale. He lived in New York in 1787 and 1788, and in these years he founded and edited the *American Magazine*. In 1793 he returned to New York and remained there until 1798. During his second stay in the city he founded *The American Minerva, Patroness of Peace, Commerce, and the Liberal Arts*, a daily paper, and *The Herald; a Gazette for the Country*, a semi-weekly. In 1796, after several changes in title, the first of these papers was renamed *The Minerva*, and in 1797 the second was renamed *The Spectator*.

From Tench Coxe [1]

[Philadelphia] Decr. 14th 1795

Sir

I have transmitted to Walter Rutherford Esqr.[2] for two years intt. on my bond to J. B. Church Esqr. the sum of Six hundred Dollars which will be delivered to you or any gentleman in your office who will exhibit to him my Bond with a receipt for that sum thereon.

I have been in the woods as I believe I informed you [3] upon the Business of Ball & Smith's contract. The advantages in favor of the Justice of our cause resulting from this inconvenient & uncomfortable exertion have been great. The Board of Property [4] after a long hearing have decided, that the warrants of Ball & Smith shall take place of those opposed to them. I have written to the Deputy Surveyor & hope now [to] get forward with the Business; tho there are some serious matters yet to remove. To secure our ground I have made a further payment of Eight hundred Dollars.

I am &ca. &ca.

Alexander Hamilton Esqr.
Atty. of J. B. Church Esqr. of N. York

LC, Papers of Tench Coxe in the Coxe Family Papers at the Historical Society of Pennsylvania, Philadelphia.

1. For an explanation of the contents of this letter, see the introductory note to Coxe to H, February 13, 1795 (*PAH*, XVIII, 262–69). See also the references cited in Coxe to H, April 13, 1793, note 3 (printed in this volume).

2. Coxe to Rutherford, December 14, 1795 (LC, Papers of Tench Coxe in the Coxe Family Papers at the Historical Society of Pennsylvania, Philadelphia).

Rutherford was a New York City merchant.

In an account dated June 18, 1797, in which Coxe wrote of his partnership with Church covering the period from May 6, 1794 to December 31, 1796, there is a debit entry which reads: "Decr. 15 [1795] To Amount of two years interest remitted to A Hamilton Esqr. thro Walter Rutherford Esqr. 600 Drs. endorsed on Bond being in full of interest to 25th Septr. 1795 225" (copy, Papers of Tench Coxe in the Coxe Family Papers at the Historical Society of Pennsylvania, Philadelphia).

3. Coxe to H, August 4, 1795 (*PAH*, XIX, 88).

4. The Pennsylvania Board of Property was established in 1782 to decide land disputes. Claimants could appeal the board's decisions to the state's courts. See "An Act to Vest Certain Powers in the President of This State, Together with the Other Officers Therein Named, and for Other Purposes Therein Mentioned," April 5, 1782 (James T. Mitchell and Henry Flanders, eds., *The Statutes at Large of Pennsylvania from 1682 to 1801* [Harrisburg, 1904], X, 408–11).

1796

To James McHenry [1]

[*New York, January 19, 1796.* Letter listed in dealer's catalogue. *Letter not found.*]

1. ALS, sold by Ben Bloomfield, New York City, 1954, List DM-2, Item 49.

To Tench Coxe

[Philadelphia, February 27, 1796] [1]

Mr. Hamilton's Compliments to Mr Coxe. An engagement which Mr. H did not recollect will not permit him to breakfast with Mr. Coxe this morning. But he will call immediately after he is released at Mr Coxe's House & afterwards at his Office.

Feby. 27th. 1796.

AL, Papers of Tench Coxe in the Coxe Family Papers at the Historical Society of Pennsylvania, Philadelphia.
1. For the purpose of H's trip to Philadelphia in February, 1796, see Robert Morris to H, February 10, 1796, note 2 (*PAH*, XX, 54).

To Tench Coxe [1]

[New York, May 16, 1796]

Sir

I am anxious to be informed how our affair now stands with Messrs. Wheelen & Co.[2] & that it be brought to an issue. How stands also the question depending before the board of the land Office? [3]

Yr. Obed ser

A Hamilton
May 16 1796

Tench Coxe Esq

ALS, Papers of Tench Coxe in the Coxe Family Papers at the Historical Society of Pennsylvania, Philadelphia.
1. For an explanation of the contents of this letter, see the introductory note
to Coxe to H, February 13, 1795 (*PAH*, **XVIII**, 262–69). See also the references
cited in Coxe to H, April 13, 1793, note 3 (printed in this volume).
2. Israel Whelen and Joseph I. Miller were grocers and merchants in Philadelphia.
3. See Coxe to H, December 14, 1795, note 3 (printed in this volume).

From Tench Coxe [1]

[Philadelphia] May 17th 1796

Sir

I mentioned to you that the Board of Property had decided in
favor of Ball & Smiths Warrants,[2] but I presume it has escaped
your Memory. After this six months are given by our laws for an
appeal to the courts of Law. I hoped that this would elaps—but
about the last day the process was served. I have apprized my council, in the former stage, of the present situation of the matter & due
care will be taken to procure all the proper means of a favorable
decision.

Sometime since I applied to Mr. Wheelen,[3] and finding a prospect
of raising the Money as soon as the other part of the concern would
expect the difference between my share of the present balance & the
value of the full third, I offered [to] repurchase one third at the first
cost & to take that undivided interest or to draw at once one third
out of Patterson's, Church's & Coxe's lands. Mr. Wheelen expressed
his willingness, but sd. Mr. G. Wescott had hesitated, & was then out
of Town. That having made the offer to you he would consider
himself bound to persuade Mr. W. to it, & I should hear on his return. Mr. Wescott has been back about a week or ten days but I
have not yet heard from them.

Mr. Anthony informs me that he has advised you [4] of his having
recd. from me the Deed of Robert Wescott for the eleven tracts of
land taken back for Mr. Church by you, & the patents for them,
which I sent him about the day of your lat[e] departure from Philadelphia [5] agreeably to your desire.

Mr. Burd [6] of our supreme Court told me on Sunday that Mr. R.

Morris had made provision for the Judgments against him so far as his own real & separate share of them.[7] This it may be useful to Mr. Church's affairs that you should hear.

I am, sir, &ca. &ca.

Alexr. Hamilton Esqr. (N. Yk.)

LC, Papers of Tench Coxe in the Coxe Family Papers at the Historical Society of Pennsylvania, Philadelphia.

1. For an explanation of the contents of this letter, see the introductory note to Coxe to H, February 13, 1795 (*PAH*, XVIII, 262–69). See also the references cited in Coxe to H, April 13, 1793, note 3 (printed in this volume).

In *PAH*, XX, 184, this letter is listed as a "letter not found."

2. See Coxe to H, December 14, 1795 (printed in this volume).

3. On May 23, 1796, Coxe wrote to Israel Whelen: "I shall be glad of the decision of Messrs. Wheelen, Miller & Wescotts about my offer to repurchase an undivided third part of the 88 tracts of the lands bought of me and of Mr. Alexr. Patterson in 1794. I informed Mr. Hamilton, that I had offered to buy in for a sixth, a fourth or a third, & he wishes for information about the same . . ." (LC, Papers of Tench Coxe in the Coxe Family Papers at the Historical Society of Pennsylvania, Philadelphia).

4. Joseph Anthony's letter to H has not been found.

5. Paltsits states that H was in Philadelphia "shortly before May 10, 1796" (Victor Hugo Paltsits, ed., *Washington's Farewell Address* [New York, 1935], 31), but no information concerning the purpose of this visit has been found in H's extant correspondence.

6. Edward Burd was prothonotary of the Supreme Court of Pennsylvania.

7. For Robert Morris's debt to Church, see the introductory note to Morris to H, June 4, 1795 (*PAH*, XVIII, 359–70). See also Morris to H, July 20, November 16, December 18, 1795; January 15, March 6, 12, 14, 30, April 27, May 17, 1796 (*PAH*, XVIII, 469–70; XIX, 430, 498–500; XX, 40, 63, 74, 74–75, 103, 141–45, 184–88).

To Tench Coxe [1]

New York May 30. 1796

Sir

Some days since I received your letter [2] in which you mention to me that Mr. Wheelen pursuant to what he said to me, was himself willing and would endeavour to prevail upon the other parties concerned with him to permit Mr Church's proportion of the land sold to be withdrawn by lot. In carrying this idea into execution, I presume it is well understood that the drawing must be confined to the Identical tract of land which was purchased by you in connection with Mr Church not from the aggregate of that and your other land sold to Wheelen & Miller. But I sincerely wish the Affair was terminated.[3]

I am   Sir   Yr humble servant   A Hamilton

Tench Coxe Esq

ALS, Papers of Tench Coxe in the Coxe Family Papers at the Historical Society of Pennsylvania, Philadelphia.
   1. For an explanation of the contents of this letter, see the introductory note to Coxe to H, February 13, 1795 (*PAH*, XVIII, 262–69). See also the references cited in Coxe to H, April 13, 1793, note 3 (printed in this volume).
   2. Coxe to H, May 17, 1796 (printed in this volume).
   3. Coxe endorsed this letter: "about the return of the residue of the Lands of Mr. Church."

To Tench Coxe [1]

[New York, June 12, 1796]

Sir

Accidental Circumstances prevented my seeing you previous to my departure [2] to know the issue of the Arbitration—proposal to Mr Wheelen. I will thank you to inform me.

I have heared that some late law of Pensylvania has put in jeopardy the property of *Aliens* where there were not actual settlements.[3] I will thank you to explain this. Is it where the Patents were originally to *Aliens?*—or does it extend to lands patented to Citizens & purchased by Aliens? Is it where there were in the patents *conditions* of settlement or have any new conditions been established? & What? &c. &c

Yr hum servant   A Hamilton

Tench Coxe Esq

ALS, Papers of Tench Coxe in the Coxe Family Papers at the Historical Society of Pennsylvania, Philadelphia.
   1. For an explanation of the contents of this letter, see the introductory note to Coxe to H, February 13, 1795 (*PAH*, XVIII, 262–69). See also the references cited in Coxe to H, April 13, 1793, note 3 (printed in this volume).

2. See Coxe to H, May 17, 1796, note 4 (printed in this volume).

3. For the Pennsylvania laws concerning the right of aliens to own land, see Coxe to H, May 10, 1795, note 3 (*PAH*, XVIII, 339).

From Tench Coxe [1]

[Philadelphia] June 13th 1796

Sir

Mr. Whelen informed me that he would call upon me soon to fix some preliminaries about the arbitration. I soon expect him but have not yet seen him on the subject.

I have not heard of any improvement condition in regard to the lands of Aliens in Pennsylvania, and am satisfied there can be none to effect Mr. Church's purchases with me. It would be an expostfact to provision—in equitable & void. Certain Lands over Allegany were granted with condition of settlement, which was illy expressed, & much neglected & attempted to be avoided by devices supposed to be legally feasible. I never thought safe or right, and therefore never meddled with them. I think this must be what you have heard of. They only regard that small part of the State which lies N. of Ohio & W. of Allegany river, and, I believe, not all that—also some part or all of triangel at Presque-isle.

I am &ca. &ca.

Col. A Hamilton New York

LC, Papers of Tench Coxe in the Coxe Family Papers at the Historical Society of Pennsylvania, Philadelphia.

1. Coxe wrote this letter in answer to H to Coxe, June 12, 1796 (printed in this volume).

From Barent Bleecker [1]

[*New York, September 12, 1796*. The description of this letter in the dealer's catalogue reads: "Reminding him that the third install-ment for the lands in Cosby's Manor would come due Oct. 4, and requesting payment." *Letter not found.*]

The Collector: A Magazine for Autograph and Historical Collectors, LXVII,
No. 1–2 (January–February, 1954), 7, Item e 44.
    1. For an explanation of the contents of this letter, see the introductory note
to Philip Schuyler to H, August 31, 1795 (*PAH*, XIX, 200–04). See also H to
Phineas Bond, September 1, 1795 (*PAH*, XIX, 216); H to Robert Morris, September 1, 1795 (*PAH*, XIX, 216–17); H to Bleecker, March 20, 1796 (*PAH*,
XX, 78–79).
    Bleecker was an Albany merchant and land speculator.

To Tench Coxe [1]

[New York, November 10, 1796]

Sir

I beg the favour of you to let me know what if any thing has
been settled with Messrs. Wheelen & Miller or whereabouts that
affair is. I expect with certain[ty] Mr. *Church* early in the spring,[2]
and should be grieved to have to inform him of an unsettled state of
this business.

I am   Sir   Yr. very hum. servant   A Hamilton

Nov 10. 1796

Tench Coxe Esq

ALS, Papers of Tench Coxe in the Coxe Family Papers at the Historical Society of Pennsylvania, Philadelphia.
    1. For an explanation of the contents of this letter, see the introductory note
to Coxe to H, February 13, 1795 (*PAH*, XVIII, 262–69). See also the references
cited in Coxe tc H, April 13, 1793, note 3 (printed in this volume).
    2. In May, 1797, John B. Church and his wife Angelica Schuyler Church,
Elizabeth Hamilton's sister, returned to the United States after twelve years
in England. While Church was out of the United States, H had acted as his
agent for his American business affairs.
    On May 26, 1797, Church wrote from New York to Coxe: "I arriv'd here a
few days since, and amongst other Papers receiv'd from Col Hamilton your
Bond for 5000 Dollars which became due the 25th September last, in the Multiplicity of Business in which he is engaged it had escaped his Notice that so
long a Time had elapsed since the Bond became due, and that he had only
received one Years Interest on the Bond, as it will not suit me to lend Money
at Interest, I must request by Return of Post a Remittance for the Principal and
Interest of the Bond, and I will thank you to furnish me at the same Time with
a State of the Sale of the Lands which you have made on my Account and
also a Remittance for the Amount you have reciv'd in Consequence of such
Sale" (ALS, Papers of Tench Coxe in the Coxe Family Papers at the Historical
Society of Pennsylvania, Philadelphia).

1797

Receipt to William Cooper [1]

[New York, March 10, 1797]

Rec'd five hundred dollars of William Cooper on account of Mr. Churchs Mortgage on lands in Otsego County.   March 10, 1797

Alexander Hamilton

Dollars	500
Some months past	
	1000
	1500

DS, anonymous donor.

1. Cooper, the founder of Cooperstown, New York, was appointed judge of the Court of Common Pleas for Otsego County on February 17, 1791. From March 4, 1795, to March 3, 1797, he was a Federalist member of the House of Representatives.

For an explanation of the contents of this letter, see H to John Chaloner, June 11, 1793 (*PAH*, XIV, 533). See also Thomas FitzSimons to H, March 21, July 14, December 17, 1795 (*PAH*, XVIII, 301–02, 464–66; XIX, 498); H to Cooper, December 16, 1796 (*PAH*, XX, 443–44).

From Oliver Wolcott, Junior

[*Philadelphia, April 13, 1797.* On April 22, 1797, Hamilton wrote to Wolcott [1] and referred to "your letter of the 13th instant." *Letter not found.*]

1. Printed in this volume.

To Oliver Wolcott, Junior [1]

Albany April 22. 1797

Dear Sir

My absence from New York to attend the Court here has put it out of my power to answer sooner your letter of the 13th instant.[2]

The characters which occur to me as proper to be considered for Collector are these—

Benjamin Walker [3]—This Gentleman you know as well as I do. He is every way qualified and fit, and had he remained in the place of naval officer he might, qualified as he is, have looked to that of Collector almost as a matter of course—but the having quit the former terminates the pretension on that score.[4] He stands a candidate at large. As such however, he equals any in the requisites for the Office, and has the peculiar advantage of Experience in relation to it. But you ought to be apprised that from his engagements in certain agencies from abroad &c, he has for a long time executed the naval office chiefly by deputy—and if he should be concluded upon for the other it ought to be well understood that his *intire personal attention* is expected and the *relinquishment* of his agencies, for I suspect they will not harmonize.

Matthew Clarkeson. [5] This is among the worthiest and best esteemed of our Citizens. Till his appointment to the Office he now holds he has had little familiarity with accounts, but I should believe his attention and care, *upon principle,* would ensure a good execution of the Office & his personal qualities would render his appointment peculiarly acceptable. I believe however he is connected in Trade—& I do not know that he would relinquish it for the Office.

Nicholas Fish.[6] I have a perfectly good opinion of this Gentleman who is also very generally esteemed and according to my ideas of him, he would execute the Office as well as any man & there is no circumstance in his situation against it. I presume he would prefer it to that which he now holds.

You however who have had the conduct of both these Gentlemen in their present Offices more immediately under your eye in different capacities, can from thence judge what that conduct promises in the other Office. There is *I know* always inconvenience in the change of a man who is in the train of a particular office. But there is also the motive (of no small consequence) of encouraging men to accept offices of less eligibility by the expectation of better when they occur.

AQUILA GILES.[7] There are few whom I should have preferred before this Gentleman, had I not been lately told that there have been some delays in bringing forward monies which came into his hands as Marshall. You probably have more light on this subject than me and can appreciate the force of the objection. He is however less a man of business than some others.

Gulian ver Plank (now President of the Bank of New York). He is a man of superior mental endowments to any of those who have been named & of superior acquirements. His moral character is of the most estimable sort. His habits have not led to a familiarity with accounts—& he is supposed not much addicted to labour. But I think he would *upon principle* apply himself closely to a good execution of whatever he should undertake. He is a man of moderate fortune & has no particular pursuit—so that I think he might be willing to accept though I am not certain.

Jonathan Burrall[8] (now Cashier of the office of Discount). According to my opinion *no man* would be *better qualified* or more *faithful*. He is respectably connected in our state by marriage[9]— and well esteemed though not of *important* standing in our community. He would however be an acceptable appointment.

James Watson[10]—would no doubt be *well qualified* & there is every ground of confidence in his fidelity. He affords the public the security of a good fortune. It must however not be omitted that by *something* in his character, by too much fondness for office, by some marks of indecision & temporising in lesser matters, he is far less well esteemed in our community than the other characters who have been named.

For qualifications relative to the Office I should prefer *Walker Fish Burrall* & Watson.

The *consideration* for the candidates in the better part of the community stands nearly thus. *Clarkeson, ver Plank, Fish = Walker, Burrall, Giles, Watson.*

I have thought it better to give you this map of Characters for the information of the President than to draw myself any definitive conclusion. It is not easy to err much in a choice among them.

I should have mentioned Col Smith [11] among the most prominent but for the late unfortunate circumstances which attend him and which would render his appointment ineligible to such an Office at this time.

Yrs truly   A Hamilton

April 22. 1797

Ol Wolcott Jun Esq

ALS, RG 59, General Records of the Department of State, Applications and Recommendations, 1797–1801, National Archives.

1. When *PAH*, XXI, was printed, only the last three paragraphs of this letter had been found.

This letter concerns candidates for the office of collector of customs at New York City to replace John Lamb, who had been dismissed for a shortage of funds in his accounts. For background to this letter, see H to Wolcott, April 22, 1797 (*PAH*, XXI, 54–55); Wolcott to H, April 4, 1800 (*PAH*, XXIV, 390–91).

2. Letter not found. H was in Albany to attend the New York Supreme Court, which met from April 18 to April 29, 1797.

3. Walker was naval officer of the port of New York. In May, 1795, he became a representative of the Pulteney Associates, a London company that speculated in lands in the Genesee country of western New York.

4. See H to George Washington, January 31, 1797 (*PAH*, XX, 498–99).

5. Clarkson was commissioner of loans for New York.

6. Fish was supervisor of the revenue for the District of New York.

7. Giles was United States marshal for the District of New York.

8. Burrall was cashier of the New York Office of Discount and Deposit of the Bank of the United States.

9. Burrall was married to Frances Amelia Wickham, great-granddaughter of Gabriel Ludlow and Sarah Hanmer. Ludlow came to America from England in 1694 and became a successful merchant in New York City. He built and owned several vessels engaged in the coasting trade, and obtained a royal patent for four thousand acres of land in what is today Orange County. He also served as clerk of the New York House of Assembly from 1699 to 1733.

10. Watson, a New York City lawyer and merchant, was a member of the Senate from 1796 to 1798.

11. William S. Smith, John Adams's son-in-law. For the "late unfortunate circumstances," see H to Wolcott, April 22, 1797, note 10 (*PAH*, XXI, 54–55).

To Robert Troup [1]

[*June 20, 1797.* The description of this letter in the dealer's catalogue reads: "on legal matters." *Letter not found.*]

1. ALS, sold by Robert H. Dodd, New York City, April, 1916, Catalogue 20.

From Cyrus De Hart [1]

Rhinebeck [New York] Augt. 2d 1797

Sir

I have just recd the enclosed Citation within twenty four hours—which leave no time for me to attend to the business. If I understand the business—the decision of the arbitrators will be consider'd as a Verdict. If the decision of the arbitrators cannot be set aside I wish you if possible to cause a delay if it can be done—So that the proprietors may have at least three months to collect the mony.

Your most Obt   Cyrus D Hart

Mr. Van Dervoort [2] will hand you this. I shall be down to attend Beachs tryal.[3]

ALS, Hamilton Papers, Library of Congress.
  1. De Hart was a resident and landowner in Rhinebeck, Dutchess County, New York.
  This letter concerns one of several related trespass cases, *Robert Williams & Cornelius C. Van Wyck* v *Cyrus de Hart,* all of whom were residents of Dutchess County. The case was heard during the January, 1796, term of the New York Supreme Court. On July 27, 1797, the Supreme Court ordered the parties to submit their controversy to arbitration and award. On July 31 the Court ordered that "it duly appearing to this Court that the said Cyrus de Hart hath not observed or obeyed the said rule or order, It is now Ordered that the said Cyrus de Hart shew cause on Tuesday next in this present Term why an Attachment should not issue against him." The court issued an attachment against De Hart on August 4, 1797 (MS Minutes of the New York Supreme Court, under the dates of January 30, 1796, July 27, 31, August 4, 1797 [Hall of Records, New York City]).
  2. This is presumably a reference to John Van Der Voort, a resident of the town of Beekman, Dutchess County, New York.
  3. The trespass case of *Cyrus de Hart, Daniel Halsey and Others* v *Joseph Beach* was entered on the calendar of the New York Circuit Court on August

8, 1797, but the trial was postponed and was not heard until October 31, 1797, when De Hart and the other plaintiffs were nonsuited because they did not appear for the trial, and the jury was dismissed (MS Account Book of Costs, New York Circuit Court, under the dates of August 8, October 31, 1797 [Hall of Records, New York City]).

An entry in H's Cash Book, 1795–1804, under the date of January 23, 1797, reads: "this sum received of Dehart v Beach 25" (AD, Hamilton Papers, Library of Congress).

H endorsed this letter: "De Hart adm Williams."

From James Monroe [1]

[*Philadelphia, August 4, 1797.* Letter listed in dealer's catalogue. *Letter not found.*]

1. ALS, sold by Stan V. Henkels, Jr., April 21, 1891, Item 393-H.

To James Monroe [1]

[*New York, August 8, 1797.* Letter listed in dealer's catalogue. *Letter not found.*]

1. ALS, sold by John Heise, Syracuse, New York, 1921, Catalogue S5, Item 9.

To Tench Coxe [1]

[New York, August 23, 1797]

Sir

I enclose you a letter from Mr Church. I must add to it my earnest request that you will exert yourself to complete the business which is the subject of it. The punctuality of his temper occasions to me no small embarrassment in reference to a delay which appears to him extraordinary. I shall receive much pleasure from the knowlege that the affair is closed.

With consideration   I am Sir   Yr Obed serv   A Hamilton

Aug 23. 1797

Tench Coxe Esq

[ENCLOSURE]

John B. Church to Tench Coxe [2]

Albany Augt. 19: 1797

Sir

I imagine this Letter will find you return'd to Philadelphia. I am much disappointed and regret that I was obliged to quit New York before I received an Account of your having arranged with Mr. Anthony [3] the Division of the Lands. I have received a Letter from him that he fears he shall not be able to effect it with you, and that I must repair to Philadelphia in Person to procure a Settlement; I hope you will be so good as to complete this Business immediately with him and spare me the Trouble of a Journey there which would at present be exceedingly inconvenient to me and as I hope that by this Time every Obstacle to a Settlement is removed I flatter myself you will not put me to the Trouble of a Journey which I should take with regret. I am very respectfully Sir   Your mo: obedt hum Servt.

J B Church

I shall return to N York in a few Days, and hope to receive an Acot of the Settlement of this Business.

Tench Coxe Exqr.

ALS, Papers of Tench Coxe in the Coxe Family Papers at the Historical Society of Pennsylvania, Philadelphia.

1. For an explanation of the contents of this letter, see the introductory note to Coxe to H, February 13, 1795 (*PAH,* XVIII, 262–69). See also the references cited in Coxe to H, April 13, 1793, note 3 (printed in this volume).

2. ALS, Papers of Tench Coxe in the Coxe Family Papers at the Historical Society of Pennsylvania, Philadelphia.

3. Joseph Anthony.

From Tench Coxe [1]

[Philadelphia] August 26th 1797

Sir

I wrote yesterday to Mr. Church, & now trouble you with this from a presumption that he is yet absent. My letter gives some information, which as it regards his Pennsa. property, it may be well for you to see immediately. I therefore recommend your attention opening my letter to him. I have just recd. Mr. Church's of the 19th.[2] & yours of the 23d or 25th.[3] In regard to the division of the tracts to give him a separate title for his interest of 17 ¾ tracts in Patterson & Co's Concerne, I want it for him to that amount & for myself for the amot. of my 18 ¾ Tracts as much as possible. Whenever Messrs. Whelen & those concerned with him are in Town I will attend to it on a minutes notice, and it can be drawn by lot in an hour. Mr. Whelen is to give me Notice when they are here. At this time the prospect of them being soon in town is bad, as you may presume, when I tell you that from my office windows I can see ten houses that are shut up,[4] between them & Mr. E. Tilghman's[5] on Chestnut Street alone, & that I shall be this Evening without a servant in my house, the two left me by Mrs. Coxe being gone on acct. of the disorder. My Clerk, who is yet with me, will proceed in all things in his power as to the papers, that are wanted in lieu of the regular details, which by preceeding papers were furnished before.[6] The tax lists made up for the safety of the property have furnished the means of a correct & detailed document, which I had the pleasure to enclose yesterday, in the letter refered to above.

A similar part shall be furnished for the other part upon a division.

The draughts or plats, now in hand, will give another view of the same property, and shall be sent on when done. If I can stand my ground in the City I shall make progress in my public & private business, and a full share of my attention shall be paid to a methodical & complete exhibit of the property founded upon my former informations, & upon such knowledge of the precise local situation of the lands, as I occasionally obtain.

Our Town is much alarmed, & a little touched with putrid fever in some cases, I believe, contagious.

No Physician, Student of Physick, Apothecary, Sexton or Grave digger has died so far as I am informed.

With consideration   I am Sir   yr. obedt. Servt.

The Offices of the Secy. comptr. Audr. & Regr. are moved to the Green House at Gray's Ferry.[7] Mr. Francis[8] has moved up to Twelfth Street permanently. His office is near Mr. Meredith[9] & I remain, as heretofore. The Atty. Genl. I saw in Town this day, &

the Secy. of State & War yesterday & the day before. Very various Views are taken of our Situation.

LC, Papers of Tench Coxe in the Coxe Family Papers at the Historical Society of Pennsylvania.

1. For an explanation of the contents of this letter, see the introductory note to Coxe to H, February 13, 1795 (*PAH*, XVIII, 262–69). See also the references cited in Coxe to H, April 13, 1793, note 3 (printed in this volume).

2. This letter is printed as an enclosure to H to Coxe, August 23, 1797 (printed in this volume).

3. H to Coxe, August 23, 1797 (printed in this volume).

4. This is a reference to the effect of the yellow fever epidemic in Philadelphia in the summer and fall of 1797. See Robert Morris to John B. Church, November 1, 1797, enclosed in Morris to H, November 1, 1797 (*PAH*, XXI, 308–09).

5. Edward Tilghman was a lawyer. He was the cousin of William Tilghman, who became a trustee of Coxe's estate after 1800 (introductory note to Coxe to H, February 13, 1795 [*PAH*, XVIII, 262–69]).

6. On September 1, 1797, Coxe wrote to John B. Church: "My Clerk has finished & sent to me . . . a draught of the lands in the concern of Patterson & Co. You will find your eleven (separated already) by the Names & quantity of acres. The original warantees Names are given in the draught with exactness, to make that easy. I am proceeding . . ." (LC, Papers of Tench Coxe in the Coxe Family Papers at the Historical Society of Pennsylvania, Philadelphia). On September 6, 1797, Coxe wrote again to Church: "I have just recd. from the city the two enclosed draughts A—being that of 5 tracts, in the concern of 30, with Steedman of Mar & April 1793

"& B being that of 25 in that concern, & of 155 in Ruston, Steedman & Co's concern of June 1793.

"In the former contract you have the latter 21 tracts, conveyed by order to Mr. Joseph Anthony, of Philada. These lands lie East of Susquehannah, West of Lehi, South of Woppohawkly & North of Mahantango in Luzerne, Northumberland & Northhampton, in Pennsa. & are included in the tax lists lately sent to you." (LC, Papers of Tench Coxe in the Coxe Family Papers at the Historical Society of Pennsylvania, Philadelphia.)

7. Gray's Ferry, or the Lower Ferry, was on the Schuylkill about a mile south of the then city of Philadelphia in an area which is now part of the modern city. It was the site of Gray's Gardens, from which Secretary of the Treasury Oliver Wolcott, Jr., wrote to his father on September 4, 1797: "I arrived here last evening and without exposure to the sickness in the city. . . . More of the houses are deserted than was the case in 1793, and business is suspended almost entirely" (George Gibbs, *Memoirs of the Administrations of Washington and John Adams: Edited from the Papers of Oliver Wolcott, Secretary of the Treasury* [New York, 1846], I, 560).

8. Tench Francis, Jr., was cashier of the Bank of North America. He and Coxe's mother, Mary Francis Coxe, were the children of Tench Francis, Sr., a lawyer in Philadelphia and Attorney General of the Province of Pennsylvania from 1741 until his death in 1755. In addition Tench Francis's grandson, Tench Tilghman, was the cousin of Tench Coxe and of the Edward Tilghman mentioned in note 5 above.

9. Samuel Meredith was Treasurer of the United States, or head of the Treasurer's Office in the Treasury Department.

To Théophile Cazenove [1]

New York, October-December, 1797. Proposes the forms which should be used for investing the one-hundred thousand dollars which Robert Morris had agreed to pay to the Seneca Indians for their lands in Ontario County, New York.

Copy, Gemeentearchief Amsterdam, Holland Land Company. These documents were transferred in 1964 from the Nederlandsch Economisch-Historisch Archief, Amsterdam.
   1. H wrote this letter in his capacity as attorney for the Holland Land Company. Cazenove was the company's principal representative in America.
   For an explanation of the contents of this letter, see H to Herman LeRoy, William Bayard, and James McEvers, December 16, 1796, note 1; March 4–July 18, 1797 (*PAH*, XX, 447–48, 530). See also Goebel, *Law Practice*, forthcoming volumes.

From Thomas Stoughton [1]

[*New York, November 11, 1797.* On June 25, 1803, Stoughton wrote to Hamilton: "I had the honor to write you on this Subject the 11th. Novre. 1797. accompanying a Statement of Facts, copy of our Articles, and my claims." *Letter not found.*]

   1. See Stoughton to H, June 25, 1803 (printed in this volume).

1798

From Theodore Sedgwick

[Stockbridge, Massachusetts, November 19, 1798. Letter not found.]

"Letters from T. S. [Theodore Sedgwick] to Genl. A. Hamilton," William Livingston Papers, Book 3, Massachusetts Historical Society, Boston.

From Michael Welsh

New York [1798–1804]. "A Series of misfortunes which have pursued me from infancy . . . make me apply to you for a Small Sum to relieve me from present embarrassment. The portrait that accompanies this letter is not offered to you in barter for the sum required. No Sir, it is my request that you would honor it with some corner in your house. . . . It is Sir the portrait of the Countess of Serang, Daughter of General Count Lacy and wife of General Welsh of the Irish Brigades now lord Serang. . . . I have Singled you out to relieve me at present and to be the Guardian and protector of the Image of the woman who cherished and nourished me with maternal care. . . . The Sum for which I apply to your bounty is about thirty five Dollars and is the amount I owe for boarding &c. . . ."

ALS, Hamilton Papers, Library of Congress.

1799

From William Duer [1]

New york. 13th. Jany. 1799.

Dear Sir

As I Owe to your kind Interposition the Permission I have obtained from the Secretary of the Treasury to reside with my Family in the Liberties 'till remanded, so I trust with Confidence that your friendly Exertions will not be wanting to insure to me a Continuance of this Priviledge.

Colo. Giles [2] the Marshall has within these few days Expressed a Doubt to one of my Fellow Prisoners, that this Permission can only be construed to be in Force during the Sickness; and under this Impression (though I have had Evidence of his friendly Disposition to me, and my Family) he may Esteem it his Duty to interfere in this Business. I Enclose you a Certified Copy of the Engagement which has been transmitted to the Secretary of the Treasury—And as no Orders for remanding me have been transmitted I conceive myself Entitled to the Priviledge of Liberties in the Suit of the United States.

You will oblige me Extremely, in seeing Colo. Giles in order to remove from his Mind the Misapprehension he Entertains in this Business. I am now on the Point of Emerging from this Abyss of Misery; let me Conjure you to Use your Influence, and kind Offices to prevent my being replunged into it. The State of my Health for these two or three months, has become truly Alarming. I labor under a Malady which requires a greater Degree of Attention than I can obtain, in this Place, and which is daily Encreasing from the Anxiety of my Mind. To this are added Family Considerations of the most Urgent Nature, which render my Return to my Family Essential to their Preservation from Misery, and Ruin. Lady Kitty [3] will do herself the Pleasure of delivering to you in Person this Letter. I am Dear Sir with Sentiments of Esteem, Your Obet. Humble servt.

W Duer

Major Genl. Hamilton

[ENCLOSURE]⁴

[New York, October 1, 1798]

The Undersigned having obtained permission from the Secretary of the Treasury of the united states by his Letter of the 19th of September last directed to the Keeper of the Prison of the City of New york—to reside within the Liberties assigned by Law to the Jail of the City and County of New york Does hereby engage not to depart beyond the said Limits and to return to Confinement when required by proper authority derived from the United States.

In Witness whereof he hath subscribed Two Engagements of the same Tenor and Date one of which is to be transmitted to the Secretary of the Treasury of the United States the other to be preserved by the Keeper of the prison of the City of New york. Dated New York October first 1798

W Duer

Signed in the presence of
Wm W Parker Goaler

I Certify that the foregoing is a true copy of an original transmitted to the Secretary of the Treasury
Given under my hand this fourteenth Day of January in the year 1799

Wm W Parker Keeper
of the Debtors Apartment

ALS, Sleepy Hollow Restorations, Inc., Tarrytown, New York.
    1. In *PAH*, XXII, 412, this letter is listed as a "letter not found."
    For background to the letter printed above, see Duer to H, March 21, 1792, note 1 (printed in this volume).
    On March 23 Duer had been imprisoned in New York City for debts which he owed to the United States (Duer to H, December 24, 1790, note 1 [printed in this volume]). H has frequently been credited with securing Duer's temporary release from prison in 1797 (Allen Johnson and Dumas Malone, eds.,

Dictionary of American Biography, V [New York, 1930], 487; Davis, *Essays*, I, 330–31; and earlier volumes of *PAH*), but no conclusive evidence has been found that he left jail—even for a short time—in 1797.

In September, 1798, Secretary of the Treasury Oliver Wolcott, Jr., at H's suggestion, permitted Duer "to reside at any place within the liberties of the Prison, during the continuance of the present contagious disease [yellow fever]." See enclosure to Wolcott to H, September 19, 1798 (*PAH*, XXII, 185–87). This enclosure is incorrectly addressed to Thomas Hazard. The letter was actually sent to William W. Parker.

As the letter printed above indicates, Duer wished to have the privileges which he had been granted in September, 1798, continued, and he even hoped that he might be permitted to leave jail and return to his family. Although evidence is lacking, it appears that Duer was not released and that he retained the "liberties" of the prison until his death there on May 7, 1799.

2. Aquila Giles was United States marshal of the District of New York.

3. Catharine Alexander Duer.

4. Copy, Sleepy Hollow Restorations, Inc., Tarrytown, New York.

From William Duer [1]

New York Jany. 17th. 1799.

Dear Sir.

I Enclose you agreably to my Promise a Copy of Mr. Wolcotts Letter to the Keeper of the Prison.[2]

On an attentive Perusal It appears clearly to me that the Indulgence granted by Mr. Wolcott was in Consequence of the Epidemic prevailing in the Jail, and it may be construed to terminate with the Extinction of the Contagion. Nevertheless, The Stipulation proposed in the Letter is, That I should return *when required* after the Contagion had Ceased—and the Engagement transmitted to the Secretary, purports, that this Requisition shall be made by proper Authority derived from the U. States.

The Fact is, That no Counter Orders have been transmitted—and the Keeper having permitted me to go on the Liberties during the Sickness (although I was still detained in private Suits) conceives himself not authorised to detain me when it can be done without Committing the United States—as to Individual Claim.

It is not difficult for me to Conjecture what Mr. Wolcotts Motives were for Expressing his Letter in the Manner which he has done. In a Government constituted as ours, whose Administration is constantly opposed and Vilified by a virulent and Wicked Faction, it is hardly possible for an Officer to be either just, or humane to one who has become the unhappy Object of public Censure without Exposing himself to the Suspicion of being actuated by base, and Unworthy Motives, and of thereby destroying his Public Utility. I cannot however persuade myself if I am once admitted to the Liberties, that Mr Wolcott on a proper Representation of the afflicting malady under which I labor, of the Security derived from Bonds given as my private Surety, and of the Ultimate Responsibility of the late Commrs. of the Treasury will judge it necessary to debar me of that Privilege. Under these Circumstances I submit it to your opinion whether it is not best that I should avail myself of the Keeper's Release, without committing either Mr. Wolcott, the Attorney General, or the Marshall in the Business.

After you have maturely reflected on this Subject, I will desire Lady Kitty to call upon you—and if you agree with me you can inform her so personally.

My days are sad beyond Description—My Nights Miserable. I am again attacked with a Complaint which soon after the Peace had nearly put an End to my Existence, a Suppression of Urine—attended with acute Pain like those Arisg from the Stones or Gravel. Unless I can be relieved by the Use of Warm Baths, and of such Medical Aid as can only be applied under my own Roof, I foresee that in the Course of this Year I shall probably terminate a Wretched Existence. On my own Account, I could meet my Fate not only with Resignation but with Complacency. But when I reflect on the probable Consequence of leaving to a merciless World, those who are dearer to [me] than my Life, the Thought drives me to Distraction—and the Agony of my Mind Encreases that which is incident to my Unhappy Complaint.

I am with Sentiments of Regard   Dear Sir   Your Obet. Hble. sert.

W Duer

Major Genl. Hamilton.

ALS, Sleepy Hollow Restorations, Inc., Tarrytown, New York.

1. In *PAH*, XXII, 422, this letter is listed as a "letter not found."

For an explanation of the contents of the letter printed above, see Duer to H, January 13, 1799 (printed in this volume).

2. See enclosure to Oliver Wolcott, Jr., to H, September 19, 1798 (*PAH*, XXII, 185–87).

From William Duer [1]

[New York, February 16, 1799]

Dear Sir.

I have risen from a Sleepless Bed, with a Mind too distracted to Write to you. Whilst my memory still serves to mention to you certain Circumstances relative to my Accounts with the United States, and the Situation of my Family I wish to see you. How long this will be the Case God only knows!—he is a better Judge of what I am than Man, and at his Tribunal only I Expect Justice. The Sympathy which Mr. Morris [2] informs me you feel for me and mine affords me Consolation in the Depth of my Misery. My Affection for yourself, and my Sensibility for whatever interested your happiness has been Ever sincere—and I have felt with Pain any Appearance of your Withdrawing from me. What Impressions have been made in your Mind I know not: whilst my Reason maintains its Ascendancy I wish to remove them: and for this Purpose I request on the Ground of our Antient Friendship that you will see me as soon as possible.

I am Dear Sir   Your Affectionate Friend & Hble servt.   W Duer.

Alexr. Hamilton Esqr.
New York. Feby. 16th. 1799.

ALS, Sleepy Hollow Restorations, Inc., Tarrytown, New York.
  1. In *PAH*, XXII, 486, this letter is listed as a "letter not found."
  For an explanation of the contents of this letter, see Duer to H, January 13, 17, 1799 (both printed in this volume).
  2. Gouverneur Morris.

From Jean Mouchon [1]

New York, March 2, 1799. Explains his actions as an agent for La Barre and Company in a dispute concerning a shipment of wine from France to New York on the ship *Chesapeake*.

ADS, Hamilton Papers, Library of Congress.
1. Mouchon was a New York City merchant at 101 Beekman Street.
This letter concerns the case of *Dominique Allard* v *John Mouchon*. In April, 1797, Mouchon, acting as an agent for the New York mercantile firm of La Barre and Company, received a shipment of wine from Bordeaux with instructions to sell the wine. In July, 1797, Allard wrote to Mouchon that the wine belonged to him, not to La Barre and Company (Mouchon to Richard Harison and Brockholst Livingston, March 4, 1799 [ADS, Hamilton Papers, Library of Congress]). Allard subsequently brought suit against Mouchon, and on February 21, 1799, with H as Mouchon's attorney, the Supreme Court of New York referred the dispute to Harison and Livingston as referees. Harison and Livingston submitted a report to the court favoring the defendant, but on April 24, 1800, the court ordered that the report be set aside, stating "The facts in this case are intricate, and there exists so much doubt and obscurity on the subject, that there is reason to apprehend that the referees did not possess all the lights which may now be afforded them, and which may lead to a more satisfactory result. We therefore think the case ought to be reviewed . . . in order to re-examine the merits" (MS Common Rule Book, New York Supreme Court, 1797–1799, under the date of February 21, 1799 [Hall of Records, New York City]; MS Minutes of the New York Supreme Court, 1797–1800, under the date of April 24, 1800 [Hall of Records, New York City]; William Johnson, *Reports of Cases Adjudged in the Supreme Court of Judicature of the State of New-York; from January Term 1799, to January Term 1803, Both Inclusive; Together with Cases Determined in the Court for the Correction of Errors, During that Period* [New York, 1808], I, 280).

To John Murray [1]

[*New York, April 2, 1799.* Letter listed in dealer's catalogue. *Letter not found.*]

1. ALS, sold in 1898 by John Cadby, Albany, New York, Catalogue 33, Item 133.
Murray, a New York City merchant, was a director of the Bank of New York from 1789 to 1794. In 1798 he was a director of the New York Office of Discount and Deposit and president of the New York City Chamber of Commerce. He owned property on Murray Hill in New York City.

From Ezra L'Hommedieu [1]

[*April 9, 1799.* ". . . I consent that you receive the four thousand Dollars which have been deposited on account of this note without prejudice to your recourse against me as Indorser." [2] *Letter not found.*]

The Collector: A Magazine for Autograph and Historical Collectors, LXXII,
No. 6 (1959), 128, Item i 299.
   1. L'Hommedieu represented New York in the Continental Congress from
1779 to 1782 and in 1788. He was a member of the New York Assembly from
Suffolk County from 1777 to 1783, clerk of Suffolk County from 1784 to 1810,
and a member of the state Senate from 1784 to 1792 and from 1794 to 1809.
   For background to this letter, see H to L'Hommedieu, April 4, 1799 (*PAH,*
XXIII, 8–10).
   2. Text taken from extract in dealer's catalogue.

From Edward Carrington [1]

[*Richmond, July 5, 1799.* The description of this letter in the
dealer's catalogue reads: ". . . about the appointment of an aide-de-
camp. '. . . Contracts are now in operation at every place assigned
as recruiting stations . . . and at them such temporary arrangements
are made as enable the Officers to be proceeding.'" *Letter not
found.*]

The Collector: A Magazine for Autograph and Historical Collectors, LXXIX,
Nos. 7–10 (1966), 4, Item J-202.
   1. Carrington was supervisor of the revenue in Virginia.

UNDATED LETTERS AND DOCUMENTS

From ——————

[n.p., n.d.]

Sir.

Mr. Duer the late Secretary of the Board of Treasury [1] having informed us that in Consequence of his having Exhibited the account of our Salaries,[2] the warrant including the same has been made out in his Favor as Secretary of the late Board. We beg Leave to inform you that we have no Objection to its issuing in that Form.

We are Sir, Your most Obet. Hble Serts.

Alexr. Hamilton Esqr.
Secretary to the
late Board of Treasury

Copy, New-York Historical Society, New York City.
   1. William Duer was secretary of the Board of Treasury from 1786 to 1789.
   2. For salaries which were still owed to employees of the Board of Treasury after H had become Secretary of the Treasury on September 11, 1789, see *PAH,* V, 382–83, 391, 403–05.

To ——————

[n.p., n.d.]

Dr. Sir

The amount due to the Bank does not appear in the papers except in a letter of Butlers in which he states it at 8900 Drs. But this was not the subject of my inquiry. I wanted to know the probable amount here of the Cargo which was assigned for our suit ought to be for that amount.

Yrs.   with respect   A H

ALS, in a grangerized copy of [William Coleman] *A Collection of the Facts and Documents, Relative to the Death of Major-General Alexander Hamilton; with Comments: Together with the Various Orations, Sermons, and Eulogies, That Have Been Published or Written on His Life and Character* (New-

York: Printed by Hopkins and Seymour, for Riley and Co. Booksellers, No. 1, City-Hotel, Broadway, 1804) in The Sol Feinstone Collection, Library of the American Philosophical Society, Philadelphia.

To ————————

[n.p., n.d.]

Dr. Sir

I have perused the declaration & approve it. I presume the 12 of Decr. last was previous to *suing out* the Writ; if not to avoid cavilling it may [be] well to antedate it.

Yrs.   A Hamilton

ALS, Yale University Library.

To ————————

[n.p., n.d.]

Dear Sir

I am mortified at the unseasonable trouble I occasion to you, but if the inclosed is in a state to admit regularly of an authentication by you I shall be glad of two copies under your seal of office.

I remain very respectfully & with great regard   Yr Obed ser

A Hamilton

I shall want one copy by tomorrow
Eight O Clock

ALS, Harvard College Library.

To ————————

[n.p., n.d.]

I will thank you for your name on the inclosed.

Yrs.   A H

ALS, New-York Historical Society, New York City.

To ——————

[n.p.] March 15

Dr. Sir

I think we must admit the special verdict. If there be any thing in it which they cannot prove otherwise, they may by a bill of discovery obtain the effect of the admission.

Yrs.   A H

ALS, Mrs. John Jay Pierrepont, Ridgefield, Connecticut.

From John Burchan [1]

[Philadelphia, n.d.] [2]

John Burchan, the Young Gentleman recommended to Col. Hamilton by Thomas Lowrey,[3] is to be found at Mr. Michael Roberts,[4] No. 32. Hanover Square.

AL, Papers of Tench Coxe in the Coxe Family Papers at the Historical Society of Pennsylvania, Philadelphia.

1. On January 3, 1793, Burchan was listed as a clerk in the office of the register of the Treasury Department (*PAH*, XIII, 466).

2. This letter was presumably written at some date between September, 1789, and December, 1792.

3. Thomas Lowrey was marshal for the District of New Jersey from September 26, 1789, to January, 1802.

4. Roberts was a Philadelphia merchant.

To Mathew Carey [1]

[Philadelphia, n.d.]

Mr Hamilton's Compliments to Mr Carey. He would readily comply with Mr Carey's request if he had any paper containing his speech;

but having none he cannot do it unless Mr Carey will furnish him with one. If this can be done Mr H will correct it this evening which indeed he would wish to do, as there are considerable errors.

Copy, Historical Society of Pennsylvania, Philadalphia.
1. Carey, an Irish printer and publisher who fled to America in 1784 to escape prosecution for his political views, was editor of *The American Museum* from 1787 to 1792. He subsequently became a publisher, bookseller, and the author of several pamphlets and books on American economic development. He was a prominent civic leader in Philadelphia until his death in 1839.

Comments on Jews

[n.p., n.d.]

& progress of the Jews and their from their earliest history to the present time has been & is, intirely out of the *ordinary course* of human affairs. Is it not then a fair conclusion that the *cause* also is an *extraordinary one*—in other words that it is the effect of some great providential plan? The man who will draw this Conclusion will look for the solution in the Bible. He who will not draw it ought to give us another fair solution.

AD (incomplete), American Jewish Historical Society, Waltham, Massachusetts.

From Peter Corne [1]

[*n.p., n.d.*]. Asks Hamilton's opinion on what steps he should take to recover his losses in New York State during the American Revolution. States that the commissioners of sequestration seized and sold all his "Stock grain Hay Farming Carriages & utensills Contrary to the intention of Congress" and that damages to his farm in Cortlandt Manor in Westchester County by the American forces amounted to at least six hundred dollars.

ALS, Hamilton Papers, Library of Congress.
1. Corne was a Loyalist from Westchester County, New York, who had

moved to New York City during the British occupation of that city during the American Revolution. He became involved in a public controversy between civilian and military officials in the city. With permission of the mayor he erected posts for scales on a wharf. Samuel Brownjohn cut down the posts as a public nuisance. When the military authorities fined Brownjohn and sent him to prison for noncompliance, many inhabitants viewed him "as a Martyr" and a symbol of opposition to military rule ("Historical Memoirs From 16 March 1763 to 12 November 1783 of William Smith," folio vol. VII, under date of February 6, 1782 [AD, Manuscript Division, New York Public Library]). It has been suggested that this incident was one of the events leading to the establishment of civilian rule in the city (Oscar Theodore Barck, Jr., *New York City During the War for Independence. With Special Reference to the Period of British Occupation* [New York, 1931], 69–70).

Draft of an Act Imposing Duties on Carriages and Servants [1]

[Philadelphia, n.d.]

An act imposing Duties on Carriages and servants

Be it enacted that every Owner or possessor of any of the carriages hereafter specified shall pay a yearly duty for the same according to the rates following viz

ADf, Hamilton Papers, Library of Congress.

1. This document presents certain difficulties concerning both the date and purpose for which it was written. In some respects it is not unlike an act which H introduced in 1787 into the New York Assembly ("New York Assembly. An Act for Raising Certain Taxes Within This State," February 9, 1787 [*PAH*, IV, 40–66]). The document printed above was not, however, written in the Confederation period, for in it amounts of money are expressed in dollars rather than in pounds (which H used in the 1787 act), and reference is made to the "office of Inland Duties."

There is a possibility—but only a possibility—that H drew up this document as a draft that he considered including (but later decided to discard) in his "Report Relative to a Provision for the Support of Public Credit," January 9, 1790 (*PAH*, VI, 51–168). If this is the case, it was written after September 1, 1789, when the House passed a resolution requesting such a report (*Journal of the House*, I, 117) and before January 9, 1790.

H may also have written this document in response to a request from a House committee which had been appointed on March 26, 1794, "to inquire whether any, or what, further or other revenues are necessary for the support of public credit, and if further revenues are necessary, to report the ways and means" (*Annals of Congress*, IV, 531). The work of this committee led to the introduction and passage of "An Act laying duties upon Carriages for the conveyance of Persons" (1 *Stat.* 373–75 [June 5, 1794]). H as Secretary of the Treasury more than once mentioned a tax on carriages (*PAH*, VI, 288; XIII,

For every carriage of the kind now called a coach fifteen Dollars

For every carriage of the kind now called a Chariot twelve Dollars

For every Post Chaise and other close four wheeled Carriage ten Dollars

For every phæton and other open four wheeled carriage 8 Dollars

Provided that this duty shall not be deemed to extend to Waggons

And be it further enacted that every such owner or possessor of any of the said carriages shall in the first week in   [2] next and thenceforth in the first week in May in each year report in writing to the nearest office of Inland Duties if within   miles of his or her chattels or place of residence such of the said carriages as he or she may have with the name and description thereof which report shall be signed by such owner or possessor. And in case there be no office of Inland duties within the said distance of   miles of the dwelling or place of residence of any such Owner or possessor he or she upon the request of any Commissioner or Commissioners of Inland Duties for the district within which he or she shall reside, or the lawful deputy of such commissioner or Commissioners, shall make to him or them the like report in writing as is above directed to be made to the respective offices of Inland duties. And every such owner or possessor for every neglect or refusal to make such report as the case may require shall forfeit and pay treble the amount of the duty payable by him or her pursuant to this act for any of the said carriages in his or her possession. Provided that the same person shall not be obliged to make more than one report of the same identical carriage or carriages; but after the first report shall be and continue chargeable each year for the duty on each carriage so reported unless notice shall be given that he or she hath parted therewith, which notice shall be given in some such first week in May.

269-70; XVIII, 91); John C. Hamilton attributes the authorship of the bill in 1794 for taxing carriages to H (*JCHW*, V, 99-103; *PAH*, XVI, 462); and William Bradford suggests or hints that H may have written the bill (*PAH*, XVIII, 396-97, and 397, note 18). On the other hand, no specific evidence has been found that H either wrote the measure or (with the possible exception of the document printed above) that he contributed to its preparation. In this connection it should perhaps also be noted that "An Act laying duties upon Carriages for the conveyance of Persons" contains no provisions for taxing servants and that its rates for taxing carriages were uniformly lower than those proposed by H in the document printed above.

2. This and subsequent spaces left blank in MS.

And be it further enacted that the said Duty shall be payable at the option of such Owner or possessor either at the time of making such report as aforesaid or within the first week of September and payment shall be made by such Owner or possessor at the same office at which his or her report shall have been made, or (where there shall be no office within the said distance of   miles of his or her residence) to any Commission[er] or Commissioners of the district or his or their deputy who shall first demand the said payment of him or her, at his or her dwelling or place of residence.

And be it further enacted that if any such Owner or possessor shall neglect or refuse to make such payment as the case may require it shall be lawful for the Commissioner or Commissioners of the district within which he or she shall reside or his or her deputy thereunto properly authorised to levy the ⟨amount⟩ of the duty payable by him or her ⟨by di⟩stress and sale of his and her goods and chattels to be conducted in manner following to Wit [3]

And be it further enacted That every person who shall retain employ or have any Male servant or servants in any of the capacities of Maitre d'hotel house steward Valet De Cham⟨bre⟩ Butler Under butler Confectioner Cook house porter waiter footman coachman groom postilion stable boy or by whatsoever name or names male servants acting in any of the said capacities may be called shall pay therefor the several yearly duties following that is to say

For one male servant the sum of one dollar

For two male servants and not more the sum of two Dollars each

For three male servants and not more the sum of three Dollars each

For four Male servants and upwards the sum of four Dollars each

And every male person of the age of 21 years and upwards never having been married who shall retain or employ any such servant shall pay for him over and above the rates aforesaid the sum of one Dollar.

Provided always, and be it further enacted that the duties hereby imposed shall not be construed to extend to any servant retained or

3. At this point H left almost a page blank in MS.

employed *bona fide* for or in the purposes of husbandry or manufactures or of any trade or calling whereby the employer of such servant shall earn a livelihood or profit or of any College or seminary of learning.

And be it further enacted that the Inhabitant householder of any house in which there shall be any lodger or inmate who shall have or keep any servant or servants liable to the duties aforesaid or any of them shall within one week after a requisition or writing list at any such house from or by any Commissioner or Commissioners aforesaid his or their deputy deliver to or leave for such Com~. or Comns. his or their deputy a list in writing of every such lodger or inmate in such house who shall at the time of delivering or leaving such Notice retain or employ any servant liable to the duties hereby imposed on any of them or shall have retained or employed any such servant or servants in any year preceding immediately preceding any period for making such report as aforesaid; which list shall express the Christian and surname of every such lodger or inmate and also of every such servant or servants to the best of the knowlege or information of such inhabitant householder and if any inhabitant householder shall refuse or neglect to deliver any such list or shall wilfully omit or misrepresent any description which ought to be contained therein he or she so offending shall for every such offence forfeit   dollars

To Elizabeth Hamilton

[n.p., n.d.] [1]

For want of having made application on time The stage waggon has been engaged so as to prevent my going in it. I must therefore take my chance by water which I shall do tomorrow and must content myself with praying for a fair wind to waft me speedily to the bosom of my beloved.

Adieu   A Hamilton

Love to Ang [2] & Marg. [3]

ALS, New York State Library, Albany.

1. On March 15, 1858, John C. Hamilton wrote the date "April 8, 1795" on this letter, but in April, 1795, both H and Elizabeth Hamilton were in Albany.

2. Depending on when this letter was written, this could be either Angelica Hamilton, Hamilton's oldest daughter who was born on September 25, 1784, or Angelica Church, who was Elizabeth Hamilton's sister. Angelica Church and her husband left the United States for England in the summer of 1783 and did not return until the spring of 1797.

3. Margarita Van Rensselaer, Elizabeth Hamilton's sister, who died in 1801. See H to Elizabeth Hamilton, March 16, 1801 (*PAH*, XXV, 348–49).

To Richard Harison [1]

[n.p., n.d.]

Dr Sir

I will thank you briefly to assign your reasons with the opinion I have requested.

Yrs   A H

ALS, Richard Harison Papers, New-York Historical Society, New York City.

1. Harison was United States attorney for the District of New York from 1789 to 1801.

To John Laurance

[n.p., n.d.]

Dr Laurence

I have lately made some Cash advances which have run me aground. I will thank you for the loan of a hundred dollars for a few days.

Yrs.   A Hamilton

Monday morning

ALS, New-York Historical Society, New York City.

To John Laurance

[n.p., February 28]

Dr Laurence

I am just now as to the command of Cash as poor as *Job:* & I do not like to go into the Bank. If you can accomodate me with 100 Dollars for ten days you will oblige Yrs   A Hamilton

Febr 28

ALS, New-York Historical Society, New York City.

To Henry Lee [1]

[*n.p., n.d.* ". . . Pray resolve my doubts. For a man in my situation ought at least to take care how he fails in his *pecuniary* duty. . . ." [2] *Letter not found.*]

1. ALS, sold by Sotheby & Company, December 15, 1953, Item 453.
2. Extract taken from dealer's catalogue.

Receipt from LeRoy and Bayard [1]

[New York, n.d.]

Hnble Alexr. Hamilton Esqr.

To Le Roy & Bayard Dr.

For 1 Sett of Exchange vizt
their Draft dated New York 23d. Ulto. at 60 ds. St
to the order of James McEvers, on P. & C. Van Eeghen [2] Amstm., pble in London, No 16 £Sty 250   Ex 4 ⅌ Ct.   £433.6.8

Dollars 1155.57

Recd. the above

LeRoy & Bayard
⅌ Jas. Chevalier [3]

DS, Hamilton Papers, Library of Congress.

1. Herman LeRoy and William Bayard were partners in the New York City mercantile firm of LeRoy, Bayard, and McEvers, which represented the Holland Land Company in the United States. The third partner was James McEvers.

This receipt was sent to H in his capacity as attorney for the six Dutch banking firms which were formally organized as the Holland Land Company on February 13, 1796.

2. P. and C. Van Eeghen was one of the four Dutch banking houses in Amsterdam which in 1789 appointed Théophile Cazenove as their agent to handle their speculations in American securities, and it was one of the six firms which formed the Holland Land Company in 1796.

3. James Chevalier was a New York City merchant. In addition, he was the publisher of the [New York] *Mercantile Advertiser* from April 22, 1799, to August 23, 1799, when he died.

To James McHenry

[New York, n.d.] [1]

My Dr. Sir

I was at Albany when your letter got here. I have snatched the first hour from my avocations to sketch to you my thoughts in a rude shape.

Yrs. Affecly   A H

ALS, New York State Historical Association, Cooperstown, New York; ALS (photostat), James McHenry Papers, Library of Congress.

1. This letter was presumably written between January 12, 1796, when McHenry was appointed Secretary of War, and May 6, 1800, when he submitted his letter of resignation to President John Adams.

To Peter Van Gaasbeck [1]

[n.p., n.d.]

Dr Sir

I learn with great pleasure the intelligence contained in your private letter.[2] I hope the good sense of our state will every day give new triumphs to good men & good measures.

With esteem & regard   Yr Obed ser   A Hamilton

P. V. Gaasbeck Esq

ALS, Lloyd W. Smith Collection, Morristown National Historical Park, Morristown, New Jersey.
1. Van Gaasbeck, a merchant in Kingston, New York, was a member of the House of Representatives from 1793 to 1795. He died in 1797.
2. Letter not found.

To Benjamin Walker [1]

[*n.p.*, *n.d.*[2] "Forward the enclosed with as much expedition and certainty as you can (I don't mean that an express should be employed) and say nothing about it." [3] *Letter not found.*]

1. ALS, sold by Parke-Bernet Galleries, Inc., December 3, 1963, Lot 2235, Item 112.
2. The dealer's catalogue dates this letter "Philadelphia, 4 April, 1799." On April 4, 1799, H was in New York City, not Philadelphia.
3. Extract taken from dealer's catalogue.

To ———— Watts [1]

[n.p., n.d.]

Dr Sir

I would advise you to close with Mr. Hobart [2] on his own terms; only fix what is a reasonable time: say three four five or six months, the longer the better. Let a fair copy of the paper inclosed be signed with a receipt at bottom for the money in specie. This may, if necessary be afterwards put more in form. Yrs.

A Hamilton

ALS, Mr. A. J. Marino, Weehawken, New Jersey.
1. This letter, which is addressed to "Mr. Watts," was presumably written to either John or Robert Watts. Both lived in New York City and were sons of John Watts, Sr., who had been a member of the provincial council and who under an act of attainder on October 22, 1779, had to forfeit his estates to New York State (Harry B. Yoshpe, *The Disposition of Loyalist Estates in the Southern District of the State of New York* [New York, 1939], 17). John Watts, Sr., left New York for England, and on June 16, 1784, his two sons purchased their father's former property (Yoshpe, *Disposition of Loyalist Estates*, 38, 131).
H was on more than one occasion associated with both sons as an attorney. For John Watts, Jr., see H *et al.* to Patrick Murdock, September 7, 1790 (*PAH*,

VII, 25–26); H to Philip Schuyler, October 12, 1795 (*PAH*, XIX, 311–13); the entry in H's Cash Book, 1795–1804, under the date of March 16, 1796 (AD, Hamilton Papers, Library of Congress). For Robert Watts, see entries in H's "Cash Book," March 1, 1782–1791 (*PAH*, III, 20, 58); entries in H's Cash Book, 1795–1804, under dates of May 9, 1796, and January 10, 1797 (AD, Hamilton Papers, Library of Congress).

2. John Sloss Hobart, who was a member of the Provincial Congress from 1775 to 1777, was a justice of the New York Supreme Court from 1777 to 1798. On January 11, 1798, he was elected to the United States Senate, but on April 12, 1798, he was appointed United States judge for the District of New York, a position which he held until his death in 1805.

To ——————— *Wooster* [1]

[n.p., August 22]

Mr. Hamiltons compliments to Mr Wooster. General Stewart[2] has been under some misapprehension respecting Mr. Hs desire to see Mr. Wooster.

Aug 22

AL, United States Military Academy, West Point, New York.

1. H wrote on the outside of this letter "Capt Wooster." Thomas Wooster of Connecticut was a captain in Webb's Additional Continental Regiment from February, 1777, to April, 1779. He was an applicant for Federal office in 1789 (*GW*, XXX, 327–28), and on August 21, 1798, H listed a Thomas Wooster from New York who "wished to serve his country once more" (*PAH*, XXII, 95).

2. Walter Stewart, a veteran of the American Revolution who was brevetted a brigadier general at the end of the war, was a Philadelphia merchant and from December 10, 1793, to January, 1796, surveyor for the District of Philadelphia and inspector of the revenue for the port of Philadelphia.

ADDENDA AND ERRATA

Volume I

Page

242–22   To William Livingston, April 29, 1777. *Additional sources:* ALS, Mr. Jon F. Hopkinson, Greenwich, Connecticut; copy, Hamilton Papers, Library of Congress. Both the ALS and the copy omit the last paragraph of this letter.

244   From Hugh Knox, date line: *For* April 31st: 1777 *read* [April–May, 1777]
     Add following note: MS is misdated April 31st: 1777.

258   To Francis Grice, source line: *For* VII *read* VIII

279–80   From Gouverneur Morris, July 4, 1777. *Additional sources:* copy, The Sol Feinstone Collection, Library of the American Philosophical Society, Philadelphia; copy, Catharine S. Crary Collection, Columbia University Libraries.

283–84   To Colonel Elias Dayton, note 2: *For* MacWhorter *read* Macwhorter

299   To Hugh Knox, date line: *For* [July, 1777] *read* [July 1–28, 1777]
     Transfer this letter to *PAH*, I, 279.

306–09   To Robert R. Livingston, August 7, 1777. *Additional sources:* copy, The Sol Feinstone Collection, Library of the American Philosophical Society, Philadelphia; copy, Catharine S. Crary Collection, Columbia University Libraries.

326–27   To John Hancock, September 18, 1777. *Additional source:* F. S. Bartram, *Retrographs: Comprising a History of New York City prior to the Revolution* . . . (New York, n.d.), 82. This version is longer than the copy printed in *PAH* and also differs in wording.
     Source line: *For* Transcript *read* Copy

329   "Bill for Expenses of George Washington's Staff," source line: *For* Hamilton Papers *read* George Washington Papers

Page

329–30 H and John Laurens to John Sullivan, September 21, 1777.
Additional sources: copy, Reel 72, Item 59, III, p. 61, Papers
of the Continental Congress, National Archives; copy, RG
93, War Department Revolutionary War Records, Miscellaneous Records, National Archives.

384 Paragraph 6, line 1: *For* sico *read* scio

409 Note 113, line 3: *For 6 read* 69

414 To George Washington, note 2, lines 1 and 2: *For* Charles
Carroll *read* Charles Carroll of Carrollton

422–23 "Remarks Concerning the Office of Inspector General,"
note 1, line 14: *For* printed *read* calendared

432 George Washington to the Board of War, line 2 and note
1: *For* Heister *read* Hiester

434 George Washington to the Committee of Congress, note 1,
line 2: *For* Charles Carroll *read* Charles Carroll of Carrollton

437–38 To James McHenry, source line: *For* ALS *read* ALS
(photostat)

442 George Washington to William Heath, line 2: *For* Heister
read Hiester

445–46 "Commission to William Grayson, Robert Hanson Harrison, H, and Elias Boudinot," March 28, 1778. *Additional
source:* copy, Reel 168, Item 152, V, p. 489, Papers of the
Continental Congress, National Archives.

454–56 William Grayson, Robert Hanson Harrison, H, and Elias
Boudinot to George Washington, April 4, 1778. *Additional sources:* copy, Reel 168, Item 152, V, p. 493, Papers

Page

481 First letter, title and note 1: *For* Thevenau Francy *read* Lazare-Jean de Francy-les-Arnay, Théveneau de Francy

485 From Edward Stevens, note 2, line 1: *For* Kings *read* King's

487 "Oath of Allegiance," May 12, 1778. *Additional source:* copy, Long Island Historical Society, Brooklyn, New York.

497–501 To William Duer, June 18, 1778. *Additional source:* ALS, Hamilton Papers, Library of Congress.
  Last two paragraphs and closing: *Delete* broken brackets. This material has been located in the Hamilton Papers, Library of Congress.

525–26 To George Washington, July 20, 1778. *Additional sources:* copy, New Hampshire Historical Society, Concord; copy, Hamilton Papers, Library of Congress.

543 Note 5, line 1: *Delete* Marquis de Choin (frequently misspelled Chouin) and *substitute* Marquis de Chouin

551–52 From James McHenry, note 1: *For* Philippis *read* Phillipus

552 George Washington to Comte d'Estaing, line 2: *For* Choin *read* Chouin

553 George Washington to Nathanael Greene, September 22, 1778. *Additional source:* LS, in the handwriting of H, Bibliothèque Municipale, Lille, France.

561 George Washington to Comte d'Estaing, line 2: *For* Comte d'Orvillier *read* Comte d'Orvilliers

566 Third letter, title, line 1, and note 1: *For* Thurston *read* Thruston

567 George Washington to Alexander McDougall, October 24, 1778. *Additional source:* LS, in the handwriting of H, the

Page

W. Wright Hawkes Collection of Revolutionary War Documents, on deposit at Union College, Schenectady, New York.

576   From Charles Armand, November 5, 1778. *Additional source:* copy, Columbia University Libraries.

591   Note 2, line 1: *For* Setouket *read* Setauket

591–92   "Commission to Robert Hanson Harrison and H," November 30, 1778. *Additional source:* copy, dated November 20, Reel 168, Item 152, V, p. 519, Papers of the Continental Congress, National Archives.

594–95   Charles O'Hara and West Hyde to Robert Hanson Harrison and H, December 12, 1778. *Additional source:* copy, Reel 184, Item 167, p. 17, Papers of the Continental Congress, National Archives.

595–97   Robert Hanson Harrison and H to Charles O'Hara and West Hyde, December 12, 1778. *Additional source:* copy, Reel 184, Item 167, p. 18, Papers of the Continental Congress, National Archives.

Volume II

Page

viii   Section III, first entry: *For Etr. Pol. read Etr., Corr. Pol.*

4   George Washington to John Jay, January 27, 1779. *Transfer to PAH*, II, 5.

6   To Henry Knox, note 2. *Delete* and *substitute:* Lewis Garanger was a captain of bombardiers in the French artillery of Major General Philippe Charles Jean Baptiste

Page

Tronson de Coudray. In 1779 he was seeking to be admitted into the service of the Continental Army. See H to Knox, March 26, 1779, note 1 (printed in *PAH*, XXVI).

8   George Washington to Alexander McDougall, February 14, 1779. *Additional source:* LS, in the handwriting of H, the W. Wright Hawkes Collection of Revolutionary War Documents, on deposit at Union College, Schenectady, New York.

25   George Washington to Philip Schuyler, line 1: *For Discusses use of Sus read* Discusses use of Sus

25–26   To Nathanael Greene, date line: *For* March *read* May. The JCH transcript is incorrectly dated.
Transfer this letter to *PAH*, II, 61.
Additional source: ALS, Library of the American Philosophical Society, Philadelphia.

40   Second letter, title, line 3, and note 1, line 1: *For* Murnand *read* Murnan

45   From Lachlan McIntosh, May 14, 1779. *Additional sources:* copy, Reel 169, Item 152, VII, p. 365, Papers of the Continental Congress, National Archives; copy, Reel 187, Item 169, V, p. 305, Papers of the Continental Congress, National Archives.

45–46   To Lachlan McIntosh, May 14, 1779. *Additional sources:* copy, Reel 169, Item 152, VII, p. 361, Papers of the Continental Congress, National Archives; copy, Reel 187, Item 169, V, p. 307, Papers of the Continental Congress, National Archives.

62   George Washington to the Marine Committee, line 2. *For* Blodget *read* Blodgett

Page

78–79 To Major General Israel Putnam, note 2: *For* east *read* west

107 To Henry Knox, source line: *For* Thoms *read* Thomas

117 Note 4: *For* Dunlop *read* Dunlap

127–28 To William Gordon, August 10, 1779. *Additional source:* copy, in William Gordon to Moses Wheelock, September 16, 1779 (ALS, The Sol Feinstone Collection, Library of the American Philosophical Society, Philadelphia).

141–43 From William Gordon, August 25, 1779. *Additional source:* copy, in William Gordon to Moses Wheelock, September 16, 1779 (ALS, The Sol Feinstone Collection, Library of the American Philosophical Society, Philadelphia).

144–45 To James Duane, August 28, 1779. *Additional source:* ALS, Lloyd W. Smith Collection, Morristown National Historical Park, Morristown, New Jersey.

161 H to ——, September 10, 1779. The addressee of this letter is Nathanael Greene.
This letter is reprinted in *PAH*, XXVI.

170 Note 3, line 1: *For* Toussant *read* Touissant

172–74 To James Duane, September 14, 1779. *Additional source:* ALS, Lloyd W. Smith Collection, Morristown National Historical Park, Morristown, New Jersey.
This letter is incorrectly printed as two separate letters. The second letter to Duane on page 174 is actually the first paragraph of the letter beginning on page 172.

183 Source line: *For* Columbia University *read* Columbia University Libraries

Page

193   George Washington to William Alexander, Lord Stirling, line 2. *Add* the following note: Lady Mary Stirling, the wife of Peter Van Brugh Livingston, was the sister of William Alexander, Lord Stirling.

200–01   George Washington to Louis Le Bèque Du Portail and H, October 10, 1779. *Additional source:* copy, PRO: C.O. 98/393–96.

217   Note 2, paragraph 2, line 3: *For* Setouket *read* Setauket

234–36   To ——. *Add* the following paragraphs to introductory note: Lucius Wilmerding, Jr., in a letter dated January 16, 1962, has suggested the following two other possibilities concerning the addressee of this letter. In the first place, it is possible that the letter was a draft that H retained. Second, James Duane might be considered a possible recipient on the ground that he was the first known person to whom H wrote in detail on finances and fiscal policy (H to Duane, September 3, 1779 [*PAH*, II, 400–18]). Mr. Wilmerding writes: "As chairman of the treasury prior to the reorganization of that department in the summer of 1779, Duane might at least expect to be mentioned for the post of minister of finance, and Hamilton, in recommending the establishment of such an office, may have thought it only polite to say, Thou art the Man."

     In addition, Mr. Wilmerding has written concerning the date of this letter: ". . . there is one piece of evidence not noticed in your [introductory] note that would appear to point, like everything else, towards December 1779. In arguing for a tax in kind [*PAH*, II, 243], Hamilton does not mention the act of February 25, 1780 [*JCC*, XVI, 196–201], founded on a resolve of December 17, 1779 [*JCC*, XV, 1391], which quoted a requisition in kind to the several states. In his later letter to Duane [*PAH*, II, 412], he says that, by that act, Congress probably intended a tax in kind but their intention had not been answered."

Page

235   Line 3: *For* 40 to 1 *read* 20 to 1

253   From Nathanael Greene, January 4, 1780. *Additional source:* copy, The Huntington Library, San Marino, California.

260   George Washington to Samuel Huntington, line 2: *For* Nevin *read* Nevins

260   Third letter, title and note 1: *For* Robert Burnett *read* Ichabod Burnet

261–62   "Poems by Colonel Samuel Blachley Webb," note 1, paragraph 2, line 4: *For* was at Beverwyck, near Morristown, New Jersey *read* was called Beaverwyck and was located in Hanover Township, Morris County, New Jersey

271–72   George Washington to Arthur St. Clair, Edward Carrington, and H, March 7, 1780. *Additional source:* copy, Reel 184, Item 167, p. 85, Papers of the Continental Congress, National Archives.

275–85   "Minutes of the Proceedings at Amboy from March 10 to March 14, 1780." *Additional source:* copy, Reel 184, Item 167, p. 43, Papers of the Continental Congress, National Archives.

288–89   From James McHenry, source line: *For* George Washington Papers *read* James McHenry Papers

289–91   "A Proposition," March 18, 1780. *Additional source:* copy, Reel 184, Item 167, p. 109, Papers of the Continental Congress, National Archives.

291–92   Arthur St. Clair, Edward Carrington, and H to William Phillips, Cosmo Gordon, and Chapel Norton, March 19, 1780. *Additional source:* copy, Reel 184, Item 167, p. 113, Papers of the Continental Congress, National Archives.

Page

295–96   Arthur St. Clair, Edward Carrington, and H to George
         Washington, March 26, 1780. *Additional source:* copy, Reel
         184, Item 167, p. 81, Papers of the Continental Congress,
         National Archives.

296–301 Arthur St. Clair, Edward Carrington, and H to George
         Washington, March 26, 1780. *Additional source:* copy, Reel
         184, Item 167, p. 93, Papers of the Continental Congress,
         National Archives.

308–09   Arthur St. Clair, Edward Carrington, and H to George
         Washington, April 10, 1780. *Additional source:* copy, Reel
         170, Item 152, VIII, p. 523, Papers of the Continental Con-
         gress, National Archives.

323   From Nathanael Greene, May 15, 1780. *Additional source:*
         copy, The Huntington Library, San Marino, California.

324   George Washington to Marquis de Lafayette, note 1: *For*
         Louis Urbain du Bouexie *read* Luc-Urbain de Bouëxic

329   Note 3: *For* Kinlock *read* Kinloch

340   George Washington to Joseph Reed, June 16, 1780. *Addi-
         tional source:* LS, in the handwriting of H, Park Collection,
         Morristown National Historical Park, Morristown, New
         Jersey.

363   Note 2, line 7: *For* Louis Urbain du Bouexie *read* Luc-
         Urbain de Bouëxic

367   Note 8. *Add:* For a full account of Franks' career, see
         Franks to George Washington, May 12, 1789 (ALS,
         George Washington Papers, Library of Congress; copy
         [undated], in the handwriting of Franks, Hamilton Papers,
         Library of Congress).

386   Paragraph 3, line 12: *For* Atkin River *read* Adkin River

Page
391   Title: *For* Count *read* Comte
        Source line: *For* Hamilton Papers *read* George Washington Papers

396   Note 11. *Delete* and *substitute:* Coos, on the Connecticut River, site of the present-day Newbury, Vermont.

440–41   To Nathanael Greene, September 25, 1780. *Additional source:* copy, Reel 175, Item 155, I, p. 443, Papers of the Continental Congress, National Archives.

443   George Washington to Anthony Wayne, September 26, 1780. *Additional source:* LS (photostat), in the handwriting of H, George Washington Collection, "Facsimiles and Transcripts," MS Division, New York Public Library.

445   To Anthony Wayne, September 28, 1780. *Additional source:* ALS (photostat), George Washington Collection, "Facsimiles and Transcripts," MS Division, New York Public Library.
        Line 3: *For* prisoner's *read* prisoners

460–70   To John Laurens, October 11, 1780. *Additional sources:* copy (incomplete), Yale University Library; copy (extract), Colonel Richard Gimbel, New Haven, Connecticut.
        Note 1, line 5: *For* New York *Evening Post read New-York Evening Post*

472–73   To Isaac Sears, October 12, 1780. *Additional source:* copy, PRO: C.O., 95/262–64.

473–75   To Elizabeth Schuyler, October 13, 1780. *Additional source:* ALS, Columbia University Libraries.

479–80   To James Duane, October 18, 1780. *Additional source:* ALS, sold by Christie, Manson & Woods International Inc., October 21, 1977.

Page

481–83 From Marquis de Fleury, note 5: *For* Louis Urbain du Bouexic *read* Luc-Urbain de Bouëxic

488 Note 1, lines 1 and 2: *For* Bonum (or Bonham) Town, New Jersey, *read* Staten Island, New York
 Note 1, line 3. *Add:* He was a member of the New York Assembly in 1777, 1778, 1779 to 1783, and 1784 to 1786.

492 Note 11, line 5: *For JJC read JCC*

494 To Richard Varick, note 2, line 2: *For* 1870 *read* 1780

495–96 "Deposition in Favor of Lieutenant Colonel Richard Varick," October 31, 1780. *Additional source:* DS, in the handwriting of H and signed by John Glover, Harvard College Library.

521 Note 5: *For* was at Beverwyck, near Morristown, New Jersey *read* was called Beaverwyck and was located in Hanover Township, Morris County, New Jersey
 Note 8: *For* Guibert *read* Gaulbert

528 To George Fisher, line 6: *For* if you assist me *read* if you can assist me

529–33 From Nathanael Greene, January 10, 1781. *Additional source:* copy (incomplete), The Huntington Library, San Marino, California.

536 First letter, line 2: *For* Lieutenant *read* Lieutenant Colonel

538–39 To Timothy Pickering, January 21, 1781. *Additional source:* LC, Hugh Hughes Letter Books, New-York Historical Society, New York City.
 Source line: *For* ALS *read* ALS, RG 93

559 George Washington to William Livingston, February 13, 1781. *Additional source:* LS, in the handwriting of H,

Page

       William Livingston Papers, MS Division, New York Public Library.

562   George Washington to James Clinton, February 16, 1781. *Additional source:* LS, in the handwriting of H, The Sol Feinstone Collection, Library of the American Philosophical Society, Philadelphia.

569   To James McHenry, source line: *For* ALS *read* ALS (photostat)

579   George Washington to Chevalier Destouches, February 27, 1781. *Additional source:* LS, in the handwriting of H, Lloyd W. Smith Collection, Morristown National Historical Park, Morristown, New Jersey. This letter has a postscript in Washington's handwriting.

582   To Samuel Blachley Webb, March 2, 1781. *Additional source:* ALS (photostat), MS Division, New York Public Library.

636   George Washington to Comte de Rochambeau, source line. *Delete* and *substitute:* Df (photostat), in the handwriting of H, George Washington Papers, Library of Congress, from the original in the Château de Rochambeau, France.

645–46   From Robert Morris, May 26, 1781. *Additional source:* LC, Robert Morris Papers, Library of Congress.

647   Note 2. *Delete* and *substitute:* This is a reference to the possibility of the selection of H by the New York legislature to serve as a member of the Continental Congress.

648   To Elizabeth Hamilton, source line. *Add:* This letter is now located in The Sol Feinstone Collection, Library of the American Philosophical Society, Philadelphia.

650   Line 3 from bottom: *For* interior *read* inferior

Page

679–82 To Marquis de Lafayette, October 15, 1781. *Additional sources:* copy, Reel 188, Item 169, VIII, p. 249, Papers of the Continental Congress, National Archives; copy, Reel 171, Item 152, X, p. 281, Papers of the Continental Congress, National Archives.

Volume III

Page

7 Note 6, line 3: *For* Pascal *read* Paschal

9 Note 10: *For* Macauley *read* Macaulay

10 Note 11: *For* Laurence *read* Laurance

30 Note 54. *Delete* and *substitute:* For Williams, see *PAH,* XXI, 389.

42 Note 92, line 2: *For* 1786 *read* 1796

59 Note 150: *For* Tillery *read* Tillary

72 Note 3, line 2: *Delete* Marquis of Lansdowne

83–86 To Vicomte de Noailles, April–June, 1782. *Additional source:* ALS, Papiers de Noailles, Archives Nationales, Paris.

86–87 From Robert Morris, May 2, 1782. *Additional source:* LC, Robert Morris Papers, Library of Congress.

90–91 From Robert Morris, June 4, 1782. *Additional source:* LC, Robert Morris Papers, Library of Congress.

98–99 From Robert Morris, July 2, 1782. *Additional source:* LC, Robert Morris Papers, Library of Congress.

Page

114   From Robert Morris, July 22, 1782. *Additional source:* LC, Robert Morris Papers, Library of Congress.

139   Note 18, line 1: *For* Laurence *read* Laurance

153   Note 7, line 2: *For* Laurence *read* Laurance

159   From Robert Morris, September 6, 1782. *Additional source:* LC, Robert Morris Papers, Library of Congress.

171   Line 2: *For* Laurence *read* Laurance

172   Note 2, line 2: *For* a congressional resolution of September 9, 1782, *read* a congressional resolution introduced on September 9, 1782

177–79   From Robert Morris, October 5, 1782. *Additional source:* LC, Robert Morris Papers, Library of Congress.

179–80   From Robert Morris, October 5, 1782. *Additional source:* copy, George Washington Papers, Library of Congress. Source line: *For* LS *read* LC

186–87   From Robert Morris, October 16, 1782, note 2, line 1: *For* Laurence *read* Laurance

187   From Robert Morris, October 23, 1782. *Additional source:* LC, Robert Morris Papers, Library of Congress.

191   From Robert Morris, October 28, 1782. *Additional source:* LC, Robert Morris Papers, Library of Congress.

202   "Committee of Continental Congress to Frederick A. Muhlenberg," date line: *For* 1783 *read* 1782

208–09   H and William Floyd to George Clinton, December 9, 1782. *Additional source:* copy, "Legislative Papers, 1780–1803," Item No. 2457, New York State Library, Albany.

Page

211–12 Second letter, title and notes 1 and 4: *For* Laurence *read* Laurance

226 Note 1, line 3: *For* 1879 *read* 1869

226–27 To Elizabeth Hamilton, note 1, line 1: *For* Parsipanny *read* Parsippany

229 "Continental Congress. Motion that Requisitions on the States Be Revised," note 2. *Add:* On February 26, 1783, the "Report on Mr Hamiltons motion for making allowances to states" was "Read & consideration postponed" (Reel 163, Item 149, III, p. 23, Papers of the Continental Congress, National Archives).

283–84 "Continental Congress. Remarks on Robert Morris," note 1, line 3: *For JJC read JCC*

290–93 To George Washington, March 17, 1783. *Additional source:* copy, Hamilton Papers, Library of Congress.

323–25 Robert Morris to H, Theodorick Bland, Thomas Fitz-Simons, Samuel Osgood, and Richard Peters, April 14, 1783. *Additional sources:* LC, Robert Morris Papers, Library of Congress; copy, Reel 149, Item 137, II, pp. 657–59, Papers of the Continental Congress, National Archives.

356–61 Robert Morris to H, Richard Peters, and Nathaniel Gorham, May 15, 1783. *Additional source:* LC, Robert Morris Papers, Library of Congress.
Note 5, lines 1 and 3: *For* Le Grand *read* Grand

365 "Continental Congress. Motion of Protest against British Practice of Carrying off American Negroes," May 26, 1783. *Additional source:* D, in the handwriting of John Rutledge, Reel 42, Item 36, II, p. 129, Papers of the Continental Congress, National Archives.

Page

376   Note 3, lines 1 and 3: *For* Kinlock *read* Kinloch

377   To George Clinton, June 11, 1783. *Additional source:* ALS (photostat), Papers of George and James Clinton, Library of Congress.

382   Note 3. *Delete* and *substitute:* The annexed papers Nos. 1 to 4, containing opinions concerning a military peace establishment by George Washington, Benjamin Lincoln, and Louis Le Bèque Du Portail, may be found in Reel 45, Item 38, p. 317, Papers of the Continental Congress, National Archives. For Lincoln's opinion, see Lincoln to H, May, 1783 (printed in *PAH,* XXVI).

408   Note 2, line 1: *For* Carbery *read* Carberry

432   From John Chaloner, source line: *Add* Philadelphia

459–60   From John Jay, September 28, 1783. *Additional source:* ADf, Windsor Castle, England.

470   From George Washington, October 18, 1783. *Additional source:* ALS, sold by B. Altman & Co., New York City (*The New York Times,* November 28, 1976).

481   Note 4, line 2: *For* share *read* shares

565   Note 4, line 2. *Add:* See "An Act to amend an Act, entitled, An Act for granting certain Privileges to the College, heretofore called King's College, for altering the Name and Charter thereof, and effecting an University within this State" (*New York Laws,* 8th Sess., Ch. XV [November 26, 1784]).

568   Note 4. *Delete* first sentence and *substitute:* In 1782 New York State appointed Samuel Jones, a lawyer from Oyster Bay, New York, and Richard Varick to collect and or-

Page

ganize the British statutes which were to remain in force under the state constitution.

Note 5, line 4: *For* a Mr. Jefferys *read* Patrick Jeffrey

576–77   To John Chalnor, note 1: *Delete* and *substitute:* James and Alexander Stewart, Philadelphia merchants in the firm of Stewart and Totten

577   From John Chaloner, August 27, 1784. *Additional source:* LC, Historical Society of Pennsylvania, Philadelphia.

585–86   To Francisco de Miranda, introductory note, paragraph 2, line 9: *For* Yorek *read* Yorck

Paragraph 3, line 2: *For* XV, 72–77 *read* XV (Caracas, 1938), 72–77

599   To Elizabeth Hamilton, first letter, date line: *For* Westchester *read* Chester

599   To Elizabeth Hamilton, second letter, date line: *For* Westchester *read* Chester

Note 2: *For* 57 *read* 58. 57 Wall Street was H's law office.

Note 3. *Delete* and *substitute:* H was in Chester, Orange County, New York, as attorney for the proprietors of Wawayanda in the case of *Wawayanda* v *Cheesecocks.* For information on this case, see Goebel, *Law Practice*, forthcoming volumes.

601   To ———, line 2: *For* Macauley *read* Macaulay

610–11   To William Duer, date line: *For* Westchester *read* Chester

Note 4. *Delete* and *substitute:* H was in Chester, Orange County, New York, as attorney for the proprietors of Wawayanda for hearings before the commissioners appointed in the case of *Wawayanda* v *Cheesecocks.* The hearings commenced on May 19, 1785. For information on *Wawayanda* v *Cheesecocks*, see Goebel, *Law Practice*, forthcoming volumes.

Page

613–14   From James Duane, John Jay, and Robert R. Livingston to H and Samuel Jones, June 9, 1785, note 3. *Add:* In Luther S. Livingston, ed., *American Book-Prices Current* (New York, 1911), 812, there is an entry which reads: "Autograph Postscript, 8 lines, signed, to a copy of an agreement between the Agents of New York and Alexander Hamilton and Samuel Jones as Counsellors in the Controversy with Massachusetts." This document has not been found.

619   To Richard Varick, line 3: *For* Macauley *read* Macaulay

621   Second title: *For* Philip Schuyler *read* Stephen J. Schuyler

622   Third letter, title, line 3 of text, and note 1: *For* Kinlock *read* Kinloch

629   Note 4: *For* Macauley *read* Macaulay

636   Note 2, line 1: *For* a New Yorker *read* a resident of Albany, New York

641   Note 2: *For* Nicholas *read* Zachariah

650   From Isaac Gouverneur, Junior, note 1. *Delete* and *substitute:* Gouverneur was the son of Samuel Gouverneur and was called Junior to distinguish him from his uncle, Isaac Gouverneur.

658   Note 6, line 2: *For* Kinlock *read* Kinloch

675   From Broome and Platt, note 1. *Add:* See Broome to H, April 18, 1786.
         Add the following note at end of letter: The endorsement on this letter reads: "Col Hamilton is requested by Mr S Broome of New H[aven] not to proceed as the within letter directs till he again hears from him. 1 Septem. 1787."

678   From Philip Schuyler, line 6: *For* lands *read* leases
         Note 2: *For* John *read* Stephen

Page

679   From Ebenezer Hazard, source line: *For* LS *read* Copy

680   To Bell and Woodmass, line 1: *For* Hamilton wrote *read* On August 4, 1786, Hamilton wrote

691   From Peter Van Schaack, date line: *For* Kindorhook *read* Kinderhook

692   To William Wickham, note 2: *For* Chesecocks *read* Cheesecocks

Volume IV

Page

111   Note 4, line 2: *For* Batcheler *read* Batchelor

125   "New York Assembly. Remarks on an Act Directing a Mode of Trial and Allowing of Divorces in Cases of Adultry," note 1. *Add:* For H's earlier interest in this bill, see "New York Assembly. Report on the Petition of Isaac Gouverneur, Junior," February 14, 1787.

155   First title: *For* Samuel Breeze *read* Samuel Breese
        Note 1: *For* Breeze *read* Breese

160   "Constitutional Convention. Motion that Representation in the National Legislature Ought to be Proportioned to the Number of Free Inhabitants," May 30, 1787. *Additional source:* D, RG 360, Records of the Constitutional Convention of 1787, Journal of the Proceedings of the Whole House, National Archives.

207–11 "Constitutional Convention. Plan of Government," note 1. *Add* the following paragraph: There are also versions of this "Plan" by David Brearley (AD, RG 360, Records of

Page

     the Constitutional Convention of 1787, Papers of David Brearley, National Archives) and William Paterson (AD [photostat], William Paterson Papers, Box 1, Library of Congress). Neither has any information not contained in the document printed above.

232   To Thomas Mullett, note 3: *For* Wooldridge *read* Wooldrige

232   From Thomas Mullett, line 3: *For* Wooldridge *read* Wooldrige

236   Note 1, lines 10–11: *For* a town in the Prussian province of Hanover *read* part of the Bishopric of Münster

242   Note 7, line 4: *For* a town in the Prussian province of Hanover *read* part of the Bishopric of Münster

278   Second title: *For* Ceasar *read* Caesar

280   Note 4. *Add* the following paragraph: The "little orphan" was Frances Antill, daughter of Edward Antill, a lawyer and a veteran of the American Revolution. In 1783 Antill bought land in New Jersey but shortly thereafter moved to New York City, where he was living and practicing law in 1786. In 1787 he went to Canada. In 1791 or 1792 Antill died in Clinton County, New York. In 1802 his estate was still unsettled and was the subject of litigation in the New York Supreme Court. For information concerning the case of *Gerrit G. Lansing, Administrator of Edward Antill* v *Isaac Cortelyou,* see Goebel, *Law Practice,* II, 303–10.

283   Note 1, last line, and note 3: *For* Brienne *read* Loménie de Brienne
     Note 6, line 2: *For* Balkans *read* Crimea

284   First title: *For* Ceasar *read* Caesar

Page

297   First full paragraph, Section I. *Add* the following note: See also James Kent to William Coleman, May 12, 1817 (ALS, Columbia University Libraries).

300   Note 36, line 2: *For Comments read Comment*

317   Title: *For* Pierre Van Cortlandt, *read* Pierre Van Cortlandt, Junior
        Note 1: *Delete* and *substitute:* Van Cortlandt had been a clerk in H's law office from 1784 to 1786.

332–33 To Benjamin Rush, November 21, 1787. *Additional source:* ALS, sold by Sotheby Parke Bernet, Inc., January 29, 1974, Item 93.

346   Note 22: *For* Cornelis Pauw *read* Cornelius de Pauw

376   Note 5, line 2: *For* French marshal and courtier *read* French marshal and courtier, was famous for his *Mémoires* and *Réflexions ou sentences et maximes morales.*

492–93 "Appointment as Delegate to the Continental Congress," note 1. *Add* the following paragraph: A copy of a resolution in the Hamilton Papers, Library of Congress, reads: "State of New York

The Senate January 22d. 1788
Resolved that the Hon. Ezra L. Hommedieu, Egbert Benson, Alexander Hamilton, Abraham Yates Junior and Leonard Gansevoort Esquires, are duly Nominated and Appointed Delegates, to Represent this State in the Congress of the United States, until the first Monday in November next; and thence forward until Ten days after the first Subsequent Meeting of the Legislatures. Provided nevertheless that the Delegates so Nominated and Appointed shall not on any account, hold their Seats in Congress longer than one Year, to be Computed from the day of their Appointment.
        "Extract from the Journal   Abm. B. Bancker Clk.

Page

"Secretarys Office of the State of New York, the 31st. Jany. 1788

"I Do hereby Certify the aforegoing to be a true Copy of a Resolution of the Senate, now on file in this Office. Examined and Compared therewith By Me

Lewis A. Scott. Secretary."

590   Note 2, line 1: *For* Kettlelas *read* Keteltas

654   Note 4, line 1: *For* Jean *read* Jacques; line 3: *For* Warville *read* Brissot de Warville

Volume V

Page

208–10   To William Livingston, August 29, 1788. *Additional source:* copy (incomplete), Columbia University Libraries.

215   To Richard Morris, September 8, 1788. *Additional source:* DS, Columbia University Libraries.
           This document is printed in Goebel, *Law Practice*, I, 257–58.

239   Note 1. *Add:* See also the entry entitled "Land Account" in H's "Cash Book," March 1, 1782–1791 (*PAH*, III, 52).

253   Note 9, line 1: *For* on January *read* in January

311   Note 2, paragraph 2. *Delete* and *substitute:* The address was circulated as a broadside. It is entitled "To the Independent Electors of the State of New-York," and is signed by Jonathan Lawrence and dated March 9, 1789 (DS, The William L. Clements Library of the University of Michigan).

Page

317   Note 2, last two sentences. *Delete* and *substitute:* The address of the Antifederalist committee was a broadside entitled "To the Independent Electors of the State of New-York," signed by Jonathan Lawrence and dated March 9, 1789 (DS, The William L. Clements Library of the University of Michigan).

342–43   To Elizabeth Hamilton, note 2. *Delete* and *substitute:* H is referring to the house at 58 Wall Street which he had rented for at least a year. See H to Elizabeth Hamilton, March 17, 1788 (*PAH*, III, 599), May 28, 1789 (*PAH*, V, 342–43); "Conveyance from James Barclay and Others," September 17, 1785 (printed in *PAH*, XXVI).

364   "Promissory Note from William Duer," note 1, lines 2 and 3: *For* Assistant Secretary *read* Assistant to the Secretary

368   Note 3: *For* Jean *read* Jacques

369   To Samuel Meredith, note 1: *For* Assistant Secretary *read* Assistant to the Secretary

376   Note 7: *For* Sweeney *read* Sweeny

378   From Sharp Delany, paragraph 2, line 1. *Add* the following note after "The Letter to Mr. Eveleigh": H's letter to Nicholas Eveleigh has not been found.

394   Note 4: *For* Louis Le Rey de Chaumont *read* Jacques Donatien Le Ray de Chaumont

394–95   "Treasury Department Circular to the Collectors of the Customs," September 22, 1789. *Additional sources:* LS, to Joseph Hiller, Mrs. Maurice A. Thorne, Tucker Hill, Virginia; copy, to Otho H. Williams, RG 46, Records of the United States Senate, Reports and Communications from the Secretary of the Treasury, National Archives.

Page

411–12 "Treasury Department Circular to the Governors of the States," September 26, 1789. *Additional source:* copy, to Jonathan Trumbull, owned by Donaldson, Lufkin, & Jenrette, Inc., New York City.

422 "Treasury Department Circular to the Collectors of the Customs," October 3, 1789. *Additional source:* LS, to Richard Harris, Hamilton Papers, Library of Congress.

427 Note 2: *For* Jean *read* Jacques

429–30 To William Short, October 7, 1789. *Additional source:* LS, Widener Library, Harvard University.

437 First letter, title: *For* To —— *read* To Catharine Greene
Add the following note to title: Catharine Greene was the widow of Major General Nathanael Greene.
Additional source: ALS, sold by Dodd, Mead and Company, New York City, November, 1903, Catalogue 69, Item 62.

448 Note 3. *Delete* and *substitute:* H to Delany, October 17, 1789 (printed in *PAH*, XXVI).

460 Note 5: *For* Linghan *read* Lingan

461 From Samuel Johnston, October 25, 1789. *Additional source:* LC, Governor's Letter Book, North Carolina State Department of Archives and History, Raleigh.

482 Note 1, paragraph 3, line 2: *For* elevated in *read* elevated to

486 Line 2 from bottom of text: *Delete* note number 9

487 Line 3: *Add* note number 9 at end of sentence

495 Note 1: *For* Louis Le Rey de Chaumont *read* Jacques Donatien Le Ray de Chaumont

Page

503–04   To Jeremiah Wadsworth, November 9, 1789. *Additional source:* ALS, The Sol Feinstone Collection, Library of the American Philosophical Society, Philadelphia.

    This letter contains a postscript which was cut from the copy printed in *PAH*, V. The postscript reads: "P.S. Our dear friend Mrs. Church sailed by the last Packet. She desired me to inform you of this with her affectionate remembrances. She goes fully determined if possible to return."

506   Title and note 1: *For* MacWhorter *read* Macwhorter

513   Note 5. *Delete* and *substitute:* H to Wadsworth, **November 8, 1789** (printed in *PAH*, **XXVI**).

544   Note 4, line 1: *For* Montague *read* Montagu

545   Note 5, line 1: *For* Montague *read* Montagu

569–70   From Tench Coxe, November 30, 1789. *Additional sources:* ADf, ADfS, LS, Papers of Tench Coxe in the Coxe Family Papers at the Historical Society of Pennsylvania, Philadelphia.

    Attached to Coxe's signed draft is a list in his handwriting which reads:

"N. 1. Enquiry   Museum & a ⟨–⟩

N. 2. An address to the friends of Amr. Mans.   do & do

N. 3. A paper on the future legislation of Commerce addressed to R. H. Lee esqr   Museum

N. 4. A Continuation of the address on the Subject of American Mans. (Museum)

N. 5. Thoughts on the future prospects of Ama. published in Dunlaps paper of 1788 about Septr. or Octr.

N. 6. An accot. of the Navn. &ca

No. 7 Spanish Wool

N. 8. Succedanea for foreign liquors."

    "N. 1" was *An Enquiry into the Principles on Which a*

*Commercial System for the United States of America
Should be Founded; to Which are Added Some Political
Observations Connected With the Subject. Read Before the
Society for Political Enquiries, Convened at the House of
His Excellency Benjamin Franklin, Esquire, in Philadelphia,
May 11, 1787* (Philadelphia: Printed and Sold by Robert
Aitken, at Pope's Head, in Market Street, 1787). This arti-
cle was printed in *The American Museum* (June, 1787), I,
432–45. "N. 2" was *An Address to an Assembly of the
Friends of American Manufactures, Convened for the Pur-
pose of Establishing a Society for the Encouragement of
Manufactures and the Useful Arts, Read in the University
of Pennsylvania, on Thursday, the 9th of August, 1787, by
Tench Coxe, Esq. and Published at Their Request* (Philadelphia: Printed by R. Aitken & Son, at Pope's Head in
Market-Street, 1787). "N. 3" was a "Letter to the Honourable Richard Henry Lee, Esq.," signed by "An American,"
which was published in the [Philadelphia] *Pennsylvania
Herald* on December 29, 1787, and printed in *The American Museum* (January 1788), III, 78–83. "N. 4" was the
"Address to the Friends of American Manufactures" dated
October 20, 1788, in *The American Museum* (October,
1788), IV, 341–46. It also appeared in *The Federal Gazette,
and Philadelphia Evening Post* on October 20, 1788, and
was reprinted in the [Philadelphia] *Pennsylvania Gazette*
on October 29, 1788, signed by "An American Citizen."
"N. 5" was "Thoughts on the present Situation and Prospects of the United States of America," signed by "A
Pennsylvanian," which was published in the [Philadelphia]
Pennsylvania Packet, and Daily Advertiser on October 31,
1788. "N. 6" and "No. 7" have not been found. "N.8" has
not been found, but it is probably similar to what became
Chapter VII of Book 11, entitled "Containing a View of the
Subject of Foreign Distilled Spirits, Extracted from a Pub-
lication in the Year 1789," in Coxe's *A View of the United
States* (Philadelphia: Printed for William Hall, No. 51,
Market Street, and Wrigley & Berriman, No. 149, Chesnut
Street, 1794), 492–95.

Page

Note 1, line 2: *For* Assistant Secretary *read* Assistant to the Secretary
Note 5: *Delete*

572   Note 8, line 5: *For* Jean *read* Jacques

575–78   "Treasury Department Circular to the Collectors of the Customs," November 30, 1789. *Additional source:* LS, Independence National Historical Park Collection, Old Custom House, Philadelphia.

Volume VI

Page
8   To Nathaniel Gorham, note 3: *For* Wykoff *read* Wyckoff

11–13   From Tench Coxe, December 16, 1789. *Additional source:* ADfS, Papers of Tench Coxe in the Coxe Family Papers at the Historical Society of Pennsylvania, Philadelphia.

30–31   "Treasury Department Circular to the Collectors of the Customs," December 23, 1789. *Additional source:* LS, sold by Charles Hamilton Autographs, Inc., Auction No. 101, December 9, 1976.

31–32   To Tench Coxe, December 24, 1789. *Additional source:* ALS, Papers of Tench Coxe in the Coxe Family Papers at the Historical Society of Pennsylvania, Philadelphia.

52   First full paragraph, line 2: *For* Montague *read* Montagu
Line 14: *For* In his alarming crisis *read* In this alarming crisis

53   Second full paragraph, line 1: *For* Hobbs *read* Hobbes

Page

113   Note 138: *For* Le Grand *read* Grand

181–83   From Gaspard Joseph Amand Ducher, note 1: *For* French consul *read* French vice consul

207–09   To Benjamin Lincoln, January 25, 1790. *Additional source:* copy, to the President, Directors, and Company of the Society for the Encouragement of Manufactures, Philadelphia, Papers of Tench Coxe in the Coxe Family Papers at the Historical Society of Pennsylvania, Philadelphia.
             Note 3, source line: *For* George Washington Papers *read* LC, George Washington Papers
             Note 4, paragraph 2: *For* Assistant Secretary *read* Assistant to the Secretary

212   Note 6: *For* Le Grand *read* Grand

213   Note 13: *For* Jean *read* Jacques

227   Note 4, paragraph 2. *Add:* On March 20, 1790, Jay sent an extract of Short's letter of December 15, 1789, to H (Reel 142, Item 127, p. 218, Papers of the Continental Congress, National Archives).

236   Note 5, line 1: *For* Le Grand *read* Grand

269–70   "Treasury Department Circular to the Collectors of the Customs," February 17, 1790. *Additional source:* LS, Papers of Elbridge Gerry, Library of Congress.

330–31   "Treasury Department Circular to the Collectors of the Customs," March 30, 1790. *Additional source:* LS, to Jonathan Fitch, Montague Collection, MS Division, New York Public Library.

346   Note 1, line 3: *For* Assistant Secretary *read* Assistant to the Secretary

Page

354 Note 2, lines 3 and 4: *For* William Loughton Smith, Federalist Congressman from South Carolina, wrote to Otho H. Williams *read* William Smith, a member of the House of Representatives from Maryland, wrote to his son-in-law, Otho H. Williams

367 "Treasury Department Circular to the Collectors of the Customs," April 16, 1790. *Additional sources:* LS, Montague Collection, MS Division, New York Public Library; copy (incomplete), Lloyd W. Smith Collection, Morristown National Historical Park, Morristown, New Jersey.

371 To Thomas Jefferson, note 2, lines 1 and 3: *For* Le Grand *read* Grand

401 To Tench Coxe, May 1, 1790. *Additional source:* ALS, Papers of Tench Coxe in the Coxe Family Papers at the Historical Society of Pennsylvania, Philadelphia.
Note 3, lines 1 and 3–4: *For* Assistant Secretary *read* Assistant to the Secretary

404 To William Webb, source line: *For* Treasury Circulars *read* 1762–1810

407–08 From Andrew Ellicott, note 2. *Delete* and *substitute:* New York ceded the lands in question to the Confederation government in 1780. For the eventual acquisition of these lands by Pennsylvania, see Thomas Mifflin to H, May 5, 1791, note 1.

411 First document, title: *For* Assistant Secretary *read* Assistant to the Secretary
Additional source: DS, Papers of Tench Coxe in the Coxe Family Papers at the Historical Society of Pennsylvania, Philadelphia.
Paragraph 1, last line. *Add* the following note: A copy of Coxe's oath of office, dated May 10, 1790, may be found

Page

in the Papers of Tench Coxe in the Coxe Family Papers at the Historical Society of Pennsylvania, Philadelphia.

415 To Israel Ludlow, title. *Add* the following note: Ludlow was a New Jersey surveyor and land speculator. He also acted as an agent on the frontier for William Duer.

416 To Timothy Pickering, note 2, line 1: *For* Assistant Secretary *read* Assistant to the Secretary

416–17 "Treasury Department Circular to the Collectors of the Customs," May 13, 1790. *Additional source:* LS, to Benjamin Lincoln, Cornell University Library.

463 Running head: *For* July 1790 *read* June 1790

477 From Benjamin Lincoln, line 1: *For* Thatcher *read* Thacher

486 Note 6, line 1: *For* Hart *read* Heart

496 Note 7. *Additional source:* PRO: C.O. 42/69 f. 16–25.

497–98 "Conversation with George Beckwith," July 15, 1790. *Additional source:* PRO: C.O. 42/69 f. 16–25.

498 From Jeremiah Olney, July 16, 1790. *Additional source:* ADfS, Rhode Island Historical Society, Providence.

501–02 From Timothy Pickering, note 1: *For* Assistant Secretary *read* Assistant to the Secretary

513–14 From Oliver Wolcott, Jr., July 31, 1790. *Additional source:* ALS, Connecticut Historical Society, Hartford.
Note 2: *For* Wylie or Wylley *read* Wylie, Wylley, or Wylly

546 From Jonathan Elmer, note 3, line 3: *For* Shureman *read* Schureman

Page

546–49 "Conversation with George Beckwith," August 7–12, 1790. *Additional source:* PRO: C.O. 42/69 f. 16–25.

550 "First Conversation of August 8–12 with George Beckwith," August 8–12, 1790. *Additional source:* PRO: C.O. 42/69 f. 16–25.

550–52 "Second Conversation of August 8–12 with George Beckwith," August 8–12, 1790. *Additional source:* PRO: C.O. 42/69 f. 16–25.

552 From William Barton, note 1, line 2: *For* Assistant Secretary *read* Assistant to the Secretary

564 From Jeremiah Olney, August 23, 1790. *Additional source:* ADfS, Rhode Island Historical Society, Providence.

591 Note 1, line 2: *For* August 3 *read* August 31

Volume VII

Page

6 To Jeremiah Olney, September 1, 1790. *Additional source:* LS, Rhode Island Historical Society, Providence.

20 From Jeremiah Olney, September 2, 1790. *Additional source:* ADfS, Rhode Island Historical Society, Providence.
Note 2: *For* Assistant Secretary *read* Assistant to the Secretary

27–28 From Jeremiah Olney, September 8, 1790. *Additional source:* ADfS, Rhode Island Historical Society, Providence.

30 To William Short, September 10, 1790. *Additional source:* ALS, The Sol Feinstone Collection, Library of the American Philosophical Society, Philadelphia.

Page

63   Note 3: *For* de Campo *read* del Campo

67   To Sharp Delany, paragraph 3, line 5: *For* indispensaable *read* indispensable

82   Note 1: *Delete* and *substitute:* Paterson, a British book-seller, cataloguer, and auctioneer, was one of London's leading book dealers until 1769 when he sold all his stock. After 1769 he prepared bibliographies of a number of England's most extensive private libraries and for some years acted as a librarian at the Bowood estate of Lord Shelburne.

86–87   From Jeremiah Olney, October 1, 1790. *Additional source:* ADfS, Rhode Island Historical Society, Providence.

110   "Treasury Department Circular to the Commissioners of Loans," October 13, 1790. *Additional source:* LS, Donaldson, Lufkin, & Jenrette, Inc., New York City.

122   From Jeremiah Olney, October 22, 1790. *Additional source:* ADfS, Rhode Island Historical Society, Providence.

127–28   "Contract for Army Rations," note 2, paragraph 5, line 4: *For* March 6 *reads* April 26

132   From Jeremiah Olney, October 29, 1790. *Additional source:* LS, Rhode Island Historical Society, Providence.

142–43   From Jeremiah Olney, November 8, 1790. *Additional source:* LS, Rhode Island Historical Society, Providence.

149   From Jeremiah Olney, November 12, 1790. *Additional source:* ADfS, Rhode Island Historical Society, Providence.

174   To Peter Anspach, December 2, 1790. *Additional source:* copy, RG 217, Miscellaneous Treasury Accounts, 1790–1894, Account No. 6595, National Archives.

Page

175–87 From William Short, December 2, 1790. *Additional source:* copy, Duke University Library.

182 Note 10: *For* von *read* van
Note 12, lines 2 and 3: *For* Le Grand *read* Grand

194 Note 4: *For* Champion and Dickerson *read* Alexander Champion and Thomas Dickason

210 To Jeremiah Olney, December 13, 1790. *Additional source:* LS, Rhode Island Historical Society, Providence.

237 First full paragraph, last line: *For* Montague *read* Montagu

348–57 From William Short, December 18, 1790. *Additional source:* copy (incomplete), Duke University Library.

372 To Peter Anspach, December 20, 1790. *Additional source:* copy, RG 217, Miscellaneous Treasury Accounts, 1790–1894, Account No. 6595, National Archives.

381 From Jeremiah Olney, December 24, 1790. *Additional source:* ADfS, Rhode Island Historical Society, Providence.

382–83 From Jeremiah Olney, December 27, 1790. *Additional source:* ADfS, Rhode Island Historical Society, Providence.

386 Title: *For* —— to William Seton *read* Ephraim Brasher to William Seton

398 From Sharp Delany, first letter, date line: *For* December, 1790 *read* November, 1790
Transfer this letter to *PAH*, VII, 171

398 From Sharp Delany, second letter, date line: *For* December, 1790 *read* December 13–31, 1790.
Add the following note to date line: This letter was

Page

written in response to H to Delany, December 12, 1790 (printed in *PAH*, XXVI).
Transfer this letter to *PAH*, VII, 210.

408   From Thomas Jefferson, date line: *For* January 1st. 1791 *read* January 13. 1791
Transfer this letter to *PAH*, VII, 425.

415   From Jeremiah Olney, January 6, 1791. *Additional source:* ADfS, Rhode Island Historical Society, Providence.

418–19   "Report on Duties Arising on Tonnage, for the Year Ending September 30, 1790," January 6, 1791. *Additional sources:* copy in French, Papers of Edmond Genet, Library of Congress; copy, PRO: B.T. 6/21.

420–21   "Report on Duties on Imports," January 7, 1791. *Additional sources:* copy in French, Papers of Edmond Genet, Library of Congress; copy, PRO: B.T. 6/21.
Notes 4 and 5. *Additional sources:* copies in French, Papers of Edmond Genet, Library of Congress; copies, PRO: B.T. 6/21.

422   From Jeremiah Olney, January 10, 1791. *Additional source:* ADfS, Rhode Island Historical Society, Providence.

424   Note 1, line 2: *For* January 1, 1791 *read* January 13, 1791

426   Note 1, line 1: *For* January 1, 1791 *read* January 13, 1791

426–27   "Treasury Department Circular to the Governors of the States," January 14, 1791. *Additional source:* copy, to Samuel Huntington, owned by Donaldson, Lufkin & Jenrette, Inc., New York City.

437–38   From Jeremiah Olney, January 17, 1791. *Additional source:* ADfS, Rhode Island Historical Society, Providence.

438–39   From Jeremiah Olney, January 17, 1791. *Additional source:* ADfS, Rhode Island Historical Society, Providence.

Page

442 Note 4. *Add:* In the correspondence of John Graves Simcoe, governor of Upper Canada, however, Elliot is identified as Andrew Elliot (E. A. Cruikshank, *The Correspondence of John Graves Simcoe, with Allied Documents Relating to His Administration of Upper Canada* [Toronto, 1923–1931], I, 21, 48; V, 163).

461 From Isaac Ledyard, note 1, line 2: *For* Newton *read* Newtown

462 "Report on the Establishment of a Mint," introductory note, paragraph 2, line 8: *For* leave *read* leaves

463 Line 9: *For* is *read* are

472 Line 6: *For* rule or intrinsic value *read* rule of intrinsic value

570 Date line: *For* Communication *read* Communicated

613 To Jeremiah Olney, January 31, 1791. *Additional source:* LS, Rhode Island Historical Society, Providence.

Volume VIII

Page

61–62 From Benjamin Lincoln, note 1: *For* Letter not found *read* Letter not found, but see H to Lincoln, January 21, 1791.

135 Second title: *For* Alexander Dallas *read* Alexander J. Dallas

138–41 "Report on the Petition of Comfort Sands and Others," February 24, 1791. *Additional source:* copy, dated February 21, 1791, Robert R. Livingston Papers, New-York Historical Society, New York City.

Note 2. *Add:* For this petition, as well as supporting documents, see "The humble memorial of Comfort and

Page

Joshua Sands and Walter Livingston for themselves and Associates," n.p., n.d. (copy, Robert R. Livingston Papers, New-York Historical Society, New York City).
Note 4, line 5: *For* Philps *read* Phelps

164 Note 1: *For* Baylis *read* Baylies

165 Title: *For* Catherine *read* Catharine

171 Note 9, line 1; note 12, line 1: *For* Le Grand *read* Grand

178 Enclosure, title: *For* Le Grand *read* Grand

179 Enclosure, title: *For* Le Grand *read* Grand

183 Note 1: *For* Baylis *read* Baylies

209 Second title: *For* Alexander Dallas *read* Alexander J. Dallas

228 Note 6, line 2: *For* Thomas T. Belote *read* Theodore T. Belote

237 Note 1: *For* Assistant Secretary *read* Assistant to the Secretary

246–48 To William Duer, note 2, paragraph 2, line 4: *For* note 1 *read* note 2
Note 2, paragraph 2, line 4: *Add* at end of sentence: Also in the New-York Historical Society is an undated document in William Duer's handwriting which is endorsed: "Memorandum of appropriation by Theodosius Fowler of 20.000 Dollars received on Acct. of the Contract. Octr 29th—1790."

253 From Pierre Charles L'Enfant, date line: *For* Maryland *read* Federal District

271–72 To William Ellery, note 1, line 5: *Delete* 56

Page

275   Note 3, line 6: *For* Venable *read* Venables

277   Note 1: *Delete* and *substitute:* For Rufus King's letter, see
           King to H, n.d. (extract, in Thomas Jefferson's handwrit-
           ing, enclosed in Jefferson to George Washington, April 17,
           1791 [ALS, RG 59, Miscellaneous Letters, January 1–
           July 31, 1791, National Archives]).

301   Note 2, line 5: *For* 1793 *read* 1796

340–41   "Treasury Department Circular to the Collectors of the
           Customs," May 13, 1791. *Additional source:* copy (mis-
           dated March 13, 1791), to Benjamin Lincoln, Causton-
           Pickett Papers, Library of Congress.

342   "Conversation with George Beckwith," date line: *Delete*
           Philadelphia

345   From Jeremiah Olney, note 1: *For* William Barton *read*
           William Barton, Jr.

354   From Henry Knox, note 1, line 1: *For* Shepard *read* Shep-
           herd (Shepard, Sheppard)

411   Source line: *For* Alexander Dallas *read* Alexander J. Dallas

460   Note 8, line 2: *For* Le Grand *read* Grand

485–86   To William Seton, June 17, 1791. *Additional source:* copy,
           RG 217, Miscellaneous Treasury Accounts, 1790–1894, Ac-
           count No. 7363, National Archives.

505   Note 1: *For* Le Grand *read* Grand

507   Second letter, title: *For* Alexander Dallas *read* Alexander J.
           Dallas

517   Note 2: *For* Assistant Secretary *read* Assistant to the Sec-
           retary

Page

522–23   To Mercy Warren, July 1, 1791. *Additional source:* ALS, Papers of the Society of the Cincinnati, Library of Congress.

532–33   From Thomas Mifflin, note 1, line 1: *For* Alexander Dallas *read* Alexander J. Dallas

Volume IX

Page

x   Line 4 from bottom: *For* (1957–1962) *read* (New York, 1957–1962)

30   From William Duer, note 1, lines 1 and 2: *For* Assistant Secretary *read* Assistant to the Secretary

35–37   "Treasury Department Circular," August 13, 1791. *Additional source:* LS, Carnegie Library of Pittsburgh, Pennsylvania.

69–70   From William Seton, August 15, 1791. *Additional Source:* copy, RG 217, Miscellaneous Treasury Accounts, 1790–1894, Account No. 7363, National Archives.

74–75   To William Duer, last line of text. *Add* the following note: On September 6, 1791, Tench Coxe wrote to Duer: "The Secretary of the Treasury has received your letter by M. de la Roche accompanying the manufacturing subscription book. He proposes to retain it here and at his request I transmit you in lieu of it three of the printed subscription papers for the purpose of procuring such additions as may offer at New York. Mr. Dewhurst having applied to Mr. Hamilton for an opportunity of writing two or three sums for himself & friends it will be well that some suitable person call upon him without delay. Papers similar to those in this inclosure will go to day into the hands of six suitable persons, which would have been done before but that it was thought expedient first to add the list of the New York

Page

Subscribers." To this letter Coxe added the following postscript: "Mr. Hamilton is not well. His old nephritic complaint has visited him tho not severely" (ALS, Papers of Tench Coxe in the Coxe Family Papers at the Historical Society of Pennsylvania, Philadelphia).

85   Note 5: *For* Assistant Secretary *read* Assistant to the Secretary

100   Note 7, line 1: *For* Le Grand *read* Grand

103   Note 12, line 1: *For* Le Grand *read* Grand

129   To Thomas Jefferson, August 31, 1791. *Additional source:* AL, Papers of James Madison, Library of Congress.

142   Note 25, line 1: *For* Le Grand *read* Grand

157   Last line: *For* Charles McEvers, Jr. *read* James McEvers

201   Note 1: *For* Charles McEvers, Jr. *read* James McEvers

217–18   "Treasury Department Circular to the Collectors of the Customs," September 20, 1791. *Additional source:* LS, The Sol Feinstone Collection, Library of the American Philosophical Society, Philadelphia.

237–38   To George Washington, line 2: To "Governor St. Clair" *add* the following note: Letter not found. On November 9, 1791, Washington sent St. Clair's letter to H to Thomas Jefferson for his consideration (Tobias Lear to Jefferson, November 9, 1791 [AL, RG 59, Miscellaneous Letters, 1790–1791, National Archives]).

255   Note 4: *For* Duval d'Esprémesnil *read* Jean Jacques Duval d'Esprémisnil

263–64   From Edmund Randolph, source line: *Delete* and *substitute:* ALS, RG 46, Second Congress, 1791–1793, Various Reports Submitted to the Senate, National Archives.

Page

319   Note 6: *Delete* and *substitute:* John Trumbull of Connecticut, the son of Governor Jonathan Trumbull, Sr., was a
veteran of the Revolution, but is best known as a painter.

341   Note 35. *Add* the following paragraphs: In the Hamilton
Papers, Library of Congress, is an undated document in the
handwriting of Roger Newberry which is endorsed
"Sample of Flax thread or Yarn Spun by Mill Machinery.
for Mr. Alexr. Hamilton Treasury Philadelphia." This
document reads: "*Warp Yarn.* Spun by Machinery on
nearly the same principle as the Cotton Mill Machinery. It
is the first effort, & was done at the House of Mr Backiss
30 miles from New Castle under Line in Engd. It is a most
ingenious & *very beneficial* discovery, as from 80 to 100
threads can be thrown of at a time, the same as with
Cotton. I have a drawing & specifications of the two
machines wch work it, one for the thread in a first state &
the second for the last stage of Spining. It is done by frames
of rollers & spindles, four to each frame, wch are so multi-
plyd by wheel work, chiefly of Brass, as to spin 80, or 100
or more threads at a time according to the Force of Water,
Steam, Horse, or Animal Force afforded to the work.
N B this thread is the first Effort, & meant for the backs
of Fustains or thicksets, but the machinery now works
thread of any fineness vizt. to that fit for 5f ⅌ yard
Linen, or Cambricks of 7 or 8f ⅌ yard.
The Cost of the two machines (wch there is great difficulty
to get a sight of, I suppose will be about sixty Guineas.)
One man & two small boys, or girls, is sufficient manual
labour for the Machine of 100 threds."

360   Line 9: *For* Hommoor Barney *read* Hanover Barney

368   Note 19, line 2: *For* Newton *read* Newtown
Note 20: *For* Cornelius J. Bogart *read* Cornelius I. Bogert

403   From George Washington, date line: *For* Maryland *read*
District of Columbia

Page

405   Note 2, line 1: *For* William G. Giles *read* William B. Giles

462   Note 16, lines 1, 2, and 3. *Delete* and *substitute:* For Lewis Tousard's pension granted on October 27, 1778, see *JCC*, XII, 1068. See also "An Act allowing Lieutenant-Colonel Tousard an equivalent for his pension for life" (6 *Stat.* 15 [April 30, 1794]), which reads as follows: "*Be it enacted,*

476   From William Ellery. At end of letter *add* the following note: See Ellery to H, October 14, 1791, note 1.

477   Source line: *For* RG 46 *read* RG 46, Second Congress, 1791–1793,

510–11   From James McHenry, note 2, line 3: *For* William Pinckney *read* William Pinkney

         Paragraph 2, line 4: *Delete* number 3 and *insert* at end of paragraph.

         Note 3. *Delete* and *substitute:* McHenry's fears proved groundless, for Maryland did not change or replace its constitution.

529   Second letter, title: *For* Alexander Dallas *read* Alexander J. Dallas

532   Note 12: *For* Cornelius J. Bogart *read* Cornelius I. Bogert

533   Note 22, line 3: *For* "Thomas Jefferson's Notes on a Conversation with Alexander Hamilton" *read* "Conversation with Thomas Jefferson"

536   Note 33: *For* west bank *read* east bank

538   "Report on Tonnage for the Year Ending September 30, 1790," November 25, 1791. *Additional source:* LS, sold by Emily Driscoll, New York City, 1957, Catalogue 17, Item 233.

547–48   To William Short, November 30, 1791. *Additional source:*

Page

LS, marked "Triplicate," Widener Library, Harvard University.

560–61 To Philip A. Hamilton, December 5, 1791. *Additional source:* ALS (facsimile), Columbia University Libraries.

Volume X

Page

xiv Line 5: *For Conseil read Conseils*

xiv Line 8: *For* (Paris, 1827) *read* (Paris, 1821–1833)

10 Last two lines of text: *For* Assistant Secretary *read* Assistant to the Secretary

20 Line 6: *For* succedance *read* succedanea

37 Line 8 from bottom: *For* succedance *read* succedanea

124 Note 107, line 4: *For* unidentified handwriting *read* Tench Coxe's handwriting

231 Note 126, paragraph 2, lines 9 and 10: *For* Assistant Secretary *read* Assistant to the Secretary

365 Note 1, paragraph 2, lines 4 and 5: *For* Hartford Manufacturing Company *read* Hartford Woolen Manufactory

376–78 From James Reynolds, note 1. *Delete* last sentence, which begins on page 377, and *substitute:* Here the affair rested until the summer of 1797, when the earlier charges of speculation with Reynolds were revived in Pamphlets V VI, dated June 26 and July 4, 1797, in a series of tracts written by James T. Callender, which were published in book form under the title *The History of the United States for 1796* (Philadelphia, 1797).

Page

389   From Jacob Sarly, note 2, lines 1 and 2: *For* Tippo *read* Tippoo

394–95   To Melancton Smith, note 1: *For* Convention in 1788 *read* Convention in 1788 and was among the first of the Antifederalists to vote for the Constitution.

408   Note 6. *Add:* For an earlier opinion which H wrote concerning Nathanael Greene's relationship with the firm of Hunter, Banks, and Company, see "Mr. Hamilton's oninion upon Banks affair," August 16, 1785 (DS, Pierpont Morgan Library, New York City).

412   Note 12: *For* Warrington *read* Warington

469   Source line: *For* Alexander Dallas *read* Alexander J. Dallas

470   Note 2, line 1: *For* Alexander Dallas *read* Alexander J. Dallas

479   Note 10, line 1: *For* Molleville *read* Moleville

487   Note 8: *For* Le Grand *read* Grand

504   Note 1: *For* Assistant Secretary *read* Assistant to the Secretary

523   Note 5: *For* Lee is referring *read* H is referring

528   To the President and Directors of the Bank of New York, date line: *For* 1792 *read* 179[3]

    Add the following note to date line: H mistakenly dated this letter 1792. See "Contract with George Dannacker and William Young," October 22, 1792. See also "Report on Rules and Modes of Proceeding with Regard to the Collection, Keeping, and Disbursement of Public Moneys, and Accounting for the Same," March 4, 1794.

    Transfer this letter to *PAH*, XIII, 506.

Page

549   Note 29, line 4: *For* 184 *read* 186

575–76   To William Short, January 28, 1792. *Additional source:* LS, marked "Third," Widener Library, Harvard University.

Volume XI

Page

18   Note 2, lines 1 and 2: *For* Assistant Secretary *read* Assistant to the Secretary

37   Note 3, line 1: *For* 1792, Blotters *read* 1792, RG 39, Blotters

39–40   To John Tayler, note 2, line 4: *For* Johnson *read* Johnstone

43   Note 1, line 1: *For* March 31 *read* March 30

122   Note 3, line 2: *For* Assistant Secretary *read* Assistant to the Secretary

126–27   From William Duer, note 2, lines 4 and 5: *For* Hartford Manufacturing Company *read* Hartford Woolen Manufactory
         Note 3, line 1: *For* Assistant Secretary *read* Assistant to the Secretary
         Note 3, last sentence: *For* 28 *read* 23

135   Note 3, line 1: *For* Assistant Secretary *read* Assistant to the Secretary

161   Note 1, line 1: *For* Church *read* Schuyler

165   To William Short, March 21, 1792. *Additional source:* LS, marked "Duplicate," Widener Library, Harvard University.

Page

168   From William Duer, note 1, line 1: *For* Church *read* Schuyler

178   Note 1, paragraph 5, line 3: *For* Molleville *read* Moleville

185   From Robert Troup, note 1, line 1: *For* Church *read* Schuyler

185–86   From Nicholas Low, note 1, line 1: *For* Church *read* Schuyler

194   To William Seton, source line: *For* on the writing *read* in the writing

205   Second letter, title: *For* John Miller *read* John Miller, Junior

207   Introductory note, line 11: *For* Roderigue *read* Roderique

208   Paragraph 1, line 4: *For* Le Grand *read* Grand
        Paragraph 3, lines 1 and 5: *For* Le Grand *read* Grand

209   Note 6, line 1: *For* Le Grand *read* Grand

209–10   Note 10, lines 4 and 5: *For Beaumarchais and the "Lost Million"* (n.p., n.d.), 34–38 *read* "Beaumarchais and the Lost Million," *Pennsylvania Magazine of History and Biography*, XI (1887), 34–38

219–22   To William Short, April 2, 1792. *Additional source:* copy (incomplete), marked "Triplicate," Widener Library, Harvard University.

227   Line 2: *For* 3,893,000 *read* 3,929,214

233   Note 3: *For* March 6 *read* March 5

262–63   To William Short, April 10, 1792. *Additional source:* LS, marked "Triplicate," Widener Library, Harvard University.

Page

266   Note 4: *For* Jean Baptiste La Roche *read* Jean Baptiste de la Roche

289–91   To William Short, April 16, 1792. *Additional source:* LS, marked "Triplicate," Widener Library, Harvard University.

328   Note 1, line 1: *For* Molleville *read* Moleville

354–55   To George Washington, date line: *For* 1792 *read* 179[4]
    Add the following note to date line: See H to George Washington, May 1, 1794; H to Otho H. Williams, May 3, 1794.
    Transfer this letter to *PAH*, XVI, 372.
    Note 1: *Delete.*

361   First letter, title: *For* From —— *read* From Samuel R. Gerry

365   Note 2. After first sentence *insert:* On January 19, 1792, the House of Representatives "*Ordered,* That a committee be appointed to consider and report whether any, and what, alterations ought to be made in the acts for establishing the Treasury and War Departments . . ." (*Journal of the House,* I, 493). The committee reported on February 29, 1792 (*Journal of the House,* I, 523).

366–67   Note 7. *Additional source:* Undated copy, Papers of Tench Coxe in the Coxe Family Papers at the Historical Society of Pennsylvania, Philadelphia.
    Add the following paragraph: "In the Papers of Tench Coxe in the Coxe Family Papers at the Historical Society of Pennsylvania, Philadelphia, are the drafts of two letters by Coxe. Both letters are undated, and neither has an addressee. Both letters criticize the powers to the comptroller in the provisions of the House report quoted in the preceding paragraphs of this note. Either letter or both of

Page

them may have been drafts of letters addressed to H, but no internal or external evidence has been found that the letters were actually sent to H.

369–70 To William Short, May 7, 1792. *Additional source:* LS, Marked "3rd," Widener Library, Harvard University.

393 Third title: *For* William Barton *read* William Barton, Junior

418 "Treasury Department Circular to the Collectors of the Customs," May 23, 1792. *Additional source:* LS, Independence National Historical Park Collection, Old Custom House, Philadelphia.

419 From Thomas Willing, line 2: *Insert* quotation marks before Mr.

431 Note 10, line 6: *Insert* quotation marks after candor
Lines 10 and 11: *Delete* Philadel*phia* and *substitute* Philadelphia

446 First letter, title: *For* To —— *read* To Samuel R. Gerry
Additional source: The Autograph Album: A Magazine for Autograph Collectors, I, No. 1 (June, 1933), Item 79.

456 From William Duer, note 1, line 1: *For* Church *read* Schuyler

477 Note 9, line 4: *For* transit *read* transmit

484–87 "Treasury Department Circular to the Collectors of the Customs," June 4, 1792. *Additional source:* LS, to Samuel R. Gerry, Widener Library, Harvard University.

502 Note 5, line 1: *For* 1796 *read* 1797

519–20 To William Short, June 14, 1792. *Additional source:* LS, marked "3rd," Widener Library, Harvard University.

Page

532 Note 3, line 1: *For* Alexander Dallas *read* Alexander J. Dallas

552 Note 3, line 2: *For* Alexander Dallas *read* Alexander J. Dallas

554 To William Short, June 23, 1792. *Additional source:* LS, marked "3rd," Widener Library, Harvard University.

560–63 Title: *For* Agreement with the President and Directors of the Bank of the United States *read* Agreement with the President, Directors, and Company of the Bank of the United States.
Additional source: copy (incomplete), Papers of Tench Coxe in the Coxe Family Papers at the Historical Society of Pennsylvania, Philadelphia.

569 Note 5: *For* 1792 *read* 1790

591 Note 4, line 5: *For* end *read* and
Note 4, line 9: *For* June 15 *read* June 14

Volume XII

Page
xi Line 1: *For* Paul Leicester Ford *read* Paul Leicester Ford, ed.,

xiii Line 12: *For* 1908 *read* 1909

90 Note 13: *For* Sylvanus *read* Silvanus

102–07 To William Short, July 25, 1792. *Additional source:* LS, marked "Triplicate," Widener Library, Harvard University.

112–17 From John Nicholson, note 1, paragraph 4, line 14: *For* Alexander Dallas *read* Alexander J. Dallas

Page

143   Title: *For* Alexander Dallas *read* Alexander J. Dallas

147   Note 3, line 1: *For* July 22 *read* July 2

162   Note 10, line 4: *For* Colonne *read* Calonne

184   First letter, title: *For* Alexander Dallas *read* Alexander J. Dallas

203   Note 4: *For* William Barton *read* William Barton, Junior

212   First letter, title: *For* Alexander Dallas *read* Alexander J. Dallas

213   Note 2, line 5: *For* Pinckney *read* Pinkney

214–15 To William Short, August 16, 1792. *Additional source:* copy, marked "Duplicate," Widener Library, Harvard University.

286–87 To William Short, August 28, 1792. *Additional source:* LS, marked "3rd," Widener Library, Harvard University.

303   To Thomas Pinckney, note 3: *For* Le Grand *read* Grand

305   To Tench Coxe, note 1, paragraph 2, line 11: *For* Conner *read* Connor

327   To James Lingan, note 1: *For* Maryland *read* District of Columbia

328–29 To William Seton, September 6, 1792. *Additional source:* ALS (photostat), Hamilton Papers, Library of Congress.

367   Note 5, line 5: *For* James Iredell *read* Jared Ingersoll

371   Note 3: *For* Le Grand *read* Grand

Page

376–77 To William Short, September 13, 1792. *Additional source:* LS, marked "Triplicate," Widener Library, Harvard University.

387   Note 3, line 1: *For* Alexander Dallas *read* Alexander J. Dallas

390   Note 6, line 1: *For* John McGantt *read* John M. Gantt

393   From Henry Van Dyke, title and note 1: *For* Henry Van Dyke *read* Henry Vandyke

409–10 From Gouverneur Morris, note 1, line 1: *For* Le Couteulx de Cantaleu *read* Le Couteulx et Cie.

416   Note 2: *Delete* and *substitute:* Presumably William Lewis, former United States judge for the District of Pennsylvania, who had resigned on April 11, 1792.

441   Note 45: *For* Le Grand *read* Grand

444   Note 56, lines 2 and 3: *For* Le Grand *read* Grand

476   Note 12: *For* Le Grand *read* Grand

494   Note 3, line 1: *For* Alexander Dallas *read* Alexander J. Dallas

520   Note 11: *Delete* reference to note 10

521   Note 14: *For* 8 *read* 5

542   Note 5, lines 1 and 5: *For* Findlay *read* Findley

598   Note 20, paragraph 2: *For* Zechariah *read* Zachariah
        Note 21: *For* 14 *read* 13

598–99 Note 22, line 5: *For* Cameal *read* Carneal

611   Last two lines. *Add* the following note after "salaries &

Page

disbursements of his office here": DS, Thomas Jefferson Papers, Library of Congress.

618 Note 7. *Delete* last two sentences and *substitute:* On August 20, 1792, he was captured by the Austrians who handed him over to the Prussians. In 1794 the Prussians returned Lafayette to the Austrians, who imprisoned him in the fortress of Olmütz in Moravia, where he remained a prisoner until September 19, 1797, when he and his family were released at the intercession of the French.

620–22 "Treasury Department Circular to the Collectors of the Customs," October 25, 1792. *Additional source:* LS, Papers of Tench Coxe in the Coxe Family Papers at the Historical Society of Pennsylvania, Philadelphia.

631 Note 2, line 1: *For* Oliver Wolcott *read* Oliver Wolcott, Jr.

Volume XIII

Page

xi Line 26: *For* Mederic *read* Médéric

9 Note 7: *For* Le Grand *read* Grand

12 Note 13: *For* John Charles Michael de Wolf *read* Charles John Michael de Wolf

16 Note 1, paragraph 2, line 9: *For* Jean *read* Jacques

19–22 To William Short, November 5, 1792. *Additional source:* LS, marked "Triplicate," Widener Library, Harvard University.

24 Note 3: *For* Sterrett *read* Sterett

115 Note 1, paragraph 3, line 8: *For* had Clingman imprisoned *read* had Clingman arrested, but Clingman secured his release on bail the same day.

Page

115   Last line: *For* Assistant Secretary *read* Assistant to the
       Secretary

117   First paragraph. After "your letter of this day" *add* the fol-
       lowing note: Letter not found.

219   Note 4, line 5: *For* Pinckney *read* Pinkney

357   Second letter, title: *For* John Miller *read* John Miller,
       Junior

358   Note 2: *For* Le Grand *read* Grand

380–81 From Jeremiah Olney, note 1, line 3: *For* December 10,
        1792, *read* December 10, 13, 1792
               Note 1, line 4: *Delete* December 13, 1792

395   "View of the Commercial Regulations of France and Great
       Britain in Reference to the United States," date line: *For*
       [1792–1793] *read* [1792–1794]

436   Note 117, line 8: *For* past *read* passed

449   First letter, title: *For* John Miller *read* John Miller, Junior

473   Note 3, line 2: *For* Laurence *read* Laurance

482   Second letter, title: *For* Alexander Dallas *read* Alexander J.
       Dallas

483   Enclosure, title: *For* Alexander Dallas *read* Alexander J.
       Dallas

486   Note 1, line 1: *For* Chevalier de Rochefontaine, *read* Che-
       valier de Rochefontaine, who later became known as
       Stephen Rochefontaine,

508   To Henry Knox, note 1: *For* John Miller *read* John Miller,
       Jr.

Page

509   Second letter, title: *For* John Miller *read* John Miller, Junior

527–28   To Thomas Jefferson, note 2: *For* Le Grand *read* Grand

534   Second paragraph, line 11: *For* $2,000,000,000, *read* $2,000,000

Volume XIV

Page

7   To William Short, February 5, 1793. *Additional source:* ALS, marked "Private," Widener Library, Harvard University.

14   Title: *For* Alexander Dallas *read* Alexander J. Dallas

78   Note 35, line 5: *For* [Ferdinand Le] *read* [Ferdinand]

137–38   "Treasury Department Circular to the President and Directors of the Offices of Discount and Deposit of the Bank of the United States," February 23–March 5, 1793. *Additional source:* copy, dated March 5, 1793, to the President and Directors of the Bank of Providence (*Reminiscences of Newport by George Champlin Mason 1884, Extended and Illustrated by His Son George Champlin Mason* [Newport, Rhode Island, 1901], III, 151A).

172   Note 8. *Delete* second sentence and *substitute:* In 1789 he was hired by the City of New York to convert the old Jacobean City Hall on Wall Street into Federal Hall, which served as the temporary capital of the new Federal Government.

181   Note 3: *For* Le Grand *read* Grand

259–60   "Treasury Department Circular to the Collectors of the Customs," March 29, 1793. *Additional source:* LS, The Sol

Page

Feinstone Collection, Library of the American Philosophical Society, Philadelphia.

264–65 "Treasury Department Circular," March 30, 1793. *Additional sources:* LS, to Henry Marchant, Rhode Island Historical Society, Providence; LS, to Robert Morris, New Jersey Historical Society, Newark.

287–90 To James McHenry, note 4: *For* James Chamberlaine *read* Samuel Chamberlaine, Jr.

304–05 Title. *Add* the following note: For an explanation of the contents of this letter, see the introductory note to Coxe to H, February 13, 1795 (*PAH*, XVIII, 262–69). See also the references cited in Coxe to H, April 13, 1793, note 3 (printed in *PAH*, XXVI).

The agreements mentioned by Coxe in this letter are in the Papers of Tench Coxe in the Coxe Family Papers at the Historical Society of Pennsylvania, Philadelphia.

The "friend" mentioned in the sixth paragraph of this letter is William Vans Murray.

310–11 From Gouverneur Morris, note 3: *For* Le Grand *read* Grand

328–29 Note 4, paragraph 2, line 6: *For* Os *read* Or

352 From Thomas Pinckney, line 1: *For* Archdekue *read* Archdekne

357 "Treasury Department Circular to the Collectors of the Customs," April 29, 1793. *Additional source:* copy, Papers of Tench Coxe in the Coxe Family Papers at the Historical Society of Pennsylvania, Philadelphia.

385 Line 6: *For* sttae *read* state

417–18 "Treasury Department Circular to the Commissioners of Loans," May 6, 1793. *Additional source:* LS, to Thomas

Page

Smith, The Sol Feinstone Collection, Library of the American Philosophical Society, Philadelphia.

427 Note 3, line 3: *For* Thomas Newton, Jr., inspector *read* Thomas Newton, Jr., former inspector

438 Note 18, line 5: *For* Manuel de Goday *read* Manuel de Godoy

464 Paragraph 3, line 1: *For* 1789 *read* 1787
Note 20, line 3: *For* Assistant Secretary *read* Assistant to the Secretary

465 Line 1. After "five hundred dollars" *add* the following note: Receipt to William Duer, n.d. (DS, signed by Christopher Gore, Andrew Craigie, and Duer, Andrew Craigie Papers, American Antiquarian Society, Worcester, Massachusetts).

478 Note 2: *For* Le Grand *read* Grand

536 From James Hamilton, date line: *For* Danish *read* British

544 Note 3, line 2: *For* Assistant Secretary *read* Assistant to the Secretary

547 Note 2: *For* Tappan *read* Tappen

549 Note 5. *Delete* and *substitute:* William Lewis, former United States judge for the District of Pennsylvania, had resigned on April 11, 1792.

Volume XV

Page
28 "Treasury Department Circular to the Collectors of the Customs," source line: *For* Lingam *read* Lingan

Page

1 18   To George Washington, July 20, 1793, paragraph 2, line 1.
             After "Capt: Dennis" *add* the following note: Patrick Den-
             nis was master of the New York revenue cutter *Vigilant.*

166–67   Note 1. *Add* the following paragraph: In the Thomas Jef-
             ferson Papers, Library of Congress, is a document in Jeffer-
             son's handwriting entitled "Alteration proposed in the letter
             to G. Morris, in consequence of an examination of the trea-
             ties between France & Great Britain." At the foot of this
             document H wrote:

"submitted *essentially* in the same words without 22	'Not *being subjects* of either crown' said to be in the same words with our 22 Article. The words of our Article are 'not apartenant' *not belonging* &c. The *sense* is the same but not the *words.* Approved with the remark which merely regards accuracy of expression.

                                             A Hamilton"
             Following H's comment, Edmund Randolph wrote: "I am
             content either way. Edm. Randolph." H's advice was not
             taken, but it concerns the wording in the sixth paragraph
             of the letter Jefferson sent to Morris. For this paragraph, see
             ASP, Foreign Relations, I, 168.

169–71   "Cabinet Meeting. Opinion on the Fitting Out of Privateers
             in the Ports of the United States," August 3, 1793. *Addi-
             tional source:* copy, Papers of Thomas Jefferson, Library
             of Congress.

178–81   "Treasury Department Circular to the Collectors of the
             Customs," August 4, 1793. *Additional source:* LS, The Sol
             Feinstone Collection, Library of the American Philosophi-
             cal Society, Philadelphia.

184   Note 11. *Add:* In the Thomas Jefferson Papers, Library
             of Congress, is a document in the handwriting of Randolph,
             H, and Jefferson, which contains another version of the

Page

last two paragraphs of the document printed above. There are few and insignificant differences in wording between the two versions.

227 Note 13, line 1: *For* Sodermanland *read* Södermanland

233 Introductory note, line 5: *For* Alexander Dallas *read* Alexander J. Dallas

270 To George Washington, note 1, line 8: *For* Packer's *read* Parker's

279 Note 1, line 2: *For* 1789 *read* 1788

311–12 From James Watson, August 30, 1793. *Additional source:* copy, in Watson's handwriting, from the original in the New York State Library, Albany.

318 Note 1. *Add* the following paragraph: In *JCHW*, VI, 35, the letter printed above is dated September 2, 1795.

320 Note 5: *For* Assistant Secretary *read* Assistant to the Secretary

324–25 From George Washington, September 6, 1793. *Additional source:* ALS, sold by Kenneth W. Rendell, Inc., Newton, Massachusetts, Catalogue 106, Item 71.

329 Note 1. *Add:* For the effect of the yellow fever epidemic on the operation of the Treasury Department, see Ezekiel Forman to Tench Coxe, September 11, 20, 1793; William Barton to Coxe, September 11, 1793; John Mease to Coxe, September 19, 1793 (all ALS, Papers of Tench Coxe in the Coxe Family Papers at the Historical Society of Pennsylvania, Philadelphia).

340 Note 2. *Add:* Coxe's draft of this letter may be found in the Papers of Tench Coxe in the Coxe Family Papers at the Historical Society of Pennsylvania, Philadelphia.

Page

349–51 From Abraham Yates, Junior, September 27, 1793. *Additional source:* ADf, The Sol Feinstone Collection, Library of the American Philosophical Society, Philadelphia.

370 Note 15, line 1: *For* Le Grand *read* Grand

383 Note 11, line 2: *For* Pennevert and Cherni *read* John Pennwert (Pennevert, Penveer, Pinevert) and Paul Arnaud Cherui

403 From Jeremiah Olney, note 2. *Add:* November 7, 1793.

417–18 From Richard Morris, note 1: *Add* in 1792 and 1793

422 Note 4: *For* Le Grand *read* Grand

436–38 To George Washington, December 2, 1793. *Additional source:* letterpress copy, enclosed in Thomas Jefferson to Edmond Charles Genet, December 6, 1793 (ALS, Thomas Jefferson Papers, Library of Congress).

518 Note 21: *For* JCC, XIX, 197 *read* JCC, III, 358–59; XIX, 197

535 Note 24, line 8: *For* August 21 *read* August 31

545–46 "Treasury Department Circular to the Collectors of the Customs," December 18, 1793. *Additional source:* LS, to William Ellery, The Sol Feinstone Collection, Library of the American Philosophical Society, Philadelphia.

549 From James Lingan, date line: *For* Maryland *read* District of Columbia

589 Note 9, line 1: *For* Lennox *read* Lenox

604 Note 2. *Delete* and *substitute:* H may have wished this information for use in the preparation of his "View of the Commercial Regulations of France and Great Britain in

Page

Reference to the United States," which is dated 1792–1793 in *PAH*, XIII, 395, but which may have been written in 1794. See Coxe to H, January 1, 1795 (printed in *PAH*, XXVI); H to Coxe, January 12, 1795 (printed in *PAH*, XXVI).

619   Note 3. *Add* the following paragraph: For additional information concerning the attachments and transfers of funds and H's role in these activities, see Théophile Cazenove to the four firms, June 11, 1793 (LS, Gemeentearchief Amsterdam, Holland Land Company. These documents were transferred in 1964 from the Nederlandsch Economisch-Historisch Archief, Amsterdam).

622   Note 4: *For* Peter T. Curtenius *read* Peter S. Curtenius

625   Note 1, paragraph 2, line 7: *For* Elijah Clarke *read* Elijah Clark

633   Note 1, line 2: *For* 1788 *read* 1786

638   Note 1, line 5. *Delete:* first

668   From George Wray, source line: *For* Segreted *read* Segregated

Volume XVI

Page

23   From James Lingan, date line: *For* Maryland *read* District of Columbia

93   Note 3, paragraph 2, line 4: *For* Udney *read* Udny

97   Title: *For* Peter pra Van Zandt *read* Peter Pray Van Zandt

126   Note 8: *For* Le Grand *read* Grand

Page

234   Note 2, line 5: *For* Francis *read* Frances

398   Note 2, line 4: After "Pennington" *insert* (Penington)

466   **Note 4, line 1:** *For* **Udney** *read* **Udny**

516   Note 3, line 1: *For* Truxton *read* Truxtun

525   Note 5: *For* Truxton *read* Truxtun

531   Notes 2 and 3: *For* Truxton *read* Truxtun

536   Note 1. *Add* to first paragraph: See also Tench Coxe to
         Miller, June 17, 21, 1794; Thomas Hartley to Coxe, two
         letters of June 24, July 8, 1794 (all ALS, Papers of Tench
         Coxe in the Coxe Family Papers at the Historical Society of
         Pennsylvania, Philadelphia).

540   Note 3, line 1: *For* Isaac Zane, Jr. *read* Isaac Zane

553–54   From Christopher Richmond, note 2: *For* Ramsey *read*
         Ramsay

Volume XVII

Page

1   Note 2, lines 1 and 3; note 3, line 1: *For* Feasch *read* Faesch

28   Note 5, line 1: *For* **Crook's** *read* **Crooks's**

38   Note 32, line 7: *For* Virginia *read* **North Carolina**

42   Note 48, line 2: *For* **Myer's** *read* **Myers's**

Page

96   Note 1. *Delete* last two lines and *substitute:* opposition"
(ALS, Papers of Tench Coxe in the Coxe Family Papers at
the Historical Society of Pennsylvania, Philadelphia). This
letter is printed in Brackenridge, *Insurrection*, 144–45; *Calendar of Virginia State Papers*, VII, 251–53.

     Note 2, line 5: *Delete* (Brackenridge, *Insurrection*, 146–
47) and *substitute* (LS, Papers of Tench Coxe in the Coxe
Family Papers at the Historical Society of Pennsylvania,
Philadelphia). This letter is printed in Brackenridge, *Insurrection*, 146–47.

215–16   To Samuel Hodgdon, source line. *Read:* ALS, Mr. Charles E.
Mather, II, Mather & Co., Philadelphia.

290–91   To Oliver Wolcott, Junior, September 29, 1794. *Additional
sources:* three copies, Papers of Tench Coxe in the Coxe
Family Papers at the Historical Society of Pennsylvania,
Philadelphia.

340   Note 8: *For* Joshua Humphreys *read* Joshua Humphreys, Jr.

379   Note 11, line 3: *For* Speer *read* Spiers

422–23   To John Quincy Adams, December 5, 1794. *Additional
source:* LS, endorsed "Triplicate," deposited in the Library
of The Phillips Exeter Academy, Exeter, New Hampshire.

430   From Timothy Hurst, note 3. *Delete* and *substitute:* William Brownjohn, Hurst's father-in-law, was a New York
City druggist.

449   From Tench Coxe, note 1: *For* Hieskell *read* Heiskell

460   From Tench Coxe, note 1, line 3: *For* John Watts *read*
John Watts, Jr.

Page
466–75   From Tench Coxe, paragraph 3, line 3: *For* gnowledge
          read knowledge
                  Note 9: *For* Truxton *read* Truxtun

537   Title, line 3: *For* Republice *read* Republic

Volume XVIII

Page
xii   Line 9 from bottom: *For* Charles R. King *read* Charles R.
          King, ed.,

41   Note 1, last line: *Delete* forthcoming. *For* III *read* forth-
          coming volumes

43–44   From George Pollock, note 3, paragraph 3, line 12: *Delete*
          forthcoming. *For* III *read* forthcoming volumes

159   Note 2, line 6: *For* Espenditure *read* Expenditure

175   Note 1: *For* Sewell *read* Sewall

178   Line 4: *For* Sewell *read* Sewall

200   Title: *For* From John Clark *read* From John Clark, Junior
                  Note 1. *Delete* second sentence and *substitute:* A major
          in the Second Battalion of the Pennsylvania Flying Camp,
          Clark was auditor of accounts for the army from February 1,
          1778, to November, 1779, when he resigned from the
          army because of ill health.

205–06   From Walter Livingston, note 4, paragraph 2, lines 4 and 5:
          Delete forthcoming. *For* III *read* forthcoming volumes
                  Note 6, line 2: *For* Assistant Secretary *read* Assistant to
          the Secretary

Page

Note 7, lines 4 and 5 and 8 and 9: *Delete* forthcoming. *For* III *read* forthcoming volumes

262–69 From Tench Coxe, February 13, 1795, introductory note, note 1, paragraph 1: *Delete* last sentence.

Note 1, paragraph 3, line 3: *For* 305–06 *read* 304–05

Note 13, paragraph 2, line 3: *For* in 1790 and 1791 *read* from 1790 to 1795

Note 22, line 4: *Delete* forthcoming. *For* III *read* forthcoming volumes

Line 3 of letter. *Add* the following note after "*Church, Coxe, Ball, Smith & ca.*": See "rough Account of Land bought by Murray, Church & Coxe of Ball & Smith. T.C.," February 12, 1795 (ADS, Papers of Tench Coxe in the Coxe Family Papers at the Historical Society of Pennsylvania, Philadelphia).

270 Note 2, line 1: *For* 1780 *read* March 1, 1782

280 Note 4, line 1: *For* Cornelis Pauw *read* Cornelius de Pauw

289 To Benjamin Walker, note 1, line 1: *For* imigrated *read* immigrated

Note 1, line 3: *For* 1788 *read* 1786

293–94 From Tjerck C. DeWitt, note 2, lines 4, 5, and 6: *Delete* forthcoming. *For* III *read* forthcoming volumes

295–300 To Robert Morris, introductory note, line 3: *For* February 15 *read* February 16

Note 14, line 2: After "New York City" *add:* (Goebel, *Law Practice*, II, 450).

304 Note 4, last line: *Delete* forthcoming. *For* III *read* forthcoming volumes

316 Note 4, last line: *Delete* forthcoming. *For* III *read* forthcoming volumes

Page

331   Note 2, last line: *Delete* forthcoming. *For* III *read* forth-
             coming volumes

333   To James Watson, note 1, lines 5, 9, and 10: *Delete* forth-
             coming. *For* III *read* forthcoming volumes

334   Note 3, last line: *Delete* forthcoming. *For* III *read* forth-
             coming volumes

335–36   Note 3, paragraph 2, lines 4 and 5: *Delete* forthcoming. *For*
             III *read* forthcoming volumes
                  Note 3, paragraph 9, line 3: *Delete* forthcoming. *For* III
             read forthcoming volumes
                  Note 3, paragraph 10, lines 5 and 6: *Delete* forthcoming.
             For III *read* forthcoming volumes
                  Note 3, paragraph 10, last two lines: *Delete* forthcoming.
             For III *read* forthcoming volumes

337   From Gerrit Boon, note 1, line 3: *Delete* forthcoming. *For*
             III *read* forthcoming volumes

338   Line 17. After "& myself" *add* the following note: See
             "Acct of Ruston & Co for J. B. Church," May 21, 1795
             (AD, Papers of Tench Coxe in the Coxe Family Papers at
             the Historical Society of Pennsylvania, Philadelphia).
                  First full paragraph, line 11. After "I have written to
             Mr. Murray" *add* the following note: Coxe to William
             Vans Murray, May 1, 1795 (LC, Papers of Tench Coxe in
             the Coxe Family Papers at the Historical Society of Penn-
             sylvania, Philadelphia). On May 17, 1795, Murray wrote
             to Coxe and declined Coxe's offer (ALS, Papers of Tench
             Coxe in the Coxe Family Papers at the Historical Society of
             Pennsylvania, Philadelphia).

340–44   From Robert Troup, note 5, paragraph 3, lines 3 and 4: *De-
             lete* forthcoming. *For* III *read* forthcoming volumes
                  Note 5, paragraph 4, lines 6 and 7: *Delete* forthcoming.

Page

For III *read* forthcoming volumes
Note 6, line 3: *For* note 5 *read* note 6

363   Note 18, last line: *Delete* forthcoming. *For* III *read* forthcoming volumes

366   Note 39, line 5: *For* 179[5] *read* 179[4]

373   Note 2, lines 4, 5, and 6: *Delete* forthcoming. *For* III *read* forthcoming volumes

384   Note 3, last line: *Delete* forthcoming. *For* III *read* forthcoming volumes

392–93   To Oliver Wolcott, Junior, note 1, line 2: *For* Gilbert Livingston, first lord of Livingston Manor *read* Gilbert Livingston, youngest son of the first lord of Livingston Manor

397   Note 18, line 3: *For* 1789 *read* 1787

452   Line 7: *For* inquieture *read* inquietude

455   To John Thurston and Company, note 1, lines 3 and 4: *Delete* forthcoming. *For* III *read* forthcoming volumes

458   Note 10, last two lines: *Delete* forthcoming. *For* III *read* forthcoming volumes

471–72   To James Nicholson, note 2, paragraph 2, line 2: *For* Udney *read* Udny

474–75   From Edmund Randolph, note 3, lines 3 and 4: *Delete* forthcoming. *For* III *read* forthcoming volumes

477   Line 3: *For* November 11, 1795 *read* November 5–11, 1795

503–07   To Robert Troup, note 6, lines 3 and 4 and 8: *Delete* forthcoming. *For* III *read* forthcoming volumes

Page

Note 8, last line: *Delete* forthcoming. *For* III *read* forthcoming volumes

Note 13, last two lines: *Delete* forthcoming. *For* III *read* forthcoming volumes

Note 14, last two lines: *Delete* forthcoming. *For* III *read* forthcoming volumes

Note 15, last line: *Delete* forthcoming. *For* III *read* forthcoming volumes

Note 17, last two lines: *Delete* forthcoming. *For* III *read* forthcoming volumes

Note 24, lines 3 and 4: *Delete* forthcoming. *For* III *read* forthcoming volumes

Note 25, last line: *Delete* forthcoming. *For* III *read* forthcoming volumes

Note 26, last line: *Delete* forthcoming. *For* III *read* forthcoming volumes

Volume XIX

Page

v   Line 10: *For* ben *read* been

vi   Line 1: *For* of *read* or

xi   Lines 2 and 5 from bottom: *For etats read états*

38   First full paragraph, line 3: *For* convinction *read* conviction

77   "The Defence No. IV," August 1, 1795. The source line for this document is incorrectly printed at the end of the preceding document.

87   Note 1, line 2: *Delete* forthcoming. *For* III *read* forthcoming volumes

88   Note 3, line 2: *Delete* forthcoming. *For* III *read* forthcoming volumes

Page

97   Note 3, line 2: *Delete* forthcoming. *For* III *read* forthcoming volumes

202   Note 16, lines 2 and 3: *Delete* forthcoming. *For* III *read* forthcoming volumes

203   Note 23, lines 2 and 3: *Delete* forthcoming. *For* III *read* forthcoming volumes

204   Note 24, line 1: *For* Catharine *read* Catherine

232   From Nicholas Olive, note 1, line 3: *Delete* which planned

232   To Nicholas Olive, note 2, last line: *Delete* forthcoming. *For* III *read* forthcoming volumes.

309–11 To James Greenleaf, note 2, line 1: *For* H's opinion *read* H's escrow agreement
       Note 2, paragraph 1, last two lines: *Delete* forthcoming. *For* III *read* forthcoming volumes
       Note 2, paragraph 2, last line: *Delete* forthcoming. *For* III *read* forthcoming volumes
       Note 3, last two lines: *Delete* forthcoming. *For* III *read* forthcoming volumes
       Note 4, lines 7 and 8, 13 and 14: *Delete* forthcoming. *For* III *read* forthcoming volumes

313   Note 8: *For* John Watts *read* John Watts, Jr.

313   To Peter Smith, note 2, last line: *Delete* forthcoming. *For* III *read* forthcoming volumes

474   Note 5, line 2: *For* Catharine *read* Catherine

507–08 Note 26, lines 17 and 18: *For* Catharine *read* Catherine

512   Note 2, line 15: *Delete* forthcoming. *For* III *read* forthcoming volumes

Page

515   Note 2, last line: *Delete* forthcoming. *For* III *read* forth-coming volumes

527   Note 15, line 15: *For* Charles R. King *read* Charles R. King, ed.,

Volume XX

Page

10   Note 1, line 2: *For* Assistant Secretary *read* Assistant to the Secretary

11–13   To Jedidiah Morse, note 3. *Add* the following paragraph: The case of *Jedidiah Morse* v *John Reid* was tried in the United States Circuit Court for the District of New York with H as Morse's attorney. In April, 1798, the Court ordered Reid, a New York City bookseller who in 1796 had reprinted Tiebout and O'Brien's edition of Winterbotham's book, "to desist and refrain from the further reprinting and publishing . . . of the Book entitled 'A Geographical Commercial and Philosophical view of the present situation of the United States of America' . . ." and to pay Morse $262.50 (RG 21, United States Circuit Court for New York, Old Equity Case Files, 1792–1827, Box 5, National Archives; RG 21, MS Minutes, United States Circuit Court for the District of New York, 1790–1808, under the dates of September 5, 1796, April 8, September 5, 1797, April 2, 4, 6, 1798, National Archives).

32   Note 30. *Delete* brackets in text and note.
      A draft in H's handwriting of the material within brackets has been found in the Hamilton Papers, Library of Congress, where it was misfiled under the date 1800. It is now filed with the remainder of the document.

Page

41   Note 1, line 2: *Delete* forthcoming. *For* III *read* forthcoming volumes

81   Note 2, line 2: *For* 1789 *read* 1788

110   Second letter, title: *For* Bollman *read* Bollmann

114   Note 5, line 3: *Delete* forthcoming. *For* III *read* forthcoming volumes

120   Note 4, line 3: *For* 1788 *read* 1786
        Note 4, line 9: *For* February 20, 1798 *read* February, 1797

169   To George Washington, note 3, line 4: *Delete* forthcoming *For* III *read* forthcoming volumes
        Note 3. *Add:* But see Coxe to H, May 16, 1796 (*PAH*, XXVI).

184   From Tench Coxe, note 1, line 3: *For* Assistant Secretary *read* Assistant to the Secretary

201   Note 3, lines 4 and 5: *Delete* this enterprise was not a success, and

203   Note 2: *For* Le Grand *read* Grand

205–06 From Tench Coxe, May 31, 1796. *Additional sources:* LC (two copies), Papers of Tench Coxe in the Coxe Family Papers at the Historical Society of Pennsylvania, Philadelphia.
        Note 3, line 4: *Delete* forthcoming. *For* III *read* forthcoming volumes

211   Note 1, paragraph 2, lines 5, 17, 21 and 22: *Delete* forthcoming. *For* III *read* forthcoming volumes

226   Note 3, line 2: *For* Sonthonnax *read* Sonthonax

Page

260   Note 3, last line: *Delete* forthcoming. *For* III *read* forthcoming volumes

325   Note 6, line 2: *For* Armand *read* Amand

334   Note 3: *For* Catharine *read* Catherine

370   Note 6: *For* Tatum *read* Tatom

390–91 From Tench Coxe, November 12, 1794. *Additional source:* LC, Papers of Tench Coxe in the Coxe Family Papers at the Historical Society of Pennsylvania, Philadelphia.

416   Note 2, line 5: *For* Siegmund *read* Sigmund

417–18 From Henry Sadler and Company, note 2. *Add:* See also an entry in H's Cash Book, 1795–1804, on November 26, 1796, which reads: "Costs & Fees received of ⟨–⟩ & Sadler for arbitration opinion   20" (AD, Hamilton Papers, Library of Congress).

432   Note 26, lines 7 and 12–13: *For* Le Grand *read* Grand

438   Note 2. *Add:* In the Hamilton Papers, Library of Congress is an undated document in Edward Carrington's handwriting which has been misfiled under the date of "August 10, 1800." In this document Carrington projected the distribution of electoral votes in the presidential election of 1796.

454   Note 2, line 6: *For* any debt *read* my debt

456–60 From Ann Mitchell, note 1, line 9: *For* staegt *read* slaegt
        Note 1, paragraph 4, last line: *For* July 11 *read* July 10

489   Note 23, lines 2 and 3: *For* George E. Hopkins *read* George F. Hopkins

Page

528 From Robert Morris, line 10: *For* of their Content *read* to their Content

536 From Robert Morris, line 1: *Add* the following note: Charles Bridgen to Morris, March 6, 1797 (copy, Hamilton Papers, Library of Congress).

538 From William Hamilton, note 1: *Delete* and Laird of Grange, Ayrshire, Scotland.

Volume XXI

Page

xiii Section IV, line 2: *For* multilation *read* mutilation

1 Note 1, line 13: *For* Jean *read* Jacques

8 From Rufus King, note 1, line 1: *For* United State Senator *read* United States Senator

14 Note 7, lines 3–4 and 15: *For* Catharine *read* Catherine

55 Note 3: *For* Daniel C. *read* Gulian

62 Note 3, line 4: *For* April 26, 179 *read* April 26, 1797

79 Note 1: *For* Laird of Grange, Ayrshire, Scotland *read* a resident of Greenock, Scotland

85 From Jeremiah Wadsworth. At end of letter *add* the following note: In the Hamilton Papers, Library of Congress, is a copy of the appraisal of the land in Salisbury, Connecticut, known as the Livingston Lot. The appraisal is dated January 10, 1795. Also in the Hamilton Papers is a description of the Livingston Lot, dated May 19, 1777,

Page

extracted from the town records of Salisbury and certified
by the town clerk.

86   Note 1, line 3: *For* Assistant Secretary *read* Assistant to the
Secretary

93–95   Jacob Mark and Company to John B. Church, H, and John
Laurance, note 3, line 6. *Delete* from "Indenture" to the
end of the paragraph and *substitute:* ("Mortgage by John
Laurance, John B. Church, and Alexander Hamilton to
Robert Gilchrist," August 21, 1802). On January 8, 1795,
Mark, who owed Robert Gilchrist and Theodosius Fowler
$70,000, gave them a mortgage on Townships 21, 15, 9, 10,
and a part of 17 (Bill in Chancery, *Robert Gilchrist* v
Jacob Mark, John Laurance, and others, May 21, 1801
[Chancery Papers, Copied Libers, Vol. 128, 469–85, Hall
of Records, New York City]; Fowler's Account Book,
Stevens Family Papers, New Jersey Historical Society,
Newark). On January 15, 1796, Laurance purchased for H,
Church, and himself Townships 21 and 15, in which Mark
retained an undivided one-fourth interest to be held in
trust (Conveyance, Mark and his wife to Laurance, January 15, 1796 [Chancery Papers, Copied Libers, Vol. 128,
507–10, Hall of Records, New York City]). On January
20, 1796, H made the following entry in his Cash Book,
1795–1804: "John Laurance Dr to Cash   for this sum dld
John Laurance towards my share of two Townships of
Land No. 21 & No. 15 in Rosevelts purchase, purchased of
Mr. Mark   1000" (AD, Hamilton Papers, Library of Congress). H recorded additional payments for this land of
$5,000 on January 21, 1796, $88.90 on March 30, 1796, and
$5,326.65 on December 12, 1796 (AD, Hamilton Papers,
Library of Congress). H also paid $226 on June 24, 1796,
and $150 on October 11, 1796, for surveying the land (AD,
Hamilton Papers, Library of Congress). By 1800 Mark
was in serious financial difficulties and was declared a bankrupt. In 1801 Gilchrist began Chancery proceedings to
foreclose on the mortgage he held, on which $41,000 in

overdue payments was owed by Mark (Bill in Chancery, May 28, 1801; Joint and Several answers of Jacob Mark and others, May 17, 1802; Answer of John Lawrance, May 17, 1802 [Chancery Papers, Copied Libers, Vol. 128, 469–85, 486–97, 499–516, Hall of Records, New York City]). In order to protect the investment which they had already made in Townships 21 and 15, H, Church, and Laurance redeemed the lands still subject to mortgage by purchasing for $43,530.33 the residue of Mark's holdings (Townships 9, 10, a portion of 17, and his one-fourth share of 21 and 15) (Master's Report, May 18, 1802; Decree, May 31, 1802 [Chancery Papers, Copied Libers, Vol. 420, 401–03, 404–06, Hall of Records, New York City]; Final Decree, March 7, 1803 [Chancery Papers, Copied Libers, Vol. 128, 522–33, Hall of Records, New York City]). As security for payment to Fowler and Gilchrist, who were business partners, of one-half the purchase price, or $21,765, H, Church, and Laurance executed on August 21, 1802, a bond and mortgage on an undivided half of the lands ("Mortgage by John Laurance, John B. Church, and Alexander Hamilton to Robert Gilchrist," August 21, 1802; "Promissory Note to Theodosius Fowler," August 21, 1802). In his "Statement of my property and Debts July 1. 1804" H wrote: "My share of townships No. 9. 10. 15. 17 and 21 in Scribas Patent in connection with J B Church and John Laurence viz

112   Note 18, line 3: *Delete* forthcoming. *For* III *read* forthcoming volumes

112–13   To Jeremiah Wadsworth, note 1, line 6: For staegt *read* slaegt

129   Line 11: *For* Assistant Secretary *read* Assistant to the Secretary

145   Line 9. After "author" *add* the following note: On October 10, 1796, John Beckley wrote to Tench Coxe: "Enclosed are Hamilton's precious confessions. Be pleased to preserve

Page

every scrap; they are *truly* original and *authenticated* by himself" (ALS, Papers of Tench Coxe in the Coxe Family Papers at the Historical Society of Pennsylvania, Philadelphia).

165   Note 1, paragraph 4, lines 6–7 and 10–11: *Delete* forthcoming. *For* III *read* forthcoming volumes

198   Line 6: *For* Twemlaw *read* Twemlow

199   Note 7, line 7: *For* 1767 *read* 1797

211–12   Certificate by James Monroe, note 1. *Add:* But on August 16, he did send the certificate to Burr with the following covering letter:

"Accept my acknowledgments for yr. attention to the affr. with Colo. H. I have been very sick but am well agn. or nearly so. I set out tomorrow on my way home.

"Now that there is no prospect of a challenge (I mean in perspective) from Colo. H., I feel myself at liberty to give a certificate which will I presume satisfy him. It wod. have done so when here. It contains a decln. that I meant to give no *sanction to* or *opinion of my own* as to the entry made by myself. Had he sought this in a conciliatory manner I wod. always have given it. But he sought it in a manner wh. left me under an impression that if I did not give it, he wod. challenge me, & therefore I wod. give none & waited his challenge. He did not take that course but used harsh language &ca as you know. If I cod. give a stronger certificate I wod. (tho' indeed it seems unnecessary for this with that given jointly by Muhg. & myself seems sufficient) but in truth I have doubts upon the main point & wh. he rather increased than diminishd by his conversation when here & therefore can give no other. I give it upon the principles you state from motives of candour & unconditionally.

"upon the other point I own to you I am not satisfied.

Page

I did not mean to give or provoke a challenge it is true, but yet I did mean to accept one if given in any form. I ask'd him a direct answer to a plain question, whether he meant his as *such* or not, & to this he does not give a direct answer; but plays upon the word *advance*, in a manner I do not like. I must therefore request you to ask him explicitly whether he meant his former letter as a challenge, under any possible state of my mind, and in case he did not accept it for me, under the accomodation stated in my former letter.

"My state of health will not permit me to pay more attention to this subject at present. I submit the whole affr. to yr. discretion being fully convincd that you will conduct it with a delicate & inviolate regard to my honor. I give you full command over it. I enclose you the whole of the correspondence assuring you that I will ratify whatever you do for me.

"Mr. Dawson remains here a week & will receive & forward any commands for me that time—my address is at charlottesville, in wh. neighbourhd. I reside." (AL, Munson-Williams-Proctor Institute, Utica, New York).

294   Last line: *For* 103 *read* 800

312   Note 3, paragraph 2, line 1: *For* John Rutledge *read* John Rutledge, Jr.
        Note 3, paragraph 3, last line: *Add* See also Goebel, *Law Practice*, forthcoming volumes.

349   Note 4, line 1: *For* 18 Fructidor *read* 18 Fructidor An V

358   Note 2, line 8: *For* Francis *read* Frances

374   Note 10: *For* 18 Fructidor Year 5 *read* 18 Fructidor An V

401   Note 5, line 2 from bottom: *For* Jean *read* Jacques

414   Note 6: *For* 18 Fructidor *read* 18 Fructidor An V

Page

483   To Elizabeth Hamilton, note 1, line 1: *For* Catharine *read* Catherine

492   Note 5, paragraph 2, line 2: *For* Flemming *read* Fleming

495   Note 3, line 2: *For* Catharine *read* Catherine

517–18   "Memorandum from Joseph F. Mangin . . . ," note 1, paragraph 3, line 9: *For* Flemming *read* Fleming

518   Note 1, line 1: *For* Bollman *read* Bollmann

Volume XXII

Page

19   Note 65, line 2: *For* Ratifying Convention *read* Federal Constitutional Convention

41   Note 1, line 5: *For* July 31 *read* July 30

49   From Theodore Sedgwick, note 1, last line: *For* 1801 *read* 1799

50   From James McHenry, date line: *For Philadelphia read Trenton*

56   From James McHenry, date line: *For Philadelphia read Trenton*

59   From Joseph Mangin, note 1, line 9: *For* Flemming *read* Fleming

64   Note 7, line 3: *For* 1788 *read* 1786
        Note 7, line 6: *For* 1798 *read* 1797

Page

89   Note 12, line 1: *For* Wilcocks *read* Willcocks

93   Note 40, last line: *For* 1784 *read* 1794

132   Note 190: *For* Sheaf *read* Sheaff

139   Note 238: *Delete* second sentence and *substitute:* A major
        in the Second Batallion of the Pennsylvania Flying Camp,
        Clark was auditor of accounts for the army from Febru-
        ary 1, 1778, to November, 1779, when he resigned from the
        army because of ill health.

141   Note 252, line 3: *For* He *read* H

178–79 To Benjamin Walker, William Inman, and William Cooper,
        note 1, last line: *Delete* forthcoming. *For* III *read* forthcom-
        ing volumes

184   Note 3, line 9: *For* Joseph Philippe Létombe *read* Philippe
        Joseph Létombe

186   Title: *For* Thomas Hazard *read* William W. Parker

187   Note 4. *Additional source:* copy, Sleepy Hollow Restora-
        tions, Inc., Tarrytown, New York
           Note 5, line 2: *For* Church *read* Schuyler
           Note 7, line 3: *For* v *read* adsm.

215   Note 7, paragraph 2, line 7: *For* orderd *read* ordered
           Note 7, paragraph 2, last line: *For* 1798–1801 *read* 1793–
        1797

223   Line 3: *For* Jeremias *read* Jeremiah

245   Note 21, line 2: *For* Du 1er aout 1791 *read* Du 1er aout
        1791

261   Note 30, last line: *For* Lord Malmsbury *read* first Earl of
        Malmesbury

Page

278   Note 27, line 1: *For* Herman *read* Heman

280   Note 38, line 1: *For* Bebee *read* Beebe (Bebee)

299   Note 83, line 1: *For* Brooks *read* Brookes

321   Note 11: *For* Thatcher *read* Thacher (Thatcher)

322   Note 18: *For* Cummings *read* Cumming

379   To James McHenry, date line: *For* Decr. 20 1798 *read*
         Decr. 26 1798
             Source line, line 2: *For* copy, in the handwriting of
         Philip Church *read* copy, dated December 20, 1798, in the
         handwriting of Philip Church
             Transfer this letter to PAH, XXII, 393

380   To James McHenry, note 2: *For* McDougal *read* Mc-
         Dougall

405   Note 4, last two lines: *Delete* Brand Whitlock, *La Fayette*,
         II (New York, 1929), 115 and *substitute* Lafayette to H,
         February 10, 1801

412   From William Duer, source line: *For* Church *read* Schuy-
         ler
             Note 1: *Delete* H to Oliver Wolcott, Jr., August 22,
         December 28, 1798

420   Line 2: *For* Truxton *read* Truxtun
             First full paragraph, line 14: *For* Truxton *read* Truxtun
             Second full paragraph, lines 9–10: *For* Truxton *read*
         Truxtun
             Note 2, line 12: *For* Truxton *read* Truxtun

422   From William Duer, source line: *For* Church *read* Schuy-
         ler
             Note 1: *Delete* H to Oliver Wolcott, Jr., August 22,
         December 28, 1798

Page

444 First letter, title: *For* Samuel Lewis *read* Samuel Lewis, Senior

Note 2. *Add:* On April 24, 1799, Peter Hagner, principal clerk in the office of the Accountant of the War Department, wrote to James McHenry: "I Certify that there is due to Alexander Hamilton Major General of the army of the United States, the Sum of Eight hundred & thirty nine Dollars and forty one Cents, being for his pay, subsistence & Forage for the months of January, February and March, 1799, including his compensation as Inspector General to the 31 March 1799 agreeably to the act of Congress of the 3rd of March 1799" (RG 217, Records of the General Accounting Office, Department of War Accountant's Office, Report Book B, July, 1797–May, 1799, National Archives). For the law concerning the pay of major generals, see Section 3 of "An Act for the better organizing of the Troops of the United States; and for other purposes" (1 *Stat.* 750–51 [March 3, 1799]).

446 First letter, title: *For* Samuel Lewis *read* Samuel Lewis, Senior

450–51 Note 26. *Delete* last line and *substitute:* John B. Church's oldest son Philip was born on April 14, 1778. Church had four other children: John B., born in 1779; Catherine, born in 1780; Elizabeth, born in 1786; Richard Stephen, born in 1798.

484–86 "Circular on Recruiting Service," February 18–19, 1799. *Additional source:* LS, in the handwriting of William LeConte and with additions in H's handwriting, to Ebenezer Huntington, The Hulbert Taft, Jr., Library, The Taft School, Watertown, Connecticut.

486 From William Duer, source line: *For* Church *read* Schuyler

Note 1: *Delete* H to Oliver Wolcott, Jr., August 22, December 28, 1798

Page
517   Line 1: *For* comliments *read* compliments
           Note 1, line 3: *For Browne read Bowne*

526   Line 1: *For* 1 *read* 2

577   Note 5, line 1: *For* Aleksanor *read* Aleksandr

584   Note 2. *Delete* third sentence and *substitute:* The officers
           already holding commissions under this act were never
           called into active service nor has any record been found
           that they were discharged.

610   Fifth letter: *For* MacWhorter *read* Macwhorter

Volume XXIII

Page
63   Note 3: *For* McDougal *read* McDougall

98   Note 2, lines 3 and 6: *For* Truxton *read* Truxtun
           Note 5, line 1: *For* Truxton *read* Truxtun

Map facing page
338   Fort Dearborn (Chicago) was not held by the United
           States Army until 1803.

379   Note 7: *For* Macniff *read* MacNiff

508   Note 2, line 1: *For* Center *read* Senter

545   Note 2, line 12 and 13: *For* Charles Maurice Talleyrand-
           Périgord *read* Charles Maurice de Talleyrand-Périgord

547   Line 3: *For* [Henry] *read* [Charles]

Page

566   Note 1, paragraph 2, line 1: *For* Mitchel *read* Mitchell

599   Note 1, line 3: *For* New Jersey Ratifying Convention *read*
         Federal Constitutional Convention

604   Note 15, line 3: *For* the [New York] *Time Piece read The*
         [New York] *Time Piece*

610   Fourth letter: *For* Truman *read* Trueman

658   Third Letter: *For* Thatcher *read* Thacher (Thatcher)

673   Sixth letter, line 2: *For* Bayley *read* Bayly

681   Eighth letter: *For* Taylor *read* Tayler

689   Eleventh letter: *For* Taylor *read* Tayler

Volume XXIV

Page

ix   Line 2 from bottom: *For Otis. 1765–1848 read Otis, Fed-
         eralist, 1765–1848*

265   Note 6: *For* Ireland *read* Scotland
           Note 7, line 1: *For* Tippo *read* Tippoo

298   Note 2, line 1: *For* Latour Longnevoué Veuve Fleury *read*
         Latour Longnevoué, marquise de Fleury

486   To William Vans Murray, note 1: *Delete* and *substitute:*
         Madame de Vaublanc was the wife of Vincent-Marie-
         Viénot, comte de Vaublanc, who was banished from France
         in 1797. See Murray to H, August 28, 1801, note 1. See also

Page

Louis Gottschalk, ed., *The Letters of Lafayette to Washington*, *1777–1799* (New York, 1944), 377–78, 379–80.

537–38   Note 6, lines 1 and 3: *For* Sewell *read* Sewall

585   Line 17: *For* July 31 *read* June 30

655   Sixth letter, line 2: *For* Leumy *read* Leamy

Volume XXV

Page

20   Note 2, paragraph 4, line 2: *For* Jedediah *read* Jedidiah

21   Note 3, line 2: *For* Angelican *read* Anglican

29   Note 8, line 1: Guérinère *read* Guérinière

38   From Philip Schuyler, introductory note, paragraph 2, line 14: *For* his executors, John B. Church, John Laurance, and Matthew Clarkson *read* John B. Church, John Laurance, and Matthew Clarkson, the trustees

45   From James Wilkinson, date line and note 2, line 4: *For* Maryland *read* District of Columbia

59   To Edward Carrington, note 1, last line: *Delete* until his death in 1810 and *substitute* until the office was abolished under the terms of "An Act to repeal the Internal Taxes" (2 *Stat.* 148–50 [April 6, 1802]).

90   Line 10 of text: *For* Your *read* Yours

91   Note 9, line 3: *For* 399–40 *read* 299–30

Page

110   Note 23, line 4: *For* St. James *read* St. James's

120–21   From Charles Wilkes, note 3: *Delete* forthcoming. *For* IV *read* forthcoming volumes.

142   Note 6, line 2: *For* for *read* from

149   Note 6, line 1: *For* Jedediah *read* Jedidiah

178   First full paragraph, line 7: *For* Jedediah *read* Jedidiah

185   Paragraph 3, line 4: *For* Jedediah *read* Jedidiah

212   Paragraph 2, lines 1 and 2: *Add* note to "French Diplomatic Agent at the Hague" to *read* Louis André Pichon

241   Note 4, line 5: *For* MacDonell *read* McDonnell

252   Note 2, line 8: *For* comte *read* vicomte

269   From Eliphalet Fitch, note 2, last line: *Delete* forthcoming. *For* IV *read* forthcoming volumes.

291   Note 3: *For* note 4 *read* note 40

296   Note 5, line 2: *For* Malcolm *read* Malcom

315   Note 2, line 2: *For* note 2 *read* note 5

336   To Edward Livingston, date line: *For February 10 [1801] read February 10 [1802]*
        Transfer this letter to *PAH,* XXV, 520

343   To Nathaniel G. Ingraham, note 1, last line: *Delete* forthcoming. *For* IV *read* forthcoming volumes

389   From John McComb, Jr., line 2 of text: *Delete* reference to note 2

404   From Eugene Lucet, note 2, paragraph 2, last two lines: *Delete* forthcoming. *For* IV *read* forthcoming volumes

415   Note 6, last line: *For* August, 1801 *read* August 20, 1801

417   From William Hornby, note 1, last line: *Delete* forthcoming. *For* III *read* forthcoming volumes

475   From James A. Bayard, note 1, last two lines: *Delete* forthcoming. *For* IV *read* forthcoming volumes

481   Note 3, line 4: *For* Hubbard *read* Hubbart
       Note 3, last two lines: *Delete* forthcoming. *For* IV *read* forthcoming volumes

495   Note 2, lines 1 and 2: *For Richard S. Hallett* v *William Houstoun, Paul Skidmore, and Gamaliel Skidmore read Richard S. Hallett v William Burrell, William Houstoun, Paul Skidmore, and Gamaliel Skidmore*

519   Note 3: *For* Joseph Howell *read* Joseph Howell, Jr.

522   Lines 4 and 5: *Add* note to "the draft of a letter" to *read* Letter not found

INDEX

COMPILED BY JEAN G. COOKE

Burr, Aaron (*Continued*)
    comments on, 324; and New Eng-
    land, 188-89, 192; newspaper attacks
    on, 14; in New York politics, 187-
    90, 191-92, 195, 205, 206-7, 207-8, 240,
    243, 245-46, 261; presidential candi-
    date, 21, 141, 239; and Republicans,
    13, 238; trip South, 20-21
—— duel with Hamilton: accusations
    against Hamilton, 241; arrangements
    for, 300-1; challenge, 256, 274-75,
    278; comments on Hamilton, 257;
    demands on Hamilton, 264-71, 272-
    73, 274-75; inquiries about Hamilton,
    312; *letters from* Hamilton, 241-42,
    247-49, 253-54; *letters to* Charles
    Biddle, 240, 334; *letters to* Hamilton,
    242-46, 249-51, 255-56; *letter to*
    David Hosack, 312; second for, Van
    Ness, William P., conversations
    with, 254, 255, 256, 258, 267, in-
    structions to, 256-57, *letters to*, 241,
    265, 266-67, 300-1, 334-35, 341, 344.
    See also Hamilton, Alexander,
    Hamilton–Burr duel; Pendleton,
    Nathaniel; Van Ness, William P.
Burr, Aaron (father), 188-89
Burr, Isaac, 319, 321
Burr, Joseph, 715; *letter to* John Phil-
    lips, 716
Burr, Theodosia, 21
Burrall, Frances Amelia Wickham
    (Mrs. Jonathan), 753
Burrall, Jonathan, 662; Hamilton's
    comments on, 752-53
Burrell, William, 871
Bush, John, 659, 660
Butler, —— (Mr.), 771
Butler, Zebulon, 416-18
Byng, John, 421, 423
Byron, William, 303, 304

Cabinetwares: duties on, 516, 645
Cabot, George: *letter from*, 610-11;
    letter from Oliver Wolcott, Jr., 35;
    letter to Tench Coxe, 610; *letters to*
    Rufus King, 12, 72
Cadiot, Jean, 11
Caines, Cornelia Johnston Verplanck
    (Mrs. George), 234-35
Caines, George, 234-35
Callender, James Thomson: and Ham-
    ilton, 36-37, 237, 830; *The History
    of the United States for 1796* . . . ,
    36-37, 830; and Thomas Jefferson,

36-37, 112-13, 141; *The political
    progress of Britain* . . . , 36; *The
    Prospect Before Us*, 37; trial of, 192;
    and "Walker Affair," 141
Calonne, Charles-Alexandre de, 837
Camden, S.C., 441
"Camillus," 117, 118
Camman, P. A., 303
Campbell, John: *letter to*, 684
Campbell, W., 386
Campo, Bernardo del, 820
Canada, 384; proposed British cession
    of, 198, 201-2, 210
Canals, 608, 640-41
Candles, 641; duty on, 513-14
Cannon: duty on, 632, 638
Cape Cod, Mass., 640-41
Capital: and manufacturing, 642
Caradeux Leycaye, —— (Mme),
    117; *letter from*, 89-92
Caradeux Lecaye, Jacques Joseph, 92
Caradeux Lecaye, Jean-Baptiste, 90,
    91-92
Caradeux Lecaye, John Baptiste, 92
Caradeux Lecaye, Comte Laurent, 89,
    91
Caradeux Lecaye, Louise Agathe
    (Mme Jean-Baptiste), 92
Carberry, Henry, 804
Carey, Mathew: *letter to*, 773-74
Carleton, Guy, 1st Baron Dorchester,
    425, 526-28, 530; *letter to* Elias Bou-
    dinot, 448; *letter to* George Wash-
    ington, 427
Carlisle, Pa., 441
Carneal, —— (Mr.), 838
Carpender, John G., 24
Carpenter, Elizabeth, 470
Carpets and carpeting: duty on, 517
Carr, William, 417
Carriages: taxes on, 116, 515, 775-78
Carrington, Edward, 140, 141, 858; *let-
    ter from*, 767; *letter to*, 870; *letter
    to* George Washington, 382-88
Carroll, Catherine, 192
Carroll, Charles (of Carrollton,) 192, 789
Carter, John, 449, 450, 457. *See also*
    Church, John B.
Carter, Jonah, 417
Carthy, Daniel, 539
Cartridge paper: duty on, 632, 638, 645
Caste, Joseph, 10
Castorland project, 41
Cathcart, James: *letter from* William
    Eaton, 28